THE PAPER OFFICE, FOURTH EDITION

THE CLINICIAN'S TOOLBOX™

A Guilford Series

EDWARD L. ZUCKERMAN, *Series Editor*

BREAKING FREE OF MANAGED CARE
A Step-by-Step Guide to Regaining Control of Your Practice
Dana C. Ackley

THE ESSENTIAL GUIDE TO GROUP PRACTICE IN MENTAL HEALTH
Clinical, Legal, and Financial Fundamentals
Simon H. Budman and Brett N. Steenbarger

OUTCOMES AND INCOMES
How to Evaluate, Improve, and Market Your Psychotherapy Practice by Measuring Outcomes
Paul W. Clement

TREATMENT PLANS AND INTERVENTIONS FOR DEPRESSION AND ANXIETY DISORDERS
Robert L. Leahy and Stephen J. Holland

REWARDING SPECIALTIES FOR MENTAL HEALTH CLINICIANS
Developing Your Practice Niche
Rona L. LoPresti and Edward L. Zuckerman

THE INSIDER'S GUIDE TO MENTAL HEALTH RESOURCES ONLINE
Revised Edition
John M. Grohol

CLINICIAN'S THESAURUS, 6th Edition
The Guide to Conducting Interviews and Writing Psychological Reports
Edward L. Zuckerman

CLINICIAN'S ELECTRONIC THESAURUS, VERSION 6.0
Software to Streamline Psychological Report Writing
Edward L. Zuckerman

THE CHILD CLINICIAN'S REPORT-WRITING HANDBOOK
Ellen Braaten

THE PAPER OFFICE, Fourth Edition
Forms, Guidelines, and Resources to Make Your Practice Work Ethically, Legally, and Profitably
Edward L. Zuckerman

The Paper Office

FOURTH EDITION

Forms, Guidelines, and Resources
to Make Your Practice Work Ethically, Legally, and Profitably

Edward L. Zuckerman, PhD

THE GUILFORD PRESS
New York   London

© 2008 Edward L. Zuckerman
Published by The Guilford Press
A Division of Guilford Publications, Inc.
72 Spring Street, New York, NY 10012
www.guilford.com

Printed in the United States of America

This book is printed on acid-free paper.

Last digit is print number: 9   8   7   6   5   4   3

Library of Congress Cataloging-in-Publication Data

Zuckerman, Edward L.
    The paper office: forms, guidelines, and resources to make your practice
work ethically, legally, and profitably/ Edward L. Zuckerman. — 4th ed.
        p. cm. — (The clinician's toolbox)
    Includes bibliographical references and index.
    ISBN: 978-1-59385-835-3 (pbk. : alk. paper)
    1. Psychiatric records—Forms.   2. Psychiatric records—Handbooks,
manuals, etc.   I. Title.   II. Series.
    [DNLM: 1. Psychotherapy—organization & administration—United States.
2. Consent Forms—United States.   3. Forms and Records Control—United
States.   4. Medical Records—United States.   5. Patient Care Planning—
United States.   6. Private Practice—organization & administration—United
States. WM 420 Z935p 2008]
    RC455.2.M38Z828 2008
    616.89'14068—dc22
                                                                2008007821

To my beloved daughter, Lilly Charlotte Lawrence Zuckerman.
This book is for the education you richly deserve.

About the Author

Born in New York City, Ed Zuckerman found his life's passion while working as a psychiatric aide at New York's Bellevue Hospital in the 1960s. He earned his PhD in clinical psychology at the University of Pittsburgh and worked in community mental health while gaining his license. He has worked with adults with developmental disabilities as well as those with severe alcohol addiction, acted as liaison with state hospitals, taught undergraduates, and been in the independent practice of general clinical psychology for many years. He now lives with his family in rural western Pennsylvania with horses, ducks, geese, chickens, and lots of mud and trees. There he consults and creates worthwhile practice tools for clinicians.

Acknowledgments

Many of my professional colleagues have generously taken the time to offer their advice, suggestions, and creations (and I hope that you, the present reader, will do the same; see p. 7). In most cases their names appear next to their contributions throughout this book, and I must restate my gratitude for their assistance in making this book as useful to our professions as it has become. Thank you all.

Joan Anderson, PhD, Houston, TX
Marc Andrews, ACSW, Pittsburgh, PA
Dorothy Ashman, MA, Bloomsburg, PA
Linda Azzi, RN, BS, Evergreen, CO
Bruce Barrett, MA, CPT, Duxbury, MA
Mitchell Berk, CSW, MA, Island Park, NY
Ginger E. Blume, PhD, Middletown, CT
Margaret A. Bogie, Chantilly, VA
Sheila Carluccio, MA, Dickson City, PA
David Clovard, MD, Raleigh, NC
Allan J. Comeau, PhD, West Los Angeles, CA
Harry Corsover, PhD, Evergreen, CO
Estelle Disch, PhD, Cambridge, MA
Steve Eichel, PhD, Newark, DE
Constance Fisher, PhD, Pittsburgh, PA
Donald J. Franklin, PhD, Bridgewater, NJ
Muriel L. Golub, PhD, Tustin, CA
Irvin P. R. Guyett, PhD, Pittsburgh, PA
Gordon Herz, PhD, Madison, WI
Ronnie M. Hirsch, PhD, New York, NY
Russ Holstein, PhD, Long Branch, NJ
Glenn W. Humphrey, OFM, PhD, New York, NY
Susan Hutchinson, DSW, LCSW, Irvine, CA
Richard E. Jensen, PhD, St. Charles, IL
Sam Knapp, EdD, Harrisburg, PA

Susan Lentulay, MA, Erie, PA
Don-David Lusterman, PhD, Baldwin, NY
Robert E. McCarthy, PhD, Myrtle Beach, SC
David A. Miller, PhD, Kansas City, MO
Ivan J. Miller, PhD, Boulder, CO
Kathleen Quinn, EdD, Cheyenne, WY
Jackson Rainer, PhD, Norcross, GA
John Roraback, PhD, Moline, IL (deceased)
Joseph Rosenfeld, PhD, Southampton, PA
Kathie Rudy, PsyD, Great Neck, NY
John M. Smothers, PhD, ABPP, Bethesda, MD
Eugene Snellings, CSW, ACP, Baton Rouge, LA
Ruth H. Sosis, PhD, Cincinnati, OH
Charles H. Steinmeyer, PhD, Warren, PA

I also wish to express my appreciation to Bob Matloff and Seymour Weingarten of The Guilford Press for their continuing support of and trust in the value of this project, as well as for their honesty and openness as friends and associates. The best thing they did for me was to provide me with an ideal editor, Barbara Watkins. She has been consistently smart, articulate, patient, enthusiastic, and a damn quick learner. I must also express my great appreciation for the tireless efforts of editorial project manager Anna Brackett and copy-editor Marie Sprayberry, whose superb sense of style, proportion, and language have greatly increased this book's readability, clarity, and value.

Contents

Note: All figures, forms, and handouts are shown in **bold**.

List of Figures, Forms, and Handouts

All the forms and handouts listed below can be found on the accompanying CD in .pdf format, so they can easily be printed out and look exactly as they do in the book. All forms except Handouts 2 and 4 are also available on the disk in .rtf format, so they can be tailored.

Introduction

Ways This Book Can Help You

This book is designed for both the novice and the experienced practitioner.

If you are a clinician just entering independent practice, who wishes to start up a practice properly, this book will help you get organized and develop good professional habits. It will make you

- less vulnerable (and therefore less anxious) when doing clinical work,

- more efficient, and

- more profitable and stable as a business.

All of this should give you more satisfaction with the career of therapist. This book cannot contain everything you should know to be in independent practice; it does contain all you need to make the correct initial decisions about office practices and paperwork, and so it will help you start out right.

If you have been in private practice for a few years, this book can help you to update your practice to conform to current legal and ethical developments. We live in a world that has become more litigious. Standards of professional practice and conduct have evolved rapidly, becoming ever more complex and subtle. Private practice has become more difficult because of the anxieties raised by malpractice cases and ethics complaints. For all of us, the remedies for this anxiety lie in increasing our coping skills (such as by acquiring particular expertise), developing fuller and more realistic understanding of the issues, and taking preventative actions. As therapists, our best defenses against malpractice are to offer high-quality and thoughtful care, use rational and effective procedures, and document our reasons and decisions thoroughly.

The resources in this book are carefully tailored to meet each of these needs. *The Paper Office* provides the basic operational "tools" needed by psychotherapists of any orientation, training level, or discipline. It should be emphasized that they are designed for the solo practitioner and the small-group practice, and may not meet the needs of a large or diverse group, agency, prison, school, or military practice. In addition, *The Paper Office's* forms and other materials are designed only for outpatient settings.

What This Book Contains

This book provides both practical information and ready-to-use resources:

- Brief guidelines and checklists alert you to the most important legal and ethical issues, and direct you in developing solid working procedures.

- Paper resources—sample documents and photocopiable forms—offer effective ways to meet specific challenges to your practice.

- This book is designed to function as "a malpractice risk reduction kit."

The forms and other materials offered are administrative and procedural, much more than clinical. They organize information to support the delivery of clinical services and to protect both clients and therapists. These materials will enable you to do the following:

- Understand and manage the financial side of practice, including fees and dealing with managed care organizations (MCOs).

- Efficiently collect such client information as demographics and insurance coverage.

- Document each client's presenting problems, mental status, and risk factors.

- Organize the intake information into diagnoses, prognoses, and treatment plans.

- Make and keep all your records so that they meet the current federal legal standards for privacy and security—those of the Health Insurance Portability and Accountability Act (HIPAA) of 1996.

- Assure that you are meeting ethical and legal standards in getting fully informed consent to evaluation, treatment, release of records, and so on.

- Respond proactively to the need for boundary clarifications/maintenance, and prevent ethical violations.

- Relate to MCOs, supervisees, students, and trainees in legal and ethical ways.

- Reduce your risk of malpractice, licensing board complaints, and liability suits.

This book assumes that you, the reader, are already a trained, practicing clinician. It assumes that you know how to do evaluations and therapy, and that you deal with clients and families. Therefore, the forms offered in this book are not forms for collecting data on symptoms or dynamics. For example, although you are offered a way of summarizing a client's mental status (Form 35), you are not given any tests or protocol of questions to collect the data the form summarizes. If you need questions to assess a client's presentation, history, symptoms, and mental status, and the words to describe these, the *Clinician's Thesaurus* (Zuckerman, 2005) contains the entire language of mental health.

Unique Features

The professions' ethical standards, principles, and guidelines have been incorporated into each form and sample document. This avoids the remoteness of reading about abstract principles, the narrowness of individual case studies, and the possibility of overlooking the necessary application of an important principle in your practice's procedures and paperwork. After the principles are learned through these applications, they can be more easily applied to new situations through your sensitized and enhanced ethical reasoning.

The forms and other materials have been designed and updated to meet current legal and ethical standards for the practice of psychotherapy by the several disciplines. As you know, there are significant differences in these standards by state, discipline, and population. To be comprehensive, this book tries to include any point or issue raised in any jurisdiction. It is very likely that concerns now raised in only a few places will eventually be applied in every location, and so these should be addressed now. The courts, the mass media, and the public have generally not paid attention to the differences among the professions, and so the book is inclusive in this respect as well.

However, you must know your local rules. Although I have made sincere and extensive efforts to be complete, I cannot guarantee that these materials will meet *all* the ethical and legal rules of *all* professions and jurisdictions. Your best sources of current and localized information are your state's and discipline's organizations. Join them, contribute to them, and participate in them; doing so will make you more aware and sophisticated, and will keep your practice up to date. For example, psychologists who belong to the Pennsylvania Psychological Association (PPA) have had a much lower rate of licensing board complaints than nonmembers (Sam Knapp, Professional Affairs Officer, PPA, personal communication, 2006).

In a similar vein, some readers have asked whether this book has been read and reviewed by lawyers. It has not, both because of the problem stated above of local and discipline differences, and because there would be some conflicting opinions that could not be resolved. Instead, I have relied heavily on published articles that have had the benefit of peer review, and on books by authorities who represent the consensus or vanguard in the field.

How to Use This Book in Your Practice

If you are an experienced clinician, read the table of contents for the forms and other materials you think are most important to the way you currently practice. Some will be ones you know you should implement to meet ethical and legal standards; others will make you more efficient and help you be better organized.

If you are a beginning practitioner, I recommend that you start with the materials offered in "Quick Start," below.

The sections of this book are generally organized as follows:

- The background you need to make use of the forms or other materials is offered first. Much of this information is displayed for rapid learning in the form of guidelines and checklists.

- The legal and ethical aspects and options for each element of the forms or sample documents, and any areas where these can be modified for your own practice, are described next.

- The model forms or other materials are then presented. (Note that the in-text discussion of each form or handout is indicated in the left margin with the form or handout number itself in a box; e.g., **FORM I** .)

Quick Start: Recommended Core Materials

These are the basic forms for any client intake:

Form 19   First-contact record
Form 21   Notice of privacy practices (unabridged)
Form 22   Notice of privacy practices (brief version)
Form 23   Consent to privacy practices
Form 24   Client demographic information form
Form 25   Client clinical information form
Form 26   Brief health information form
Form 28   Financial information form
Form 43   Structured progress note form
A form or handout for establishing informed consent to treatment, various methods for
    which are described on Chapter 4.

Depending on what you learn about the client during the intake, any of the following could be appropriate:

Form 27   Chemical use survey
Form 30   Adult checklist of concerns
Form 31   Child checklist of characteristics
Form 49   Briefer form for requesting/releasing confidential records and information

If you expect the client to use health insurance that is managed, the MCO is likely to want the information from these forms:

Form 35	Mental status evaluation and checklist
Form 37	Suicide risk assessment summary and recommendations
Form 38	Intake summary and case formulation
Form 39	Individualized treatment plan for managed care organizations

The materials above can be produced for your practice in just a few minutes for a few cents. The forms will photocopy clearly and look quite professional. On these forms, a space at the top is provided for your own letterhead. If you anticipate using a small label on your paperwork to identify the client by name, ID number, barcode, or something similar, you can offset your "letterhead" information to the left and leave room for the label on the right side. If you want to modify them or use ones that must be tailored to your practice, the CD contains the text of almost every form in a modifiable (.rtf) format.

Use the forms for 3 months with every new (and some old) clients. Mark the end of the 3-month period in your appointment book when you start. Then relax and focus on doing a fine job as a therapist. After 3 months, review how the forms are working for you. Decide which additional forms you want to incorporate into your practice or what changes you need to make to fit them better into your practice. Make any modifications or additions, and write to me with your suggestions and criticisms. If you make changes, please see the section below on sharing your changes.

Availability of Materials on CD

To save you time and effort, all the forms and handouts you might use in your practice are available on the CD inside the back cover. The materials are word-processed documents in several formats, so any computer can open and display them. Instructions for using the CD are on the last page of this book.

A Cautionary Note and Disclaimer

Although the publisher and I have made reasonable efforts to assure that the contents of this book are both accurate and up to date, we cannot be responsible for matters beyond its scope or level of detail, local variations, or future developments. For example, the laws and regulations that apply to your work as a clinician may be federal, state, or local, or they may pertain specifically to drug and alcohol clients, clients of mental health/mental retardation programs, clients of specific government programs, or patients with HIV/AIDS. In addition, special rules may govern practitioners working in schools, health facilities, outpatient clinics, or the like. Your local professional societies and experts on the scene are the best sources for information about current and applicable rules, both ethical and legal.

All of my comments about HIPAA and its regulations are my own interpretation from reading the Act and other resources and have not been reviewed by lawyers. The wording of the HIPAA forms is my own and is designed for small practices. HIPAA offers no text or suggestions and encourages practitioners to use language tailored to their setting, clients, and practices.

The listing of websites in this book does not constitute an endorsement by the publisher (The Guilford Press) or by me (Edward L. Zuckerman) of those websites, or of the information, products, or services contained therein. Other than at sites authorized and maintained by the publisher or by me, we do not exercise any editorial control over the information you may find at these other locations. Neither the publisher nor I assume responsibility for any loss incurred as a result of the application of any of the information contained in this book, or for any incidental or consequential damages in connection with or arising out of the furnishing of the materials in this book. No representation is made that they are the only or best ways to practice as a professional psychotherapist. This book is intended to assist an informed intermediary in the treatment of clients and patients—that is, the professional psychotherapist. It is neither recommended nor appropriate for use by amateurs or for self-help.

This book is sold with the understanding that the publisher, distributors, and I are not attorneys, accountants, or ethicists; nor are we engaged in rendering legal, financial, ethical, or other professional consulting services. If materials other than those presented here are needed to manage the purchaser's professional practice or a specific clinical case in any respect, we advise you to engage the services of a competent professional. Any forms that create a contract between the practitioner and the client should be reviewed by your legal counsel and should be modified to conform to local law and practice.

No warranty is expressed or implied, and in no event shall the publisher, I, or any reseller be liable for consequential or incidental damages.

About Reproducing Materials in This Book

One of the main advantages of this book over other books on ethics or practice is the high quality of the materials—the forms, checklists, patient education handouts, and so forth—and it was probably for these materials that you purchased it. However, before you begin using these materials to enhance your practice, I must remind you of the legal context of copyright in which they exist. **I have legal copyright to many of the forms and handouts in this book,** but I want you to be able to use them in your practice. Thus, I ask the following:

1. You, the individual professional who purchased this book, may photocopy or print from the CD any of the forms and handouts in the book for which photocopying rights are expressly granted in the form's or handout's caption, but only for use in your individual clinical practice and with your own patients.

     This means you cannot give copies to your associates, supervisees, friends, or other professionals for their own use. Why? Because a professional should not use these forms without understanding fully their ethical and legal underpinnings, context, and implications. Not owning the book will significantly limit that understanding and expose him or her to increased malpractice risk. If others want to use these materials, they must purchase a copy of *The Paper Office* for themselves.

2. You may modify the reproducible forms and figures to suit your practice or your needs. In fact, **you should modify them** for the specific legal or other conditions that apply to your practice, and in any way that will further your clients' understanding.

However, modification does not invalidate my copyright. Again, the modified version can only be used in your individual clinical practice with your own patients.

3. If you work in a group practice and want to use these materials in that setting, you must buy a copy of this book for each individual who will use the materials. Multiple-copy discounts are available.

4. If you are leading a class, workshop, or other educational program and want to distribute copies of some of these materials, you should do the following:

   - Review the law regarding copyright restrictions on what is and is not "fair use." For example, decide whether providing copies of the materials in this book would in any way reduce the sales of the book, which would then make your distribution illegal.

   - Consider requiring students to purchase copies of this book, because the use of these materials without the legal and ethical guidance contained in this book may get them into trouble.

5. Some materials in this book are copyrighted by individuals who did not grant reproduction rights beyond their publication in *The Paper Office*. Therefore, such materials may not be reproduced without the written permission of the copyright holder indicated on the form itself.

6. In addition, all materials for which photocopying rights are not given in a caption, and that are not copyrighted by other individuals, are copyrighted by Edward L. Zuckerman. Their reproduction is forbidden without prior written permission from The Guilford Press.

Your Forms and Other Contributions: A Nice Offer

- If you're disappointed with any part of this book, don't keep it a secret. Be a good customer, citizen, and therapist: Complain. Send in your criticisms and improvements.

- If you need forms or materials not offered here, let me know.

- If you design or find better or additional forms that you think should be included here, please send them to me for the next revision of this book or for specialized versions of *The Paper Office*. You will receive full credit for your contributions and comments if they are used, and you will receive **a free copy of the next version or edition** if your valuable contributions have been included.

Send your contributions to me at this address:

Edward L. Zuckerman, PhD
P.O. Box 222
Armbrust, PA 15616-0222

Or send an e-mail to me (mail@thepaperoffice.com).

Future Developments

As this field develops, this book will be revised to meet the needs of practicing clinicians. The publishers and I will be very grateful for your comments, suggestions, and criticisms. There is a feedback form at the back of the book to make your contributing easier.

It is my hope that by sharing the best efforts and ideas I have been able to borrow, modify, and devise, this book will make your professional life easier and more productive, and will further the professional development of all practitioners of the craft of therapy. Ideally, it will help therapists of all disciplines to strive for the goals expressed in the following oath, which the graduate program in psychology at Adelphi University requires of all entering students:[1]

OATH

As I embark on a career as a psychologist, I vow to respect the dignity and worth of the individual and honor the preservation and protection of fundamental human rights. I will be committed to increasing knowledge of human behavior and of people's understanding of themselves and others, and to utilizing such knowledge for the promotion of human welfare. While I pursue these endeavors, I will make every effort to protect the welfare of those who seek my services or of any human being or animal that may be the object of my study. I will use my skills only for purposes consistent with these values, and will not knowingly permit their misuse by others. While demanding for myself freedom of inquiry and communication, I accept the responsibility this freedom requires: competence, objectivity in the application of skills, and concern for the best interests of clients, patients, colleagues, and society in general. I accept with pride these commitments I have made and will cherish this day of entry into the profession of psychology.

---

[1]This oath is reprinted by permission of the Chair, Derner Institute of Advanced Psychological Studies, Adelphi University, Garden City, NY.

CHAPTER 1

Basic Paperwork and Communication Tools

1.1 Basic Paperwork Tools: An Overview

I must create a System or be enslaved by another man's.
—WILLIAM BLAKE

Your psychotherapeutic skills and personal resources are the basis of your effectiveness as a therapist. But practice also requires the effective operation of your professional office, and this is based on specialized paperwork. This book presents the essential paperwork tools to help you operate a solo or small-group psychotherapy practice ethically, legally, and profitably.

Therapeutic practice has ethical dimensions. Mental health clinicians have been in the forefront of the development of professional ethical guidelines. Concepts such as confidentiality, informed consent, and boundary issues have been articulated through careful deliberations. Professional ethics safeguard patients, enhance therapists' trustworthiness, and improve the climates of communities.

Therapeutic practice also has legal dimensions. Therapists live and work in a complex and rapidly developing legal context designed to protect the individual and reinforce socially approved behaviors. The United States is a nation under laws, and social policies are incorporated into laws.

Finally, in the United States, therapeutic practice has financial dimensions. The delivery of health care services is inescapably intertwined with commerce, and mental health services are no exception. Therapists must be paid for services, and so financial functions such as income, expenses, fees, billing, and taxes must be attended to. Therapists operate in offices and meet for appointments, and so they use standard business resources and office equipment.

Thus there are four aspects of a psychotherapy practice: the therapeutic, the ethical, the legal, and the financial. These four dimensions interact, intertwine, and may compete with one another. We, as professional therapists, need to take account of all of them. We must also respond effectively to their continually evolving interactions. Sometimes the demands of doing so seem burdensome, but we cannot ignore them. This book is one carefully reasoned response to this burden and obligation.

Each tool in *The Paper Office* has a primary function in one of these four areas, but each tool also has ramifications that extend into the other areas. For example, stationery and business cards are important business tools. But the professions have important legal and ethical rules about how therapists present themselves. Similarly, the making and keeping of financial and treatment records are basic administrative office tasks. But rules of confidentiality mean that treatment records cannot be handled and copied like documents in other kinds of business. Also, ensuring payment for services is essential, but the way this is done can affect treatment in many ways that are unique to the practice of psychotherapy. **This book's photocopiable forms, sample documents, guidelines, checklists, and step-by-step procedures will help you integrate the relevant legal and ethical principles and current practices into your ordinary paperwork, thus lightening both your worry and your administrative burdens.** The adoption of just those tools and procedures appropriate for your practices will reduce your malpractice and ethics violation risks substantially. Review the materials described in the following chapters, and evaluate for yourself how much they will lower your anxiety over your practices.

This first chapter covers some office administration basics: What needs to go on a letterhead and in a resume, and what should not? What records do you need to keep? Where and how should you keep them, and for how long? Chapter 2 takes a detailed look at financial tools and procedures, from tracking income and expenses to procedures for billing and for getting paid. Chapters 3 and 4 explore practical ways to meet the ethical and legal requirements of practice, including methods for reducing malpractice risk, and a range of specific tools for obtaining informed consent. Chapters 5 and 6 offer detailed forms and procedures for recording treatment from intake through termination. Chapter 7 offers methods for ensuring confidentiality and offers many forms and form letters for releasing and obtaining client records. Appendices are guides to further resources.

1.2   Presenting Yourself on Paper

Ethical Aspects of Self-Presentation

In choosing the wording that presents you and your practice to the public, it is important to recognize that there are legal, ethical, and rational differences between competence, credentials, and titles. The American Psychological Association's (APA, 2002, Standard 5.01b) code of ethics states that a psychologist must not misrepresent himself or herself in regard to training, skills, or credentials. Furthermore, it is solely the professional's responsibility to assure the absence of confusion, ambiguity, or falsity. **Be certain that your credentials are stated accurately and precisely every time.**

Guidelines for Clear and Accurate Self-Presentations

- Always use your highest degree. Earlier ones are unnecessary, and their use suggests pomposity (always inappropriate in a therapist) rather than extra training. However, it *is* appropriate to use two degrees if the degrees are in different but relevant fields (e.g., a forensic psychologist's possession of a PhD and a JD). Use the exact degree's abbreviation rather than "Dr."; this lessens confusion. Do not use both, as in "Dr. Joe Rorschach, PhD." This is redundant; it also confounds the social title of "doctor" and the professional educational qualification "PhD," a rampant boundary crossing (see Section 3.6). "Ph.D." and "PhD" are both acceptable styles because they do not mislead. "PhD" is a more modern style.

- The use of "Doctor" for nonphysicians is acceptable in casual conversations and nonmedical settings, where it is not misleading. Those having a doctorate from a nonpsychological program (such as biochemistry) should not use "Doctor" in psychological settings.

- A professional title is optional but often clarifying. However, depending on the state, some titles have legal definitions. Check your state's definition of the following to ensure legitimacy: "consultant," "evaluator," "clinical psychologist," "counselor," "therapist," "psychoanalyst," and "psychotherapist." Similarly, to prevent both misrepresentations and misunderstandings, clarify your status (in addition to giving your degree) as "Psychologist in training" or "Supervised by . . . " on reports.

- No one can use the title "psychologist" in any state unless he or she is licensed or similarly credentialed. "Licensed psychologist" (or "certified psychologist") is now considered acceptable, but this was not always the case. Using both words together was seen as redundant. It was also seen as misleading, in that it seemed to suggest that a *"licensed* psychologist" was somehow better than just a "psychologist," or even that there were *unlicensed* psychologists. "Licensed psychologist" is currently permissible, however, and you could include your license number for clarity.

- Specialties of practice (e.g., "practice confined to children" or specialty in "forensic evaluations") are useful to introduce yourself to other professionals or possible referrers, and to convey your areas of competence. However, beware of creating false impressions, because you will have to deliver what you advertise at a high level of expertise. When clinicians present themselves to clients as having certain areas of competence, the courts have generally held them to the standards that professional organizations set, even if the clinician is not a member of such organizations or qualified for membership. Evidence of competence differs by specialty (e.g., certification by the Academy of Certified Social Workers or the National Register of Health Service Providers in Psychology), so know and use only the ones appropriate for your profession, and be scrupulous about your qualifications. There are "boards" whose only requirement for membership is paying a fee. Do not bother to join such boards, because other professionals know which are real credentials and which aren't. They will think less of you and your real credentials if you indicate membership in such "vanity boards" (Dattilio, 2002).

- "Member/Fellow [as appropriate] of the American Psychological Association" is now acceptable. For years it was frowned on because it suggested a credential where there was none; there is no special training or particular skill required for APA membership. However, it does represent conformance to the APA's ethical code, and so is quite important.

The Name of Your Practice

Your practice's name is up to you. The simplest option is to be yourself: "First name Last name, Degree," or, more traditionally, "John Doe, PhD."

You may also create a name for your practice, such as the professional-sounding "Associated Associates" or the grandiose "The American Research Foundation for Interpersonal Therapeutics." This is called a "doing business as" (D/B/A) name. Descriptive terms such as "Therapy" or "Counseling" may be useful pegs to keep you in others' memories, but some have been used so often that they offer no identity. Check phone books for examples, and try for some uniqueness. Location names are assumed to stick in memory (e.g., Allegheny, Gateway, and Three Rivers are popular in Pittsburgh), and they may be helpful, as patients (or at least referrers) seem to prefer a local therapist.

If you are going to operate your practice under anything other than your real name, you need to register this D/B/A name with your state government for legal reasons. Usually the appropriate government office is called something like the Corporation Bureau of the Department of State. You can call your practice anything except a name someone else has already taken or something a government official finds improper. You will need to fill out a simple form that identifies you as the person behind the facade, pay a small fee, and publish the name in your local newspaper of record. The newspaper's classified ad department will help you with the procedure, and the fee for this is modest.

Your Stationery and Cards

Checklist for Necessary Information for Letterheads

❑ Use your legal name without nicknames (unless you live in the South, in a small community, or in some other locality where nicknames are acceptable). If there is a similarly named professional in your area, add initials or, better yet, a distinguishing subtitle or practice name.

❑ Include your highest clinical degree, specializations, and other credentials.

❑ Include your complete address with zip code. Use all nine digits. (Remember, the referral or check lost in the mail is worse than worthless; it's a hassle.) If you have multiple addresses, indicate them, but make it clear to which address mail (especially payments to you) is to be sent. Do not use abbreviations (e.g., Bldg.), as they are tacky and do not save space on a letterhead. In particular, avoid using erroneous or outmoded abbreviations (e.g., Penna. is archaic for Pennsylvania).

❑ An e-mail address should be included on all your forms, both for its convenience and for the image it conveys of someone who is up-to-date. If you have a website, indicate it as well.

❑ Your telephone number should always include your area code. If you will be getting a separate fax line, and are getting new phone numbers, order both numbers at the same time and you can get them in sequence for simplicity.

❑ There is no consensus on making your home phone number available to your clients. Some therapists report that calls are rare, are almost always justified by a true emergency, and when not are grist for the therapy mill. Others do not want to involve their family members inside the boundaries of therapy and are concerned about violent or harassing patients. An unlisted number may be worth the added cost. If you ever make calls from home to clients, you should consider arranging for blocking of caller ID, because without this a client will be able to discover the number from which you called.

❑ You should also decide whether you want to be available on a 24-hour basis (is that part of your responsibility to your patients, or is your privacy part of maintaining boundaries?), and then make your rules clear in your client information brochure (see Section 4.2).

❑ List your tax identification number (TIN) or national provider identifier (NPI) and license number (with type and state) on anything that will become a bill or accompany a bill, because insurers need these to pay you.

❑ Check and recheck the accuracy of *every word and number* before you print hundreds of any card or paper. I once had to rewrite my area code on 1,000 cards.

Logos

Logos are popular but not yet standardized. Orthopedists are using a braced-tree design, podiatrists a foot in a winged serpent (Aesculapius) design, and psychologists and psychotherapists the Greek letter "psi" (Ψ), but these devices have no meaning for the uninitiated. Most stationery printers offer at least one other logo you might consider, or you could use a simple letter monogram. You may want to design a logo suitable for the name of your practice (tree motifs are nonthreatening). You could have the printer do it for a small charge, or actually hire a professional who has done this before and have a really good job done. (Therapists are notorious for their resistance to using other professionals.) If you can't find an experienced artist, call the owners of a funeral home that has a nice text/logo and ask who did theirs. (This is a good tip—really!)

Phrases such as "We care for you" are tacky. You don't really care for the people who may see your card until they become patients, and we should presume that all therapists care for their patients (as noted by Constance Fisher, PhD, of Pittsburgh, PA).

Type Style and Size

You cannot go wrong with a typeface from one of the large medical stationery printers. Roman is preferable to *italic*. **Bold** in small sizes is not sharp and uses more space. Serif and **sans serif** faces are equally acceptable these days for professionals. Larger type is easier to read for seniors (over 40 and also your likely referrers) and for anyone struggling with a seventh-generation photocopy: This is 10 point, this is 12 point, this is 14 point.

Paper and Envelopes

When I receive it, I always notice crisp, heavy, linen-textured, laid, 100% cotton rag, water-marked, ivory-colored bond paper. I fiddle with it and admire it, but am not impressed by the professional behind it—only curious about how much extra this person has to charge me or my clients for this affectation. Are there any documents created by therapists that deserve or need anything but ordinary 20-pound white paper? If the client's records are to be destroyed in a few years to prevent misinterpretation, why use archival acid-free paper that will last 200 years?

If you use a word processor, you may not need printed stationery at all. You can print the letterhead on each page as it comes out of your laser or inkjet printer (minimum 300-dot-per-inch resolution).

You need envelopes with your name and address, because if a letter is undeliverable it will be returned to you only if the return address is on the envelope. Your computer's printer may be able to print a return address on blank envelopes, or you can buy a label printer.

For sending out bills, you will need envelopes imprinted with your name and address, or you can use a "two-window envelope" that shows your address through the upper window and the patient's address through the lower window. Save a tree: If you decide on imprinted envelopes, you need buy only a year's supply of #10 window envelopes for billing and regular imprinted envelopes for correspondence (a box of each, usually 500). No business occasion requires fancier stationery, so spend your money on your well-earned pleasures.

Business Cards

Business cards are essential. Carry a few in your wallet and in your datebook, because they have many purposes. You can offer a card to introduce yourself tactfully; the recipient can easily make conversation by inquiring about your location or what you have listed as your specialties. When you make presentations, always bring lots of cards to give to audience members so that they may call on you for professional services. You can also use them for small notes to others, or can use others' cards to note your promises to call or send something to them.

Plain black ink, slightly raised, roman lettering on a firm (but not too stiff), very white card is always acceptable. The catalogs of the major medical printers offer dozens of designs, typefaces, and colors. After you have made some contacts in your practice area, you can discover the local standards of good taste by examining the cards for which you have traded and then follow these examples. Even so, wait until you have been in practice a few years before ordering 5,000, baby blue, translucent smoky plastic, gold-foil-lettered cards with a logo of doughboy figures hugging each other. (Yes, I received these from a therapist.) Remember the old rule about dressing for a party: You can always dress down from formal attire, but you can't dress up from jeans.

Some business cards incorporate an appointment card on the back. These can provide for single or multiple appointments and different formats; these features make the card even more useful and not much more expensive. Medical Arts Press offers a card that has "Questions to ask my doctor" or "Special instructions" printed on the back. Local printers could do the same for you if this makes sense for your way of practicing. If you have two related positions (e.g., a clinic staff job and a private practice), you can have each printed on one side of a card. If you do business in another language or country, you can have cards printed with translations or addresses on each side.

Do-it-yourselfers can buy sheets of precut business cards for a laser printer (e.g., Avery 8371) at any office supply store. Templates for layouts can be downloaded from www.avery.com. Clip art can be added from them or from hundreds of collections on the Web. In fact, many business forms are available online. For example, Office Depot has perhaps 200 forms at www.officedepot.com under the "Free Business Forms" link.

Announcement Cards

Announcement cards are usually heavy cardboard ("pasteboard"), paneled cards about 4" high and 5" wide, which you are supposed to send to anyone who might conceivably refer a patient to you. They simply announce the opening of your office, your specialties, and your location, or the fact that you have taken on a partner or moved. I don't keep the ones I receive because they do not fit into any filing system. The addresses are more easily found in the phone book, anyway. A better method might be to send a letter, which allows a fuller description of your work with some personalized elements, and include a few business cards (which *can* be filed) or perhaps a preprinted Rolodex™ card (see your local printer or run them off on your photocopier).

Your Resume and Curriculum Vitae

A resume usually presents your current job functions or future goals, the strongest of your educational and vocational accomplishments, or other relevant experiences. Two pages is the maximum length, and one page is often all that others expect to read. A curriculum vitae (Latin for "course of life," usually abbreviated as CV) is more formal and professional in orientation. It is usually sequential and emphasizes any activities that bear on your career development (education, honors, scholarships, professional experiences, grants received, publications, memberships, licenses, etc.). The distinctions between a resume and a CV are often blurred these days.

Any bookstore will provide several books of samples and guidelines for writing a resume or CV and for phrasing one's accomplishments attractively. There are several from a small publisher called Ten Speed Press (www.tenspeed.com), which I like for their simplicity and efficiency, but which are not as polished and professional as some others.

Keeping your resume or CV on a word processor permits you to add new information easily and to reorganize and tailor information to the recipient's needs. For example, you might emphasize your teaching experience for a school consulting job, your clinical work and training for a hospital, or your publications for a research position. Always date it currently. As an effective alternative that will get more attention when many people apply to the same job, you can write up your resume as a letter, describing your skills and history together.

Many professionals keep a file folder labeled "Resume" (or "CV" or "Professional Development") in which they place any paper that documents activities to be added to the resume or CV, such as presentations made, publications, all training received, continuing education unit credits, or anything that mentions them by name. Periodically, they then update the resume or CV from this folder. (Such a file will also serve as a defense if a complaint alleges that you are untrained or unqualified to practice some technique or procedure.)

Keep copies of your resume or CV available and up to date, so you can give it to potential consultees, other professionals, referrers, credentialing groups, hospital medical staffs, and potential employers. It should function as an expanded business card. In particular, if you do any public speaking, bring a full resume or CV (as a resource for those who hired you) and a one-paragraph narrative presentation of your relevant credentials and experiences, printed or typed in large letters. Ask the person introducing you to read it to the group. Remember, your peers (and an ethics committee) will hold you alone fully responsible for assuring that the media present you correctly.

Many situations require full documentation of your history and training: applying for jobs, joining certain professional organizations, applying for licensure, responding to legal matters (e.g., complaints) or testifying in court, and applying to certifying boards. The Association of State and Provincial Psychology Boards (www.asppb.org and 800-448-4069) offers two excellent tools for these situations. Its Credentials Bank will hold transcripts, records of supervision, continuing education records, and similar materials that may be very hard to produce at a later time. And becoming licensed in another state is greatly simplified by the Association's Certificate of Professional Qualification in Psychology (CPQ).

Checklist for Your Resume or CV

☐ Plain white paper is sufficient unless you are applying for a job where your sense of style matters.

☐ More than two pages may seem like bragging, so unless you are applying for an academic position where your history of publications and presentations matter, keep it skimmably short.

☐ Use one typeface, and only a few **boldfaced** words. Boldface is a tasteful emphasizer if used with discretion. Use underlining instead of italics only if you are typewriting. Using ALL CAPITALS is like shouting, so be judicious. Do not use fancy layout or display typefaces.

☐ Your resume or CV must be scrupulously accurate—no lies, distortions, exaggerations, or other misrepresentations. These are ethical violations and reportable as such, which might cut short your promising career. Careful readers who find inappropriate statements will lose faith in your competence.

☐ Both resumes and CVs are business forms, and so there is no room for your sex, marital status, age, children, hobbies, musical interests, charitable or religious activities, or the like. If in doubt, leave it out. However, many people offer both a work and home address and phone, because professional contacts often overlap social ones these days.

Creating a Different Version of Your Resume or CV

It is helpful to have at least two versions of your resume or CV. The "maximum version" should have every heading and entry, name and date. New material can be added, and selections from it can be tailored to specific audiences. A single-page "synoptic version" can be used for others less fascinated with *all* of your accomplishments.

Figure 1 shows a partially filled-in sample CV, to illustrate the headings and layout for a maximum version.

1.3   Your Appointment Book

We all need a simple way to keep track of our obligations. Call it an "appointment book," "datebook," "calendar," "schedule," "little black book," or *"vade mecum,"* but it is a necessity of every practitioner. I have found it practical to operate by the rule "If it is not in my book, it does not exist," and so I write down all plans and appointments, both personal and professional. However, it appears to be a universal law that anything written in your datebook in ink will have to be changed.

Your appointment book is a record of your business; thus, it should be kept indefinitely. It not only documents your activities, but also records the services you rendered. It can be of value with the tax people or in court, and can be used to reconstruct your day even years later, so keep your old ones.

What an Appointment Book Should Include

Look for a book that covers an 8 A.M. to 9 P.M. schedule. The diary should also include a phone/address book (removable for transfer to the next year's book).

The National Psychologist (www.nationalpsychologist.com) sells an appointment calendar that has a 13-hour-per-day, 6-day-per-week schedule, with 15-minute intervals to meet the needs of even the most "workaholic" clinician. It also includes DSM codes, a listing of psychotropic medications, and other useful sections. It is 8½" × 11" and lies flat when open.

A List of Current Clients

Keeping a list of your current or recently active clients in your datebook may be very helpful if you need to cancel or reschedule appointments, or reach clients in an emergency. Of course, such a roster could be an obvious breach of confidentiality and a significant risk. One way to reduce the risk is to write only a client's initials and phone numbers and employ a simple encryption that will baffle most people: Simply substitute the next (or second or third) letter in the alphabet or digit in sequence for the true initials and phone num-

Curriculum Vitae

SIGMUND J. THERAPIST
1001 Spectacular View Lane
Terrific City, Supreme State 12345-6789
(900) 555-1212

January 15, 2008

EDUCATION

1995   PhD in Clinical Psychology—Distinguished University, Sovereign State
1991–1992   Internship in Clinical Psychology (American Psychological Association-approved)—Psychology Department, Splendid Health Center, Altered State University, Altered State

ADDITIONAL EDUCATIONAL EXPERIENCES

HONORS

CREDENTIALS

1995   Licensed as a Psychologist in Supreme State, Number 12345
1997   Entered into National Register of Health Service Providers in Psychology, Number 12345
1998   Fellow, American Psychological Association, Number 1234-5678

TEACHING EXPERIENCE

1990–1999   Superb University, Department of Psychology, Terrific City, Supreme State 12345
            Adjunct Associate Professor since 1993

CLINICAL PRACTICE

1995–2002   Independent Practice of General Clinical Psychology at Excellent Hospital, Terrific City, Supreme State 12345

RESEARCH/CONSULTATION EXPERIENCE

1990–1991   Research Assistant (half-time)—Project Champion, Psychology Department, Magnificent University, Marvelous City, Ecstatic State 54321

PUBLICATIONS

TRAINING PROGRAMS PRESENTED

REFERENCES

Professional, business, and personal recommendations are available.

FIGURE 1. Sample curriculum vitae, partially filled in.

ber. For example, for your client Jan Grimly whose phone number is (123) 456-7890, write "kh2345678901." Using an earlier letter or number is an alternative, and you could make a little graphic (perhaps on the first page of your datebook) to jog your memory of the encryption method you have chosen. If you use an electronic device for your information, you can use a password or encryption method.

1.4   Basics of Record Keeping

One of the attractions of private practice is the freedom from agency-imposed requirements, and one of those most eagerly dispensed with is elaborate record keeping. Although you cannot escape the need for records, you can adopt record-keeping methods that are simpler and more closely tailored to your needs.

You will need to keep both business or financial records and case or clinical records. Keeping them separate is necessary. Business records consist of your income and expense records, checkbook, payrolls, tax forms, business and professional licenses, billing forms, and so forth. Your accountant can help you set these up efficiently. (Get an accountant; it's a good investment.) For a detailed discussion of financial record keeping, see Chapter 2.

Clinical records (whose confidentiality must be protected) include your datebook or schedule, case records (including intake forms, treatment plans, progress notes, referral notes, periodic summaries, discharge plans, etc.), correspondence with clients and with others about clients, and the like. It is also a good idea to keep telephone and office visit logs in the event that a lawsuit calls for a reconstruction of events.

For guidance in recording the intake and initial evaluation of a case, see the forms in Chapter 5. Chapter 6 covers treatment plans and how to record the progress of treatment. For a full discussion of confidentiality concerns, see Chapter 7.

The remainder of this chapter provides an overview of clinical records, including the reasons to keep them, the nature of their contents, and their physical structure and organization. It also includes a discussion of how to maintain the security of your records, and how long to retain them.

Why Keep Records?

First, records must be kept to comply with your profession's ethical expectations. For example, Standard 6.01 of the APA ethics code (APA, 2002) states: "(a) Psychologists create . . . records and data relating to their professional and scientific work in order to (1) facilitate provision of services later by them or by other professionals, . . . (3) meet institutional requirements, (4) ensure accuracy of billing and payments, and (5) ensure compliance with law." On the basis of these guidelines, many states (e.g., Pennsylvania) are *requiring* licensed mental health practitioners to keep records. You cannot disregard these requirements on the basis of expediency, concern for confidentiality, or a feeling that "My notes are only about process or are illegible, so they would be of no use to anyone else." If challenged by an ethics committee or in court, you will be held to your profession's standards, simply because you present yourself as a practitioner. **Not keeping records is now grounds for a malpractice claim.** Having no records is illegal and unprofessional, thus demonstrating poor care. "An inadequate record will itself be seen as evidence of substandard care, no matter what care was actually provided" (Weiner & Wettstein, 1993, p. 179). Reid (1999, p. 12) phrases this as "Skimpy notes imply skimpy care."

Adequate record keeping allows you to defend yourself. Records will be your best defense in the event of a malpractice or ethics complaint or other litigation. See Soisson et al. (1987) for the specific advantages of having good records in defending a malpractice claim.

In addition, your records document your provision of services. This is a legal obligation and is necessary to receive payment from anyone. "Courts and external review bodies view the absence of documentation in the record about an event as evidence that it never occurred, no matter what the subsequent claims of the clinicians" (Weiner & Wettstein, 1993, p. 179).

Records document the thoroughness of your assessment if the untoward should happen. They help you to organize your thoughts about a patient and case. Your records establish a baseline of current functioning for structuring treatment or for evaluating progress and the impact of providing services.

Records have many additional uses. Your records can show whether and when a client met an eligibility requirement (e.g., disability). They are needed for supervisory review, consultation, peer review, quality control, and statistical reporting. They may be needed to maintain the client's continuity of care in future therapy or with other therapists. They provide clues as to which treatments have been successful and which are to be avoided. They offer crucial information for interdisciplinary communication. They allow you to review past successes at a future time. They replace memory, which is often inaccurate. Records are useful for self-education and student education, or for research. Lastly, you need to keep records because you are being paid to.

To summarize, **keeping records is not optional.** If you currently do not take notes or take insufficient ones, you are playing with fire as well as doing your clients a disservice. Change now; set up your record-keeping practices before the sun goes down again.

A caution is in order, however: Making records risks exposing confidential information to being misplaced, and subjecting yourself to being subpoenaed and coerced into self-incrimination in licensing board procedures. In a groundbreaking research project, Miller (2001) surveyed Colorado psychologists and found 517 who objected to rules that clients must have records that could be viewed by a third party. These results supported the presence of a standard of practice for therapy that included keeping records without a diagnosis, identification, and reasons for treatment, but that was not consistent with most ethics advice and board practices. It therefore created the legal basis (as a standard of practice) for a different set of record-keeping practices that could be defended (see also p. 47). Incidentally, since records must be kept to protect the therapist, other options include the use of an alias for a client, an inexact shorthand, and the omission of sensitive information.

What Should Be in the Records?

You cannot record all you observe, say, or hear, and so you must select. In almost all cases you should focus on what is significant for the treatment of the client, and not primarily to secure payments, protect yourself from malpractice claims, or deceive anyone (Dwyer & Shih, 1998).

I believe there are 10 categories of information we need to keep on each client. Each of these categories is described below.

Intake and Assessment

1. *Intake forms.* The client's record should contain basic information on the client, the reasons for referral, and the client's chief concerns. Section 5.3 offers three examples: the first-contact record and two client information forms. In addition, the Health Insurance Portability and Accountability Act (HIPAA) of 1996 requires that the client see your "notice of privacy practices" (NPP) at first contact. Section 1.5 explains this further. This notice can be included in the preappointment package mailed to the client if there is time, or it can be given to the client before the intake interview.

2. *Histories.* The record can include personal and family histories, as well as histories of previous interventions or treatments. Sections 5.4 and 5.5 include an interview guide and a form for parents to fill out on a child's developmental history.

3. *Evaluations and assessments.* The client record needs to include clinical assessments, previous evaluations, and any testing. Section 5.4 offers two problem checklists (one for adults and one for children). Focused guides for the evaluation of chemical use, mental status, health information and medication, and suicide risk can be found in Section 5.6.

4. *Diagnoses and case formulations.* Each client record should include formal diagnoses and a case formulation. Offered in Chapter 5 is an intake summary, which can help in case formulation and treatment planning.

Treatment Planning, Progress, and Termination

5. *Treatment plan.* Each client's record should document the treatment plan. The plan should include the target problems, methods of intervention, reviews, and outcomes. Chapter 6 offers several plan formats.

6. *Progress notes.* These might include regular summaries of treatment sessions. See Section 6.2 for more possibilities for progress notes. Under the HIPAA Privacy Rule, you can create separate psychotherapy notes that receive special privacy protection. By definition, these are not part of the client's medical chart (see Section 6.2).

7. *Termination summary.* This should consist of a summary of treatment provided, the progress made, any remaining problems, the client's prognosis, the reasons for termination, and any clinical recommendations. (See Section 6.3.)

Other Important Client Record Contents

8. *Correspondence.* This might include correspondence and records from past treaters and notes of nontrivial phone calls with the client or with other professionals about the client.

9. *Financial records.* These might include a signed agreement to pay; the dates of services; the charges, payments, bills, and collection phone calls; and notes to the client, insurance companies, and managed care organizations (MCOs) about bills and payments.

10. *Legal documents.* These would include any releases signed by the client (such as the HIPAA consent form; see Section 5.4), and documentation of informed consent through contracts or the client information brochure (see Chapter 4).

I agree with Knapp (1992a) that records should be the following:

- **Comprehensive.** All the relevant data should be included: names and addresses, fee arrangements, dates and kinds of services rendered, results of consultations and testing, correspondence, releases, reports prepared, notes of phone calls and meetings, progress notes, and discharge summary.

- **Objective.** Facts need to be separated from opinion; observable behaviors need to be included.

- **Substantive.** The diagnosis, presenting problem, treatment plans, and your rationale for each of these should be contained in the records.

- **Consistent.** Your behavior should match your treatment plan and diagnosis, or you should document the reasons for any inconsistencies.

- **Retrievable.** Your notes need to be readable, your records findable, and your charts organized.

- **Current.** You should make your notes in a timely fashion.

- **Secure.** You must make certain that your records are inaccessible to unauthorized others. All of these characteristics are discussed below.

The Physical Structure for Organizing Your Case Records

As indicated above, each client must have a range of specific information in his or her record.

HIPAA states that if you keep psychotherapy notes, they must be kept "separate" from the rest of the medical record, so be sure to adapt the records system you choose to meet this requirement. See Section 6.2 on keeping psychotherapy notes.

The Basic Manila Folder Method

FORM 1

You can use an ordinary manila folder for each client. Although this format is simple and cheap, it has liabilities: Loose pages can get lost or misplaced; also, pages and entries are kept in the sequence in which they were created, and so information is not organized by topic or relevance. This traditional, even classic approach to record keeping can be improved by developing a checklist of the contents (see Form 1), which can be printed on the outside of each manila folder. There is no indication of the client's name on the outside, for privacy reasons. You should tailor Form 1 to your own office procedures and forms.

The Folder with Sections

The major medical publishers have systems specifically designed for recording of patient care efforts. For example, these may have dividers preprinted with various headings ("Intake," "Treatment Plan," "Legal Stuff," etc.) in a standard hospital or medical office chart. Different colors of paper can be used for each section, with the most frequently used pages in ordinary white. Look at all the options before you decide. Even if it costs more, a more usable record-making system will pay for itself very soon. How much do you charge other people for your time? How much of it do *you* waste each month searching in your folders?

The Three-Ring Binder Method

Allow me to introduce Zuckerman's Unpretentious Clinical Keeping-of-Records System (ZUCKRS). It is a simple three-ring binder that holds all the materials about each active patient in a separate section and can be carried to the office each day. Although this system is almost embarrassingly low tech, it has been adopted by many of the therapists who have seen it.

The Binder. A plain vinyl-over-board binder without lettering or logo, in a dark color (like a dark blue suit), is always acceptable. Taste enters here: Neon pink will probably assure that you do not leave your book behind, but it may (or should?) clash with your office decor. If your ego decides the binder is a good idea, use your therapy talents to overcome your feeling that binders are not for adults, or to curb your grandiose inclination to buy the alligator leather version. Different colors for different settings or offices do make sense. If your accountant encourages you to make capital investments, there are heavy-duty designs with piano-hinged covers and other features for tech lovers. Buy the best quality, because the rings will meet evenly and the pages will not get caught.

Paper. Cheaper filler paper is 8" × 10½", slightly smaller than a regular 8½" × 11" page, such as you would use for a form. Forms will then show at the outside margin or edge of the page, and this may be useful. Whatever kind of paper you choose, make it your standard. Use it for writing all your professional work, and always keep a supply of it everywhere you write. You will save great effort and time. This method allows you to keep all your professional work (teaching notes, consultations, bestseller-in-progress, etc.) in separate three-ring binders cleanly and efficiently. Using colored paper for different parts of the client's record is trendy, but, except for yellow, it won't photocopy as well as white. You will also need a three-ring punch for your forms and paperwork received.

Checklist for Client Records

Client # _____ Intake date _____

1. Informed consent materials

	Date	By whom?
❑ NPP and consent given and signed*		
❑ Information brochure for clients given and signed*		
❑ Risks, benefits, outcome, alternatives of treatment discussed and noted		
❑ Handout on limits of confidentiality given and signed*		
❑ Duty to warn, danger to self/others discussed and noted		
❑ Requests for records from others signed and sent*		
❑ Payment policy discussed, agreement to pay signed*		
❑ Consent/contract to treatment given and signed*		
❑ Consent for follow-up given and signed*		
❑ Consent to evaluate without commitment to treat discussed and noted		
❑ Other consents discussed and noted (research, recordings)		

2. Further evaluations or consultations needed—indicate questions to be addressed

❑ Medical: _____   ❑ Psychiatric: _____

❑ Vocational/educational: _____   ❑ Other: _____

3. Case management information

a. Referral received: Date _____   By whom? _____

b. First contact: Date _____   By whom? _____

c. Intake completed: Date _____   By whom? _____

d. *Initial* treatment plan sent to MCO: Date _____   By whom? _____

Consultation with MCO reviewer named: _____   Authorization number: _____

Number of sessions authorized: _____   Review scheduled for: _____

e. *First reauthorization* request: Date _____   By whom? _____

Consultation with MCO reviewer named: _____   Authorization number: _____

Number of sessions authorized: _____   Review scheduled for: _____

Second reauthorization request: Date _____   By whom? _____

Consultation with MCO reviewer named: _____   Authorization number: _____

Number of sessions authorized: _____   Review scheduled for: _____

Third reauthorization request: Date _____   By whom? _____

Consultation with MCO reviewer named: _____   Authorization number: _____

Number of sessions authorized: _____   Review scheduled for: _____

f. Forms and records requested and released*

Req. date	Form/record	Sought from/sent to	On date	By

FORM 1. Checklist for client records. Asterisked (*) items are materials that can be found in this book.

Dividers. The common Mylar-reinforced dividers, especially with colored tabs, are usable. But better are the very wide dividers (9" × 11") made of the heaviest paper material or solid plastic. It is probably best not to write patients' names on the tabs or the edges of your forms for security reasons. Many people can easily read upside down. The few seconds spent searching for the record can be a way for both the patient and therapist to focus mentally on what is going to be their work in the hour.

Checklist for the Contents of Each Client's Section. The following are listed in sequential order, not in order of importance. These contents are discussed and specific forms or sample documents are provided later in *The Paper Office* as indicated.

❑ A billing form (see Section 2.3).

❑ First-contact record (Form 19) and similar records (see Section 5.2).

❑ Paper for notes. You can use blank filler paper, or print up the structured progress note form (Form 43) or the HIPAA-protected psychotherapy note if you decide to use it. See Section 6.2.

❑ Documentation of informed consent—for example, a signed copy of the client information brochure (see Section 4.2), and other forms and materials regarding treatment and consent to evaluation that appear in Chapter 4.

❑ Psychological testing done by you.

❑ Previous records (medical, psychological, educational, etc.) that you obtain (see Section 7.4). These would include copies of release forms you have used.

❑ Correspondence from, to, and about the client.

❑ Newspaper or other clippings about the client, or clippings that the client brings in.

❑ Anything else you think is relevant at present or in the future.

Computerized Client Records

The simplest way to keep clinical records on a computer is to create a folder or directory for each client, and to add a file for each visit. You can do this by creating a blank progress note (see Forms 43 and 44 for formats you can adopt) as a "template" or "stationery," and opening it each time you want to make a record. Fill in the current information, save it to the client's folder or directory, and entitle it with the client's initials and today's date. If you don't want to write so much, you can just open a file in each client's folder or directory called "Progress Notes" and add to what you have written before. Many of the computerized billing programs also now offer some way to incorporate progress notes.

Electronic medical records (EMR) are the wave of the future because of legal pressures (such as HIPAA requirements), infatuation with all things computerized, and the self-interests of the business community. Do not jump into this complex area without due consideration, because programs are continually being developed and upgraded. As an introduction, see the list of programs at www.nationalregister.org/development_Zuckerman; however, no list will be complete. Below are some widely recommended programs that include many functions:

1. Therascribe, from John Wiley & Sons Publishers, is based on Arthur E. Jongsma, Jr.'s, model of treatment planning (see more at www.wiley.com/legacy/therascribe/default.htm).

2. ChartEvolve, from CIMS Group, is based on James A. Kennedy Axis V model (described briefly in Section 6.1).

3. ICANotes, from ICANotes, Inc. (www.icanotes.com), is a well-regarded program that is easy to use.

4. QuicDoc, from DocuTrac, Inc. (www.quicdoc.com), is a complete office management program for therapists.

5. TheraManager, from TheraManager Software, Inc. (www.theramanager.com), is a very complete and functional program.

When a Case Is Closed

After termination, or if the records become too bulky, a client's pages can be transferred from other formats to a manila folder and filed for "permanent" storage in a locked cabinet. If you indicate the dates of service provision on the outside, it will make it easier to prune your records after 15 years or whatever number of years you select as a disposal date (as suggested by Constance Fisher, PhD, of Pittsburgh, PA). See Section 1.6, below, on retention of records and their disposal.

1.5   Record Security

Privacy of information is the goal; the methods of achieving it are security. "Security applies to the spectrum of physical, technical and administrative safeguards that are put in place to protect the integrity, availability, and confidentiality of information" (Gue, 2002). HIPAA set minimum standards for protecting the privacy of health and mental health records, as well as standards for the security of electronic and other health information. It also established a set of clients' rights regarding their health and mental health information.

HIPAA's rules apply to five kinds of "covered entities" (CEs): recognized health care providers; health plans (e.g., health maintenance organizations [HMOs], MCOs, other insurers); health care clearinghouses (companies that translate your bills and CMS claim forms for payment); administrators of health savings accounts (HSAs); and Medicare discount drug card providers. All of these collect, store, and transmit health care information, and so are subject to HIPAA. Parenthetically, financial institutions that may process client payments (such as banks or credit card processors) are not required to comply with HIPAA, since they see only the client's and clinician's names, the date, and the charges for "professional services," none of which are considered PHI.

HIPAA and Privacy

The regulations of relevance to therapists concern clients' PHI. This is an individual's health information that "relates to the past, present, or future physical or mental health or condition of an individual; the provision of health care to an individual; or the past, present, or future payment for the provision of health care to an individual" (HIPAA Section 164.501).

HIPAA's privacy and security regulations concern how client information is safeguarded when it is collected, created, stored in your office, shared with other treaters, used in teaching, training. consultation, or research, and sent to insurers. It is the *information* in the record that is protected by this law, and so it not only applies to electronic records (e.g., word processor documents, faxes, data entry), but also to paper records and even oral communications (e.g., conversations, telephone calls, and messages). Most consultations and teaching are also covered. The full text of the Act can be found at www.hhs.gov/ocr/hipaa.

HIPAA, though large and detailed, can be divided into three sections, each with a number of rules and standards.

1. The Electronic Health Transactions Standards concern health insurance programs, eligibility for benefits, coordination of benefits across different insurers, payments, and so forth. These require the adoption of "Standard Code Sets" for each kind of transaction to describe persons, services, and disorders. This very complex set of computer programs is provided to you by your billing service, billing program's developers, or the insurers you deal with.

2. The Security and Electronic Signature Standards concern verification of identity and accuracy of electronically transferred data. Passwords and encryption are essential.

3. The Privacy Standards concern the maintenance of confidentiality and the access to an individual's "protected health information" (PHI).

A client's PHI is used in "treatment, payment, and health care operations" or TPO. Exact definitions can be found in HIPAA Section 164.501, but here are some simplified versions.

Treatment is when a provider offers or manages health care or related services, consults with other providers, or makes a referral.

Payment includes what a health care plan does to obtain premiums, determine eligibility and exact benefits (coverage), and provide payment or reimbursement. These can include activities such as coordination of benefits with other insurance, assessment of the patient's health, determining the medical necessity of care, and reviewing utilization.

Health care operations is a very general term that includes at least the following activities conducted by the CE: quality assessment and improvement activities; review of the performance, competence, or qualifications of health care or non-health-care professionals; training of students or practitioners; accrediting, licensing, or credentialing of health care professionals; activities relating to health insurance or health benefits; medical review, legal services, and auditing functions, including fraud and abuse detection and compliance programs; as well as a variety of actions to support business administration, planning, sales and marketing, customer service, grievance resolution, due diligence, and so forth.

As you can see, almost every kind of activity is addressed by these regulations, which allow a great deal of freedom to share information about the individual.

Under HIPAA, a simple notification—an invitation to read the NPP—to a patient during intake about your ways of handling his or her PHI is all that is needed to allow you to share his or her PHI among all CEs, such as treaters, treating agencies, those in training, health insurers, MCOs, and others (see Section 164.506). Once notified of his or her rights, the psychotherapy client signs a "consent" form, and treatment may begin. PHI can be "used" (within your organization) and "disclosed" (shared) with other participants in the patient's TPO. No "accounting" (record) of these uses and disclosures is required. If the PHI ever needs to be used for other than TPO or disclosed to anyone outside the organization, a written release (authorization) is required. You must keep a record of these (rare) disclosures (but not of those common ones made for TPO). Note that this is not informed consent, because the consent document is signed before any PHI is collected, and thus it may be shared without the client's knowledge of its contents. The consent's signing does not signify consent to any particular thing, especially not to treatment or evaluation. It indicates only that the client agrees that he or she has been exposed in some way to your office's practices on handling PHI.

Your state's laws preempt HIPAA if they more stringently protect the patient's privacy. In the regulations, there are so many exceptions and exclusions to these requirements for control over a patient's PHI that the result is a very, very basic level of privacy protection.

Steps for Becoming HIPAA-Compliant

1. Select someone in your practice to be the "privacy official" for implementing HIPAA. In a small practice, this will be you. Using your office manager in this role may not ensure that all clinical and legal considerations will be adequately integrated, and if this person should leave, continuity will be compromised.

   a. Your first task is to become informed about the Act.

   b. Second, understand how PHI is currently created, used, accessed, disclosed, and stored in your practice.

   c. Third, discover, from reading, consultation, and continuing education programs, how much of HIPAA you will actually have to implement, considering that your local laws are likely to be more stringent and that HIPAA allows you to tailor safeguards to your risks and setting.

2. Create a written set of policies for implementing the procedures of HIPAA (a HIPAA

policies and procedures manual, or HP&PM). The rationale for creating an HP&PM offered by the APA Practice Organization lawyers is that such a manual would become crucial if an investigation were to be launched because of an accusation of an unauthorized release of PHI or electronic PHI (EPHI)." This manual and the documentation that its practices are being followed would be the only way to show that the leak of information could not have come from your office.

FORM 2   The checklist offered as Form 2 is not an substitute for an HP&PM, but it can guide your implementation of privacy and security practices and provide some documentation of your efforts and their effectiveness, especially if it is completed every 6 months or more often.

3. If you have any staff members who see clients' PHI, you must train them in HIPAA's rules on privacy. This is an opportunity to review ethical and local legal rules as well as your office's practices with them. (See Section 7.2 for more on training staff on privacy.)

4. Develop the following paperwork:

   a. An NPP, within which clients should be told that they can complain about your privacy practices or an unauthorized disclosure of their PHI. (See Section 5.4, Forms 21 and 22.)

   b. A HIPAA consent form for disclosure of PHI for TPO. (See Section 5.4, Form 23.)

   c. A HIPAA-informed authorization form for disclosures of PHI. (See Section 7.4.)

   d. A business associate contract. Business associates are non-CEs who perform non-TPO services (such as doing your billing or answering your phone) on your behalf and also have access to your clients' PHI. They must agree, in a contract, to safeguard the privacy of this PHI.

   e. Keep records of your HIPAA efforts and compliance, and monitor adherence.

5. Develop policies and procedures concerning PHI to allow patients to do the following:

   a. Access, inspect, and copy their records.

   b. Amend their PHI.

   c. Complain about privacy violations (see Section 7.8).

   d. Revoke an authorization to disclose their records.

Tips for Record Security

Keep all your case records, including the identifying data in your billing system, in a locked and secure place (APA Guideline 6, 2007). But remember that no place is totally

A Checklist of Security Procedures for a Small Psychotherapy Practice

To the privacy/security officers,

For each statement below, circle T (true), F (false), or ? (don't know), and take any immediate actions necessary to block potential threats to privacy. Write notes on the back. Repeat at least yearly.

Date completed: _____ by _____, who is the privacy officer/security officer/systems administrator of _____.

1. Personnel

a. Privacy and security officers (who can be the same person) have been made responsible for data security. This person or persons keep informed about legal developments (such as HIPAA) and technical issues (such as hardware and software); train all current staff members, new hires, and temporary workers; make necessary changes when an employee leaves the practice; and so on.   T   F   ?

b. We conduct background checks on all new hires and comply with all laws about employees.   T   F   ?

c. All employees have been trained in all our office rules and the consequences of breaking them.   T   F   ?

d. All employees receive initial training in privacy and security, periodic security reminders, in-service training, and monitoring from the privacy/security officer(s).   T   F   ?

e. These training efforts and their outcomes are documented and evaluated.   T   F   ?

f. All staff members have access to only the information and records they need to perform their job functions.   T   F   ?

2. Physical controls over information

a. The staff areas are locked at the end of the workday and whenever no staff member is present.   T   F   ?

b. Former employees do not have keys or access to the office, files, or computers.   T   F   ?

c. Passwords and IDs are not written in any easily accessible locations or on the computers.   T   F   ?

d. All office computers are in areas with no client access, or have hoods or are arranged so that no client can see the screen.   T   F   ?

e. We do not call out clients' names in the waiting room and do not have them sign in on a sheet that other clients might see.   T   F   ?

f. All papers with protected health information (PHI) are placed in locked files or are shredded on the premises by the time the office is closed for the day.   T   F   ?

(cont.)

g. Only bonded records destruction companies are employed, and records of all destruction are maintained.   T   F   ?

h. A privacy/security officer keeps records of all PHI-containing equipment that we own, lease, or operate. The officer monitors this equipment at regular intervals and whenever it is sent for maintenance, repair, or replacement, to ensure against accidental unauthorized releases of PHI.   T   F   ?

i. We do not use Social Security numbers for record-keeping purposes or identification purposes. When these need to be recorded, they are not easily visible or accessible.   T   F   ?

3. Security of electronic data

a. Each staff member needing access to records has a different, unguessable, sufficiently long, regularly changed password.   T   F   ?

b. All computers (including our networked computers) have malware protection, which is updated at least every 48 hours.   T   F   ?

c. When we use the Internet, we have a software firewall and similar protections, which are updated and tested regularly.   T   F   ?

d. Staff members have been trained never to leave a monitor unattended. We use "sleep" programs, password-activated automatic screen savers, timed log-off programs, or other means as appropriate to make access to PHI unavailable when a computer is not being used.   T   F   ?

e. Portable computers are locked down in the office or used only in secure locations.   T   F   ?

f. Encryption is used for all messages transmitted from employees' homes or from outside the office to the office's computers.   T   F   ?

g. Passwords are used on portable digital assistants, personal organizers, and similar devices.   T   F   ?

h. Automatic encryption programs are used to prevent the storage or transmission of all client information in any readable format.   T   F   ?

i. If we use e-mail for any kind of PHI, we encrypt it.   T   F   ?

j. Backups of all client data are frequent, regularly scheduled, checked for accuracy and availability, stored off-site, and destroyed at regular intervals.   T   F   ?

k. The systems administrator or a privacy/security officer has prepared a written plan to handle emergencies and recover our PHI from disasters.   T   F   ?

l. The computer system will not allow any new software to be added. Only the systems administrator can overcome this restriction.   T   F   ?

m. All computer drives, magnetic tapes, diskettes, CDs, and other devices that hold confidential data are either physically destroyed or wiped with proven utility programs before they are junked, sold, donated, or otherwise disposed of or serviced (on the premises or off).   T   F   ?

4. Telephones, answering machines, and facsimile machines

a. Staff members keep their voices low, so that their phone conversations cannot be overheard by patients or uninvolved employees.   T   F   ?

b. All staff members are trained about what questions to ask and what to tell or not to tell callers about clients we see.   T   F   ?

(cont.)

c. A privacy officer regularly arranges calls that ask for client information, to test our telephone security measures.　　T　F　?

d. Employees are trained to leave only nonspecific messages on clients' answering machines unless a client has previously agreed to the leaving of confidential messages.　　T　F　?

e. The office's answering machine's volume is turned low when incoming messages are recorded and when the message is picked up, so that no one else can hear.　　T　F　?

f. All fax transmissions have a cover sheet with the phone numbers, number of pages, and a note about contents' confidentiality and what to do in case of mistakes.　　T　F　?

g. Users of the fax check the intended recipient's phone number against the one stored in the fax and do not use numbers not stored in the fax (so as to prevent dialing errors).　　T　F　?

h. When there is any concern, the recipient is called to confirm reception of the fax.　　T　F　?

i. No confidential information is ever discussed on portable, cordless, wireless, or cellular telephones.　　T　F　?

5. Releasing records

a. Records are reviewed by a single designated person before being released.　　T　F　?

b. Nonessential information is deleted, obliterated, or masked.　　T　F　?

c. Only the HIPAA-compliant "minimum necessary information" is sent out.　　T　F　?

d. The recipient is always verified.　　T　F　?

e. The authorization/request for records is examined for legal compliance, completeness, and so forth.　　T　F　?

f. No records are released until all uncertainties are resolved.　　T　F　?

6. Administration

a. We have HIPAA-compliant business associate contracts with all appropriate entities.　　T　F　?

b. A privacy/security officer tests all safeguards at irregular, unpublicized, but frequent intervals and document the results.　　T　F　?

c. Changes and improvements to these safeguards are budgeted and implemented in a timely fashion.　　T　F　?

7. Other points unique to our office or practice (add these here):

secure. A three-ring binder (see above) can be kept in your personal possession, which is sometimes better.

Computerized records, even billing information, must be secured as well. Many therapists quaintly insist on a paper "hard copy" backup of computerized records, without realizing that by printing out their records they have increased the risk of disclosure from almost zero to fairly high, because many more people can read paper than can access your computer. Some word processors include encryption, but if yours does not, buy and *use* an encryption program such as the courageous Philip Zimmermann's PGP (Pretty Good Privacy), which is easy to use, unbreakable, and public. It is downloadable from www.pgp.com/downloads/desktoptrial.html (the trial is permanent and so is free), and you can learn more about the history of this valuable program and encryption at www.philzimmermann.com/en/background/index.html. The site www.epic.org/privacy/tools.html offers tools for encrypting telephone calls, e-mail, your hard drive, and anonymous e-mailers.

An unresolved issue at present is the "probative value" of computerized records. How much trust can we place in a document that can be as easily altered as notes kept on a computer? Methods for authenticating documents such as digital signatures are just becoming available, and we should adopt them for our records as soon as practical. For a start, see the Digital Signature Guidelines from the American Bar Association (www.abanet.org/scitech/ec/isc/dsgfree.html).

HIPAA requires you to secure your computerized records from disasters as well as prying eyes. Design a simple-to-use and practical-to-implement regular backup program for your computer records. Many computer programs' manuals will teach you how to set up one. (Yes, I know we all say we do this, and most of us still don't. I do now, but only after a painful disaster.) The simplest backup method is to make a copy each week of your clinical files to a floppy disk or CD and store it off-site in a secure place. More sophisticated programs allow this to be done automatically on a schedule and only for those files that have changed.

If your computer ever needs service or upgrading, anyone at the repair facility can read your clinical files if you have not password-protected them, so this is a must. Finally, when you sell or give away your old computer, you should erase the files on your hard drive. Deleting the files or putting them in the Trash/Recycle Bin is not enough; when you do this, only their addresses are removed. You need to use a program like Burn Disk Utility (Macintosh), or Eraser (for Windows), to make them truly unrecoverable.

A somewhat simpler alternative is a "vault" program, which creates a separate section on your hard drive whose contents are encrypted. Such programs are inexpensive, easy to set up, and very secure. Because there are so many and they continue to add features, do a search and visit some developers' sites (such as www.truecrypt.org, www.axantum.com/AxCrypt/, www.jetico.com, and www.finecrypt.net). These all work on Windows up through XP. Mac users have FileVault built into OSX, of course, but programs like FileGuard X4 will do more (www.intego.com/fileguard).

Records can be lost, stolen, damaged, or destroyed. An article in *Practice Strategies* ("Tips from an Attorney . . . ," 1988) suggests the following: (1) Don't panic. (2) You may not need the records of clients you saw years ago. (3) Copies of your reports may exist in the files of others (such as insurance companies, attorneys, school systems, etc.), and you can request these. (4) Notify your professional insurance carrier and ask whether it will pay the costs of recovery. (5) Inform current clients of the problem. Review their treatment plans and status with them. (6) Write a synopsis for clients who are likely to need their records, such as those in litigation.

1.6   Retention of Records

When therapy ends and the case is closed, the records need to be preserved so that you can do the following:

- Comply with laws and ethics.

- Assure continuity of care (such as patient transfer).

- Defend yourself from some belated accusation. Despite statutes of limitations, the laws are in flux, and court decisions have extended the client's time to sue (e.g., "2 years after the discovery of damage").

- Qualify the client for some services in the future (e.g., Social Security disability, a special college program for a person with a learning disability).

- Restart a case because a patient returns for treatment.

- Cope with some other situation that is presently unforeseeable.

How Long Should Records Be Kept?

The rules for retention of records are complex, overlapping, and dependent on a host of variables—such as type of services, location, professional discipline, contractual obligations, and contents of the record. Partly to eliminate some confusion, HIPAA set a minimum of 6 years for retaining all PHI, and this is often the best simple rule. However, the Internal Revenue Service expects you to keep financial records for 7 years, as do the recently revised guidelines from APA (2007). Social Security disability can be awarded 5 years retroactively. Malpractice suits may have short time limits, but breach of contract may go back further, depending on state tort laws and even criminal laws. However, suits alleging later discovery of harm done to a child in treatment can go back much further. Generally, complaints to licensing boards have no time limit, and your records will be your main (and probably your only) defense.

Suggestions on Retaining Records

- If you have a secure space, keep the whole record forever for your own protection.

- Children's records should be retained until 5 years after they reach their majority, even though their findings may become out of date. Write that "discard date" on the outside of the folder when you close the case and store the record.

- Keep adults' records for at least 12 years, or keep a summary forever. Write the 12-year "discard date" on the outside of the folder when you store the record.

- At your established "discard date," destroy the records (see below) or offer to give them to another professional caring for the client. Design a mechanism to find a current address at some specified future time, and to send each patient a letter giving him or her the choice of having records transferred to a successor therapist whom they have seen or are seeing or another practitioner (or anyone who would understand the issues) chosen by the patient. Do not offer clients the choice of receiving the records directly or of destroying the records, because (1) they cannot anticipate the needs for the records; (2) they do not own the records; (3) they do not have the training to understand the records; and (4) the records may be needed by you.

- Whatever procedures you choose, be sure to document it in sufficient detail in your HP&PM (see Section 1.5), and keep copies where your attorney, your family, or another therapist can find it. Also, be absolutely consistent in using your procedures, because any exceptions would suggest to a malpractice attorney that you have something to hide. Lastly, develop some standard form for recording which records you disposed of, when, and how, for both documentation and defense. I recommend that you keep only a list of the names of clients and the beginning and ending dates of your treatment.

- An additional consideration concerns changes in technology. Old records may not be readable on newer word processors, or the media they were recorded on may no longer even be in use. Therefore, save your records as ASCII code ("plain text" or "text only"), which will never be unrecognizable. Similarly, storage media such as zip drives, floppies, and tape are disappearing from computers now, and so records maintained on them will soon be inaccessible. It does appear that the CD format will be usable for some years, but devise a plan to remind yourself to transfer all old records when you update your computer.

Disposal of Your Records

Even when destroying records, you have to maintain their confidentiality. You can't just throw them in the trash. A simple shredder isn't expensive but takes time. You might organize a group of your peers with old records to take them all to a professional disposal firm (look in the Yellow Pages under "Records Management") and get a "Certificate of Destruction."

Preserving Your Records When You Close Your Practice, Retire, or Die

You are ethically and legally responsible for protecting the confidentiality of and access to your records if you should become unable to care for them, according to Standards 3.12 and 10.09 of the APA ethics code (APA, 2002). McGee (2003) further describes the ethical points and other considerations in a highly recommended article. Closing of your practice because of your moving, disability or incapacity,[1] temporary or permanent retirement, loss

---

[1]This term is preferable to "incompetence" for its precision.

of license to practice, or "untimely demise" requires assuring the well-being of your patients, and so there are significant ethical, legal, and practical matters to be addressed.

There do not appear to be any official guidelines for a "professional will" for closing psychological practices, so the suggestions below have been gathered from many sources and the guidelines of other professions. I have organized them into two large sections. The first addresses closing your practice over a period of time, as would happen when you retire or move. The second section addresses what to do now to prepare for the possibility of unexpected death or sudden incapacity. Because you cannot foretell your demise, I recommend that you negotiate all these arrangements with your colleagues, THIS MONTH.

Closing Your Practice

Despite what you may have heard, practices are rarely worth much, as they are so personal (Woody, 1997). Rather than selling my own practice when the time comes for me to retire, my preference would be to pay another professional to assume the duties of safeguarding my records and responding to calls and mail, and to explicitly allow a "bridge therapist" to refer or to accept as clients any who might call expecting to reach me.

Your Obligations to Clients: Continuity of Care. If you retire or otherwise close your practice, you have obligations to current clients. With some, you will finish up therapy if you have the time. You may need to transfer other clients. All will need to be informed that you are leaving practice, when your office will close, and how they may obtain their records should they need them. They must be given sufficient time to make the best resolutions and least traumatic alternative arrangements (I would think not less than 60 days, depending on how often you are seeing them, but the earlier the better). You should make clear recommendations for those you believe require continued services. You simply cannot discontinue with clients in need, because this can be seen as "negligent abandonment"—which is both unethical and grounds for a malpractice suit. Of course, make sure those practitioners to whom you refer clients are both available and offer appropriate and high-quality services, in order to avoid problems with "negligent referrals." It is entirely appropriate for you to make the initial calls to these successor therapists.

If you are retiring, indicate when you will stop taking new patients and let your caseload wind down, which will be easier on you and others. But, because you may not have the time, prepare, **this week**, a termination letter to be sent to your current and recent clients (the last 18 months seems reasonable to me) notifying them of why you are closing up shop; exactly when the office will close; who will have your records, and how to reach them; whom clients can call in an emergency; what other therapists and community resources (agencies, professional organizations) are available if they want more services; and so on. Make it clear that it is the clients' choice to pursue additional services and that the confidentiality of their records will be preserved. A copy of this letter (and any returned mail) should be placed in each client's file. Post a copy of this letter in your office and any other suitable places. Have your staff remind clients of the date of your closing your practice. Finally, place copies with your will, your life insurance policy, and other places your successor might look.

Legal consultants have recommended to physicians an even stricter policy. They suggest sending the above-described letter by registered mail (return receipt requested) for high-risk patients. They suggest that you enclose a medical record release authorization form (for requesting copies and transferring records to another physician), state the length of time (in years) that the records will be retained, and provide a permanent mailing address or post office box number for all future record requests. You must arrange for someone to maintain the address and respond to requests for records, for the time periods mentioned below.

The Duties of the Custodian of Your Case Records. You must protect your records' confidentiality and security (against theft, prying eyes, accidental discarding, etc.), preservation (against fire, rodents, water damage, etc.), and access (for a successor therapist, defense against a complaint or suit, response to a subpoena, etc.). These needs will be present even after your death or a client's. The following checklist will help you address them.

❑ Devise a letter of explanation for your successor therapist or custodian about your files. The letter should cover such items as how client records are filed and named (by last name, by date of last contact or discharge,[2] by a case number,[3] etc.) where they are kept,[4] the shorthand or abbreviations you have used in your notes, and destruction schedules and procedures. It may be appropriate to explain where to find the office keys and your appointment book (Spayd & Wiley, 2001).

❑ Close out case records with summaries, and bring all case notes up to date. Respond to any unfinished correspondence.

❑ Destroy some out-of-date records, following your usual procedures, so there will be less to transfer.

❑ Microfilming your records may make sense. Look under "Document Management" or "Records Management" for companies in the Yellow Pages.

❑ Actually transfer the records physically to your records' custodian, or contract to have this done.

❑ Send copies of the termination letter described earlier about closing your practice and who will have custody of your records to the following:

  ❑ Your state licensing board. If you wish either to surrender your license or to become inactive, request this as well.

  ❑ Your state, national, and other professional associations, and any other professional committees, groups, or organizations to which you belong or pay dues. Resign or choose an inactive status rather than letting your membership lapse for lack of dues.

---

[2]So that the files can be pruned regularly by destroying files older than the number of years they legally must be kept.

[3]And, if so, where to find the cross-index of names and numbers.

[4]With the keys for your locked files and the locations and passwords for your computerized records, both clinical and financial.

❑ Your referral resources, and those who refer to you.

❑ Your professional friends.

❑ Your professional insurance carrier.

❑ Your billing service, if you use one.

❑ Your business and personal lawyers.

❑ All health plans with which you have done business (prepare a list of these organizations). Note that the letter described earlier may not be sufficient for such organizations if you must also address the issues of unpaid bills.

Your Financial and Contractual Obligations. The following checklist will aid you in resolving any outstanding financial or contractual issues.

❑ Meet with your lawyer, banker, accountant, financial advisor, and others to review any unmet obligations you have. Draft any needed letters, notifications, forms, or agreements.

❑ Review the procedures for dissolution that are written into any partnership, professional corporation, or professional association agreements. Take the appropriate legal, financial, or other actions.

❑ Deal with all your rental agreements and leases—office space, cars, equipment, utilities, telephone, Internet access, advertising contracts (Yellow Pages), websites/pages, cleaning contracts, and so on.

❑ Devise a plan for the formal dissolution of your business entity (i.e., distribution and liquidation of assets; notification of the appropriate state authorities, such as the Secretary of State; business account dealings). Your professional lawyer should handle this along with your accountant, so make sure they are notified of your circumstances.

❑ Arrange to dispose of your real assets. Used office equipment typically brings 10 to 50 cents on the dollar, depending on age and condition. Decide who is to receive it, or donate, sell, or otherwise dispose of your office equipment, supplies, and any other real property or real estate.

❑ Decide about your accounts payable and accounts receivable. Decide on an appropriate collection process and assign responsibility for it.

❑ Create a plan to make timely payments of federal, state, local, and other taxes; employee insurance; workers' compensation premiums; and the like.

❑ Make arrangements for ethical disposal, sale, or transfer of your psychological tests, library, biofeedback equipment, or other professional materials.

❑ Make arrangements for your professional liability insurance. Purchase a "tail" for your professional liability insurance if you have a "claims-made" policy (see Section 3.3). You (or your estate) can still be sued or complained against after you close up shop, and a tail protects against future complaints about your previous actions. Some insurance companies offer this at no cost if you have been a client for a while, but they must be notified. If you have the time and have had a number of high-risk cases, consider raising your coverage significantly for the last year of your practice, as your tail's limits will be based on the coverage limits in force during this time.

❑ Do not cancel premises insurance when you move out; wait until you are no longer the legal tenant.

❑ Consider cancelling your journal subscriptions. What professional roles do you intend to maintain in retirement?

If You Should Suddenly Become Incapacitated or Die

If you become incapacitated, there are at least three professional roles for which you should leave instructions so these can be filled by one or more persons. A **successor professional** will provide at least emergency or brief services (as a "bridge therapist") to your clients and may take on their cases. It would be best to have several named successors, in case one is unavailable when an emergency arises. Second, the **executor of your professional will** is the one responsible for carrying out its provisions. Last, the **custodian of your records** maintains their security and legal release. This may be the same person as either of the others, but can be different for reasons of practical access and longevity. Do not simply ask a friend or friends to assume these obligations as a personal favor; too much is involved. Select and negotiate these functions with trusted colleagues. Arrange remuneration for each role out of your collectibles or estate. Pay the custodian for the costs of storage and the burdens of maintaining the security and potential access as a necessary expense of your retirement or estate.

Devise now a contingency plan for your practice. Then discuss it with your family, some colleagues, and your staff, and arrange for your lawyer to incorporate it into your personal will. Assure that your plan, which is called here a **"letter of instructions,"** is very readily accessible to all those who must carry out your directions. It should address all the concerns and issues raised above, as well as some that arise because of sudden loss. The checklist that follows can guide you in devising a contingency plan.

❑ Arrange for a staff member, specific friend, or family member to notify others of your disability or death. Besides those described above, rapid notification should be given to your professional and family lawyers and your accountant. You should include all the ways of reaching each of these persons in your letter of instructions.

❑ Because a situation might arise suddenly in which you are unavailable, a list of all of the ways and places in which you could be contacted by those concerned about your well-being should be easily available to your staff and family. Your staff should have "all contact information for [your] spouse, life partner, adult children, or anyone else who would likely know of [your] whereabouts or sudden health problems" (Tracy, n.d.). Tracy suggests that staff members should be formally permitted to make such calls and be told to wait no longer than an hour after your unexplained absence before making such calls. Train your staff in all these procedures.

❑ Since I have recommended that all records be maintained indefinitely, your custodian will have to make a similar "professional will" for the maintenance of your records in the event of his or her own retirement, disability, or death. (This could lead to an infinite regress; 25 years after treatment should cover all but infinitesimal risks.)

❑ If you have not prepared a termination letter (see above), your executor should be instructed to write a brief letter explaining your death or incapacity and the closing of your practice. This can be given to all current clients and mailed to all recent clients so that all are informed rapidly, explicitly, and simultaneously. It should address the relevant issues described here, such as access to records and referrals. In addition, the executor should place a notice of your demise in the local newspaper of record.

❑ You should also write an obituary for yourself, rather than burdening others with this responsibility. It should contain at least the facts of your life. See your current newspaper for guidelines. Keep it in your strongbox at home or with your lawyer.

❑ Arrange a method to remind yourself regularly to review and update your letter of instructions as necessary. Your practice or that of your executor may have changed.

❑ If you should die unexpectedly, a brief message should be placed on your voice mail or answering machine, or with your answering service, for future potential clients who call your office when referred by friends, colleagues, or advertisements. Try to arrange for these messages to be available for the next 12–18 months.

❑ Prepare a brief version of your termination letter for your successor professional to send to those who call and in reply to any professional mail you receive. This letter should explain the circumstances and suggests options.

❑ You must be explicit about your accounts receivable. Make sure your executor can legally accept monies due you and pay your bills.

❑ Create a plan for your professional successor to make timely payments of federal, state, local, and other taxes; employee insurance; workers' compensation premiums; and the like.

There are a number of resources for creating a professional will. Ragusea (2002) is fairly complete. Eric Marine (n.d.) has an online article on this from a risk management perspective, and the book by Pope and Vasquez (2005) has a chapter on this topic as well.

CHAPTER 2

Financial Tools and Procedures

2.1 Setting Financial Policies for Your Practice

Money matters will be treated by cultured people in the same manner as sexual matters, with the same inconsistency, prudishness, and hypocrisy. The therapist must be determined not to concur in this attitude, and in his [sic] dealings with patients to treat money matters with the same matter-of-course frankness that he wishes to induce in them in matters relating to sexual life.
—SIGMUND FREUD (1913/1958, p. 131)

The provision of therapy is both a business and a profession. As a business, it involves unavoidable dealings with money, and this is often problematic for therapists. They enter the field with a commitment to human service. Many have been trained at public expense or have worked in a public service setting; they may believe that making a profit from the misery in others' lives is unjust. However, the simple truth is that a therapist who does not succeed as a businessperson will not be able to work independently.

As a therapist, you *must* make decisions about many aspects of the business relationship with your clients. Choose options that seem fair, protective of both parties, and enforceable; then communicate them clearly, both orally and in writing. You will need policies to answer the following questions:

- When will you discuss money with the client?

- How much will you charge?

    Will you have different charges for different activities, or a per-hour charge for everything you do?

    Will you give discounts, do free therapy, or use a sliding scale of charges based on income?

    Will you charge for broken appointments, and if so, how much?

- How will you handle insurance coverage?

    Will you accept only what the client's insurance will pay, and not collect anything from the client? (The insurers view this as potential fraud; see below.)

    Will you require "assignment of benefits" and be paid directly by the insurance company, or will you trust the client to pay you?

    Will you prepare insurance claim forms for patients, or simply supply a bill they can submit?

    Will you join managed care organizations' (MCOs') "panels" of providers and "participate" (i.e., agree to provide services at the rates set by third-party payers)?

- How will you handle delinquent accounts and when?

    Will you only send reminders and rebill, or use collection letters?

    At what point will you use collection agencies? Lawyers? Small-claims court? When will you write off bad debts?

    When will you discontinue seeing a patient for not paying your fees?

When you have made these decisions, incorporate them into your means of gaining informed consent (see Section 4.2, the client information brochure).

About Fees

Because few professional training programs teach about fees, some basics are covered here.

One of the "professional pleasures" offered by private practice is the freedom to take on a case that interests you without regard to the client's ability to pay. Do not let greed or fear take away this freedom. As you might guess, the belief that "paying for therapy is therapeutic" is endorsed most strongly by psychoanalysts and least strongly by social workers. It has repeatedly not been scientifically supported, and its popularity is generally declining. Reviews of the literature found no clear relationship between fee paying and outcome (Pope et al., 1975; Herron & Sitkowski, 1986). Ethically, free therapy cannot be of a lesser quality than paid therapy, so do not try to cut corners; learn to live with this, or do not do *pro bono* (unpaid) work at all. The American Psychological Association (APA) strongly recommends that all psychologists do some unpaid work. The amount of such work is left to the conscience of the individual clinician. Many therapists dedicate a percentage (5–15%) of their practice to *pro bono* services as part of their responsibility to society. If a client has an unexpected and long-lasting loss of income, and neither termination nor transfer is desirable, you might consider your work *pro bono* and bite the bullet.

Finally, if you are terminating a client for lack of payment, be cautious and thorough, and try to get a payment plan agreed to. If it appears that it will be a sticky situation, consult with a colleague about issues of abandonment, client welfare, and the like, and note the consultation in your records. See also Section 6.3 on termination.

Ethical Guidelines on Fees

Pope (1988c) has examined the laws and ethics pertaining to fee policies and procedures. The following discussion is based on his suggestions for avoiding common pitfalls.

Ethically, you must make financial arrangements in advance of treatment, so that consent to treatment is fully informed. Standard 6.04a of the APA ethics code (APA, 2002) requires that "As early as feasible in a professional or scientific relationship, [the psychologist] and the client/patient or other recipient of psychological services reach an agreement specifying the compensation and the billing arrangements." It is best to have clients know your charges before you even meet for the first time, so that they are not seduced by your interview into forming a relationship that then imposes financial hardship or is even exploitative.

Tell the client your policies on raising fees during the course of treatment, charging for missed appointments, the maximum balance due you will tolerate, your use of a collection agency, and so forth. Make certain that the financial arrangements are fully understood by the client. For this a written fee policy is essential, and this policy should be stated in your client information brochure.

You should know by the end of the first evaluation hour, from the social history information you have obtained, whether a client is able to pay you. **Therefore, give no "free initial consultations,"** because the client is by then committed to you, having revealed his or her personal issues. (This is called "undue influence" by lawyers.) Also, charging from the beginning of therapy sets a positive and equitable expectation that the client will indeed get and has a right to "what he or she paid for."

You may decide for marketing or clinical reasons to offer a "free introductory consultation" to allow the client to get a sense of "how well we may work together." Harry Corsover, PhD, and Linda Azzi, RN, BS, of Evergreen, CO, offer a nice option they term "Intro+." This is "the free intro and time in our schedule to move right into a session if that is what [potential clients] choose. We say on the phone that most people choose the latter, since if they come here and decide to work with us, they would rather get started right away than have to go home and come back another day" (H. Corsover, personal communication, September 22, 2007).

Fee splitting—that is, taking a fee or paying a percentage or dollar amount solely for making a referral—is still open to interpretation. Although payment in other businesses for referrals is common and accepted, it creates a conflict in human services: Did you refer the client to Dr. F because he or she was the best clinician for that client, or because you were paid a fee by Dr. F? In an agreement with the Federal Trade Commission (APA, 1992), the APA agreed not to prohibit paying for referrals. The rules in psychology (APA, 2002, Standard 6.07) allow fee splitting when the dividing of payment is based on the services provided (such as evaluation and recommendations) and not simply on making the referral. However, this is too vague to enforce, local rules differ, and arrangements are often complex. It is best to avoid even the appearance of fee splitting. Do not take payment of any kind for a referral, and be careful that you can justify the clinical appropriateness of a referral to a specific clinician—especially when you share an office, are friends, or have any kind of business connections.

Accepting payment for your services in anything but money is "**barter.**" Barter is an ancient, flexible, and honorable method, and gives more people access to your services. The APA code of ethics (APA, 2002, Standard 6.05) allows barter and offers some minimal standards and guidelines. Woody (1999) offers a thoughtful discussion of the risks and guidelines if you wish to use barter. However, barter presents great potential for abuse, exploitation, conflicts, and distortion of the professional relationship. I strongly recommend that you **do not barter** or exchange therapy for either goods (whose value can be questioned) or services (as this creates a dual relationship—i.e., that of employer–employee). Barter is a frequent source of ethics complaints. If a client has no money and you wish to help, offer your services *pro bono.*

Setting Your Fee

Your "fee" is the amount you are willing to sell your services for. This should be the same as the amount you actually charge every client. Routinely accepting a lower fee by waiving insurance copayments is seen as fraud by third-party payers; when you do this, your actual, collected fee is not the stated amount you are charging the insurers. If you decide to accept a lower payment from a client in financial distress or for any other reason, do so only occasionally, with good reasons, and document your rationale in detail in your notes. Make sure you can justify the fee you set for each client; you may have to.

There is no standard method for setting fees; but here are some options:

- **Cost-plus pricing** is determining your fee by adding together your fixed and variable costs plus a profit. This is the traditional pricing method in many businesses, although not in private practice. If you take the time to compute your costs (your "nut"), it will allow you to know whether you are really making a go of your practice. However, do not try to add, say, 10% for "administrative expenses" when a patient requires billing or add on 20% for "extended contacts with MCOs and authorization." First, your contract with an MCO will clearly state that you may not bill any of its clients separately for any other charges and that the MCO will not pay such charges. Second, the MCO will see this as illegal because you will be charging insurance-covered patients a higher fee, not your agreed-to fee.

- **Competitive pricing** is setting your prices to match, exceed, or underprice your competition, depending on whom you see as your competitors. Psychiatrists charge the most, with psychologists charging 80–90% of that, and social workers charging 70% or less. Counselors and psychiatric nurses charge about 50%. The newsletter *Psychotherapy Finances* publishes a fee survey each year, with enlightening information and comparisons.

  One last point about comparative fee setting deserves mention. Because of antitrust laws, professionals cannot conspire with each other in order to fix rates. You cannot say to another practitioner, "I won't accept less than $75 an hour, and you shouldn't either." On the other hand, professionals are free to exchange information about rates (as above), just as "advertising one's rates in the Yellow Pages, in brochures, or as part of written practice policies is okay. In fact, it may be very helpful to the competitive process" (Sahid, 1998). Sahid offers these basic rules: "1. Practitioners should not discuss their fees with competitors. 2. Never suggest a fee as a line-in-the-sand that would prompt a boycott or refusal to contract with a managed care firm. 3. If you sign a contract with a managed care firm, the rate agreed to is your fee."

- **Pricing by negotiation** is accepting a price that is arranged in the marketplace of buyers and sellers. With private-pay patients, be mindful that they are needy and therefore not your equals in negotiating a fee. The negotiation process requires self-esteem and autonomy, which patients often lack. They also usually lack an appreciation of your (quite high) costs in providing your services. As you know, the actual buyers of mental health services for many clients are their employers or their employers' delegates—the whole panoply of MCO contractors. They do not appear to lack self-confidence and negotiation resources. Although there are alternatives to managed care (see especially Ackley, 1997; LoPresti & Zuckerman, 2004) developing a knowledge base in this area will be essential for most therapists.

- **Pricing by time** is charging for your time, regardless of the services provided (therapy, consulting, teaching, supervising, etc.). Because it is rarely possible to charge for preparation, teaching and lecturing tend to be underbilled. You can try to reduce these costs by specializing in only a few topics at a time and by selling these preparations to several audiences.

- **Pricing by setting an income goal** is choosing a yearly income goal, dividing it by the number of hours you want to work, and calculating your hourly charge. This is worth considering for life or financial planning. Is this a self-esteem test? Is this a test of how role-socialized you are? Did you pass?

Other Fee Arrangements

Offering Discounts

Discounts can take several forms. First, MCOs demand a lower fee, with the rationale that it is a discount for a bulk order. They promise to send you many referrals, keep you busy, and fill your empty hours, and so they contend that they deserve a lower price than if you had to recruit and negotiate with one client at a time. See Section 3.11 for more on managed care.

You can offer discounts for various reasons, and most businesses do. However, you must make the rationale perfectly clear to the client and any insurance company, make it consistent with your state's insurance and business laws, and be entirely consistent in its application. It is altogether proper to offer clients who need less of your time a lower fee. A 20% discount for clients who pay by check, cash, or credit card at the time of service and do not need any paperwork or phone calls for insurance or any other reason is justified. Clients usually feel that they got a bargain and earned the discount. Sending a yearly statement indicating only dates of service and payments made without a diagnosis or procedure code and to be used for the client's income taxes or medical savings account is the only paperwork provided. This is the policy of the Boulder, CO, Psychotherapists' Guild (www.psychotherapistsguild.com). Another inventive, successful, and encouraging option has been developed by Volunteers in Psychotherapy of West Hartford, CT (www.ctvip.org/scripts/index.asp), which describes itself as "a community nonprofit organization that provides truly private psychotherapy for no fee (or a low fee). Clients 'pay for' their therapy by doing independent volunteer work for the charity of their choice," and the more they volunteer the less they pay. With this plan, all managed care intrusions are avoided—no reports, no confidentiality issues, no limits on treatment length or type (e.g., medications may be offered too). Others have tried this as well, so it may work for your setting.

Charles H. Steinmeyer, PhD, of Warren, PA, offers what he calls "no-nonsense fees" for therapy and consultations, which make the discounts more specific. From his established fee, he deducts dollar amounts for no phone calls to MCOs or insurance companies, for no filling of claims forms, for no reports or treatment plans sent, and finally for no bills sent. If any of these are needed later, he charges for them at the rates indicated originally. The results are complete confidentiality, no nasty surprises if an MCO refuses to pay, and a predictable cash flow for both parties.

Sliding Fees

Sliding fee scales provide discounts, but often awkward ones. Unless their use is proceduralized, they are discriminatory, and any rule will be unfair to some clients because everyone's circumstances are different. Also, since you are no longer charging everyone the same fee, insurers may see this as at least a violation of your contract. See below.

Treating an MCO Patient without Using MCO Benefits

Making arrangements for payment with an MCO patient is complicated by your contract with the MCO. If you are on the panel and the patient wants to use MCO coverage, you are obligated to accept the MCO fee you agreed to as full payment and not to bill the patient for the difference between that fee and your (usually much higher), regular fee (this is called "balance billing"; see Section 2.5). However, if the patient does not wish to use his or her MCO coverage, or if the service you will provide is not covered by your or the client's MCO contract, or if the benefits have been used up or have been denied, then you and the client can work out any mutually agreeable financial arrangement.

Self-Pay Arrangements for Confidentiality

If you offer clients the option of not using their health insurance, the records you create (which you must keep both to be ethical and to protect yourself) need never leave your office. However, the clients are very likely to be asked in the future, "Have you ever been treated for a mental disorder?" or something similar. Should they say no, knowing that your records will not then be requested? What about some future legal proceeding that brings their current mental state into question and for which your records may help them (or not)? When I have raised this question with my peers, I have received several suggested courses of action.

If a client wants to consult you about a "problem in living" and you work on that, with no mention of a "psychological condition," then the client can answer honestly that no such condition was diagnosed or treated. Similarly, Miller (2001) has indicated:

> I consider a diagnostic evaluation to be a separate service that I only conduct if the patient requests it. Therefore, when I see a self-pay client, I do not record a diagnosis. . . . for the vast majority of my clients, I am providing psychological consultation for personal and interpersonal issues. In other words, my clients are merely exercising their right to talk with or consult with a psychologist, and there is no reason that they need to carry a DSM-IV diagnosis because they wanted to exercise that right. Therefore, if I have not diagnosed them, they can say that they have never been treated for a psychiatric condition. (Miller, 2001, p. 78)

Miller (2001) also reports on a survey of psychologists that supported this position in hearings by the Colorado licensing board, which was considering requiring a DSM-IV diagnosis and other clinical information on each case.

> Consumers only want a diagnosis when it will clearly lead to better treatment or some benefit greater than the potential discrimination or stigma. In psychotherapy, many times the DSM-IV diagnosis does little to guide treatment, and it is often not necessary. Moreover, there is no clear dividing line between psychotherapy and the processes of problem solving, consultation, or coaching—services that do not require a diagnosis. Considering the negative repercussions of a mental health diagnosis, it is not surprising that in many situations consumers wish to be able to talk with a professional or use the tool of psychotherapy without either a diagnostic evaluation being conducted or a diagnosis being recorded. The petition documents that a large portion of psychologists support the right to talk with a mental health professional without receiving a formal diagnosis. (Miller, 2001, p. 78)

Pricing Forensic Services

Forensic testifying is commonly billed at double your clinical rate and includes all time out of the office (i.e., travel time), because your time to testify is so unpredictable that you should not schedule any clients afterward. Charging for half a day is a common minimum, as is requiring to be paid several days before testifying. Of course, never either accept or defer a fee contingent on the case's outcome, because this will be seen as compromising the independence of your opinions. (Expect to be asked about this by opposing counsel.) You are likely to be asked to meet with "your" attorney beforehand and should bill for this time, as for any other services to clients. Be careful with any notes you might take at this meeting, as they are "discoverable" (i.e., subject to a subpoena) by the other side.

Providing a deposition in your office is simpler than actually testifying, and so charging your usual clinical fee, plus the time needed to review your files or other related activities, is reasonable. For any deposition, negotiate with the attorney the number of hours, keeping in mind the number of clients you must cancel and reschedule. To be sure of maintaining your independence and being paid in advance, ask the lawyer involved to pay you a retainer fee in advance. Ask for more than you expect, and promise to return any unused amounts. Formal retainer agreements vary greatly in detail and size, from half a page (see "retainer agreement" under "the therapy investment" at www.cullagunabeach. com/ti.php) to 12 pages (at www.lawandpsychiatry.com). Reading these documents is a cheap education before signing one.

Again, make certain to be paid in advance, and stop when the paid time is up. It is not uncommon for depositions to take longer than expected, and for attorneys to try to get you to bill opposing counsel for the additional time, so be assertive. Any case materials you bring to a deposition are likely to be copied for the other side, so be very selective and don't let an attorney have any originals.

Pricing School Services

If you plan to do school consultation or training, develop a letter explaining your services (in nontechnical terms, if possible) and fee schedules. Give it to any school personnel who inquire about your services, and provide an estimate of the amount of your time required. Their response should be an authorizing note and signature on the estimate, or a letter agreeing to accept responsibility to pay for the services.

If a parent wants to use some insurance or agency resources to pay your fees, make it clear that you will bill the parents; that they must talk to a case manager to arrange payment for your several hours of consulting; and that this service is not testing or therapy and will not be billed at a discounted rate under any MCO or health maintenance organization (HMO) plan. You may have success in getting the school to pay for your staff training services after you have done your work with the child (and thus make your fees a worthwhile cost to the parents), especially if the previously provided school services have been unproductive.

Discussing Fees

The resistance to setting up a fee arrangement in the first session comes almost completely from the therapist. If you say, "We can worry about the money later," you are increasing your uncollectable fees by 20%. It is also unethical because it prevents informed consent. One simple way of discussing fees is to raise the issue toward the end of the first session, after you have discussed the length of treatment. I have used phrasing like this:

> "There is one more issue we must talk about, and that is fees. My regular fee is $_____ per session. Take a minute and consider what I have said about how long your treatment should take, and weigh your income and expenses, and tell me if you can afford that."

I find that most clients agree to pay this amount. If they say they cannot or appear very reluctant, I usually say, "Well, in light of your situation, tell me what you can afford and I will accept that."

I have used this policy for years with few abuses or regrets. If you adopt it, be aware that you are at risk even if you do not put anything like this in your client information brochure, because a patient may complain. It is better to develop a credit policy for all patients. This is also a good time to introduce or reinforce paying for each session at its end. Note that these policies do not apply to those who have you bill their insurers or use MCOs.

If someone other than the client pays the fee, make that responsibility clear to the payer with a formal agreement (see Form 29). Also make it clear that this arrangement does not entitle the payer to confidential information. When the client is a child, however, parents do have the right to general information on progress. This should be spelled out in detail in your client information brochure (see Section 4.2).

Tips on Collecting Fees

- **Simply do not allow clients to run up large unpaid bills.** You should allow no more than two sessions without payment to elapse before you raise the issue with a patient, because you cannot terminate a client in great psychological need just for financial problems. If you extend credit, you should set a dollar limit, such as $1,000, on a maximum balance. Do not try to charge interest on the balance, as you then have to complete state and federal legal agreements as a creditor (according to the Truth in Lending Act of 1968), which are quite burdensome. There is also an ethical aspect of extending credit by allowing an unpaid bill. As Gordon Herz, PhD, of Madison, WI, notes (personal communication, August 27, 2000), you are in effect entering into a dual relationship with the client: both therapist needing care and creditor/collector, with very different goals, rules, and methods.

- Big balances may tempt patients to devise malpractice suits or ethics complaints to escape them. This is a major source of such complaints.

- The longer the delay, the smaller the collection. The established wisdom of collection agents is that if a payment is over 90 days late, you will collect 50% or less.

- If you allow a patient not to pay, you will both feel rotten. Your not handling disagreeable and important issues or delaying their handling sets a poor example. The patient may come to believe that you are not a good therapist.

- You may need a simple book of two-part receipts for the few patients who pay cash. Don't waste your money on custom-printed receipts unless you use the form for other purposes (see Form 4).

- If a client gives you a check that makes you suspicious, cash it *immediately* at the client's bank. If the account does not have sufficient funds, don't try again until you know the check will clear—you can call the bank every day or two and ask if the funds are there. When the account has the funds, cash the check immediately.

2.2   The Income and Expense Records

A record of your income is essential and can be as simple as a single page of inexpensive, ruled 8½" × 11" accounting paper for each month with appropriate column headings. Figure 2 shows the type of income record I use, shortened here for space reasons. Most of it is self-explanatory, but a few details require comment. Initials are added for names that are common. The columns of income correspond to tax needs. I have two offices in different communities, so taxes are paid to two municipalities. Paychecks, from which taxes have already been deducted, are recorded in the third column. The "Other" column is reserved for special income that does not fit these labels. I cluster the checks in each deposit with a large bracket, and write the total amount and date of deposit in the last column. You should adapt the form to your style and needs.

Monthly Income Record

For: _July 2008_

Date	Check #	Source of income	Office 1	Office 2	Paychecks	Other	Deposits
4	207	Lenin	100				
	456	Nixon	75				
6	129	Stalin		100			575.00 (7/10)
8	567	Hoover, J. E.		200(I)[1]			
	130	Stalin		100			
11	—	Lenin	100($)[2]				
	459	Nixon	75				
12	938	Bonaparte		68			1,064.33 (7/17)
14	004	Lecture to CIA				100	
15	888	Lecture to NSA				100	
15	996	NIMH			621.33		
Subtotals			350	468	621.33	200	
Grand total							1,639.33

[1]If it was an insurance payment, a letter "I" can be inserted to clarify the source.

[2]If a client pays you in cash, you can insert "$" to keep your records clear.

FIGURE 2. Sample monthly income record.

Your Checkbook

There are two components to recording your professional expenses. The first is your business checkbook, and the second is an expense summary, completed on a monthly or quarterly basis. A checking account used exclusively for your practice is crucial in business record keeping. A checking account is also essential for paying your business-related obligations. Try to avoid getting a business account, which has all kinds of fancy expenses associated with it. A personal account may also make it easier to get a card to use automatic teller machines for convenient deposits. Choose the least expensive account possible.

Remember that every legitimate and necessary business expense (because it is deductible against income) is really very valuable to you. The true cost of purchases for your business is about 50% of what you pay, because they are tax-deductible, and you are probably in the 50% tax bracket (federal income tax of 28%, state and perhaps local income taxes of about 5%, FICA of 15.7%, sales tax of about 6%, etc.). This is the way the U.S. Congress, in its wisdom, has set up the country. Enjoy it. Buy whatever will make your business easier and more efficient.

Choosing a Business Credit Card

Although the issue of a business credit card is not directly connected with that of a business checking account, I'd like to mention it briefly in passing. It makes sense to get a separate credit card for your business and avoid using it for personal purchases. If you have more than one business, get a card for each. Write a note on an adhesive slip on each card to keep each card's use clear. Get bank cards (Visa or MasterCard) for all your accounts to save costs. The "Gold" versions are as good as the private cards in terms of offered services you really can use, such as rental car insurance coverage. If you maintain a large balance each month, look for the lowest interest rates; if you pay off your balance, look for no yearly fees, and lowest costs for advances and other fees.

Monthly/Quarterly Expense Summary

FORM 3

The second step in systematic recording of expenses is having a running summary of your expenses. Form 3 offers headings in standard accounting format that match the categories on business and personal income tax forms. You need enter only each expense's date and amount, and so you can place many checks, receipts, bills, and so forth on the same horizontal line. The line and section totals (e.g., auto expenses) can be entered into your federal and state quarterly estimated income tax forms, so that you do not overpay or underpay your taxes. When you have completed a year's worth of these, you will also have a good sense of where your money is going, feel more comfortable with the business side of your practice, and be able to plan better.

2.3   Methods of Billing

To save yourself grief, find a billing method that works for you in terms of your resources (time, secretarial help, computer access, size of your practice), and use it until something *markedly* better comes along. The common options are covered below.

Whichever of the following options you choose, **you should bill often**. I know this is a burden, but you will collect more money in the long run.

The simplest and cheapest method of billing is *not* having to bill: Have clients pay at the time of each session.

Credit Cards

The second simplest method of billing is to accept credit card payments. This ensures full payment, avoids the delay of billing, and makes payment certain. Business supply stores and banks can help you become a "vendor" or open a "merchant account" to accept credit cards. Be warned, however, that credit card companies have sold their lists of transactions, so you should inquire about the card issuer's privacy policies to avoid embarrassing your clients in the future.

For charging clients' cards, have them sign a credit/debit card payment consent form, so you can then indicate that you have their "signatures on file." For an example of this form, see www.therapymatch.com (then "Office Management" at the top, and then "Our Merchant Solutions" at the bottom).

Costs for becoming a credit card "merchant" vary greatly. You should consider the length

Business Expenses

Month: _____ or Quarter: 1 2 3 4 of Year: _____

	1	2	3	4	Total
Prof. services: Accounting					
Legal expenses					
Secretarial					
Supervision/consultation					
Professional liability insurance					
Professional licenses					
Professional library					
Professional dues					
Advertising					
Auto expenses: Loan					
Fuel					
Insurance					
Repairs					
Supplies					
Registration fees					
Other					
Bank fees, checks					
Business entertainment					
Business gifts					
Office expenses: Supplies					
Supplies					
Equipment					
Subscriptions					
Rent(s)					
Telephone					
Answering service					
Utilities					
Repairs					
Postage					
Printing					
Refunds given					
Taxes paid (on business):					
Business privilege					
Property					
Sales					
Training/Prof. development					
Travel, meals					
Miscellaneous (small amounts):					
Other (specify reason & payee):					
Cash expenses (total and staple receipts on back):					

FORM 3. Monthly/quarterly expense summary. From *The Paper Office*. Copyright 2008 by Edward L. Zuckerman. Permission to photocopy this form is granted to purchasers of this book for personal use only (see copyright page for details).

of the contract, the likely total amount you will be charging per month, the set-up fees and account fees, and the costs of equipment. The level of service is important for those not sophisticated about business, so check for telephone support and online access to your account. Investigate business memberships at Sam's Club (www.samsclub.com, then "Services" at the top, and then "Merchant Credit Card Processing") and Costco (www.costco.com, then "Business," at the top, then "Business Services," and then "Merchant Credit Card Processing"). Each of these can make you a vendor with little hassle and low fees, and each offers other low-cost services, such as business printing and websites. Your profession's associations may also have good credit card processing arrangements and the vendor will be familiar with therapists' practices. If you want to avoid these connections, PayPal can allow you to accept credit cards online with a "virtual terminal" (www.paypal.com, then "Merchants," then "accept credit cards online").

Offering the convenience and payment deferral of credit card charging has become very popular and productive for therapists, and this should increase with the use of flexible spending accounts (FSAs) for health care. For more on these, see www.fsaplan.info, for example.

Statements

Most clients need records of the services received and of their payments to you, for tax purposes or for reimbursement from health insurance.

If your office help is cheap and reliable, sending out statements could work for you. Use a statement card, writing in each month's contacts, charges, and payments, and then compute a balance due. Then send out a photocopy of this 5¾" × 8½" card each month in a #9 window envelope. Medical printers offer the materials needed.

FORM 4   Some therapists, in lieu of a bill, provide the patient with a form like Form 4 after every visit. Professional billers call it "a walk-out statement." It has the advantages of (1) replacing a monthly cumulative "statement"; (2) providing a reminder at the end of the session to pay and a receipt for payments made; (3) indicating and reminding the client of the next appointment; and (4) being a record of services provided for client-submitted insurance claims.

Form 4 also documents each visit with a signature and confirms the client's consent to receiving services. You can use this form when you think a client has some undefined or unarticulated reluctance about treatment; have the client sign the form as soon as he or she comes in. Clients will go along with almost any procedure if you make it seem matter-of-fact and customary. Lastly, the form reinforces the client's assumption of financial responsibility for your fees.

This form is based on one used by Irvin P. R. Guyett, PhD, of Pittsburgh, PA. If you want to print it up by the hundreds, it can be made into a no-carbon-required form, which will create a copy for the client and one for you or your bill-generating person. In the space after "NPI," put your national provider identifier (see Section 2.5). You can replace "State license" with another indication that you are a credentialed and payable professional, if you so desire. On the line for diagnoses, you can enter either the name or ICD code number or both. Using only the code number may increase confidentiality. Under "Services performed," you can print appropriate codes and their titles as well, although none are

Record of Services Provided

NPI: _____ State license #: _____

Client: _____ Date of service: _____

Diagnoses: _____

Services performed (CPT or other codes):   Service location (if different from above):

_____   _____

_____   _____

This is session number _____ of a total of _____ visits authorized by your managed care organization on _____.

Fee	Adjustment	Charges	Amount paid	Balance due

Signature of client, which indicates consent to services and acceptance of final responsibility for payment, regardless of any third-party benefits: _____

Therapist's signature: _____

Date of our next appointment: _____, the _____ of _____, at time _____ A.M./P.M.

FORM 4. Record of services provided. Adapted from a form devised by Irvin P. R. Guyett, PhD, of Pittsburgh, PA, and used by permission of Dr. Guyett.—From *The Paper Office*. Permission to photocopy this form is granted to purchasers of this book for personal use only (see copyright page for details).

offered here because they change fairly often (for a discussion of *Current Procedural Terminology* [CPT] codes, see Section 2.5).

Any client submitting an MCO insurance claim will need to have a CMS-1500 form completed (see Section 2.5) or a similar form devised by his or her MCO. However, for "self-pay" clients, Form 4 can be modified to meet the client's information needs for tax purposes or reimbursement by simply adding a column at the left side for the dates of service.

Each session gets its own line. It may seem distrustful, but when you complete the form, routinely initialing or signing under the last visit entry will discourage the client from adding sessions to increase a deductible medical expense or illegally recover additional reimbursement.[1] You can use the back of your original to record when you mailed the last copy of this form or any special financial arrangements you made. Keeping the original in the front of the client's case file can help you know the client's balance and address any payment problems early.

SuperΨbills

Some therapists have adopted the SuperΨbill approach. It has a three-part "no-carbon-required" form with diagnostic codes, patient insurance submission instructions, service codes, and your practice's identification imprinted on it. You only have to make checkoffs and mail it out. Medical printers can supply these, and some computerized billing programs will print a kind of "superbill."

Completing the CMS-1500 Standard Billing Form

If all you need is to complete the CMS-1500 form to send to insurance companies, you can do so easily. Some companies will accept photocopies of this red form, but if not, you can make up a master copy for each patient and photocopy it. Each time you submit a claim, add session dates and other information, and photocopy the master to send out. Blank forms are available cheaply from online suppliers such as www.filerx.com and pmiconline.com—search for "CMS-1500." Computer programs that keep track of your clients' information and then print it onto blank red forms are big time savers and cost about $100. The following were available at this writing: *Just Claims* from www.medisoft.com; *EZClaim* from www.ezclaim.com; *EASYCMS-1500 Form Filler* from www.littleguysoftware.com; and *HCFA Form Manager 2007* from www.econsoft.com/generic30.html.

Computerized Billing Programs

Mental health billing is the most complex area of medical billing. To meet the needs of practitioners, there are about 25 computerized billing programs publicly available. Some are slightly adapted from medical programs designed for large practices, and some have been in the mental health field for more than 10 years. Price depends on features and sup-

---

[1] If you are concerned with this kind of fraud, and if you complete bills on a computer, try to choose a font not widely available so that your bill cannot be added to without making the additions obvious. Thousands of fonts are available on the Internet at no cost.

port, not the size of your practice, so buy what works for you after you test their demos. Those called "office management" programs do scheduling, note making, and similar tasks, as well as billing. All are compliant with the Health Insurance Portability ands Accountability Act (HIPAA) by now. Programs construct a bill to give to clients, track MCOs' session limits, bill multiple payers separately, keep progress notes, send out reminders, and help with treatment planning. The evaluation of these programs is beyond the scope of this chapter, but if you bill more than 25 clients a month and do not have an ace billing person working for you, you should investigate them. Most are advertised in your professional newsletters.

Billing Services

There are companies that will do your billing for you. Look under "Billing Services" in the Yellow Pages or ask around. Billing services will provide a variety of valuable services, including allowing you to accept credit card payments, as well as electronic claim submission. They can bill all kind of insurers and third parties, using these parties' current forms, procedures, and policies, and with faster turnaround on your accounts receivable. They offer help with audits by payers, verification of benefits, and toll-free assistance, and they can save you postage (although your telephone bill may go up a little if you fax). They send nicely printed bills to the client, bills to third parties with all the needed information ("clean claims"), and monthly reports on the status of your accounts receivable. Because they receive your protected health information (PHI), you will need to have a business associates agreement with them to comply with HIPAA; they will usually supply the form. The cost to therapists is based on a percentage of the amount collected, usually between 6% and 8%. Before signing up, ask how they deal with billing mistakes—they should have at least a big "errors and omission" insurance policy. Evaluate the forms they want you to use, and how they deal with insurance company denials (do they simply pick the "low-hanging fruit" of easy cases, or are they persistent but not too aggressive?). Be sure to get and check some references, and to confirm how long they have been in business and how many clients they have. Remember, you will be held responsible for their actions—if not legally, then ethically (APA, 2002, Standard 6.06).

2.4   Collecting Overdue Fees from Clients

Note. Collecting from insurance companies is covered in Section 2.5.

Regular billing gives you a good grasp of your accounts, so that you will know when someone slips from 30 to 45 days behind. The later a client is in paying, the less likely it is that you will collect the full sum owed you; the curve is steep and negatively accelerated.

If you are squeamish about dunning your clients for money or think that it negatively affects the intimate therapeutic relationship, find another way to assure that you will be paid, or you will have to leave private practice. You can work it through with your own therapist (more work and more costly), hire someone to dun clients (cheaper and easier), use a paperwork solution such as that described below, or have your secretary (or spouse, calling as your office manager) call the slow payers.

However, keep in mind that collection efforts are a frequent cause of ethics complaints (see Section 3.1). Whichever method you choose, proceed with caution.

Calling the Client

A face-to-face discussion with you is the best, but a phone call is a good way to assure payment. A second choice is a personal call from a secretary or office manager. This has been shown to be many times more productive than using the mail. Be sure, though, that whoever makes the call understands the limitations on what he or she can do and say. Read up on the federal and state laws and practices in this area before starting. In general, the caller must always be polite, show concern for the client's best interests, listen to explanations, offer to work out a payment schedule, and follow up methodically. Calls may be made only between 8 A.M. and 9 P.M. The caller should carefully note his or her efforts and the client's response on a 3" × 5" "tickler card," which can go into your "tickler file."

The most common version of a tickler file is a set of index cards with spaces for the client's name and today's date. As of today, indicate the days the account is past due, the action taken, its results, and the follow-up date. Last, indicate the final action taken (amount paid, sent to collection, etc.). These cards are filed, and, after the action is performed, refiled behind 105 dividers: 3 sets of 31 for the days of the next 3 months, and 12 for the months of the year.

Sending a Note on the Bill

When there is a larger-than-expected unpaid balance, or a payment is more than 30 days late, I attach a yellow Post-it Note (removable so the bill can still be submitted to the insurance company) to the bill. Since such a client's case is usually closed, the note usually says something like "Is there some problem with this account?" or "Are you having a money problem?" or "Is there some trouble with your insurance company?" It then requests or informs the client of action: "Please call/talk to me if there is some difficulty with this," or "Can you pay me something on this account?" or "I will call you next week about this."

Sending Collection Letters

Collection letters seem to work better than notes on the bill. Meek (1987) provides an excellent discussion of such letters in just three pages. For those of you who have never received them, collection letters come in increasing intensity of wording (and often of paper color as well). The "first-level" notes are increasingly demanding in tone, but all indicate a willingness to talk and work out a payment plan. The "second-level" letter informs the client that you will no longer provide services until payment is made. The "third-level" letter threatens legal action.

Other Methods

If a bill is several years old, and you don't want to sue now but might in the future, you can extend the debt's payment time. Try to get an acknowledgment of the debt (by a dated signature on a letter), a small payment, or even a promise to pay. Sometimes people's financial situations change and they will actually pay their debts off. Ask; it's cheap to try.

As the third-level collection letter suggests, you can use small-claims court in your district. It is simple and cheap, and no lawyer or other professional is required. It is almost always successful, but you need to decide the following: (1) Have you tried all other methods first? (2) Is there anything to collect? Does the client have the money? and (3) Do you want to make an enemy for this much money?

The APA's ethics code allows the use of collection agencies, but you must inform the client first and provide him or her with the opportunity to pay before proceeding (APA, 2002, Standard 6.04e). Indeed, never turn over a debt to a collection agency without first having spoken with the client. Surprising the client with a call from a collection agency may provoke a retaliatory ethics or malpractice complaint. Hussey (1986) has good advice on collection agencies.

Investigate and carefully read your contract with a collection agency, to reduce problems. Some problems I have heard of include being locked into a single agency for collecting your money; being required to pay a fee if you discontinue having an agency collect for you; having collection activities dropped if you or the agency is sued or threatened with a suit by the client; receiving very limited (and often ineffective) investigation to find a client who has "skipped out"; and having to supply a lot of material to support your bill. Overall, some agencies are clearer and fairer than others, so be thorough and ask lots of questions.

As a final reminder, if patients are not allowed to get behind in their payments to you, sophisticated collection methods will not be needed. Have clients pay upon receipt of services, or bill early and often. **Don't let patients get behind in their payments to you!**

2.5   Billing Third Parties—and Getting Reimbursed

In the old days, you had a professional relationship only with the client (first party) and not with the insurance company (third party). The client paid you and then might recover payment from the indemnity insurer with whom he or she had a contract. These days you are more likely to have a contract with an MCO, a preferred provider organization (PPO), or an HMO, and so you *do* have a professional relationship with a third party.[2] Your contract will stipulate all the billing procedures and limitations.

Before you provide any services, you should confirm that the client is indeed covered for your services. This is called "verification of coverage." Both indemnity policies and an MCO's procedures are invariably complex and time-consuming. See the behavioral health insurance benefits questionnaire (Form 6) in Section 3.11, for a list of questions to guide you through your calls to an insurer or MCO.

---

[2]The term "MCO" ("managed care organization") will be used from this point onward in this book to encompass all similar legal, financial, and organizational structures, which may be called preferred provider organizations (PPOs), health maintenance organizations (HMOs), or the like. For all practical purposes they are the same for the mental health clinician, because in each case a third party (the MCO) is making decisions that restrict treatment of the client (the first party) by the clinician (the second party).

What You Need to Know for Insurance Processing

If you do not have the following information and skills, learn them from private seminars, other billers, training programs provided by the larger insurers (e.g., Blue Cross/Blue Shield), or national training organizations.

- Know which of your services are reimbursable and for what amounts. *Physicians' Current Procedural Terminology* (CPT) is revised yearly (see www.ama-ass.org/ama/pub/category/3113.html). It is an enormous multivolume publication defining all recognized health treatment practices. You will need CPT code names and numbers to bill for your services. As a therapist you only need to know a dozen codes, but these must be current. Two codes, 96150 and 96151, cover assessments and reassessments, respectively, to identify the biological, psychological, and social factors important to the prevention, treatment, or management of physical health problems. Four codes (96152, -3, -4, and -5) can be used to reflect services (to an individual, group, and family with and without the client present) to modify the psychological, behavioral, cognitive, and social factors affecting the client's psychological functioning, health, and well-being. They do not apply to patients with psychiatric diagnoses, and cannot be reported on the same day as the psychiatric codes.

- ICD diagnostic codes are required by HIPAA regulations (see Zuckerman, 2007). If you are treating a psychological condition related to a medical one, or if you are doing neuropsychological evaluations or treatments, use the medical ICD codes. They are reimbursed more routinely, with less resistance, and often at higher rates by Medicare, Medigap policies, commercial carriers, and MCOs. The parallel CPT codes may allow you more hours for assessment or services. If you are treating a psychological condition and using psychological methods, use both a psychological CPT code and an ICD diagnostic code. Do not use the psychological procedure codes with a medical diagnosis, and vice versa. Different procedures can be provided to the same patient for different diagnoses—that is why there is a space on the CMS-1500 form for a diagnosis code next to each procedure code's space. There may be limits on similar procedures performed during the same visit.

- Know what forms and terms to use. You will need the CMS-1500 or the insurer's own billing form. Be familiar with the jargon of billing (e.g., "duration of session," "place of service," "coinsurer," "verification of benefits," etc.). Understand deductibles, copayments, coordination of benefits, and percentage coverages, as well as how they are computed. A book by Small and Barnhill (1998) is an excellent resource and guide to all these aspects and details.

- Be sure to obtain an NPI, explained later in this section.

- Understand how to get around companies that deliberately delay payment and devise obstacles, or at least know how to pursue these organizations energetically. Payment of some of your perfectly legitimate claims is likely to be refused, and so to get paid, you must appeal those "denials." This topic is too detailed and changeable for discussion here.

- This may seem obvious, but given the behavior of MCOs, make certain to get (even if you have to make many calls) the "certification letter" that authorizes you to bill an

MCO for the services you are going to perform. This is the only support you have for a claim that might be "lost in the mail," "never received in this office," or just has "no record of that contact or agreement."

- Obtain precise information concerning the lifetime and annual deductible or limitations.

- Be sophisticated about how to use time of billing to your advantage. For example: are yearly deductibles based on calendar years or on 365-day periods from diagnosis or initiation of service?

- Make arrangements for the "physician referral" issue.

Billing for Medicare Patients

The various government programs are confusing, but do not reject the provision of services to Medicare-covered clients too quickly. Although there are some bureaucratic complexities, there are many benefits—reliable and fast payments; billing on additional codes for more complete and realistic reimbursement; and grateful patients and families. What each Medicare program means for psychotherapists is beautifully explained by Norris et al. (1998).

The APA Practice Directorate has a free and very comprehensive *Medicare Handbook*, which can be ordered from 202-336-5889 and is also provided online (www.apa.org/practice/medtoc.html). This is the single best source of information for psychologists, and reading its approximately 35 pages will be well worth your time. The APA Practice Directorate's site (www.apa.org/practice/prof.html) has other relevant resources, such as *The Basics of Medicare Audits*, *State Medicaid Reimbursement Standards for Psychologists*, and *Medicare Private Contracting: Plus or Minus?*

According to the 1989 Medicare law, you must notify the patient's primary physician after treatment has begun unless the patient specifically requests that no notice be given. You should discuss the desirability of this notification, carry it out by letter or phone if the patient agrees, and document these steps and this decision in your notes (see Section 4.2).

National Provider Identifier

You, whom managed care changed from a therapist into a generic "provider," and whom HIPAA turned into the even more anonymous "covered entity" (CE), can now become a plain 10-digit number without "intelligence" (it doesn't identify your discipline or location, etc.). It costs nothing, and lasts a professional lifetime. You will need this number—your NPI—in order to be paid by health insurance companies. Each provider needs one, so you may get one for yourself and an additional one for your business. Once you get your NPI keep it secure but handy, as you will enter it on each CMS-1500 billing form and will probably share it with other CEs. You must furnish updates to its database within 30 days of any changes, such as moving. It is not yet clear who will have access to this database and for what purposes.

More information can be obtained at the CMS site for the NPIs (www.cms.hhs.gov/ NationalProvIdentStand), by phone (800-465-3203 or TTY 800-692-2326), by e-mail (customer service@npienumerator.com), or by U.S. mail (NPI Enumerator, P.O. Box 6059, Fargo, ND 58108-6059). You can apply for an NPI on paper or via the Internet. The Internet application takes 15–30 minutes, and you will get your number in a few days by e-mail. The website is nppes.cms.hhs.gov, and the phone number is 800-465-3203.

Before you apply, you will need the following information:

- A permanent **mailing address** and a single **practice location**.

- All the numbers you have previously used to bill insurers, such as your **unique provider identification number (UPIN)**, and your **Medicare and Medicaid numbers**, as well as the **state** you practice in for each.

- The "taxonomy/provider type" is what we call a **professional discipline**.

- The "taxonomy selection" is what we call a **practice area or specialty.** It has nothing to do with paying your taxes. The categories seem to me an odd selection and have changed; you can select as many as you like, and you can always change these later. For each one chosen, you must enter your **license number and the state in which you are licensed for that specialty.**

- Enter a permanent **phone number** and **e-mail address** for the provider, and (if you like) enter a name and credentials for an "alternate contact person."

Checklist for Avoiding Illegal and Unethical Billing Procedures

The APA code of ethics (APA, 2002) states simply that "Psychologists' fee practices are consistent with law" (Standard 6.04b) and that "Psychologists do not misrepresent their fees" (Standard 6.04c). This makes accurate billing an ethical responsibility and subject to ethical as well as legal risk. Kovacs (1987) examines billing practices that put you at legal risk. Here is a checklist of ways to avoid such risks:

❑ Bill only for services actually rendered, not for missed or shortened appointments. (You can collect for these from the patient under most conditions, but read your MCO contract. See Section 4.2.)

❑ Bill only in the name of the patient. Bill members of a therapy group for group therapy, not as if they were individual therapy patients. If you see a couple, do not bill both members as individuals. Billing for only one person when you are doing relationship therapy is fraudulent.

Miller (2000), in an online article, states:

> Insurance companies generally refuse to pay for couples therapy claiming that their policies do not cover marriage counseling. Although many clinicians and patients have assumed that there is nothing that can be done, in most cases, there is a way to obtain reimbursement for couples therapy. The key to overcoming the denials is understanding the

issues and how the denials involve "downcoding to avoid payment." Armed with this information, assertive clinicians can do something to stop managed care's erosion of mental health services.

I strongly recommend this article (and other materials on the same site, www.psychotherapistsguild.com/refusal.html).

❑ Do not mislead the insurance company into believing that you provided a service when in fact a trainee or assistant did, even if the insurance company will not pay for services provided by others (as it should). This is an issue we should take up with lawmakers.

❑ Charge the insurer only the fees you and the client agree upon. If the patient really cannot afford your fee, (1) lower it or (2) refer him or her to another provider or clinic.

❑ Do not bill for double your usual fee, so that the insurance company will pay half and you will then receive your usual fee.

❑ Do not try to collect more than 100% of your fee by billing two insurers when a patient is covered by his or her own and a spouse's plan (Knapp, 1994). However, it may be acceptable to bill the second insurer for the part not paid by the first; read the contract under "coordination of benefits."

❑ Accepting the actual amount paid by a third party as full payment of your fee when it is not your agreed-on, posted fee is fraud. If you have told the third party your fee is x dollars, and now you in effect accept less as full payment and do not collect the patient's part (the copayment), this is submission of a false claim, or violation of the anti-kickback provisions of your contract with the payer. Do not advertise or state in your client information brochure that "Medicare is accepted as payment in full" or "Insurance is accepted as full payment." State in writing your financial policy concerning waiving the copayment only for the indigent, and define your criteria for "indigent." Do not offer the waiver; let the client ask for it. Do not routinely claim to the third party that a patient's financial hardship prevents his or her payment. Investigate and document the client's income and insurance coverage before waiving the copayment. Do not fail to make a good-faith effort to collect the client's part of the fee unless you have documented his or her indigence. Document your collection efforts. These are burdens, but the risks are high.

❑ It is common practice to collect part of your fee from the client's health insurance and copayment, and, if that does not cover your fee, to bill the client for the rest. In fact, this practice is incorporated into several of the forms in this book. With indemnity policies this is reasonable and legal, but with an MCO contract this "balance billing" is likely to be forbidden. Such contracts require you to agree not to charge the client for the part of your regular fee that you have forfeited to become a managed care provider. They usually go further to indicate that if the MCO rejects your claim for payment for services you have rendered, you can only collect the copayment and not the rest of the fee (for which you had billed the MCO). Read your contracts very, very carefully.

❑ Do not change the diagnosis or the CPT code so that the insurance company will pay for your services or pay more (this is called "padding the bill" or, more currently, "upcoding"). For example, do not label what is truly a V-code diagnosis an "adjustment disorder," or turn "adjustment disorder" into "dysthymia," or change "biofeedback" into "psychotherapy" if these are not accurate. Do not bill for two 45-minute sessions for 1 hour of your work. "It's dishonest, and you're telling the patient that you think it is fine for both or you to become criminals for the price of a few sessions" (Reid, 1999, p. 63).

❑ Don't "cream and dump." That is, don't see those with insurance until their coverage is exhausted and then refer them away.

❑ Do not pretend that you were "too busy with clinical issues to worry about the paperwork," or say that you "trusted your assistant," or use other excuses for fraudulent billing.

Failure to follow these rules can result in your being prosecuted. You may then be convicted of insurance fraud, perjury to commit fraud, or collusion with the patient; you can subsequently be fined and jailed (I have heard that psychologists have served time for insurance fraud). Fraud, perjury, and collusion are all felonies and will usually cost you your license and livelihood. The federal government has cracked down on fraudulent health care billing, and the Office of the Inspector General has elaborate rules on compliance.

Late Payments from Insurers

Insurers must either pay or deny a claim within a limited time period (usually 30 days) after it is submitted. You can threaten to report insurers to the state insurance commissioner if they are too slow. If you can do so, and it is worthwhile to you, monitor the progress of all claims you submit, and keep after the insurers on old claims. Computerized billing programs can often do this automatically.

Insurance companies have been almost universally delaying payment by asserting that the forms submitted are incomplete—are not "clean claims." It has become so severe a problem that Pennsylvania finally passed a law (Act 68 of 1998) compelling timely (within 45 days) payment of "clean claims" or payment of interest on the balance due. Your state may have similar laws and procedures. If your state does not, pursue such legislation. If it does, enclose a copy with your claims. Do not assume that an insurance company or MCO is either competent or honest. However, if company personnel tell you that information is missing, remedy the situation immediately (a fax machine is very handy here). If what they ask is confidential, write to them supplying alternative information (see Section 7.5).

Authorization of Benefits

Sometimes patients may receive payments from their health insurance for services you have provided and then fail to pay you. You can prevent this, as well as simplify the financial part of their lives, with the very standard procedure that the sample letter below supports. In addition, when you experience problems with receiving payment, having such a letter may allow you legitimate access to a client's benefit information and previous records to respond to denials based on "preexisting conditions"[3] if the client has left treatment, as is likely.

[Letterhead]

[Date]
[Name of insurer]   [Name of patient or insured]
[Addresses]   [Patient's or insured's identification number or Social Security number]

Dear _____:

Your health insurance may cover part of the costs of your treatment here. I would prefer that the insurance company pay its obligations directly to me, rather than paying you and then having you pay me. In order to make that arrangement, I need your signature below. Please read the next two paragraphs and sign where indicated. If you have questions or would like to discuss this, please give me a call.

This is a direct assignment of my rights and benefits under this policy. I hereby request that payment of authorized Medicare, Medigap, and/or other health insurance plan benefits be made on my behalf to the therapist named above for services provided. I authorize this therapist to release to my third-party payer/insurer and/or to the Centers for Medicare and Medicaid Services and its agents, as necessary, any medical information needed to determine the benefits payable for related services. This authorization shall be considered valid for the duration of the claim. A photocopy of this authorization will be considered as effective and valid as the original.

I understand that I will be personally responsible for any amount denied, or any remaining amount owed for services partially covered by my third-party payer/insurer. This payment will not exceed my indebtedness to the above mentioned assignee, and I agree to pay, in a current manner. I agree to pay any costs incurred by this therapist in collecting such fees.

_____   _____
        Signature of patient (or insured, parent, or guardian)   Date

_____ Copy received by client   _____ Copy held by therapist

2.6   Marketing Your Practice Ethically

Marketing is required for the independent practice of psychotherapy. Clients will not just walk in off the street, and so you must either approach them directly (advertising, giving presentations, etc.) or have clients referred to you (by other professionals, insurers, ex-clients, agencies, etc.). There are many ways to get your practice known to others (see the list of books in Appendix A), but the best marketing for professional services is word of mouth, and so this section will focus on reaching ex-clients and the professionals ("gatekeepers") who might refer patients to you.

---

[3]Like the term "preauthorization," which means "authorization," use of this term by insurance companies demonstrates the failure of their employees' education. They mean, of course, "existing conditions."

Ex-clients are the best sources for referrals, because they have already been persuaded that you can help them. Using testimonials from ex-clients is considered proper, but psychologists have generally frowned on such testimonials because they are so easily distorted. Only those who liked your services would be asked to testify, although few testifiers have had any experience with competing services. Bear in mind also that Standard 5.05 of the APA's code of ethics (APA, 2002) forbids asking or using current clients for testimonials, because it would be potentially exploitative. Traditionally one does not approach active clients of other therapists. Some view this injunction to be both paternalistic (after all, these are adult and experienced consumers who can make informed choices) and not in the best interest of the clients, who may receive better services from you than from their current therapists. The APA ethics code (APA, 2002) offers guidance that emphasizes consideration of the client's welfare, full discussion of these issues to minimize confusion and conflict, and proceeding with caution and sensitivity (Standards 10.04 and 5.06).

Physicians (not "doctors," please) are often good referral sources. Some specialties have enormous caseloads (10,000 patients in an internal medicine or gynecology group is common), have many patients with psychological problems, and often want to refer their troubled or troublesome cases. Their offices may even call and make the appointment if you are easily accessible. When you visit (as you should), ask whether you can leave educational brochures in a rack in their waiting rooms.

As noted in Section 2.1, beware of fee-splitting arrangements. Paying for referrals is common and ethical in many businesses, but psychologists' practices are not purely businesses. The APA ethics code (APA, 2002) specifically forbids this (in Standard 6.07), because being paid for making referrals to one service provider and not to another is likely to distort the referrer's views of what is best for patients. You may have to clarify this point with some potential referrers.

Your fellow clinicians can be an excellent source of referrals if they are simply (and repeatedly) informed of your availability and specialties on a regular basis. Below, you will find several means for making your services better known.

As required by Standards 5.01 to 5.04 of the APA ethics code (APA, 2002), you must be accurate in representations of your credentials, qualifications, and promises in mass media advertisements, in all forms of publicity, and when offering workshops for the public. Ads in the Yellow Pages generate many referrals, but they are sometimes of lower quality: People often call in the heat of an argument or crisis and may not show for the appointment. They do not cancel, as they think they will have to explain, feel guilty, apologize, or even get talked into coming. Or they may not understand the "rules of the game" of therapy and need socializing into the way this special relationship is conducted. As the "gatekeeping" function becomes more professionalized by MCOs and the like, fewer people will use the ads in the Yellow Pages. Referrals will be almost exclusively by networks and websites.

If you want encouragement, information, and guidance on various marketing activities (e.g., surveying community needs and resources; writing and placing advertisements; creating newsletters; designing and presenting workshops to the community, peers, and businesses; etc.), see the books listed in Appendix A on practice development and marketing.

Practice Announcement Letters

A letter is a simple and effective way to tell potential referrers that you are available. Below is a copy of a letter I sent to the medical staff when I joined a local hospital's adjunct medical staff. It will need to be tailored to your orientation, professional situation, methods, audience, and comparative advantages, but it is a useful model of how to approach physicians. Keep the letter undated, as you should not send this announcement to every staff member at one time; if you do, you will be inundated with referrals to which you cannot respond. Try five per month for those you meet at the hospital. Indicate what you *don't* do (e.g., testing or child therapy) or treat, as well as what you do, or you will get inappropriate referrals and annoy your referral sources. I believe it is crucial to identify one or two specialties, so that the referrer has a "hook" to "hang your name on." Without these, you will blend into the undifferentiated mass of "service providers" and be ignored. With physicians, I have used "collaboration" or "consultation" to describe my practice model and found ready acceptance. Additions to this letter might address costs by indicating which MCO panels you are on; whether you offer a sliding fee scale and/or do *pro bono* work; and whether you have a waiting list, or will refer any who cannot afford to see you to appropriate community resources. For some settings, if you are a psychologist, you may have to explain the APA's ethics code's opposition to fee splitting.

[Letterhead]

[*No date*]

Dear Dr. _____ :

May I take a moment of your time to briefly introduce myself? I've just joined you on the staff here at _____ Hospital and opened an office for the general practice of clinical psychology in the Medical Arts Building.

I treat adults (but not children) for depression, anxieties, phobias, and similar emotional disorders, using behavioral and cognitive methods that have clear scientific support of their effectiveness and efficiency. They do not involve extensive exploration of a patient's childhood or unconscious mind. Instead, my methods are active, directive, and educative; I aim at solving the problems the patient faces here and now.

I am keenly interested in treating conditions such as _____, _____, and _____ in close cooperation with physicians, who would of course retain the overall medical responsibility for their patients.

My background includes a PhD in clinical psychology from the University of Pittsburgh and a year-long full-time internship, both of which were approved by the American Psychological Association for training in specifically *clinical* psychology. I have worked for more than a dozen years in psychiatric hospitals, community mental health centers, and centers for the treatment of mental retardation, as well as in consultation/liaison and independent practice. Because I am a fully licensed psychologist, my fees are often partly covered by a patient's health insurance.

The research on the psychological needs of medical patients has uniformly indicated a high level of benefit from psychotherapeutic services, so if I can be of any assistance to you or your patients, please do not hesitate to call on me.

I have been warmly welcomed here and eagerly anticipate productive years of providing effective services to patients. Since my office is close by, I would be happy to come to meet with you, even briefly, at your convenience.

Sincerely,

_____

[Signature]

P.S. I have been very active in the psychotherapeutic community in Pittsburgh, and so if a patient of yours needs a specialized service, I may be able to refer him or her to someone who can meet this need. I would be happy to answer your questions or your patient's questions at any time and will respond to all phone calls very promptly.

Referrals from Physicians

It has been repeatedly established that physicians, do not refer their medical patients for the psychotherapy their patients need. One way to overcome this obstacle is to educate physicians about the criteria for appropriate referral and effective treatment. This could be in the form of a list or as a brief assessment questionnaire that a physician can use with a patient. One such questionnaire was developed by Charles H. Steinmeyer, PhD, of Warren, PA. It has physicians assess patients on the following six criteria: insight (patient's understanding of the nonmedical problem as having psychological roots); reality testing (patient's ability to perceive and respond to consensual reality); memory functioning (patient's ability to retain learning); communication ability (patient's verbal skills); abstraction or conceptual function (patient's ability to generalize across situations); and thinking processes (patient's ability to participate in problem solving). Patients are rated on a 4-point scale, with 4 indicating normal to high functioning. Patients with high ratings (3 or 4 on all the criteria) are "appropriate" for verbal psychotherapy with psychological methods very likely to be effective for major problems.

Referrals for Group Therapy

We all know that group therapy can be very productive, can be time- and cost-efficient, and can address and resolve unique issues. Why don't mental health clinicians make better use of groups? The main reason is that they don't have a sufficient flow of clients. How then can you increase the flow of suitable referrals? By "publicizing" your groups to all potential referrers. A letter or notice can be circulated often and widely that explains what the group is about and for whom it is appropriate. It should provide enough information so that the referrer can made intelligent recommendations. Include the following types of information:

- Group's general purpose: Therapy? Support? Supervision? Education? Training?

- Group focus: A psychiatric diagnosis? A medical condition? A common problem in living? Other?

- Group's status: Is it a potential group or definite? Is it newly forming or ongoing? Is it time-limited or open-ended?

- Criteria for both inclusion and exclusion: Age? Sex? Individuals or couples? Other?

- Group leader credentials: Highest degree, license information, relevant special training.

- Leadership style or orientation: Cognitive? Behavioral? Psychoeducational? Psychodynamic? Other?

- Meeting logistics, if set: Meeting location, day of the week, time, session length, frequency.

- Contact information for referrer questions: Name, address, phone (with best times to call), e-mail.

- Contact information for group leader(s) if different from above.

"Thanks for the Referral" Notes

Thank-you notes for referrals are sent as a professional courtesy, to document continuity and comprehensiveness of care, and to encourage more referrals.

During the first session with a referred patient, discuss and decide with the patient, how much he or she wants the referrer to know about the treatment. A "Yes" response to the appropriate question in Section B of Form 24 (the client demographic information form) is a sufficient release to inform the referrer that the patient showed up and is being evaluated. When it would be better to send a report of your findings, diagnosis, duration and nature of treatment, progress notes, and the like, then get a signed release-of-information form (Form 52) before calling or writing to the referrer. See the next section on progress notes.

If the client does not show up, you should inform the referring professional, because this is important information about the client's compliance with the referrer's treatment recommendations. Although you won't have the client's permission to release information about the client's status, I think that since the referrer knew of the referral (having made it), the client knew of it (having agreed to the appointment), and you knew of it (having set up the appointment), there is no breach of confidentiality.

You do not need to give any notification to former or current clients who refer others, because of general reasons of privacy. Also, a nonprofessional's recommendation to a friend or associate is only personal advice, and the recipient is free to ignore it.

A common and professional format is to send a note like this:

[Letterhead]

[Date]

Dear Dr. _____:

Please accept my thanks for referring _____ to me for professional services.

If it is appropriate, and with a signed release from the client, I will provide you with a written or telephone summary of my clinical impressions and recommendations soon after our meeting. If for some reason the appointments are not completed, I will let you know.

If you have any questions or other concerns that you would like me to respond to in this client's case, please contact me immediately.

I sincerely appreciate your confidence in my services, and again thank you for this referral.

Very truly yours,

_____

[Signature]

The contents of your letter should be tailored to the referrer's involvement in treating the client and the client's needs for privacy. If the referrer is no longer involved in the client's care, a simple thank-you note may be all that is needed.

Sending Progress Notes to the Referrer or Cotreater

Any referrer wants to know, at a minimum, whether a client contacted you and entered into treatment. That is why the client demographic information form (Form 24) has a question to get permission to tell the referrer that the referral was completed. Medicare requires that you inform the client's physician of your providing treatment (see Section 4.2), and as a courtesy, you should keep all those who are continuing to provide care informed of progress and problems. The APA ethics code (APA, 2002) no longer specifically requires you to coordinate your treatment with the client's physician, but does strongly suggest it.

If you are actively collaborating with the referrer and sharing interventions (e.g., having a physician write the client's psychiatric medications), more details about changes in symptomatic behaviors, side effects of medications, failure to adhere to regimens, changes to treatment plans, advice on management, and the like would be appropriate, as would more frequent correspondence.

Checklist for the Contents of a Progress Letter

Since you will be treating all kinds of patients, I have not offered a form here, but the contents could include these:

❑ Name and identifying numbers.

❑ Dates of service.

❑ Diagnosis or diagnoses, with ICD numbers and labels (see Zuckerman, 2007), and especially any changes to these.

❑ Brief case formulation.

❑ Target symptoms, goals, etc.

❑ Kind(s) of treatment(s) you provided.

❑ What information you have given to the patient.

❑ Problems or information of relevance to the referrer or cotreater in managing the case.

❑ Response to treatment.

❑ Cooperation, motivation, adherence.

❑ Prognosis and expected duration of treatment.

❑ A closing expression of appreciation, hope that the information is of value, indication of your continued availability for consultation, and the like. (See Zuckerman, 2005, for many alternative phrasings for closing a note or report.)

Suggestions

- Keep it brief. Most professionals avoid reading more than a page.

- A progress note can be created during a session with the client. This can become an opportunity to review progress and goals, as well as getting informal permission.

- Since you are sending information to another professional, you need your patient's written permission. It is better to get a current release-of-information form (Form 52) signed near the time you send this information than to rely on an older one from the intake, when the client did not know what you might send or say.

- For convenience, get permission to make telephone consultations with the referrer or collaborator by including this option on the release form.

Tracking Where Your Referrals Come From

The value of collecting information on the sources of your referrals can be expressed in terms of the old "80/20 rule": 80% of your patients come from 20% of your referrers.[4] The problem is that you may not know who those 20% are, and so may not be able to work

---

[4]How do I know? It is a universal rule—just as 20% of your patients cause 80% of your billing problems, or 80% of your joy comes from 20% of your companions. The 80/20 rule is usually attributed to Vilfredo Pareto (1848–1923), an Italian economist.

better with them to increase those referrals. Creating a client log or form with the general headings provided below will help you to clarify the situation and understand which networks include you. It will give you a clearer and more objective picture of your practice's perceived orientation and visibility, so that you can decide whether you wish to change to meet your goals. When you create your own log, please adapt the headings below to the categories that suit your practice best.

If you keep this client log with your billing forms, you can fill it out monthly for all new patients. Alternately, you can complete it at intervals, perhaps when you file your quarterly estimated taxes. The referral source can be coded as follows: Yellow Pages, newspaper ad, MD, attorney, MH professional (names or disciplines), ex-patient, agency, ex-training setting, peers, public speaking engagement, etc. Age, sex, zip code, and problem/diagnosis categories should be modified to suit the goals of your practice. Note that zip codes can inform you of the geographic range of your client base, can indicate how far people will travel, and can guide your placement of advertisements or other marketing efforts.

Characteristics of New Clients

Client's initials	Date called	Referred by/ code	Age	Sex	Zip code	Problem/ diagnosis	

In addition, for collaborative or marketing purposes, you might reorganize these data by referral source or by diagnosis to shape your marketing efforts.

Analyzing and Using the Data on Referral Sources

At intervals, you should examine your log of client characteristics and collect some simple totals and percentages. Entering these numbers into a database will allow you to pose interesting questions such as these:

- Does the referrer who sends me the most cases with X diagnosis also have a lot of clients with Y diagnosis whom he or she is not sending to *me*?

- Has referrer R begun to send me lots more clients or ones with different diagnoses than he or she did a year ago because of my marketing efforts with him or her?

- Am I getting a lot of new clients who live or work in a particular area, and so might I consider opening an office for their convenience?

- Am I getting a lot of new clients with diagnosis *D*, and so might I get more training in, advertise, or teach this specialty?

- Which of my advertisements and other marketing efforts are most and least productive?

Examining the patterns will allow you to answer questions about your practice that will help you achieve your personal and professional long-term aims. For example:

- What is the number of new referrals I need to meet my practice/income goals?

- Compared with last month and with last year, am I meeting my goals?

- What are my new goals for next quarter?

- What are some new methods to meet these goals?

Clement (1999) is an excellent resource for more ideas on the practical value of such information.

Collecting Feedback on Your Psychological Reports

The essential reason for doing evaluations—whether they involve testing, interviewing, or observations—is to collect information that shapes the decisions to be made about the treatment of individuals. And if you do any kinds of evaluative reports, the essential information you need to do your best evaluations is feedback on the value of your reports from their consumers.

The list of questions below can be used to structure a simple letter, which will demonstrate that you care about satisfying the needs of the recipients of your reports and will provide you with information to improve them. You should send it at least yearly to school personnel, therapists, the courts, or other colleagues/professionals who make referrals to you. Modify the words if you evaluate children or are sending this to parents or other consumers. If you do educational evaluations, you might review Ownby's (1991) form for some language.

1. Did the report give you information beyond what you already knew?

2. How helpful and realistic were . . . (here offer a list of sections and contents of your reports, such as recommendations for therapy or training, coping with symptomatic behaviors, etc.)?

3. Did the report fail to address areas of concern to you? If so, which?

4. Do you have any suggestions or comments?

Conclude the letter by expressing gratitude for the recipient's time and concern.

Your Website, or "Hanging Out Your Shingle in Cyberspace"

With the huge increase in Internet use over the last decade, a large percentage of potential clients will now look for a therapist on the Internet. Even when given your name by a referral source, many possible clients will search for information about you and your practice on the Internet. A website can convey so much about you and your practice that it saves your own and would-be clients' time, reduces no-shows and inappropriate referrals, and educates clients for better work. No matter what kind of services you offer, every clinician can benefit from having a website. And developing one can be creative and fun.

A single-page "Web presence" can be set up in a few minutes for little or no cost without requiring you to learn any new skills. A simple website, of five pages, can be set up in a few hours for a few dollars a month. You can find more advice and solid information on websites for professionals at www.therapymatch.com.

There are only a few steps to the process. Here they are, followed by more detailed explanations.

> **Step 1. Collect, write, and organize what will be on the site.** It must meet ethical and legal guidelines, as well as convey in plain English what you want to say and to have possible clients hear. Other materials suitable for referrers, peers, the news media, or other audiences that suit your work can also be included.

> **Step 2. Select a website design or a web designer.**

> **Step 3. Select a website hosting service and get the site up on the Internet.**

Step 1. Collect, Write, and Organize What Will Be on the Site

Include basic information on you and your practice:

- Demographics: Name, degrees, professional memberships, awards, certifications, credentials, and so on.

- Contact information: Addresses of all offices, all phone numbers, all e-mail addresses, emergency procedures.

- Map and directions to your office (Yahoo Maps, etc.).

- A photo or two of you and perhaps your office or building.

- The logo or letterhead of your practice, and a motto if you use one.

- The domain name you would like to use, as well as some alternatives. Check at www.directnic.com to see whether a name is already taken.

Include descriptive content:

- A "Welcome to my practice" message or brochure.

- Descriptions of your practice in plain English, such as the problems you treat and an explanation of your approach.

- Descriptions of your specialties, with names/URLs of websites related to these specializations. It may be best to include some professional sites, but most should be for potential clients and other laypersons.

- Descriptions of your background, training, experience.

Consider also content like this:

- Your intake procedures and how to make an appointment.

- Forms, handouts, and information such as those that would be included in your preappointment packages (see Section 5.4).

- Your HIPAA-required notice of privacy practices (NPP; see Section 5.4).

- Declaration of conformance to codes of ethics, and appropriate links.

- A list of your publications and presentations, preferably with links to the contents.

- Professional areas in which you are an authority and are available for public speaking or media contacts.

- Links to news feeds in mental health or sites with similar information.

- Anything else that makes you and your practice distinctive and memorable.

Step 2. Select a Website Design or a Web Designer

Designing your site can as simple as using a template provided by your website hosting company and doing it yourself. Or, in order of increasing costs, you can do the following: Use the designers at your Web host, find a local Web designer, or use one of the national firms. If you are comfortable with the Internet, there are fairly easy-to-use website-designing programs (such as FrontPage, Freeway, Sandvox, and RapidWeaver). An alternative is to use a blogging program (such as WordPress). A small practice can hire a designer and get an attractive and functional design for less than $1,000. Plan to spend a few hundred dollars more a year on updates and hosting.

Step 3. Select a Hosting Service for Your Website

Many organizations will keep your website (its pages) on their servers, which are basically collections of hard disks for storage connected to the Internet. Anyone typing your website's URL (a hypothetical example would be www.edstherapyshack.com) into a browser (e.g., Mozilla Firefox, Internet Explorer, Safari) will have the pages downloaded from the server to his or her computer. Although your Internet service provider (e.g., mac.com, aol.com, or verizon.com) may offer a free site, it will be pretty basic and will use your sign-in name, not a unique URL. It is better to get a free-standing site, and some are free and worth exploring. Offers and features change so often that I can only suggest a few now. Do a search when you create your site. By the way, you can move your site (pages) to a different hosting service pretty easily.

Google offers free hosting and design templates, but you will not have your own domain name (it will be something like www.edstherapyshack.google.com). Microsoft's Office-LiveBasics offers free sites and a free domain name. Sam's Club offers 5-page sites when you have a business membership. The upgraded "Business" level is only $60 a year at this writing and has so many options it will take you hours to choose. Costco (www.valueweb.com/costco) offers sites at $15 and $18 per month with a domain name and lots of room. Yahoo! GeoCities (geocities.yahoo.com) offers a free "Web presence," which is too basic, but its geocities.pro is quite complete and costs about $100 a year. The APA offers a single attractive template of six pages and site for $99 per year to members of the Practice Organization. Intelligently, it allows you to offer forms, a photo, and a resume, and it includes a news feed from APA of psychology stories. Because it does not include a domain name, your site's URL would be, for example, apapo.org/edstherapyshack. I could not determine whether it will show up in searches using Google or other search engines, or whether it uses valuable keywords, which will raise your site's position in the search results.

As an alternative to a free-standing website, you might consider getting a page in a directory of therapists. For example, *Psychology Today* magazine offers a national directory that is easily searchable from its website (www.therapists.psychologytoday.com). The cost is about $300–$350 a year. The format is not changeable, but it allows you to include an introductory narrative about your approach, experience, modalities, specialties, languages, fees, insurance panels, and contact information. It also allows a photo, a map to your office, and other features. You will not have a URL, but instead a page in the directory, which can be found by using your zip code, last name, or 10 other variables. Other directories (e.g., www.networktherapy.com, www.findcounseling.com, and www.therapy-site.com) are similar. For a table comparing directories go to www.websitesforclinicians.com. These will build your site for you, maintain it, and host it, which is an excellent approach to getting a good site up efficiently. Costs vary, but all provide good value for about $500–1,000.

One directory (www.webpsytes.com) has two unique features. First, it can set up a site for a group practice; second, it reminds you to post your NPP, a legal requirement of any provider's site. It offers the usual e-mail options, and apparently five pages for individuals and eight for groups.

Carol Goldberg, PhD, is a psychologist who does much in the media and designs websites for psychologists. Check out her site (www.websitesandsoundbites.com) for examples and readings. Another designer familiar with the needs of clinicians is Linda Chapman (www.therapistwebsites.com).

www.therapymatch.com will create a very complete site. For the first year, it will include (among other things) a logo, hosting, a domain name, a video of you talking, and help with selecting keywords. All support is by phone, and its description of its website development process is detailed and reassuring. It also has a practitioner directory, which is simple but complete.

If you decide to create your own site, you want to buy a "hosting package" at a low price per year and a website design program (a set of templates for the design of the pages of your site). Some host services to compare are www.doteasy.com, www.netfirms.com, www.fastermac.com, www.homestead.com, www.directnic.com, www.fatcow.com, www.godaddy.com, and www.1and1.com.

CHAPTER 3

Reducing Malpractice Risk
by Operating Ethically

3.1   Ethics and Malpractice

Study widely.
Question thoroughly.
Deliberate carefully.
Analyze clearly.
Act conscientiously.
—The sage kings Yao and Shun,
as described by YAMAZAKI ANSAI

Why Are Ethical and Legal Issues So Complicated?

Abstract ideas of right and wrong can be simple. Unfortunately, the real world can be quite complicated:

- Principles must be stated abstractly to be comprehensive, and yet each case and situation is unique. "Should" and "must" are often too vague to direct specific actions; actions require precise answers (when, how, where, etc.).

- Ethics and laws can sometimes conflict, such as when the client's best interests require confidentiality but the law requires disclosure. Two ethical imperatives can also be in conflict in a particular situation.

- Therapy's goals may conflict with ethical guidelines. For example, full disclosure of a treatment's risks is necessary for informed consent, but may weaken a client's motivation for therapy. Offering success rates may make him or her disappointed with the therapist or hopeless about therapy's outcome.

- There are many ways to view a case and its issues; some views may be in conflict, and we cannot know all of them. Even experts will differ in their interpretations, recommendations, and judgments, as each can have different conceptual bases.

- The field of psychology keeps evolving. Laws and court decisions keep changing. Each state has different laws; departments within a state government can have different rules; and there are gaps and overlaps in the laws and rules.

In addition to the points made above, keep in mind that written standards for ethical behavior can be of two kinds: "ethical standards," which are mandatory, with punishment for violations; and "general principles," which are aspirational and do not involve punishment for violations, but toward which we are expected to strive. Furthermore, Haas et al. (1986) found that "When psychologists are faced with a variety of ethical dilemmas, they will often make decisions based on their personal value systems and not on the basis of defined ethical principles" (p. 321). Such decisions may "feel right," but how can we be sure that this is good enough to protect us legally and ethically? How can we do better? As professionals committed to empiricism, let's look at the data.

The Major Malpractice Risks for Clinicians

Pope (1989a) reviewed the data on malpractice against psychologists from January 16, 1986, to July 1, 1988, and found 27 major causes for successful suits. His findings are summarized in Table 1. The major issues are indicated in boldface, and the causes are ranked by the percentage of claims each represents. Note how few "failure to warn" cases there were (ranked 23rd), although such cases generate a lot of therapist anxiety. Note also how relatively many problems were related to fee collection (ranked 5th), despite which many therapists vigorously pursue monies owed them. More specific data appear to be unavailable, because insurance companies consider it proprietary information and the state boards are concerned about confidentiality.

Other data come from a report by the American Psychological Association (APA) Committee on Ethics (1988). This committee reviewed complaints over a 5-year period and found a pattern similar to that found by Pope. The majority of ethics complaints came from the following small number of issues:

- Dual relationships, including sexual intimacies (23%).

- Violations of various APA practice and research standards and guidelines, or of governmental laws and institutional regulations (16%).

- Therapist behavior that violated or diminished the legal or civil rights of others (8%).

- A professional's failure to preserve appropriate confidentiality of patients or students (4%).

There are additional areas of concern (Sam Knapp, personal communication, October 2, 1996). First, child custody evaluations, which by their nature leave someone unhappy, have produced a large number of complaints on the issues of breach of confidentiality, and violations of the ethics of assessment. Second, the treatment of adult survivors of childhood abuse using recovered memories has resulted in high awards in malpractice cases.

TABLE 1. Major Causes of Successful Malpractice Suits against Psychologists

Cause	% of costs	% of claims
1. **Sexual impropriety**	53.2	20.4
2. **Incorrect treatment** (i.e., using treatments the therapist was not qualified to perform by lack of training or experience)	8.4	13.2
3. Loss (to the patient) from evaluation (performed by the psychologist)	2.6	8.5
4. **Breach of confidentiality or privacy**	1.3	6.4
5. **Countersuit for fee collection** (improper fee setting, billing, or fee collection methods)	1.3	6.2
6. **Suicide of patient**	11.2	5.8
7. **Diagnosis: Failure to or incorrect**	3.7	5.4
8. Defamation: Libel/slander	0.7	4.4
9. **Improper death of patient or others**	2.0	3.2
10. Miscellaneous (the meaning of this category was unclear to Pope)	0.8	3.1
11. Premise liability (e.g., a client was hurt in the office by falling)	0.1	2.4
12. Violation of legal regulations	0.5	2.6
13. Bodily injury	1.6	2.2
14. Loss of child custody or visitation	0.2	2.2
15. Violation of civil rights	1.1	2.1
16. Licensing or peer review	0.2	2.1
17. Poor results	0.1	1.7
18. Undetermined (i.e., the causes of action were undetermined)	7.9	1.5
19. Breach of contract	0.1	1.4
20. Assault and battery	1.5	1.2
21. Failure to supervise properly	0.3	0.9
22. **Undue influence (these are basically dual relationships)**	0.4	0.6
23. **Failure to warn**	0.6	0.4
24. Abandonment	0.1	0.3
25. False imprisonment/arrest	11 cases, average cost $935	
26. Failure to refer	1 case, cost $2,141	
27. Failure to treat	2 cases, average cost $38	

Note. The data are from Pope (1989a).

The best advice may be simply to avoid this approach, and if you do use it, to be very clear about boundaries. A third but murky and developing area concerns the risks of seeing managed care patients; in response to this. Section 3.11 offers ways to (at a minimum) obtain and document informed consent to treatment within the limitations imposed by managed care. Lastly, a survey by Montgomery et al. (1999) indicated that issues of supervision may be a largely unrecognized area of increased risk (see Section 3.12 for ways to reduce this risk).

This may seem like a long list. Do you have to worry about everything you do as a therapist? The answer is no. Nearly all malpractice complaints stem from just a few issues, and most are in areas over which you have excellent control. Over 60% of the claims in Table 1 and the majority of complaints noted by the APA Committee on Ethics originated in sexual improprieties, dual relationships, substandard diagnosis or treatment, lapses in the duty to protect, and poor office administration. You can reduce or eliminate the vast majority of risks in these areas if you are clinically competent and self-aware, if you consult fully with others, and if you create an adequate written record to document your actions and the reasons for them. Here is the good news in all this: **Almost all malpractice cases arise not from unforeseeable problems, but from ones that could have been avoided if only they were recognized and anticipated** (Bennett et al., 1990).

In some cases, the issues are so clear that lists of dos and don'ts can be created for them. I have included these in this book where appropriate. More importantly, some principles are so clearly formulated that they can be incorporated into your practice simply by using the forms, sample documents, guidelines, and checklists in this book. In fact, that is a major concept underlying this book: If you build the ethics into your paperwork, you greatly reduce your risk of malpractice.

Four Steps toward Ethical Self-Protection

1. **Be realistic.** Ethical dilemmas can and may happen to you.

   One barrier to improved ethical practice is arrogance. "Pride goeth before a fall," but arrogance is hard to avoid when capable people are asking your advice every day, listening carefully, paying you, and being grateful. Do not let false pride, denial, panic, ignorance, or rumors cause you to avoid acting to protect yourself and your clients.

2. **Learn the rules.** The fact that you have the client's best interests at heart, are well intentioned, or like the client doesn't ensure that you are acting ethically. Don't assume that ethical niceties and picky little rules can be ignored because you are a "good guy/girl." These rules have usually been carefully worked out after painful experiences.

   First, get, read, and keep available copies of your state's licensing law and all the ethical codes or principles you operate under. You need to be mindful of the legal context in which you operate. There are many codes of ethical standards. Which ethical standards apply to you? It will be the code of the group you align with by education or by the title or description you offer of your services. You will also, perhaps surprisingly, be held to the standards of any group an ordinary citizen would see you as belonging to. Even if you are not certified by the American Association for Marriage and Family Therapy, a court is likely to hold your practice to this group's standards if you identify yourself as a "marriage counselor" or "family therapist."

   Second, buy a new book on ethics every once in a while. Skim it, and especially note new risks and threats among other developments. This is especially important when your discipline's code has been revised. Here are some dates for current ethics codes by discipline—psychologists, 2002; social workers, 1999; counselors, 2005; psychiatrists, 2006—so you can know what to expect in the future. You can most easily find links to all relevant codes at Ken Pope's site (www.kspope.com/ethcodes/index.php).

   In addition, join your profession's associations. Their newsletters and listservs will keep you ahead of changes in laws, regulations, and court decisions. Their boards, ethics committees, and professional staffs are available to offer useful guidance.

3. **Develop an ethical consciousness.** Ethics education should result in feeling a "learned dis-ease." This is an awareness of vulnerability, complexity, and multiple perspectives. It is almost an operational definition of an ethical consciousness. It will give you a "gut feeling" to guide and warn you. This anxiety should motivate thoughtfulness, consultation, conservatism, foresight, contingency planning, and empathy. The development of an ethical sensitivity will help alert you to the ethical aspects and implications of all your professional activities. For practice, a book by Stromberg et al. (1988,

pp. 235–271) contains a table of more than 100 situations in which the practice of psychology raises legal or ethical questions. For documentation concerns, a book by Moline et al. (1998) has similar vignettes.

To develop and maintain an ethical awareness, repeatedly evaluate the ethical implications of your decisions. Ask yourself "What if . . . ?" questions from a "worst-case scenario" perspective and from the perspective of a hostile complainant (patient, peer, or lawyer). Be especially careful about novel or uncommon practices. If what you are doing with a client, or are considering doing, is unusual among your peer professionals, get at least one consultation on its ethical correctness *before* proceeding. My own rule is this: If you don't personally know anyone else who is doing what you are considering doing, be extraordinarily cautious.

4. **Tighten up your procedures.** By using checklists and similar procedural devices, you can anticipate problems and head them off. Such procedures can remind you of legal obligations, shape the questions you ask, and offer easily incorporated risk management strategies. Read each section of this book that applies to your practice, evaluate the forms and sample documents, modify them as necessary, make photocopies, and *use them* with every one of your patients.

3.2   Legal Aspects of Malpractice

When Do Patients Sue?

Lawsuits represent about the last stage of breakdown in human relationships. They tend to occur in therapeutic contexts under the following conditions:

- When patients are disappointed with the outcome of treatment.

- When patients think they have had a bad outcome and attribute it to the therapist's incompetence or negligence.

- When patients believe they have been exploited or "used" financially, emotionally, or sexually.

- When patients are presented with a bill larger or later than they expected.

What Is Malpractice?

Negley (1985) offers this definition: "Malpractice is a deviation (by omission or commission) from the standards of professional care which then results in an injury" (p. 243). From the viewpoint of a plaintiff's attorney, a potentially successful case must have these three elements: a serious injury, regardless of the extent of the violation of the standards; a "deep pocket" belonging to an insurance company or an institution; and someone's behavior that caused the injury.

Soisson et al. (1987) summarize what a plaintiff must demonstrate to support a malpractice claim as follows:

"a. The practitioner owed a duty to the plaintiff that was based on an established therapeutic relationship" (p. 498). That the relationship was "therapy" is the simplest part to demonstrate and is not of much concern here.

"b. The quality of care provided by the practitioner fell below the standard of care expected of the average practitioner" (p. 498) This standard used to be determined on a local basis, but is now interpreted by the courts on a regional or national basis. The comparison may be based on the specialty advertised or offered to the patient, or the care offered by other practitioners of a particular school of thought (Knapp et al., 1998, p. 88).

"c. The patient suffered or was caused harm or injury" (Soisson et al., 1987, p. 498).

"d. The practitioner's dereliction of duty was the direct cause of the harm or injury" (p. 498).

Many kinds of behaviors can result in liability: negligence, breach of contract, intentional misconduct, defamation, invasion of privacy, failure to prevent an injury, and so on (King, 1977). Wilkinson (1982) adds liability for self-inflicted injuries and suicide, harm by the client to third parties, errors in judgment concerning patient management, harmful treatment methods, and sexual misconduct. Perhaps it should be emphasized that neither a bad outcome nor a mistake is proof of malpractice (Knapp, 1994).

The real risk is of complaints to licensing boards, not of malpractice liability suits. Complaints are much more common for many reasons. The complainant does not have to spend much time or any money (the board will do the investigation and prosecution); also, he or she does not have to prove damage or loss, but only a violation of your state's licensing law's rules. A complaint can provide the same satisfactions as a suit could bring without the risks of losing the suit. Furthermore, in states that may incorporate your profession's national code of ethics into the licensing law, an ethics violation can be grounds for revoking your license.

The Good News (for Us): The Real Risks Are Small

Reviewing the data, Van Horne (2004) concluded: "It appears that about 40 in 10,000 licensed psychologists will face any action by a licensing board [in a year], while fewer than 13 in 10,000 licensed psychologists will face a formal discipline reported to the ASPPB [Association of State and Provincial Psychology Boards] Disciplinary Data System" (p. 175). This is a real-world rate of almost 4 psychologists in 100 who are disciplined in a 30-year career. Even so, almost 10% of psychologists will be complained against, and that is a major stressor.

Data on the outcomes for sued mental health practitioners were not readily available, but medical malpractice suits are rarely successful; the risk of a loss at trial is surprisingly small. Although 100% of patient's consulting malpractice attorneys are angry at their doctors, only 20% have sufficient facts to file complaints (and some of these are mistaken).

Only 10% of lawsuits against physicians go to trial, and in them defendants are exonerated 70–90% of the time; 75% of suits filed are won by the physicians and 60% are resolved without payment to the patients (Barge & Fenalason, 1989). Charles (cited in Barge & Fenalason, 1989) has reported that four of five cases are settled without payment to the plaintiffs, and that in three-fourths of those that go to trial, the physicians are vindicated. Furthermore, "For those who do win . . . the median award is $36,500" (Charles, in Barge & Fenalason, 1989).

The Bad News (for Us): Malpractice Accusations Hurt

As the saying goes, "You can't win a malpractice lawsuit, but you sure can lose one." And you can do so very badly. The actual costs, losses, and hassles pale before the self-doubt, public humiliation, and anxiety. You can be sued for more money than you have or will ever have, or than your spouse has or will earn, or than either of you might inherit. Your insurer will at best pay only part of the judgment (but generally most of your defense), and will try to settle the case early (if this is successful, you may be seen as guilty by your peers even if you are innocent). You will spend countless hours sitting in court (where you *are* on trial), giving depositions, having conferences with lawyers, getting support from friends, and engaging in endless self-reproaches and tears. If you are convicted of a felony, you will lose your license and have to find a new line of work. Yet another consequence of malpractice is being entered into the National Practitioner Data Bank/Healthcare Integrity and Protection Data Bank (P.O. Box 10832, Chantilly, VA 20153-0832; www.npdb-hipdb.com). Maintained by the U.S. Department of Health and Human Services, it lists those practitioners who have had medical malpractice payments made on their behalf; actions taken against their licenses or clinical privileges; actions taken by professional societies against them; and judgments or convictions for health care fraud, criminal convictions, and similar decisions. Although those entered can get information on their entries for $16 and notary fees, the public cannot and may never be able to. However, health care organizations, licensing boards, and insurers can access this list, and so entry may greatly limit your future ability to practice.

There are very sensitive portraits of the effects of just being accused in Charles (1985), Charles et al. (1988), Lewis (2004), and Schoenfeld et al. (2001). Indeed, Charles et al. (1985, 1988) have described the "malpractice stress syndrome"—a pattern of behaviors, feelings, and thoughts that is much more likely to appear in those involved in a malpractice case than in those not so involved. The sued are more likely to feel depressed, ashamed, misunderstood, defeated, tense, angry, and frustrated. They experience headaches, insomnia, and similar symptoms; drink alcohol excessively; and have suicidal ideation. They stop seeing certain kinds of patients, consider retiring earlier, and discourage their children from entering their profession.

What to Do If You Are Complained Against: A Checklist

The following checklist concerns lawsuits, but also generally applies to having a complaint alleged against you with an ethics or licensing board. It is based on recommendations from Wright (1981a, 1981b), Woody (2000), the American Professional Agency (1992), and others.

❑ **It is likely that you will be surprised by a licensing board complaint,** because administrative law's rules do not include the same protections as those of the U.S. Constitution (Williams, 2001). The board can investigate you without telling you about the investigation, and you do not have to be given a copy of the complaint until later.

❑ **If you are served a summons or a subpoena, accept it, but don't overreact to it.** Control your anxiety; don't panic. Keep these points in mind:

If a large number of allegations are made, this "shotgun" approach is standard practice, and most of the time they are all settled at once.

Exaggeration and "legalese" are to be expected.

Lawsuits are not unusual in our society. The vast majority of complaints and lawsuits are frivolous and go nowhere.

Resolution will take years (from 1 to 3 years, usually).

❑ **Call your professional liability insurance agency immediately and supply the information its staff members request.** They will open a file, assign a claims manager at their office, and call a local lawyer. Meet with this attorney as soon as possible. Remember that these contacts with a lawyer *are* privileged communications. But do not make any notes until you have established a relationship, as these documents are *not* privileged unless done for an attorney.

❑ **Consider hiring your own lawyer,** since your goals and those of the insurance company may not be identical in many regards—such as the energy to be invested in investigation or discovery, or the timing of an offer to settle the case. Understand that the insurance company in the employer of the lawyer they sent you to. Having your own lawyer does not indicate wrongdoing and will not worsen your situation, although it may have in the past, when board processes were less structured. Your lawyer can serve as a consultant to monitor the case and advise you on options, even if he or she does not represent you at the hearing, negotiations, or trial.

❑ **Assemble all relevant documents and records.** Do not alter, add to, or destroy any documents. Show them to no one except your lawyer. Do not release any documents unless your attorney instructs you to do so. Make and keep copies and originals of everything. Do not offer more than is relevant.

❑ **Read the relevant literature.**

❑ **Educate your lawyer about the strengths and weaknesses of your case.** If this is a complaint to the licensing board, consult with your lawyer and prepare a carefully considered reply to the board. The client is likely to read this reply, so be circumspect. Do not divulge confidential information unless you have the client's consent or a subpoena from the board.

❑ **Assume a defensive stance.** Admit nothing and make no self-incriminating statements to *anyone* not covered by confidentiality. Do not attempt to "therapeutically resolve" the issues or to "negotiate" a resolution. These communications are not privileged and can be used against you. If it is a current client, end the therapy immediately with a letter (created with the help of your attorney) advising the client to transfer and offering a few referral names. See Section 6.3 on termination.

❑ **Do not communicate with the client or the client's lawyer by mail or in person,** but only through your lawyer.

❑ **Do not talk openly to the investigator of the complaint.** These conversations are not privileged or confidential and can be used against you. At least in Pennsylvania, there is no requirement that you even meet with the investigator, so you may choose to handle the case by paper and through your lawyer.

❑ **Do not play lawyer and attempt to settle the matter.** Don't meet or talk with the client or the opposing lawyer unless your attorney is present. If you do meet with the client's attorney, be sure the client has consented to that conversation. Follow this rule even if you are told that another therapist is the target of potential litigation. Inform the patient's attorney and "Bill the [patient's] attorney for your time, just as you would bill the patient. To not bill might imply that you owe the patient something because of improper care" (Barge & Fenalason, 1989).

❑ **Do not discuss your claim with** *anyone* **(except perhaps your legal spouse) without the agreement of your personal attorney.** Consultation with a trusted colleague or close friend may seem valuable, but such conversations are *not* privileged and can later be used against you. If you do talk to experts in ethics, any lawyers other than your own, or any institutional colleagues, do so only in hypothetical terms. Limit discussions with colleagues to the process of being sued or ways to cope with the stress, and do not discuss details of the case, the care you provided, or any other confidential information. **Personal therapy** for the stress and other personal issues related to a claim, however, may be valuable, and such conversations *are* considered privileged communications because you are then a client.

❑ **Continue to work at your profession to the same high standards.**

Do not feel ashamed because you are sued. Remember (as you have no doubt told clients), the fact that someone didn't like what you did does not prove you did anything wrong.

Don't let yourself get depressed or overly concerned. Control your anger as well. Learn to compartmentalize your life.

Remember that being complained against doesn't mean you are a jerk, stupid, or incompetent.

❑ At some point, attorneys will start to talk about **a settlement**. Discuss any proposals fully with your personal attorney, and weigh the many factors and implications carefully. Do not rush, and make sure you have the resources before you "do the right thing." Review your insurance policy's terms about consenting to a settlement, which may greatly affect your choices. (See also point 17 of "Guidelines and Issues to Consider When Purchasing Liability Insurance," below.)

❑ When it is all over, **create a summary of the case and its outcome**. You will need this in later years, when you apply for panel membership and other opportunities. "When the ordeal is over and the dust settles, celebrate your survival and get on with your life. Acknowledge the lessons you've learned, make amends where you need to, and move on" (Boedecker, 1995, p. 3).

❑ If you are accused, read Wright (1981a, 1981b) and Pope and Vasquez (2005, Ch. 7). If you are sued for malpractice, read Cohen (1979, pp. 274–283). It would even be wise to read these in advance.

3.3 Professional Liability ("Malpractice") Insurance

Disclaimer: These issues are complex; needs are individual; and policies differ in many details. The following is intended as an overview, so do not base your insurance decisions solely on this summary, but examine the policies and ask questions.

Introduction

You may ask, "Do I really need professional liability insurance?" It covers more than "malpractice," the name that is often used by clinicians. You could buy no insurance (called "going bare"), which *might* reduce your risk of some kinds of suits (because plaintiffs' lawyers look for those with "deep pockets" to make a case worth taking on), and it will save a few hundred deductible dollars a year. However, such a plan offers no protection for your personal assets or assistance with the expenses of defending yourself in either a suit or the much more likely licensing board complaint. Without insurance, you assume all the risks of practice by yourself. Buying insurance is a way of risk sharing. If you are considering "going bare," read more about the risks, assess your exposures, and consult your lawyer. If a court judgment goes against you, you can lose all your current assets and future resources (inheritance, future income, spouse's income, etc.). You could also lose your license and thus your profession.

Occurrence-Based versus Claims-Made Policies

Professional liability insurance changed in many ways in the 1990s because of competition among insurance companies, patterns of suits and settlements, and the cyclic nature of the insurance business. The standard form of coverage, called "occurrence-based," was almost completely replaced by one called "claims-made." However, both are still available, and either one may be a better fit for your needs. Most of us had the occurrence-based plans, and most of us, to save money, have switched to the claims-made plans without much to worry about. Problems generally arise only if we wish at a later date to switch back to an occurrence-based plan or wish to switch carriers (insurance companies). As we go through this discussion, refer to Figure 3.

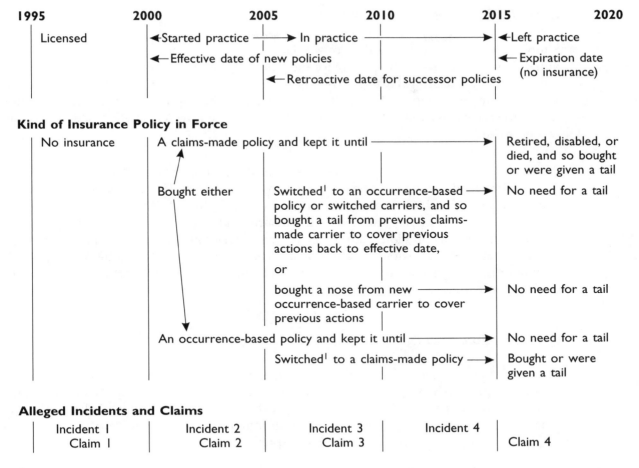

Kind of Insurance Policy in Force

Alleged Incidents and Claims

[1]Or were canceled/dropped, or the claims-made policy's company stopped writing professional liability coverage or went bankrupt or was bought out and changed its business, or any other reasons.

Incident 1 would be covered only if you had bought prior-acts "nose" coverage in 2005. It would not be covered under the occurrence-based policy or even a claims-made policy bought in 2000, because it occurred before the effective dates of either kind of policy.

Incident 2 would be covered under either the claims-made policy (if the claim was made after the effective date, 2000, and before the expiration date, 2015, of the policy) or the occurrence-based policy (no matter when the claim was made).

Incident 3 would be covered under either claims-made policy (the 2000–2015 policy or the 2005–2015 policy) but only if the policy were in force when the claim was filed (after the retroactive date—2005). If it were reported after 2015, it would only be covered under the tail coverage bought in 2015. It would be covered under the occurrence-based policy bought in either 2000 or 2005.

Claim 4 would be covered by an occurrence-based policy, or only if you bought or received a tail (since you last had a claims-made policy).

FIGURE 3. An illustration of your coverage in claims-made and occurrence-based policies over time.

Claims-Made Policies

Simply put, a claims-made policy covers claims (accusations of malpractice) made against you during the years you are paying for the policy. It does not matter when the incident on which a claim is based occurred, only when the claim is made. More technically, it covers most of your professional activities that occurred after the effective date of your initial policy (or the retroactive date of the successor policy), or after the termination date if you purchased a "tail."

A "tail" or "extended reporting period" covers the time period starting with the end of your claims-made coverage and moving forward in time. The language is confusing, because we usually think of a tail as being behind us in time, but here it is understood as the continuing tail of risks assumed by the insurer and it moves forward in time. You can buy a tail from your previous claims-made carrier. These are often free or not very expensive if you have been insured for a few years. The reason they cost so little is that you will no longer be adding risks by seeing clients, and the risk assumed by the insurer actually declines over time.

Occurrence-Based Policies

Simply put, an occurrence-based policy covers incidents that occurred during the time the policy was in force (being paid for), without regard to when a claim is made or reported. If you are accused of an incident that is alleged to have occurred after your policy's effective date (first day of coverage) and before its termination date (when you canceled it or stopped paying for it), an occurrence-based policy will cover it.

If you choose or are forced to switch from a claims-made to an occurrence-based policy, you will need coverage for the previous years of practice no longer covered by a claims-made policy. You may be able to buy a tail from the claims-made carrier that you are leaving, or you can buy "nose" coverage from your new occurrence-based carrier. The "nose" (the opposite of a tail), called a "prior-acts rider," covers those actions you took before being covered by the new occurrence-based policy. When you buy prior-acts coverage, make sure its effective date is extended backward to the effective date of your previous claims-made policy.

Changing from One to the Other

Generally, you are likely to switch to or maintain your claims-made policy, because all other features being equal, the cost of buying the tail is delayed (and so costs less). The cost of buying this policy is smaller because it is, in effect, "built into" an occurrence-based policy.

However, a change may be forced upon you by a policy's cancellation, a carrier's withdrawal from the professional liability business, or other changes in the world of insurance, so it is worth considering. You will need coverage for the previous years of practice no longer covered by your old claims-made policy. You will need a nose from your new carrier or a tail from your old carrier.

Points of Comparison and Advantage

Costs

In the long run, the two types of policies will cost nearly the same; in the short run, however, a claims-made policy costs less over the first few years and may stay lower over time. The premiums will always be higher for occurrence-based coverage, because you are essentially paying for a built-in tail coverage (see below). On the other hand, after you end your occurrence-based coverage, there is no need to spend money to buy a tail whose price you cannot anticipate years in advance.

The first few years' premiums (your costs) for claims-made coverage are less than those for an occurrence-based policy. This is true simply because the current premium covers only this current year's risk exposure, which is less than that accumulated in the collective previous years of your practice because you will see fewer patients this year than the total you saw in all the previous years. In addition, the full cost of a claim is rarely paid during the year it is reported. Thus the policy "matures" (rises in cost) over 4 to 7 years' time to reflect the increased risk exposure and likelihood of claims accumulated over the years. Claims-made premiums may stay lower than those of occurrence-based policies, as the premiums are more tightly linked in time to the actual loss experience of the insurer.

To compare costs, compute the costs for at least 5 and preferably 10 years. Add the premiums of each year until a claims-made policy matures, average them, and add the costs of a tail when comparing the claims-made policy to an occurrence-based policy. These figures are available from each company, no matter what the person who answers the phone says, because all companies are registered with your state's insurance commissioner.

Limits of Liability Coverage

An advantage of claims-made policies is that you can purchase higher liability coverage (more dollars) at any year's renewal to protect you against the rising size of awards. Of course, this additional coverage will cost you more, but the flexibility is valuable in the face of the inflation in settlement costs and the size of claims awards. With an occurrence-based policy, there is no way to make your coverage for past incidents retroactively larger; you specified the limits for each year each time you renewed the policy.

The two types of policies are not equivalent, so evaluate your needs and risk tolerance. Here is a large difference, as described by Bogie (2002):

> Say you have a $1 million occurrence[-based] policy which you renewed each year for ten years. You would have $1 million coverage for each and every one of those ten years. Compare it to a $1 million claims-made policy with the unlimited tail . . . which you renewed for ten years. You would have $1 million in total covering the entire ten-year period.

That is, if many claims are made in a single year, even for acts over several years, they could exceed the limits of such a policy.

A major disadvantage of occurrence-based policies is that a claim may be made against you many years after an alleged act occurred, and therefore it would be covered under a policy written many years ago. This has several limitations: (1) The policy probably had lower liability limits, and so fewer dollars are available to pay all the claims made under your policy; (2) it may have had different features, no longer matching today's types of risks and claims; and (3) it may have been with a carrier no longer in this market and not eager to defend a claim from a nonpayer of premiums.

Guidelines and Issues to Consider When Purchasing Liability Insurance

1. **Never lie or omit anything on an application,** as the insurer can easily deny coverage because of false statements or failure to stay within policy limitations (such as your not really being in "part-time" practice).

2. **Become well informed. Read your current policy or that of a friend.** Review the materials listed in Appendix C of this book.

   - Policies are only a few pages long but very educational.

   - Policies differ greatly, and if there is a problem, you will be held to the language of your policy. Some polices seem to be almost unchanged from a general business liability form or one for all professions, whereas others understand and speak to therapists.

   - **Examine the differences between the policies** to see which small differences, if any, are highly significant for your practice, history, and future professional plans. Later in this section, I offer checklists on which to compare plans' features, and Appendix C lists the sellers of such insurance for psychologists.

   - **Do ask each insurer you are considering for a "specimen" policy,** because their marketing materials and "summaries" may not give you enough information for your particular practice, may make misleading yes–no comparisons, and may incorrectly describe their competitor's products.

   - **If you call with more than routine questions, talk to a "licensed agent"** and not just the person answering the phone, because only licensed agents are legally required to provide complete information.

3. **Liability limits numbers are stated as two dollar amounts**—for example, "$1 million/$3 million." The first is the maximum to be paid for a single claim (even if it includes more than one person), and the second is the maximum to be paid for all claims filed against the policy in any one policy year. Buy the coverage limits to protect your life's assets. Evaluate your personal assets, present and future, in need of protection as well as the risks of your practice activities.

   - Higher coverage is not much more expensive than the lower coverage.

   - The most commonly purchased coverage is the $1 million (per claim)/$3 million (aggregate—multiple claims in one policy year) form.

- Check to see whether the (substantial) costs of defense may be deducted from the limits the company will pay. If so, consider buying higher coverage

- If you need even higher limits (e.g., for a group practice), talk with the agency.

4. **Choose the program administrator or agency that provides the best service,** because you will almost never deal with the actual insurance company—the "carrier" or "insurer" that would pay a covered claim against you. The "program administrator" or "agency" is the office that sells the policy you buy, bills and collects your payments (premiums), evaluates claims made against you, etc. For psychologists, the two largest agencies are (a) the American Professional Agency and (b) Trust Risk Management Services for the APA Insurance Trust (APAIT), which is the insurance-selling arm of the APA. Call and ask a few simple questions.

- Can you reach informed and experienced persons when you have questions? Are their answers accurate and complete? Are they educating you or just selling insurance? Are they forthcoming about any limitations?

- When you have legal questions, can you speak to a licensed agent or only to a salesperson? Are there delays and barriers in gaining access to these persons?

- Can you understand the answers? Can you use the answers in your decisions?

- Do they answer promptly? Repeatedly?

- What do they say about the other companies' policies? Do they know the differences?

- Do they send you any materials they promised?

- Are their bills and forms clear and not too burdensome (because you will be filling them out at each policy renewal year)?

Then call the other companies and see how they do.

5. **Consider the stability and size of the insurance company (the "carrier")** that actually provides the coverage.

- Look for A. M. Best ratings of A+ or A, and similar high ratings by others.

- Evaluate the years the carrier has been insuring your kind of professional, the number of states it operates in, and the number of professionals it insures; longer, larger, and more will make the carrier more skilled in handling such claims and less likely to pull out of the business.

- Insurance companies new to malpractice can offer lower rates because they have fewer payouts. This must be balanced against such a company's ratings of size and financial security.

- You will need to buy tail or nose coverage if you change carriers (insurance companies).

- You may want to stay with the same carrier and program administrator out of loyalty to the professional association, or in order to avoid a reexamination of a closed complaint against you.

6. **Check into the availability or size of discounts** offered to the following:

    - Those who have taken continuing education courses, especially courses in ethics or risk management.

    - Part-time practitioners (usually working 20 hours per week or less). Find out how this status is determined by each insurance carrier, as it can differ.

    - Members of the National Register, the American Board of Professional Psychology (ABPP), or other certifying boards.

    - Professional employees of yours. (Generally, such professionals should have their own liability coverage as well.)

7. If the premium is substantial, **evaluate the availability of periodic payments** throughout the year (especially when there is no finance charge).

8. **Investigate the costs and availability of coverage for agencies, facilities, or other organizations for which you work** (called "additional insureds") and which require you to have insurance to protect them.

    - Generally, if you are the sole employee of a professional corporation, you do not need to buy additional coverage for the corporation; however, if there are other practitioners, discuss your situation with the agency. There may or may not be an additional charge for partnerships or corporations.

    - What is the size of the additional costs to add independent contractors or consultants to your coverage?

    - If you are in a partnership or joint practice that has a claims-made policy, and you then leave the practice, you should be covered by the policy. Check with the program administrator to see how this is actually arranged.

9. Even if you are not near retirement, you might have to quit practice due to disability or other reasons. Therefore, **investigate the cost of a tail** and the guarantee of its availability. If you will be practicing for only a few years, consider an occurrence-based policy, which will save you the costs of buying a tail—but do the math. For the last few years of your practice with a claims-made policy, consider increasing policy-limits: These will be the levels of coverage offered in the tail you will buy, and reason and inflation will be well served.

10. **Most policies will not pay fines, penalties, or damages (punitive, exemplary, or multiplied).** These are simply excluded and will be levied against your assets if

awarded (the bad news). These are very, very rarely imposed in our area, as malice and repetition are required (the good news).

11. **Weigh the absence or size of a deductible** for awards made against you. To evaluate the cost of a deductible, multiply its dollar amount by the probability of a suit in 1 year (on the order of 4–8% for psychiatrists, about half that for psychologists), and subtract this amount from the yearly cost of any policy that does not have a deductible.

12. **See how the policy pays the actual defense costs in a suit** (investigation, bonds, legal fees, court costs, costs of expert testimony), as well as defenses before licensing and other regulatory bodies.

   ▪ The options are as follows: "without limit" (best); "above the liability limit," with some limit (typically $15,000 to $25,000—acceptable); "deducted from your liability limits" (not good); or pays none of them (worst). You should know that these payments only last up until admission of guilt or conviction.

   ▪ Low limits of payments (e.g., $5,000) are easily exceeded. (How many hours of attorney time would those dollars cover?) When costs exceed your limit because the case is or becomes complex or longer, you will have to pay the attorney yourself, and it is unlikely that you will want to switch to another attorney and start all over at your expense.

   ▪ The coverage for defense in a hearing before a state licensing board may not be as advantageous as it seems. In my opinion, it will tend to involve lawyers from the beginning of the process; this may make the process, which might have been collegial, more adversarial and litigious. Remember, many complaints are dismissed or resolved at this early stage. On the other hand, having an attorney may support some due process and adequate investigation, which the board may not offer you otherwise.

   ▪ As soon as you notify your plan administrator of a complaint or suit, the administrator will select an attorney from their list of attorneys near you who have the appropriate experience. You should ask about how the attorney is being paid by the insurer (capitation, discounted fees to get the referral [managed legal care], bill against a retainer, salary, fee-for-service billable hours, etc.). Use this information to evaluate how much service you will get before you use up your coverage, and ask what will happen then. Also evaluate any financial pressures on the attorney to settle.

13. **Will the policy pay you for the income lost** when you are defending a claim against yourself by giving depositions, consulting with your lawyer, and attending hearings or a trial? What is the limit to these payments per day or in total? Some policies will pay only if you are a defendant in a criminal case, and some when you are before a board of inquiry.

14. **Does the policy offer coverage when you act as a supervisor** (to nonemployees), and if so, what is its cost? Claims for negligent supervision can be made against you even if you never saw a patient. Is the number of your supervisees larger than the policy allows? Do you have to see a patient to be covered?

15. **Examine statements about location of your services.** If you practice in several states, or outside the United States, make sure your activities are covered.

16. **The policy should cover "all your professional activities"** and exclude none. In particular, examine the coverage for "Good Samaritan" acts if you might provide this kind of service during a disaster or emergency.

17. **Evaluate each policy's "consent to settle" aspects.**

    - The best policies require your agreement before settling, which is called "unlimited consent to settlement."

    - Generally, if you refuse to accept a settlement that the insurance company recommends (and that the plaintiff, suing you, accepts), the carrier will not cover any further defense costs and you will have to pay those. Furthermore, if you then lose the case, the company will not pay more than it could have settled for.

    - In the worst case, you may have no choice but to accept a settlement your carrier agrees to (a "hammer clause"). Try for some language that allows you some leeway and power.

18. **Does the insurer or agency offer high-quality, low-cost risk management seminars** and educational efforts? Do these offer continuing education credits? Is telephone "legal" or risk consultation available when you are worried? If so, how good is it?

19. If you are a psychologist, **the APAIT "endorsement" is a value that is difficult to weigh.**

    - As noted above, APAIT is the insurance-marketing arm of APA. It is a significant profit center for APA, and so its interests are not identical with those of clinicians in practice.

    - By the way, you will not see booths from other professional insurance companies at the APA conventions, because APA will not allow competition for any "member benefits" it offers. APAIT's costs of advertising in APA journals are also not the same as those charged to its competitors, and so you will have to make the effort to get information from other providers. See Appendix C.

    - You won't have to pay APA dues if you select a policy other than from APAIT. Ask yourself if you would otherwise belong to APA, and if not, reduce the yearly cost of the policy by your APA dues when comparing policies.

20. Having **tail coverage** is becoming more important, because the courts are now accepting suits beyond the old statutes of limitations, and if you work with children they may file claims when they become adults. Note that when you buy a tail, the size of the tail fixes the total amount of money available to pay all the claims that may be made against you in the future. Since the tail's size depends on the liability limits you chose in your last renewal, consider raising these limits substantially.

21. If there is any doubt that a company will still be solvent in 15 years, do not consider its occurrence-based policy.

Checklists for Comparing Professional Liability Insurance Policies

Specific information on policies is not easy to acquire. The two largest "insurers"—the American Professional Agency (a true broker) and APAIT (the insurance-marketing arm of APA, with Trust Risk Management Services as the broker)—offer nonoverlapping information, and the other agencies (listed in Appendix C) vary in their enthusiasm for providing information before you sign up. Below are listed the main questions you should ask when examining the offerings of an insurer; there may be others, depending on your practice, local laws, history, and projected needs.

What Kinds of Activities Are Covered?

There are dozens of possible exclusions for actions and situations not covered. Read the actual policy (not a summary) carefully, and evaluate which exclusions you can live with. Are the following included?

- ❏ "All professional activities" (best), or only those specified or those not excluded? Check the coverage for special treatments (hypnotism, biofeedback, divorce mediation, group therapy, or whatever you do). Other complex risks are collaborating with physicians and forensic testimony.

- ❏ If you serve as a peer reviewer or on an ethics panel, make certain you are covered against claims of negligence or maliciousness by either the sponsoring organization's policy or your own malpractice policy.

- ❏ Sexual misconduct liability (not just the costs of defense before a licensing board or in a civil suit, but payment of judgments against you) coverage, if any, is usually small— a "sublimit" of $25,000. Your employees should be covered, as well as yourself.

- ❏ "Vicarious liability" for students, supervisees, employees, and independent contractors. This is most important in group practices and in collaboration with other professionals. If you have any uncertainties, seek professional guidance.

- ❏ Personal injury (slander, violation of rights of privacy, malicious prosecution, etc.).

- ❏ Advertising injury (false advertising, libel, copyright infringement).

- ❏ Premises ("slips and falls") liability. Try to get this included.

- ❏ Contractual or fee disputes (e.g., breaking a contract, with a managed care organization [MCO]).

- ❏ And others: employment practices liability; discriminatory acts; nonprofessional administrative activities; cases against another professional with the same insurance carrier; dishonest, criminal, fraudulent, or malicious acts; and any business relationship.

Note. Confirm the availability and cost of any of these risks that are of interest to you, and evaluate whether the coverages are in addition to the policy's usual limits.

Payment for Costs of Defending a Claim

❑ Are there limits per incident, per year, or lifetime? (My advice: Act on your fears and buy the bigger coverage.)

❑ Are lost wages while defending a claim or board hearing covered ($ _____ per day, to a limit of $ _____)?

❑ Are your other costs included (hotels, transportation, etc.)? This is not really much money, so it is not an important coverage.

Support

Look for the following:

❑ Free, anonymous, convenient, unlimited ability to talk to a lawyer, psychologist, or other appropriate professional for advice on prevention and risk management. (Perhaps make a test call?)

❑ The educational value, usefulness, and cost of risk management seminars or other materials.

❑ The educational value and usefulness of mailed or online materials.

Agency

Ask yourself these questions:

❑ Does the person who answers the phone exhibit general knowledge of the field, quality of explanations, sensitivity to your concerns, responses that are valuable to your decision making, and knowledge of other companies' policies?

❑ Can you speak to a licensed insurance agent, or just the unlicensed (though trained) sales/clerical/administrative person who answers the phone?

❑ Did the agency send a "specimen" policy when specifically asked?

❑ What is the agency's experience (years, number of policy holders) in dealing with therapists?

Application Form

Examine the application form for these characteristics:

❑ Complexity and burden (because you will be redoing it every year).

❑ Specific language of history questions, especially if you have had an ethical problem.

❑ Intrusiveness and history requested. (Some states allow questions to discover whether your "personal habits" constitute a "moral hazard.")

Specimen Policy

You will be bound by the terms of the actual policy, not the simplified description of it that agencies all send. Ask yourself these questions about the specimen policy:

❑ Is it in "plain English"?

❑ Is it tailored for therapists versus generic professionals, or (worse) is it a generic liability policy?

❑ Is it written to exclude (by naming) or designed to include all your professional activities?

Insurer, Carrier, or Insurance Company

Ask the following questions:

❑ What is the carrier's A. M. Best rating? (A+ to C–; A or A+ is fine.)

❑ What is its experience (years, number of policy holders) in dealing with therapists?

❑ In which states does it sell policies? (New York's laws are generally considered the most thorough)?

Rates and Costs

Warning: Cost should not be a determining factor in your insurance purchase.

❑ Get prices for $1 million/$3 million coverage.

❑ To compare costs, compute the costs for at least 5 and preferably 10 years.

❑ Consider also the costs of APA membership for APAIT coverage if you are a psychologist but do not have other reasons to be an APA member.

❑ Can premium payments be spread over a year with no finance charge?

Tail or Nose Coverage

Ask these questions:

❑ Is there guaranteed availability of a tail? Are there limitations on availability (e.g., if you had a sexual misconduct accusation, or perhaps were not insured for the last 5 years with the company)?

❑ Is the tail for a limited number of years or unlimited?

❑ What is the cost (if any) of a tail upon death, retirement, or disability (i.e., how many years must you have been insured to get it free)?

❑ What is the cost of prior-acts coverage (a nose) if you are switching from a claims-made policy or switching insurance agencies or carriers (in which case you can buy either a nose or a tail, but noses are cheaper than tails)?

Credits and Discounts

Look for credits and discounts (percentages) on your rates for the following:

❑ Being new to practice (first- and second-year discounts).

❑ Part-time practice.

❑ Continuing education courses and credits.

❑ Ethics or risk management continuing education courses.

❑ Board certification (National Register, ABPP, etc.).

Other Issues

❑ If you work in different states or areas, is coverage "worldwide" or at least "in the United States," or is it confined to your office or offices?

❑ How much control over a settlement do you have?

Issues for Group Practices

For group practices (partnerships, general business corporations, professional corporations, or professional associations), consider the following issues:

❑ Is your (and your employees') work outside your main employment setting covered? This matters if you (or they) do some "moonlighting," such as consulting or teaching outside your office.

❑ What is the cost of coverage for "additional insureds" (consultee organizations, part-time employees, etc.)? Do you have to cover MCOs on your policy?

❑ Are there different rates? You may be charged the "insured" rate; employees with a master's degree or higher may be charged a "professional" rate; and any others a "paraprofessional" rate. Clerical workers are not usually charged separately, but look at the application form. These are all for W-2 employees; your independent contractors ("1099s") are not covered and need their own policies.

❑ If you hire staff members before the next renewal date, are they automatically covered?

❑ Can you get different limits for each therapist ("severability of limits")? If one member of the group has a practice that requires high-limit coverage, he or she can get that without having everyone else pay the same (higher) premiums.

❑ Are there discounts for multiple MDs or PhDs?

❑ Can you keep your coverage if you leave the group?

❑ If you have 15 or more employees, you may need employment practices liability insurance coverage.

Note. If you do have more complex arrangements, consult a licensed agent or broker.

Other Kinds of Insurance You Might Need

Disability or Income Protection

You are much more likely to become disabled than to die, and your disability will disrupt your finances almost as much as an adverse malpractice judgment, so prepare for it with disability insurance. Be aware that loss of income if your license is revoked due to malpractice is not covered by this insurance. Disability insurance is moderately expensive, but less so if you buy it at a younger age.

Premises Liability

If anyone (not just a patient) is injured while in your office, premises liability insurance can protect you. Most professional liability policies often offer this coverage as a component, and the better ones include it free of charge, but do ask.

- Some include premises liability coverage with a policy for office property (see "Office Property," below), for business interruption (due to damage to the office), or the like. Your office or renter's insurance policy probably already covers this.

- You will need a separate policy for a home office; see your home insurance's agent about a "rider," which is inexpensive.

Office Overhead/Expense

If your office expenses (rent, loans, advertising, car, staff) are a large part of your income, and you *must* pay them because of contracts you signed, you can buy insurance to pay these expenses if you are ill or injured. Such insurance is moderately expensive.

Office Property

Finally, consider insurance to cover your office equipment, such as computers and furniture. Select more than you think you'll need, because prices rise and the process of replacing is costly. "Replacement cost" is much better than "current value" when you have a loss. If you work at home, you will need a separate policy or a rider on your homeowner's policy to cover the cost of replacing your office equipment. Such insurance is inexpensive.

3.4   Ways to Reduce Your Risk of Malpractice

Note. For a discussion of reducing your risk of malpractice in billing, see Section 2.5.

Twenty-Two Steps for Risk Reduction

As long as you are practicing, you can never totally eliminate your risk for malpractice, but here are 22 concrete steps that can very significantly reduce your risk. Note that these steps pertain to psychotherapy with *adults.* The assessment and treatment of children raise other issues. An excellent yet brief introduction to how the ethical principles play out for children and adolescent clients can be found in Barnett et al. (2001).

1. **Assure the continuity of each patient's care.** You do not have to accept everyone as a patient, but once you have accepted a patient, don't neglect or abandon him or her. See Section 6.3 on termination.

2. **Practice competently.** The central protective rule of ethics is to stay within what we know. It is hard to know exactly what we don't know, or to know beforehand what we don't know well enough. Clinical knowledge comes from direct training by experienced teachers (supervisors); from work at regionally and professionally accredited educational institutions (e.g., internships); from training workshops by leaders in the field; from relevant and prolonged consultations; from your own well-considered experience over substantial time; and from thoughtful reading, writing, and teaching. In general, always keep the following guidelines in mind:

   - Never do what you are not legally entitled to do. Do not practice medicine, law, or pharmacy if you are not so credentialed.

   - Do not try to do everything you *are* legally allowed to do. You are *not* competent to handle everything that walks in the door.

   - Moreover, you are probably not really competent to do some things you were exposed to if you did not receive the necessary quality and intensity of training.

   - Make clear the real areas of your competence in your communications to patients, both orally and in writing. Inaccurate expectations can be the basis for treatment failure and a complaint.

   - If you do assessments, use "a well-defined and systematic method of interpreting test findings and be able to support your findings in court" (Cohen, 1983/1990, p. 660). See also Section 3.5 on malpractice in testing.

   - Don't use shortcuts (sending tests home with clients, or depending excessively on computerized test interpretations).

■ Do not do custody evaluations without considering the inherent conflicts and the potential for dissatisfied clients. Take many precautions. Glassman (1998) reviews the issues and makes many useful suggestions. The publication of APA's guidelines for custody evaluations (APA, Committee on Professional Practice and Standards, 1998) includes many resources and definitions as well as suggested behaviors. The APA code of ethics (APA, 2002) requires the psychologist to "clarify at the outset . . . the probable uses of the services provided or the information obtained" (Standard 10.02). The received wisdom is that doing custody evaluations will result in a high frequency of licensing board complaints.

■ If you operate in the area of "health psychology" or "behavioral medicine," be especially careful not to "practice medicine without a license." Maintain full, continual, and two-way communication with physicians, and define your roles and knowledge base carefully (Knapp & VandeCreek, 1981).

3. **Get fully informed consent.** Require competent, informed, and voluntary consent for everything you do. Inform clients fully about the limits of confidentiality, *before* they reveal something you cannot keep confidential. See Chapter 4 on obtaining consent.

4. **Maintain confidentiality.** Know the limits of the confidentiality you can offer, and do not promise more than you can deliver. See Chapter 7 on confidentiality.

5. **Communicate fully.**

   ■ Communicate completely. Keep your patients' expectations reality-based.

   ■ Communicate openly. Become curious about difficulties and failures of communication. Be willing to hear complaints nondefensively.

   ■ Communicate honestly. Don't pretend to clarity you don't have; the best direction is not always clear, and each case is a little different. Issues and decisions can remain clouded. We can only use our best judgment based on our knowledge, skill, and experience, but we can use all of it and share our concerns.

   ■ Communicate clearly, especially in regard to money, fees, and insurance.

   ■ Communicate regularly. Your patient handouts, forms, and regular feedback on progress are crucial here.

   ■ Don't be distant. Be kind and warm where appropriate. Show that you care about the client's welfare and are "doing everything in [your] power to help" (Pressman & Siegler, 1983, p. 109).

6. **Supervise fully.** When you supervise, be thorough and be available. Monitor your students, teammates, and employees closely. Supervision is always a difficult balance between paternalism and the encouragement of autonomy, between risk assumption and self-protective fears. Have your supervisees obtain their own professional liability insurance, if possible. If not, you must provide it under your policy; in either case, remember that you will be held responsible for their actions. Bear in mind that your employees can commit malpractice. Prevention should include training in confidenti-

ality, collections, filing, scheduling, and any other areas that occur to you. See Section 3.12 for more guidance.

7. **Keep abreast of new developments on both the clinical and legal fronts.** You must know what is considered high-quality in the field, so you have to keep up with current developments. Put aside time and money for professional development (more than the minimum required for continuing education credits). Continuing education on both your methods *and alternative ones* is essential; go to the presentations of those you disagree with. Keep aware of the development of the legal aspects of professional work as well. Remember that the half-life of the knowledge base gained in a PhD program is (at the very most) 10 years.

8. **Consult frequently and formally.** Get consultation when things aren't going well with a patient, whenever you have some unease about something, and definitely when you are considering breaking any rule. Do not delay! If you have doubts or are uncomfortable about your conceptualization or treatment, consult with a colleague and/or your attorney. "Consult" with clients' former therapists by getting records and asking questions. Thomas Gutheil, the renowned clinical ethicist, has put this most succinctly and memorably: "Never worry alone" (quoted in Reid, 1999, p. 9). Nonmedical therapists (and many medical therapists) should consult clients' physicians about any medical questions.

9. **Take seriously and evaluate thoroughly any evidence of suicidal ideation or intent.** See Sections 3.9 and 3.10.

10. **Have a contingency plan.** It is much more difficult to plan after a client becomes dangerous to self or others. Your plan should include resources for family or support system contact, special consultations for both you and the client, medications, referrals, hospitalization, police contacts, contacts with your lawyer, and so on. Tell your client about your options and your duty to warn (see Section 4.2). It may be too late to do this when the client is dangerous, so write this need into your datebook this minute.

11. **Refer carefully.**

   ▪ Refer clients when the problem they present is one with which you have little experience or training.

   ▪ Refer only to others who have the necessary areas of competence. Get feedback from those clients you refer and respect, so that you know who is competent and who is not among your possible referral resources. There is a kind of malpractice called "negligent referral."

   ▪ Ethically, a client who does not improve under your care should be referred elsewhere, even when a colleague with the necessary competence seems hard to find or the client is reluctant to start again. At the minimum, the client must be informed and allowed to choose. Document the options, the choices made, and their rationales.

12. **Be conservative in your treatments.** You are required by the ethics of your profession

to act prudently and reasonably. If you do not, you are exposing yourself to risk, because you are exposing your patient to substandard treatment.

Having a theoretical rationale for a treatment does not make it ethical; nonetheless, base all your psychotherapeutic interventions on a well-established theory (Woody, 1988, p. 211). This does not mean that you must *always* follow a recognized "school" with at least a minority of adherents, but courts are likely to move in that direction. Your treatment does not have to have an empirical justification, but it must be seen as acceptable by a significant number of your peers. In general, it will be hard for a court to find fault with the prudently reasoned use of a new and professionally or scientifically supported method by a therapist with strong credentials and no personal gain in sight.

If your treatment lacks this prudence, call it "experimental," tell the patient of other treatment options, get more detailed informed consent, and discontinue it at the first sign of harm to the patient. It is a continuing and difficult professional struggle to balance the use of a scientifically tested method, which (in theory) protects the patient, against the need to tailor any method to the unique client and the need to innovate (for future clients' benefit). This balancing is an inescapable ethical dimension of high-quality practice.

13. **Don't promise a cure.** Be careful when discussing the effectiveness of your treatment approach, and do not allow a client to develop expectations that will not be fulfilled. Promote realistic expectations of treatment outcomes, not overly optimistic expectations of success, by utilizing standardized conceptualizations and classifications and by making probabilistic statements (Cross & Deardorff, 1987, p. 75).

14. **Document.** Get a relevant case history, especially of substance use, violence, homicide, suicide, all previous episodes and treatments, lawsuits, and the like (see the intake materials in Chapter 5). Keep clear, concise, and complete records. Use behavioral descriptions, not just diagnoses, labels, or shortcut jargon. Record the essentials. Pressman and Siegler (1983) suggest: "One way to think about what the medical record should contain might be to think about what you would want to see if you were called in as a new consultant on the case in order to understand the history and to start a course of treatment" (p. 109).

    Document your thinking, reasoning, and judgments as well. Record diagnoses, prognoses, progress, and evaluations of outcome. Record your instructions to clients, handouts given to clients, and after-hours calls. Document no-shows (and your responses), consultations, and your arrangements for another professional's covering for you, and for which patients. See Chapters 5 and 6 for a full discussion of clinical record keeping.

15. **Diagnose.** If a case should come to a courtroom, a therapist cannot "hide behind the notion that since his or her theory of therapy does not rely on psychodiagnostics, [no diagnostic evaluation was performed]" (Woody, 1988, p. 211). A good history may be all that is necessary and *reasonable* (the key word). The extent and nature of this evaluation process depend on your professional discipline as well. Malpractice claims for "misdiagnosis [negligent or improper diagnosis] generally require the use of egregiously inappropriate" methods (Stromberg et al., 1988, p. 453).

A care provider has an obligation (a) to diagnose accurately and thus treat properly; (b) to ensure that a patient who presents with an emotional problem does not suffer from an undiagnosed and untreated coexisting or contributing medical illness; and (c) to provide adequate biological treatment. This burden is especially heavy on care providers who are biased against, lacking proficiency in, or reluctant to obtain consultation for such treatment. In a representative and most instructive case with a negative outcome, the court stated that "the question is not whether the physician made a mistake in diagnosis, but rather whether he failed to conform to the accepted standard of care" in his procedures and judgments (Stromberg & Dellinger, 1993, p. 7). In order to document your own clinical judgments, administer psychological tests as necessary.

16. **Avoid fee disputes and the accumulation of a large debt.** Never turn a debt over for collection without a personal conversation by you (not your secretary or office manager) with the client (not a spouse or other).

17. **Be alert to a patient's dissatisfaction with you.** This may be why the patient is not paying your bill, attending sessions regularly, or complying with treatments. Other early warning signs of dissatisfaction may include a patient's being overconcerned with your fees; being overly critical of a previous therapist or treatment (and therefore likely to be dissatisfied with yours); and having unrealistically high expectations of therapy's outcome (which are bound to be dashed). Of course, all of these should be dealt with as issues in therapy. In addition, factors such as lack of "psychological-mindedness" and entering therapy under external pressure may direct a patient to seek a way out of therapy, to gain revenge, and to make a profit all at the same time—by filing a complaint or suit. Of course, any patient's dissatisfaction should be responded to immediately, but this may also be the first warning of a complaint or suit.

    Pay careful and immediate attention to any patient's disappointment or to failure of any expectations. If you are distant, arrogant, not readily available, or hard to talk to, then a patient may begin to question your competence. Remember that patients are usually not qualified to judge your clinical competence. This is why testimonials from patients were forbidden until the 1992 revision of the APA code of ethics, and even now testimonials from current patients are not allowed (APA, 2002, Standard 5.05).

18. **Respect the complexities of families and couples.** Be aware that family and marital therapies raise sticky complexities regarding the therapist's responsibility to each person, particularly regarding confidentiality and informed consent. The therapist's own values (about preserving a marriage, extramarital affairs, sex roles, etc.) add to the complexities. Margolin (1982) addresses these issues sensitively and clearly, and advises being open and straightforward with the clients. Her article is required reading for anyone who is designing consent procedures for couples or families.

19. **Don't work if you are impaired.** Exhaustion, drugs and alcohol, personal crises, illness, and many other stressors and reactions can severely lessen the ability to do good work. Stop work or restrict your workload, and seek appropriate rest and help. If you engage in malpractice, it will be much more damaging than poor functioning. Most professional organizations have "colleague assistance" programs that can help you recover and are kept confidential. For APA Practice Organization members, there

is a superb manual for effective programs, *Advancing Colleague Assistance in Professional Psychology* (APA, 2006; this can be downloaded from www.apa.org/practice/acca_monograph.html).

A significant risk factor for unethical practice is therapist burnout. If you identify with several of the items on this short list, read some of the books on therapist burnout (e.g., Grosch & Olsen, 1994; Pearlman & Saakvitne, 1995), and seek consultation.

- Do you feel pessimistic or even cynical toward clients?

- Have you experienced persistent and interfering daydreams during sessions?

- Have you had hostile thoughts toward any client?

- Are you bored with your clients? Are they beginning to sound the same?

- Do you find yourself overly quick to diagnose?

- Are you overusing medication as treatment for the client or yourself?

- Are you blaming the client?

20. **Terminate properly.** See Section 6.3 for guidance in avoiding abandonment and other problems.

21. **Consider screening clients for litigiousness.** You might think about excluding from your practice clients you believe are likely to file lawsuits at some point.

22. **Consider limiting the scope of your practice.** You might limit or plan in the future to limit your practice to a single or a few specialized clinical domains.

Sensitivity to Differences in Culture, Religion, Gender, and Other Dimensions

In no other profession do culture, socialization, roles, and world view matter more than in clinical work. We should be aware and respectful of clients' customs, parenting styles, acculturation, expectations of therapy and healing, and any other factors that play major roles in our work. We have both an ethical obligation (APA, 2002 [Principle E] and 2003) and a clinical need to be sensitive and competent in dealing with those with different backgrounds. It goes without saying that we should be aware of the common cultural, ethnic, religious, racial, and sexual orientation differences. However, we also need to examine our beliefs about fat and body size, age, gender, income and social class, disabilities, illiteracy and language use, and other such areas of difference. We must work for insight into our own values, biases, and prejudices, and our expectations of roles and obligations, likely conflicts, and communication styles. (Goode, 2000, offers a fine checklist to raise awareness.) We must enlarge our sensitivities to cross-cultural issues of institutional oppression, racism, sexism, elitism, ageism, beautyism, and similar distortions, so as to avoid limiting our clients' potentials.

Lists of culture-specific characteristics that affect psychological functioning are available for many subcultures and ethnicities (Paniagua, 2005; D'Avanzo & Geissler, 2003). Although such information is often valuable, assuming that all members of a group will have all these characteristics is stereotyping; there is much variation within any group. It is probably best to use these characteristics as hypotheses to be modified or discarded during treatment.

General resources for developing cultural competence include a chapter by Barnett and Polakoff (2000), which is a brief overview, and books by Sue and Sue (1999) and Paniagua (1998). More specifically, a book by Orlandi et al. (1992) deals with substance abuse/ dependence, and books by McGoldrick et al. (1996) and Okun (1996) deal with family therapy.

- Becoming more multiculturally competent is difficult (Hansen et al., 2006, is highly recommended), but many resources are available for assessing and altering beliefs that limit effectiveness with clients of all cultures. Besides general resources such as Sue and Sue (2003) and Paniagua (2005), others address personality assessment (Dana, 2005), substance abuse treatment (Straussner, 2001), and family therapy (McGoldrick et al., 2005), so seek out materials suited to your practice. For difficult self-change, see Sue (2003).

- Review and read all your paperwork and handouts for clients, with an eye to cultural assumptions and possible stereotypes. Although clearly racist, ethnocentric, and unscientific content is unlikely, insensitivity to all the variations of the human condition may make your practice less comfortable to diverse populations. In addition, materials in larger typefaces, efforts to reduce background noise and other distractions, larger or different seating, and other modifications for clients with physical differences will be appreciated. See www.w3.org/WAI for a website on meeting standards for accessibility online.

- Those for whom English is a second language may be able to participate in therapy in English, but would be better informed about legal and ethical details by reading some materials in their primary language. Look online for versions of the "notice of privacy practices" (NPP) and Consent forms, and for educational materials on disorders and substance abuse, from the Substance Abuse and Mental Health Services Administration (SAMHSA), the National Institute of Mental Health (NIMH), and hospitals serving minorities. Programs on the Web can translate your materials or others into workable versions (see, e.g., babel.altavista.com).

Other Risk Areas for Malpractice

A risk area of increasing frequency is the counseling of HIV-positive clients who engage in high-risk activities, such as needle sharing and unprotected sexual intercourse. See Section 3.9 for more on this issue.

In your writing and publishing, you should be alert to the ethical and legal consequences of scientific fraud, misinformation, plagiarism (uncredited taking of words), duplicate publication (publishing the same or essentially the same findings more than once in order to get more publication credits on your resume), piecemeal/serial publication (unnecessarily separating your findings so you can publish them in several articles to get more publications), and failure to credit authorship properly. An excellent guide to the last of these problems is provided by Fine and Kurdek (1993).

3.5 Avoiding Malpractice in Psychological Testing

Psychological assessment can be ethically problematic in a variety of ways: It is difficult to gain fully informed consent without revealing tests' nature; consent to use or release the results must be given before any results are available; biases can come from many directions; there are legal issues with using tests results, and so forth. The best easily available resource is the section on assessment at Ken Pope's site (www.kspope.com/assess/index.php). Along with much other material are two papers on avoiding malpractice in testing (Pope 1988d, 2003), whose recommendations are loosely adapted for this section.

Require the Client to Give Consent

The APA code of ethics (APA, 2002) specifically requires informed consent for testing (Standard 9.03) and refers to a fuller discussion of the meaning of informed consent in Standard 3.10. For more on components of consent, see Section 4.1.

Consent must be all of the following:

- **Competent.** The client must be both old enough and sufficiently intellectually competent to understand the consequences of giving consent, to understand the choices, to make a consistent decision, and to act in his or her best interests. Obviously, for children, persons with mental retardation, and others, the substitute consent of a competent and appropriate adult needs to be obtained. This issue is of greater ethical concern when the purpose of testing is to determine competence (e.g., to make a will or life-planning decisions).

- **Voluntary.** Clients must know that they have the option to refuse or discontinue testing without suffering negative consequences. They must also know the situational consequences if they do not participate (such as loss of disability benefits, promotions, etc.; Sweet, 1990). You and an unbiased peer should be able to agree that a client is not feeling threatened or just being agreeable in consenting.

- **Informed.** Clients must know the purposes, nature, and consequences of the assessment and of the tests you will use. Specifically, tell clients that they have a right to know the test results, along with the conclusions and recommendations, They must also be told all the significant consequences of the testing that can be anticipated, and they must understand the issues, such as conflicts of interest or the ramifications of the results. These are especially important in forensic evaluations. The issues must be explained in terms familiar to the clients. Also, you must be sure to document that these explanations have been given. Make certain that you know, and fully inform the clients about, *all* those who will have access to the test report and the raw data. And, lastly, all of this should occur before the testing begins, so you will be in compliance with all laws and your conscience will be clear.

Know the Rules

First, you must know the appropriate standards and guidelines of your discipline. Professional organizations have published many guidelines (see Appendix D) with which you should be familiar. Generally, you will be held to the national standards, so learn them and provide services at a high level of quality and integrity.

In addition, you must know the current state and local laws. Conflicts between what you promise a client (such as confidentiality of some information divulged to you) and what the governing laws require can be avoided if you know all the applicable laws (such as those concerning clients with both substance abuse and developmental disabilities). Another example: Which takes precedence—workers' compensation law or mental health law? Lastly, if your state's rules are less stringent in protecting privacy, the Health Insurance Portability and Accountability Act (HIPAA) rules and procedures will apply, so you must be familiar with them as well.

Stay within Your Areas of Competence

Weiner (1989) has argued that it is possible to be competent at psychological testing without being ethical, but that it is not possible to be ethical without being competent. Don't do everything you are licensed, trained, or even degreed to do. Make certain you are fully trained and practiced in administering, scoring, and interpreting each test you use. If you were last trained in test administration years ago, a consultation with a colleague who observes you may be very enlightening and may improve the validity of your testing. Don't use a test if your administration will be invalid, or if your knowledge is insufficient to interpret *all* potential findings validly and fully.

A severe impediment to good practice is that we usually cannot know what we do not know. In a series of experiments, Kruger and Dunning (2002) found that the least capable individuals greatly overestimate their abilities and the most capable slightly underestimate theirs. More striking is that unless we are highly competent in an area, we cannot judge our own or others' competence accurately. Let this serve as a humbling warning.

Administer Tests the Way They Were Designed

- You must understand the technical aspects of measurement, validation, and evaluation design; the tests, procedures, and materials used; and their limitations and appropriateness for the subject.

- Follow the standardized procedures *exactly* when you are administering and scoring a test, to ensure validity, or you will "unstandardize" a standardized test (Pope, 2003).

- Use only tests whose manuals have the necessary and currently appropriate reliability and validity data. The manuals should also have detailed procedural descriptions of the methods of administering, scoring, and interpreting the tests' results.

- Use the most current, reliable, and valid version of a test. Although the APA code of ethics (APA, 2002) specifically forbids the use of obsolete or outdated tests (Standard

9.08), Sam Knapp (personal communication, October 2, 1996) reminds me, "It can be justified to use an earlier version of a test under some circumstances, for example, in doing a test–retest with a particular patient."

- Test security is required by the APA code of ethics (APA, 2002) in Standard 9.11. For this reason, do not quote the questions asked (especially from copyrighted tests) in your reports; instead, describe the stimuli in general terms. Similarly, keep the tests, materials, and manuals unavailable to potential clients and to unsophisticated users. Do not let clients take a test home (this ensures that no one will assist the clients in answering as well). Because of HIPAA, a major test publisher, Pearson Assessments, has issued a set of guidelines on client access to test materials (including test booklets, computer generated reports, scoring keys, answer sheets, etc.; see www.pearsonassessments.com/catalog/hipaa.pdf). Pearson asserts that these are protected from disclosure to clients and to other covered entities (CEs) as trade secrets, and that they are not protected health information (PHI). On the other hand, test *data* (results, interpretations, scores, protocols) would be PHI and can be disclosed. These guidelines have not yet been legally tested, but are likely to apply.

Interpret and Report Your Findings Carefully

- It is probably a good idea to write your report as if persons besides the referrer will someday read it. If you are not fully comfortable justifying (perhaps in court and to a hostile opposition) any statement, either leave it out or modify it.

- Don't go beyond your findings: Do not, in your report through defensiveness or arrogance, go beyond your data. The APA ethics code reminds us that psychologists must recognize the "limitations of their interpretations" of assessment results (APA, 2002, Standard 9.06).

- Treat test results as hypotheses, not factual pronouncements. After all, they are only behavior samples from the universe of possible behaviors. When you use an automated scoring and interpretation service, you must understand the decision rules that transform the raw data into interpretative statements, as well as the psychometric properties of the program (especially its reliability and validity).

Be Alert for Biasing Factors

- Know and keep in mind the assumptions behind your orientation, and struggle to understand how these can blind you to evidence, shape your expectations, and bias your results. Again, the APA code of ethics (APA, 2002) gives guidance for sensitivity and circumspection in test administration and interpretation in Standard 9, especially Standard 9.06.

- Seek out and attend to personal, social, and cultural factors that can bias your results. As noted earlier, these may include ageism; "beautyism" (the influence of weight, height, coloring, and prettiness); ethnic preferences and beliefs; racism; sex-role stereotypes; your social class; "personal allergies" to some people; your financial gain from some findings or diagnoses; sympathy with the "victim"; hostility to the "aggressor";

blaming the "victim"; supporting the "downtrodden"; your personal liberalism or conservatism; feelings about those who smoke, drink, abstain, and/or are "in recovery"; biases for or against various religions or degrees of religiosity; and other less well-recognized feelings that can interfere with careful analysis.

- Understand and always give full weight to the "low base rate" phenomenon, which can severely limit the accuracy of any variable's identification. Similarly, appreciate the effects of a high base rate, and know the local base rates of the phenomena of interest.

- In your report, state clearly all possible limitations of and reservations about reliability and validity:

    Environmental factors: room lighting, a client's poor hearing or need for glasses, interruptions, noise.

    Communicational factors: the client's hearing, speech, and facility in English (written, read, heard, and spoken). For example, the Minneapolis Multiphasic Personality Inventory (MMPI) requires an eighth-grade reading level.

    The client's personal aspects: age, sex, education, and ethnic/cultural background.

    Any differences between the client and the norming population, which might invalidate the use of a test for this client. When such differences exist, weight them.

Be Aware of Forensic Issues

As noted in Chapter 2, never either accept or defer a fee for forensic evaluations contingent upon the outcome of the trial (because doing so appears to compromise your professional independence), and do not base custody evaluations on less than full evaluations of all parties. Anderten et al. (1980) add several other considerations for forensic evaluations:

- Be especially careful to be objective and impartial, resisting pressure to support the position of the side that hires you.

- Work with your attorney to assure that *all* of your relevant findings will be heard in court.

- Make your first priority the client's well-being, not your loyalty to the attorney or agency.

Be Thorough

- Consider possible physical causes of any and all findings, and pursue their investigation.

- Always obtain and review previous testing and treatment records.

The APA code of ethics (APA, 2002) requires providing feedback to clients in Standard 9.10. The best brief overview of the ethical obligations one assumes when providing clients with feedback on tests results is provided by Pope (1992). Fischer (1994) also addresses feedback and all aspects of tailoring assessment to the individual. For a release form, see Section 7.5 and Form 52. Finally, as always, you should stay current on the literature, the issues, and the evolving state of the assessment arts.

3.6   Boundary Issues

A role, such as being a therapist, comes with rules—what is to be done and not done in performing that role. Some of those rules create boundaries: a circumscribed time frame (meeting only for the therapy "hour"); a particular place (meeting only in the office); restrictions on touch (only handshakes, no hugs); limits on self-disclosure (none or only with careful consideration); restrictions on gifts (rare and of small extrinsic value) and money (for therapy, not investment advice or tips); and so on. When these boundaries are respected and not crossed the relationship is made predictable and safe. Accidental or incidental *crossings* may occur, such as at a public musical event, without causing harm to a client. Crossings may also be deliberate but justified, such as a longer therapy meeting during a crisis. Boundary *violations* are conceptualized along many facets: the therapist's intent (such as self-interest and benefit); the relevance of the action to the treatment (outside meetings as part of *in vivo* desensitization vs. socializing); the client's interpretation of the behaviors (a hug intended by the therapist to be congratulatory may be seen as intrusive or sexual by a client); current, evolving, and local professional standards (first-name-basis conversations used to be considered inappropriate); and others. Furthermore, a crossing may be seen as a violation if the client feels it is unwelcome; if it harms the client; or if the client's history, diagnosis, or values shape it as stressful.

In light of these considerations, Barnett et al. (2007b) suggest that before acting,

> psychologists should work to be sure that (a) their intention is motivated by the client's treatment needs and best interests and not by their own needs; (b) the boundary crossing is consistent with the client's treatment plan; (c) the boundary crossing is sensitive to the client's diagnosis, history, culture, and values; (d) the boundary crossing—and the reasoning supporting it—is documented in the client's record; (e) the boundary crossing is discussed, if possible, with the client in advance to ensure his or her comfort with the plan and to prevent misunderstandings; (f) the power differential present is considered, and the client's trust is not exploited; and (g) consultation with a respected colleague is used to guide the psychologist's decision. (p. 403)

Several of models of decision making in terms of ethics have been devised. Sonne's (2006) appears to be the most inclusive. A very good self-educational questionnaire exploring the consequences of boundary confusion is the Exploitation Index (Epstein & Simon, 1990). Boundary issues stemming from "dual relationships" in general, and from client–therapist sexual intimacy in particular, are discussed in detail in the next two sections.

Take the time to answer the questionnaire presented in Figure 4. To gain most from it, consider all your clients when answering if; not just the one it asks about. The questions are likely to raise your consciousness of how these issues can distort your work. I am indebted to Estelle Disch, PhD, of Cambridge, MA, for her permission to reprint it, and to Sam

Are You in Trouble with a Client?

The purpose of this checklist is to alert you to boundary issues that might be interfering with your ability to work effectively with a particular client. Be particularly attentive if the situation persists even after you have attempted to change it. Answer either true or false to each question and add any explanations or details.

Client's initials or pseudonym: _____   Date: _____

1. This client feels more like a friend than a client.   ☐ True ☑ False

2. I often tell my personal problems to this client.   ☐ True ☑ False

3. I feel sexually aroused in response to this client.   ☐ True ☑ False

4. I want to be friends with this client when therapy ends.   ☐ True ☑ False

5. I'm waiting for therapy to end in order to be lovers with this client.   ☐ True ☑ False

6. To be honest, I think the good-bye hugs last too long with this client.   ☐ True ☐ False

7. My sessions often run overtime with this client.   ☐ True ☑ False

8. I tend to accept gifts or favors from this client without examining why the gift was given and why at that particular time.   ☐ True ☑ False

9. I have a barter arrangement with this client.   ☐ True ☑ False

10. I have had sexual contact with this client.   ☐ True ☑ False

11. I sometimes choose my clothing with this particular client in mind.   ☐ True ☑ False

12. I have attended small professional or social events at which I knew this client would be present, without discussing it ahead of time.   ☐ True ☑ False

13. This client often invites me to social events and I don't feel comfortable saying either yes or no.   ☐ True ☑ False

14. This client sometimes sits on my lap.   ☐ True ☑ False

15. Sometimes when I'm holding or hugging this client during our regular therapy work, I feel like the contact is sexualized for one or the other or both of us.   ☐ True ☐ False

16. There's something I like about being alone in the office with this client when no one else is around.   ☐ True ☐ False

17. I lock the door when working with this client.   ☐ True ☑ False

18. This client is very seductive and I often don't know how to handle it.   ☐ True ☐ False

19. This client owes me/the agency a lot of money and I don't know what to do about it.   ☐ True ☑ False

20. I have invited this client to public or social events.   ☐ True ☑ False

21. I am often late for sessions with this particular client.   ☐ True ☑ False

22. I find myself cajoling, teasing, or joking a lot with this client.   ☐ True ☑ False

23. I am in a heavy emotional crisis myself and I identify so much with this client's pain that I can hardly attend to the client.   ☐ True ☑ False

(cont.)

FIGURE 4. Are you in trouble with a client? Questionnaire for assessing boundary issues, devised by Estelle Disch, PhD, of Cambridge, MA, and reprinted here by permission of Dr. Disch. (Items 48–51 were suggested by Sam Knapp, EdD, of Harrisburg, PA.)

Figure 4 (*cont.*)

24. I allow this client to comfort me. ❑ True ☑ False

25. I feel like this client and I are very much alike. ❑ True ☑ False

26. This client scares me. ❑ True ☑ False

27. This client's pain is so deep I can hardly stand it. ❑ True ☑ False

28. I enjoy feeling more powerful than this client. ❑ True ☑ False

29. Sometimes I feel like I'm in over my head with this client. ❑ True ☑ False

30. I often feel hooked or lost with this client and supervision on the case hasn't helped. ❑ True ☑ False

31. I often feel invaded or pushed by this client and have a difficult time standing my ground. ❑ True ☑ False

32. Sometimes I hate this client. ❑ True ☑ False

33. I sometimes feel like punishing or controlling this client. ❑ True ☑ False

34. I feel overly protective toward this client. ❑ True ☑ False

35. I sometimes drink or take drugs with this client. ❑ True ☑ False

36. I don't regularly check out what the physical contact I have with this client means for the client. ❑ True ☑ False

37. I accommodate to this client's schedule and then feel angry/manipulated. ❑ True ☑ False

38. This client's fee feels too high or too low. ❑ True ☑ False

39. This client has invested money in an enterprise of mine or vice versa. ❑ True ☑ False

40. I have hired this client to work for me. ❑ True ☑ False

41. This client has hired me to work for her/him. ❑ True ☑ False

42. I find it very difficult not to talk about this client with people close to me. ❑ True ☑ False

43. I find myself saying a lot about myself with this client—telling stories, engaging in peer-like conversation. ❑ True ☑ False

44. If I were to list people in my caseload with whom I could envision myself in a sexual relationship, this client would be on the list. ❑ True ☑ False

45. I call this client a lot and go out of my way to meet with her/him in locations convenient to her/him. ❑ True ☑ False

46. This client has spent time at my home (apart from the office). ❑ True ☑ False

47. I'm doing so much on this client's behalf I feel exhausted. ❑ True ☑ False

48. I have given this client a ride home. ❑ True ☑ False

49. We have had lunch/dinner during sessions. ❑ True ☑ False

50. This client has performed minor favors for me, such as returning library books or picking up dry cleaning. ❑ True ☑ False

51. I have accepted valuable gifts from this client. ❑ True ☑ False

Knapp, EdD, of Harrisburg, PA, for suggesting the addition of the last four items. Dr. Disch has a more extensive and specific list of boundary crossings that may be violations and that indicate poor treatment, entitled "Is There Something Wrong or Questionable in Your Treatment?" (www.advocateweb.org/basta).

3.7   Dual (or Multiple) Relationships

What Are Dual Relationships?

"Dual relationships" exist whenever a therapist interacts with a client in more than that one role, such as also being a business partner, teacher, consultant, or sexual partner. The relevant portion of the APA code of ethics (APA, 2002) is Standard 3.05.

Why Avoid Dual Relationships?

Performing any role besides that of therapist can create goals, needs, and desires that are yours and not the client's. Dual relationships may lead to conflicts between your interests and the client's, and so you may not put the client's interest first. **Thus dual relationships impair your unselfish judgment, which is the essence of being a professional.** In addition, such relationships can have these negative effects:

- They limit the effective handling of the relationship variables.

- They usually close the door to future therapy if it is needed.

- The power differential inherent in the therapy relationship may be exploited through seducing or intimidating the client into the other relationship.

- In addition, when clients are exploited in dual relationships, complaining about it is much more difficult for them than complaining about most other issues, like fees. The clients must overcome the power differential and positive feelings in order to assert their own needs. The risks to a client are usually much greater than the risks to a therapist. For example, in a complaint, confidentiality may be broken and the therapist can say, allege, or deny almost anything about the client's life, thus putting the client on trial.

Harmful dual relationships usually stem from "subtle, gradual, and innocuous beginnings" (Pope, 1988a, p. 17). They may arise from inattention to the dynamics of the therapeutic relationship, or from a desire to be of even more help to a patient. They can also arise from the patient's own manipulation (because of pathology, transference, or other sources); in these cases, "dual" relationships often become "duel" relationships.

Types of Dual Relationships

There are many types of dual or multiple relationships, and therapists must be alert to all the possibilities. Pope (1988a) lists 18 real-life scenarios (and I have added some others), which can be simplified into the following general kinds of relationships.

Double Roles

Double roles include being a therapist as well as a supervisor, teacher (see below), dissertation committee member, evaluator, or research supervisor to the same person. Another example of double roles is providing therapy to current social acquaintances or business contacts, or to former ones when the old relationship was intense. Any such double roles are likely to distort the therapy relationship.

Being both a therapist and a friend is a third example of double roles. A "friend" is defined as someone with whom one socializes outside the therapy office. There are many distinctions between friendship and therapy, and the patient handout provided a little later (Handout 1) describes some of them. A policy is also included in the sample client information brochure (Section 4.2), and you may wish to make additions to this list from your own experience. You may even wish to expand upon the list in Section 4.2 for a separate handout; if you do so, please share the results with me.

Other examples of double roles include the following:

- Having any kind of sexual relationship with a former or current client (see Section 3.8).

- Having any kind of business relationship with a former or current client (that of employer, coauthor, consultant, advisor, mentor, partner, lender, debtor, etc.).

- Providing any kind of psychological services to the children of your employees; to children of colleagues, friends, or frequent social, political, or business contacts; or to children you coach in an athletic activity.

- In regard to students (see above), always refer your current students seeking therapy, and be careful about relationships with those who might become your students. It may even be better to remain somewhat distant, have only casual contacts, or meet only at social events associated with the university until a student graduates and one of your roles terminates, before entering a closer friendship with this person (Koocher & Keith-Spiegel, 1998).

Double Professions

The term "double professions" means serving in a second professional capacity with your patients, such as practicing law/medicine/financial advising (or any other profession) without a license (Pope, 1988a).

Double Financial Relationships

Double financial relationships are a third type of dual relationships. Trading or bartering therapy for legal or professional services (e.g., tutoring), goods, or discounts—either on a dollar-for-dollar value or on a task-for-task basis—puts you into an additional commercial role. In this role your goals are, or appear to be, in conflict with those of your clients. That is, you seem to be providing services at the lowest cost to you but the highest cost to them.

When Dual Relationships Are Not Avoidable: Weighing Their Effect

Multiple relationships are unavoidable in rural areas, in the military, and in most small communities (Campbell & Gordon, 2003). The central issue is the avoidance of *conflicting* roles. The APA ethics code (APA, 2002) notes that "Multiple relationships *that would not reasonably be expected to cause impairment or risk exploitation or harm* are not unethical" (Standard 3.05; emphasis added). Thus the code does not forbid dual or multiple relationships, but puts the burden of keeping them harmless on the psychologist. Eleven guidelines for doing so are offered by Barnett and Yutrzenka (1994).

In an intelligent and thoughtful article, Gottlieb (1993) proposed that since dual relationships are often unavoidable and are not prohibited outright, their variable effects ought to be weighed on three dimensions: "power," "duration," and the clarity of the time limits of the relationship, which he calls "termination." Essentially, relationships with low power differentials, briefer contacts, and clear time boundaries are less risky for exploitation, require less consultation, require less extensive and detailed informed consent, and so on. For example, vocational testing is lower on all three dimensions than intensive psychotherapy. For carefully reasoned arguments and suggestions about defining which multiple relationships are harmful and which are not, see Younggren and Gottlieb's (2004) elaboration of Gottlieb (1993), as well as Sonne (2006). Also useful is the website of the Markkula Center for Applied Ethics (scu.edu/ethics/practicing/decision). Staal and King (2000) have adapted Gottlieb's model for military psychologists, and Younggren's (2002) article is helpful in evaluating the ethics of a dual relationship.

If you recognize that you are deep in conflicting and risky dual relationships with a patient, Kaplan (1990) recommends that you do the following:[1]

- Don't wait until the patient makes it clear that a problem has developed. Act.

- Get consultation about (1) the dynamics of the dual relationships, (2) how best to end the dual relationships, and (3) how to create the least harm to the patient.

- Review your malpractice insurance policy and inform your carrier. Talk to an attorney to learn how to limit your liability.

- With the patient's agreement, try to get a mediator to devise a "mutually agreeable, constructive solution which works toward restoration of a healthy therapeutic relationship or, in the alternative, develop a means to terminate both . . . relationship[s] without harming the patient through abandonment" (Kaplan, 1990, p. 30).

- "Arrange for an independent evaluation of the patient to determine whether the patient has been harmed and to develop future treatment recommendations" (Kaplan, 1990, p. 30).

---

[1]This list is adapted from Kaplan (1990). Copyright 1990 by the Illinois Psychological Association. Adapted by permission.

- Document all interactions with the patient and your memories of how the dual relationship arose.

- Document any agreements with the patient, and have them reviewed by both your own counsel and the patient's.

Preventing Trouble

HANDOUT 1   A handout on dual relationships is presented as Handout 1. It is intended to be used for patient education, and thus to lessen troubles in this area. It can be left in your waiting room or handed to a patient when questions or a potentially risky situation occurs.

3.8   Sexual Intimacies in Therapy

Sexual relationships with patients are a particularly toxic type of dual relationship, and they constitute a plague in the health professions. We must greatly extend our efforts to prevent them through consciousness raising, training, supervision, investigation, and punishment. The APA code of ethics (APA, 2002) says flatly in Standard 10.05 that "Psychologists do not engage in sexual intimacies with current therapy clients/patients," and in Standard 10.08 that they do not do so "with a former client/patient for at least two years after cessation or termination of therapy." (See later in this section for clarification of this latter prohibition.)

What Is Meant by "Sexual Intimacies"?

Although there is no precise agreement on the definition of "sexual intimacy," the following statements are made in the professional liability insurance policies of several professional organizations.

The American Professional Agency's policy defines "sexual misconduct" this way:

> any type of actual, alleged, attempted, or proposed physical touching or caressing, or suggestion thereof by *You* or any person for whom *You* may be legally responsible, with or to any of *Your* past or present patients or clients, or with or to any relative or any person whom regularly resides with any such patient or client, or with or to any person with whom such patient or client or relative has an affectionate personal relationship, which could be considered sexual in nature and/or inappropriate to any psychological services being provided. (American Professional Agency, 2006, p. 6; emphasis in original)

Rockport Insurance, with policies for all the mental health professions except psychiatry, phrases it this way:

> "Sexual misconduct" means any: a. Action or behavior; or b. Physical contact or touching; that is intended to lead to or which culminates in any sexual act, arising out of the professional treatment and care of any client, patient, or any other person whose care has been entrusted to an insured. "Sexual misconduct" includes such action, behavior, physical contact or touching

Limits of the Therapy Relationship: What Clients Should Know

Psychotherapy is a professional service I can provide to you. Because of the nature of therapy, our relationship has to be different from most relationships. It may differ in how long it lasts, in the topics we discuss, or in the goals of our relationship. It must also be limited to the relationship of therapist and client *only*. If we were to interact in any other ways, we would then have a "dual relationship," which would not be right and may not be legal. The different therapy professions have rules against such relationships to protect us both.

I want to explain why having a dual relationship is not a good idea. Dual relationships can set up conflicts between my own (the therapist's) interests and your (the client's) best interests, and then your interests might not be put first. In order to offer all my clients the best care, my judgment needs to be unselfish and professional.

Because I am your therapist, dual relationships like these are improper:

- I cannot be your supervisor, teacher, or evaluator.
- I cannot be a therapist to my own relatives, friends (or the relatives of friends), people I know socially, or business contacts.
- I cannot provide therapy to people I used to know socially, or to former business contacts.
- I cannot have any other kind of business relationship with you besides the therapy itself. For example, I cannot employ you, lend to or borrow from you, or trade or barter your services (things like tutoring, repairing, child care, etc.) or goods for therapy.
- I cannot give legal, medical, financial, or any other type of professional advice.
- I cannot have any kind of romantic or sexual relationship with a former or current client, or any other people close to a client.

There are important differences between therapy and friendship. As your therapist, I cannot be your friend. Friends may see you only from their personal viewpoints and experiences. Friends may want to find quick and easy solutions to your problems so that they can feel helpful. These short-term solutions may not be in your long-term best interest. Friends do not usually follow up on their advice to see whether it was useful. They may *need* to have you do what they advise. A therapist offers you choices and helps you choose what is best for you. A therapist helps you learn how to solve problems better and make better decisions. A therapist's responses to your situation are based on tested theories and methods of change. You should also know that therapists are required to keep the identity of their clients secret. Therefore, I may ignore you when we meet in a public place, and I must decline to attend your family's gatherings if you invite me. Lastly, when our therapy is completed, I will not be able to be a friend to you like your other friends.

In sum, my duty as therapist is to care for you and my other clients, but *only* in the professional role of therapist. Please note any questions or concerns on the back of this page so we can discuss them.

---

whether it is committed by, caused by, or contributed to by an insured or any other person for whom an insured may be legally liable. (Everest Reinsurance Company, 1999, p. 7)

As you can see, current policies are very broadly written. In addition, state laws differ in defining sexual behaviors; some indicate only heterosexual genital intercourse, while others include kissing and sexual touching but may be silent on other kinds of sexual expression.

With Whom Are Sexual Intimacies Prohibited?

Sexual intimacies are not allowed with "clients" of any kind, including supervisees, trainees, students of yours, or any persons in a professional relationship with you (e.g., business partners or employees). In parallel, the APA ethics code (APA, 2002) says that you should not do therapy with former sexual partners (Standard 10.07).

Standard 10.06 of the APA code (APA, 2002) also forbids sexualized relationships with "individuals [whom psychologists] know to be the close relatives or significant others of current clients/patients." This definition includes all members of a client's household, and it may even include anyone (such as an ex-spouse or a boyfriend or girlfriend) with whom any of these persons has or had a close emotional relationship. Although this is the most stringent exclusionary approach, it may be better to be safe than sorry, in light of the direction the field is going.

Stromberg and Dellinger (1993) raise the question of how state regulations define "patient" or "client." This may be of considerable importance to psychologists, who often have a wider spectrum of possible professional relationships than do psychiatrists or social workers. For example, psychologists see assessment subjects, organizational clients, research participants, employment counseling clients, and coaching clients. Obviously, psychologists have to know the answer to this question and be circumspect; regulators tend to think in polarities, whereas psychologists may evaluate patienthood in terms of the intensity, duration, and intimacy of the relationship. Haspel et al. (1997) provide both excellent discussions of the definitional issues and quoted definitions from many states' laws.

Who Is Prohibited from Engaging in Intimacies?

You as the therapist are prohibited from engaging in sexual intimacies, of course, but those you employ or supervise are also prohibited.

The Damage to the Client and to Therapy

Therapist–client sexual intimacies are universally prohibited because they betray the trust the client has in the therapist's putting the client's needs first. The harm to the client can be extensive (Pope, 1988b). There have been problems with the collection of empirical data in this area; as a result, we have only the upper and lower limits of occurrence rates, and descriptions of some of the damage from these relationships (Williams, 1992).

Frequently reported consequences to clients (Bouhoutsos et al., 1983) include ambivalence, distrust of men or women, and distrust of therapy. The victims become "therapeutic orphans." They may have flashbacks, nightmares, and other recollections, and/or depression, hospitalizations, and suicides. They may exhibit relationship problems, with confusion about identity, boundaries, and roles. They may experience feelings of anger, abandonment, exploitation, devastation, guilt, emptiness, and isolation; they may also show suppressed rage, emotional dyscontrol, and mood swings.

Pope (1988b) has described the "therapist–patient sex syndrome" as similar both to posttraumatic stress disorder and to the sequelae of child or spouse abuse, rape, and incest. According to Pope, this syndrome involves "(a) ambivalence, (b) a sense of guilt, (c) feelings of emptiness and isolation, (d) sexual confusion, (e) impaired ability to trust, (f) identity, boundary, and role confusion, (g) emotional lability . . . , (h) suppressed rage, (i) increased suicidal risk, and (j) cognitive dysfunction . . . " (1988b, p. 222). Folman (1990) has suggested that 11 psychotherapy processes are all affected negatively by sexual contacts: transference, countertransference, trust, confidentiality, resistance, privacy, intimacy, boundaries, self-disclosure, use of touch, and termination. Theory suggests that the effects may differ for men and women, may be worse if the therapist initiates the intimacies and is married, and may also be worse if the client has been victimized before. In summary, if any of the negative consequences described here is likely to occur, they are so serious that taking the chance that a patient *won't* be harmed is unethical. As clinicians, we do have a minimal ethical duty: "At least do no harm."

Negative Consequences to the Clinician

The helping professions no longer ignore sexual relations with clients. It appears that, in fact, the trend is toward greater enforcement, condemnation, and punishment. If you need reinforcements for abstaining from sexual intimacies, here are some from Keith-Spiegel (1977) and others:

- Subsequent therapists will support and encourage your ex-client to complain.

- Your client/lover will expect commitment, or at least a continuation of the relationship, from you; you will then have to deal with a spurned lover, not a helped client.

- The mass media love these cases. You will be publicly pilloried.

- Some states make ethical violations illegal, so you can lose your license.

- As of 2003, 24 states have criminalized sexual contact between therapists and clients (McArdle, 2003). It is a felony, and the maximum sentence is often 20 years in prison and a fine of $150,000.

- Intimacy with a client is likely to result in multiple legal problems. Gary Schoener, an expert in this area, says, "I call it a triple whammy. First, a criminal case can result in a prison term or probation and a large fine. Second, a criminal conviction makes it more likely that a therapist will lose a civil case and have to cough up monetary damages. Third; criminal conviction usually makes it an easy and fast job for a state board to revoke professional licenses" (Schoener, quoted in Foster, 1996, p. 25).

- You cannot really win if you are sued; you will experience excruciating stress, lost money, and conflict with your significant others. Your professional liability insurance probably won't cover the damages awarded: Insurers generally cover only up to $25,000 for sexual cases, and many will not cover these at all. Current practice is for the insurance company to offer the $25,000 only for the defense of the claim, and nothing to settle the claim or pay any damages awarded. Therefore, you alone will be fully responsible for any damage awards. Insurance companies use the rationale that their policies don't cover intentional or knowing misconduct, and that your ethics code and the literature have put you "on notice" that these are wrong (Stromberg & Dellinger, 1993). Moreover, you can even be sued by the patient (and his or her significant other, if any) for such things as intentional infliction of harm (Stromberg & Dellinger, 1993, p. 9).

Not Me! I Would Never!

Misconceptions and distortions abound about sexually intimate and abusing therapists. Pope (1989b) has identified categories and scenarios for therapists who became sexually intimate with patients. On the basis of his work and that of others, we can debunk a number of erroneous ideas as follows:

- It is not true that only poorly trained therapists get sexually involved with patients.

- It is not true that only jerks get sexually involved; respected, influential, successful, or prominent therapists also do the same.

- It is not true that the sexually active therapist is seen as a hero. Such a therapist's sexual behaviors will be seen as exploitative and motivated by feelings of inadequacy (Keith-Spiegel, 1977).

- It is not true that sexual intimacies can be simply an extension of sex education or sex therapy.

- It is not true that sexual intimacies can be a component of trailblazing or innovative therapy.

- It is not true that sexual intimacies may be justified if the consequence of refusal would be the client's suicide or something else as serious. (If this idea even flickers though your mind, consult a peer to examine this rationalization and find ethical alternatives.)

- It is not true that abusing therapists will only abuse one sex, so confining their practice to the other sex will safeguard their clients.

- It is not true that the termination of therapy legitimizes the intimacy. You cannot simply discharge or refer a patient and then pursue a relationship.

- It is not true that waiting 2 years after discharge means "it can't be transference" and thus it is all right.

- It is not true that "anyone can get carried away with passion." You will be held responsible for your behavior.

- It is not true that sincerely believing that sexual attraction is totally inappropriate and harmful protects a therapist from being sexually attracted (Bennett et al., 1990).

- The Group for the Advancement of Psychiatry (GAP, 1990) offers some common rationalizations that have led therapists into trouble:

  "If we had met socially I'm sure we would have had a great relationship right from the start. Why should we be penalized by our bad luck in meeting this way?"

  "We are both mature people, and basically healthy, so we can handle the relationship despite any transference distortions."

- It is possible that real true love—not just transference—can happen in therapy, but it is not at all certain that a client and a therapist can accurately distinguish it. Therapists and clients have married after the therapeutic issues are resolved, but the burden of demonstrating that such a relationship is not exploitative rests completely on the therapist. See below.

Is Sexual Intimacy with a Client *Ever* Acceptable?

The Safest Course: "Never"

Sexual intimacy with a client is *never* acceptable, even if the therapy is over. **It is always your responsibility to say "No." "Never—without time limits"** is the safest course. For example, the American Psychiatric Association (2006) says, "Sexual activity with a current or former patient is unethical" (Section 2, No. 1), and other professional groups have gone further.

For psychologists, the code of ethics (APA, 2002, Standard 10.08) sets a 2-year posttherapy time limit, but after that the psychologist is responsible for demonstrating that the relationship is not exploitative (Standard 10.08b). This is slippery; a therapist in love/lust/loneliness is likely to be a poor judge of these issues. It is educational to read the APA code's list of criteria for evaluating potential exploitativeness: the length of time since termination; the nature, duration, and intensity of the treatment; the circumstances of termination; the client's personal history and present mental status; the chances of adverse impact on the client; and any statements or actions by the therapist during the course of therapy *suggesting or inviting* the possibility of a posttermination sexual *or romantic* relationship with the patient (APA, 2002; modified and emphasis added).

Individual states, however, are enacting laws concerning the time limits. Florida (Fla. Stat. Chapter 21U-15004) considers the therapy relationship "to continue in perpetuity," whereas California believes in a 2-year limit (Cal. Civil Code Section 43.93), as do Ohio and Minnesota. There is also much uncertainty about the statute of limitations for suing. Generally it has run from the time of the incident, but courts are now accepting the idea that the statute may not start until the harm is discovered or recognized, and this may be years later. "Thus, in essence, most courts are bending over backwards to permit patients to proceed with suits against abusive therapists—even if their mental state caused considerable delay in doing so" (Stromberg & Dellinger, 1993, p. 10).

Because of the many options and factors involved, therapists who are sexually involved with clients or ex-clients can never be sure that they will not be sued for sexual intimacies, no matter how long it has been since the termination of therapy. For all these reasons, "never" is safest for both you and your clients.

Other "What If . . . ?" Situations

- Sex with a client is not allowed even if you believe it is in the client's best interest (as sex therapy, as a means of raising his or her self-esteem or sexual confidence, as a restitutive emotional experience, etc.).

- Sex is not allowed even if the client is a consenting adult who wants to have sex, initiates it, authorizes it, says it's OK, promises it will be no problem for you, pleads, or the like. In the laws making therapist–client sex a felony, consent (by the client) is specifically ruled out as a defense to be used by the therapist. The point here is that such laws remove from consideration the defense that the client consented to the sexual relationship, and make this kind of relationship a statutory crime like statutory rape. So if you and a client have sexual intimacies, you are guilty *de jure.*

- Even if what you feel for a client is "true love," sex is not allowed. Sorry, but your feelings do not count here. It is probably unethical even when you fully intend to marry a client or ex-client. Plans change; promises don't.

- Sex, of course, is not allowed with force, seduction, drugs, threats, or intimidation.

- If you think, "Sex outside the office is OK because it is not therapy," think again. Sex is not allowed even if you never discuss therapy, because it is the role conflict—not the actions or location—that is harmful.

- Sorry, but even *flirting* is out. This is not a legitimate or reliable way to raise the self-esteem of a patient.

- *No* kind of sex is allowed. Remind yourself that sexual activities are not just limited to intercourse, not just genital, not just heterosexual.

- Regarding touching: The safest rule, "Never touch," may seem too conservative and crippling to both parties. Durana (1998) and Downey (2001) review the literature and offer legal and clinical guidelines. Smith et al.'s (1998) book is comprehensive and authoritative. Some guidelines from Meiselman (1990, p. 138) were originally devised for treating adult women who were sexually abused as children, but seem sensible and well reasoned:

  "Wait for the client to spontaneously initiate touch or indicate a willingness to be touched." This allows the client to retain control and security.

  "Specifically ask for the client's permission before touching her in any way." This allows cognitive reinforcement of affects and supports the client's control of her (or his) body.

"Avoid falling into a routinized pattern of touching," because "establishing a custom of touching can cause the client to feel coerced into allowing touching . . . when she would prefer to avoid it."

"Decline any form of touch that seems likely to be sexually stimulating to either party." Be aware that *any* touch can be sexualized, and the contact may be erotic only to the patient. This rule reinforces boundaries and the rule that both parties have the right to say "No."

A Checklist of Preventive Measures

❑ Inform clients early in therapy about ethical limits. (See Handout 1 and Section 4.2.)

❑ Reduce your vulnerability by doing nothing but therapy in the office, keeping the office businesslike, and perhaps never being alone in the office suite with some clients.

❑ Be sensitive to how each client may interpret your nonsexual or affectionate behaviors, conversation about sexual topics, jokes, efforts to be helpful, and so forth. Even simple touches and expressions of concern can be misinterpreted. Think how the patient will interpret your touching him or her. Explain what you are doing and why before you do it, so that it will not be seen as a sexual overture (Bennett et al., 1990).

❑ Monitor your feelings throughout the therapy. If your attraction or fantasies become strong or distracting, consult immediately.

❑ Ask yourself: What effects will a sexual relationship with this client have on my other important relationships?

❑ Remind yourself: You really need this career. You have worked hard and long for it, and you are, or will be, very good at it. Don't throw it away for a little "fun." There is an old saying (and not only for men): "Don't let the little head do the thinking for the big head."

What to Do If a Client Asks You for Sex

If a client asks you for sex, plan your reaction carefully, because this is a high-risk situation for you and a high-vulnerability time for the client. Maintain the client's self-esteem (perhaps say that you are flattered), and clarify the request. In particular, explore the issues therapeutically:

- Is the client attracted to your role or power, or to you as a person?

- Are there transference, avoidance, authority, abuse, or parental issues?

- Is the client subverting the therapy to avoid confrontation and change?

- Is the client setting up another defeat of a therapist, failure of treatment, or failure of his or her own efforts?

Rutter (quoted in Foster, 1996, p. 27) offers this observation:

> A client trying to seduce a therapist may be repeating past injuries, but is also most likely searching for a response that will discourage this repetition. The client is doing exactly what patients are supposed to do when they see their doctors: bringing her [sic] illness to her therapist, her self-destructive pattern, in the only way she knows how, by repeating it with her therapist, right there in the room. Along with her hunger for warmth and affection, she is showing her therapist that she has always been out of control of her own sexual boundaries. The therapist can either victimize her as others have, or he can offer her a way to begin recovering from her past injuries.

When you say "No" to the client (as you must), make the "No" solid. Do not be ambiguous. Don't say "Only if . . . ," or "When . . . ," or even "No, but . . . ". Say, "It is unethical and would be harmful to you. Not after therapy is over. Never, under any conditions." Set and keep rigid boundaries, but also use this incident as grist for the therapeutic mill.

Consciousness Raising

In an appendix to their book, Pope and Bouhoutsos (1986) offer a list of situations in which the risk of sexual intimacy with a client is high. Their list is rephrased below, with some additions, for consciousness-raising purposes.[2]

You are at increased risk when you are:

- Preoccupied with your personal problems when in therapy.

- Playing the authority on everything and becoming angry when challenged.

- Dressing, talking, or acting in a flirtatious or seductive manner with a patient.

- Prescribing that a client dress, talk, or act in a flirtatious or seductive manner. You are at some increased risk of the patient's misunderstanding when you prescribe seductive behavior (as in dating skills training or sexual therapy), or especially when you have him or her rehearse with you. Therefore, be extra careful to get fully informed consent. Also, you might want to involve a consultant or a witness to your therapy plan and methods.

- Prescribing sexual behaviors for your vicarious pleasure, curiosity, voyeurism, or sense of power.

- Prescribing abstinence or proscribing some relationship because you are jealous.

- Discussing sexual material because of your own interests rather than the patient's clinical needs.

- "Dating" your patient—taking him or her out for lunch, a drink, a film, or an art gallery. Treating agoraphobia *in vivo* might lead to these situations.

[2]Most of this is adapted from Pope and Bouhoutsos (1986). Copyright 1986 by the Greenwood Publishing Group, Inc. Adapted by permission.

- Scheduling a patient so that you have lots of time with him or her (last patient of the day), or can be alone together, or can have extra sessions with him or her.

- Wallowing in a "mutual admiration society": giving or receiving excessive compliments, basking in the glow of the client's appreciation while ignoring or minimizing the distortion, and rationalizing away either party's limitations.

- Not examining your attraction or arousal in light of the therapy's dynamics and your own psychological state and needs, and not offering an appropriate and therapeutic response.

- Isolating the patient from other sources of assistance so that you become his or her "life-line," and he or she is less likely to tell another professional of your sexual relations.

- Isolating yourself from consultation, peers, supervision, and education.

- Believing that in the case of this patient, there are special mitigating factors that make sex OK (GAP, 1990, p. 58).

By far the most common scenario in which sexual improprieties arise is one in which a male therapist (or, rarely—5–10% of the time—a female therapist) has personal problems that temporarily distort his (or her) judgment. Therefore, if you are compromised by such problems, do not work. Rest and recuperate; get consultation and education. Everything is more difficult to get out of than into. If you discover or even suspect that you are at risk, **get help immediately!** Seek consultation, personal therapy, time off, or whatever you need.

What to Do If You Are Attracted to a Client

"Attraction" means finding a client strikingly physically attractive, amazingly witty or sensitive, alluringly comfortable for you, or the like. Here are some guidelines for what to do if you find yourself feeling attracted:

- Step back mentally and ask yourself whether this presentation has previously been a strategy of the client's for getting his or her needs met. Ask how such a strategy plays into your own needs and situation. Consider your own issues, such as rescue fantasies and needs to be admired, found attractive, be in control, or be depended upon. In addition, how are your intimate relationships going now?

- How have you previously resolved such attractions? Remember, therapists should meet clients' needs, not vice versa.

- Irvin P. R. Guyett, PhD, of Pittsburgh, PA, advises: If you find yourself fantasizing about the client outside the session, or your fantasies are amplified in the next session, consult a peer.

- If you are attracted, do *not* discuss this attraction with the client until you have consulted a peer first. You must fully understand your side before putting anything more on the client.

- It is still your responsibility to deal with both your own and the client's urges, fantasies, and attractions in a therapeutically productive way, or you may be at risk of malpractice even without the sexual contact. That is, you may be ignoring or not meeting the client's needs but meeting your own, and so you are providing inadequate or even incompetent services.

- Some advise immediately referring a client to whom you develop romantic feelings; however, besides resembling abandonment and punishing the client, this is avoidance of your or the client's feelings. It is likely to be better in the long run to process these feelings with your supervisor or consultant and to resolve them.

- Ask yourself: Can I control my impulses? Can I be open about this problem and my feelings with a colleague? If you cannot resolve the feelings, terminate the therapy and refer the client, before you get into deeper trouble.

- Pope (1987) outlines a successful case treatment of a therapist who was highly attracted to a client. This may be useful reading. The best overview of the facts, consequences, and issues is also by Pope (2000).

Reporting Another Therapist

What if you recognize the damage done to a patient by a previous sexual relationship with a therapist, but the patient does not? Of course you will work with the patient on this issue, but do you have to report it? Generally, the answer is yes (APA, 2002, Standards 1.04 and 1.05), because you have a duty to care for the patient. Unfortunately, fewer than 3% of such cases are reported to licensing boards (Parsons & Wincze, 1995).

What if a client *falsely* accuses a previous therapist of sexual misconduct? Good starting sources for some information about false accusations of sexual improprieties are Gutheil (1992), Sederer and Libby (1995), and Williams (2000).

Client–Therapist Intimacy: Appropriate and Inappropriate Conduct

HANDOUT 2   The purposes and functions of Handout 2 are as follows: (1) to reduce the rate of inappropriate sexual behaviors on the part of clients; (2) to increase the rate of clients' reporting of sexual exploitation by all kinds of professionals; and (3) to protect you if you are misunderstood or even accused of sexual improprieties, because this form states your rules of practice. The handout is valuable because it is written for consumers, in a narrative and casual style. Its message and tone are empowering; it addresses questions of ethics, harm, love, and discomfort with sexual behavior in therapy; and it offers options for reacting, taking action, and handling the emotions stirred up by sexual behaviors in therapy.

This handout is not suitable for routine distribution to every client, because the reading may be burdensome for those who have not had ideas or experiences along these lines.

Client–Therapist Contact: Proper and Improper Conduct

This brochure has been written to help you understand what is proper and improper conduct for a therapist, and what responses are available to you as a consumer. It may raise issues that you have not considered before. However, if you are well informed, you will be better able to make sure your needs get met in therapy.

Although almost therapists are ethical people (that is, moral and law-abiding people) who care about their clients and follow professional rules and standards in their practice, there are a very few who do not consider what is best for their clients and who behave unethically. These issues apply to any mental health worker: psychologists, psychiatrists, social workers, counselors, clergy, nurses, or marriage and family therapists.

Therapist Behaviors That May Not Be OK

There will be times in your therapy when it might be important, even if it is very uncomfortable for you and your therapist, to discuss your feelings and concerns about sex. In fact, such discussions may be needed if you are to benefit from your therapy. **However, sexual contact is never a proper part of any sex education or sex therapy.**

Many caring therapists sometimes show their feelings through touch. These forms of physical contact in therapy, such as a handshake, a pat on the back, or a comforting hug, may not concern you. But you are the best judge of the effects that any touching may have on you. If your therapist engages in any type of physical contact that you do not want, tell him or her to stop, and explain how you feel about that contact. A responsible therapist will want to know about your feelings and will respect your feelings without challenging you.

If your therapist makes sexual comments or touches you in a way that seems sexual to you, you are likely to feel discomfort. Trust your feelings. Do not assume that your therapist must be right if it feels wrong to you.

There are warning signs that a therapist may be moving toward sexual contact with you. The therapist may start talking a lot about his or her own personal problems, giving you gifts, writing letters to you that are not about your therapy, or dwelling on the personal nature of your relationship. Or the therapist may create the idea that he or she is your only source of help by criticizing you for standing up for yourself, or by telling you how to behave with a sexual partner. A red flag should definitely go up if your therapist discusses his or her own sexual activities or sexual attraction to you. Other signs include making remarks intended to arouse sexual feelings, or forms of physical seduction, such as sexual touching.

(cont.)

Attraction to Your Therapist

It is normal for people in therapy to develop positive feelings, such as love or affection, toward a therapist who gives them support and caring. These feelings can be strong and may sometimes take the form of sexual attraction. It can be helpful to discuss these feelings with your therapist in order to understand them. A caring, ethical therapist would never take advantage of your feelings by suggesting sexual contact in therapy or by ending therapy to have a romantic relationship with you.

Though sexual feelings sometimes occur, and discussion about them is often useful, sexual contact with your therapist cannot be helpful. Sexual contact in therapy has been found to be harmful to the client in many ways, including damaging the client's ability to trust. The harmful effects may be immediate, or they may not be felt until later. For this reason, sexual contact with clients is clearly against the rules of all professional groups of mental health workers (psychologists, psychiatrists, social workers, counselors, and so on).

Actions You Can Take If You Believe That Your Therapist's Actions Are Not OK

Any time you feel uncomfortable about a part of your therapy, including therapist behavior that you think is improper, consider discussing this with your therapist. Your therapist should not try to make you feel guilty or stupid for asking questions, and your therapist should not try to frighten, pressure, or threaten you. If your therapist will not discuss your concerns openly or continues to behave in ways that are not OK with you, you probably have reason to be concerned.

When a discussion with your therapist about these behaviors does not help, you have the right to take some further action. You may wish to find another therapist and/or file any of several types of complaints. It is important for *you* to make the final decision about what course of action is best for your concerns and needs.

It may be very hard for you to think about making any kind of complaint against your therapist. You may worry that he or she will eventually find out about your complaint and be angry or hurt about it. You may also be concerned about possible harm to your therapist. There are several points to consider when you are trying to decide what is the best thing to do:

- Sexual contact between a therapist and a client is never a proper form of treatment for any problem. A therapist who suggests or engages in sexual contact in therapy is showing a lack of concern for you.
- Sexual contact in therapy is never your fault. Regardless of the particular things that have happened, you have placed your trust in the therapist, and it is his or her duty not to take advantage of that trust. If the therapist does this, you have been betrayed.
- A therapist who engages in sexual contact with a client might do so more than once and with more than one client. If no one reports this behavior, other people may be harmed by the same therapist.

Specific Courses of Action

Remember that you have the right to stop therapy whenever you choose. At the same time, you may also wish to make some type of complaint against the therapist who has acted improperly.

If you choose to make a complaint against your therapist, the process may become long and difficult. Other clients taking such action have felt overwhelmed, angry, and discouraged. It is very impor-

(cont.)

tant that you have support from people you can depend upon. Good sources of support might be family members, friends, support groups, a new therapist, or some type of advocate. Identifying and using good sources of support will help you feel more secure about the plan of action you have chosen.

You may wish to see another therapist to help you continue with your therapy, including dealing with problems resulting from the experience with the unethical therapist. It would not be unusual for you to have confusing thoughts and feelings about your experience and your previous therapist. It would also be understandable if you felt frightened about seeking, or had difficulty trusting, a new therapist.

You may also want an advocate to actively help you in making and pursuing plans. Try to locate a mental health worker who has had experience with other clients who have been victims of therapist sexual misconduct. He or she will be able to understand your situation, provide you with important information, and support you in your choice of action.

Many therapists work in agencies or other offices with supervisors. Consider talking to your therapist's supervisor or agency director to see what can be done.

You may want to contact the state and/or national professional group to which your therapist belongs. For example, many practicing psychologists are members of this state's Psychological Association and the American Psychological Association. These organizations have specific rules against sexual contact with clients, and each has an ethics committee that hears complaints. State and national professional associations do not license their members to practice psychotherapy; however, they can punish an unethical therapist, sometimes by expelling that person from membership in the organization. Such an action may make it more difficult for the therapist to get or keep a license to practice.

If your therapist is a licensed professional, you may want to contact this state's licensing board of the profession to which your therapist belongs. It has the power to take away or suspend the license of a professional found guilty of sexual misconduct.

Another option is to file a civil suit for malpractice, which would be done through a lawyer. To get a referral to an advocate or therapist experienced in working with victims of sexual misconduct, or to obtain information on filing a complaint, call or write to this state's professional organization.

Here are the addresses of some of the organizations mentioned above:

American Counseling Association
5999 Stevenson Avenue
Alexandria, VA 22304
800-347-6647
www.counseling.org

American Psychiatric Association
1000 Wilson Blvd., Suite 1825
Arlington, VA 22209-3901
703-907-7300
www.psych.org

American Psychological Association
750 First Street, N.E.
Washington, DC 20002-4242
800-374-2721
www.apa.org

National Association of Social Workers
750 First Street, N.E., Suite 700
Washington, DC 20002-4241
202-408-8600
www.socialworkers.org

There are groups in many communities to help victims of sexual abuse, and you can usually find them through the telephone book's "Human Services" section.

Please write your questions on the back of this handout so we can discuss them. Thank you.

Also, it may stimulate inappropriate thoughts in clients who are diagnosed as borderline, psychotic, or dependent.

You should be the one to ask or bring up the subject of this handout, because the client may be feeling too ashamed, confused, or guilty to do so. It can be given to a patient when it is topically appropriate, or it can be made available in a three-ring binder, along with other patient education materials and some of your forms, in your waiting room. You might suggest that a client "look through the book when you have a chance, because I want you to have this information." Perhaps 3–5% of new female clients will have had a sexual relationship with a previous therapist or other trusted professional. Although you should ask about this possibility in the first interview's history taking (this is why questions about it are included in the intake interview questions and guide—see Form 33), the client may not be ready to reveal this. You generally cannot ask this question repeatedly, but by leaving Handout 2 on your waiting room table, you have "normalized" the question, done some education, and told the client you are ready to hear about this relationship whenever the client is ready to reveal it. The same applies to domestic violence and battering.

Thorn et al. (1993) found that the use of a brochure or handout such as Handout 2 raised clients' consciousness about specific kinds of sexual abuse, and was very likely to prevent such abuse by therapists. Furthermore, Thorn et al. (1996) showed that the use of this brochure did not decrease trust in therapists or increase the likelihood of filing a false complaint, as some might fear. Some patients who read this or similar materials may come to recognize that a previous therapist was sexually exploitative. You should be prepared to deal with this contingency legally, emotionally, and professionally through education or through referral.

This handout is based on one authored by the Alabama Psychological Association's (P.O. Box 97, Montgomery, AL 36101; phone 334-262-8245) Committee to Prevent Sexual Misconduct. This was in turn adapted from a longer brochure published by the APA's Committee on Women in Psychology (1989), entitled "If Sex Enters the Psychotherapy Relationship." A version is also available online (www.apa.org/pi/therapy.html).

Insert the names, addresses, and phone numbers of your state's associations on page 3 of the handout, above the associations listed there, before you copy the handout for distribution.

3.9 The Duty to Protect (and Warn)

In addition to the ethical duties discussed previously, therapists also have ethical and legal obligations to prevent their clients from physically harming themselves or other persons. If you believe a client is dangerous, you have to use all reasonable care to protect the potential victim of your client's violence. You must use your professional judgment and position to *protect*, not just the more narrow duty simply to *warn*. Actually, your duty is to take appropriate action, which is not confined to warning. You have a less clear but more general obligation as a citizen to protect your fellow citizens.

The Legal Basis

The court's two decisions in the famous *Tarasoff* case (*Tarasoff v. Regents of the University of California*, 1976) established therapists' duty to protect. Since then, court cases have sent mixed messages about the limits of therapists' liability and required behaviors. But they have rarely held a therapist liable, and never when a professionally proper response was made. (This is good news for therapists.) **You will not be held responsible for a negative outcome if you have done what a good clinician should have—proper evaluation, planning, and implementation.** A review (Appelbaum, 1996) of suits against clinicians for warning others concludes that therapists should warn potential victims in order to avoid liability for subsequent violence, even though doing so opens the therapist to allegations of breach of confidentiality.

When adopting *Tarasoff,* the courts have usually followed three basic principles in assessing liability. These principles are (1) "foreseeability" of harm (a verbal threat or action taken), (2) identifiability of a victim, and (3) feasibility of therapist intervention. On the other hand, about 15 states have adopted "anti-*Tarasoff*" (or proconfidentiality) legislation or immunity statutes, which hold a therapist not liable if he or she fails to warn a victim. Furthermore, if therapists do break privilege in order to protect life, they generally will not be held liable for this breach under a doctrine of "qualified privilege" (i.e., if they can prove that there was a necessity to breach confidentiality). Some states have passed laws to limit a mental health practitioner's liability to situations where the therapist has actual knowledge of a danger to a specific person; even then, the liability is avoided if the therapist warns the target person and notifies the police. About half the states have some law about warning an identifiable victim of a serious threat. In some states you must notify the identifiable victim; in one, you must notify police only when you can't reach the victim; in another, you must notify if the client is just "considering" (the client need not say he or she "intends" to kill). Still other states offer you a choice among responses for protecting a victim. Obviously, you must know your state's rules in detail. Every state with a requirement to warn also protects you from any liability for warning.

When Do You Have a "Duty to Warn"?

You have a duty to warn, and should reveal the threat of violence, when you have reasonable cause to believe that the patient is dangerous to a specific person. But what are the characteristics of "reasonable cause" that trigger your duty? Here are the most common criteria.

First, the threat must be toward *a specific and identifiable target*. This must be a particular person, identifiable persons, or sometimes property, rather than a general group or category. The threat may arise through the patient's contemplation of a criminal act; so be attentive to all the consequences of such statements. The threat may also be toward the client's self, as in self-mutilation, suicide, or even self-neglect (such as failing to eat or drinking alcohol to the point of unconsciousness). Second, the threat has to be *believable*. It should be explicit, not vague; motives count, as does history, in assessing the potential for violence. Third, the threat has to be *imminent*, so that you must take action and cannot wait for others to learn of the risk and act to prevent the damage. Fourth, the threat must be by or to a *client* of yours. Your state's statutes and case law qualify all of these. See also the list of risk factors for violence in Section 3.10.

In determining whether reasonable cause exists, you must use good judgment, professional skill, and knowledge at levels usually provided by your peers. However, you are "not liable for simple errors made in good faith and with reasonable professional judgment" (Brodsky & Schumacher, 1990, p. 668). You do not need to be a perfect predictor of dangerousness—only to exercise a standard of care that a reasonable member of your discipline, in your local community and in these particular circumstances, would use. Such a professional should have current knowledge in the areas of evaluating dangerousness and violence. You must "take whatever other steps are reasonably necessary under the circumstances" (*Tarasoff v. Regents*).

What to Do When You Decide to "Warn"

"Discharging your *Tarasoff* duties" (as the lawyers call it) depends on many factors. You must take "reasonable" and "necessary" steps to protect the potential victim or victims. These will, of course, vary with the circumstances and the local laws, but *may* include the following options. Good sense suggests that you should implement as many of these options as possible, based on local rules and consultation:

- Warning the intended victim.

- Notifying local law enforcement authorities.

- Contacting people who can apprise the potential victim of the danger.

- Initiating voluntary or involuntary commitment. (This will shift the burden of decision making to the legal and medical systems.)

- Taking whatever other steps seem appropriate and necessary under the unique circumstances.

- Documenting all your thoughts and efforts. "Think out loud for the record."

State laws vary from offering specific steps (reasonable efforts to communicate the threat to victim and police) to simply warning the victim. In New Jersey, the therapist must do "any of the following: (1) arranging for the patient to be admitted to a psychiatric facility; (2) initiating procedures for involuntary commitment of the patient; (3) notifying local law enforcement authorities; (4) warning the intended victim; or (5) in the case of a minor who threatens to commit suicide or injury to herself, warning the patient's parents or guardian" (Stromberg et al., 1993b, p. 10).

Note that "dangerousness" and "duty to warn" may apply to HIV-positive patients in some situations and jurisdictions, but this has not been widely supported. As always, you must know your local laws.

Suicide

The duty to protect often extends to protecting patients from themselves. Although courts have rarely held therapists responsible for outpatient suicides, this situation is now changing, especially where the situational facts are clear. In general, the therapist is protected by performing the proper professional activities—thorough evaluation, careful consideration, and appropriate interventions. See Section 3.10.

Family Violence and Abuse

Cervantes (1992) indicates specific steps therapists can take to respond to their ethical and legal responsibilities to protect spouses and children from abuse:

- Developing a safety plan with clients.

- Knowing the legal protections available.

- Assessing for and reporting child abuse.

- Assessing for and reporting cruelty to animals.

The ethics of family therapy in cases of violence are considered by Willbach (1989). The APA's Committee on Professional Practice and Standards (1996) has offered guidance (but no formal guidelines) for those who treat abused children.

If you even suspect that a client has either endured or perpetrated abuse, you may have a legal duty to report the situation and an ethical duty to protect the abused person(s) (see Section 7.1). Precautionary measures should include the following:

- Examine all situations coming to your attention that might involve abuse.

- Just as people with hypochondria can get sick, even people with paranoia and people who lie can be victims. Be thorough.

- Keep your assumptions about perpetrators open (people of all classes, races, ages, etc., assault other people). In particular, be alert to your negative reactions to a possible perpetrator. If these continue to interfere with your objectivity, refer the case. Similarly, attend to your rescue fantasies.

- Know in detail, and obey, local laws' requirements about reporting abuse, and prepare your response thoughtfully. You must also know about the statute of limitations on child sexual abuse for your state. See www.smith-lawfirm.com for information.

- Get consultation if you are not familiar with the perpetrator's or other family members' personality patterns and choose not to refer.

- Document fully and sensitively the claims, your evaluation, and your actions. Because perpetrators or other family members may pressure abused persons to recant or modify their statements, be certain to record verbatim the information offered to you (about occurrences, circumstances, sequences, etc.).

3.10 Assessing a Client's Dangerousness to Self and Others

The preceding section has described your ethical duty to protect your client and potential victims of his or her violence. This section covers assessing dangerousness. If you have *any* reason to suspect any risk, a comprehensive evaluation of the risks of violence is necessary. Be sensitive to your feelings, which may lead you toward or away from full and accurate assessment. Kleepsies et al. (1999) offer a superb analysis and recommendations. For assessment through skilled interviewing, Shea (2002) is highly recommended, especially Appendix A on documentation. The books by Bongar (2002) and Maris et al. (2000) are comprehensive and well written. Some ideas from Jobes and Berman (1993) on risk documentation have been incorporated here. For the management of suicidal patients, Jobes (2006) is both informative and supportive.

Here are the steps you should ideally take in dealing with the risk of violence.

Prepare Ahead of Time

Monahan (1993) urges therapists to become educated in risk assessment, stay current with developments in the field, and be conversant with the laws of their jurisdictions. For example, you should obtain continuing education and otherwise keep up to date on working with spousal abuse.

In addition, indicate the limits of confidentiality in your educational procedures at the beginning of therapy (see Sections 4.2 and 7.1).

Gather Information to Assess Risk

"Obtain reasonably available records of recent prior treatment and carefully review current treatment records" (Monahan, 1993, p. 243). Note the use of "reasonably"; this is meant to exclude "all possible" records. If a record is very old, if it concerns problems irrelevant to the risks at hand, or if it is likely to be unobtainable, you do not need to obtain it to be seen as acting like a responsible professional. However, it is advisable to obtain any record known to be relevant to violence, and to obtain usual records and read them for violence-related information. In addition, it may be advisable to ask the client for a release to question others who may know of the client's behavior, history, or motives (you can amend Form 49). If the client refuses, document this refusal.

In your deliberations, attend to the client's motivation. Beck (1990, pp. 702–703) suggests asking, "Are you angry at anyone? Are you thinking of hurting anyone?" If the answer is yes, it is important to follow this up with questions about specific thoughts the patient is having; about whom these thoughts are occurring; when, where, and how long these thoughts are occurring; whether the patient is worried about the control of these impulses; and whether the patient has acted on them or come close to acting on them. Bennett et al. (1990) suggest also assessing for beliefs in justified revenge or in the appropriateness or efficacy of violence.

Evaluate the Risk Factors Present

The Issue of Suicide

If people are responsible for their own behavior, why are mental health workers held responsible when their patients commit suicide? "Courts often conclude that suicide occurs within the context of 'diminished capacity' or diminished functioning; therefore customary views that patients are responsible for their own behavior do not always apply" (Knapp & VandeCreek, 1983, p. 18). However, courts usually recognize that suicide cannot be well predicted, but "professionals have been held liable when they ignored or failed to assess indicators of suicide" (Knapp & VandeCreek, 1983, p. 18). "Courts usually consider two fundamental issues: (a) did the professional adequately assess the likelihood that a patient was suicidal? and, (b) If an identifiable risk of harm was determined, did the professional take sufficient precautions to prevent suicide?" (Knapp & VandeCreek, 1983, p. 18).

The assessment of a client's suicidality must be an ongoing process throughout treatment, because many factors can rapidly raise or lower the chances of a suicide attempt. To perform ethically, you must collect all the relevant information, weigh this information to the best of your ability, and document your conclusions and decisions. *You are not expected to predict the future perfectly, only to do your job well.* Your assessment can be based most securely on different sources of information and different ways of acquiring it. For example, you can assess known risk factors, which produce a general probability or likelihood of suicide but can't predict the specific likelihood for an individual. The checklist of suicide risk factors (Form 5; see below) facilitates the recording of the most widely recognized risk factors. A second source of information, and obviously most crucial, is your interviewing of the client. What the client tells you may be distorted for a variety or reasons (a wish to avoid hospitalization, cognitive deficits, inability to assess future impulses, etc.), and so additional sources of information should be consulted, such as family members, previous treaters, or old records. Efforts to gather such information and its results should be indicated in your records. Finally, you can integrate all the information you have obtained on the suicide risk assessment summary and recommendations (Form 37). It is designed not only to summarize the risk factors and interview information, but to document your professional judgments about suicide. You may not need to use both of the forms, especially when early indications are that the suicide risk is not great, but they are desirable when the risk appears to be high.

The Assessment of Suicide Potential: Risk Factor Analysis versus Predictions of Suicide. Summarizing much research, Hillard (1995) stated that "none of these studies has identified factors that successfully predict suicide by an individual." Why not? The main obstacle is well recognized: Suicide is quite uncommon. Only about 11.5 in 100,000 persons per year commit suicide in the United States (National Center for Injury Prevention and Control, 2005). It is so rare that even a highly accurate test for suicide potential results in unacceptably high levels of false positives (which mean that time and money are wasted in investigating these cases) or false negatives (which mean, tragically, that interventions are not offered when they might help).

Although we can't predict suicide, we can assess risk. Risk factors are those variables that are significantly correlated with suicide, according to grouped data, though they cannot predict individual cases. Using them, we can design levels of intervention appropriate to the level of risk. For example, risk factors of race and sex are significant: 72% of suicides are white males; there are about 20 per 100,000 age-adjusted deaths for males, as opposed to 4.84 for females; nonwhite males make up 7% of all suicides, and nonwhite females 2% (Allen et al., 1994).

Risk Factors for Suicide among Psychiatric Patients. Among psychiatric patients, however, the suicide rates are much higher—about 6% on average, and as high as 20% among those with panic disorder (Rudd et al., 1993). These figures indicate that having a psychiatric disorder is a significant risk factor. Bongar (1992) and Hirshfeld and Davidson (1988), summarizing several studies, found the following points relevant:

- A psychiatric history (diagnosis, treatment, hospitalization) increases the risk of completed suicide. Having a psychiatric disorder/diagnosis raises the rate for males 8–10 times; having depression raises the male rate 80–100 times (and severe depression raises it 500 times). Risk is also increased with a diagnosis of schizophrenia or substance abuse. Caldwell and Gottesman (1990) report a lifetime suicide rate of approximately 15% for those with mood disorders (which is over 30 times the rate of the general population), and a rate of 10–13% for those with schizophrenia.

- Having been an inpatient increases risk from 5 to 40 times the risk in the general population.

- In the general population, males have a greater risk for attempts than females by a ratio of about 2.5:1; however, this ratio falls to about 1.5:1 for psychiatric inpatients because of the increase in female suicide completers.

- Older white males are the greatest risk group outside institutions, but the riskiest inpatient age groups are 25–40 for males and 30–50 for females.

- Alcohol use is implicated in increased risk in several ways:

    One in five victims of completed suicide is intoxicated, and many more attempters have used alcohol immediately prior to their attempts.

    Persons with alcohol use disorders are more likely than individuals with other diagnoses to communicate suicidal intent.

    The rate of completed suicide is increased for those with alcohol use disorders if there is a concurrent depressive disorder.

- A history of previous suicide attempts greatly increases the risk for completion, except among those with psychotic disorders, who may offer little or no warning.

- Refusal or inability to cooperate with treatment increases risk.

FORM 5

There are a number of other clusters of risk factors for suicide (see Zuckerman, 2005), and many of these have been incorporated into Form 5. Bear in mind that the factors have to be weighted; they change over time; and, of course, they have different meanings for different

Checklist of Suicide Risk Factors

Client: _____ Date: _____

The following ratings are based on my:

❑ Review of records (specify): _____

❑ Interview with staff, friends, relatives (circle and name): _____

❑ Observations of this individual over the last ❑ interview ❑ day ❑ week ❑ month

❑ Other (specify): _____

Demographic risk factors

❑ European American or Native American   ❑ Male   ❑ Protestant

❑ Lowest socioeconomic class   ❑ Suicidal partner   ❑ Never-married or widowed status

❑ Divorced status (especially repeated divorce or divorce in last 6 months)

❑ Age: Young adult (15–24) or very elderly (75–85 or older)

Historical risk factors

❑ Relative or close friend died by suicide   ❑ Criminal behaviors   ❑ Poor work history

❑ Checked "suicide" on intake form or other assessments   ❑ Self-mutilating behaviors

❑ History of substance abuse or dependence   ❑ History of abuse (physical, sexual, of long duration, etc.)

❑ Suicidal behaviors: ❑ Multiple threats/attempts of ❑ high lethality ❑ high violence ❑ high pain
  ❑ Clearly intended death ❑ Secretive attempts ❑ Anniversary attempts

❑ Chronic psychiatric problems ❑ Frequent accidents

❑ _____

Recent specific risk factors

Check applicable boxes and enter a code for time period at the "____" as follows: 24 = within last 24 hours, ds = last few days, w = last 7 days or week, m = last 30 days or month, ms = last few or 2–4 months, y = last 12 months or year.

❑ Had passive death wishes T: ____   ❑ Experienced fleeting ideation T: ____

❑ Experienced persistent ideation T: ____   ❑ Made threats T: ____

❑ Made gestures T: ____   ❑ Engaged in actions, rehearsals T: ____

❑ Made suicide plans that involve a highly lethal method and a time without interruption T: ____

❑ Made an attempt of ❑ high ❑ medium ❑ low lethality T: ____
  with ❑ high ❑ medium ❑ low potential for rescue

❑ Seen recent/relevant media reports T: ____   ❑ Current recent substance abuse

❑ Talked with therapist or other staff about suicide intentions/thoughts T: ____

(cont.)

❏ Made a clear statement of intent to others   T: _____   ❏ Written a suicide note   T: _____

❏ Described a practical/available method or plan   T: _____   ❏ Made a will   T: _____

❏ Given away an important personal possession   T: _____   ❏ Made funeral arrangements   T: _____

❏ Established access to means/methods   T: _____   ❏ Other (specify): _____

Current psychological risk factors (circle a number)

❏ Hopelessness	Absolutely hopeful	1	2	3	4	5	Absolutely hopeless
❏ Psychological pain	Little	1	2	3	4	5	Intolerable
❏ Vegetative symptoms (sleep disturbances, restlessness)	Mild	1	2	3	4	5	Severe
❏ Agitation, irritability, rages, violence	Low	1	2	3	4	5	High
❏ Stressors (major or irrevocable losses, failures)	Low	1	2	3	4	5	High
❏ Social support system (nearby friends, therapist, spouse/ partner)	Strong	1	2	3	4	5	Weak
❏ Problem-solving ability	Low	1	2	3	4	5	High
❏ Involved in treatment, progressing, adherent	Yes	1	2	3	4	5	No
❏ major physical illness	Well	1	2	3	4	5	Sick
❏ Self-regard	Extremely positive	1	2	3	4	5	Extremely negative
❏ Impulsivity (low self-control, distractibility)	Low	1	2	3	4	5	High
❏ Depression (blunted emotions, anhedonia, isolation)	Low	1	2	3	4	5	High
❏ Cognitive disorganization (organic brain syndrome, psychosis, intoxication, head injury)	Low	1	2	3	4	5	High
❏ Other factors (homicidal intent, few/weak deterrents, motivated by revenge): _____	Low	1	2	3	4	5	High
❏ _____	Low	1	2	3	4	5	High
❏ _____	Low	1	2	3	4	5	High

Additional information on the items checked can be found in/at: _____

Protective factors

❏ Married or in committed relationship   ❏ Consistent employment or schooling

❏ Enjoys leisure, friendships, activities, family   ❏ Has young children

Additional factors for a child or adolescent

❏ Female (more likely to attempt)   ❏ Male (more likely to succeed)

❏ Age above 15   ❏ Rural resident   ❏ Strained family relationships

❏ Other stressors (legal difficulties, unwanted pregnancy, change of school, birth of a sibling, etc.)

Therapist: _____   Supervisor: _____

This is a strictly confidential patient medical record. Redisclosure or transfer is expressly prohibited by law.

individuals. Also, remember (1) that low risk never means *no* risk; and (2) that risk factors are not simple predictors, have no established weights in a predictor equation, and must be integrated with other data. Form 5 is only a guide.

The purposes of this form are (1) to evaluate the recognized risk factors for suicide, (2) to ensure and document the thoroughness of this evaluation for ethical and protective purposes, and (3) to initiate appropriate treatment of the suicidal client.

More formal assessment measures include scales of suicidal ideation (Beck et al., 1979; Reynolds, 1991), suicidal intent (Beck et al., 1974), and hopelessness (Beck, 1986). There are many other suicide evaluation scales, most with good empirical support. For example, Western Psychological Services (www.wpspublish.com) sells the Suicide Probability Scale (Cull & Gill, 1988), which has 36 questions that map onto four scales—Hopelessness, Suicide Ideation, Negative Self-Evaluation, and Hostility. There are norms for normals, psychiatric patients, and attempters, and it can be hand- or computer-scored. A version of the Reynolds (1991) Suicidal Ideation Questionnaire for adolescents is available from Sigma (www.sigmaassessmentsystems.com).

Responding to a Suicidal Crisis. There is no one foolproof treatment plan to follow in dealing with a suicidal patient, but make certain to act aggressively by implementing the plan you choose. When you realize that a patient is suicidal, take precautionary measures such as the following:

- Hospitalization.

- Close, repeated, and continuing observation.

- Referral for appropriate services.

- Preventing access to means of self-harm (e.g., letting the patient have only small doses of risky medications, removing guns from the patient's home).

- Providing backup services when you are unavailable.

- Consultation.

- Reviewing and keeping complete records.

Having collected the information on Form 5, you can use Form 37 to summarize your recommendations and plans for coping with this risk situation.

"No-suicide contracts" are simple, but lack evidence that they reduce suicides (Miller et al., 1998). They have no legal validity and have not protected professionals (Simon, 1999) in suits. In the context of a strong therapeutic relationship, however, proposing open communication about suicidality and restating shared goals and commitments can strengthen the "alliance for safety."

For a suicidal patient who (you believe) understands the issues and is competent to sign, you might consider a note with wording like the following:

I accept and acknowledge that I am responsible for my own actions. I do want to continue to live and improve my life. If I come to feel and believe that my life situation has become too difficult or painful, I will contact you, _____, my therapist, by phone at _____ or at _____. If I cannot reach you, I will call _____ at _____, or I will go to the emergency department of _____ Hospital.

This should be signed and dated by both of you. The wording should be expanded and tailored to the individual client, and should be subject to ongoing discussion and revision.

The Risk Factors for Interpersonal Violence

The following variables, according to Monahan et al. (2001) and Beck (1990, p. 702), are associated with increased interpersonal violence:

- Being male.

- Being 16–25 years of age.

- Moving frequently.

- Being unemployed.

- Living or growing up in a violent subculture or family.

- Abusing substances.

- Having lower intelligence.

- Having a history of violence (this is the best indicator)—fighting, hurting others, and violence against animals. Violence against property has to be separately evaluated for motivation and degree of control.

- Having appeared in court for violence, or having had inpatient psychiatric treatment for violence.

- Reporting own acts of violence.

- Committing more severe, recent, and frequent violent acts.

- Having weapons (or other means) available, or actually having used weapons.

- Having previously identified potential target persons who are available or accessible.

- Having multiple stressors (which may lessen frustration tolerance).

Obviously, there are no normative weights available for these factors, and they are based on grouped data rather than data on individuals, so use them with circumspection. An article by Tishler et al. (2000) addresses management of the violent patient, and Monahan et al.'s (2001) book is the definitive resource on the prediction of violence, being based on the masterful MacArthur Foundation research program.

Analyze the Information Gathered

Consider what additional information is needed and obtain the assessments. Examples may include assessments of paranoia or sociopathy, or of membership in a social grouping that condones or promotes violence. Richard E. Jensen, PhD, of St. Charles, IL, helpfully suggests considering all potential problematic behaviors: aggression, arson, elopement, suicide, robbery, property destruction, terroristic threats, and any other situation-specific behaviors. Jensen also suggests attempting, from records or other data, to assess these intervention-relevant factors: the "triggers" of the negative behaviors; the client's compliance with previous treatment and likely compliance with future treatment; and the client's attitude toward therapists, programs, staff, members, and so on.

In addition, assess the client for lessened internal controls. For example, psychosis, paranoid suspiciousness, organic brain syndrome, and substance use can all cause lessened control (Beck, 1990, pp. 702–703). Bennett et al. (1990, p. 66) note that the following may also lower internal controls: a history of impulsiveness or volatile temper; affective illness; beliefs in justified revenge or the appropriateness or efficacy of violence; and medication interactions.

Be alert to threats. If the client makes any threats, Bennett et al. (1990) advise evaluating their purpose. Is a threat real or manipulative? Is it self-justifying or self-protecting, or is it made in order to avoid some other consequence? Be especially alert to threats with specific details. Beck (1990) cautions that mention of time, method, contingency, location, victim, and use of the active voice are all indicators of greater likelihood in a threat.

Get consultation as well. The demonstration of a consensus, especially among professionals of several disciplines, proves that your care did not fall below a reasonable standard. You may need someone's assistance if pharmacotherapy or hospitalization is necessary.

Finally, it may be valuable, but is not generally necessary, to consider other foreseeable victims (such as coworkers) beside those identified by the patient.

Document the Situation and Your Actions

"Record the source, content, and date of significant information on risk and the content, rationale, and date of all actions to prevent violence" (Monahan, 1993, p. 246). Your notes should show that you "understood the nature of the situation and that reasonable steps were taken in light of the facts" (Fulero, 1988, p. 186). Take full and thoughtful notes about any threat. Quote the patient's statements and answers to your questions; note your conclusions, your course of action, your rationale for choosing this course, and reasons you believe it is better than any other available choice. Your records should show how you thought out the issues in an ongoing way, what happened, your evaluation, the options you considered, risk–benefit analyses, your judgments, the patient's involvement, the treatment plan to reduce risk factors, and so on.

Manage the Risk

Make any environmental manipulations (e.g., removing guns) that may reduce the danger of impulsive actions.

Before you break confidentiality, weigh the costs against the benefits, such as protecting a possible target. The costs can include losing the trust of the client or even the opportunity to continue to work with the client and help him or her. Discuss the issues with the client before disclosure. This is rarely unproductive when it is handled as a part of therapy, and harm seems more likely when it is not discussed. Beck (1982) suggests involving the client in warning the potential target. It may even be possible to involve the potential target in the therapy (Knapp, 1994). But be cautious and modest in considering your resources.

This may sound strange, but you should attempt to get a release (see Form 49) to break confidentiality if a serious threat is made. Most violent people are desperate and ambivalent about their aggression, and are still competent to consent. Violent behavior does not, in and of itself, justify breaking confidentiality. In addition, do not break confidentiality when you have only suspicions but no client words or deeds. If you are uncertain, use judgment, consultation, and thorough, honest documentation. Do not act to warn just out of fear of a *Tarasoff* suit.

As an alternative to breaking confidentiality, **consider intensifying the therapy** and documenting the alteration and its rationale. The following are good ideas:

- Increase the frequency of sessions.

- Focus on anger, aggression, controls, consequences, alternatives to violence, and topics that stimulate violent thoughts.

- Pay more attention to minor threats.

- Work with the client to attend to the "triggers" and to change the violent behaviors and risks, but be aware that the client may lie to you about his or her changes.

- Follow up on any lack of compliance with treatment (Monahan, 1993).

- Do anything that will increase the "therapeutic alliance."

In addition, it is wise to **develop various protective interventions**:

- Develop a safety plan for both the potential target and the perpetrator.

- If the spouse is a target, consider couple therapy, but only if safety issues can be adequately addressed and documented.

- Know your community's resources for targets of abuse and violence (shelters, support groups, police, etc.).

- Work with family members who can more closely observe the client.

- Consider hospitalizing the client or notifying the police—actions that would serve to incapacitate the client (Monahan, 1993).

- Monahan (1993) also suggests "target hardening," or making the target less vulnerable (by decreasing salience or accessibility, hiring bodyguards, etc.). This is not a therapy area, so get consultation.

- "Communicate information and concerns about violence to the person responsible for making decisions about the patient, and make important items salient" (Monahan, 1993, p. 245).

Gather your resources now; do not wait for an emergency situation. I suggest that you determine *right now* what your referral and support resources are in your community; trying to find them with a crisis on your hands may be too late and is certainly more stressful. Make it a goal for this week to ask all your peers and anyone else who would know about who can help in *any* crisis (suicide, violence, abuse, homicide, etc.), and get their exact names and phone numbers. Collect names, phone numbers, addresses, and any procedural details for contacting the following: police in your and the client's area; psychiatric or other appropriate inpatient facilities; consulting psychiatrists; the local mental health authorities who can authorize hospitalization; lawyers and legal organizations you can consult with; colleagues familiar with the local scene and with the treatment of potentially violent individuals; and any other persons who, or agencies that, may be helpful.

For a specific client, routinely gather information on who is medicating or can medicate him or her; on friends and family members who can intervene, house the client, or separate him or her from potential targets; and on insurance coverage for emergency hospital care and/or other intensive treatment.

It is always possible that the client will not agree to your efforts to reduce the likelihood of violence. In these cases you might consider getting a more specific **waiver of your responsibility** any time a patient refuses to cooperate with an important treatment recommendation (Liberman, 1990). You could create a letter to be signed by the client to the effect that (1) he or she has been fully informed about your treatment recommendations; (2) refusing your specific treatment recommendation(s) may seriously compromise his or her health or have other adverse personal, social, vocational, medical, or other consequences, some of which have been discussed fully with the client and others of which may be as yet unforeseeable; and (3) the client voluntarily and with full understanding is choosing to refuse or not to cooperate with your recommendation(s). Examples offered by Liberman (1990) include a patient with severe bipolar disorder who refuses or discontinues mood-stabilizing medications; a patient with severe anorexia nervosa who refuses inpatient treatment; and those with signs of serious medical conditions who refuse evaluation, consultation, or treatments.

Do Damage Control

If violence has occurred, do not make public statements of responsibility, and do not tamper with the record (Monahan, 1993). See Section 3.2.

Limit Your Personal Vulnerability to Violence

Therapists are as vulnerable to violence as others are. Guy et al. (1992) found that about half of all the psychotherapists they studied had been threatened, harassed, or physically attacked by patients during their careers. These unwanted behaviors and fears included unwanted calls to their offices or homes; threats of malpractice suits; verbal threats; destruction of the contents of their offices; physical attacks on therapists or on their loved ones; threats against their loved ones; destruction of their homes; and even murder of therapists or their loved ones (Guy et al., 1992). More recently, Purcell et al. (2005) have discussed the dangers posed by clients who stalk psychologists.

As a result of such experiences, many therapists have taken protective measures. These include refusing to treat certain clients or to disclose personal data to patients; prohibiting clients from appearing at one's home; relocating one's office to a "safe" building; specifying intolerable patient behaviors; discussing safety issues with loved ones; having no home address listing in the telephone directory; developing contingency plans for summoning help at the office; avoiding working alone in the office; hiring a secretary; terminating a threatening client; obtaining training in management of assaultive behaviors and self-defense for oneself and one's loved ones; installing a home security alarm system; developing a contingency plan for family members if a client appears at the home; avoiding solo practice; installing an office alarm system (you can add a hand-held remote control "panic button" to such a system at small cost—keeping this in public display as well as reach makes good sense); keeping a weapon at home and/or at the office; hiring a security guard; and other measures (Guy et al., 1992). It may be in your best interest to consider each of these for yourself and implement some of them today, before trouble strikes.

3.11 Ethical and Legal Issues in Working with Managed Care Organizations

Managed health care is pervasive, multifaceted, and evolving. Originally designed primarily to increase access and quality, and secondarily to control costs, it has done neither while deconstructing a world-class American enterprise—health care. Mental health has suffered disproportionately, in that no distinctions have been made between inpatient services (high cost and lesser effectiveness) and outpatient services (lower immediate and long-term costs with more effectiveness for almost all conditions).

The impacts of managed care on mental health services are complex, and they are addressed in detail in this section. The issues include ethical conflicts, the complexities of contracting with MCOs,[3] threats to confidentiality, dealing with MCO reviewers and restrictions on treatment, maintaining continuity of care, and the administrative burdens of treating MCO patients.

[3]As noted in Chapter 2 (see footnote 2 there), "MCOs" is used here as a blanket term for all similar organizations, such as preferred provider organizations (PPOs) and health maintenance organizations (HMOs).

Conflicts and Concerns

Working in an MCO environment raises ethical conflicts, some of which are no doubt familiar to you:

- Your loyalties can often be divided between your patient's needs and those of the controller of funding that employs you (the MCO). Neither you nor your patient chose the MCO (the patient's employer did), and yet you are under contract to the MCO.

- Decisions about care are often based on cost control (and reduction), and not on quality of services, long-term client benefits, the research on treatments' effectiveness, or your or your client's informed preferences. Thus you may be pressured to provide care you know (or should know) to be inadequate.

- You may be induced to treat problems and diagnoses beyond your expertise in order to prevent the income losses and costs of referral to more expensive specialists, inside or outside the "network of providers."

- Your client has essentially no confidentiality. You must either omit information from your records (which you may later need to demonstrate your thoughtful decision making if you are complained against or sued), or force the client to trust the MCO (which does not operate by your ethical standards or any other recognized, legal, or enforceable code of ethics). See below for more specifics.

- If you are not a psychiatrist, you should explain to clients that their MCO will very often require them to see a psychiatrist for medication evaluations (and almost always prescriptions), no matter what the clients or you believe is best. Noncooperation with this will lead to nonauthorization for your payment and their care.

Miller (1998), in just a few downloadable pages (at www.nomanagedcare.org/eleven.html), offers more information on these and other ethical lapses from a client's point of view; I consider it essential reading. Other resources for understanding the ethical issues with MCOs include revealing testimony to Congress by a physician who worked for MCOs, Linda Peeno, MD (www.nomanagedcare.org/DrPeenotestimony.html), and "13 Things Your Health Insurer Doesn't Want You to Know" at a commercial site (www.insure.com/articles/healthinsurance/knowledge.html). Because these concerns must be described to potential clients before treatment begins (in order to obtain their informed consent to treatment), Handout 3 is provided at the end of this section for the purposes of patient education. The following discussion covers these and other practical ethical issues that arise in working with an MCO.

Joining an MCO Panel

If you wish to be paid by an MCO for providing clinical services to the employees (and their families) of companies that have hired the MCO, look in the Yellow Pages under "Health Maintenance Organizations" or contact the national offices of the handful of major MCOs. Call their provider relations numbers and ask for the application materials you will need to join their "panels" of approved "providers."[4] You will find that almost all MCOs have full panels of providers and are not interested in your applying, unless you have a specialty they want or are located in an underserved area (yet with many "covered lives" living there). Before you apply, consider that MCOs generally will not accept onto their panels, or will simply not make referrals to, those who practice styles of therapy they disapprove of. MCOs that seek you out and ask you to join their panels are likely to be setting up a "network of providers" before bidding on employers' MCO contracts. The panel application paperwork is very detailed and time-consuming, as is the often yearly "recredentialing" process. You may find that entering your credentials and other information into a database maintained by the Council for Affordable Quality Healthcare (caqh.geoaccess.com/oas) is worthwhile, because you can then make them available to MCOs, licensing boards, or hospitals, others you choose. Additional practice information can be included, and there is no cost.

If you join a panel, you are agreeing to take clients they refer to you (in almost all cases) and be paid only what the contract allows—a payment from the MCO and a payment from the client (a "copayment"). You may not bill anyone for any more (no "balance billing"). You will be accepting clients at a much lower fee than is customary in your setting, but will hope to come out ahead by filling empty hours. You should be aware that MCOs' fees for therapy have not been raised in the last 20 years, although inflation has doubled the cost of living. No one expects fees to be raised.

Try to use a name with a first letter that is early in the alphabet, as MCO staff members usually go down an alphabetical list when making referring phone calls. Never pay a fee to join a panel or to be recertified—a sure sign of a weak company. You may find some MCO criteria burdensome such as completing clinical evaluations and the paperwork for "initial certification for treatment" within a day or two, or being able to see referred clients "immediately." MCO staffers have been known to make calls to clinicians presenting themselves as patients and asking to be seen as soon as possible, to check on your compliance with the latter point.

Complexities in Your Contract with the MCO

You must understand every part of the contract you sign. This may seem obvious, but you will need to do repeated readings, as well as obtain the assistance of peer consultation and your lawyer to grasp the implications of the contract's language (see Stout et al., 2001, for an introduction to the language of MCOs). Here are some examples:

- Do not assume that you are offered the identical contract other psychologists have been offered in your area, or that this year's is identical with the one you signed last year. Note that "evergreen renewals" allow an MCO to renew your contract without any negotiation on your part.

- Read not only the contract but all of its "attachments," such as the provider manuals in which more obligations and responsibilities are spelled out. These are in "incorporation by reference" statements.

[4]You did go to "provider" school, didn't you? The entire language of managed care is that of a business model like manufacturing (with completely interchangeable parts). Although this model has been successful in many areas of American life, it seems completely inappropriate for providing health care.

- Understand the ways you are assuming risks by agreeing to "withholds" (payments for your services that are not paid to you unless you provide services the way the MCO wishes).

- An indemnification or "hold harmless" agreement states that if the MCO is sued by a patient for the actions of the provider, then the provider cannot hold the MCO responsible in any way for the outcome. Generally, your insurance will cover your actions and those of any employees you have included in your insurance application, but not the actions of your nonemployees. Common sense would indicate that you should avoid signing an indemnification agreement that holds you responsible for the acts of nonemployees.

- Beware of "noncompete" or "exclusivity" clauses, which prevent you from having business relationships with competing programs, even after you have left the first MCO.

- "No-disparagement" and "gag" clauses prevent you from criticizing the MCO, discussing treatment options that the MCO won't pay for, mentioning financial incentives given to you or other providers, criticizing adverse decisions made by the MCO, or the like. These limit your ability to practice as you believe best, advocate for your client, and appeal a denial of payment. These "gag" rules may be disappearing because of new laws, but do read your MCO contracts carefully. The risk to you is that you may be sued or complained against for failure to treat properly when you knew or should have known that a different kind of service was needed, and yet you could not recommend or refer for it because of your MCO contract. You are still responsible for your client's care.

- "Termination without cause" provisions allow an MCO to remove you from its panels with 60 or 90 days' notice for any reason. Of course, this could be a financial disaster to you, would limit the continuity of your care, and might not be in the client's best interest. Best would be allowing only termination with a list of specified causes, but also ask about the MCO's appeals process for these types of termination, and try to make them work both ways.

- "Severability" clauses keep the rest of the contract binding, even if one part is declared illegal or unenforceable.

- As noted above and in Section 2.5, most if not all contracts forbid your doing "balance billing." Therefore, you cannot collect from the client for uncanceled appointments, any part of your agreed-upon fee not paid by the MCO, and for other costs. This will lessen your income. By the way, you cannot deduct your losses due to missed appointments from your taxes.

- In evaluating your profit from MCO cases, add your administrative time in dealing with the MCO over authorizations, lost paperwork, case reviews, and appeals of denials.

- Be aware that MCOs do **retrospective case reviews** as well as the ongoing ones (though continuing authorization requirements). An MCO can, after examining paid-for (often closed) cases, decide that you should not have treated some of its referrals; if so, it will require you to return money paid to you. If you have a large MCO caseload, prepare for such demands.

■ Beware of contract language that requires your obligations to survive contract termination but does not require the same of the MCO, allows the MCO to interpret your nonresponse to contract changes as acceptance of them, defines your case records as its proprietary information, or requires you to provide burdensome 24-hour/7-day coverage. In some cases, the MCO may require you to employ only other panel members in your organization, or to provide coverage when you go on vacation or are otherwise unavailable.

The list above is not exhaustive, and other issues may arise over time. A review by your business attorney is highly recommended before you sign any managed care contract.

Beginning to See MCO Clients

Clients will call their MCO and the MCO staff will refer them to you (and probably several other providers), or clients will call you because they see your name in the MCO's pamphlet of providers' names. Those referred by the MCO have had a session or two "preauthorized," but before you see self-referred clients, you must obtain preauthorization for being paid for the MCO. This will involve at least one phone call to "certify or verify their benefits"—that is, to determine whether the mental health services they are seeking are currently covered by a particular MCO contract. Failure to accurately confirm coverage of a particular person, by a specific insurance plan, for the specific services provided by you (considering your credentials and panel membership status) is a common cause of nonpayment to you and disruption of services. Errors can be made in phone contacts; insist on a written verification of coverage and treatment authorization being faxed to you before starting treatment. See "Verification of Coverage," below.

After meeting a self-referred client, you will have to complete and submit an assessment and treatment plan—often called an "initial treatment plan" or "individualized treatment plan" (see Form 39)—with a great deal of information on the client's history and functioning. An MCO typically requires a clinician to provide a diagnosis, treatment plan, evaluation of the patient's level of performing activities of daily living, assessment of substance use/abuse, and evaluation of the lethality of any suicidal plans, so that the "medical necessity" (see below) of treatment may be determined. It is not uncommon for MCOs to take some time to decide to accept (or even refuse) your proposed treatment plan, during which time you may suffer financial risk and your client emotional hardship. If your proposed treatment is acceptable to the MCO, you will have a small number of visits "authorized." Before these are used up, you must decide whether your client will need more treatment; if so, you must submit an "outpatient treatment report" (OTR), which is a kind of progress note on how the client is functioning and a revised treatment plan. Generally, you must indicate progress toward treatment goals for the authorization of further services. Because you ethically may not lie about levels of function, treatment may be denied to those who could benefit from it but who are not severely incapacitated. After all, MCOs' therapeutic goal is only a "return to previous level of functioning," by which they mean reduction of symptoms to a baseline level before treatment began or similar baseline. This is not what we mean by "mental health" or even "remission."

After you begin seeing clients (which may not be soon—most clinicians receive only a few referrals per year), the MCO will start a "profile" on how many sessions you typically use per case (and perhaps how frequently you see clients); how much difficulty you cause the MCO when seeking authorization for services; and how you meet many other undisclosed criteria. This profile will be used to decide whether or not to offer you referrals and "recredentialing."

Lastly, despite your timely submission of forms and information to the MCO, there may be extensive delays (1) before decisions are made and (2) before you receive payment, even after authorization. The first type of delay places you and your client in anxious limbo, and the second is solely your burden.

Initial Discussions with the Client about MCO-Related Ethical Issues

Securing informed consent involves discussion with any potential client prior to treatment about its risks and benefits (see Chapter 4). Managed care brings additional risks beyond the clinical ones, such as those concerning confidentiality and continuity of care. Having a client read and review an OTR form will make more concrete and believable the information sought by MCOs and the concerns you raise in your discussion. The form will also be a stimulus for the client to weigh the use of MCO benefits. Although some forms are fairly simple (e.g., Magellan's current one), some are quite intrusive requiring the collection (and, effectively, the disclosure) of a great deal of information not clearly relevant to treating the presenting issues. Value Options offers two OTR forms Outpatient Registration Forms 1 and 2; see www.valueoptions.com/providers/Forms/Clinical/Outpatient_Registration_Form_ORF2.pdf).

Confidentiality

The lack of confidentiality in managed care treatment has received wide publicity, but the potential client must be informed in advance of the specific implications for mental health treatment, to give him or her the ability to refuse such treatment.

Appelbaum (1993) notes that you must disclose to the patient the "nature and extent of information that may have to be released to managed care reviewers" (p. 254), as well as the lack of ethical and legal limitations on the disclosure of this information within the MCO and possibly the client's employer. Similar sensitive information will be regularly required for treatment reauthorizations, internal reviews, and in-your-office reviews. The fate of this information and its consequences for the client are almost always uncertain.

This information is often transferred to the MCO by fax or electronic methods. Under HIPAA, all MCOs are CEs (as part of "Health Plans") and must conform to the Privacy and Security Rules. However, CEs are allowed to design their own processes within the general HIPAA privacy and security regulations. Also, investigations of HIPAA compliance occur only upon a complaint of an "unauthorized disclosure." The almost universal experience of the "loss" of PHI materials sent by clinicians to MCOs should constitute the presumption of an unauthorized disclosure, but this has not been pursued legally. In addition, the training and skills of the MCO personnel receiving and evaluating this information are uncertain. These people are not controlled by the laws and ethics that apply to licensed psychotherapists. Reviewers are not (at least at the initial levels) mental health professionals; even at higher levels, they may not be clinicians or therapists. Only a few MCOs require even a professional of your discipline to review your treatment. Given these factors, I advise the following:

- You should have a more detailed discussion with the client of the issues described here, have the client read Handout 3, and get a more specific release-of-information form signed (you can use Form 49) before talking to an MCO reviewer.

- You should discuss with the client the probable consequences of releasing this information to the MCO, where it will become part of a permanent medical record.[5] It is likely that this record will be accessible to many other organizations over time, such as when the client applies for health or life insurance, security clearances, mortgage loans, or jobs. Of course, this information will not be shared for these purposes without the client's signature. The issue here is that once recorded, it *must* be disclosed, or the client will have to forgo ordinary opportunities like getting a job or a mortgage. Such honest discussion may or may not lessen the tendency of clients to be forthcoming and self-disclosing when advised of an MCO's confidentiality rules (Kremer & Gesten, 1998).

- Releasing detailed information may be countertherapeutic with some borderline or paranoid patients, as well as with those in the public eye. You should decide what to do and may have to forgo MCO payments with these patients.

Informing the Client about MCO Coverage, Benefits, and Limitations on Treatment

Clients must be informed of the limits of the payments available to them under their MCO coverage. This should include both the written limits and your own experience of the services frequently authorized (which are nearly always less than optimal). They should be fully informed about the limitations on those from whom they can receive treatment without having to pay more out of pocket.

- The client must accept the MCO's intention to pay only for treatment to return the client to *baseline* levels of functioning. When this has happened, you and the client must renegotiate your contract, including goals, methods, and payment for further services.

- MCOs tend to approve only very brief treatment, which may not be clinically appropriate for all patients. Their present and apparently universal philosophy of treatment is that briefer is better. In the experience of many clinicians, this seems to prevail no matter what the diagnosis, history, or need, but I have seen no good data on this point. MCOs' definition of "brief" is often too short (6–10 sessions) to be effective for many diagnoses, according to the literature (which suggests 20–30 sessions for effectiveness with anxiety disorders and depression). See Steenbarger (1994) for a brief but comprehensive review of the "dose (sessions)–response (outcome or change) relationship" in therapy. Yet MCO personnel themselves have little or no valid research support for requiring brief therapy (see Miller, 1998). Because they are usually not clinicians, they

---

[5]Consider the following. The Medical Information Bureau is the most likely repository, but the information is not in your words or in a narrative format. It is coded and simplified for the use of insurers, and thus open to distortion. Also, when MCOs and similar organizations merge, their data systems must merge too, and so data may be distorted. Lastly, when mental health data are recorded in medical databases, the level of confidentiality may be lowered to that of the medical data.

are not your consultants or your supervisors, and therefor legally unable to offer direction for treatment. (However, as you will see in Form 39, it is often useful for later discussion to record their comments and suggestions.)

- MCOs restrict the range of clinicians a client may see to those on their approved "panel" of providers. MCOs represent to employers and their "covered lives" that these providers are highly qualified and so raise the quality of care provided. Panel members are certainly clinicians who accept MCOs' lower-than-customary fees and possess some credentials, but this says nothing about the appropriateness or quality of care delivered.

- Some plans will reimburse for services provided by those not on their panels. If you are not on an MCO's panel, and if no empaneled provider is available in the area, or none has your specific skills, and if the client assertively seeks the service, then you could be paid at higher than the empaneled rate. You must negotiate each case with the MCO and would be authorized as an "out-of-network provider," but only if the client's contract allows such an arrangement.

- A client's insurance coverage and MCO may change during your treatment; reviewers and other staff members at the MCO may give you inaccurate information; or they may later deny payment for previously authorized service ("retroactive denials")—all of which change the true costs of treatment for the client. The client should be informed of these possibilities and, in your experience, their likelihood.

Verification of Coverage

An MCO will not authorize an "episode of treatment" (your services) unless a client's policy specifically covers the particular services (defined by *Current Procedural Terminology* [CPT] codes) and, of course, the MCO believes the services to be "medically necessary" (discussed later in this section). Most clients are woefully uninformed or misinformed about their actual coverage, and so you must decide first whether you or they will make the arduous calls to the MCO. Clients are also not in the best position to learn the intricacies of behavioral health insurance when they come for help, and many simply give up (which MCOs apparently count on). You or your staff are usually better motivated, informed, and persistent, and your clients will be grateful for your relieving them of this **FORM 6** burden. The questions in Form 6 address all the variables in MCO policies (as well as of indemnity insurance policies) of which I am currently aware. When you are calling to ask about excluded diagnoses or other issues, try to ask about several, even if not all of them are appropriate for the client you are calling about. This is both for your information and for confidentiality purposes, so that an MCO staffer cannot associate a particular client with a particular condition. If you wish to have clients gather this information, you can give them Form 28 (the financial information form) instead of Form 6.

Dealing with MCO Reviewers

Some MCOs "micromanage" therapy by requiring frequent, detailed telephone consultations with their "care coordinators" or reviewers and submission of OTR forms in order for you to receive reauthorization for a small number of continuing treatment sessions.

Questionnaire for Determining Behavioral Health Insurance Benefits

Try to get an answer to each question, and make longer notes if you need to, so you can be clear about the coverage. You will need to have this information before you call:

Patient's name: _____

Patient's date of birth: _____   Patient's ID/SS #: _____

Policy holder's name (if different from patient): _____

Policy holder's date of birth: _____   Policy holder's ID/SS #: _____

Policy holder's employer: _____

Address of policy holder's employer: _____

Name of MCO or other insurer: _____

Policy #: _____   Group #: _____   Renewal date: _____

Name of any behavioral health subcontractor: _____

Phone #	Buttons or prompts	Date(s) called	Name(s) of representative(s) spoken with

1. Is this specific patient covered under this policy? ❑ Yes ❑ No

2. Are services for treating "mental and nervous disorders" covered? ❑ Yes ❑ No

   Are services for treating "drug and alcohol disorders" covered? ❑ Yes ❑ No

3. Is "outpatient psychotherapy" or "outpatient mental health/behavioral health treatment" for these disorders covered? ❑ Yes ❑ No

4. Will the insurance pay for these kinds of treatment?

   Individual psychotherapy ❑ Yes ❑ No

   Family therapy ❑ Yes ❑ No

   Psychological testing ❑ Yes ❑ No

(cont.)

FORM 6. Behavioral health insurance benefits questionnaire (p. 1 of 3). From *The Paper Office.* Copyright 2008 by Edward L. Zuckerman. Permission to photocopy this handout is granted to purchasers of this book for personal use only (see copyright page for details).

Group therapy ❏ Yes ❏ No

Drug and alcohol treatment ❏ Yes ❏ No

Medication prescription and monitoring ❏ Yes ❏ No

❏ Other: _____

5. Is this coverage current ❏, or has it ceased as of _____, 20____ ❏, or won't it start until
   _____, 20____ ❏?

6. Are services provided by a licensed psychologist, social worker, or other mental health professional covered?

    a. Are additional credentials required? ❏ No ❏ Yes
   If yes, which? _____

    b. Is referral by a physician required? ❏ No ❏ Yes

    c. Is supervision by a physician required? ❏ No ❏ Yes

    d. Is consultation with a physician required? ❏ No ❏ Yes

7. Is this therapist a "participating" or an "eligible" provider under this particular ❏ Yes ❏ No
   insurance plan?

8. Will the insurance plan pay out-of-network providers? ❏ Yes ❏ No
   If not, what are the additional costs involved? _____

9. Is there an exclusion for "preexisting" conditions? Are these present in this case?

10. Are there excluded diagnoses? (Ask about ADHD and learning disorders, ODD, borderline personality dis-
    order, conduct disorder, chronic pain, or others as relevant.)

11. Is there a "copayment" that the client must pay for each treatment session? ❏ No ❏ Yes
    (If yes, how is it calculated? _____)

12. Is there a deductible that must be paid by the patient before the insurance company ❏ No ❏ Yes
    will pay anything? (If yes, how much is it? $ _____)

    Is this deductible per year, per calendar year, per person/client, per family, per diagnosis (underline which)
    or some combination of these? _____

13. Will the insurer pay the entire amount of allowable charges (after the deductible) for ❏ No reduction
    mental health services, or does it reduce the coverage for mental health services? ❏ Yes
    (If yes, how much? $____ or ____%)

(cont.)

14. Is there a limit on the amount the insurance will pay for mental health services in a year   ❑ No   ❑ Yes
     or a lifetime? (If yes, $_____ per year and/or $_____ in lifetime. How much of this remains available? $_____)

15. Is there a limit on the number of visits/sessions per year or by diagnosis?   ❑ No
                 ❑ Yes, _____ per year.   ❑ Yes, by diagnosis: _____

16. If the spouse, the parents of a child patient, or the whole family is seen are these visits   ❑ No   ❑ Yes
     covered differently than visits of the patient alone?   (If yes, how? _____)

17. Will the policy pay for sessions longer than 1 hour?   ❑ Yes   ❑ No

18. If we must meet for two sessions on a single date, will insurance pay for it or for   ❑ Double
     only a single session per day?   ❑ Only one session

19. Will insurance pay for more than one session per week?   ❑ No
              ❑ Yes, but only _____ sessions per week   ❑ Yes, as decided by the professional

20. Coordination of benefits: What rules apply if more than one insurance company is providing coverage for this patient and claims are submitted to both companies? (Which has priority?)

21. Are there any other rules, requirements, forms, or procedures that we should be aware of?

22. Treatment authorization number: _____ Authorizer: _____
     Starting date: _____   Number of sessions: _____   Dollar limit: _____
     Authorization renewal date: _____

23. Authorization to be faxed. Received? ❑ Yes, Date: _____   ❑ No

24. Where are claims forms to be sent?

To protect yourself against MCO disorganization, mistakes, and deceit, the late John Roraback, PhD, of Moline, IL, suggested that clinicians tape-record their calls to MCO reviewers. If you decide to do so, notify the MCO at the start of the call; otherwise, your taping will be illegal. Obviously, this approach may well be seen as hostile by the MCO, but it should serve to protect you in cases of legal actions over adverse consequences to a patient, so you might be selective. Although doing so is burdensome, always get the full name(s) and any other identifier(s) of the reviewer(s) you speak to, use these during the call, and record the date and time of the call and the number(s) called. You can record wait times as well. Note the contents of the call for later support or negotiations. Reviewers generally cannot make changes, but supervisors can.

From the other side, the guidelines below are from Bruce Barrett, MA, CPT, of Duxbury, MA, who was a medical reviewer. They are reproduced with his kind permission.

1. Always assume that reviewers really do have patients' interests in mind. They really believe that short-term treatment in the least restrictive setting works best, and that they have the research studies to support their position. They also see payments to you as the patients' money (which it is—it's part of the compensation package at their employment).

2. Don't confuse a life-threatening diagnosis with life-threatening patient status. For example, bulimia nervosa is a life-threatening disorder, but the status of a patient with bulimia nervosa may not be currently life-threatening. You'll need to document the current facts to show that the patient's present condition warrants the treatment you're planning now.

3. Failure in outpatient treatment is often necessary before inpatient treatment will be approved. Documenting patient behavior that shows this failure (rather than therapists' impressions, feelings, or anticipations, accurate as they may be) is what reviewers look for.

4. Make sure you really do what you tell a reviewer a patient really needs. You remember your reviewers—they remember you, too, and they keep notes.

5. Be ready to appeal decisions of payment denial. It may be that your patient has to do this, but you can help by knowing the procedure. Insurance companies have higher-skilled professionals to review denials and appealed claims, although in my experience the first-line reviewers are pretty sharp, too. Overturned denials are typically the result of clearer documentation of the need for treatment.

6. Don't bother trying to get or keep the patient in the hospital because you or some other key treater is away, busy, on vacation, or sick. Hospitals don't charge your patient's health care treasury less for the slow weekends, so discharge on Friday, not Monday.

7. Learn the criteria for admission, continued stay, and the various other levels of treatment (partial hospitalization, outpatient care, etc.) for the various conditions you treat. Learn them as well as you would if you were a reviewer, or a consultant to an insurance company. Then learn (from the reviewers, if possible) what manner of documentation—what type and quality of case facts—they use to make their decisions.

8. Rely on objective and behavioral data in your case notes. "Spouse reports patient binged and purged three times in last 24 hours" is much more useful than "This patient is getting worse and needs an inpatient stay." Patient self-report helps, too, even when there is clear evidence of denial (e.g., "Patient reports feeling better than ever, despite relapse of purging").

9. Psychological denial and other forms of patient-based unreadiness for treatment can be tricky, but reviewers know that, too. Showing evidence that a patient's degree of denial is colossal, and might be broken through with intensive (inpatient or partial hospitalization) treatment, can be impressive to a reviewer.

10. Make sure it all fits together—diagnosis, need for treatment (patient condition), intensity of treatment planned, and intensity of treatment delivered. Hyperbole in the need for treatment, when coupled with routine scheduling of appointments (or even scheduled gaps in treatment), stands out like a sore thumb. A life-or-death patient condition calls for urgent action and timing from the therapist.

Continuity-of-Care Concerns

As soon as you accept patients, you have a duty to provide high-quality care until you discharge them. But, because of MCOs' limitations on treatment you are likely to have patients for whom MCOs refuse to authorize more treatment but who are not ready for discharge. Therapists have the ethical obligation—and may, under managed care, have a contractual obligation—to continue to treat patients whose benefits become unavailable or exhausted. There are three other aspects of maintaining continuity of care.

First, "If managed care refuses payment, you are legally required *at least* [to] (1) provide clinically necessary *emergency* services regardless of payment" (Stromberg & Dellinger, 1993, p. 13; emphasis added). Ethically, you cannot abandon a patient in crisis, regardless of the financial situation.

Second, a therapist has the additional obligation to appeal an MCO's decisions to deny services that the clinician has recommended. If your client could benefit from more treatment but is not severely incapacitated, authorization may be denied, and ethically you may not falsify levels of functioning. Appelbaum (1993, p. 254) notes the "possibility that payment for therapy might be terminated before either the patient or the clinician believes that the goals of treatment have been achieved." If the client continues to need care, in the clinician's opinion, the clinician must appeal the MCO's decision. Note, however, that this process is entirely under the auspices of the MCO, which makes all the rules. Appelbaum (1993) says, "At a minimum, a clinician whose patient has been denied payment for care that he or she believes is indicated, may have an ethical obligation to contest, on the patient's behalf, the decision of the managed care entity" (p. 253). Stromberg and Dellinger (1993) make this point even more strongly: "If managed care refuses payment, you are legally required [to] (2) energetically seek approval for additional services the patient genuinely needs" (p. 13). The clinician should make some effort at the initial appeal level. A decision on whether to continue to secondary levels of appeal needs to be made after "consultation with the patient, taking into consideration the likelihood of success, whether the patient still desires to proceed with treatment, and the availability of alternative means of paying for care" (Appelbaum, 1993, p. 253).

Third, since an appeal is rarely successful, alternative treatment resources must be considered. You should ask yourself and the client:

- Can the client afford to obtain care from an out-of-network provider at higher cost?

- Can the client pay out of pocket for your therapy?

- Is the client willing to proceed with your therapy during the appeals process, risking being held responsible for all the charges accrued in the interim?

- Are there free or less expensive alternative sources of care to which the client can be referred, if you find them competent to treat, and the client finds this referral acceptable?

- Are you willing to continue your care at a reduced rate or without payment?

- Are you willing to terminate the client?

However, read your MCO contract carefully. It may in fact require you to discharge the patient. Or it may require you to continue to treat the patient after benefits are exhausted, if he or she still needs treatment; it may even prevent you from charging the patient for this treatment.

Educating Clients about Managed Care

HANDOUT 3   Handout 3 is designed to inform clients of the practical, financial, legal, and ethical implications of managed care. Before using it, read and decide whether it is accurate for your location, contracts, profession and experience. For example, if a patients' bill of rights is passed in your state or nationally, or your state has legal precedents like the *Jaffee v. Redmond* (518 U.S. 1, 1996) case (see www.jaffee-redmond.org, DeBell & Jones, 1997, and Shuman & Foote, 1999), you should modify the statements about confidentiality in this form. Some sentences in the handout that are highly critical of managed care are offered in italics, and you might choose to delete them if your practice is dependent on MCO. The next-to-last paragraph offers clients the possibility of paying you directly and thus not creating any records outside your office; this may not be allowed under your MCO contracts when the MCO has made the referral and "covers" a client's life. A few sentences are adapted from Higuchi (1994), who provides a good review of the legal issues. I must thank Jackson Rainer, PhD, of Norcross, GA, and Charles H. Steinmeyer, PhD, of Warren, PA, for improving this section and handout through their reviews.

Therapists have an ethical responsibility to inform clients of the main issues in using managed health care, despite the fact that some of the research is not very encouraging. For example, an analogue study reported by independent practitioners informed student nonclients of the impacts of managed care on therapy. It had negative effects: "Participants were significantly more likely to believe that managed care would have a negative impact on treatment and significantly less likely to see an independent practitioner, use insurance benefits, expect to benefit from treatment, expect to form a strong working relationship, and trust that the practitioner would work in their best interest" (Pomerantz, 2000, p. 159). These results suggest that therapists should make certain to provide accurate, current, and

What You Should Know about Managed Care and Your Treatment

Your health insurance may pay part of the costs of your treatment, but the benefits cannot be paid until a managed care organization (MCO) authorizes this (says they can be paid). The MCO has been selected by your employer, not by you or me. The MCO sets some limits on us, and you need to know what these are before we go further.

Confidentiality

If you use your health insurance to help pay for psychotherapy, you must allow me to tell the MCO about your problem and give it a psychiatric diagnosis. You must also permit me to tell the MCO about the treatment I am recommending, about your progress during treatment, and about how you are doing in many areas of your life (functions at work, in your family, and in activities of daily living). I am not paid separately for collecting, organizing, or submitting this information, and I cannot bill you for these services. All of this information will become part of the MCO's records, and some of it will be included in your permanent medical record at the Medical Information Bureau, a national data bank that is not open to the public. The information will be examined when you apply for life or health insurance, and it may be considered when you apply for employment, credit or loans, a security clearance, or other things in the future. You will have to indicate that you were treated for a psychological condition and release this information, or you may not get the insurance, job, loan, or clearance.

All insurance carriers claim to keep the information they receive confidential, and there are federal laws about its release. The laws and ethics that apply to me are much stricter than the rules that apply at present to MCOs. *There have been reports in the media about many significant and damaging breaches of confidentiality by MCOs.* If you are concerned about who might see your records now or in the future, we should discuss this issue more fully before we start treatment and before I send the MCO any information. You should evaluate your situation carefully in regard to confidentiality. For some people and some problems, the privacy of their communications to their therapist is absolutely essential to their work on their difficulties. For others, their problems are not ones that raise much concern over confidentiality.

Treatment

The MCO will review the information I send it and then decide how much treatment I can provide to you. *The MCO can refuse to pay for any of your treatment, or for any treatment by me. Or it may pay only a very small part of the treatment's cost, and it can prevent me from charging you directly for further treatment we agree to.* Finally, it can set limits on the kinds of treatments I can provide to you. These limited treatments may not be the most appropriate for you or in your long-term best interest. The MCO will approve treatment aimed at improving the specific symptoms (behaviors, feelings) that brought you into therapy, but it may not approve any further treatment. The MCO will almost always

(cont.)

require you to see a psychiatrist for medication evaluations (and prescriptions), *whether you or I think this is appropriate.*

When it does authorize our treatment, the MCO is likely to limit the number of times we can meet. Your insurance policy probably has a maximum number of appointments allowed for outpatient psychotherapy (usually per year, though there may be a lifetime limit as well), but the MCO does not have to let you use all of those. It may not agree to more sessions, even if I believe those are needed to fully relieve your problems, or if I believe that undertreating your problems may prolong your distress or lead to relapses (worsening or backsliding).

If the MCO denies payment before either of us is satisfied about our progress, we may also need to consider other treatment choices, and they may not be the ones we would prefer. We can appeal the MCO's decisions on payment and number of sessions, but we can only do so within the MCO itself. We cannot appeal to other professionals, to your employer, or through the courts. This state does not have laws regulating MCOs—that is, laws about the skills or qualifications of their staff members, about access to medical and psychological records by employers and others, or about the appeals process.

You should know that my contract or your employer's contract with a particular MCO prevent us from taking legal actions against the MCO if things go badly because of its decision. *My contract may prevent me from discussing with you treatment options for which the MCO will not pay.* I will discuss with you any efforts the MCO makes to get me to limit your care in any way.

The particular MCO in charge of your mental health benefits can change during the course of your treatment. If this happens, we may have to go through the whole treatment authorization process again. It is also possible that the benefits or coverage for your treatment may change during the course of our therapy, and so your part of costs for treatment may change.

Lastly, even if we send all the forms and information to the MCO on time, there may be long delays before any decisions are made. This creates stressful uncertainty and may alter our earlier assumptions about the costs and nature of your treatment.

Our Agreement

If, after reading this and discussing it with me, you are concerned with these issues, you may have the choice of paying me directly and not using your health insurance. This will create no record outside of my files. This possibility depends on my contract with your MCO.

I have read and understood the issues described above and willingly enter treatment accepting these limits. I give my therapist permission to submit information in order to secure payment for the mental health services to be provided to me.

❏ Yes, I want to review and/or receive copies of any written materials you send to my MCO.

❏ No, that is not necessary.

_____   _____   _____
Signature of client   Printed name of client   Date

unbiased information about managed care, and that they should be especially sensitive to the effects of managed care on the therapeutic relationship.

If you have a managed care arrangement that involves capitation[6] (payments to you by the MCO of a fixed amount—the PMPM rate—to provide for all the mental health needs of the "covered lives") or a case rate system (in which you are paid a lump sum per case, usually regardless of diagnosis, and no matter what kinds of care the client needs), you should disclose this to all new clients. Why? Because these arrangements, just like MCOs' excessive paperwork, use of "medical necessity" criteria, limited or even "phantom" panels of providers, and other cost controls, serve to constrain and ration the care available (Miller, 1998), and clients should be informed of these limitations to be able to consent to enter treatment. For example, Rosenthal (2000) found that case rate payments resulted in reduction of numbers of sessions by 20–25%, compared to sessions for clients seen on a fee-for-service basis (payments for each session).

The Concept of "Medically Necessary" Care

"Medical necessity" is a concept created by MCOs and has no history or basis in economics, insurance, medicine, psychiatry, or psychology. It was based on the belief that services were being overused (i.e., treatment was being provided when it was not necessary), and that this was the cause of the great increases in health care costs in the 1970s. (More recent research has called this into question.) MCOs sold employers the idea that they could substantially reduce health care costs by limiting care to "medically necessary" services. The concept is used to control access to different kinds of services by the MCOs. For about a decade, health care costs to employers did indeed grow more slowly or level off. Providers, especially hospitals, were paid a lot less, and MCOs made huge profits. Cost cutting peaked in the early 1990s, and so did the profits of MCOs and similar arrangements.

However, "medical necessity" is still universally used to control payments to providers. The criteria for "medical necessity" vary among disorders and also across MCOs; are considered business secrets and so are not generally publicly available; and have never been subjected to empirical evaluation. (One list of such criteria is available at www.magellanprovider.com/MHS/MGL/providing_care/clinical_guidelines/MNC.asp?leftmenu=5&sub=child5_4. Note that outpatient, office-based treatment is addressed in just 2 of the 105 pages. The definition is crucial for payment and patient care decisions, and so has been argued without much agreement. See mentalhealth.samhsa.gov/publications/allpubs/SMA03-3790/content03.asp for an overview. The whole report from 2003 is at mentalhealth.samhsa.gov/publications/allpubs/SMA03-3790/default.asp.) The MCO reviewers' opinions of what is "medically necessary" care will be based on their training in the MCO and is unlikely to match your professional views or your clients' expectations of kind or duration of treatment.

FORM 7 Form 7, a medical-necessity-for-psychotherapy checklist, is modified from one by Allan J. Comeau, PhD, of West Los Angeles, CA, and is used with his kind permission. It was designed to improve documentation to third-party payers and to assist with thinking through decisions about continuing or reducing/ending treatment. Because MCOs use the criterion of "medical necessity," in dealing with their reviewers it may be advantageous to

[6]From, perhaps, either the German *kaput* for "finished and done," or the Latin, as in "to capitulate" or "decapitation."

Checklist for Assessing the Medical Necessity for Psychotherapy

Patient:_____ Identification number: _____

Based upon my ongoing assessment, the above-named patient requires continued psychotherapy and or psychotherapeutic case management for the following reasons:

❑ This patient has a history of regression to a lower level of functioning without ongoing psychotherapy services.

❑ This patient has improved considerably in the past, but his or her functioning and condition deteriorated following a reduction of frequency in therapy visits.

❑ This patient has a history of noncompliance with other essential components of his or her care (medications, day treatment, attendance, sobriety, etc.), and psychotherapy helps this patient to improve his or her level of adherence to planned treatment.

❑ This patient's current level of functioning is such that psychotherapy and/or case management services are needed to support maintenance at this (lower) level of functioning.

❑ This patient's current Global Assessment of Functioning (GAF) score is below 70 (with difficulties in social, occupational, or school functioning, etc.). Psychotherapeutic treatment is essential to support stabilization.

❑ This patient's GAF score is below 60 (with moderate or greater difficulty in social, occupational, or school functioning, etc.). Psychotherapeutic treatment is essential to promote stabilization.

❑ This patient's GAF score is below 50 (with severe difficulty in social, occupational, or school functioning, etc.). Psychotherapeutic treatment is essential to assist with stabilization.

Additional information:

_____

_____

I therefore recommend these methods and frequency of treatment:

❑ Individual psychotherapy at the rate of _____ sessions per week/month.

❑ Group psychotherapy at the rate of _____ meetings per week/month.

❑ Collateral therapy at the rate of _____ meetings per week/month.

❑ Clinical case management at the intensity of _____.

❑ Other: _____

Thank you for your attention to this matter.

Sincerely,

_____   _____

(Signature of clinician)   Date

FORM 7. Medical-necessity-for-psychotherapy checklist. Adapted from a form devised by Allan J. Comeau, PhD, of West Los Angeles, CA, and used by permission of Dr. Comeau.—From *The Paper Office*. Permission to photocopy this form is granted to purchasers of this book for personal use only (see copyright page for details).

discuss a case from this perspective. Presumably a reviewer will have a good deal of clinical information at hand, and this form summarizes your conclusions and (ideally) will lead the reviewer to see the case in the way you indicate.

Coping with Administrative Burden, Fees, and Payments

MCOs have been able to shift the administrative burdens of insuring clients to clinicians. A provider now has to determine whether a potential client has current coverage for the proposed services; determine whether a required referral from the client's primary care physician has been formally made; keep track of the number of sessions authorized and received; renew the authorization before that number has been used; provide a claim (billing) form that perfectly matches the MCO's needs (a "clean claim"); send it to the MCO's preferred and current staff and addresses; and so on. Clinicians routinely report that they (or their office staff) spend about 30% of their work time on such paperwork issues. Some offices have found calling in the early mornings to be more time-effective. Also, because you will usually be put on hold, the use of a speakerphone will allow you to do other work while you wait.

It is clear that MCOs have not developed equivalently efficient administrative practices. They routinely "lose" the papers mailed and faxed to them; give incorrect information on coverage, clients, and fees to clinicians; or delay or simply do not respond by mail, phone, fax, or e-mail. They routinely fail to notify providers of changes in their procedures, and then refuse payment when these new rules are not complied with. On occasion they pay less than what was accurately billed (and rarely even apologize for these "errors"). They have been stretching out the time they take to pay their bills. Their staff turnover, mergers, and inadequate training interact to make them extremely inaccurate. They obviously have no incentive to improve their functioning, and have changed only when compelled to by laws such as those requiring timely payment for claims (with interest being charged—of course, the interest rates are less than the costs of improving their services). Many clients and clinicians simply give up on pursuing claims, and there are no criminal or civil penalties for this sort of inefficiency by an MCO.

What Can a Clinician Do?

1. Get paid more?

    - The fees MCOs have been paying have generally been going down, so you will not be able to raise your fees to cover these additional costs, or to keep pace with inflation and your costs of doing business.

    - Join only panels that pay a fee that allows you to make a reasonable profit. For some clinicians, this may not be possible or may become impossible.

    - A particularly nefarious MCO practice has been documented in several locations and is likely to be widespread. MCO plans have many fewer providers actually available than their lists appear to offer, and these have been called "phantom panels." In a courageous and groundbreaking effort, Holstein (2007) called all psychologists and psychiatrists in two counties in New Jersey and asked: (1) "Are you still on the panel?", (2) "Are you taking new patients?", (3) "If so, when is an appointment available?", and (4) "Do you treat children, adults, or both?" He found very few resources for patients.

You can do your own data collection using this model in just a few hours (I did it for western Pennsylvania). When you find deficiencies, you can approach an MCO and ask for higher fees to provide services, using the argument that they need you. For example, a provider whose client may need medications and cannot get an appointment is at great professional risk, and the client is being very poorly served. You can tell an MCO that your practice is busy, that you are a member of other panels, and that you will (just as good business logic) prefer to take clients from the better-paying plans. Only speak to someone at the MCO who has the power to negotiate. Be armed with data, such as that the panel listing has 50 psychologists and 5 psychiatrists, but only 7 of the psychologists and 1 psychiatrist are taking patients—a situation that is clearly not serving the needs of the community or the plan. Do not expect the MCO to agree with your data. If you decide to collect these kinds of data, consult your state association, because the official APA position is that sharing such information is an illegal restraint of trade practice. Also, be aware that some MCOs will not or cannot negotiate fee changes. However, in an underserved area, you only need be a member of a small number of panels.

MCOs have routinely not paid for treatment of couples by claiming that their policies do not cover marriage counseling. Ivan Miller, PhD, has offered guidance for responding to this irrational obstacle (see www.psychotherapistsguild.com/refusal.html).

- Locate your practice where there are few providers but many "covered lives," so you will get many referrals from MCOs and can make a profit because of your practice design.

- Provide services that MCOs value highly but cannot find providers to perform. If you specialize in newer or rarer services, explore with the MCOs whether they are in need of such services before applying for their panels. Try to negotiate a higher fee for these unusual services. Reviewers may be, and their supervisors usually are, authorized to negotiate fees.

- See MCO patients, but only as an out-of-network-provider (not on the patients' MCO's panel, although you may be on other MCOs' panels). Again, the MCO must want your services and be willing to pay a higher fee than it pays to its panelists.

- Discuss the true costs and risks of using "extremely basic/minimal MCO coverage" before accepting a person as your client. If it is legal to do so, offer the client a discount of, say, 25% for services without MCO paperwork, no diagnosis, and payment at the time of service.

2. Recover your administrative costs?

- Your MCO contract generally will not permit you to bill the MCO or the client for the additional time needed to complete paperwork, call the reviewers, and similar administrative burdens, or for using client time to fill out OTRs and other MCO forms, but check. If you routinely have clients sign a form agreeing to accept financial responsibility for all nonreimbursed costs (such as Form 28), you might consider billing the client for your administrative costs, where this is legal.

3. Complain to your state's insurance commissioner and to your legal representatives?

- An MCO is only vulnerable to laws with teeth. Your state is unlikely to have laws like these (the insurance lobby has been very strong), so join with your state professional organizations, clients, and consumers to lobby. Call and write to your representatives.

- When you have to resubmit a bunch of OTRs (outpatient treatment reports) or similar documents, consider sending an explanatory cover letter with the date you sent the first (now "lost") OTRs, and a copy of this letter to the insurance commissioner of your state.

4. Complain better to the MCOs?

- Document all calls and paperwork sent (to whom, when, where, for what, length of call, etc.). After the first call, ask to speak to a supervisor,

- After a few discussions with supervisors, try to arrange a face-to-face meeting to discuss problems and solutions with someone at the MCO.

- If it is harder for the MCO to drop you (by simply not sending your referrals) than it is to deal with the additional paperwork your complaints to the insurance commissioner will generate, the MCO's personnel may deal more efficiently with you.

- Have one of your staff members call each MCO on each claim submitted more than 2 weeks ago and not yet paid. This is burdensome and costly, but it will be so to the MCO as well.

- When you are told that client paperwork was "not received," you could become very concerned or even frightened that a document with "confidential medical information" has gone astray. Confirm that you have mailed it correctly, and conclude that it must have been lost in their office. Because the "not received" gambit is so widespread, MCO staffers will not admit to finding the paperwork if you propose calling back later to check on their search efforts. Instead, point out that if they do not have this paperwork, it has *by definition* fallen into the wrong hands. Think out loud that perhaps it is time for you to speak to the client's employer about the large number of similar incidents you have documented of shabby, almost negligently careless mishandling of "sensitive and legally protected confidential medical information." The least you should accept as a response is the name and number of an individual who will receive the copy you send next, and who will immediately call you back to confirm its receipt. (These ideas are from Russ Holstein, PhD, of Long Branch, NJ, and are presented here with his permission.)

5. Enlist your clients in these efforts?

- Complete authorization forms with the clients present. When they see what is being asked, they will be fully informed, and many will resent the invasion of their privacy.

- If you can work with your clients on this, have them write letters of appeal to the MCO, with copies to the insurance commissioner.

- Educate your clients and prospective clients about MCOs and how to complain. Complaints about inefficiency, delays, and privacy issues directed to their employers' benefits office are usually more effective than those directed to an MCO. However, beware that you might be seen as recruiting your clients for your own or guild issues, so be selective about which clients you approach and over which issues.

6. Ask the MCO for a better procedure for your practice?

- Ask that you be given initially 12 visits and routinely receive reauthorizations for 12 more.

- Ask whether there are simplified procedures available, such as checkbox OTRs (see Section 6.1), special fax numbers with receipts, or other modern business practices.

- Do not accept any offers to assist MCOs in developing better procedures (perhaps unless you are paid in advance). Look up "coopted" in the dictionary.

7. Resign from panels that cause you hassles?

- Figure out your true costs of serving a client of each MCO. Include not just your clinical time and office overhead and staff time, but all the costs of dealing with them as described above. You may find, as some therapists have found, that you are losing money seeing an MCO's clients.

- If you decide to resign from a panel for any reason, you are likely to find that your name is not removed from its list of members for a very long time, and you will get calls for appointments for years. These are opportunities to do some public education on managed care; make it clear to callers that the fault for this misinformation lies with the MCO and not with you. You might explain why you have resigned.

Finally, see Appendix E for a list of online and other resources for becoming more informed about coping with MCOs.

3.12 Legal and Ethical Aspects of Supervising and Being Supervised

As clinicians, we all participate in clinical supervision during our careers, often both as supervisees and as supervisors. We do this because of our faith in the necessity of face-to-face assessing, teaching, monitoring, and mentoring to raise skill levels, model sophisticated skills and attitudes, socialize the novice into a profession's world view, and so on.

Being supervised is like an apprenticeship with a master to integrate the theory learned in training (in school as well as self-education) with the development and application of skills to the needs of real-world patients. In contrast to "consultation" with an independent peer or organization, "supervision" suggests the monitoring and control of the supervisee's practice by the supervisor. In the professions, there is an expectation that the supervision is educational and the relationship will terminate when the skills have been passed on. Formalizing the supervision relationship by contract with peers, associates, or others from whom you can learn or to whom you teach is a small step but a legally protective one, and it is implied by Standard 7.06 of the APA ethics code (APA, 2002). See Form 8 below for an example of such an agreement.

Most supervision takes place either on a one-to-one basis or in a seminar format. However, it can also include the use of cotherapy and team therapy, formal assignments and teaching, modeling by the supervisor, and formalized mentoring outside the classroom. The Internet is bringing other possibilities.

Risks and Responses

1. **Supervising is a special skill.** Some circumspection is needed by clinicians who are considering becoming supervisors. A high level of clinical skill is a necessary but not sufficient qualification for a supervisor, because students need more than demonstrations to learn sophisticated procedures. Some clinicians may be well able to do, but not to explain or teach. Furthermore, knowledge alone is insufficient to assure its being passed on, because "telling is not teaching," and showing does not address the situation of the learner. Also, clinicians may approach supervising from the perspective of their favorite school of therapy, which may not be appropriate or sufficiently flexible for the demands their supervisees face. Lastly, supervision based on a supervisor's own training experiences may simply pass on poor-quality or out-of-date skills. It is clear that being an effective supervisor requires more than a high level of professional skills as an experienced clinician. A brief but sophisticated overview is provided by Barnett et al. (2007a).

    Advice: Training in supervision can be very enlightening and beneficial, and is probably necessary to reduce risk as well.

2. **Be aware of vicarious liability.** There is an old legal concept, *respondeat superior*, in which the master is held responsible for the actions of the servant; thus some clinicians may shy away from supervising, fearing its uncontrolled consequences. The law has held that the clients treated by your supervisee under your supervision are *your* clients. Although it is true that a supervisor can be held responsible for some actions of the supervisee ("vicarious liability") even when the supervisee is a licensed professional, incidents of this type have not been a significant professional liability risk factor, which should be reassuring.

    Advice: A careful selection process, comprehensive discussions and training, continual monitoring, a clear contract, and inclusive liability insurance can reduce your risk to an insignificant level. Supervision should be timely, frequent, and of sufficient duration to allow competent monitoring of the supervisee, sufficient mutual under-standing of the case, and evaluation of treatment.

3. **Do not exceed your areas of competent practice.** Just as you would not employ a method you didn't know well or treat a diagnosis you were unfamiliar with, you should not attempt to supervise in a clinical area in which you do not have demon-strated competence, or to perform supervision for which you lack sufficient skills. Supervisees must have been adequately trained to execute each treatment prescribed by the supervisor, even though the supervisor will be held responsible.

   Advice: This may require you to refuse some supervisees or some clients for a supervisee, so plan ahead.

4. **Be aware of informed consent issues.** There are two issues here: the client's consent to be treated by a clinician who is being supervised, and the supervisee's consent to be supervised. First, according to Standard 10.01c of the APA ethics code (APA, 2002), cli-ents must be informed about, understand the consequences (risks and benefits) of, and voluntarily agree to treatment by your supervisee. Specifically, they must be told that you are supervising, what your credentials are, that you will be reviewing the supervisee's records (and probably recordings of the sessions), and so on. This is part of their consent to treatment. HIPAA regulations allow the supervisees full access to the client's record, because they are providing health care services ("treatment") to a client who had consented to share PHI during the intake process. Second, your supervisee must be fully informed and consent to the supervision process you will pursue. A full discussion of this issue and many others can be found in a highly rec-ommended article by Thomas (2007). According to Standard 7.06 of the APA ethics code (APA, 2002), the processes for evaluating performance and providing feedback to students and interns are required to be specified.

   Advice: The best ways to reduce these risks is simply to have a very clear contract. Form 8 addresses these issues. A few examples of contracts are also available online. For example, the Saskatchewan College of Psychologists has posted its 2003 Supervi-sion Agreement for Provisional Practice Psychologists on its website (www.skcp.ca/forms/supervision-agreement.pdf). A major writer in the area of clinical supervision, Carol A. Falender, PhD, has also generously placed a sample outline contract online (www.cfalender.com/super.pdf). (Note that Dr. Falender's form is copyrighted—as you should assume all online materials are, unless the fact that they are not is specifi-cally indicated.) Vespia et al. (2002) offer a list of 52 supervision behaviors from which you could develop your own rating forms. In addition, use the best evaluation meth-ods available. Share them with the supervisee and negotiate their use, frequency, interpretation, and so forth.

5. **Consider confidentiality issues.** Understand that neither consultations nor supervi-sion are privileged communications, so you and your notes could be dragged into court.

   Advice: If a supervisee needs assistance on a case with significant legal implications, refer him or her to a lawyer. If he or she needs therapy for anxiety or depression, per-haps due to a stressful legal case, arrange for a therapist with the usual privacy protections. Do not become your consultee's "therapist," as this is a dual relationship. See below.

6. **Avoid exploitation.** Avoid dual relationships with a supervisee. The supervisor must be careful in relations with the supervisee that there is no possibility of exploitation. Obviously, sexual relationships are forbidden (by Standard 7.07 of the APA ethics code; APA, 2002), but others that are possible (such as supervising with business partners, relatives, spouses, friends, or prior clients) should also be avoided.

Advice: Stick to doing only supervision with supervisees. Moreover, a supervisee should pay a fee for each hour and not use a percentage of the fees received from the clients, as this is fee splitting and still (usually) unethical.

Advice to supervisees: Your sessions should be constructive, so if you are not sure you are getting your money's worth, seek out another consultant. You can outgrow your teacher, you know.

A Formal Agreement

FORM 8   Because of the pressures to formalize the context of supervisory relationships, Form 8, an agreement for professional supervision, addresses various issues of relevance to the supervision relationship. This form incorporates some ideas from one developed by Kathleen Quinn, EdD, of Cheyenne, WY, for which I am most grateful.

Since supervision can be at many levels, some of the terms in the form have been placed in parentheses where they would apply only to those being supervised for pre- or postdoctoral internships or for licensure. It is written for psychotherapy supervision, so other clinical functions (such as diagnostic testing, case management, school consultation, mentoring and group supervision) will probably require additional or substitute paragraphs. If the supervision is for licensure or to meet some other formal goal, make sure that the frequency, duration, and intensity are sufficient to meet the requirements by incorporating them into the form's text. The means of emergency contact could include home phone numbers, cell phone, pager, answering service, or institutional switchboard. The form deliberately does not address the model of therapy, school, discipline, or approach, as these are likely to differ widely across supervision situations. The following points have also been omitted from Form 8 because they are too dependent on the circumstances, but should be articulated for informed consent and clarity: the purposes of the supervision; the work the supervisee is to perform (such as assessment, counseling, consulting, etc.); the location of the services; and the payment to be received for services rendered to the clients of the supervisor. This form would be inappropriate for online or peer-to-peer supervision. Lastly, it is not designed for specialized supervision, such as that of "burned-out," traumatized, or otherwise impaired professionals, or of professionals who are being rehabilitated or under supervision required by their licensing boards.

A Record of Supervision Meetings

A format for recording supervision is offered below, but you should create a customized form for your goals, methods of practice, and types of contacts. This form should be agreed to

Agreement for Professional Supervision Services

Introduction

This agreement has been created to address the legal, ethical, practical, and clinical issues of the supervision relationship. It can be added to or modified as the supervision process unfolds over time and across cases, and these addenda are indicated on the last page. This agreement is intended to articulate and clarify the complex mutual responsibilities of the parties involved, the procedures of the supervision, and the personal development needed to become a capable and responsible professional (deserving of independent professional practice).

Parties

We, _____, (hereinafter called the "supervisee") and _____ (hereinafter called the "supervisor"), agree that the supervisor will provide professional supervision services as outlined below.

Meetings and communication

The supervisee agrees to meet with the supervisor in person as mutually arranged or at these locations and times:

_____   _____
Location   Days, hours

_____   _____
Location   Days, hours

It is the supervisee's responsibility to initiate meetings as often as necessary to meet the goals of supervision, to meet his or her training needs, provide high levels of care to the clients involved, and to address other needs that may arise.

Besides our face-to-face meetings, we may use postal mail, telephone, video, e-mail, or other means to communicate. If we use e-mail messages or wireless phones to discuss cases or other confidential information, they must be encrypted. Electronic recordings will require the written consent of the clients involved.

Because we need to be able to reach each other easily and because emergencies may arise, the following arrangements for contact are made.

Supervisee

_____   _____
Days and hours of availability   Means of emergency contact

_____   _____
Days and hours of availability   Means of emergency contact

_____   _____
Days and hours of availability   Means of emergency contact

(cont.)

FORM 8. Agreement for professional supervision (p. 1 of 4).   Incorporates some ideas from a form devised by Kathleen Quinn, EdD, of Cheyenne, WY, and used by permission of Dr. Quinn.—From *The Paper Office*. Permission to photocopy this form is granted to purchasers of this book for personal use only (see copyright page for details).

Supervisor

Days and hours of availability	Means of emergency contact
Days and hours of availability	Means of emergency contact
Days and hours of availability	Means of emergency contact

When the supervisor is unavailable due to vacation or other events, the supervisor will assure adequate availability of a substitute supervisor and will inform this person of the supervisee's needs and situation.

Frequency and Financial Concerns

The supervisee agrees to pay for services provided, up until the time either of us informs the other (in person or by written means) of his or her plans to end the relationship. The supervisee agrees to pay the fee of $_____ per session for these services, starting on or about _____ and continuing at about the rate of about _____ meetings per _____. Vacations and other planned absences from supervision will be negotiated at least 30 days in advance.

Records and Confidentiality

1. We both agree to keep records of our meetings, which will document the following:

   - The dates and times we met face to face or otherwise communicated.

   - The cases involved by name or case number.

   - The results of previous clinical efforts and interventions, the progress of each case, the client's needs, and similar concerns.

   - Other relevant issues, such as ethical, legal, procedural, interpersonal, or organizational ones.

   - The supervisee's areas or skills in need of enhancement and progress toward mastery.

   - The recommendations and assignments given by the supervisor and assumed by the supervisee.

   - Discussion of the supervision process, procedures, and progress.

2. We will maintain these records in the same ways as we maintain clinical case records (as to confidentiality, availability, security, etc.).

3. We are both aware that these records are not privileged.

Supervisee's responsibilities

1. Presentations to clients and informed consent.

   - The supervisee agrees to not misrepresent or advertise himself or herself in any way that might imply a competence or credential he or she does not have.

   - The supervisee agrees to explain to clients his or her professional achievements, status, or title, and to make it clear that he or she is being supervised. The supervisee will explain the supervision process and the supervisor's activities, profession, and credentials. The supervisee will explain that clients in therapy with the supervisee are legally considered to be clients of the supervisor. Clients will read and agree to the supervisor's client information brochure and other client educational materials as needed.

   - The supervisee will obtain informed consent of clients to the information and record sharing involved in this supervision. Where direct observation and/or audio or video recordings will be made, the supervisee will obtain fully informed consent. Consent forms will be completed as appropriate.

2. Risk management.

   - The supervisee will inform the supervisor of any problems with any clients or cases as soon as possible. Any interactions with a client that raise any level of concern about risk to the client, family, peers, or others must be discussed with the supervisor immediately.

(cont.)

- The supervisee will abide by the appropriate national code of ethics for his or her profession and its guidelines and other similar materials, as appropriate to the kinds of services being rendered to clients and the characteristics of those clients.

- The supervisee will abide by the current rules and regulations of this state's professional licensing board.

- The supervisee will adhere to the policies and procedures of the employers of the supervisor and supervisee.

- The supervisee will obtain and maintain his or her own professional liability insurance coverage.

3. Supervisee's education.

- The supervisee recognizes that a major value of supervision is the learning of professional roles and associated behaviors.

- The supervisee agrees to use his or her best abilities to remain responsive to suggestions and recommendations.

- The supervisee agrees to bring to the attention of the supervisor any deficits the supervisee recognizes in his or her ability to perform the clinical functions involved in therapy or other clinical activities with clients.

- The supervisee agrees to complete readings and other educational assignments made by the supervisor. The supervisee may be asked to summarize or in other ways demonstrate the learning of the contents of these materials.

4. Clinical procedures.

- The supervisee agrees to meet with clients and perform psychotherapeutic or other clinical functions in a professional, reliable, and responsible manner.

- The supervisee agrees to implement to the best of his or her ability the recommendations made by the supervisor for the handling of each case.

- The supervisee agrees to develop adequate, appropriate, and current written treatment plans and will remain responsible for such. These will be reviewed at scheduled times with the client(s) and supervisor, and changes will be incorporated as needed.

Supervisor's responsibilities

1. Sensitivity, responsiveness, and flexibility.

- The supervisor agrees to try always to bear in mind issues of diversity, particularly their many dimensions and influences, and to be sensitive and respectful of all differences among the client(s), the supervisee, and himself or herself.

- The supervisor agrees to attend to the boundaries, balances, and potential multiple relationships between the supervisor and supervisee. In all cases, the interests of the supervisee will be held primary.

- The supervisor agrees to maintain awareness of the sometimes fine line between doing supervision and providing psychotherapy. If the supervisor should decide that the supervisee can benefit from psychotherapy, he or she will make referrals.

2. Evaluation.

- The supervisor agrees to conduct an initial evaluation of the supervisee's knowledge, attitudes, and skills concerning the clinical activities that the supervisee intends to undertake and the supervisor to supervise. Other areas, as proposed by either party, may be assessed as well. Based on this comprehensive evaluation, both parties will formulate specific goals and methods for the content and nature of the supervision.

- The supervisor agrees to explain and obtain fully informed consent of the supervisee to any and all methods and procedures for the evaluation of the supervisee, their nature and timing, and any other persons who will also review the evaluations and results, before implementing any of them.

- If disagreements should arise that the supervisor and supervisee cannot resolve, they will take these difficulties to the supervisee's educational supervisor if the supervisee is in supervision as part of an educational program and if not they will consult with staff members of the local or state professional association.

(cont.)

3. Monitoring and risk management.

- The supervisor will review the supervisee's treatment plans, written notes, and audiotapes and/or videotapes of selected treatment sessions on a periodic basis as decided by the supervisor. Direct observation of the services provided by the supervisee will be arranged if at all possible.

- The supervisor has legal responsibility for the supervisee's clients and will take all appropriate actions in their best interests.

- Supervision will include examination of and education in legal and ethical issues, as well as patient treatment issues.

- The supervisor agrees to abide by the appropriate national code of ethics for his or her profession and its guidelines and other similar materials as appropriate to the kinds of services being rendered to clients and the characteristics of those clients.

- The supervisor agrees to abide by the current rules and regulations of this state's professional licensing board.

- The supervisor agrees to adhere to the policies and procedures of employers of the supervisor and/or supervisee.

- The supervisor will maintain current professional insurance coverage and include the supervisee as required by law, regulation, or the insurer.

4. Supervisor's education.

- The supervisor agrees to continue to learn about supervision.

- The supervisor agrees to remain current in the model(s) and methods of assessment, therapy, legal and ethical issues, and similar clinical concerns.

5. Administrative responsibilities.

- The supervisor will maintain appropriate and necessary records of the experiences and services provided to and by the supervisee for licensure or certification, and will ensure that the criteria are met.

- The supervisor will provide evaluations, letters of recommendation, and similar documents about the supervision and supervisee as requested by the supervisee.

Modifications to this agreement can be made with consent of both parties and shall be made in writing.

I, the supervisee, have read the supervisor's office policy statements as well as the supervision statement above. I agree to act according to everything stated there, as shown by my signature below. I understand that this agreement can be terminated if either party does not live up to his or her responsibilities as outlined above. I agree to adhere to the contents of this agreement, until otherwise negotiated and formalized as addenda to this agreement.

_____   _____
Signature of the supervisee indicating agreement   Date

I, the supervisor, have discussed the issues above with the supervisee. I hereby agree to adhere to the contents of this agreement, until otherwise negotiated and formalized as addenda to this agreement.

_____   _____
Signature of the supervisor indicating agreement   Date

_____ Copy accepted by supervisee   _____ Copy kept by supervisor

Addenda or modifications to this agreement   Date

1.

2.

3.

by both the supervisor and supervisee. If the supervisee completes it, a copy should be furnished to the supervisor, so that everything is on the table and changes can be negotiated.

Notes can be written into the spaces provided, or the numbers can be used to organize narrative notes recorded on plain paper. This format provides a space for the supervisor's name and location, but it is best if more detailed information is also recorded. For example, you could indicate the following for each supervisor in full on the back of the first of these forms you use: the supervisor's agency, type of agency, or setting (e.g., private practice); full business address; telephone numbers (regular, home, emergency, fax, pager, e-mail, etc.); Social Security number; and any other information that might be needed in the future to substantiate that the supervision occurred.

Supervision Record

1. Supervisor: _____ Agency/location: _____

2. Session's date: _____ Meeting number: _____ Duration: _____

   Individual or group? _____ Live or case consultation? _____

3. Preparation: (a) Supervisee's progress on tasks or homework from last session with client; (b) client case materials collected (paper and electronic records, genogram, consultations); (c) other materials collected (literature); (d) supervisee's concerns/issues to be raised (personal, family, case, theoretical, practical, organizational, ethical, conflicts); and (e) goals for the session.

4. Patients discussed (use initials): For each, discuss (a) problematic behaviors or concerns/main issues/progress/questions; (b) themes; (c) hypotheses; (d) treatment decisions made/tasks assumed.

5. Supervisor's comments/evaluations about: Supervisee's conceptualization of case/treatment/problems; interventions/implementation of treatments; handling of issues; self-awareness; process, clinical, or theoretical areas; evaluation of treatment; etc.

6. Skill development/training recommendations or suggestions made. If supervisee's performance is deficient, this must be made clear, and a remediation plan must be developed and implemented.

7. Signature of supervisor: _____

   Signature of supervisee: _____

Consulting

Continuing professional consultations are essential for good clinical care; no one knows everything. Without consultations, you are less likely to ask advice when a question (clinical or ethical) comes up. Going it alone in murky waters is risky, if not self-destructive. Indeed, as noted earlier in this chapter, frequent and formal consultation with a respected peer is powerful protection against a malpractice verdict.

Consultation differs greatly from supervision. A consultant offers his or her expertise to an independent fellow professional who is not obliged to comply with any advice and retains full responsibility for his or her patients. Because there may be misunderstandings, get a letter of agreement about roles and responsibilities.

It is in your best interest to keep notes on your consultation sessions. These are separate from any case notes that would go into a patient's chart. I recommend keeping a separate three-ring binder in which you keep notes, photocopies, notes on readings, diaries, handouts, and anything else to support your consultation relationship and learning. These document the sessions (perhaps for a credential) and their content for defense if you are accused of an ethics or malpractice violation.

Please see Appendix F for a list of books, articles, and journals on supervision and consultation.

CHAPTER 4

Getting Informed Consent

4.1 The What and Why of Getting Informed Consent

> *Informed consent is actually a statement about the moral atmosphere of the relationship between clinician and patient. In more practical terms, informed consent is a dyadic process, or dialogue that begins at the moment of eye contact and continues throughout the relationship."*
>
> —GUTHEIL (1993, p. 1005)

The relationship of therapist and client is complex and multidimensional. It evolves therapeutically, economically, and interpersonally. If this relationship is not spelled out, the client, therapist, ethics committees, insurance companies, and courts are all quite likely to interpret it differently. The relationship should thus be clarified as soon as clinically feasible; this process of clarification and of obtaining informed consent is not optional, but essential. The relevant parts of the American Psychological Association ethics code (APA, 2002) are primarily Standards 3.10 and 3.11, as well as 9.03 for assessment and 10.01 for therapy.

Please note that this chapter does not deal with consent for forensic evaluations or services, including custody and legal competence. These and similar issues are large and complex; they simply cannot be dealt with briefly or in an overview. Before working in these areas, obtain suitable training and experience.

How can you be sure you have obtained informed consent? What specific methods can you use to obtain it? This chapter answers these questions and offers five fully developed paths, or methods, you can use with clients to secure their informed consent. Any of these methods, however, requires that four basic conditions be met.

What Informed Consent Requires

Informed consent requires a **mentally competent** person who has a good **knowledge** of what will occur in treatment, freely **chooses** to be treated, and is **documented** in the record as such. If any of these is lacking, its absence must be documented, explained, and responded to. Let's look more carefully at each of these elements.

Mental Competence

Mental competence is presumed for all adults unless a court has decided that an adult is incompetent, or the adult has manifested clear signs of incompetence to you. Receiving a severe diagnosis or even being involuntarily hospitalized does not automatically presume incompetence. Some indicators of possible incompetence are psychosis, dementia, severe depression, suicidal behavior, and the like. In such cases, consult and/or refer if you lack the professional skills to evaluate the impact of these symptoms on the client's competence. Also note that the rationality of a decision is unrelated to the competence to make it (Group for the Advancement of Psychiatry [GAP], 1990, pp. 87 ff.) An "irrational" decision is defined as one that results in the person's suffering foreseeable harms without adequate reason (GAP, 1990, p. 87). If you need formal assessments of competence to make decisions about psychiatric treatment, the three scales developed by the MacArthur Treatment Competence Study are sophisticated and specific. They address denial of symptoms, assessment of cognitive functioning, and understanding of the explanations offered of treatments. The scales and manuals are free at the MacArthur Archive (macarthur.virginia.edu/treatment.html), and their use is also described by Grisso and Appelbaum (1998).

"Competence" and "incompetence" are the common legal terms and so are used often in this discussion, but the term "capability" is often recommended by experts in mental health law in discussions of "competence"—both because of its appropriately narrowed focus (the presence of a mental disorder does not make one unable to make all decisions) and its suggestion of empirical determination (assessing the abilities to state a choice, to understand relevant information, to appreciate the nature of one's own situation, and to reason with information). A related point to keep in mind is that competence is not "all or nothing." The extent of someone's competence depends on the issues of concern at the moment. A client may be competent to consent to some treatments and not to others; the latter may require resources he or she does not possess, now or at any time, such as the ability to foresee specific consequences in detail.

Competence is generally denied to minors, but local laws differ. A minor is usually anyone under 18 years of age. By law and presumption, minors cannot give consent or waive privilege because they are considered incompetent due to age. Consent must therefore be obtained from their parents or guardians. Residing with a child does not make an adult that child's legal guardian, and being a parent does not assure the parent's having legal custody to consent. If you need consent for a minor, determine who can give it.

In order to reduce barriers to treatment of minors, there are some legal exceptions concerning their competence to consent to treatment. For example, minors can generally seek treatment for sexually transmitted diseases or pregnancy without parental consent. Some states have extended this to drug and alcohol treatment and other diagnoses, or have allowed treatment in some settings. Consent to treatment by adolescents is complicated by their not-quite-adult legal and psychological status. The tendency is to give more weight to the thinking abilities of later adolescents and less to those of early adolescents. **You must know your local laws.** To illustrate, in Pennsylvania, the following questions need to be considered in deciding whether you need parental consent to treat a child (Orlow, 2001):

(1) Are the parents together or separated/divorced, and if the latter, is there joint or sole legal custody? (2) If a single parent brings the child for treatment, is the mate deceased or unavailable, or is this information undisclosed? (3) If the child comes alone, is the child between 14 and 18 years of age or under? Each of these questions needs to be evaluated differently for therapy of the family or the child alone; for evaluations for custody, therapy, or in an emergency; and when a release of information is sought for testimony, to authorities, or by parental request. There are some smaller distinctions to be considered as well.

Knowledge

Consent is "informed if all the risks and possible consequences of the procedure . . . along with alternatives have been explained . . . and . . . [the client] understands" (Cohen, 1979, p. 248). Note that this has two aspects: (1) giving adequate information and (2) ensuring that the client understands it. We need to examine each aspect in turn. First, how much information needs to be disclosed? Must every *possible* effect be described?

"If a doctor *knows (or should know)* of possible complication[s] of the treatment, he [*sic*] is under a legal duty to disclose that information to his patient" (Cohen, 1979, p. 248). Not every possibility must be covered, but "only those risks which *a reasonable man* would consider material to his decision whether or not to undergo treatment" (Cohen, 1979, pp. 248–249; in both quotes, I have italicized terms that have legal definitions). Reid (1999, pp. 27 and 77) suggests balancing significance and likelihood. Although the rare or benign effects of treatment may not require discussion, the more dangerous or more common an effect is, the more weight and time its discussion will deserve. Haas and Malouf (1995) recommend that if in doubt, it is probably better to give information and thus support the autonomy of the patient, than to withhold it and be accused later of failing to support such autonomy. This is clearly subtle and complex in real-life practice, but some effort must be made in this direction with every patient.

Full knowledge involves giving the information that a rational person would want to have before making a decision. This usually requires you as the therapist to explain the following:

- Your approach and your qualifications.

- All procedures to be used, and any changes during treatment.

- The purposes of treatment—both the long-term and the short-term or immediate goals.

- Discomforts to be expected (e.g., conflicts with family members when a patient becomes more assertive).

- Foreseeable negative consequences, or "harms." "The harms which concern rational persons are death; pain (physical and mental); various disabilities; and loss of freedom, opportunity, or pleasure" (GAP, 1990, p. 80). They may also include some side effects of treatment.

- The anticipated benefits of this treatment.

- The option of no treatment and its consequences.

- Alternative treatments. A useful guideline for alternatives is to ask yourself whether some very differently trained but fully competent therapist might suggest some other treatment in this situation (GAP, 1990, p. 81).

Clients, even those without previous therapy experience, generally understand the ethical principles of therapy (e.g., beneficence, autonomy) but are uncertain about more specific points (Claiborne et al., 1994). Furthermore, Jensen et al. (1991) found that clinicians and parents tended to agree on the content of informed consent discussions. Parents understood these purposes of therapy: to "talk things out"; to help problems get better; to get help for complex or very difficult problems; to improve parenting skills; and to improve relationships. They also understood the limits and risks of confidentiality (e.g., the mandatory reporting of child abuse, the possibility of having family secrets revealed). However, parents were more concerned than were clinicians with iatrogenic risks: the chance that problems might fail to improve or might get worse, as well as the effects of labeling (e.g., the children's being called "mentally disturbed" by others, the parents' being seen as inadequate) and other stigma-related issues (e.g., the possibility that the children's having been in therapy might cause problems in employability, school admission, etc.). It is important to note that in this study, demographics did not affect these issues' rankings of importance. Therefore, a uniform approach, such as a handout plus a discussion that is relatively standard but that can be tailored to the particular needs of clients, is empirically justified.

Clients' needs and therapists' approaches differ, and so different information needs to be provided accordingly. For example, the scheduling of therapy is often more problematic for clients at lower socioeconomic levels, so it should be discussed more fully (Graziano & Fink, 1973). Similarly, a study found that when those with more pathology were given more information on the limits of confidentiality, they revealed less than those given less information; those with lower pathology revealed most (Taube & Elwork, 1990). Labeling and other stigma-related issues are more important for some patients or families with a history of being stigmatized or a high risk of being stigmatized (Lidz et al., 1984). Inpatients and outpatients need discussion of different issues (Lidz et al., 1984). Families have different concerns from those of single adults or minors (Gustafson & McNamara, 1987).

Discussions of different therapeutic approaches may also require different content. For example, Widiger and Rorer (1984) argue that disclosure of therapeutic methods may cripple free association. If specialized techniques (such as biofeedback or hypnotherapy) are later introduced, additional informed consent is appropriate, even though a more general informed consent to treatment was obtained early in treatment. Those who use paradoxical methods should proceed with caution; these methods raise some serious questions about consent and require a more extensive consent-getting process.

As mentioned above, the offering of adequate information is not sufficient to ensure that a patient has knowledge sufficient for consent. The second requirement now comes into play; that is, the client must understand how the information applies to him or her. Such competence has two aspects: the comprehension of the meaning of what has been told, and its appreciation—that is, the realization that what has been said applies to him or her at the present time (GAP, 1990, p. 13).

To assure the client's understanding, it is important to remember these guidelines:

- Use simple, declarative sentences.

- Give explanations in language that is free of jargon (clinical, legal, or bureaucratic) and adjusted for the client's education or reading skills. Handelsman et al. (1986) suggest sixth- to eighth-grade language skill for consent forms. The forms in the field have not improved, and one study of forms to consent to participate in research (LoVerde et al., 1989) indicated that things were getting worse, not better: In the 7 years studied, the forms got 58% longer, and they still required too high a level of education to be understood (22% required graduate school!).

- Low levels of literacy are common, as the preceding point suggests. Conversational ability is not always an indication of the ability to understand and use written health information. You should become suspicious of low literacy when dealing with clients or their patients who have had fewer than 8 years of schooling; are over 60, and so may have had less or lower-quality schooling; are members of any "minority" group; were imprisoned; have a limiting chronic condition; and/or have experienced repeated work failures. Obviously, these are not determinative. But bear in mind that about a quarter of the population will not understand (much less remember) common written materials in health care, as various parts of the 1992 and 2003 National Assessments of Adult Literacy indicate (see www.nifl.gov/nifl/facts/facts.html).

- Communicate that any questions that occur to the client will be answered at any time.

- Respect the client's levels of cognitive functioning (especially memory abilities). One pitfall is "that information overload can prevent the obtaining of informed consent, perhaps as much as underdisclosure" (Haas & Malouf, 1995).

- Ask questions that probe the client's understanding, in addition to inviting and answering his or her questions.

- Make special efforts if English is the client's second language, or if there are hearing or cultural barriers.

- Understanding may be enhanced by the use of analogies and metaphors or even case vignettes, but beware of the client's drawing unrealistic conclusions from the parallels between the client in the story and himself or herself. Visual aids and graphics such as Venn diagrams and flow charts may help explain how things have worked and will work in causal terms.

- Couch your risk–benefit statements to the patient in terms like these (GAP, 1990, p. 10):

  ". . . while no completely satisfactory statistics are available, [I] believe that this combination of treatments offers the best chance of success."

  "The success rate of this treatment is about ____%. That is, about ____% of all patients receiving this treatment experience complete or substantial relief of their symptoms."

The best overview I have read of the issues involved in informed consent for psychotherapy with guiding wisdom on how to address them is an article by Beahrs and Gutheil (2001). Among other points, they note that addressing this process deliberately is likely to have at least these benefits: enhancing the patient's autonomy, responsibility, and self-therapeutic activity, and thus improving the likelihood of treatment success; lessening the patient's dependence, passivity, and tendency to put the therapist on a pedestal; reducing the therapist's liability because of clarification of responsibilities; and reducing the likelihood that the therapy will fall victim to therapeutic fads and cultishness.

Choosing Freely

Treating patients without their consent is one type of what used to be called "paternalistic behavior"—that is, behavior that limits autonomy (the right to decide for oneself) (see GAP, 1990, pp. 27–44). Freely choosing to be treated, or "voluntariness," requires that the consent must be free from coercion—that is, free from powerful negative incentives such as "threats of severe pain or significant deprivation of freedom" (GAP, 1990, p. 12), which a rational person would find hard or unreasonable to resist. There should be a clear absence of coercion on your part. Bear in mind that others, as well as social reality, may exert coercion; this is not your responsibility unless you have control over the coercer (see GAP, 1990, p. 16, which is based on Mallory et al., 1986). Pressure is not the same as coercion; arguing forcefully for a course of action and voicing a degree of challenge may be quite appropriate at times (GAP, 1990, p. 82), especially when you feel the client's best interests are not being attended to.

The other side of the coin is that the client must know that he or she can withdraw from treatment at any time without being punished or suffering any consequences other than the loss of any benefits derived from the treatment. If there are other consequences, they must be described fully.

Patients (except children) can, of course, refuse treatments. Liberman (1990) wisely suggests obtaining a "written waiver" for situations where a patient's refusal to follow a treatment recommendation would threaten his or her health (see Section 3.10).

Documentation

All of this therapist–client communication and rapport are consummated in the signing of a form, but the form cannot substitute for the interpersonal process of gaining informed consent. The form is not itself the consent; it is only the written evidence of the discussion and agreement. The APA code of ethics (APA, 2002) now requires that "Psychologists appropriately document written or oral consent, permission, and assent" (Standard 3.10d). If you do not get a signed form, you must carefully document in your notes what you have told the client about treatment, to demonstrate that you have indeed obtained informed consent.

If you cannot obtain consent before beginning treatment, document the reason why not (e.g., emergency, incompetence/proxy consent, court-ordered treatment, etc.) Then, if possible, get consent as soon as the crisis has passed. Everstine et al. (1980) recommend obtaining consent even in cases where treatment is compelled. The reason is that, though "legally empty, [consent] in many cases will very likely have clinical usefulness" (p. 832). The APA ethics code (APA, 2002) recognizes this issue and details responses in Standard 3.10b. When "consent" does not apply, this kind of agreement is termed "assent." Consent (or assent) forms can include clinically valuable leverage, as noted by Beahrs and Gutheil (2001): "Optimally, they also should mention the necessary role of patients' self-therapeutic activity, which in certain cases can be elaborated to include voluntary abstinence from specific problem-maintaining behaviors such as abuse of controlled substances" (p. 8).

Remember also that a signed form, by itself, is not a guarantee that informed consent has been obtained. Vaccarino (1978) reported that "legal actions for lack of informed consent have been brought despite the existence of a signed consent form" (p. 455). He emphasizes that **consenting is an interpersonal, face-to-face, rapport-based, continual discussion process, and not a mechanical, paper-based one.** Furthermore, studies of medical patients given written consent forms suggest that at best 60% of the information is retained, and so the discussion process is essential (Grunder, 1980; Ley, 1982).

Ken Pope, PhD, has generously assembled hundreds of resources about informed consent into an invaluable resource at (see www.kspope.com/consent). In addition, his collection of links to ethics codes, guidelines, and standards (www.kspope.com/ethcodes/index.php) is an excellent starting point for any questions about the codes of different organizations in therapy, assessment, and forensics.

The Three Steps to Obtaining Informed Consent

The discussion above emphasizes that informed consent is an ongoing process, not a single act. How can you be sure you have obtained it? The following three-step process offers the best procedures.

The first step is to have discussions covering the issues, because discussion is the essence of informedness. Use either your memory, or, better, one of the following as a basis for the topics to cover in your discussion:

- The topics covered in the client information brochure (see Section 4.2).

- The questions in "Information You Have a Right to Know" (see Section 4.3).

- The contents of clients' rights statements (see Section 4.4).

- The contents of treatment contracts (see Section 4.5).

- A checklist made up from the materials above and your own understanding and ideas about the nature of your treatment and the client as an individual.

The second step is to document the client's agreement with one (or, in complex situations, both) of the following:

1. A signed consent form. Use one of these:

    ■ The client information brochure (see Section 4.2).

    ■ A treatment contract (see Section 4.5).

    ■ A consent-to-treatment form (see Section 4.6).

2. Your notes concerning each of the relevant issues. The notes must document the following about both the discussions and the client's consent:

    ■ That you and the patient discussed all the relevant issues (for informedness).

    ■ That you answered all the patient's questions (again for informedness).

    ■ That the patient signed the form voluntarily.

    ■ That the patient was competent to consent. Use a statement such as the following: "In my professional judgment as a [psychologist or other type of mental health professional] and after interacting with the patient for _____ minutes, observing his or her behavior and discussing many topics, I found no reason to suspect that the patient was not competent to consent to treatment."

The third step is to keep the discussions about your treatment and their documentation ongoing. This is especially important when there are difficulties or when you change the treatments you offer.

Do Written Consent Forms Have a Negative Effect on Clients or Treatment?

Some clinicians are reluctant to use specifically worded consent materials such as those offered in this book, for fear they might turn away clients. They fear that the materials will create obstacles to (or distract clients from) treatment, or that their use will make a humane activity too formal and legalistic. Fortunately, empirical data are available to address these issues.

Handelsman (1990) has researched the effects of materials like these, in various combinations, for many years. He found that their use increased readers' positive judgments of the therapist's experience, likability, and trustworthiness; increased the readers' likelihood of recommending the therapist; and even increased self-referral by the (nonclient) subjects. More recently, Handelsman's team found that offering more readable forms with more specific information about the therapist "increased ratings of the attractiveness of the therapist, and of the relevance of and satisfaction with the forms. Personalized forms also tended to increase recall" (Wagner et al., 1998, p. 115). In an analogue but prospective study, Gustafson et al. (1994) found that providing information about risks and benefits did not affect parents' decision to seek psychological treatment for their children. Sullivan et al. (1993), in an analogue study, reported that subjects "gave higher ratings to a therapist who used an informed-consent procedure and reported more willingness to recommend him [*sic*] to a friend and go to him themselves" (p. 160).

In a study with university students in counseling, Dauser et al. (1995) found that providing a great deal of information on ethical issues (such as the limits of confidentiality, right to terminate, etc.), on the therapist's professional experience, and on what to expect in therapy (anticipated results, risks, alternatives, etc.) had no negative effects. There were no differences in no-shows or client-initiated terminations between those receiving more and those receiving less information. Those receiving more information felt they had a better understanding of what counseling would be like than did those receiving less information.

The limits of confidentiality constitute the topic of most concern to patients (Braaten, Otto, & Handelsman, 1993). Beeman and Scott (1991) found that therapists believed that pursuing informed consent enhances autonomy and control, enhances the therapeutic relationship, satisfies ethical requirements, increases motivation for therapy, ensures appropriate expectations, views older adolescents as adults, satisfies legal requirements, results in fewer divorced-parent complaints, and selects only those wanting therapy. It appears that a majority of therapists do seek informed consent, although almost exclusively through discussions, which are of course very vulnerable to the pressures of current interests and the vagaries of memory.

To summarize, **the research does not support any negative effects of using consent forms, and suggests many benefits.** Yet, despite these findings, many therapists do not use a form for obtaining informed consent to treatment (Handelsman et al., 1986). It can be argued that a form has the advantages of being (1) a defense against malpractice; (2) a patient education tool; (3) an aid in socializing the patient into therapy; and (4) a means of therapist self-development. In my experience, about 60% of psychologists now use some paper form (usually a single page) for informed consent purposes. The main reason offered by the others for not doing so is the effort it takes to research its contents. This chapter offers the fruits of just such a research effort.

Finally, consider this: Psychotherapy and psychotherapists are almost universally portrayed in film and on television both negatively and erroneously, so clients new to therapy are very likely to have assumptions and beliefs that will distort and limit the therapy if not addressed (Orchowski et al., 2006). A discussion of clients' expectations as these relate to the points raised in the informed consent materials can be both informative and liberating. And such a discussion can clarify points about a client or a proposed course of therapy for you as well. O'Neill (1998, as quoted in Pope, n.d.) puts it this way:

> While most therapists recognize that negotiation can clear up clients' misconceptions, fewer recognize that negotiation is also a vehicle for clearing up the therapist's misconceptions. An open dialogue can make the therapist aware of features of the case that depart from both the therapist's model and his or her previous experience, and thus it serves as a corrective to the representativeness and availability biases.

The Five Paths to Informed Consent

We have now examined the basic requirements for obtaining informed consent: that your client be mentally competent to consent to treatment; that you communicate information about your qualifications and the treatment; that you make certain the client understands these; that the client choose freely to be treated; and that you document the entire ongoing process.

The remainder of this chapter offers five methods for conducting this process. In essence, they are five differing *paths* to consent. These are (1) giving and discussing a client information brochure; (2) offering clients a list of questions to guide discussion (here called "Information You Have a Right to Know"); (3) offering a list of clients' rights as a basis for discussion; (4) using a psychotherapy treatment contract; and (5) using a consent-to-treatment form.

4.2   The First Path to Informed Consent: The Client Information Brochure

Kinds of Brochures

There are at least three kinds of brochures in wide use. Each is tailored to a specific purpose—namely, to market your service; to give patients specific information on specific conditions, procedures, and topics; or to initiate patients into, and assure informed consent for, therapy. Table 2 offers a more detailed description of each type.

In the table, I have named each of the brochure types according to its purposes. Other writers have called the marketing brochure, aimed at potential clients and possible referrers, a "practice" brochure; I find this ambiguous because it describes only some aspects of the

TABLE 2. Types and Purposes of Brochures Used in Psychotherapy

Type	Purpose	Possible contents
Marketing brochure	Describing your services in a very positive light so as to attract new clients.	Your resources, addresses, staff, credentials, ways to reach you, and so on. May also include testimonials (from ex-clients), invitations to visit, maps, photographs.
Topical brochure	Educating clients about specific topics. This is sometimes called "patient education."	Treatable conditions and the methods and benefits of therapy; health insurance, costs, and procedures; medications; child development and conditions; and many other common concerns.
Client information brochure	Assuring informed consent; conforming to ethical and legal concerns; creating a therapeutic alliance or contract; reducing malpractice risks; socializing clients into therapy; modeling openness; and so on.	Office procedures, such as intake, financial arrangements, appointments, clinical records, and the release of records. Also, the nature of therapy, appropriate goals, treatment planning, and assessment of progress.
Combination	Simplifying your paperwork or reducing its costs.	Various combinations of the contents described above.

practice. The marketing brochure could be the core of a package sent to potential referrers. You might add a cover letter explaining how you work with other professionals, your background and training, a letter-sized poster for their offices' bulletin boards, some business cards, a faxable referral form, and the like. Note that though the topical and client information brochures both provide factual information (which sometimes even overlaps), their goals and approaches are quite different. The fourth kind, the combination brochure, is quite common but I do not recommend it. Designing separate brochures for each purpose will avoid confusing the readers with extraneous details and assure that all issues have been addressed.

I concentrate here on the third type, the client information brochure. This needs to be as comprehensive and protective as possible in order to achieve the goals listed in Table 2. A comprehensive client information brochure is the *core document of the treatment relationship*. It establishes the boundaries of your way of practicing, and is a therapeutic contract between you and your client. It should be thoughtfully constructed because it initiates and structures your relationship, which is the heart of therapy. You will generally be seen as having obtained initial informed consent if your client has read your client information brochure and has acknowledged in writing that he or she has done so.

Besides being a legal/ethical contract, the client information brochure can also enhance the process of therapy. Based on open exchange, it models an ongoing negotiation process. Collaboration with an informed client not only satisfies legal requirements, but facilitates trust therapeutically. The process of informing clients through a marketing brochure alone can elicit their fantasies and erroneous beliefs; if these are not addressed, they could hinder therapy (Cross & Deardorff, 1987, p. 64). The client information brochure permits handling of these issues earlier. Finally, this document serves to "socialize" or introduce clients into the procedures and expectations of therapists, and can be tailored to this aim. If you develop particularly fine efforts at socialization, please share them with me.

How to Use the Model Client Information Brochure

At the end of this section, I offer an exhaustive model client information brochure. I have tried to include the full range of topics, not all of which may be relevant to your practice. It is designed to allow you to create a comprehensive and detailed brochure tailored for your own practice in just an hour or two. Spending the time to tailor a brochure to your needs will be a good investment, both ethically and professionally. Even weighing the parts you finally conclude are inessential can raise your awareness. To help with this task, I offer suggestions and commentary at appropriate points throughout the model brochure's text.

This brochure is very highly detailed, so as to be legally and ethically correct. It is written in standard U.S. grammar and word choice to make it widely applicable. Terms unfamiliar to the average client are explained in language the client can understand (APA, 2002). Note also that I have chosen a personal "I" style over an institutional, passive voice or a formal "we" version. You may prefer one of the other two; choose what feels most comfortable for you, but be consistent across all your documents.

If you are using the CD of forms and figures from this book, you can import this text and make the changes to it. You should pick and choose sections from this long version to match your specific practice needs. You can also change the format or margins, and add suitable wording to tailor it to your working methods, your locality, your clients, and your understanding of your practice. I generally call the model brochure "Information for Clients," but alternative titles might include "Welcome to the Psychological Practice of [Name]," "Introduction to the [Name] Clinic," or "New Client Introductory Information." Meek et al. (1985) use "Office Policy Statement," and I have seen "Service Agreement," but both seem too formal and somewhat dated. The brochure could also be titled by goal, such as "Ensuring Fully Informed Consent for Counseling." Others might prefer "Starting Our Work Together" or "How I Do Therapy."

Having the brochure conveniently available on your word processor is advantageous, because you can then print copies when needed and update it as your practice evolves. As a rule, when you find yourself telling three clients the same information, you should probably add it to your version of the brochure.

Other model brochures are available online at therapists' websites. For example, Laura Brown, PhD, ABPP, provides one on her site (www.drlaurabrown.com/resources.php#forms), along with other relevant materials. Various brochures are also available in print resources. Doverspike (1997) offers several forms.

I recommend the use of the client information brochure as the most comprehensive method for getting informed consent. However, the use of even a very complete brochure for informing clients of the nature of therapy and of your practice's procedures has some drawbacks:

- There is no way to be certain that a client has understood what he or she has read, or even that he or she has read the brochure, unless you open a discussion.

- Risks and alternative treatments for an individual's particular difficulties are very difficult to convey in a generic, preprepared document.

- The client has effectively lost the right to refuse information.

- Most of these brochures require too high a level of psychological sophistication and reading skill (see Wagner et al., 1998, for a review and current findings). A recent evaluation of the readability levels of "notices of privacy practices" (NPPs) required by the Health Insurance Portability and Accountability Act (HIPAA) found that almost all were in a difficult range (Walfish & Ducey, 2007). You can get an idea of the reading demands your brochure makes by using Microsoft's Word program. Under Preferences, go to "Spelling and Grammar," and under "Grammar," click on "Check grammar with spelling" and "Show readability statistics." Then open your document and select "Spelling and Grammar" under the "Tools" menu. Click through your document, ignoring all the items the checker finds and making no changes. At the end of this task, among the statistics about your document that are displayed are the Flesch Reading Ease Score (aim for 60–70) and the Flesch–Kincaid Grade Level (below 8 is excellent if possible).

Therefore, it is worth considering the alternative methods presented later.

The Model Client Information Brochure

The model brochure now begins, indented between vertical lines. The headings can be used in your own brochure. As you will see, my comments and suggestions are interwoven throughout.

INFORMATION FOR CLIENTS

Welcome to my practice. I appreciate your giving me the opportunity to be of help to you.

This brochure answers questions that clients often ask about therapy. I believe our work will be most helpful to you when you have a clear idea of what we are trying to do.

This brochure talks about the following:

- What the risks and benefits of therapy are.

- What the goals of therapy are, and what my methods of treatment are like.

- How long therapy might take.

- How much my services cost, and how I handle money matters.

- Other important areas of our relationship.

After you read this brochure, we can talk in person about how these issues apply to you. This brochure is yours to keep. Please read all of it. Mark any parts that are not clear to you. Write down any questions you have, and we will discuss them at our next meeting. When you have read and fully understood this brochure, I will ask you to sign it at the end. I will sign it as well and make a copy, so we each have one.

About Psychotherapy

I strongly believe you should feel comfortable with the therapist you choose, and hopeful about the therapy. When you feel this way, therapy is more likely to be very helpful to you. Let me describe how I see therapy.

My theoretical approach is based on . . .

The most central ideas in my work are . . .

The goals of my treatment are . . .

Here you should create a general statement about therapy as you see it. Woody (1988, p. 207) calls this communicating your "standard of care." "The Therapy Process" by Meek et al. (1985) is an outstanding example of such a statement; it raises questions while asserting an approach. Eimer (1988) uses a three-stage model of therapy, the description of which is designed as a patient handout. Tailor your statement to your conception of the impact and value of your psychological services. It can include the general aims appropriate to therapy as you understand it. Include your model of working with patients (e.g., collaboration, education, problem solving, insight into dysfunctional patterns, redeciding, primal release, relearning through transference, working with outside groups, etc.). It is also appropriate to describe, under a separate heading, other services you offer (such as court testimony, relationship counseling, or psychological assessment). If these service descriptions become quite detailed, you should make them into separate handouts. Services you do *not* offer can also be specified, such as custody evaluations for relationship therapy patients.

It may be useful to indicate, if applicable, that you are not a physician (or "medical doctor," not just the ambiguous "doctor"), and so you do not use physical interventions such as medications. When discussing the kinds of treatment you offer, you can indicate that when medications are appropriate, you will work closely with the client's physician. This is completely appropriate, as about 80% of prescriptions for psychotropic medications are written by nonpsychiatrists (see Goodwin et al., 2001). A more recent study (Harpaz-Rotem & Rosenheck, 2006) reported that "there were no significant differences between PCPs [primary care providers] and psychiatrists in either the proportion of patients who received psychotropic medication, the frequency of clinical contacts, or the dosages or types of medications prescribed" (p. 225). Note that both studies focused on children and adolescents, but there is no reason to believe that these patterns differ greatly for adult patients. It may be helpful in discussing medical care to evaluate the client's attitude toward psychotropic medications. Irrational fears, overly optimistic expectations, and general ignorance (e.g. "chemical imbalance") are widespread, and having information about your client's thoughts (from a discussion of your brochure or from responses on your intake forms) may usefully guide in later treatment.

Hawkins and Bullock (1995) suggest that it would be proper to **indicate here any moral values you hold** that might conflict with clients' religious beliefs. Because psychiatrists are the least religious of medical specialists (and psychologists are not likely to be very different), a gap in religiousness between a client and clinician would not be uncommon (Curlin et al., 2007). Hare-Mustin et al. (1979) suggest specifying and elaborating on any technique that might be at odds with clients' values. For example, if you do relationship counseling, you might indicate your views on divorce as a response to marital distress, or make it clear that your obligation is to the mental and emotional health of the individuals, not to the relationship. A relationship cannot be a client, according to Koocher and Keith-Spiegel (1998), but Margolin (1982) differs on this point. If your treatment methods are experimental or even controversial, you should make this section even more detailed or prepare a special consent form.

Another aspect of fully informed consent arises when you are asked whether you do "Christian counseling" (or have "Christian values" or something similar). It is both ethically appropriate and may be therapeutic to clarify what is meant before you reply. The "clinical integration" of religious and spiritual values into psychotherapy has grown rapidly. This is a complex area, so see Pargament (1997, 2007), Richards and Bergin (2000), and Sperry and Shafranske (2004), among many others. The caller may be seeking a Bible-based therapy (involving prayer, references to Bible stories, the teachings of Jesus, etc.). This is pastoral counseling, and you should either be so qualified or refer the client if he or she is uninterested in therapy involving any secular theories, principles, or research.

For those of us who are psychologists, there are several concerns in discussing "Christian values." First, we have an ethical requirement to respect the values of others (Principle E of the APA ethics code; APA, 2002). Second, we must make our own values and beliefs very clear to clients from the beginning, so that clients can give informed consent to treatment.

Third, we have an ethical requirement for cultural competence (Principle E). It seems very clear that evangelical Christians constitute a true subculture, so we must have the same level of cultural competence we require for working with other special populations. Lastly, the research shows that therapy is more successful when the client and therapist share more expectations. This suggests the benefits of exploring values early in the therapy process.

Potential clients seeking a therapist with "Christian values" usually want someone who is able to work within their world view. Note that being "a psychologist who is also a Christian" is not a sufficient response, because there are so many kinds of Christians with so many value systems and so many issues on which they differ. Is a client concerned with going to hell for an unforgivable sin, struggling with Biblical condemnations of homosexual behaviors, seeking a morally acceptable resolution of an affair, unwilling to consider a divorce or an abortion, or suffering through a spiritual crisis because of a loss of faith? In light of the discussion above, you should, as part of your intake procedures, take a religious history (see Zuckerman, 2005, pp. 264–266) and then discuss the issues bringing clients for therapy and the religious context of their lives. Clarifying areas of difference between your own and your potential clients' beliefs that are likely to affect treatment seems essential for informed consent.

The following is the way my own brochure describes my approach, its central ideas, and its goals to clients:

> The type of therapy I do is called "rational–emotive behavior therapy," or REBT. It was developed by Albert Ellis, PhD, and is described in his dozens of books.
>
> We often believe that our behaviors and feelings are caused by what happens in the real world. However, this is not quite true. When we have any kind of experience, it does not affect us directly. Rather, we first give it a meaning through our beliefs about it. For example, if I hear a sound in the kitchen and believe it is made by my wife, I am not bothered at all. But if I believe I am alone in the house, the same sound can bother me a great deal. Here we see that feelings and behaviors (my actions about the sound) flow from the active process of thinking and adding meaning to the actual event (the sound).
>
> Dr. Ellis separates beliefs into two kinds: "rational" beliefs, or ones based on reality and logic, and "irrational" beliefs, or ones based on false or unrealistic ideas. When we have irrational beliefs, we suffer from strong negative emotions (like rage, depression, and anxiety). When we act on the basis of irrational beliefs, our actions are often not effective and can even be harmful. If we have rational beliefs, we will experience more of the positive emotions (like pleasure, hope, and joy). We can still feel the mildly negative emotions, like irritation, sadness, and concern, but our behaviors will be more effective.
>
> I think of my approach to helping people with their problems as an educational one. Anyone can learn to recognize irrational beliefs, dispute them, and replace them with more rational beliefs. We can, with practice, unlearn irrational beliefs and become happier persons who function better in the world. This is what I mean by an educational approach.
>
> I want you to be able to use REBT without me. I encourage you to learn more about what methods are used in REBT, how well it works, and what possible problems or side effects it may have. I can lend you books and articles that explain how it works. Please return them when you no longer need them so I can lend them to other clients. I may also give you copies of articles or handouts that are yours to keep.

You may want to include the URLs of websites that explain and document your methods. This is not only educational, but supportive therapeutic optimism and client motivation. For example, the National Association of Cognitive Behavior Therapists has a three-page overview suitable for clients (www.nacbt.org/whatiscbt.htm). You can include a link to it on your own website.

> I usually take notes during our meetings. You may find it useful to take your own notes, and also to take notes outside the office. You could also tape-record our meetings to review at your leisure at home.

As to a client's note taking, I have found this useful for the same reasons I take notes myself: It is an opportunity to mull over what has been said; it aids my (or the client's) focusing as I decide (or the client decides) what to note; and it provides a record of what has happened and been said that I (or the client) can review. Occasionally, I have encouraged clients to keep a three-ring binder called "My Therapy" for notes, diaries, questions, clippings, photos, or any other relevant materials. It may be necessary to mention that these notes should be kept in such a way as to maintain their privacy, and even that clients might wish to destroy these at some future date.

Consider carefully before including the suggestion, as I do, that the client tape-record sessions. We all say things that we might later modify or withdraw, but a recording is fixed. You cannot ask a client to destroy recordings he or she has made, because they belong to the client. Also, such recordings would have to be maintained by the client in a secure manner and perhaps over a long time period. On the other hand, I have encouraged audiotaping by some patients when the educational content bears repeating, with the rationale that they have "had two sessions for the price of one." Be sensitive to the magical qualities of your taped voice for some clients. In most cases, when a client does not find making recordings beneficial, he or she usually simply stops bringing the equipment to sessions. See Section 4.6 and Form 16 if you are considering making tape recordings. Remember, recordings you make become part of your records and so can be "discovered" by an unhappy client's lawyer, and you must make arrangements for their continued confidential maintenance. In any case, do not tape-record without the client's informed consent.

> By the end of our first or second session, I will tell you how I see your case at this point and how I think we should proceed. I view therapy as a partnership between us. You define the problem areas to be worked on; I use some special knowledge to help you make the changes you want to make. Psychotherapy is not like visiting a medical doctor. It requires your very active involvement. It requires your best efforts to change thoughts, feelings, and behaviors. For example, I want you to tell me about important experiences, what they mean to you, and what strong feelings are involved. This is one of the ways you are an active partner in therapy.
>
> I expect us to plan our work together. In our treatment plan we will list the areas to work on, our goals, the methods we will use, the time and money commitments we will make, and some other things. I expect us to agree on a plan that we will both work hard to follow. From time to time, we will look together at our progress and goals. If we think we need to, we can then change our treatment plan, its goals, or its methods.

You might want to indicate that minor, major, and multiple problems take different amounts of therapy time (both frequency of sessions and duration of the therapy).

> An important part of your therapy will be practicing new skills that you will learn in our sessions. I will ask you to practice outside our meetings, and we will work together to set up homework assignments for you. I might ask you to do exercises, keep records, and read to deepen your learning. You will probably have to work on relationships in your life and make long-term efforts to get the best results. These are important parts of personal change. Change will sometimes be easy and quick, but more often it will be slow and frustrating, and you will need to keep trying. There are no instant, painless cures and no "magic pills." However, you *can* learn new ways of looking at your problems that will be very helpful for changing your feelings and reactions.

In my brochure, I do not address goals except to suggest that they involve the reduction of symptomatic or distressing behaviors. I address the client's other specific goals during our interviews and in the treatment plan.

> Most of my clients see me once a week for 3 to 4 months. After that, we meet less often for several more months. Therapy then usually comes to an end. The process of ending therapy, called "termination," can be a very valuable part of our work. Stopping therapy should not be done casually, although either of us may decide to end it if we believe it is in your best interest. If you wish to stop therapy at any time, I ask that you agree now to meet then for at least one more session to review our work together. We will review our goals, the work we have done, any future work that needs to be done, and our choices. If you would like to take a "time out" from therapy to try it on your own, we should discuss this. We can often make such a "time out" be more helpful.
>
> I will send you a brief set of questions about 6 months after our last session. These questions will ask you to look back at our work together, and sending them to you is part of my duty as a therapist. I ask that you agree, as part of entering therapy with me, to return this follow-up form and to be very honest about what you tell me then.
>
> ### The Benefits and Risks of Therapy
>
> As with any powerful treatment, there are some risks as well as many benefits with therapy. You should think about both the benefits and risks when making any treatment decisions. For example, in therapy, there is a risk that clients will, for a time, have uncomfortable levels of sadness, guilt, anxiety, anger, frustration, loneliness, helplessness, or other negative feelings. Clients may recall unpleasant memories. These feelings or memories may bother a client at work or in school. In addition, some people in the community may mistakenly view anyone in therapy as weak, or perhaps as seriously disturbed or even dangerous. Also, clients in therapy may have problems with people important to them. Family secrets may be told. Therapy may disrupt a marital relationship and sometimes may even lead to a divorce. Sometimes, too, a client's problems may temporarily worsen after the beginning of treatment. Most of these risks are to be expected when people are making important changes in their lives. Finally, even with our best efforts, there is a risk that therapy may not work out well for you.

The statement above presents a list of some risks in accordance with the requirements of informed consent. For example, Hurvitz (1976) found that progress in individual therapy may often disrupt a marital relationship. If you do this kind of work, you should include this point.

John Kachorek (1990, pp. 106–109) offers a very complete and well-reasoned handout of this type. It includes this statement:

> In therapy, major life decisions are sometimes made, including decisions involving separation within families, development of other types of relationships, changing employment settings and changing life-styles. These decisions are a legitimate outcome of the therapy experience as a result of an individual's calling into question many of their [sic] beliefs and values. As your therapist, I will be available to discuss any of your assumptions, problems, or possible negative side effects in our work together. (p. 107)

Some other possibilities for risks, according to Soreff and McDuffee (1993), are that

> symptom[s may be intensified;] the conflict may not be resolved; the emotional experience may be overwhelming or too intense to deal with at this time; the targeted behavior may not change; the patient may not be any more aware of himself [sic] than when therapy commenced; in spite of therapy, the patient still may not accept or forgive himself [sic]; the interpersonal experience may not be successful or corrective; the therapeutic experience may activate or reactivate conflicts, thoughts, or emotions that may in turn lead to disruptive behavior; new and different symptoms may develop during therapy; the patient may have difficulty in terminating therapy. (p. 491)

The next paragraph of the model brochure describes therapy's benefits.

> While you consider these risks, you should know also that the benefits of therapy have been shown by scientists in hundreds of well-designed research studies. People who are depressed may find their mood lifting. Others may no longer feel afraid, angry, or anxious. In therapy, people have a chance to talk things out fully until their feelings are relieved or the problems are solved. Clients' relationships and coping skills may improve greatly. They may get more satisfaction out of social and family relationships. Their personal goals and values may become clearer. They may grow in many directions—as persons, in their close relationships, in their work or schooling, and in the ability to enjoy their lives.
>
> I do not take on clients I do not think I can help. Therefore, I will enter our relationship with optimism about our progress.

In your description of the benefits of psychotherapy (either orally or in writing), be careful not to promise a cure, or benefits so substantial that they approach a complete cure. Again, you are not in control of all or even most of the factors determining the outcome, and you especially do not wish to cause disappointment. You might also want to cite the meta-analysis of Smith and Glass (1977), or Martin Seligman's (1995) *Consumer Reports* research on the effectiveness of psychotherapy. (A summary of Seligman's study, written for clients by Larry M. Friedberg, is available at (www.michpsych.org/index.cfm?location=3&subsectionid=4). However, recommending (even energetically) is not insisting and is not coercion, so don't be shy about the therapy you offer. Everstine et al. (1980) also discuss the benefits of personal growth and maturity.

Consultations

Depending on your practice, you might indicate here that you sometimes will suggest the need for psychological or educational testing, or for medication evaluation and prescription. If so, note the approximate cost of such referrals, and your usual arrangements for these referrals. If you are likely to refer clients to other professionals for services such as nutrition evaluation and counseling, exercise or martial arts training, vocational guidance, cosmetic surgery, credit counseling, shelters and protection agencies, or the like, this would be a good place to describe those options briefly as well.

> If you could benefit from a treatment I cannot provide, I will help you to get it. You have a right to ask me about such other treatments, their risks, and their benefits. Based on what I learn about your problems, I may recommend a medical exam or use of medication. If I do this, I will fully discuss my reasons with you, so that you can decide what is best. If you are treated by another professional, I will coordinate my services with them and with your own medical doctor.
>
> If for some reason treatment is not going well, I might suggest you see another therapist or another professional for an evaluation. As a responsible person and ethical therapist, I cannot continue to treat you if my treatment is not working for you. If you wish for another professional's opinion at any time, or wish to talk with another therapist, I will help you find a qualified person and will provide him or her with the information needed.

Try to present alternative treatments evenhandedly for two reasons: (1) to present yourself as truly having the client's best interests at heart, and (2) to keep the client from thinking that, because you are discussing other helping programs so enthusiastically, you do not really want to work with the client (Hare-Mustin et al., 1979).

What to Expect from Our Relationship

Sam Knapp, EdD, of Harrisburg, PA, offers the following wording as an introduction to this topic: "Psychological services are best provided in an atmosphere of trust. You expect me to be honest with you about your problems and progress. I expect you to be honest with me about your expectations for services, your compliance with medication, and any other barriers to treatment."

> As a professional, I will use my best knowledge and skills to help you. This includes following the standards of the American Psychological Association, or APA. In your best interests, the APA puts limits on the relationship between a therapist and a client, and I will abide by these. Let me explain these limits, so you will not think they are personal responses to you.
>
> First, I am licensed and trained to practice psychology—not law, medicine, finance, or any other profession. I am not able to give you good advice from these other professional viewpoints.
>
> Second, state laws and the rules of the APA require me to keep what you tell me confidential (that is, just between us). You can trust me not to tell anyone else what you tell me, except in certain limited situations. I explain what those are in the "About Confidentiality" section of this brochure. Here I want to explain that I try not to reveal who my clients are. This is part of my effort to maintain your privacy. If we meet on the street or socially, I may

> not say hello or talk to you very much. My behavior will not be a personal reaction to you, but a way to maintain the confidentiality of our relationship.
>
> Third, in your best interest, and following the APA's standards, I can only be your therapist. I cannot have any other role in your life. I cannot, now or ever, be a close friend to or socialize with any of my clients. I cannot be a therapist to someone who is already a friend. I can never have a sexual or romantic relationship with any client during, or after, the course of therapy. I cannot have a business relationship with any of my clients, other than the therapy relationship.

In the paragraph above, it would be appropriate to add any rules you have that the client might inadvertently break or misinterpret. For example, some therapists have a rule never to touch a patient, mainly to avoid miscommunication (see Section 3.8). See Kertay and Reviere (1993) for a full discussion of and guidelines about touch. Or you may have a rule that the client establishes (perhaps with some assistance) the goals of therapy, and that you serve as his or her consultant in providing the means for those ends. Such clarifications are especially useful for patients with borderline and personality disorders and those with a history of manipulation.

It is possible that a client or couple that you see may become involved in a lawsuit in the future. Serving as both a therapist and a forensic expert witness (even if so qualified) to the same client creates a dual relationship, with conflicts of priority and mixed obligations, and you should clarify this here.

The APA code of ethics (APA, 2002, Standard 10.02b) suggests that you address the next point:

> If you ever become involved in a divorce or custody dispute, I want you to understand and agree that I will not provide evaluations or expert testimony in court. You should hire a different mental health professional for any evaluations or testimony you require. This position is based on two reasons: (1) My statements will be seen as biased in your favor because we have a therapy relationship; and (2) the testimony might affect our therapy relationship, and I must put this relationship first.

You might also want to add more specific information on the following points:

> Even though you might invite me, I will not attend your family gatherings, such as parties or weddings.
>
> As your therapist, I will not celebrate holidays or give you gifts; I may not notice or recall your birthday; and may not receive any of your gifts eagerly.

Haas and Malouf (1995) offer excellent guidelines on the subject of gift receiving: Express positive and caring feelings; do not immediately clinically process the giving; suggest an alternative (such as a gift to charity); and relax about most of these situations.

If you treat clients for addiction, they are likely to show up intoxicated at some point. Handling this is best done with paragraphs in your brochure (1) having them agree to attend treatment uninebriated and to give consent to random drug or alcohol tests, and (2) emphasizing the value of and need for honesty. On that basis, you can immediately confront them when you suspect substance use and then explore it therapeutically, rather than dismissing them from therapy (temporarily or permanently)—or, worse, ignoring slips.

About Confidentiality

The section of the brochure on confidentiality is one of crucial legal concern. The APA ethics code (APA, 2002, Section 4.02) requires that the limits of confidentiality be communicated explicitly and in advance to all clients (clinical and organizational). It requires that you discuss the limits of confidentiality at the beginning of treatment and as any new circumstances warrant. The HIPAA Privacy Rule requires that you furnish clients with an NPP; see Section 5.4 for more on this form. Several states, including Colorado and Massachusetts, require therapists to furnish a handout to each client explaining the limits of confidentiality, so this section of the brochure addresses this issue in detail. You might want to provide your clients (or selected clients) with a separate handout concerning only this issue; see Section 7.1 for such a handout and for more information.

> I will treat with great care all the information you share with me. It is your legal right that our sessions and my records about you be kept private. That is why I ask you to sign a "release-of-records" form before I can talk about you or send my records about you to anyone else. In general, I will tell no one what you tell me. I will not even reveal that you are receiving treatment from me.
>
> In all but a few rare situations, your confidentiality (that is, our privacy) is protected by federal and state laws and by the rules of my profession. Here are the most common cases in which confidentiality is *not* protected:
>
> 1. If you were sent to me by a court or an employer for evaluation or treatment, the court or employer expects a report from me. If this is your situation, please talk with me before you tell me anything you do not want the court or your employer to know. You have a right to tell me only what you are comfortable with telling.
>
> 2. Are you suing someone or being sued? Are you being charged with a crime? If so, and you tell the court that you are seeing me, I may then be ordered to show the court my records. Please consult your lawyer about these issues.
>
> 3. If you make a serious threat to harm yourself or another person, the law requires me to try to protect you or that other person. This usually means telling others about the threat. I cannot promise never to tell others about threats you make.
>
> 4. If I believe a child has been or will be abused or neglected, I am legally required to report this to the authorities.

Under the second exception above, you might consider noting that your records may be brought into custody or adoption proceedings (this is important if you see couples or families), or any other legal case in which a judge decides that a client's mental or emotional condition is an important element. Disability cases, workers' compensation hearings, psychiatric hospitalization, and criminal cases are some possibilities.

In the fourth exception above, I use the phrase "If I believe a child . . . ". State laws differ in their language, and the word "believe" may not be accurate in your state. For example, if the legal criterion is "what a reasonable person would suspect," this means that the level of evidence for reporting is lower than if the law were to say "believe." You must know your local rules. You might post a copy of the law in your waiting room, as suggested by David Clovard, MD, of Raleigh, NC. Moreover, note that a therapist is not required to investigate or validate allegations of abuse; only suspicion or belief is necessary for a report. This is not a judgment call, but a mandate placed on therapists to protect children and other vulnerable persons by a society that values such protection more than confidentiality.

An alternative phrasing for the third and fourth exceptions above is this: "As a therapist, my legal and moral duty is to protect your confidentiality, but I also have a duty under the law to the wider community and to myself, if there is harm, threat of harm, or neglect."

Obviously, you need to tailor the confidentiality section of your brochure to your specific situation, locality, and practice. For example, does your state have other exceptions to confidentiality besides those listed above, such as elder abuse or neglect? Be sure to modify this statement in light of your title, your profession's legal status, the state in which you practice, and the type of therapy you are doing. For example, if you see neuropsychology or rehabilitation clients and your state requires you to notify it of impaired drivers, you should indicate this rule. There is no substitute for exact knowledge and caution.

The statements above are not suitable for the treatment of minors. Set the ground rules with minors and their parents before therapy. See also Forms 10 and 11 for treatment contracts for minors, and Form 14 for a consent-to-treatment form for a child.

A different or fuller statement of the law in your locality, or for your profession, may be appropriate concerning consultations. You may use the patient handout on the limits of confidentiality (Handout 6) as a basis for your version.

> There are two situations in which I might talk about part of your case with another therapist. I ask now for your understanding and agreement to let me do so in these two situations.
>
> First, when I am away from the office for a few days, I have a trusted fellow therapist "cover" for me. This therapist will be available to you in emergencies. Therefore, he or she needs to know about you. Of course, this therapist is bound by the same laws and rules as I am to protect your confidentiality.

When you are away, your "covering" colleague may need more information on and plans for handling clients with serious problems. Have your colleague document any calls received and actions taken, and have him or her send this to you for your case file. It is probably best never to be completely unreachable, but you cannot provide all services from a distance, so carefully document your thinking, decision making, and actions in an emergency. You will save your travel documentation such as tickets and hotel receipts when on professional business, but save evidence of personal travel for a while as self-protection in case a malpractice problem develops.

> Second, I sometimes consult other therapists or other professionals about my clients. This helps me in giving high-quality treatment. These persons are also required to keep your information private. Your name will never be given to them, some information will be changed or omitted, and they will be told only as much as they need to know to understand your situation.

Knapp (1992b) has made a number of suggestions about communicating with a client's primary care physician (PCP), both in general and when the client is a Medicare patient. He suggests discussing the desirability of notifying the PCP, doing so in the most efficient way, and documenting this in the chart. If the client has refused, note this and the reasons offered. Knapp suggests this wording for your brochure:

> It may be beneficial for me to confer with your primary care physician with regard to your psychological treatment or to discuss any medical problems for which you are receiving treatment. In addition, Medicare requires that I notify your physician by telephone or in writing, concerning services that are being provided by me unless you request that notification not be made.
>
> Please check ONE of the following:
>
> ❑ You are authorized to contact my primary care physician whose name and address are shown below to discuss the treatment that I am receiving while under your care and to obtain information concerning my medical diagnosis and treatment.
>
> ❑ I do not authorize you to contact my primary care physician with regard to the treatment that I am receiving while under your care or to obtain information concerning my medical diagnosis and treatment. I am providing you with the name and address of my primary care physician only for your records. (1992b, p. 7)

He then asks for the name, address, and phone number of the PCP.

I believe that HIPAA regulations allow the sharing of protected health information (PHI) with peer mental health clinicians or physicians without any other consent beyond the initial NPP. Note, however, that patients have some ability, under HIPAA, to restrict the sharing of their information (see below).

An alternative phrasing for consultation is offered by Constance Fisher, PhD, of Pittsburgh, PA: "We consult with colleagues and specialists about our ongoing work. This pursuit of quality assurance never involves your name or any specifics through which you might be identified."

> For the purpose of these consultations, I may want to make audio or video recordings of our sessions. I will review the recordings with my consultant to assist with your treatment. I will ask your permission to make any recording. I promise to destroy each recording as soon as I no longer need it, or, at the latest, when I destroy your case records. You can refuse to allow this recording, or can insist that the recording be edited.

You should have the client sign a formal release (such as Form 16) if you are going to videotape sessions for consultations.

> Except for situations like those I have described above, my office staff and I will always maintain your privacy. I also ask you not to disclose the name or identity of any other client being seen in this office.
>
> My office staff makes every effort to keep the names and records of clients private. My staff and I will try never to use your name on the telephone, if clients in the office can overhear it. All staff members who see your records have been trained in how to keep records confidential.

Make sure you fulfill this promise by designing a training program for all current and new staff members. See Section 7.2 for some guidance on this.

> If your records need to be seen by another professional, or anyone else, I will discuss it with you. If you agree to share these records, you will need to sign an authorization form. This form states exactly what information is to be shared, with whom, and why, and it also sets time limits. You may read this form at any time. If you have questions, please ask me.

You might want to add the following, again suggested by Constance Fisher, PhD, of Pittsburgh, PA: "We do not divulge the fact that you are a client or anything about you or your sessions to anyone, unless you request us (in writing) to do so."

Because you cannot foretell the needs for your records, I suggest retaining them for many years, or forever (see Section 1.6 on retention of records), and your clients should be advised of your policy. Here is my own statement:

> It is my office policy to destroy clients' records 15 years after the end of our therapy. Until then, I will keep your case records in a safe place.

There are two sides to this coin. Keeping records forever may protect you, but they are discoverable by opposing lawyers. The information in records can become very outdated and invalid, and so useless or even misleading. I think that therapists cannot automatically refuse to furnish records just because they might be invalid, so I suggest adding a statement to your cover letter warning of this issue (see Form 51).

Because your records must be available even when you cannot provide them (see Section 1.6), include a statement like this in your brochure:

> If I must discontinue our relationship because of illness, disability, or other presently unforeseen circumstances, I ask you to agree to my transferring your records to another therapist who will assure their confidentiality, preservation, and appropriate access.

The APA ethics code (APA, 2002, Standard 10.02) addresses confidentiality issues in treating couples or families. Therefore, you might want to insert a notice like the following, before going on to address the topic of the information you give to insurance companies:

> If we do family or couple therapy (where there is more than one client), and you want to have my records of this therapy sent to anyone, all of the adults present will have to sign a release.

Family therapy and couple therapy may result in divorce and custody hearings, and this may bring your records into an open court. Secrets may be revealed, or irrelevant but damaging information may be made public. The most protective record keeping is to generate separate records for each adult and for the family as a whole. This allows some privacy but does not guarantee it in a legal contest. Both parents must release family records, but each can release his or her own records, as for seeking life insurance or a security clearance.

In 15 years of practice, I was contacted twice by the FBI when patients sought security clearances. However, this is not the only risk of receiving mental health treatment; other situations should be fully explored before a record is created and it is too late. For example, when all patient records are computerized, there is likely to be no way of segregating old records, created under assumptions of confidentiality, from new ones or even from old medical records with different protections of confidentiality (as, for example, those created in different states). In addition, most medical diagnoses and treatments received have been recorded in the Medical Information Bureau's (www.mib.com) files and are accessed whenever one applies for life, health, disability, or long-term care insurance, as well as for other purposes. Routinely, diagnoses of depression affect one's eligibility for life insurance and the cost of such insurance, hiring for security-sensitive jobs, and political ambitions. You should decide if you need to educate your clients about this issue before creating a record which would become eligible for inclusion in the files at the Medical Information Bureau (MIB).

> As part of cost control efforts, an insurance company will sometimes ask for more information on symptoms, diagnoses, and my treatment methods. It will become part of your permanent medical record. I will let you know if this should occur and what the company has asked for. Please understand that I have no control over how these records are handled at the insurance company. My policy is to provide only as much information as the insurance company will need to pay your benefits.

These are lively issues and of great concern. Federal laws like the HIPAA regulations and the Employee Retirement Income Security Act of 1974 (ERISA) interact with state laws, regulations, and our codes of ethics concerning privacy issues. The computerization of medical records, storage in multiple data bases with very different access rules, the use of encryption, and other pressures and events not foreseeable at present will shape your way of practicing. You will have to craft (and update) guidelines for your practice that you believe are in your and your client's best interest.

Many states have laws concerning clients' **access** to their own records, but few of those apply to private practice. For example, federal law is silent on drug and alcohol clients' inspection of their records (Drug Abuse Office and Treatment Act of 1972, Public Law 92-255), even when such clients are seen in private practice. But it defers to stricter state laws. These laws usually concern the following points: A client has a right to inspect records; to request corrections of inaccurate, irrelevant, outdated, or incomplete information; and to submit rebuttal information or memoranda. If your state laws do not offer clients the opportunity to review and modify your records, the HIPAA regulations on accessing and amending records (164.524 and 164.526, respectively) are very likely to apply (see Section 7.1).

> You can review your own records in my files at any time. You may add to them or correct them, and you can have copies of them. I ask you to understand and agree that you may not examine records created by anyone else and sent to me.

You can charge a reasonable fee for copies, but usually not for just locating records; the accessibility of records is part of the ethical responsibility of record keeping. When a client asks me to send copies of records to another treater, I do so and do not charge, but when the records are sent to a lawyer or used in any other situation that might benefit the client, my policy is to provide a copy to the client and have him or her make copies for others. No authorization is needed to give clients their own records, but I note exactly what has been copied and sent. This make the contents known to the clients and places the responsibility for release with the clients.

HIPAA allows a professional or an agency manager to remove part of the record temporarily, if he or she determines that it might be detrimental to the client. This person must document the removal and its rationale. The client may appeal any limitation of access. If you design your procedures to work within these guidelines, and indicate your rules in your brochure, you will reduce your risk exposure greatly.

> In some very rare situations, I may temporarily remove parts of your records before you see them. This would happen if I believe that the information will be harmful to you, but I will discuss this with you.

HIPAA gives clients the right to ask for some very limited restrictions on the disclosure of their records, but since this applies very narrowly, it need only be mentioned.

> You have the right to ask that your information not be shared with family members or others, and I can agree to that limitation. You can also tell me if you want me to send mail or phone you at a more private address or number than, say, your home or workplace. If this is of concern to you, please tell me so that we can make arrangements.

As an alternative to a discussion, you could provide spaces on the intake data form (see Form 24) for the client to supply a different address or different phone, answering machine, or voice mail numbers for contacts.

My Background

This section of the brochure gives your clients information about your professional experience and training. Mention only your clinically relevant background; do not list social or political accomplishments, if these are irrelevant to being a therapist. You can include your areas of special professional interest, your publications, your supervisor status, and/or positions you hold in your professional organizations. If you present yourself as having any specialty, you will have to perform at, and conform to, the standards of others with full certification in that specialty. See Section 1.2 on the ethics of credentials. Few people are knowledgeable about therapists' credentials, so it may be helpful to offer explanations of such matters as licensure or levels of certification. You can also mention training, such as internships, qualifications, supervision, education, and positions held.

If you are being supervised, the APA code of ethics (APA, 2002, Standard 10.01c) requires that you inform clients of this fact and of the supervisor's name where the supervisor has legal responsibility. I would suggest also including the supervisor's address and phone number as well, with the intention of heading off problems.

It is not unethical to include a statement of experience such as this: "I have over 20 years of experience in the delivery of psychotherapy, psychological assessment, and consultation to children, adults, and families." You can also list the full range of services you offer such as group, individual, relationship, and/or family therapy; evaluations of various kinds; consultations with schools, other clinicians, or lawyers; hospital and home visits; and so on.

I am a psychologist with 25 years of experience. For the past 12 years, I have had my own office for the general practice of clinical psychology. I am trained and experienced in doing one-on-one and couple therapy with adults (18 years and over). Earlier in my career, I worked in clinics and similar settings. I hold these qualifications:

- I have a doctoral degree in clinical psychology from the University of Pittsburgh, whose program is approved by the American Psychological Association (APA).

- I completed an internship in clinical psychology, approved by the APA.

- I am licensed as a psychologist in Pennsylvania.

- I am a member of the APA.

- I am a fellow of the Pennsylvania Psychological Association.

I am a psychologist and I like the phrase "general practice of clinical psychology." But you might prefer to call yourself a "health psychologist," a "counselor," or another explanatory title. Just make certain that it is accurate, supported by credentials, and not misleading. I have avoided the term "private practice," but an acceptable alternative phrase is "independent practice."

Although memberships do not certify competence, listing them informs the client of your adherence to that organization's codified ethical standards. Thus the client has recourse to the professional organization's ethics committee. You might consider stating in the brochure here that you accept and practice in conformity with the code of ethics of your license or certification in your state. This model brochure makes such a statement in a later section (see "Statement of Principles and Complaint Procedures").

One last point about explaining your situation to the client for fully informed consent concerns financial conflicts of interest between the client's needs and your professional relationships. For example, if, in your independent practice, you recommend or refer the client to a program or agency of which you are an owner (or even an employee who might benefit indirectly from the program's or agency's profitability), you are bound to disclose this relationship. See also the discussions of fee splitting in Sections 2.1 and 2.4.

About Our Appointments

The very first time I meet with you, we will need to give each other much basic information. For this reason, I usually schedule 1–2 hours for this first meeting. Following this, we will usually meet for a 50-minute session once or twice a week, then less often. We can schedule meetings for both your and my convenience. I will tell you at least a month in advance of my vacations or any other times we cannot meet. Please ask about my schedule in making your own plans.

The paragraph above describes the general time frame for brief therapy. You might want to be more detailed about the first session. It could be called an "initial evaluation session," for example, and you could specify that it includes open discussion of problems and concerns, history gathering, testing or questionnaires, and completion of forms (e.g., Form 28, the financial information form).

The scheduling of weekly appointments is traditional but not empirical. In a fascinating article, Zhu and Pierce (1995) suggest that, to the degree that the learning in therapy resembles the learning–forgetting curves seen in laboratory studies, the schedule of meetings ought to be negatively accelerated. As an example, they suggest meetings at 1, 3, 7, 14, and 30 days for optimal prevention of relapse. I would very strongly encourage you to consider such a schedule.

I suggest above that appointments can be scheduled for "both your and my convenience." An alternative wording might be "Changes in appointments should be made with as much advance notice as possible, as a sign of our mutual respect." Or "While I am willing to be flexible, I have found that therapy is more effective when it occurs at a regular time each week. I hope we can work toward this regularity of schedules." Or "Appointments can be scheduled during my office hours, Monday through Friday, 11:00 A.M. to 9:00 P.M." If you use this last format, you could indicate that appointments or calls outside these times will be charged at twice your usual rate.

Be careful not to use "session" and "hour" interchangeably (unless your session length truly is 60 minutes). Doing so may mislead some clients. Do not choose the length of your session on the basis of the client's needs and what your peers are doing; choose it on the basis of your particular style of doing therapy. Keep in mind your need for breaks, for time to write notes, and for moving around, as well as your office location. Therapists often schedule 1-hour sessions for individuals and 1½-hour sessions for couples. If you treat both individuals and couples, you can include both lengths at this point in your brochure.

> An appointment is a commitment to our work. We agree to meet here and to be on time. If I am ever unable to start on time, I ask your understanding. I also assure you that you will receive the full time agreed to. If you are late, we will probably be unable to meet for the full time, because it is likely that I will have another appointment after yours.
>
> A cancelled appointment delays our work. I will consider our meetings very important and ask you to do the same. Please try not to miss sessions if you can possibly help it. When you must cancel, please give me at least a week's notice. Your session time is reserved for you. I am rarely able to fill a cancelled session unless I know a week in advance. If you start to cancel sessions, I will have to charge you for the lost time unless I am able to fill it. Your insurance will not cover this charge.

For the paragraph above, you can substitute the following:

> I will reserve a regular appointment time for you into the foreseeable future. I also do this for my other patients. Therefore, I am rarely able to fill a cancelled session unless I have several weeks' notice. You will be charged the full fee for sessions cancelled with less than 72 hours' notice, for other than the most serious reasons.

Repetition of this point on your appointment cards, on your bills, and on a sign in the office is recommended.

The quite reasonable charging for **missed sessions** can be complicated by your agreements with managed care organizations (MCOs), which generally forbid your charging a client for anything but the copayment. Read your contracts before including such a statement. Recently Medicare has allowed a client to be charged for missed sessions, as long as you also charge all your other clients for missed session. See CMS Transmittal 1279 (www.cms.hhs.gov/Transmittals/downloads/R1279CP.pdf) and the MedLearn Matters bulletin regarding this recent transmittal (MLN Matters Number MM5613; www.cms.hhs.gov/MLNMattersArticles/downloads/MM5613.pdf).

By the way, Medicare clients can be billed for any services not covered by Medicare, and these will include no-shows and recommended further evaluations. Also, you might consider offering treatments which would be beneficial and affordable when not billable. The form to do this is the Advanced Beneficiary Notice (CMS-R-131-G; see www.cms.hhs.gov/BNI/02_ABNGABNL.asp).

If you are able, should you charge no-shows, late cancellers, or late arrivers the full amount? Licensed psychologist Sheila Carluccio, MA, of Dickson City, PA, has made some excellent suggestions about this issue:

> Although it specifically states in my guidelines for treatment that I reserve the right to charge for cancellations, I reduce the charge for a missed session to $40.00 and am very specific that the charge is (1) not reimbursable through insurance and (2) charged in the event of frequent cancelling/no-shows, etc. We talk about the circumstances for missing the session. [For instance,] you'd rather go to the mall/keep forgetting to show up/don't "feel like" coming to a session? Then I'd have to charge. You have a sick child/got called to work mandatory overtime/you're snowed in and can't make it? No charge. The guidelines are then signed as a treatment contract. In the event that difficulties arise, I refer back to this contract and we discuss it. Clients know from the beginning that being charged is something that they are choosing; at the same time I am giving clients the clear message that they need to be responsible for their own benefit (consistent treatment), that I have a respectable boundary, and that my time and their treatment is valuable. For most families living in my area $40.00 is nothing to sneeze at.

Another option for a cancelled session is to make it up in the next few days by scheduling an additional session and, of course, billing for both. This is both therapeutically justifiable and financially just. What if you yourself are unable to make it to the session? A free makeup session would seem fair.

Constance Fisher, PhD, of Pittsburgh, PA, suggests having a clear, specific policy, such as the following: "Except for unpredictable emergencies (or because of a situation that would be seen by both of us as an unpredictable emergency), I will charge you 50% of the regular fee for any missed sessions." She chooses to implement this only with the second missed session.

Another possible statement is "If the appointment is not kept or is cancelled with less than 24 hours' advance notice, you can expect me to charge you for it." Some therapists add, "A retainer against such sessions, or for the closing session, will be requested at the initial meeting." For some therapists, the minimum advance notice for cancellation is 24 hours; this might then make a provision for weekends necessary, such as "Cancellations for a Monday appointment should be made no later than Thursday morning."

Note that the cancellation policy above is addressed to an individual client. If you treat families or couples, you need to make clear what you will do when everyone does not attend. (See Section 4.5 for some points concerning family therapy contracting.)

If you see children or adolescents, you should modify the following statement to suit your practice:

> I request that you do not bring children with you if they are young and need babysitting or supervision, which I cannot provide. I do not have toys, but I can provide reading materials suitable for older children.

You might also want to include a statement such as this: "You will be charged for any damage to, or theft of, property in this office by you or anyone for whom you are legally responsible." To this you might add, "I cannot be responsible for any personal property or valuables you bring into this office."

Depending on your methods, you might supply other information for clients, such as suggesting comfortable dress, requesting no smoking, asking that they avoid bringing food or drinks, or offering a note about your dog's or cat's presence (if you have an "office pet").

Fees, Payments, and Billing

Payment for services is an important part of any professional relationship. This is even more true in therapy; one treatment goal is to make relationships and the duties and obligations they involve clear. You are responsible for seeing that my services are paid for. Meeting this responsibility shows your commitment and maturity.

My current regular fees are as follows. You will be given advance notice if my fees should change.

Regular therapy services: For a session of _____ minutes, the fee is $_____ Please pay for each session at its end. I have found that this arrangement helps us stay focused on our goals, and so it works best. It also allows me to keep my fees as low as possible, because it cuts down on my bookkeeping costs. I suggest you make out your check before each session begins, so that our time will be used best. Other payment or fee arrangements must be worked out before the end of our first meeting.

Telephone consultations: I believe that telephone consultations may be suitable or even needed at times in our therapy. If so, I will charge you our regular fee, prorated over the time needed. If I need to have long telephone conferences with other professionals as part of your treatment, you will be billed for these at the same rate as for regular therapy services. If you are concerned about all this, please be sure to discuss it with me in advance so we can set a policy that is comfortable for both of us. Of course, there is no charge for calls about appointments or similar business.

Extended sessions: Occasionally it may be better to go on with a session, rather than stop or postpone work on a particular issue. When this extension is more than 10 minutes, I will tell you, because sessions that are extended beyond 10 minutes will be charged on a prorated basis.

Psychological testing services: $_____ per hour. Psychological testing fees include the time spent with you, the time needed for scoring and studying the test results, and the time needed to write a report on the findings. The amount of time involved depends on the tests used and the questions the testing is intended to answer.

Reports: I will not charge you for my time spent making routine reports to your insurance company. However, I will have to bill you for any extra-long or complex reports the company might require. The company will not cover this fee.

Other services: Charges for other services, such as hospital visits, consultations with other therapists, home visits, or any court-related services (such as consultations with lawyers, depositions, or attendance at courtroom proceedings) will be based on the time involved in providing the service at my regular fee schedule. Some services may require payment in advance.

I realize that my fees involve a substantial amount of money, although they are well in line with similar professionals' charges. For you to get the best value for your money, we must work hard and well.

You may want to specify different fees for activities with different time needs or costs. For example, fees for supervision may be lower. Fees for conducting in-service or other training sessions may be higher because of the preparation time involved. Court testimony may be priced by the half-day, since schedules may be uncertain. If you write reports for lawyers or others, you may want to state that these "must be fully paid for before they are provided in legally signed form or released to any third party." See also Form 53 for a release and contract with a lawyer.

You may wish to offer variations in your fee structure, but be careful to avoid seeming to have two fees—one for those who have health insurance and a lower one for those who do not—because the insurance company will see this as fraud. Instead, you can offer a discount on your regular fee, just as you do when you sign onto a panel of an MCO. You must, however, make this explicit on your bills by showing your regular fee, the adjustment, and the resulting charge. You could offer a discount to self-paying clients for payment in full at the time of billing or for payment in advance, but not for those who pay slowly. All of this must be explicitly stated in your information brochure for clients.

Other points that may need clarification can be included here:

- Will you accept a portion of the fee at the time of services, with the rest to be paid by the insurance company at a future date? If so, make this clear.

- Will you raise a client's fee during the course of therapy? The brochure has mentioned above that clients will be given advance notice of fee increases; this alerts them to the possibility. But if you anticipate a long treatment period and significant inflation, you should state your policy—for example, "I examine my costs yearly, and so may change my fees each new year." It may be too cautious, but consider never raising your charges to an individual client over the course of therapy, because it may appear that you are inflating your changes to gain more insurance reimbursement or in some other way exploiting the relationship (and this may trigger a complaint).

- Will you lower your fee if the MCO changes the amount it pays you, if a client's insurance coverage is exhausted, or if a client's financial circumstances change? (See Section 2.1 on financial policies.) You should decide and include a statement here.

- It is a good idea to place in your brochure and on all other relevant stationery, in large lettering, "You, the client, are responsible for paying all charges for our services at the fees listed, regardless of payments from health insurance or any other sources." Among other benefits, it deals with a situation where you see a client before your receive an authorization and yet his or her MCO policy requires preauthorization of services or they will not be covered.

- It's also a good idea to repeat that payment is due at each session by hanging a sign about this in your waiting room. You can also have it printed on your appointment cards. Susan Hutchinson, DSW, LCSW, of Irvine, CA, advises clients in her office policy statement that she does not bill for the copayment; she thus reinforces payment for each session.

- If you offer payment by credit card, say so in this section. If you don't offer it, you may want to consider doing it (see Section 2.3).

- If your fee varies with the patient's MCO contract, you must indicate that this is so, or you may be misrepresenting your fee.

- If you make any other extra charges, such as a double rate outside your usual hours, it is helpful to put it here. This is the section clients will refer to when they check on charges.

> I will assume that our agreed-upon fee-paying relationship will continue as long as I provide services to you. I will assume this until you tell me in person, by telephone, or by certified mail that you wish to end it. You have a responsibility to pay for any services you receive before you end the relationship.

If you decide to bill some clients, you probably should put something like the following paragraphs into your brochure:

> Because I expect all payment at the time of our meetings, I usually do not send bills. However, if we have agreed that I will bill you, I ask that the bill be paid within 5 days of when you get it.
>
> At the end of each month, I will send you a statement. The statement can be used for health insurance claims, as described in the next section. It will show all of our meetings, the charges for each, how much has been paid, and how much (if any) is still owed. At the end of treatment, and when you have paid for all sessions, I will send you a final statement for your tax records.

The paragraphs above obviously should fit your office procedures. If you provide a "walk-out" receipt (see Section 2.3) at the end of each session, this is what a client should submit to the insurance company, and you won't need to send a statement. As regards tax deductibility, you could add, "Depending on your financial circumstances and total medical costs for any year, psychotherapy may be a deductible expense," and "Consult your tax advisor." Cost of transportation to and from appointments and fees paid may be deductible from the client's personal income taxes as medical expenses.

You may want to advise some clients to look into medical or health *savings* accounts (MSAs or HSAs), because they can cover psychotherapy costs. The clients or their employers buy high-deductible health insurance (like the old Major Medical policies), and then establish MSAs or HSAs. A flexible *spending* account (FSA) for medical expenses cannot be used to pay insurance premiums, but it can pay for deductibles, copayments, and most medical expenses not covered by insurance, which could include psychotherapy. HSAs allow clients to save money for future expenses, whereas MSAs and FSAs forfeit unspent money back to the employer each year. The costs are low and the tax advantages are high for any client who can afford to pay several thousand dollars a year into such accounts.

> If you think you may have trouble paying your bills on time, please discuss this with me. I will also raise the matter with you so we can arrive at a solution. If your unpaid balance reaches $_____, I will notify you by mail. If it then remains unpaid, I must stop therapy with you. Fees that continue unpaid after this will be turned over to small-claims court or a collection service.

A simpler alternative to the last sentence above is offered by Sam Knapp, EdD, of Harrisburg, PA: "Patients who owe money and fail to make arrangements to pay may be referred to a collection agency." Another alternative is to set a session limit on the amount owed.

For informed consent about confidentiality, it is also a good idea to indicate the kinds of information you will provide to those you hire to collect your old bills. A collection agency may get only the client's name, address, phone number, the amount owed, and the name of the therapist. (Collection agencies usually want more information if they need to locate an ex-client.) Small-claims court will get only the client's name, address, proof of services, and the amount owed to you.

Charging of interest or offering of credit requires you to comply with federal and state laws and forms. Therefore, use late fees or charge no interest. You can use "A late fee of 1½% of the unpaid balance will be charged each month" or "A late payment fee of $_____ will be charged each month that a balance remains unpaid."

You may want to indicate that you do not give refunds to unsatisfied customers (or to explain when you do give refunds).

> If there is any problem with my charges, my billing, your insurance, or any other money-related point, please bring it to my attention. I will do the same with you. Such problems can interfere greatly with our work. They must be worked out openly and quickly.
>
> ### If You Have Traditional (or "Indemnity") Health Insurance Coverage
>
> Because I am a licensed psychologist, many health insurance plans will help you pay for therapy and other services I offer. Because health insurance is written by many different companies, I cannot tell you what your plan covers. Please read your plan's booklet under coverage for "Outpatient Psychotherapy" or under "Treatment of Mental and Nervous Conditions." Or call your employer's benefits office to find out what you need to know.

> If your health insurance will pay part of my fee, I will help you with your insurance claim forms. However, please keep two things in mind:
>
> 1. I had no role in deciding what your insurance covers. Your employer decided which, if any, services will be covered and how much you have to pay. You are responsible for checking your insurance coverage, deductibles, payment rates, copayments, and so forth. Your insurance contract is between you and your company; it is not between me and the insurance company.
>
> 2. You—not your insurance company or any other person or company—are responsible for paying the fees we agree upon. If you ask me to bill a separated spouse, a relative, or an insurance company, and I do not receive payment on time, I will then expect this payment from you.

You should insert here whatever procedures you will perform (such as doing all the verification of coverage, billing insurers, billing for copayments, etc.) and what procedures are expected of the patient.

> **If You Have a Managed Care Contract**
>
> If you belong to a health maintenance organization (HMO) or preferred provider organization (PPO), or have another kind of health insurance with managed care, decisions about what kind of care you need and how much of it you can receive will be reviewed by the plan. The plan has rules, limits, and procedures that we should discuss. Please bring your health insurance plan's description of services to one of our early meetings, so that we can talk about it and decide what to do.

It may be helpful to list in your brochure the panels of MCOs and similar organizations to which you belong, and then describe the procedures they require you to follow. Managed care issues are complicated (see Section 2.5), and to get informed consent you might want to use Handout 3.

> I will provide information about you to your insurance company only with your informed and written consent. I may send this information by mail or by fax. My office will try its best to maintain the privacy of your records, but I ask you not to hold me responsible for accidents or for anything that happens as a result.

If you think that the loss of confidentiality, lessened professional control of treatment, and the impact of a psychiatric diagnosis are significant concerns for clients, consider giving them Handout 3. Ackley (1997) also has excellent educational handouts about fees and insurance and about payment plans.

If you do not participate in managed care programs, you might want to substitute something like this:

> I am not a member of any health insurance plans or panels. Health insurance is a contract between you (or your employer) and your insurer; I am not part of that contract. However, I will supply you with an invoice for my services with the standard diagnostic and procedure codes for billing purposes, the times we met, my charges, and your payments. You can use this to apply for reimbursement.

If You Need to Contact Me

I cannot promise that I will be available at all times. Although I am in the office _____ through _____, from ____ to ____, I usually do not take phone calls when I am with a client. You can always leave a message with my secretary or on my answering machine, and I will return your call as soon as I can. Generally, I will return messages daily except on Sundays and holidays.

If you have an emergency or crisis, tell this to my secretary, who will try to contact me. If you have a behavioral or emotional crisis and cannot reach me or my secretary immediately by telephone, you or your family members should call one of the following community emergency agencies: the county mental health office at _____, or the crisis center at _____, or the _____ Hospital emergency room.

Reid (1999, p. 65) intelligently reminds us that we should not "equate constant personal availability with good care." Setting boundaries appropriate to the client, the circumstances, and your own needs is fully reasonable and therapeutic. You might include a statement that there may be times that you will be unavailable because of circumstances and that your staff knows what to do in case of problems or emergencies. The professional providing your coverage at these time will need access to records, phone numbers, and other resources of the practice. See Section 1.6 for more on making records available to successors.

You might indicate (only if it is true, of course) that you return all calls within 24 hours. The rule of immediate return is a good one to make, even if you have to work hard to keep it. You might also indicate hours for regular phone calls, such as 10 A.M. to 8 P.M., and say that calls outside these hours are treated as emergencies and charged accordingly. If it fits your style of practice, you could offer a regular hour each day during which you will be available to receive calls such as questions about homework. To reduce "telephone tag," you could specify a particular time each day during which you will return calls. Callers can then leave a number where they can be reached during that time.

For emergencies, you should add specific information for your situation. You might say, "In case of an emergency, call my answering service at _____. Tell the person who answers that you urgently need to speak with me, and ask him or her to locate me." Or, "In emergencies outside of my regular office hours, call me at home at _____. If you cannot reach me in a dire emergency, call your own medical doctor or go to the nearest emergency room." If you use a wireless phone or paging device, explain that here.

The following are some additional phone policies: "I find that telephone therapy does not work as well as face-to-face therapy, and so I discourage it. I will generally suggest our meeting if you call with a problem that is not critical." Or "I have found that brief telephone calls work quite well for some purposes, and I am willing to arrange this." Or "If I feel that our work together calls for it, I will make special arrangements for telephone contact, and this service will be charged at my usual rate."

If you have a voice mail box to which only you know the password, you might offer its use to clients but caution them that it is not for emergencies, because you may not pick up the messages the same day and calls may not be returned for 24 hours, especially if left in the evening. These limitations may lead you not to use voice mail for clients, but instead to use an answering machine or service.

Many therapists have instructions on their answering machines that in emergencies clients should call 911 or go to a hospital emergency department. Simon (2008) has criticized this practice as "worse than useless" because (1) it is likely to be perceived as creating a barrier ("Don't bother me!"), (2) it won't be implemented because of (a) the embarrassment of having the police arrive as a result of a 911 call or (b) the inability of a patient in crisis to follow directives, and (3) emergency departments often fail to provide rapid enough care. He indicates that continuous availability (or arranged competent coverage) is the standard of care and that phone calls be returned rapidly to assess and intervene to preserve and enhance the therapeutic alliance as well as manage the risk, avoid legal abandonment, and reduce suicide. He suggests making a pre-need plan with a safe place for the client to go to while awaiting the return call and including the use of suicide hotlines.

If I Need to Contact Someone about You

If there is an emergency during our work together, or I become concerned about your personal safety, I am required by law and by the rules of my profession to contact someone close to you—perhaps a relative, spouse, or close friend. I am also required to contact this person, or the authorities, if I become concerned about your harming someone else. Please write down the name and information of your chosen contact person in the blanks provided:

Name: _____

Address: _____

Phone: _____ Relationship to you: _____

Other Points

If you share office space with other therapists under any kind of financial arrangements, and especially if you operate together under an assumed business name (D/B/A) such as Therapy Associates, you will need to make clear to every client that you operate separately as a professional. This is mainly to avoid becoming involved in a complaint or suit against one of your "partners" but also to assure your clients of confidentiality.

As a professional therapist, I naturally want to know more about how therapy helps people. To understand therapy better, I must collect information about clients before, during, and after therapy. Therefore, I am asking you to help me by filling out some questionnaires about different parts of your life-relationships, changes, concerns, attitudes, and other areas. I ask your permission to take what you write on these questionnaires and what I have in my records and use it in research or teaching that I may do in the future. If I ever use the information from your questionnaire, it will always be included with information from many others. Also, your identity will be made completely anonymous. Your name will never be mentioned, and all personal information will be disguised and changed. After the research, teaching, or publishing project is completed all the data used will be destroyed.

The next paragraph is protective of both you and the client (Berkowitz, 1995). A rare patient may ask you to remove or destroy some materials with the intention of removing your means of defense, and then complain against you or institute a lawsuit.

> If, as part of our therapy, you create and provide to me records, notes, artworks, or any other documents or materials, I will return the originals to you at your written request but will retain copies.

You can also indicate in this section any special rules you have—for example, about treating patients with active substance abuse/dependence, criminal or court-referred patients, spouse/child abusers, suicidal patients, patients with paranoid disorders, and so on.

Finally, you can leave a space here to write in any additional issues that bear on each individual case.

Statement of Principles and Complaint Procedures

> It is my intention to fully abide by all the rules of the American Psychological Association (APA) and by those of my state license.

The APA's rules include its ethical principles and code of conduct, its standards for providers of psychological services, its guidelines for delivery of specialty services by clinical psychologists, and others you care to mention. If you are not a psychologist, give the applicable rules and codes of your profession here.

> Problems can arise in our relationship, just as in any other relationship. If you are not satisfied with any area of our work, please raise your concerns with me at once. Our work together will be slower and harder if your concerns with me are not worked out. I will make every effort to hear any complaints you have and to seek solutions to them. If you feel that I (or any other therapist) have treated you unfairly or have even broken a professional rule, please tell me. You can also contact the state or local psychological association and speak to the chairperson of the ethics committee. He or she can help clarify your concerns or tell you how to file a complaint. You may also contact the state board of psychologist examiners [note that this name differs across states], the organization that licenses those of us in the independent practice of psychology.

Some would consider it unnecessary, pessimistic, or even masochistic to tell clients how to lodge a formal ethics complaint. But this information is essential for fully informing the consumer, and it is required by the HIPAA regulations. (See Section 7.8 for more on this, and Form 55 for a sample complaint form) reframed as "Is there a problem?" Vinson (1987) found that the low level of reporting of sexual and other abuses by therapists was not attributable to lack of motivation, but to lack of information on how to file a complaint. Hare-Mustin et al. (1979) say that clients need to know what the legitimate grounds for complaints are, as well as what options are available for resolving them. Brown (personal communication in Branscomb, 1996) reported that in the state of Washington, where providing such information has been required since 1987, there has been no increase of complaints (frivolous or otherwise). This is, however, a complex clinical as well as ethical issue, with complicated options that are not well addressed in a small brochure. If a concern or complaint of any sort arises, document it. Do this even if you think it trivial or baseless.

In my practice as a therapist, I do not discriminate against clients because of any of these factors: age, sex, marital/family status, race, color, religious beliefs, ethnic origin, place of residence, veteran status, physical disability, health status, sexual orientation, or criminal record unrelated to present dangerousness. This is a personal commitment, as well as being required by federal, state, and local laws and regulations. I will always take steps to advance and support the values of equal opportunity, human dignity, and racial/ethnic/cultural diversity. If you believe you have been discriminated against, please bring this matter to my attention immediately.

In the list above of groups that can be discriminated against I have tried to be comprehensive—including, for example, "health status" as an indicator of HIV-positive individuals; "place of residence" in regard to low-socioeconomic-status areas or community mental health center catchment areas; and some other less usual factors. You should add to, or delete from, this list anything not applicable to your practice.

Our Agreement

I, the client (or his or her parent or guardian), understand I have the right not to sign this form. My signature below indicates that I have read and discussed this agreement; it does not indicate that I am waiving any of my rights. I understand that any of the points mentioned above can be discussed and may be open to change. If at any time during the treatment I have questions about any of the subjects discussed in this brochure, I can talk with you about them, and you will do your best to answer them.

I understand that after therapy begins I have the right to withdraw my consent to therapy at any time, for any reason. However, I will make every effort to discuss my concerns about my progress with you before ending therapy with you.

To be sure you haven't promised a cure, you might want to insert language like this at the end of the brochure:

I understand that no specific promises have been made to me by this therapist about the results of treatment, the effectiveness of the procedures used by this therapist, or the number of sessions necessary for therapy to be effective.

I have read, or have had read to me, the issues and points in this brochure. I have discussed those points I did not understand, and have had my questions, if any, fully answered. I agree to act according to the points covered in this brochure. I hereby agree to enter into therapy with this therapist (or to have the client enter therapy), and to cooperate fully and to the best of my ability, as shown by my signature here.

_____   _____
     Signature of client (or person acting for client)   Date

_____
                    Printed name

Relationship to client:
    ❏ Self ❏ Parent ❏ Legal guardian
    ❏ Health care custodial parent of a minor (less than 14 years of age)
    ❏ Other person authorized to act on behalf of the client

Besides the signature, for your additional protection and assurance that the client has read every page, you could ask the client to initial each page at the bottom by including a statement like "Initial here to show that you have read this page."

I, the therapist, have met with this client (and/or his or her parent or guardian) for a suitable period of time, and have informed him or her of the issues and points raised in this brochure. I have responded to all of his or her questions. I believe this person fully understands the issues, and I find no reason to believe this person is not fully competent to give informed consent to treatment. I agree to enter into therapy with the client, as shown by my signature here.

_____   _____
Signature of therapist   Date

I truly appreciate the chance you have given me to be of professional service to you, and look forward to a successful relationship with you. If you are satisfied with my services as we proceed, I (like any professional) would appreciate your referring other people to me who might also be able to make use of my services.

❑ Copy accepted by client   ❑ Copy kept by therapist

4.3   The Second Path to Informed Consent: The Question List as a Guide to Discussion

The second method for obtaining informed consent comes from Pomerantz and Handelsman (2004). This method is to provide the client with a list of questions as a guide for discussing the points the client raises. In an earlier publication, these authors described the advantages of their approach as follows:

> First, it informs clients what information they have a right to [ask about] but preserves their right to request it or not. Second, it may be less overwhelming for clients. . . . Third, because the answers are not spelled out, the form requires a conversation between therapist and client to take place. . . . Fourth, the form has a fourth-grade readability level. (Handelsman & Galvin, 1988, p. 224)

In short, this approach is an admirably creative, flexible, and sensitive solution to a thorny problem.

The give-and-take of discussion incorporated into this approach is the essence of the process of getting informed consent. In practice, you can give the questions to the client at the end of the first session to take home and read. The client can then be asked for questions during the second session, and the form can be signed. (If, as is fairly often the case, the client has forgotten it, a new copy can be offered, discussed, and signed.) This, then, is **a structured interview the client conducts with you.** After answering the client's questions, you can write a note such as this: "I believe I have obtained fully informed, voluntary, and competent consent to proceed with treatment because we have covered everything on my [question list]." This procedure simultaneously (1) meets your legal responsibility to get an informed consent form signed; (2) meets your ethical responsibility to have the dialogue (questions and answers) that must logically and technically underlie informed consent; and, most importantly, (3) is clinically elegant, as it starts therapy off with openness— putting everything on the table not only by answering the client's questions, but by even giving the client the questions to ask.

Because the questions are in simple English and the client signs the list to affirm that he or she has had a discussion of the points and understands them, I believe that this procedure makes a legal challenge to the effect that the patient simply signed a form, and that therefore the consent was not really informed, far less likely to succeed.

HANDOUT 4   The questions offered below and in Handout 4 at the end of this section are adapted with permission from the list by Pomerantz and Handelsman (2004), which is based on several earlier researched versions. You may want to discuss some questions with your clients besides those based on Handelsman and colleagues' work. For example, if you think it is important to have your clients know more about your way of practicing, their insurance, or other services you can offer, you can add questions designed to elicit this information. Similarly, you can add questions about clinical issues (e.g., homework expectations), cultural differences, values, or diagnoses. You could review the points raised in the client information brochure (see Section 4.2) for topics to include in these questions. Do rehearse your answers so that they flow easily, to convey your professional expertise.

Some key questions based on Pomerantz and Handelsman's work are now discussed. For clarity, the questions are set off from the text below in the same way as segments of the model client information brochure have been in Section 4.2. A more complete question list is presented later as Handout 4.

Information You Have a Right to Know

When you come for therapy, you are buying a service. Therefore, you need information to make a good decision. Below are some questions you might want to ask. You are entitled to ask me any of these questions, and I will give you the best answers I can. If my answers are not clear enough, please ask me again.

1. Tell me about yourself.

    a. Are you a psychologist? Psychiatrist? Family therapist? Counselor?

    b. What are the advantages and limitations of your credentials?

Be prepared to compare the different mental health disciplines in an evenhanded and nondefensive way, with some indications of their respective strengths. Do not either brag or be too humble, but be confident in your areas of competence. Clarity will build hope in the client or lead to a referral to someone better able to serve the client's needs.

As noted in Section 4.2, some clients seek out religious therapists, believing that such therapists will share their values. All therapists have a moral philosophy, as do all therapies. It may be useful to discuss this and other value-related issues that are most relevant to the presenting problem (e.g., family loyalty, openness despite the fear of consequences, gender roles and preferences, respect for age and authority, etc.).

Information You Have a Right to Know

When you come for therapy, you are buying a service. Therefore, you need good information to make the best decision. Below are some questions you might want to ask me. You can ask me any of these questions, and I will give you the best answers I can. If my answers are not clear or not complete enough, please ask me again.

1. Tell me about yourself.

   a. Are you a psychologist? Psychiatrist? Family therapist? Counselor?
   b. What are the advantages and limitations of your credentials?
   c. What is your training and experience? Are you licensed by the state? Supervised? Board-certified?
   d. What is the name of your kind of therapy?
   e. How did you learn how to do this therapy? Where?

2. Tell me about therapy.

   a. How does your kind of therapy work?
   b. What percentage of clients improve? In what ways? How do you know?
   c. What percentage of clients get worse? How do you know?
   d. What percentage of clients improve or get worse without this therapy? How do you know?
   e. Are there negatives or possible risks in this therapy?
   f. About how long will it take?
   g. What will I notice when I am getting better?
   h. What should I do if I feel therapy isn't working?
   i. Is there someone I can talk to if I have a problem or a complaint about therapy that we can't work out?
   j. Will I have to take any kind of tests or questionnaires?
   k. Do you follow a therapy manual with planned steps?
   l. Do you do therapy over the phone? Over the Internet?

3. Tell me about other kinds of therapy and help.

   a. What other types of therapy or help are there for my kind of problems?
   b. How does your kind of therapy compare with other kinds of therapy?
   c. How often do they work? How do you know?
   d. What are the risks and benefits of these other approaches?
   e. What are the risks and benefits of no therapy?
   f. Do you prescribe medication? Do you work with others who do?

4. Tell me about appointments.

   a. How do we arrange appointments?
   b. How often to we meet?

(cont.)

    c. How long are sessions? Do I have to pay more for longer ones?

    d. How can I reach you in an emergency?

    e. If you are not available, is there someone I can talk to?

    f. What happens if the weather is bad, or I'm sick?

5. Tell me about confidentiality.

    a. What kinds of records do you keep?

    b. Who can see them?

    c. When do you have to tell others about the things we discuss?

    d. Can members of my family, or the group [in group therapy], see my records?

    e. What do the laws and government regulations say about the privacy of my records?

6. Tell me about money matters.

    a. What is your fee?

    b. Will you ever charge me more?

    c. How do you want to be paid?

    d. Do I need to pay for missed sessions?

    e. Do I need to pay for telephone calls, letters, or e-mails?

    f. If I lose my job or my source of income, can my fee be lowered?

    g. If I do not pay my fee, what will you do to collect?

7. Tell me about health insurance and managed care.

    a. What kind of information do you have to give my health insurance company about our treatments?

    b. What will the insurance company decide about my therapy?

    c. What if you disagree with the insurance company about the best treatment?

    d. How would therapy be different if I did not use insurance and just paid you myself?

I have already given you some written information. This has included a contract, privacy statement, brochure, and/or consent form. We have also talked about some aspects of our work together. This information has dealt with most of these questions. I will be happy to explain them, and to answer other questions you have. This will help make your decision a good one. You can keep this information. Please read it carefully at home. We will also look this over from time to time.

I, the client (or his or her parent or guardian), have gone over this list with the therapist, and I understand these questions and the therapist's answers.

_____   _____

Signature of client (or parent/guardian)   Date

_____

Printed name

I, the therapist, have discussed these issues with the client (and/or his or her parent or guardian). I believe this person fully understands the issues, and I find no reason to believe that this person is not fully competent to give informed consent to treatment.

_____   _____

Signature of therapist   Date

❑ Copy accepted by client   ❑ Copy kept by therapist

2. Tell me about therapy.

   a. How does your kind of therapy work?

Obviously, your answer should be tailored to your approach. You can emphasize your theory of change and what each of you will do in therapy. You might say something along these lines: "We will discuss fully what brought you to see me; explore your history and background to understand where problems may have originated and what might be maintaining them; talk about all areas of your life, especially when, with whom, and in what settings you have problems; and discuss anything else that is important so that I can fully understand your situation." You could then describe various treatment approaches.

You could describe your expectations as follows: "I will expect you to be open and honest about your thoughts and feelings; to help design homework and practice to change things; to complete the homework to the best of your ability; to try out new ways of dealing with your feelings, thoughts, and other people; to keep records of your feelings and behaviors . . . " (add anything else you think appropriate).

   e. Are there negatives or possible risks in this therapy?

This question and the next few open discussion of possible risks and of the effectiveness of therapy. You might include the following: the risks of not changing, of feeling worse temporarily, or of a true worsening of the client's condition; possible conflicts with spouse/partner, relatives, or peers; more stress in, or even a breakup of, a relationship; or increased fears, doubts, and depression. Almost every therapy client is concerned about these things, but most clients do get better—even much better.

Having outcome data based on your clients and your setting is ideal and its collection might be considered an ethical requirement for high-quality practice (see Section 6.5). In its absence, do not paint too rosy a picture or promise a cure. Many studies have demonstrated the effectiveness of therapy. You might offer a few statistics that you can explain easily. Do explain the costs and losses associated with not entering therapy. DSM-IV-TR (American Psychiatric Association, 2000) has information on the life course of some diagnoses, which you can drawn upon for this discussion.

   f. About how long will it take?

The response to this question will depend on the client's presenting problems and prognosis. Be realistic. Don't try to offer a low number of sessions just because that is all the client's insurance will pay for, especially if you know that a low number will be insufficient to relieve the client's distress or improve functioning. You can discuss this in terms of long- and short-term goals.

   g. What will I notice when I am getting better?

I have often told my clients that they should feel increased optimism in a few sessions; increased self-confidence, energy, and courage in a few more; and consistently less anxiety or depression in 10–15 sessions. I have also told them that others may notice changes before they do. You can also focus the client's attention on specific areas chosen for their clinical utility. You might suggest that symptoms change in frequency, duration, intensity, or latency, but which will change first cannot be predicted.

> h. What should I do if I feel therapy isn't working?

You might say this: "You should discuss this with me first. We may be able to change our treatment, or our expectations might be inappropriate. We may need to add more treatment sessions or different methods. If we are not making progress, I will consult other professionals, and I may ask you to go to another therapist for a consultation." You might add that you do not take clients you don't think you can help, and that you have an ethical obligation to refer those who are not benefiting.

Being sophisticated about therapy, you will know about "flight into health," "buyer's remorse," and the placebo effect, so decide how much of this to explain to maintain motivation and momentum.

> i. Is there someone I can talk to if I have a problem or a complaint about therapy that we can't work out?

If you are being supervised, this is an opportunity to explain that. HIPAA requires you to have a complaint process for breaches of confidentiality and to explain this to clients. (See Section 7.8.) Your state or your ethics code may require you to explain complaint procedures.

> j. Will I have to take any kind of tests or complete questionnaires?

Obviously, the answer to this depends on your approach and discipline, but symptom checklists may be useful for assessing and documenting progress and outcome for both insurers and clients.

> k. Do you follow a therapy manual with planned steps?

You have an ethical obligation to use the most appropriate and effective treatments, and so you should know about them and adopt those manualized approaches suitable for your clients.

> l. Do you do therapy over the phone? Over the Internet?

For some situations where weather or transportation limit attendance, you might offer these as options.

> 3. Tell me about other kinds of therapy and help.
>
> a. What other types of therapy or help are there?

This is often a hard question for a therapist to answer, because of interdisciplinary rivalry, ignorance of others' approaches, and fears of one's own inadequacy in regard to training and skill. However, this is the kind of information you would want in choosing therapy for yourself or a member of your family. If you become informed and share openly, clients will appreciate your honesty and trust you more, and therapy will be more effective. You can describe counseling, medications, group therapies, support groups, self-help, readings, agencies, clinics, schools, and other practitioners.

f. Do you prescribe medication? Do you work with others who do?

Explain how you handle the need for psychiatric medication. Explain how managed care may require an assessment and push for prescriptions, how adherence is crucial, and what your role will be in relating to the client's prescriber. Delay discussions of the relative value of medications versus therapy and combined treatment, of the misuse of drugs, and of their limitations ("Pills don't teach") for clinically determined teachable moments.

4. Tell me about appointments.

This should be a straightforward presentation of how you run your practice.

5. Tell me about confidentiality.

a. What kinds of records do you keep?

Describe your records, or, better yet, show them the forms you use.

b. Who can see them?

Some possibilities to be explained are these: how the client can see (and can also amend) his or her own records; what MCOs have the right to know; what (minimal) information is provided to credit cards and collection agencies; and how lawyers and courts might become involved. This may be a good time to explain the process and form for authorizing the release of records, and how these are protective of privacy. If you have not given the client your NPP and gotten the consent form signed, this should be done at this point. (See Section 5.4.)

c. When do you have to tell others about the things we discuss?

It is essential that you explain the limits of confidentiality, because what is revealed in confidence cannot be unsaid. The usual situations are suicidal or homicidal threats, child or elder neglect and abuse, and court-referred cases. Your intake may suggest other areas worth exploring.

6. Tell me about money matters.

You should provide a straightforward presentation of your practice's rules about money. Rehearse this, so that you can be comfortable asking for money.

7. Tell me about health insurance and managed care.

    a. What kind of information do you have to give my health insurance company about our treatments?

You can explain this by showing Form 40 or 43. Section 3.11 concerns dealings with MCOs.

    b. What will the insurance company decide about my therapy?

Your answer can be as simple as recounting some recent experiences. You can review some key points of your contracts with the MCOs to whose panels you belong.

    c. What if you disagree with the insurance company about the best treatment?

It is widely accepted that you have an ethical obligation to appeal MCO decisions with which you disagree, at least to the first level.

    e. How would therapy be different if I did not use insurance and just paid you myself?

This is an invitation to discuss the clinical advantages of a fee-for-service practice in terms of confidentiality, additional treatment options, and expanded goals. Be aware that most managed care contracts forbid you to see their clients on a fee-for-service basis.

Be sure to ask at the next session—and, indeed, periodically throughout treatment—whether any new questions have arisen.

Handout 4 now presents the questions discussed above as a complete, two-page list.

4.4 The Third Path to Informed Consent: Lists of Clients' Rights

The third path to informed consent is less formal and more fluid, and therefore better suited to some therapists and clients than the question list. It is the offering of a list of clients' basic rights in psychotherapy.

If you are going to use this approach, you should review the available online lists cited below, as well as the list in Handout 5. Add your own ideas, and then devise a list tailored to the style and needs of your practice. You must also modify these rights statements to fit your local and current circumstances before you distribute the list, and you should keep it current by consulting with your local ethics committee.

As of this writing, a national Patient's Bill of Rights has not been made law. However, if some version does pass, you should examine it for parts that apply to your way of practicing and incorporate or at least address those issues. The Mental Health Consumers' Bill of Rights as endorsed by all the mental health professions is available online (mentalhealth.samhsa.gov/consumer survivor.billofrights.asp). It has also been published by Cantor (1999).

HANDOUT 5 The list in Handout 5 is modified from a publication of the California Department of Consumer Affairs entitled *Professional Therapy Never Includes Sex* (Quinn, n.d.). This free, 20-page booklet describes the California laws and details how to report abuse, take legal and administrative actions, and find help for the victim.

In addition, the Psychology Clinic at Western Illinois University has posted its excellent clients' rights statement online (www.wiu.edu/users/psyclin/Client_Rights.html). A long but complete listing with attention to the therapist's side has been written for physical therapists, but can be adapted (with permission, of course) and is posted at the site of the Work Confederation for Physical Therapy (www.wcpt.org/policies/principles/rights.php). It is based upon the World Medical Association's "Rights of the Patient" (see www.wma.net/e/policy/l4.htm). Another list with good formulations can be found at the site of the Visiting Nurse Association of Wallingford, CT (www.vnawallingford.org/rights.asp). Still others can be found with an Internet search.

Please examine each rights statement and modify it to suit your locale and style of practice. For example, telling a client that he or she cannot refuse court-ordered testing or therapy may insert you into a conflict between the client and the court, which would be better handled by them (Sam Knapp, personal communication, October 2, 1996).

4.5   The Fourth Path to Informed Consent: Psychotherapy Contracts

> *All treatment proceeds with a contract or a series of contractual agreements between therapist and patient that are either explicit or implicit in therapeutic discourse. The danger of an unarticulated contract is that it can be misunderstood, tacitly reconceptualized, or inconsistently applied, and thus misused. Such misunderstandings can increase exponentially in their impact, meaning and consequence over the course of treatment, resulting in an unexamined diffusion of and diversion from the therapeutic work.*
> —Lipman (1995, p. 996)

Contracts are not substitutes for a client information brochure. But they can establish a different therapeutic relationship from that established by the brochure alone. Contracts focus on more specific aspects of therapy activities. Some of the contract forms offered here expand information on the techniques or methods of therapy, and some focus more on the goals of treatment, the "rules" for therapy, or the risks of treatment versus the probability of success.

The treatment contract can be one component of the process of getting informed consent. The form is evidence of consent, but it is not a substitute for it; as mentioned earlier, courts have held in some cases that consent was not obtained despite the signing of a form. The client must be fully informed through discussions if consent is to be effectively and legally given. Only then should a contract form be completed and signed. As treatment evolves, the contract should also be renegotiated and redrafted. If you prefer less legalistic-sounding terminology than "contract," you can call such a form an "understanding" or an "agreement."

Client Bill of Rights

You have the right to:

- Get respectful treatment that will be helpful to you.

- Have a safe treatment setting, free from sexual, physical, and emotional abuse.

- Report immoral and illegal behavior by a therapist.

- Ask for and get information about the therapist's qualifications, including his or her license, education, training, experience, membership in professional groups, special areas of practice, and limits on practice.

- Have written information, before entering therapy, about fees, method of payment, insurance coverage, number of sessions the therapist thinks will be needed, substitute therapists (in cases of vacation and emergencies), and cancellation policies.

- Refuse audio or video recording of sessions (but you may ask for it if you wish).

- Refuse to answer any question or give any information you choose not to answer or give.

- Know if your therapist will discuss your case with others (for instance, supervisors, consultants, or students).

- Ask that the therapist inform you of your progress.

HANDOUT 5. Clients' rights form.   Adapted from Quinn (n.d.). This document is in the public domain.—From *The Paper Office.*

The Nature of Contracts

Contracts have many advantages, as pointed out by Hare-Mustin et al. (1979):

- They reinforce equality, mutuality, and cooperation because they require negotiation.

- They clarify the relationship's goals, boundaries, and expectations.

- They "prevent misunderstandings about the responsibilities, methods, and practical arrangements of therapy" (p. 8).

- They clarify the roles of each person in the relationship: the therapist as possessing special skills, the client as offering personal knowledge.

- They increase both parties' accountability.

Contracts can also be made therapeutic for some clients by the planful placement of ideas under headings such as "Responsibilities" (e.g., completing all homework assignments) or "Possible Negative Effects of Treatment" (e.g., disappointment with therapy for not making the client's life better without the client's making any efforts). As an illustration, see a treatment contract for working with those with a bipolar disorder (www.manicdepressive.org/contracts.html). In phrasing a contract, as in phrasing a client brochure, do not underestimate the difficulties of therapy or promise change over which you have little control. Continually reevaluate progress and modify the goals as issues become better understood.

I want here to make a distinction between a "treatment contract" and a "consent-to-treatment form." A consent-to-treatment form is a negotiated agreement that leaves out many of the goals, problem definitions, methods, and tactics; only the most critical items are stated. However, this should not be considered a psychotherapy contract. These pared-down consent forms constitute the fifth path to consent and are covered in the next section. Here I offer the more detailed and specific contract approach.

Contracts should be tailored to your practice and to the client's individual situation. Sample contract forms are offered in the following pages: a contract for individual psychotherapy, two for treating children and adolescents, and one for group therapy. I also discuss important issues for contracts with families and couples.

Checklists for a Psychotherapy Contract: Elements and Options

The contracts offered here do not cover all possible variations, and as written they may not suit your way of practicing. Below, I provide lists of the basic elements that a contract should include, together with a few additional options. These checklists are designed to help you create your own contracts. You can use one of the forms as a general model, then pick and choose items from the lists below. Any items included in the client information brochure (see Section 4.2) could also be incorporated into a contract; I have not, however, duplicated all these possible inclusions here. These checklists are partially based on ideas developed by the Health Research Group (Adams & Orgel, 1975), as modified in Kachorek (1990, p. 105). They also incorporate ideas from Stromberg et al. (1988, pp. 164–165), Hare-

Mustin et al. (1979), Bennett et al. (1990, p. 54), and Stuart (1975). The checklists' items are worded as questions about the content of the contract form.

Agreement and Consent

❏ Does the form indicate clearly that this is an informal "agreement"? It is not an exhaustive, complete specification of all treatment variables and issues. Its purpose is to indicate an understanding, or set of mutual expectations, between the client and therapist; its ultimate goals are clarification and communication.

❏ Does the form fully inform the client of all relevant aspects and decisions, so that the client can consent to treatment as an autonomous adult?

❏ Does the form state that the client's consent to treatment is voluntary, and that he or she is free to withdraw from or discontinue treatment without penalty?

❏ Does the form tell the client that the contract will become part of the treatment record?

❏ Does the contract provide space for the signatures of both client and therapist indicating agreement, and the dates signed?

Goals

❏ Are the goals of the psychotherapy with this client stated?

❏ Are they based on assessment of, and consultation with, the client?

❏ Have both long-term goals and short-term objectives been developed?

Description/Listing of Techniques

❏ Does the form describe treatment techniques, or confirm that the client has been informed of them through discussion with the therapist or reading materials?

❏ Has the client been informed of any techniques that might be at odds with his or her values?

Risks and Benefits

❏ Are the benefits to the client described fully, accurately, and without any promise of specific outcomes, results, cures, or guarantees?

❏ Are the risks to the client described, including contraindications, side effects, and undesirable or negative effects?

❏ Are the likely outcomes for the client (and the consequences for his or her family) of delaying or receiving no treatment stated?

Client Responsibilities

❑ Does the form state that the client will "cooperate fully" and "to the best of my ability"?

❑ Are specific client responsibilities indicated? These could include being on time for appointments, paying on a timely basis, doing homework, reading patient education materials, cooperating with educational efforts, and the like. On a more therapeutic level, responsibilities could include acting "as if" when initiating new behaviors, not canceling appointments when afraid, examining resistances to doing homework, and working courageously to overcome shame or humiliation.

Therapist Responsibilities: Treatment

Does the form state that the therapist will:

❑ Use his or her best efforts, skills, resources, training, experience, in good faith?

❑ Make use of the specific techniques in which he or she has been trained in the best interests of the client?

❑ Continually monitor the progress of the therapy?

❑ Operate responsibly, such as being on time, responding promptly to calls, being prepared, and the like?

❑ Fulfill other therapeutic responsibilities, such as encouraging the client's independence or rights to self-determination, not siding with one partner in couple therapy, and so forth?

Therapist Responsibilities: Confidentiality

Does the form indicate that:

❑ Professional standards and ethics will be respected?

❑ There are exceptions to confidentiality (see Chapter 7)?

❑ Permission is granted to the therapist to take notes and to record the sessions (see Form 16)?

❑ Permission is granted to the therapist to collect and publish anonymous and grouped treatment data?

❑ Written permission will be needed to disclose information about any specific clients?

Meetings and Fees

❑ Are the location, frequency, and length of meetings indicated, together with how they are arranged?

❑ Is the client's assumption of financial responsibility stated?

❑ Are fees and charges explicitly stated, including fees for missed sessions?

❑ Is the form clear about when payment is expected?

❑ Are future adjustments to the fee, if they will be made, specified?

Changing the Contract and Terminating Treatment

❑ Does the form state that any of the contract's contents may be renegotiated, but must be honored until changed? Specifics may be mentioned, such as changing the nature, priority, or definition of the goals.

❑ Are the conditions of termination of therapy made clear? Specifically, the contract may be terminated by either party, but with some explicit advance notice.

Provisions When Treating Families or Couples

❑ Does the form state your policy on nonattendance by a family member or one member of a couple?

❑ Does the form state your policy on how you will handle family secrets?

Provisions When Treating Children or Adolescents

❑ Have you included a statement on parents' or guardians' legal rights to certain information?

❑ Does the form address a minor's right to a private life and your use of discretion in communicating with parents?

❑ Does the form state your policy on disclosing a minor's drug use, sexual behavior, or illegal actions, as well as confessions and similar privacies?

Provisions for Group Therapy

❑ Does each group member agree to keep other group members' identities and information confidential? (*Note*: A client's information revealed in group therapy is generally not considered to be legally privileged. Do not assert that it is unless you know that it is in your state.)

Other Issues

❑ Are remedies for client dissatisfaction stated?

❑ Is a statement that the professional believes the client is fully competent to consent to treatment included?

A Contract for Individual Therapy with an Adult

FORM 9   Form 9 is a generalized agreement for adult clients. Modify it to suit your way of working.

About Contracts for Couples and Families

When you go from individual to couple and family therapies, the number of ways of interacting, and thus the number of ethical complexities, increase enormously. Although these complexities cannot be detailed here, there are two excellent reviews available: those by Patten et al. (1991) and by Hansen et al. (1989). The two most common ethical problems are the situations when only one partner comes for therapy and when there are secrets in the family. The provisions below can be incorporated into any of the paths to informed consent you select.

Nonattenders

What can you do when one partner comes in without the other(s)? Here are some options:

- Do an individual therapy session in which you explore family-of-origin issues.

- Refuse to meet.

- Make a tape recording for the missing individual(s).

- Do a session and review it when you all meet next. You must decide what is to be shared, so as to prevent revelation of secrets and the development of an unfair alliance with the person who was present.

Deciding which option is best depends on the specific circumstances: If the session is early in therapy, before a full commitment and therapeutic alliance have been established, it may be best not to meet. You can explain how it would not be fair, describe how it could be counterproductive for the relationship with all parties, and ask the person present to trust you that this is better in the long run.

Although the treatment of choice in family therapy is to have all the family members attend, this may not be realistic for many families. Teisman (1980) has several suggestions: offering a single individual session to the nonattender(s), in exchange for attending a single family session; having short family sessions whose only goal is developing plans for engaging the nonattender(s); taping parts of sessions for review by the nonattender(s); having only one to three sessions for the attender(s); using leverage from the referral source; and cancelling sessions at which all are not present.

Agreement for Individual Therapy

I, _____, the client, agree to meet with the therapist named below at the appointment times and places we agree on, starting on _____, _____, for about _____ sessions of _____ minutes each.

I have read the following materials on therapy, which have been provided to me by this therapist:

1. _____   3. _____
2. _____   4. _____

I believe I understand the basic ideas, goals, and methods of this therapy. I have no important questions or concerns that the therapist has not discussed. In my own words, I understand the following:

1. According to this therapy, the causes of my problems lie in: _____

    _____

2. The main methods to be used in this therapy are: _____

    _____

3. During these sessions, we will focus on working toward these goals:

    a. _____   b. _____

    I understand that reaching these goals is not guaranteed.

4. I understand that I will have to do the following things/take the following actions:

    a. _____   b. _____

With enough knowledge, and without being forced, I enter into treatment with this therapist. I will keep my therapist fully up to date about any changes in my feelings, thoughts, and behaviors. I expect us to work together on any difficulties that occur, and to work them out in my long-term best interest.

At the end of _____ meetings, we will evaluate progress and may change parts of this agreement as needed. Our goals may have changed in nature, order of importance, or definition. If I am not satisfied by our progress toward goals, I will attempt to make change in this agreement, and I may stop treatment after giving this therapist at least 7 days' notice of my intentions and meeting with the therapist for one last time.

This agreement shows my commitment to pay for this therapist's services. It also shows this therapist's willingness to use and share his or her knowledge and skills in good faith. I agree to pay $_____ per session, and to pay at the end of each session. I agree to pay for uncancelled appointments or those where I fail to give enough notice that I will not attend. The only exceptions are unforeseen or unavoidable situations arising suddenly. I understand and accept that I am fully responsible for this fee, but that my therapist will help me in getting payments from any insurance coverage I have. I understand that this agreement will become part of my record of treatment.

I also give my permission for the therapist to audiotape/videotape our sessions for personal review and use with a consultant, who is also bound by the legal framework of privacy and confidentiality. I understand that any information in this recording that could identify me in any way will not be published or given out without my written consent.

My signature below means that I understand and agree with all of the points above.

_____   _____
Signature of client   Date

I, the therapist, have discussed the issues above with the client. My observations of this client's behavior and responses give me no reason, in my professional judgment, to believe that this person is not fully competent to give informed and willing consent.

_____   _____
Signature of therapist   Date

❑ Copy accepted by client   ❑ Copy kept by therapist

This is a strictly confidential patient medical record. Redisclosure or transfer is expressly prohibited by law.

In couple therapy where one partner refuses to attend, Wilcoxon and Fenell (1983) suggest the clever use of a letter to the nonattender summarizing the research on one-partner therapy (which has a negative prognosis for the relationship), proffering an invitation to attend, and requesting a signed statement by both parties accepting the risks of one-partner therapy.

Secrets

A couple's secrets typically concern an affair, wanting a divorce, or sexual attraction to another. There are several schools of thought on secrets:

- Wendorf and Wendorf (1985) argue that the therapist's position should be similar to the following: "I will decide when and how any information I become aware of is to be shared amongst all of us. I will do so in the best interests of the family."

- Hines and Hare-Mustin (1978) advise the therapist not to keep secrets, and to refuse between-session calls that might reveal secrets. They do offer another policy: The therapist will keep the secret only with the intent of helping the individual divulge the secret.

- Margolin (1982), respecting the needs of the individuals present, argues for keeping secret only what one is asked to keep secret.

You will need to decide on a policy and communicate it to your patients *before* they reveal secrets.

Don-David Lusterman, PhD, of Baldwin, NY, includes this phrasing in his client information brochure:

> I will sometimes see you as a member of a family; if so my task may be to facilitate or improve your communication. At other times I may meet with one or another of you alone. If we do meet this way, the normal rules of confidentiality will apply. If issues come up in these sessions which you believe importantly concern your whole family, I generally will not communicate this information for you but will help you to speak to your family about any of these issues.

Contracts for Therapy with Minors

A Contract for Parental Consent to Therapy with a Minor

Before treating minor children, you should have the consent of both parents, but in many cases this can become problematic. What if one parent refuses consent or withdraws it after treatment has been initiated? What if a parent plans to use your assessments and notes for a custody fight? Does your state's board have rules about this issue, or does your setting have relevant laws defining minors or about minors seeking treatment on their own? What effect would a custody decree or an accusation or finding of abuse have on treatment?

When one parent brings a child to your office, always ask about the other parent's involvement. You need to consider whether the other parent might have any objections; this can help you prevent later disagreements and perhaps legal/ethical complaints by feuding parents. My advice about the various possibilities in this situation (keep in mind that I am not a lawyer) is as follows.

Always ask about separation, divorce, and custody on intake. If there has been a custody decision, require the parent to bring the paperwork to the first meeting. It may be sufficient to get an oral agreement to treatment from the other parent (and document this in your notes), but if the parents seem litigious or conflicted about this issue, get both parents' formal written consent to their child's treatment. Laws and regulations differ, but in general, you can evaluate or treat children from intact families with the permission of either parent and can do so until there is a custody decree. The one with the legal authority to agree to treatment may be a parent or relative with sole legal custody, a state agency with custody, a guardian *ad litem*, or others. Clarify this by reading the legal agreements; if these are old, call a representative of the court to confirm that they are still in force and have not been superseded.

If only one parent asks for treatment, you might consider seeing the parent and child for just a single evaluation session to help clarify the issues, with the understanding that you will be allowed to contact the other parent and discuss his or her perceptions and the request for your services. Do not offer any findings or recommendations, but perhaps discuss how you might help both parents to work with their child around adapting to custodial changes and visitation. Be sensitive to the likelihood that you may be being contacted with the agenda of supporting a custody battle. Make an effort to clarify and resolve the issues with all involved parties. Weigh the impact of treatment on the family versus its possible benefits to the child (e.g., providing a safe haven) and your own legal and ethical risks before proceeding. What are the likely consequences of proceeding and the risks of not treating the child? Which options are going to be more distressing to the child and which less? It may be best to refuse to treat the child during a custody struggle or divorce proceeding unless you get a court order to do so (always the best risk management strategy).

After a divorce or custody decree, you must get the permission of the child's legal custodian, who may or may not be the physical custodian (if there is a difference in your state). Shared legal custody, which is by far the most frequent arrangement will require permission from both parents. If both originally agree to treatment and one later objects, the picture is cloudy. Generally, you can proceed with treatment, but be very careful. Do not initiate treatment of a child over the objections of a parent unless there is an emergency.

As long as the other parent's rights have not been terminated, you should get the agreement of both parents that you will provide the noncustodial parent with general information (such as that and when you are seeing the child, his or her overall functioning and progress, treatment goals and plans, etc.). What if the other parent cannot be located due to homelessness or abandonment? You or the custodial parent must make reasonable efforts, such as sending certified mail to the other parent's last known address, or making some calls to find out whether anyone has a more recent address. Social Security can assist in cases where the parent is using its services. What if the other parent refuses to consent, refuses to pay, or sets up other barriers to treatment? This is a time for consultation and judgment. Always document the facts, your observations, and your thought processes leading to your decisions. After a custody decree, it will be best to have the court write your treatment into the custody decree. (See also "Consent to Counseling for a Child of Divorce" in Section 4.6.)

FORM 10   Form 10 includes the minimum for written parental consent to assessment and/or treatment of a child, as suggested by Morris (1993). He indicates the need for a written consent unless the evaluation is court-ordered, the situation is a true emergency, or the child is committed to an institution employing you. Another sample child therapy contract with a good introduction is available from the APA Insurance Trust (APAIT) at www.apait.org/apait/download.aspx.

A Contract for Therapy with an Older Minor

FORM 11   When you are dealing with a minor, the parent/guardian needs to be properly informed and to consent. In addition, the APA code of ethics (APA, 2002) encourages seeking minors' assent and considering their preferences (Standard 3.10b). Form 11 is a contract for older minors themselves and their parents to sign.

A major concern in treating minors, especially older children and adolescents, is balancing the degree of legal confidentiality available (little or none) with a minor's needs for privacy and trust in the professional. No perfect solution exists, but clarity about your rules, stated at the initiation of therapy, is essential. Taylor and Adelman (1989) encourage reframing the problem as finding ways to establish a working relationship in which information can be best shared. A discussion with parents and the child about the confidentiality issue should be a minimum. The parents can consent and the child can assent to the treatment and some ground rules about confidentiality. A signed and negotiated "letter of agreement" concerning specifics of confidentiality is advantageous at the onset of treatment, but is difficult to construct before the issues are explored. If you later discover explosive or high-risk behaviors, you can discuss and modify this agreement. A well-worded consent form for adolescents, with good examples of behaviors of concern, has been developed by Sherry Kraft, PhD; it can be found at www.centerforethicalpractice.org/Form-AdolescentConsent.htm.

Young people may become "emancipated" or be "mature minors" and have adult rights when they marry, graduate from high school, or live on their own. It is important to clarify the legal status of young people in your community and your caseload. Likely exceptions to the need for parental consent are emergencies, treatment for drug/alcohol abuse, some sensitive medical conditions, married status, or military service.

Form 11 is designed to be understood and signed by an older child or adolescent. It was originally written by Glenn W. Humphrey, OFM, PhD, of New York, NY, and is adapted here with his kind permission. To make it fit the client, replace or select the gender pronouns, and perhaps replace "the therapist" with your name and title.

A Contract for Group Therapy

Orienting a client to a group experience is complex, and only the legal and ethical issues are addressed here, not the clinical ones. You may want to construct one or more additional handouts (about the "ground rules," ways members "work" to promote growth, the roles of leaders, contacts with member's partners, use of drugs/alcohol, violence, permission to make recordings, etc.) to support your initial evaluation and orienting efforts.

There are some unique risks and benefits you might discuss with the group or add to the

Agreement for Psychotherapy with a Minor

I, _____, the parent/legal guardian of the minor, _____, give my permission for this minor to receive the following services/procedures/treatments/assessments:

1. _____
2. _____
3. _____

These are for the purpose(s) of:

1. _____
2. _____
3. _____

These services are to be provided by the therapist named above, or by another professional as the therapist sees fit. The fees for these services will be $_____ per session of service, or $_____ for the full services.

This therapist's office policies concerning missed appointments have been explained to me. I have been told about the risks and benefits of receiving these services and the risks and benefits of *not* receiving these services, for both this minor and his or her family.

I agree that this professional may also interview, assess, or treat these other persons:

1. _____   3. _____
2. _____   4. _____

Because of the laws of this state and the guidelines of the therapist's profession, these rules concerning privacy will be used:

1. _____
2. _____
3. _____

A report or reports concerning the therapist's findings will be available after this date: _____. Progress in this minor's treatment will be reviewed on or about this date: _____ and on a regular basis after that.

I am the legal custodian of this child, and there are no court orders in effect that would prohibit me from consenting to the treatment of this child.

My signature below means that I understand and agree with all of the points above.

_____   _____
Signature of parent/guardian   Date

I, the therapist, have discussed the issues above with the minor client's parent or guardian. My observations of this person's behavior and responses give me no reason, in my professional judgment, to believe that this person is not fully competent to give informed and willing consent to the minor client's treatment.

_____   _____
Signature of therapist   Date

❑ Copy accepted by parent/guardian   ❑ Copy kept by therapist

This is a strictly confidential patient medical record. Redisclosure or transfer is expressly prohibited by law.

FORM 10. Contract with parent/guardian for psychotherapy with a minor. From *The Paper Office*. Copyright 2008 by Edward L. Zuckerman. Permission to photocopy this form is granted to purchasers of this book for personal use only (see copyright page for details).

Agreement for Meetings with My Therapist

I, _____, agree to meet with the therapist named below, _____ time(s) per week starting on _____. Our meetings will last about _____ minutes. When we meet, we may talk, draw pictures, play games, or do other things to help this therapist get to know me better and understand my problems, strengths, and goals.

I understand that my parent (or parents) or my guardian has a right to know about how I am doing in therapy. I agree that this therapist may talk with my parent/guardian to discuss how I am doing. They may also talk about concerns and worries they may have about me. Or they may talk about things the therapist and I decide my parent/guardian needs to know about. Sometimes this therapist may meet with my parent/guardian without me. At other times we may all meet together.

The things I talk about in my meetings with the therapist are private. I understand this therapist will not tell others about the *specific* things I tell him or her. He or she will not repeat these things to my parent/guardian, my teachers, the police, probation officers, or agency employees. But there are two exceptions. First, because of the law, the therapist *will* tell others what I have said if I talk about seriously hurting myself or someone else. This therapist will have to tell someone who can help protect me or the person I have talked about hurting. Second, if I am being seriously hurt by anyone, this therapist has to tell someone for my protection.

I understand that sometimes I may not feel good about some things we may talk about in our meetings. I may feel uncomfortable talking to this therapist because I don't yet know him or her very well. I may feel embarrassed talking about myself. Some of the things we talk about may make me feel angry or sad. Sometimes coming to meetings may interfere with doing other things I enjoy more. But I also understand that coming to therapy should help me feel or act better in the long run. I may find that I will trust this therapist and can talk about things that I can't talk to anyone else about. I may learn some new, important, and helpful things about myself and others. I may learn some new and better ways of handling my feelings or problems. I may feel less worried or angry and come to feel better about myself.

Any time I have questions or am worried about the things that are happening in therapy, I know I can ask this therapist. He or she will try to explain things to me in ways that I can understand. I also know that if my parent/guardian has any questions, the therapist will try to answer them.

I understand that my parent/guardian can stop my coming to therapy if he or she thinks that is best. If I decide therapy is not helping me and I want to stop, this therapist will discuss my feelings with me and with my parent/guardian. I understand that the final decision about stopping is up to my parent/guardian.

Our signatures below mean that we have read this agreement, or have had it read to us, and agree to act according to it.

_____   _____
Signature of child   Date

_____   _____
Signature of parent/guardian   Date

I, the therapist, have discussed the issues above with the minor client and his or her parent/guardian. My observations of their behavior and responses give me no reason, in my professional judgment, to believe that these persons are not fully competent to give informed and willing consent.

_____   _____
Signature of therapist   Date

❑ Copy accepted by client and parent/guardian   ❑ Copy kept by therapist

This is a strictly confidential patient medical record. Redisclosure or transfer is expressly prohibited by law.

FORM 11. Contract for psychotherapy with an older child or adolescent.   Adapted from a form devised by Glenn W. Humphrey, OFM, PhD, of New York, NY, and used by permission of Dr. Humphrey.—From *The Paper Office*. Permission to photocopy this form is granted to purchasers of this book for personal use only (see copyright page for details).

FORM 12   contract in Form 12. Some possible risks, according to Soreff and McDuffee (1993, p. 492), include "disclosure of one's name or other information by a group member; emergence of extreme reactions, including disruptive behavior, in response to the intensity of the group experience; acquisition of others' symptoms and behavior from exposure to their psychopathology." Some possible benefits, also according to Soreff and McDuffee (1993, p. 492), include "insight into one's relationships; opportunity to practice interpersonal communication skills; recognition of how [one affects] others (group feedback); diminished isolation; increase in sensitivity to the reactions and feelings of others."

Many of the issues are the same in group therapy as in other therapy formats, but there are some important differences. **The legal and ethical rules of confidentiality** do not apply to group therapy, because the members are not professionals (or even cotherapists in the professional/ethical sense). The legal model in most states (except where there are laws specifically addressing confidentiality in groups) is that information shared with anyone besides a therapist, or a therapist's employee, is no longer protected. Therefore, the central issue of ethical concern in groups appears to be the maintenance of confidentiality.

To increase the likelihood of confidentiality's being maintained, you can stress the rationale and importance of maintaining it from the first meeting onward, and model it in the discussions of earlier group interactions. Repeat the rationale when any new member joins or the topic comes up in a session, even in an indirect way. Offering many examples of breaking confidentiality seems to help people control their natural desire to gossip. If you see a member of the group in individual therapy as well, be especially cautious when raising issues with this person in the group to make certain the information was not given to you in the confidence of the individual session. If it was, do not share it or act on it in group sessions. Keep separate records for each kind of therapy.

Form 12 is a contract designed for groups. For various reasons, it may need to be modified or amended to be appropriate for a particular group:

- This contract is designed to be used with the other paths to informed consent, because it does not cover issues of emergency contact, consultations, and the qualifications of the leader(s).

- There is a provision prohibiting socialization outside the group meetings, but this may not be appropriate for some support groups. Or you might alter it to require full disclosure of all members' relationships to the group.

- If the group concerns domestic violence, you might want to add a paragraph giving permission for your full and continuing contact with the group member's partner.

- If you charge a down payment to reserve a place in the group, you may want to include that in your discussion of costs. You may also want to indicate that some fees are not refundable.

- You may want to require each individual to meet separately with the leaders on a regular basis.

- The provision for a monetary payment for damages in rule 5 is to support a breach-of-contract suit in the future if a member should reveal the contents of group discussions,

Agreement for Group Therapy

As a group member, I have rights and benefits as well as duties, and I understand that some of them are described in this agreement.

This group will be called _____ and will meet from _____ to _____ on _____ at _____. The total cost of this group is $_____, or $_____ per session. I agree to pay this fee even for group meetings I do not attend, unless I make other arrangements in advance.

The purpose of this group is to provide me with the opportunity to achieve the following goals:

1. _____

2. _____

3. _____

I agree to work in this group. This means openly talking about my thoughts and feelings, honestly reporting my behaviors, keeping my promises, and exchanging helpful feedback with other members of the group.

I will attend all meetings of this group from start to finish, even if I do not always feel like it. If I cannot attend, I will tell the group a week in advance (at the beginning of that meeting), or, if it is an emergency, call one of the leaders as soon as I know I cannot attend. If I decide not to go on or am unable to go on with the group, I will discuss my reasons with the group and its leaders, and I will give 2 weeks' notice to the group.

I will not socialize outside the group with any of its members or leaders. This is needed so that everyone will be equals in the group. If I happen to meet a member outside, I will tell the group at our next meeting.

I understand that this group experience is not a replacement for individual therapy. If issues arise that are not suitable for the group's process, I may benefit from individual therapy sessions, for which I will have to pay separately from the cost of the group therapy. I will discuss this with the group's leader(s).

I understand that the leaders are required by law to report any suspected child or elder abuse, or credible threats of harm to myself or another person, to the proper authorities.

With full understanding of the need for confidentiality (that is, privacy) for all group members, I accept these rules:

1. We will use only first names. I promise to tell no one the names of the group members, or in any other way allow someone not in the group to learn their names.

2. We will permit no children, spouses, journalists, or other visitors in our sessions.

3. We will not permit any kind of recordings of our sessions, even by our members or leaders.

4. I promise not to tell anyone outside the group about any of the problems, history, issues, or other facts presented by any group member, even if I conceal the name of the member.

(cont.)

FORM 12. Contract for group therapy (p. 1 of 2).   From *The Paper Office.* Copyright 2008 by Edward L. Zuckerman. Permission to photocopy this form is granted to purchasers of this book for personal use only (see copyright page for details).

5. I understand and agree that if I break rules 1–4 often without meaning to, or if I ever break one of these rules on purpose, I will be asked to leave the group. I will also face a possible lawsuit in which I may have to pay damages. If I reveal private information, I give the offended person or persons the right to recover for damages to his, her, or their reputation. Also, this person or persons may recover for any other damages that can be proven.

6. I understand and agree that the leaders will keep a clinical case record on each individual member, and that this record will not contain information by which any other members can be identified. This record, kept in each member's name, can be shared with other professionals only with the member's written consent or to meet legal requirements.

7. I understand that the leaders will keep another record about the group's meetings and the interactions of the members, and that this record will not be included in any member's records. This record may not be shown to anyone without the written agreement of all the members and the leaders involved.

8. Other points:

_____

_____

_____

_____

_____

I have read the points stated above, have discussed them when I was not clear about them, and have had my questions answered fully. I understand and agree to them, as shown by my signature below.

_____	_____
Signature of member (or parent/guardian)	Date

_____
Printed name

Please return a completed and signed copy of this agreement to one of the group's leaders, and you will receive a copy for you to keep.

I, a leader of this group, have discussed the issues above with the client (and/or his or her parent or guardian). My observations of this person's behavior and responses give me no reason to believe that this person is not fully competent to give informed and willing consent.

_____	_____
Signature of leader	Date

_____
Printed name

_____	_____
Signature of leader	Date

_____
Printed name

❑ Copy accepted by group member   ❑ Copy kept by leader

This is a strictly confidential patient medical record. Redisclosure or transfer is expressly prohibited by law.

identity of group members, or other confidential matters. This paragraph is loosely based on one from Morrison et al. (1975) as quoted in Bindrim (1980).

- You might consider adding to rule 5 a clause that if a group member sues another member for breaching confidentiality, the one being sued will "hold harmless" the therapist for any consequences of the breach. I cannot provide the language for this agreement, because state laws vary; consult your lawyer for the proper terms.

- For patient education, you might wish to flesh out this form with some of the rationales for group therapy, or have patients agree that they have read your patient education handouts. You could emphasize the processes of member-to-member interactions; feedback from multiple perspectives, and from peers as well as therapists; the potential for exploring socially uncomfortable topics; discovering that you are not alone; trying out interactions that are possible only in a group; and the like. You might indicate what the leader will do (e.g., serve as "referee" and coordinator, interrupt some kinds of criticism and attacks) and will not do (e.g., take sides, play "the authority").

- As to attendance, you might add more on the effects on the group of missing members, tardiness, leaving early, vacation arrangements, and so forth. Discussing expected attendance as a personal commitment one makes to others, each member's irreplaceability, and so on, may be useful at this early point.

- Similarly, the impact on the group's process of adding a new member or having one leave is usually an important clinical topic and may be noted here as such.

- Some may benefit from explanations of the normality of feelings of reluctance and concerns with exposure, and the roles of members as audience or "witness bearers" even when they have little to contribute.

- Rule 6, about access to the group notes, might be modified so that this record could be reviewed by any member without needing specific permission of the other members. If so, you would need to write the record in such a manner that it did not identify members or their issues, but recorded the topics and conclusions, interaction patterns, and other aspects you deemed important to record. However, you might choose to record the group's process so that you can hypothesize and test dynamics, recall significant statements or important interactions, and so forth, entirely for your own use as a therapist. This kind of record would be protected as a psychotherapy note under HIPAA (see Section 6.2 on psychotherapy notes).

4.6   The Fifth Path to Informed Consent: Consent to Treatment and Other Services

I use "consent-to-treatment forms" when a contract would be too detailed or comprehensive, but agreement to participate in treatment must be documented for legal or therapeutic reasons. These consent forms leave out many of the goals, problem definitions, methods, and tactics, and they state only a few of the most critical items.

This section offers several different consent forms, covering the following:

- Generic consent to the treatment of an adult.

- Generic consent to the treatment of a minor child.

- Consent to counseling for a child whose parents are divorcing.

- Permission to make electronic recordings of sessions, and to make various uses of case material.

- Consent to psychological testing and evaluations.

No doubt other occasions would benefit from a written consent form. If you have developed such a form, please share it with me for the next edition (see the introduction to this book).

Generic Consent to an Adult's Treatment

FORM 13   Form 13 is a brief form for obtaining consent to the treatment of an adult. It may be useful as a preliminary agreement for a client who would be frustrated and likely to abandon treatment if confronted immediately with a longer and more complex form such as the client information brochure. Pope and Vasquez (2007) note:

> *Nothing blocks a patient's access to help with such cruel efficiency as a bungled attempt at informed consent.* . . . The doors to our offices and clinics are wide open. The resources are all in place. But not even the most persistent patients can make their way past intimidating forms (which clerks may shove at patients when they first arrive), our set speeches full of non-informative information, and our nervous attempts to meet externally imposed legalistic requirements such as the Health Insurance Portability and Accountability Act. A first step is to recognize that informed consent is not a static ritual but a useful process. (p. 135; emphasis added)

As with all of the photocopiable forms in this book, you can use Form 13 "as is" or modify it to suit your own setting and practice.

Generic Consent to a Minor Child's Treatment

FORM 14   Form 14 is a brief form for generic consent by a parent or legal guardian to the treatment of a child. Essentially, it certifies that you and the parent have had discussions on the issues relevant to the treatment.

Consent to Counseling for a Child of Divorce

The roles of therapist and forensic evaluator (e.g., of custody issues) are different, because the clients are different. As a therapist in court, you are an advocate for the child even when the legal client is the parent. As a forensic evaluator, you may try to place the child's interests first, but you are in a conflictual legal area and your duty is to the court. Never try to serve in both capacities—it is the classic dual relationship with all its risks.

Consent to Treatment

I acknowledge that I have received, have read (or have had read to me), and understand the "Information for Clients" brochure and/or other information about the therapy I am considering. I have had all my questions answered fully.

I do hereby seek and consent to take part in the treatment by the therapist named below. I understand that developing a treatment plan with this therapist and regularly reviewing our work toward meeting the treatment goals are in my best interest. I agree to play an active role in this process.

I understand that no promises have been made to me as to the results of treatment or of any procedures provided by this therapist.

I am aware that I may stop my treatment with this therapist at any time. The only thing I will still be responsible for is paying for the services I have already received. I understand that I may lose other services or may have to deal with other problems if I stop treatment. (For example, if my treatment has been court-ordered, I will have to answer to the court.)

I know that I must call to cancel an appointment at least 72 hours (3 days) before the time of the appointment. If I do not cancel and do not show up, I will be charged for that appointment.

I am aware that an agent of my insurance company or other third-party payer may be given information about the type(s), cost(s), date(s), and providers of any services or treatments I receive. I understand that if payment for the services I receive here is not made, the therapist may stop my treatment.

My signature below shows that I understand and agree with all of these statements.

_____   _____
Signature of client (or person acting for client)   Date

_____   _____
Printed name   Relationship to client
                                                                        (if necessary)

I, the therapist, have discussed the issues above with the client (and/or his or her parent, guardian, or other representative). My observations of this person's behavior and responses give me no reason to believe that this person is not fully competent to give informed and willing consent.

_____   _____
Signature of therapist   Date

❑ Copy accepted by client   ❑ Copy kept by therapist

This is a strictly confidential patient medical record. Redisclosure or transfer is expressly prohibited by law.

FORM 13. Form for generic consent to treatment of an adult.   From *The Paper Office*. Copyright 2008 by Edward L. Zuckerman. Permission to photocopy this form is granted to purchasers of this book for personal use only (see copyright page for details).

Consent to Treatment of a Child

Name of child client: _____

The therapist named below and I have discussed my child's situation. I have been informed of the risks and benefits of several different treatment choices. The treatment chosen includes these actions and methods:

1. _____
2. _____
3. _____

These actions and methods are for the purposes of:

1. _____
2. _____
3. _____

I have had the chance to discuss all of these issues, have had my questions answered, and believe I understand the treatment that is planned. Therefore, I agree to play an active role in this treatment as needed, and I give this therapist (or another professional, as he or she sees fit) permission to begin this treatment, as shown by my signature below.

_____   _____

Signature of parent/guardian   Date

I, the therapist, have discussed the issues above with the child's parent or guardian. My observations of this person's behavior and responses give me no reason, in my professional judgment, to believe that this person is not fully competent to give informed and willing consent to the child's treatment.

_____   _____

Signature of therapist   Date

❑ Copy accepted by parent/guardian   ❑ Copy kept by therapist

This is a strictly confidential patient medical record. Redisclosure or transfer is expressly prohibited by law.

The children of divorcing parents often have an obvious need for treatment. Yet a therapist can easily stumble into a minefield of accusations. By definition, about half of the persons involved in a custody dispute will be dissatisfied with the outcome, and this area has been a very frequent source of ethics complaints and suits. Knapp and Tepper (1992) offer this preventative suggestion:

> If it appears that a child custody dispute may emerge, then the treating psychologist should inform the parent(s) that a court-appointed child custody evaluator, or an independent psychologist, may be a better person to provide psychological expert testimony. Treating psychologists may be accused of being biased since they have a therapeutic alliance with one of the parents. The psychologist also may fear that the courtroom testimony would jeopardize the quality of the needed psychotherapy. (p. 16)

FORM 15 Garber (1994) offers the agreement given below (Form 15) as a means of educating the parents and informing them about the role you will assume. Although the language of Garber's form may be a bit difficult for some parents, it does an admirable job of covering the important points. If the parents endorse this agreement beforehand, this should greatly reduce your risk exposure, in addition to supporting meaningful therapeutic interventions. I have modified numbered paragraph 4 to describe psychoeducational groups generically.

If it is too late to warn parents about the difficulties of a therapist's providing testimony in a custody case, Saunders (1993), in a very worthwhile article, offers these "practical steps a psychologist can take if he or she has been a therapist to one or more of the parties" (p. 55) to avoid additional problems:

1. Directly inform all parties of pertinent facts. E.g., the therapist, has no opinion on the matter before the Court; formulation of such an opinion may jeopardize the treatment relationship; the parties have had no opportunity for informed consent.

2. Suggest an independent evaluation of all parties, and make a referral where necessary.

3. Invoke the privileged communication statute if applicable in that state.

4. Have the existing record redacted by a trial judge, to exclude potentially harmful clinical material.

5. File a motion to quash the subpoena.

6. If called as a witness, withhold any expert opinion. (Serve only as a fact witness.) (p. 55)

Steve Eichel, PhD, ABPP, of Newark, DE, suggests the following clarifications of the distinction between the therapist and evaluator roles.

1. Add the following to your contract with the client about treating children:

> I am aware that requesting the release of treatment notes or plans, reports, or evaluations (which you made as this child's therapist) for forensic purposes (such as in separation, divorce, or custody actions), or subpoenaing them or your testimony about the content of my child's treatment, will interfere with the therapy relationship so necessary for progress and so will greatly jeopardize my child's health and well-being. Therefore, I knowingly and freely waive my right to request the release of information (beyond the

Agreement for Parents

Psychotherapy can be a very important resource for children of separation and divorce. Establishing a therapeutic alliance outside of the home can:

- Facilitate open and appropriate expression of the strong feelings which routinely accompany family transitions, including guilt, grief, sadness and anger.

- Provide an emotionally neutral setting in which children can explore these feelings.

- Help children understand and accept the new family composition and the plans for contact with each member of the family.

- Offer feedback and recommendations to a child's caregivers based on knowledge of the child's specific emotional needs and developmental capacities.

However, the usefulness of such therapy is extremely limited when the therapy itself becomes simply another matter of dispute between parents. With this in mind, and in order to best help your child, I strongly recommend that each of the child's caregivers (e.g., parents, stepparents, daycare workers, guardian *ad litem* [GAL], etc.) mutually accept the following as requisites for the child's participation in therapy.

1. As your child's psychotherapist, it is my primary responsibility to respond to your child's emotional needs. This includes, but is not limited to, contact with your child and each of his or her caregivers, and gathering information relevant to understanding your child's welfare and circumstances as perceived by important others (e.g., pediatrician, teachers, other psychologists, social workers). In some cases, this may include a recommendation that you consult with a physician, should matters of your child's physical health be relevant to this therapy.

2. I ask that all caregivers remain in frequent communication regarding this child's welfare and emotional well-being. Open communication about his or her emotional state and behavior is critical. In this regard, I invite each of you to initiate frequent and open exchange with me as your child's therapist.

3. I ask that all parties recognize and, as necessary, reaffirm to the child, that I am the child's helper and not allied with any disputing party.

4. I strongly recommend that all caregivers involved choose to participate in psychoeducational groups in which separating and divorced parents learn basic strategies for conducting a divorce in the best interests of the child. I can refer you to such programs.

5. Please be advised regarding the limits of confidentiality as it applies to psychotherapy with a child in these circumstances:

   - I keep records of all contacts relevant to your child's well-being. These records are subject to court subpoena and may, under some circumstances, be solicited by parties to your divorce, including your attorneys.

   - Any matter brought to my attention by either parent regarding the child may be revealed to the other parent. Matters which are brought to my attention that are irrelevant to the child's welfare may be kept in con-

(cont.)

FORM 15. Agreement for parents regarding limitations and goals of psychotherapy with a child of divorce (p. 1 of 2). Adapted from Garber (1994). Copyright 1994 by Division of Psychotherapy (29) of the American Psychological Association (APA). Adapted by permission. The APA grants purchasers of *The Paper Office* the right to make photocopies for personal use only. Further use of this material without the express written permission of the APA is strictly prohibited.—From *The Paper Office.*

fidence. However, these matters may best be brought to the attention of others, such as attorneys, personal therapists or counselors.

- **I am legally obligated to bring any concern regarding the child's health and safety to the attention of relevant authorities. When possible, should this necessity arise, I will advise all parties regarding my concerns.**

6. This psychotherapy will not yield recommendations about custody. In general, I recommend that parties who are disputing custody strongly consider participation in alternative forms of negotiation and conflict resolution, including mediation and custody evaluation, rather than try to settle a custody dispute in court.

7. Payment for my services is due in full at the time of service. Any outstanding balance accrued (for example, in conference with attorneys, the GAL, or teachers), must be paid promptly and in full. An initial retainer of $_____ will be required prior to commencing this therapy, to be held against charges incurred and subject to reimbursement at the conclusion of this therapy, as appropriate.

Your understanding of these points and agreement in advance of starting this therapy may resolve difficulties that would otherwise arise and will help make this therapy successful. Your signature, below, signifies that you have read and accept these points.

_____   _____
Caregiver name   Date

_____
Printed name

_____   _____
Caregiver name   Date

_____
Printed name

_____   _____
Caregiver name   Date

_____
Printed name

_____   _____
Caregiver name   Date

_____
Printed name

_____   _____
Child's name   Date of birth   Age

_____   _____
Mental health professional   Date

❑ Copy accepted by client   ❑ Copy kept by therapist

This is a strictly confidential patient medical record. Redisclosure or transfer is expressly prohibited by law.

attendance, dates, and length of our meetings and your charges) to my attorney or any other officer of the court. I understand that release of clinically significant information to any officer of the court shall only be in response to a court order signed by a duly appointed judge. (This paragraph is adapted from one by Steve Eichel, and is used here with his kind permission.)

2. As a way to discourage being dragged into legal proceedings over a child you are treating, even after parents sign an agreement not to do so, you can inform them that you will bill them for all your time spent on legal issues (e.g., responding to the attorneys to explain why you will not be providing information, answering phone calls and mail, writing reports and case note documentation, traveling from your office to the court, etc.).

3. An elaboration of Saunders's (1993) point 1 above: Explain to the parents' attorneys that your testifying could easily harm or lead to termination of the therapeutic relationship. The "offended" parent would end his or her consent to treatment, and the consent of both parents is needed to treat (in the absence of a sole legal custody decision). Causing such termination might be embarrassing to that parent's attorney in court.

4. If you are compelled to testify, ask to receive and answer questions in writing.

5. As an alternative to Saunders's (1993) point 4 above, ask the judge to limit your testimony to only the questions the judge and you agree are appropriate to your role as therapist.

6. Make it clear that you can only testify about the child's needs. You cannot make any comments on parenting, because you have not evaluated the parents' skills (i.e., done a custody evaluation).

7. An elaboration of Saunders's point 6 above: Attorneys may try to get you to testify at the tiny flat fee given to fact witnesses. If you do so, you can only report dates of service, note costs, and affirm that you provided the services to the client. If you are testifying to more than this, all your statements are professional judgments, and so you are testifying as an expert witness and deserve the higher fees. Make it clear what you will and won't say as a fact witness.

Authorization to Record Sessions and Use Case Materials

FORM 16

If you think you will ever use any of your clinical notes or cases in any future professional work, you should probably get Form 16 signed during treatment (but not at the beginning, because the client will not be able to give informed consent without knowing what will come up in therapy). For the same reasons, it is inadequate to ask for the client's consent as you are starting the recording; this is not likely to provide the client with sufficient information about what will be discussed or revealed to give informed consent. Use this form afterward.

Form 16 combines a consent-to-record form with a consent to use any materials for any professional purposes. Although separate forms are often offered to clients during treat-

Release and Permission to Record Sessions and to Use Case Materials

As a therapist, I naturally want to know more about how therapy helps people. To understand therapy better, I must collect information about clients before, during, and after therapy. Therefore, I am asking you to help by allowing me to record our sessions, and also perhaps by filling out some questionnaires about different parts of your life—relationships, changes, concerns, attitudes, and other areas. Video and audio recordings are sometimes used as aids in the therapy process, in the education of mental health professionals, and in research. I need to have your written permission to make and use these recordings and materials for these purposes.

I would also be grateful for your consent to use your case material in my other professional activities. Your material may help in the development of the mental health field or in the training of health care workers. It is possible that I could use your material in teaching, supervision, consultation with other therapists, publishing, or scientific research. For these purposes, I might use any of the following:

- Clinical or case notes I or other professionals have taken during or after our sessions.

- Psychological test responses and scores, questionnaires, checklists, and similar data collection forms.

- Electronic or other recordings (such as audio and/or video recordings, transcriptions, case notes, physiological monitoring, or any other recording method) of any interview, examination, or treatment with me, my employees, or other professionals. These recordings may include clients, therapists, or others, and may be made in my office or in similar settings by other professionals.

- Other materials that are similar to those mentioned above but whose specifics I do not know at present.

- Observation of our meetings by professionals or student professionals, using video recordings or adjacent observation rooms.

For simplicity, everything listed above will be referred to as "materials" in the rest of this form.

When I use materials from my testing or therapy work, I do not want anyone who hears, reads, or sees it to be able to identify the clients involved. Therefore, I would conceal your identity by one of the following methods:

1. Reporting the results as grouped data (that is, publishing only numbers like averages, and not publishing any individual's scores or names).

2. Removing (or, if this is not possible, greatly changing) all names, dates, places, descriptions, or any other information by which you or anyone else involved could be identified. In particular, I will not use, or allow anyone else to use, your real name in any presentation of any of these materials.

3. Using any other methods for maintaining confidentiality appropriate to the medium, such as electronically concealing someone's face or altering his or her voice.

4. Using other methods (including those not yet available) that would be consistent with my professional code of ethics and professional guidelines for the maintenance of confidentiality.

(cont.)

FORM 16. Release/permission form for recording sessions and using case materials in research, teaching, and professional publishing (p. 1 of 2). From *The Paper Office*. Copyright 2008 by Edward L. Zuckerman. Permission to photocopy this form is granted to purchasers of this book for personal use only (see copyright page for details).

These materials will be presented only to other health care professionals and to their students. All of these persons are bound by federal and state laws and professional rules about clients' privacy. I will keep all these materials in a safe location, and destroy them as soon as they are no longer needed.

Therefore, I am asking you to read and sign the following:

I, the client (or his or her parent or guardian), consent to the recording of sessions for the purposes described above. The purpose and value of recording have been fully explained to me, and I freely and willingly consent to this recording.

This consent is being given in regard to the professional services being provided by the therapist named below. I agree that I am to receive no financial benefit from the use of the materials. I understand that if I do not agree to the uses of these materials or the recording of meetings as indicated, I will not be penalized in any way, and it will not affect the care I am to receive in any way. I understand that I may ask for the recording to be turned off or erased at any time during my sessions. I also understand that within 5 days following a session, I may choose to request a viewing of the recording with the therapist. I further understand that I may then ask for the recording to be destroyed. If I choose to ask this, I will deliver a written statement to this effect to the therapist within 5 days following the viewing.

I understand that I am fully responsible for my own participation in any and all exercises and activities suggested by the therapist. I agree not to hold the therapist legally responsible for the effect of these exercises on me, either during the session or later.

I give the therapist named below my permission to use the materials for research, teaching, and advancing other professional purposes. I understand that they will be used as an aid in the process of improving mental health work or training health care workers. I agree that the materials may be sold or otherwise made available to health care professionals for educational, training, and/or research purposes. These professionals and their students are bound by state laws and by professional rules about clients' privacy.

I hereby give up my rights to any and all interests that I may have in the materials. I agree to let the therapist be the sole owner of all the rights in these materials for all purposes described above.

_____   _____
Signature of client (or parent/guardian)   Date

_____
Printed name

I, the therapist, have discussed the issues above with the client (and/or his or her parent or guardian). My observations of this person's behavior and responses give me no reason to believe that this person is not fully competent to give informed and willing consent.

_____   _____
Signature of therapist   Date

❏ Copy accepted by client   ❏ Copy kept by therapist

This is a strictly confidential patient medical record. Redisclosure or transfer is expressly prohibited by law.

ment, a form combining these functions gives you more options for future use of case materials while addressing the confidentiality concerns of clients. In addition, the form includes patient education materials that explain how confidentiality will be maintained; these are designed to assist clients in giving their permission to allow you to use their clinical materials. Other points regarding this form are as follows:

- Most situations are covered through simply making identification impossible by altering the facts of the case, but sometimes these cannot be changed, and sometimes information slips through. So the use of this signed form may be double protection for little additional effort.

- According to the rules of the Federal Communications Commission (Rule 64, subpart E), you may record telephone conversations without using a beep tone every 15 seconds if you simply inform the other party that you are recording the conversation. There may be state or other regulations as well as the federal ones, however, and so you should check locally.

- If you are going to use videotape or show the client in such a way that he or she can be recognized, you will probably need to explain, in detail and in writing, exactly what is to be done with the materials (by whom, for what purposes, etc.). Form 16 can assist with that process.

Form 16 is based on ideas from the "Release and Permission to Tape Form" by Elizabeth A. Schilson, PhD, and from "Client Informed Consent for Videotaping." Both forms are in Piercy et al. (1989). Piercy et al.'s book also includes model release forms in legal language for the commercial use of photographs.

All of the above are very likely to continue to apply to your situation unless your state's laws or the regulations of your profession do not address these issues, in which case the HIPAA Privacy Rule would apply.

Under HIPAA, you must distinguish PHI for use in treatment or training from PHI for use in research. The former does not require a separate authorization, because such use is covered under normal "treatment, payment, and health care operations" (TPO), and consent would have been obtained with the NPP (see Section 5.4) during the intake process. To use a recording in research you will need both the general consent for use of PHI in TPO and a signed research authorization, which goes beyond the core elements of the authorization described in Section 7.1 to addresses other issues raised by research participation.

Consent to Psychological Testing

The APA code of ethics (APA, 2002) specifically requires obtaining "informed consent for assessments, evaluations, or diagnostic services, . . . except when (1) testing is mandated by law or governmental regulation; (2) informed consent is implied because testing is conducted as a routine . . . organizational activity . . . or (3) one purpose of the testing is to evaluate decisional capacity" (Standard 9.03a). Neither Form 17 nor 18 refers to the confidentiality of the test materials and results such as protocols and scores. Their legal protection from disclosure resides with your state's laws and court decisions. HIPAA does not specifically address these materials. However, one might argue that these should be included in "results of clinical tests" and thereby go into the general medical record rather than into psychotherapy notes (see Section 6.2).

Younggren (1995) reminds us:

> Patients have a right to know what a test is designed to measure, whether it is reliable and valid for the expected use, how the data will be used, how they will be stored and who will have access to the results. Psychologists who use scoring services and various electronic devices in conducting assessments should outline how these systems are constructed and what protections are provided. (p. 7)

On a related note, you should always ask clients you are testing whether they have been tested before, when, with what tests, by whom, and for what purposes. If a client is not very aware, delay these questions until the Wechsler Block Design subtest and then ask, "Have you seen these designs before?" In forensic and disability testing, you should expect that a client is likely to have been coached (sometimes extensively) by his or her lawyer or relatives, and so you should ask, "What have you been told about these tests, who told you, and what did they tell you?" Of course, the client does not have to tell the truth, but at least you can document what he or she says.

FORM 17   Form 17 is both a consent form for testing and an agreement to pay for such evaluations; it covers the most common and simplest cases. This form is based on one created by John M. Smothers, PhD, ABPP, of Bethesda, MD.

Consent to Being Evaluated for a Third Party

Problems may arise when either a child or an adult is referred for an evaluation whose results are to be used by the referrer (such as a court, lawyer, or disability agency) for its own purposes, which may not overlap with the client's preferences or even best interests. If you take such a case, you may be placed in a position where your obligations (to the client, to the referring agency, to the payer, to principles of beneficence, etc.) conflict. For fully informed consent, you should probably advise clients whom you are testing in such cases that the results may not be in their favor. A form is needed that combines the ele-
FORM 18   ments of consent to be evaluated and release of the results of the evaluation; Form 18 does this. Some of the wording in this form has been provided by David A. Miller, PhD, of Kansas City, MO.

When evaluating a client sent by the courts, you must consider a different aspect of confidentiality—confessions. If guilt has been established in court, through conviction or an accepted plea bargain, then the client can feel free to discuss the crime and his or her role in it. However, if you are doing an examination before conviction, you must warn the client *at the start of the interview* specifically not to tell you what he or she did or did not do concerning the charges. Explain that if he or she were to tell you about this, you would have to include those statements in your report to the court; that this might be incriminating; and that, of course, he or she has a constitutional right not to make such admissions. Make it clear that if the client wishes to discuss any details of the case, this must be entirely voluntary, and it is likely to have consequences. You may need to clarify your role as employee or consultant to the court or to an attorney. In parallel, you should ask the defense attorney whether there are kinds of information he or she would like left out of

Consent and Agreement for Psychological Testing and Evaluation

I,_____, agree to allow the psychologist named below to perform the following services:

❑ Psychological testing, assessment, or evaluation   ❑ Report writing

❑ Consultation with school personnel   ❑ Consultation with lawyers

❑ Deposition (that is, written or oral testimony given to a court, but not made in open court)

❑ Testimony in court

❑ Other (describe): _____

This agreement concerns ❑ myself or ❑ _____

I understand that these services may include direct, face-to-face contact, interviewing, or testing. They may also include the psychologist's time required for the reading of records, consultations with other psychologists and professionals, scoring of tests, interpreting the results, and any other activities to support these services. If I have questions or concerns about this assessment, the evaluator agrees to be available to discuss these after completion of the testing and interview.

I understand that the fee for this (these) service(s) will be $_____ per hour, and that this is payable in two parts: a deposit of $_____ payable before the start of this (these) services, and a second payment of the balance due on the completion and delivery of any report (or, for depositions, testimony, or other services, at the time these services take place). I understand that I am fully responsible for payment for these services.

I understand that this evaluation is to be done for the purpose(s) of:

1. _____

2. _____

I also understand the psychologist agrees to the following:

1. The procedures for selecting, giving, and scoring the tests, interpreting the results, and maintaining my privacy will be carried out in accord, with the rules and guidelines of the American Psychological Association and other professional organizations and with the applicable state and federal laws.

2. Tests will be chosen that are suitable for the purposes described above. These tests will be given and scored according to the instructions in the tests' manuals, so that valid scores will be obtained. These scores will be interpreted according to scientific findings and guidelines from the scientific and professional literature.

3. Tests and test results will be kept in a secure place to maintain their confidentiality.

4. The report of the findings of this assessment will be sent to _____.

I agree to help as much as I can, by supplying full answers, making an honest effort, and working as best I can to make sure that the findings are accurate.

_____   _____
Signature of client (or parent/guardian)   Date

I, the psychologist, have discussed the issues above with the client (and/or his or her parent or guardian). My observations of this person's behavior and responses give me no reason, in my professional judgment, to believe that this person is not fully competent to give informed and willing consent.

_____   _____
Signature of psychologist   Date

❑ Copy accepted by client   ❑ Copy kept by psychologist

This is a strictly confidential patient medical record. Redisclosure or transfer is expressly prohibited by law.

FORM 17. Consent form and contract for psychological testing and evaluation.   Adapted from a form devised by John M. Smothers, PhD, ABPP, of Bethesda, MD, and used by permission of Dr. Smothers.—From *The Paper Office*. Permission to photocopy this form is granted to purchasers of this book for personal use only (see copyright page for details).

Consent to Evaluation

I agree to undergo (or I give consent for this person, _____, to undergo) a complete psychological/psychiatric/mental health/family evaluation at the direction of this third party: _____
_____. I understand and agree that the results of this evaluation are to be the sole property of this third party. I agree that I will not hold this third party legally responsible for any events resulting from this evaluation or the records created by it.

I understand that the purpose(s) of this evaluation are:

1. _____

2. _____

3. _____

I understand and agree that no doctor–patient or therapist–client relationship exists or will be created between myself (or the person being evaluated) and the evaluator.

I understand that I may withdraw my consent to this evaluation and to the transfer of information at any time by means of a written letter. However, I also understand that my withdrawal will not be retroactive (that is, it will not apply to testing and information transfer that have already taken place). If I do not withdraw my consent, it will automatically expire in 90 days from the date I signed this form.

I agree that a photocopy of this form is acceptable, but that the photocopy must be individually signed by me and a witness. I understand I have the right to receive a copy of this form upon my request.

_____   _____
Signature of client (or custodial parent/guardian of young child)   Date

_____
Printed name

_____   _____
Signature of adolescent client   Date

_____
Printed name

I, the psychologist, have discussed the issues above with the client (and/or his or her parent or guardian). My observations of this person's behavior and responses gives me no reason to believe that this person is not fully competent to give informed and willing consent.

_____   _____
Signature of psychologist   Date

❑ Copy accepted by client   ❑ Copy kept by psychologist

This is a strictly confidential patient medical record. Redisclosure or transfer is expressly prohibited by law.

FORM 18. Form for consent to being evaluated for a third party.   Adapted from a form devised by David A. Miller, PhD, of Kansas City, MO, and used by permission of Dr. Miller.—From *The Paper Office*. Permission to photocopy this form is granted to purchasers of this book for personal use only (see copyright page for details).

your report. For example, you may—through reviewing records, gathering history, or interviewing the client—learn of previous convictions, which might not be admissible in court. You can state that you read the records, but should not indicate this content.

If the attorney asks you to remove potentially damaging statements from your report, you will be in a potentially deep conflict. The proper way to deal with this is prevention. In any communication between you and the attorney, insert the phrase that the communication is "a work product, produced specifically for attorney–client activity, at the direction of the attorney." Such a "work product" can legitimately be omitted from any materials discoverable by the other side.

CHAPTER 5

Intake and Assessment
Forms and Procedures

5.1   Creating the Client's Chart

Most clinicians dislike the burden of paperwork, but the keeping of clinical records is not optional. How, then, should it best be done? How can you be sure your records are legally and ethically adequate to protect you? How can you best document your effectiveness for supervisors or third-party payers?

The Chronology of Record Making

This chapter and the next one offer standards for making clinical case records, and detailed suggestions for how to meet those standards. **They follow the natural chronology of recording a case.** I cover various types of records at the places in the chronology where you need to give them attention.

- I start where you will start with a case—at the first telephone contact and the agreement to meet as therapist and client. I call this Phase 1 of the intake.

- Next, in Phase 2, I collect the basic intake information, or make other types of preappointment contact. I offer materials that can constitute a preappointment package, to be mailed before the first meeting. If time is short, these can be completed by the client in the office before the first meeting (Phase 3).

- Phase 3 occurs during the client's first office visit, just before I interview the client. This is the time for filling out informational forms (histories, financial data, reasons for seeking services) that must precede the face-to-face interview.

- Then, for the actual interview (Phase 4), I offer forms for structuring the collection of more detailed data. This information is often sensitive, and its collection requires face-to-face interaction with the client. Examples include information on suicide risk, physical or sexual abuse, and mental status. The interview should also include screening questions, where the client's reactions may suggest to the clinician that clinically significant information may be obtained by probing further.

- In Phase 5, the last phase of intake, the data collected are integrated and summarized. I offer forms for summarizing suicide risk, drug and alcohol use, and the formulation of the client's case. These form the basis for the next chapter, Chapter 6, which continues the chronology by looking at treatment planning, treatment progress notes, and termination.

The Contents of the Record

It is a challenge to keep all of this information logically separated and yet easily accessible. See Section 1.4 for more on structures for organizing your records, and Section 6.2 for more on structuring the contents of what you record in your notes.

5.2   Phase I: The Initial Telephone Contact

Nobody, as long as he moves about among the chaotic currents of life, is without trouble.
—CARL JUNG

The client's record should begin at the beginning—with your first contact with him or her as a prospective client. This is almost always by telephone. This initial conversation should have the following goals:

- To assess whether you are an appropriate clinician to treat this person and problem.

- To discover whether there are reasons for refusing this person as a client (see below).

- If you discover no such reasons for refusal, to make efforts to increase the likelihood that the person will show up for treatment. (Section 5.3 discusses this in greater detail.)

- To begin the chart or record of your treatment so that it is professional, usable, and effective.

Your first contact with future clients can be a source of both satisfaction and income; do it right. Ideally, you should sound competent, efficient, and knowledgeable, as well as eager to listen. As the saying goes, you have only one chance to make a good first impression. Practice until you are comfortable, smooth, and confident when offering information and answering common questions. Be prepared to give information about office hours, insurance accepted, fees, and your credentials. Practice until your statements are anxiety-free and almost routine, so that your mind can attend to the clinical aspects of the call.

Remember, confidentiality extends to this first contact, so make sure no one can overhear you. If you suspect that some highly sensitive information is about to be revealed, make sure to defer it until you can meet with your caller and discuss the implications of its disclosure more fully.

Reasons for Refusing a Caller as a Client

A caller may not be an appropriate client for you for a variety of reasons:

- You do not have the time available, and placing the caller on a waiting list is inappropriate or unacceptable. Note that placing someone on a waiting list may entail some liability for harm. "Unless you know the prospective patient well (such as when a former patient requests to return to treatment) or have taken adequate precautions to evaluate their [*sic*] needs, it would be best to refer them away immediately if you cannot take them into treatment. If, after an evaluation and intake, you place someone on a waiting list, to protect yourself, you must follow the minimal standards of the field in making that decision," says Sam Knapp, EdD, Professional Affairs Officer of the Pennsylvania Psychological Association (e-mail list posting, November 6, 2006). He goes on to suggest that a written policy may be helpful and could include at least two points. First, you could state your decision-making criteria: For example, "Priority for being given appointments is based on patient need (life-threatening emergencies are given the highest priority) and length of time on the waiting list." Other criteria (severity, appropriateness, etc.) should also be stated. Potential clients should be told to "call if they are experiencing an emergency." Second, you could indicate how long a client on a waiting list might expect to wait for service, as an estimate. If so, make it clear that this date "is contingent upon the volume of emergency requests," and that it does not take "staff illnesses or resignations" into account.

- You and the caller are not able to establish a working relationship for some reason (e.g., your personalities or belief systems differ sharply).

- The caller is a relative, coworker, trainee, or the like. (See Section 3.7 on dual relationships.)

- The client cannot afford your fees (and your low-fee and *pro bono* hours are filled).

- The client may not be suitable for voluntary treatment because he or she has a significant or recent history of violence, is in an acute medical crisis, has active and severe substance abuse/dependence, is unable to consent to treatment, has repeatedly discontinued treatment against professional advice, or has refused prescribed treatments.

- The client has problems outside your area of expertise. Remember, you are not a master of every effective treatment, and therefore you are not competent to treat every problem or every person seeking treatment (because of his or her special needs, language skills, etc.).

Getting the Essential Data

FORM 19

The simplest way to ensure the collection of basic data is to fill out the first-contact record (see Form 19) as you talk to the caller. You might keep blank copies in your briefcase or datebook, so as to have one available when you get a referral.

First-Contact Record

Date: _____ Time: _____ A.M./P.M. Case record #: _____

Identification

Name of caller: _____ Name of client: _____

Caller is ❑ client ❑ spouse/partner of client ❑ parent ❑ legal guardian ❑ legal custodian

   ❑ other: _____ **Usable phone number** (day/eve/work/call): _____

Client's address: _____

_____

Referral source ("How did you get my name?"): _____

Chief complaint (in client's exact words): _____

_____

_____

Urgency estimate: ❑ Emergency; immediate interventions ❑ Serious disruption of functioning; act in next 24 hours ❑ Treatment needed; act soon/routine ❑ Wait for: _____

Triage

❑ Referral to: _____ for: _____

❑ First appointment scheduled for: _____ at _____ A.M./P.M. at (location): _____

Given: ❑ **Goals for first meeting?** ❑ **Directions? Map?** ❑ **Cancellation costs and method?**

Any questions? _____

_____

_____

Financial information

Credit card: Name on card: _____ Card #: _____ Exp. date: _____

Social Security #: _____ Driver's license #: _____

Things to do before first appointment

Call: _____ at: _____ about: _____

❑ Send preappointment letter, client information brochure, and these forms: ❑ Client demographic and clinical information forms ❑ Adult/child concerns checklist ❑ Developmental history ❑ Financial information form

❑ Agreement to pay ❑ NPP ❑ Other: _____

Performance monitoring

Return call: Date: _____ Time: _____ A.M./P.M. Initials of call returner: _____

Call response latency: Days: _____ Hours: _____

Appointment response latency: Days: _____ Hours: _____

This is a strictly confidential patient medical record. Redisclosure or transfer is expressly prohibited by law.

Form 19 will help you to cover these essential points:

1. Get the client's name, address, and phone number, spelled correctly (ask). Clarify the relationship to the identified patient if the caller is not the client, and get a practical telephone number. This is essential later if the client does not show or fails to keep the appointment, and you have to contact the client (or other person) to cancel, reschedule, or respond. (See Section 5.3.) Since confidentiality begins here, when you ask for a phone number, also ask whether it is all right to call that number and ask for the client by name. If the client wants to keep your appointments unknown by a coworker, boss, family member, or anyone else who might answer the phone, clarify this and make some arrangement (perhaps calling only during certain hours). Since you will be sending a preappointment package or letters or a bill for your services, confirm that the address is similarly confidential, or make alternative arrangements.

2. Identify the referrer by asking, "And how did you get my name?" This answer is needed for many insurance companies; more importantly, however, it tells you about your reputation and professional network, and perhaps the client's understanding of the problem. When appropriate later, you can ask for permission to send thanks to the referrer and confirmation that the referral was completed (see Section 2.6). Having the caller offer a name may also increase the likelihood of his or her coming in. If the referrer is someone the client will see again, such as a physician, he or she may be likely to ask about the referral. If the client got your name from an advertisement or presentation you made to a group, it may be helpful to ask, "What most appealed to you?", "What moved you to call?", or "Why did you call me in particular?" These are the clinically important "Why now?" questions. The answers are also central to your marketing efforts. All of these questions are natural bridges to discussing the presenting problem.

3. Focus on the chief complaint or chief concern. This information is needed so that you can decide whether the client has reached the wrong helper, and you can then make a better referral. It also gives you insight into the level of the client's understanding of his or her difficulties, which can guide your interventions. Elicit this information by asking the caller, "Please tell me briefly what problem has caused you to call me," or "Please tell me about what is troubling you" or "Please try to tell me the problem in one sentence."

4. Determine the urgency of the problem. Get enough information about the situation so that you can decide how urgent the problem is, and can then set the first appointment, refer, or add other treatment resources.

5. Schedule the first appointment, and write its date and time in your appointment book. The longer the caller has to wait to see you, the less likely he or she is to come in (see the discussion of reducing dropout in Section 5.3). Less than 24 hours is ideal service (you would want that for yourself), but it does not allow enough time to mail out the preappointment package.

6. Tell the client you want to use the first meeting to get an understanding of his or her situation, history, and problem, and the ways the client has been coping with the situation. A useful phrasing is "This will be an opportunity for you to find out if I can

understand your situation in a way that is useful to you." You can ask the client to bring a "list of issues" to provide some focus.

7. Tell the caller that "This time is set aside exclusively for you," and that if he or she cancels it will be "impossible to fill this time." Indicate what a loss it would be to the caller (delay in resolving problems, getting clarity or relief, taking action, etc.) if this appointment is not kept. It may be helpful to ask whether the client has any "reservations" or "reluctance" about entering treatment with you now. This is accepting, sensitive, and normalizing of resistance; builds rapport; allows you to address misconceptions; and is very likely to lower the rate of cancellations.

8. Briefly tell the caller how to cancel if an absolute emergency arises, so you won't be waiting in your office at 10 P.M. You can try to charge the caller if he or she cancels or fails to show, but it won't usually work and it creates bad feelings.

9. Ask whether the caller needs directions to your office. Keep in mind the time of day (for light, landmarks, and safety), the parking situation, and public transportation specifics. You can easily produce either a general map of the area around your office, or even a map with driving directions from the client's home to your office, from your computer (use www.maps.google.com or www.maps.yahoo.com) and mail this as part of your preappointment package (see Section 5.3).

10. Ask, "Do you have any questions?" The most usual question is about fees. Prepare a short and simple explanation and rehearse it several times, *today*. Most of us are uncomfortable talking plainly about money.

11. Consider asking for the financial information indicated in Form 19. This is optional, but it can serve two purposes: (a) If you suspect that something is not quite right in this call or that there is unstable or insincere motivation for treatment, it is wise to gather this information as a means of screening the client, as well as to state clearly that you will charge the client the full fee if he or she does not show up for the appointment. (b) Raising these questions and making this statement will indeed enable you to charge for your (lost) time and effort if the client fails to keep the appointment.

12. The bottom of Form 19 reminds you of what needs to be done before the first meeting. Make notes here and follow up immediately by making calls, sending your preappointment package, or whatever is most appropriate to each case.

After the first interview, in which the client information forms (see Forms 25, 26, and 27) are completed, place the first-contact record at the back of the new chart. The form has a place for entering a case number. If you file records by name, you don't need to use a number; however, if you want to keep all the records for members of a family together, or if the client's name changes, then an anonymous case number may be useful. If you need more room for responses, you can use the back of the form.

To recap, the purposes of Form 19 are to enable you to gather data (both demographic and clinical) for the initial appointment, and to support clinical decision making (triage) as early as possible. In addition, when completed, it can be used for "performance monitoring" of your practices at a later time. You can discover how long it takes to set up an appointment after an inquiry—information that MCOs believe to be important. You can also evaluate the distributions of your clients by age, gender, location, presenting problem, referral source, and so forth, in order to expand or focus your practice.

5.3   Phase 2: The Preappointment Package and Other Types of Preappointment Contact

The purposes and functions of sending the client some paperwork (including forms to fill out) before the first appointment include the following:

- It provides material evidence of your response to the client's needs; it solidifies the relationship and demonstrates your caring.

- It confirms the existence of an appointment and the beginning of treatment.

- Because it provides this evidence, it is likely to reduce the rate of no-shows.

- It can present you in a very professional manner—as organized, attentive, responsive, and thorough.

- It can help you to collect the basic information you need about the client.

- Sending the financial information form (Form 28) can get the client used to the idea of paying directly for your services, and can provide necessary information about insurance coverage. Other forms that are discussed in Section 5.4 could also be included in a preappointment package.

- Seeing how the client fills out the forms you send can give you information on motivation and competence for therapy.

- Sending your client information brochure (see Section 4.2) can help to socialize the client into the role of patient, answer unasked questions, and give him or her permission to express further concerns. It can also teach about informed consent, confidentiality, and your way of doing therapy.

The preappointment package and other ways of making preappointment contact are discussed next.

Ways to Respond before the Initial Appointment

The Appointment Confirmation Letter

The simplest response to a new client is to do nothing after the initial call. However, if there is time, confirming the appointment by means of a form letter allows you to add more information than just the phone call or than is possible on a small card. It can indicate how to cancel, how long to expect the appointment to take, and other possibilities. A letter also gives you the opportunity to give detailed instructions or to express your feelings.

FORM 20   Form 20 is an appointment confirmation letter that you can use or modify for your practice. It includes language designed to prevent a no-show because of ambivalence and anxiety. It incorporates some ideas from Browning and Browning (as applied in a book of forms by Berk et al., 1994).

A Personal Letter

You may want to use a more personal response to new clients than this form letter. Marc Andrews, ACSW, formerly of Pittsburgh, PA, does not schedule initial appointments during the first phone contact. He tells callers, "I feel it is in your best interest if you first have some information about who I am and how I conduct my private practice." He then sends them a long letter, modeled on the client information brochure. It outlines questions that might come up in the first several meetings. He feels that clients can make better decisions without the pressure to decide on the phone. He believes that this method has reduced his level of no-shows and increased the commitment of those who do follow through.

The Preappointment Package

Sending a confirmation letter can also allow the enclosure of other information to create a package. Mention of any specific enclosures can be added to the letter. As noted earlier, the client information brochure (see Section 4.2) may be useful to enclose, and several of the preliminary assessment forms provided in Section 5.4 can also be included with instructions for the client. The notice of privacy practices (NPP) required by the Health Insurance Portability and Accountability Act (HIPAA), and the related consent form, could be included (see Section 5.4).

For example, the letter might say, "In order to get a head start on our work, I would like some information. Please complete the enclosed forms and bring them to our first meeting," or "Please read through the 'Information for Clients' brochure and note your questions on it." Specific enclosures might include the adult concerns checklist or the child characteristics checklist, the financial information form, and the client demographic information form. If these forms are not sent in advance, they should be given at the first session. Again, see Section 5.4 for these forms and more detailed discussions of them.

Including a self-addressed stamped envelope with the package, or instructions to bring the forms to the first meeting (if time is short), will increase the likelihood that the client will complete the forms.

Ways of Dealing with No-Shows and Early Dropouts

When patients drop out of treatment even before the first appointment, it wastes time and energy, depresses new therapists, limits the interpretation of therapy research, and (of course) fails to benefit the patients. Patients who do not show, or who drop out early, often can be encouraged to continue into therapy with appropriate interventions like those described below. Also, at a minimum, you need to protect yourself legally from complaints of abandonment. *(Note:* For issues of termination and procedures for managing it, see Section 6.3.)

Dear _____,

First, let me thank you for choosing me for help with your problems. I intend and expect to provide you with high-quality professional services.

Your first appointment is scheduled as follows:

Day: _____ Date: _____ Time: _____ A.M./P.M. With: _____.

Please note the location of your appointment: _____.

Your first appointment may take 2 hours or more, because my office staff and I will ask you to fill out some forms. So plan your schedule with this in mind.

If you are absolutely unable to keep this appointment, please reschedule it at least 72 hours in advance by calling _____.

It is common for those new to therapy to feel both eager to get going and uncomfortable about starting the process of therapy. Do not let some awkwardness keep you from beginning what you know will be in your long-term best interest. If you have some questions and you feel you need answers before this appointment, please call and let us discuss these. I hope that, as in most situations in life, you will find that if you forge ahead, your worries will soon greatly lessen.

Over the years, my clients have found it very helpful to think about what they want to get from treatment or therapy. Please make some notes about your goals and what is most important to you, so that we can discuss these when we meet.

In order for us to serve you best, please bring *all* of your health insurance cards, so my staff and I can help determine your coverage, find out whom to bill, and give you some idea of what your costs will be.

The fee for this first visit will be $_____. My office policy is that payment must be made or insurance coverage must be arranged at the time of each visit. Even when you or the person legally responsible for the bill gives information about insurance coverage or other methods of payment, paying the charges for therapy is your responsibility.

I look forward to a productive and successful relationship.

Yours truly,

FORM 20. Letter of appointment confirmation.   From *The Paper Office*. Copyright 2008 by Edward L. Zuckerman. Permission to photocopy this form is granted to purchasers of this book for personal use only (see copyright page for details).

Following Up No-Shows

If a client does not show for a first appointment, there is not yet a treatment contract or a *strong* legal obligation upon the therapist. Making a phone call is better than sending a note. If you reschedule the initial appointment and the patient again fails to show, a simple note such as that below is all that is necessary; more than this may be seen by some patients as harassment.

Dear _____,

You, or your child, _____, did not keep your appointment on _____ or the rescheduled appointment you agreed to on _____. I believe you or your child can benefit from treatment. Because of my concern for your health and well-being, I will be available to you in the future. Or, if you like, I can refer you to another professional, therapist, or agency. If you no longer desire my services, and do not wish me to make a referral, I suggest you seek out another therapist immediately.

Yours truly,

_____

(Signature)

Although the following discussion goes somewhat beyond the preappointment context, I feel it is helpful and even essential to include it here. Of relevance at this point is Beckham's (1992) finding that missed and cancelled early sessions were highly predictive of treatment dropout. This suggests that therapists should make great efforts to build high rapport and to respond intensively to missed sessions.

Many therapists will not call a client who did not show for a regular appointment (or failed to keep or cancel an appointment), out of fear that they will hear complaints about their competence, helpfulness, or methods. Therapists should be more tough-skinned and realistic, and should follow up on every missed appointment. There are many reasons for doing this, including the ethical responsibility for continuity of care, and the need to avoid the possible abandonment of a patient. You can say, "I understood [or thought or believed] that we had an appointment at [date/time]. What happened?" Even though you are frustrated, if you express not hostility but acceptance of the client's anxiety, you will always be remembered fondly. Of course, you should not then try to solve large (or even medium-sized) problems on the phone. Lastly, calling is a way to practice your assertiveness (just what a therapist usually preaches) in the face of (fears of) rejection and overconcern with others' opinions, anger, or disappointment.

If the problem was not a simple mixup, ask why the client did not come in. If you sense some resistance, try using one of these responses:

- "Almost everyone would like to solve his or her problems without depending on someone else. This is the universal human need for independence. But there are times when you can't do it alone."

- "We therapists sometimes say that 'everyone wants to be happy but no one wants to change.' Change is always painful, no matter how desirable or necessary it may be. Perhaps this may be a reason why you missed our recent appointment."

- "Sometimes we think we're ready to start to change, but find we have underestimated the forces holding us back. What is true, however, is that if you face a fear, the fear shrinks. If you understand that it is the right thing to do but still feel afraid, pushing yourself to come to therapy can really work."

In my experience, about 50% of no-show cases can be attributed to a mix up in appointment times or some other easily resolvable or nonrecurring cause. A call is best for a missed appointment, and it should be made as soon as you realize a client hasn't shown—perhaps 20 minutes. Never wait more than 24 hours to make this important contact. If you call a no-show, he or she will usually come in, and the result will be a good course of treatment. The client may have had an attack of resistance or reactance, forgotten, "felt better," had an emergency, or simply been ashamed of not showing up and too embarrassed to call.

Other than missed early sessions, research seems to indicate that the only predictor variables for treatment dropout are lower socioeconomic class, initial negative impression of the therapist, and therapist–client differences in understanding of the disorder and its therapy (Beckham, 1992; Corning et al., 2007). You can change all but the first of these. Sattler (1977) found the following *not* to predict dropout: age, sex, psychiatric diagnosis, level of education, and patient–therapist racial similarity. This last has been researched more thoroughly (see Maramba & Nagayama Hall, 2002, for a meta-analysis) and findings have been quite consistent (Sparks et al., 2003). Research aimed at identifying predictors of premature termination has been less consistent, most likely because of methodological–analytical deficiencies (Corning, Malofeeva, & Bucchiarini, 2007) and conflicting operational definitions of premature termination (Hatchett & Park, 2003).

Other Strategies for Preventing No-Shows and Dropouts

Getting clients to show up, to attend longer, or not to drop out can also be aided by the following methods (Pekarik, 1985; Kobayashi et al., 1998):

- Shortening the waiting time until an appointment or between appointments.

- Offering services at alternative hours or days (e.g., seeing clients on Sundays or at 7 A.M. or 10 P.M.).

- Using letters (not postcards—too public) and telephone calls as prompts for future appointments.

- Rapidly promoting a therapeutic alliance.

- Setting a focus of treatment.

- Writing contracts and treatment plans with a range of assignments.

- Contracting for a specific time limit to therapy (say, 12 sessions).

- Involving significant others in treatment efforts.

- Supporting and directing the self-monitoring of symptoms, contexts, responses, and so forth with checklists and diaries.

- Demonstrating greater therapist activity. Passivity, awaiting the best time to intervene, or using anxiety-arousing techniques may be counterproductive.

- Providing usable feedback (videotapes can demonstrate progress) and positive reinforcement for attendance.

- Providing pretherapy socialization or preparation. In particular, two sets of strategies have been found very useful in reducing dropout rates, especially among those most at risk. The first set includes psychotherapy preparatory techniques such as role induction, vicarious therapy pretraining, and experiential pretraining (Derman & Connors, 1999, p. xx; see also Orne & Wender, 1968, Katz et al., 2004, and Reis & Brown, 2006). Second, motivational interviewing methods (Rollnick et al., 2008; Swartz et al., 2007) have been found effective because they reduce ambivalence and enhance commitment to therapy.

However, bear in mind that therapists and clients may view "dropping out" differently. Patients seem to expect significant improvement in only a few sessions. Some 40% of community mental health center patients attend only 1–2 visits, and less than a quarter attend even brief therapy's minimum of 10 visits (Ciarlo, 1979). In private practice, over half of the patients do not attend for 10 visits (Koss, 1979). Although those who attend for only 1–2 sessions have poor overall therapy outcomes (Gottschalk et al., 1967), a substantial percentage report being satisfied with the improvements gained in 4–6 sessions. Clients apparently expect therapy to last for fewer than 10 sessions, and anticipate improvement within 5 visits (Garfield & Wolpin, 1963).

5.4   Phase 3: The New Client's Arrival for a First Meeting

Ways of Collecting Further Client Information

The initial telephone call with the new client should give you guidance for the additional information you need to gather. You can note the specific forms you want to have completed at the bottom of the first-contact form. If the client has not been mailed these forms in advance, they can be filled out in the waiting room before your first meeting. Using your notes, you or your receptionist can have the forms ready and waiting for the client on his or her arrival for the first appointment. The client can be asked to arrive 20–30 minutes before the interview "to complete some necessary paperwork while you wait for the therapist."

Having this information before you first meet the client face to face is very desirable. For example, without the financial information, you might start a relationship with a client whom you really cannot afford to see. Also, the client clinical information form (Form 25) will tell you whether you need to ask the client to fill out more detailed information on his or her drug/alcohol use or legal problems.

An alternative, but less reliable, procedure is to give these forms to the client after the first session and ask him or her to return them by mail the next day. Include a self-addressed stamped envelope, to increase the likelihood of return.

Information materials and forms suitable for completion by the client in the waiting room (or in the preappointment package) include the following:

- Clients must be told how you will handle their information *before* they provide it, both for informed consent and because HIPAA requires this. Your NPP (Forms 21 and 22) must be provided, and the privacy practices consent form (Form 23) must be signed at the first contact between client and clinician. In fact, if your practice has a website, your NPP must be posted there for the same reason.

- The client demographic information form (Form 24) collects basic factual identifying information. It expands on and will replace the first-contact form.

- The client clinical information form (Form 25) is for more personal information, and so it may be better in some situations to offer it when the client is alone in the waiting room, or even to wait until the interview to give it.

- The brief health information form (Form 26) collects information on health problems, medications, and treatment sources. The chemical use survey (Form 27) collects more specific data on alcohol and drug use.

- The financial information form (Form 28) collects essential information about insurance and other resources.

- For those clients who do not use insurance, or for whom insurance will not cover the entire fee charged, the agreement to pay for professional services (Form 29) clarifies payment obligations.

- Problem checklists efficiently survey the client's functioning and understanding of problem areas; they also encourage the identification of difficulties, which the client may be reluctant to state during the initial call. I offer two forms—an adult checklist of concerns (Form 30) and a child checklist of characteristics (Form 31). For children, there is also a child developmental history record (Form 32). You could add to this package symptom checklists (e.g., the Symptom Checklist 90, or SCL-90), specialized questionnaires (say, for attention-deficit/hyperactivity disorder), or pre–post measures (e.g., the Beck Depression Inventory). However, do not give clients these standardized clinical questionnaires or other tests to take home, because of test security and ethical considerations.

Let us now look at each of these in more detail.

The Notice of Privacy Practices (NPP) and the Related Consent Form

As noted throughout this book, HIPAA requires all covered entities (CEs) who provide treatment to tell clients how they will safeguard the client's protected health information (PHI) from unauthorized disclosures, and how it is used in your practice and disclosed to other CEs for purposes of treatment, payment, and health care operations (TPO). Your

NPP is designed to inform the client about your policies and procedures designed to maintain privacy. It is to be made available as early as possible in the relationship, so that no PHI is shared unless the client knows what you might do with it. The consent form that the client signs is not necessarily an agreement to your privacy policies or a consent to release of information; it simply indicates that the client agrees that he or she has been exposed to your NPP.

What Your NPP Must Contain

The NPP is an official and legally required document, and so it should reflect your way of working just as your practice brochure does. It should be integrated into your client intake, education, and orientation forms. The U.S. Department of Health and Human Services (DHHS), which sets rules for HIPAA, says: "Covered entities are encouraged to provide individuals with the most specific notice possible." The NPP must present and explain at least the following required items if it is not to be considered legally defective.

The NPP must be headed with this statement: "THIS NOTICE DESCRIBES HOW MEDICAL INFORMATION ABOUT YOU MAY BE USED AND DISCLOSED AND HOW YOU CAN GET ACCESS TO THIS INFORMATION. PLEASE REVIEW IT CAREFULLY." It must then contain statements that do the following:

- Describe all the uses and disclosures of PHI that you are permitted or required to make for TPO without authorization, including those uses or disclosures subject to the consent requirements, such as to law enforcement and public health agencies. You must include at least one example of each type of uses and disclosures you can make in terms of TPO.

- List the client's rights to do these things:

  - Request restrictions on certain uses and disclosures, including the statement that you are not required to agree to a requested restriction.

  - Receive confidential communications of PHI. This means that the client can arrange for you to send mail or bills to certain addresses, or limit phone calls to retain privacy. (In practice, we are accustomed to making these arrangements, so I have not included a form for documenting them; continue to mark in your progress notes any arrangements to which you agree.)

  - Inspect and receive a copy of his or her PHI.

  - Amend his or her PHI.

  - Receive an accounting of disclosures of PHI beyond those used for TPO.

  - Receive a paper copy of the NPP upon request. You could explain that you have the option to change the terms of the NPP and are not obligated to tell clients when you do change your NPP, and explain how the client may obtain a copy of your revised NPP in the future.

- Explain your legal duty and practices to maintain the privacy of the client's PHI and inform the client that you will abide by the terms of the current NPP.

- Describe how to lodge a complaint if the client comes to believe that his or her privacy rights have been violated.

- State that you will not disclose the PHI for other purposes without the client's written authorization.

- Inform the client that your business associates will comply with the HIPAA regulations and procedures.

- Show the date on which the NPP became effective.

These privacy protection rules interact with your state and other laws, court decisions, local practices, and professional ethics. The versions of NPPs presented in this book are based on HIPAA and have to be considered in light of other, more stringently protective state or federal laws and regulations, as required by Section 164.520(b)(1)(ii)(C) of HIPAA. Please keep in mind that this cross-walking of federal and state rules is an evolving process as new laws, court decisions, unintended consequences, and ramifications come to light. Therefore, I recommend that you schedule a reexamination and possible revision of your NPP at 6-month intervals for the next year or two.

Other Required Procedures

- **Separate the NPP from the consent form.** The HIPAA Privacy Rule prohibits the NPP and consent form from being combined into a single document. Therefore, put your consent form (Form 23) on a separate page, and give it a title making it clear that it is not a continuation of the NPP.

- **Post the NPP prominently in your office.** You must post your entire NPP in a clear and prominent location. Placing it in your waiting area is probably sufficient. Although you might make a large chart, alternatively you could place the pages in a binder inside sheet protectors, or laminate the pages. You could offer the binder or the laminated pages to all new clients and tell them that copies are available from your receptionist or in a rack in the waiting room. This will reduce copying costs and simplify your providing the latest versions to returning clients.

- **Post the NPP prominently on your website.** If you maintain a website for your practice, you must "prominently" post your NPP at the site. You must indicate that clients can obtain a paper copy of the NPP and tell them how to do so. If your site offers or explains any of your clinical services (not, I believe, just information—say, about disorders), you must direct clients to read your NPP before receiving your service.

- **The client must review the NPP and sign the consent form by the first meeting.** This must be done "no later than the date of the first service delivery." Ideally, you could supply the NPP before you see the client by making it part of your client introduction package, thus giving him or her time to receive what the regulations call adequate notice. In any case, the client should be made to review the NPP and sign the consent form before you see him or her.

- **Provide any revised NPP to active clients within 60 days.** CEs are required to "provide a revised notice to individuals then covered by the plan within 60 days of a material revision" (see www.hhs.gov/ocr/hipaa/guidelines/notice.rtf). If you change it, you do not need to mail copies to your continuing clients or even furnish it to them unless asked to do so. Of course, you would provide the revised version to new clients. When you change your NPP, you do *not* have to get a new acknowledgment of receipt of the notice. Note that this rule does not specify any kind of acknowledgment or evidence of your having provided the revised version.

- **Use understandable language.** HIPAA requires the NPP to be written in "plain language," so that an average reader will understand his or her rights. It does not state a reading level. It does not state "in English," nor does it require versions in any other language or alternative form of communication. However, other laws do mandate foreign-language versions (e.g., Title VI of the Civil Rights Act of 1964). Without these, the goal of having clients understand their rights may not be achieved, and the clients' confidence in your commitment to privacy may be weakened; therefore, so you should make the effort to provide a version your clients can understand. Versions in many languages are available from many organizations, which you can find by searching the Web.

- Although you are not required by law to do so, you should print the NPP in at least 12-point type (like this) or 14-point type (like this) for those likely to have weaker vision, so that everyone can read it.

An Unabridged NPP

FORM 21 An unabridged version of an NPP can be found in Form 21. I have simplified and condensed the required language for the clients of a typical mental health professional and a small practice. Please do not adopt it uncritically; your NPP should be tailored to the way your office actually works, so only promise what you will deliver. The regulations specifically require this and so offer no standard NPP.

- In this version, I have used the plural "we" to refer to your practice, but you may want to substitute a less formal "I" where appropriate or a more formal practice name. Also, this version does not include disclosures for fund raising, but does include some on marketing.

- The initial paragraph in all capitals is required to be included verbatim and prominently displayed near the top of the page.

- There are two places in this NPP where you should mention whether or not you allow clients access to your psychotherapy notes if you have decided to keep them (see this book's Section 6.2 for more on this subject). The first is in Form 21's section B. In the last paragraph is the sentence "In some very rare situations, you cannot see all of what is in your records." This might be followed by a mention of your notes. The second instance is in section E (item 3).

Notice of Privacy Practices

THIS NOTICE DESCRIBES HOW MEDICAL INFORMATION ABOUT YOU MAY BE USED AND DISCLOSED AND HOW YOU CAN GET ACCESS TO THIS INFORMATION. PLEASE REVIEW IT CAREFULLY.

Privacy is a very important concern for all those who come to this office. It is also complicated, because of the many federal and state laws and our professional ethics. Because the rules are so complicated, some parts of this notice are very detailed, and you probably will have to read them several times to understand them. If you have any questions, our privacy officer will be happy to help you understand our procedures and your rights. His or her name and address are at the end of this notice.

Contents of this notice

A. Introduction: To our clients
B. What we mean by your medical information
C. Privacy and the laws about privacy
D. How your protected health information can be used and shared
   1. Uses and disclosures with your consent
      a. The basic uses and disclosures: For treatment, payment, and health care operations
      b. Other uses and disclosures in health care
   2. Uses and disclosures that *require* your authorization
   3. Uses and disclosures that *don't require* your consent or authorization
      a. When required by law
      b. For law enforcement purposes
      c. For public health activities
      d. Relating to decedents
      e. For specific government functions
      f. To prevent a serious threat to health or safety
   4. Uses and disclosures where you have *an opportunity to object*
   5. An *accounting* of disclosures we have made
E. Your rights concerning your health information
F. If you have questions or problems

A. Introduction: To our clients

This notice will tell you how we handle your medical information. It tells how we use this information here in this office, how we share it with other professionals and organizations, and how you can see it. We want you to know all of this so that you can make the best decisions for yourself and your family. If you have any questions or want to know more about anything in this notice, please ask our privacy officer for more explanations or more details.

B. What we mean by your medical information

Each time you visit us or any doctor's office, hospital, clinic, or other health care provider, information is collected about you and your physical and mental health. It may be information about your past, present, or future health or conditions, or the tests and treatment you got from us or from others, or about payment for health care. The information we collect from you is called **"PHI,"** which stands for **"protected health information."** This information goes into your **medical or health care records** in our office.

(cont.)

FORM 21. Notice of privacy practices (unabridged) (p. 1 of 5). From *The Paper Office*. Copyright 2008 by Edward L. Zuckerman. Permission to photocopy this form is granted to purchasers of this book for personal use only (see copyright page for details).

In this office, your PHI is likely to include these kinds of information:

- Your history: Things that happened to you as a child; your school and work experiences; your marriage and other personal history.

- Reasons you came for treatment: Your problems, complaints, symptoms, or needs.

- Diagnoses: These are the medical terms for your problems or symptoms.

- A treatment plan: This is a list of the treatments and other services that we think will best help you.

- Progress notes: Each time you come in, we write down some things about how you are doing, what we notice about you, and what you tell us.

- Records we get from others who treated you or evaluated you.

- Psychological test scores, school records, and other reports.

- Information about medications you took or are taking.

- Legal matters.

- Billing and insurance information

There may also be other kinds of information that go into your health care records here.

We use PHI for many purposes. For example, we may use it:

- To plan your care and treatment.

- To decide how well our treatments are working for you.

- When we talk with other health care professionals who are also treating you, such as your family doctor or the professional who referred you to us.

- To show that you actually received services from us, which we billed to you or to your health insurance company.

- For teaching and training other health care professionals.

- For medical or psychological research.

- For public health officials trying to improve health care in this area of the country.

- To improve the way we do our job by measuring the results of our work.

When you understand what is in your record and what it is used for, you can make better decisions about who, when, and why others should have this information.

Although your health care records in our office are our physical property, the information belongs to you. You can read your records, and if you want a copy we can make one for you (but we may charge you for the costs of copying and mailing, if you want it mailed to you). In some very rare situations, you cannot see all of what is in your records. If you find anything in your records that you think is incorrect or believe that something important is missing, you can ask us to amend (add information to) your records, although in some rare situations we don't have to agree to do that. If you want, our privacy officer, whose name is at the end of this notice, can explain more about this.

C. Privacy and the laws about privacy

We are required to tell you about privacy because of a federal law, the Health Insurance Portability and Accountability Act of 1996 (HIPAA). HIPAA requires us to keep your PHI private and to give you this notice about our legal duties and our privacy practices. We will obey the rules described in this notice. If we change our privacy practices, they will apply to all the PHI we keep. We will also post the new notice of privacy practices in our office where everyone can see. You or anyone else can also get a copy from our privacy officer at any time. It is also posted on our website at [URL].

D. How your protected health information can be used and shared

Except in some special circumstances, when we use your PHI in this office or disclose it to others, we share only the **minimum necessary** PHI needed for those other people to do their jobs. The law gives you rights to know about

(cont.)

your PHI, to know how it is used, and to have a say in how it is shared. So we will tell you more about what we do with your information.

Mainly, we will use and disclose your PHI for routine purposes to provide for your care, and we will explain more about these below. For other uses, we must tell you about them and ask you to sign a written authorization form. However, the law also says that there are some uses and disclosures that don't need your consent or authorization.

1. Uses and disclosures with your consent

After you have read this notice, you will be asked to sign a separate **consent form** to allow us to use and share your PHI. In almost all cases we intend to use your PHI here or share it with other people or organizations to provide treatment to you, arrange for payment for our services, or some other business functions called "health care operations."

In other words, we need information about you and your condition to provide care to you. You have to agree to let us collect the information, use it, and share it to care for you properly. Therefore, you must sign the consent form before we begin to treat you. If you do not agree and consent we cannot treat you.

a. The basic uses and disclosures: For treatment, payment, and health care operations

Next we will tell you more about how your information will be used for treatment, payment, and health care operations.

For treatment. We use your medical information to provide you with psychological treatments or services. These might include individual, family, or group therapy; psychological, educational, or vocational testing; treatment planning; or measuring the benefits of our services.

We may share your PHI with others who provide treatment to you. We are likely to share your information with your personal physician. If you are being treated by a team, we can share some of your PHI with the team members, so that the services you receive will work best together. The other professionals treating you will also enter their findings, the actions they took, and their plans into your medical record, and so we all can decide what treatments work best for you and make up a treatment plan. We may refer you to other professionals or consultants for services we cannot provide. When we do this, we need to tell them things about you and your conditions. We will get back their findings and opinions, and those will go into your records here. If you receive treatment in the future from other professionals, we can also share your PHI with them. These are some examples so that you can see how we use and disclose your PHI for treatment.

For payment. We may use your information to bill you, your insurance, or others, so we can be paid for the treatments we provide to you. We may contact your insurance company to find out exactly what your insurance covers. We may have to tell them about your diagnoses, what treatments you have received, and the changes we expect in your conditions. We will need to tell them about when we met, your progress, and other similar things.

For health care operations. Using or disclosing your PHI for health care operations goes beyond our care and your payment. For example, we may use your PHI to see where we can make improvements in the care and services we provide. We may be required to supply some information to some government health agencies, so they can study disorders and treatment and make plans for services that are needed. If we do, your name and personal information will be removed from what we send.

b. Other uses and disclosures in health care

Appointment reminders. We may use and disclose your PHI to reschedule or remind you of appointments for treatment or other care. If you want us to call or write to you only at your home or your work, or you prefer some other way to reach you, we usually can arrange that. Just tell us.

Treatment alternatives. We may use and disclose your PHI to tell you about or recommend possible treatments or alternatives that may be of help to you.

Other benefits and services. We may use and disclose your PHI to tell you about health-related benefits or services that may be of interest to you.

Research. We may use or share your PHI to do research to improve treatments—for example, comparing two treatments for the same disorder, to see which works better or faster or costs less. In all cases, your name, address, and other personal information will be removed from the information given

(cont.)

to researchers. If they need to know who you are, we will discuss the research project with you, and we will not send any information unless you sign a special authorization form.

Business associates. We hire other businesses to do some jobs for us. In the law, they are called our "business associates." Examples include a copy service to make copies of your health records, and a billing service to figure out, print, and mail our bills. These business associates need to receive some of your PHI to do their jobs properly. To protect your privacy, they have agreed in their contract with us to safeguard your information.

2. Uses and disclosures that require your authorization

If we want to use your information for any purpose besides those described above, we need your permission on an **authorization form.** We don't expect to need this very often. If you do allow us to use or disclose your PHI, you can cancel that permission in writing at any time. We would then stop using or disclosing your information for that purpose. Of course, we cannot take back any information we have already disclosed or used with your permission.

3. Uses and disclosures that don't require your consent or authorization

The law lets us use and disclose some of your PHI without your consent or authorization in some cases. Here are some examples of when we might do this.

a. When required by law

There are some federal, state, or local laws that require us to disclose PHI:

- We have to report suspected child abuse.

- If you are involved in a lawsuit or legal proceeding, and we receive a subpoena, discovery request, or other lawful process, we may have to release some of your PHI. We will only do so after trying to tell you about the request, consulting your lawyer, or trying to get a court order to protect the information they requested.

- We have to disclose some information to the government agencies that check on us to see that we are obeying the privacy laws.

b. For law enforcement purposes

We may release medical information if asked to do so by a law enforcement official to investigate a crime or criminal.

c. For public health activities

We may disclose some of your PHI to agencies that investigate diseases or injuries.

d. Relating to decedents

We may disclose PHI to coroners, medical examiners, or funeral directors, and to organizations relating to organ, eye, or tissue donations or transplants.

e. For specific government functions

We may disclose PHI of military personnel and veterans to government benefit programs relating to eligibility and enrollment. We may disclose your PHI to workers' compensation and disability programs, to correctional facilities if you are an inmate, or to other government agencies for national security reasons.

f. To prevent a serious threat to health or safety

If we come to believe that there is a serious threat to your health or safety, or that of another person or the public, we can disclose some of your PHI. We will only do this to persons who can prevent the danger.

(cont.)

4. Uses and disclosures where you have an opportunity to object

We can share some information about you with your family or close others. We will only share information with those involved in your care and anyone else you choose, such as close friends or clergy. We will ask you which persons you want us to tell, and what information you want us to tell them, about your condition or treatment. You can tell us what you want, and we will honor your wishes as long as it is not against the law.

If it is an emergency, and so we cannot ask if you disagree, we can share information if we believe that it is what you would have wanted and if we believe it will help you if we do share it. If we do share information, in an emergency, we will tell you as soon as we can. If you don't approve we will stop, as long as it is not against the law.

5. An accounting of disclosures we have made

When we disclose your PHI, we may keep some records of whom we sent it to, when we sent it, and what we sent. You can get an accounting (a list) of many of these disclosures.

E. Your rights concerning your health information

1. You can ask us to communicate with you about your health and related issues in a particular way or at a certain place that is more private for you. For example, you can ask us to call you at home, and not at work, to schedule or cancel an appointment. We will try our best to do as you ask.

2. You have the right to ask us to limit what we tell people involved in your care or with payment for your care, such as family members and friends. We don't have to agree to your request, but if we do agree, we will honor it except when it is against the law, or in an emergency, or when the information is necessary to treat you.

3. You have the right to look at the health information we have about you, such as your medical and billing records. You can get a copy of these records, but we may charge you. Contact our privacy officer to arrange how to see your records. (See below.)

4. If you believe that the information in your records is incorrect or missing something important, you can ask us to make additions to your records to correct the situation. You have to make this request in writing and send it to our privacy officer. You must also tell us the reasons you want to make the changes.

5. You have the right to a copy of this notice. If we change this notice, we will post the new one in our waiting area, and you can always get a copy from the privacy officer.

6. You have the right to file a complaint if you believe your privacy rights have been violated. You can file a complaint with our privacy officer and with the Secretary of the U.S. Department of Health and Human Services. All complaints must be in writing. Filing a complaint will not change the health care we provide to you in any way.

You may have other rights that are granted to you by the laws of our state, and these may be the same as or different from the rights described above. We will be happy to discuss these situations with you now or as they arise.

F. If you have questions or problems

If you need more information or have questions about the privacy practices described above, please speak to the privacy officer, whose name and telephone number are listed below. If you have a problem with how your PHI has been handled, or if you believe your privacy rights have been violated, contact the privacy officer. As stated above, you have the right to file a complaint with us and with the Secretary of the U.S. Department of Health and Human Services. We promise that we will not in any way limit your care here or take any actions against you if you complain.

If you have any questions or problems about this notice or our health information privacy policies, please contact our privacy officer, who is _____ and can be reached by phone at _____ or by e-mail at _____.

The effective date of this notice is _____ [April 14, 2003, or whatever date your practice became HIPAA-compliant.]

- Under the "For treatment" heading in section D (part 1a) is the sentence "We are likely to share your information with your personal physician." You may want to clarify or constrain this statement.

- Under the "Other uses in health care" heading in section D (part 1b), is a paragraph on "Other benefits and services." This marketing use of PHI is controversial and rare for mental health work. You may decide to delete this.

- You may need to make a number of adjustments to section D (part 3). In regard to mandatory reporting of various abuses (part 3a), note that some states use a suspicion standard and others a belief standard, so make the appropriate alterations.

- Regarding lawsuits and legal proceedings (section D, part 3a), when you are contacted by the client's lawyer or subpoenaed by a court order, you as the professional are required to assert, on clients' behalf, their right to privileged communications.

- You might consider omitting "Relating to decedents" (section D, part 3d). This is a rare situation for therapists, as are the situations relating to public health and law enforcement. But you should be clear on these points. On preventing a serious threat to health or safety (section D, part 3f), you should review your state's handling of duty-to-warn situations and then decide on your phrasing of this point.

- Medicare's HIPAA website now has a suggested and sample NPP, *but only for Medicare clients* (see at www.medicare.gov/privacypractices.asp). It is about two pages long and has a reading level of 9th–10th grade. If you intend to use it, you will need to add any variations imposed by more stringent laws in your state and adapt it to your office procedures.

- A long and formal version of the required contents, entitled *HIPAA Privacy Rule Checklists, Section 164.520, Notice of Privacy Practices for Protected Health Information*, can be found at www.nchica.org/HIPAAresources/samples/portal.asp. This checklist can be very helpful if you are designing your own NPP or struggling to integrate the NPP's contents with your current client information brochure.

- Since NPPs must be posted to CEs' websites, doing a Web search with "notice of privacy practices" (not just NPP) will allow you to see how others are coping with this regulation.

A Shorter NPP

The government recognizes that an unabridged NPP can be intimidating to clients and allows you to use **a shorter version,** which must be accompanied by the longer version. I recommend mailing the shorter version with your introductory packet to new clients, and offering them the longer version when you first meet.

FORM 22   The second, briefer version can be found in Form 22. This may be more suitable when your local rules are more stringent and protective than HIPAA's, but you still need to comply with HIPAA by furnishing an NPP. The shorter version is also suitable if you do not want to offer clients more text that might confuse, distract, or alarm them, but it

Notice of Privacy Practices (Brief Version)

THIS NOTICE DESCRIBES HOW MEDICAL INFORMATION ABOUT YOU MAY BE USED AND DISCLOSED AND HOW YOU CAN GET ACCESS TO THIS INFORMATION. PLEASE REVIEW IT CAREFULLY.

Our commitment to your privacy

Our practice is dedicated to maintaining the privacy of your personal health information as part of providing professional care. We are also required by law to keep your information private. These laws are complicated, but we must give you this important information. This is a shorter version of the attached, full, legally required notice of privacy practices. Please talk to our privacy officer (see the end of this form) about any questions or problems.

How we use and disclose your protected health information with your consent

We will use the information we collect about you mainly to provide you with **treatment**, to arrange **payment** for our services, and for some other business activities that are called, in the law, **health care operations.** After you have read this notice we will ask you to sign a **consent form** to let us use and share your information in these ways. If you do not consent and sign this form, we cannot treat you.

    If we want to use or send, share, or release your information for other purposes, we will discuss this with you and ask you to sign an authorization form to allow this.

Disclosing your health information without your consent

There are some times when the laws require us to use or share your information. For example:
1. When there is a serious threat to your or another's health and safety or to the public. We will only share information with persons who are able to help prevent or reduce the threat.
2. When we are required to do so by lawsuits and other legal or court proceedings.
3. If a law enforcement official requires us to do so.
4. For workers' compensation and similar benefit programs.

There are some other rare situations. They are described in the longer version of our notice of privacy practices.

Your rights regarding your health information

1. You can ask us to communicate with you in a particular way or at a certain place that is more private for you. For example, you can ask us to call you at home, and not at work, to schedule or cancel an appointment. We will try our best to do as you ask.
2. You can ask us to limit what we tell people involved in your care or the payment for your care, such as family members and friends.
3. You have the right to look at the health information we have about you, such as your medical and billing records. You can get a copy of these records, but we may charge you for it. Contact our privacy officer to arrange how to see your records. See below.
4. If you believe that the information in your records is incorrect or missing something important, you can ask us to make additions to your records to correct the situation. You have to make this request in writing and send it to our privacy officer. You must also tell us the reasons you want to make the changes.
5. You have the right to a copy of this notice. If we change this notice, we will post the new version in our waiting area, and you can always get a copy of it from the privacy officer.
6. You have the right to file a complaint if you believe your privacy rights have been violated. You can file a complaint with our privacy officer and with the Secretary of the U.S. Department of Health and Human Services. All complaints must be in writing. Filing a complaint will not change the health care we provide to you in any way.

Also, you may have other rights that are granted to you by the laws of our state, and these may be the same as or different from the rights described above. We will be happy to discuss these situations with you now or as they arise.

    If you have any questions regarding this notice or our health information privacy policies, please contact our privacy officer, who is _____ and can be reached by phone at _____ or by e-mail at _____ .

    The effective date of this notice is _____ .

should not be used as a substitute for the longer version, which you must offer or make available.

Because of concerns raised by practitioners that an unabridged NPP is too long for routine use, too complex for most contacts, and confusing for many, DHHS has stated that a *layered* notice is acceptable. This means using a shorter version as a top page of the longer version; however, it cannot substitute for the longer version and must be written in plain language as well. The version in Form 22 should be suitable and still fits on one page. The paragraph in capitals cannot be altered and must be displayed prominently near the top of the page.

Your shorter versions can be tailored to the population of clients you see in your practice. For example, if your population has lower reading skills, a simplified version might be more appropriate, along with the offer of a fuller (documented) discussion of their questions. If you see a population whose information is likely to be highly sensitive, you can emphasize or expand the sections (and incorporate local laws) about what information is shared with whom under what conditions. The NPPs in Forms 21 and 22 have both been reorganized and reworded from the way the contents are presented in the regulations, to make reading and understanding them easier for clients.

Documenting Consent to Privacy Practices

After clients have been notified of their rights (though reading the NPP or having it read or explained to them), a formal acknowledgment of having been informed of your procedures and their rights is sought. This is accomplished by having them sign what is called a "consent" form—but it is *not* a consent to treatment or an authorization for having PHI used or disclosed. It is simply an indication that the client has been exposed to your rules for handling PHI. It would more properly be called an "assent" or "acknowledgment" form. According to DHHS no more is required because clients' consent to the sharing of information is implied by their seeking treatment. HIPAA incorporates this common-sensical view.

The HIPAA regulations do not provide a model consent form, but Section 164.506(c) does specify the information to be included:

- The client's PHI may be used and disclosed by the CE to carry out TPO. Actually, you have to specify which uses and which disclosures your office requires to perform specific parts of TPO.

- For more information on uses and disclosures, the client is referred to the NPP.

- The client has a right to review the NPP before signing the consent form.

- The client has a right to request restrictions on uses and disclosures of PHI for TPO (see below). The client must be told that you do not have to agree to these requests, but that if you do, the agreement is binding,

- The client can revoke the consent in writing, but not retroactively.

- The consent form should be signed and dated.

Other points about HIPAA consents:

- Because clients have to read the current version of your NPP, there is a space on the consent form to indicate what version (by date) of the NPP they have seen.

- The consent form must be visually and organizationally separate from the NPP, as noted earlier. Putting it on a separate page should do. And it must be signed and dated separately from any other consents, such as a consent for assignment of benefits, or the more traditional release/request for records.

- You must retain this consent form for 6 years from the last date it was in effect—the date of your last treatment.

- Consents do not have a specified duration, and so should be considered to be in effect for at least the duration of an episode of treatment. However, they can be revoked.

FORM 23   Form 23 is a sample consent form written to be a more explicit agreement to the procedures in the NPP. I have written it in plain language, which you can and should tailor to your own practice and needs. The fourth paragraph, which begins in **boldface,** may cause some patients to hesitate or even refuse; they may not want so little control over their information, especially when they do not yet know what information you will be collecting. It may be best to draw every client's attention to this paragraph and explain how you always ask clients for an authorization to release information and do not rely solely on this consent. In this way, they will know exactly what will be released and to whom.

The regulations concerning the consent form can be found at Section 164.506(c) of HIPAA, which specifies all the required contents of such a form. Form 23 incorporates all of these. A consent form in Spanish is available online (www.mda-ltd.com/privacy_notice1.htm).

Obtaining Client Demographic Information

FORM 24   When completed, the client demographic information form (Form 24) replaces the first-contact form, because it is more complete and can be placed first in the client's file, thus becoming the "face sheet." Again, it can be included in the preappointment package to be completed at home or given to the client in the waiting room at the first meeting. As its name implies, it is straightforward, is primarily demographic, and can easily be filled out by the client alone. By contrast, the client clinical information form (see Form 25, below) seeks more private and detailed information that may need your guidance, and it may be better to complete this form with the client during your first interview. Both of these forms are designed for those over 18 years of age.

Note: If you include Section C in Form 24, it may be useful also to include here the "no discrimination" clause from the client information brochure (Section 4.2 of this book).

Consent to Use and Disclose Your Health Information

This form is an agreement between you, _____ and me/us, _____. When we use the words "you" and "your" below, this can mean you, your child, a relative, or some other person if you have written his or her name here: _____.

When we examine, test, diagnose, treat, or refer you, we will be collecting what the law calls "protected health information" (PHI) about you. We need to use this information in our office to decide on what treatment is best for you and to provide treatment to you. We may also share this information with others to arrange payment for your treatment, to help carry out certain business or government functions, or to help provide other treatment to you.

By signing this form, you are also agreeing to let us use your PHI and to send it to others for the purposes described above. Your signature below acknowledges that you have read or heard our notice of privacy practices, which explains in more detail what your rights are and how we can use and share your information.

If you do not sign this form agreeing to our privacy practices, we cannot treat you. In the future, we may change how we use and share your information, and so we may change our notice of privacy practices. If we do change it, you can get a copy from our website, www._____, or by calling us at _____, or from our privacy officer.

If you are concerned about your PHI, you have the right to ask us not to use or share some of it for treatment, payment, or administrative purposes. You will have to tell us what you want in writing. Although we will try to respect your wishes, we are not required to accept these limitations. However, if we do agree, we promise to do as you asked.

After you have signed this consent, you have the right to revoke it by writing to our privacy officer. We will then stop using or sharing your PHI, but we may already have used or shared some of it, and we cannot change that.

_____   _____
Signature of client or his or her personal representative   Date

_____   _____
Printed name of client or personal representative   Relationship to the client

_____
Description of personal representative's authority

_____
Signature of authorized representative of this office or practice

Date of NPP _____   ❏ Copy given to the client/parent/personal representative

---

FORM 23. Consent to privacy practices. From *The Paper Office*. Copyright 2008 by Edward L. Zuckerman. Permission to photocopy this form is granted to purchasers of this book for personal use only (see copyright page for details).

Client Information Form 1

Today's date: _____

Note: If you have been a patient here before, please fill in only the information that has changed.

A. Identification

Your name: _____ Date of birth: _____ Age: _____

Nicknames or aliases: _____ Social Security #: _____

Home street address: _____ Apt.: _____

City: _____ State: _____ Zip: _____

Home/evening phone: _____ e-mail: _____

Calls or e-mail will be discreet, but please indicate any restrictions: _____

_____

B. Referral: Who gave you my name to call?

Name: _____ Phone: _____

Address: _____

May I have your permission to thank this person for the referral?   ❏ Yes   ❏ No

How did this person explain how I might be of help to you? _____

_____

_____

C. Religious and racial/ethnic identification

Religious denomination/affiliation: ❏ Protestant   ❏ Catholic   ❏ Jewish   ❏ Islamic   ❏ Buddhist

    ❏ Other (specify): _____

Involvement: ❏ None   ❏ Some/irregular   ❏ Active

How important are spiritual concerns in your life? _____

Which (if any) church, synagogue, temple, or meeting are you involved with? _____

Ethnicity/national origin: _____ Race: _____

Or other similar way you identity yourself and consider important: _____

D. Your medical care: From whom or where do you get your medical care?

Clinic/doctor's name: _____ Phone: _____

Address: _____

If you enter treatment with me for psychological problems, may I tell your medical doctor so that he or she can be fully informed and we can coordinate your treatment?   ❏ Yes   ❏ No

(cont.)

FORM 24. Client demographic information form (p. 1 of 3).   From *The Paper Office.* Copyright 2008 by Edward L. Zuckerman. Permission to photocopy this form is granted to purchasers of this book for personal use only (see copyright page for details).

E. Your current employer

Employer: _____ Address: _____

_____

Work phone: _____ Calls will be discreet, but please indicate any restrictions: _____

_____

F. Emergency information

If some kind of emergency arises and we cannot reach you directly, or we need to reach someone close to you, whom should we call?

Name: _____ Phone: _____ Relationship: _____

Address: _____

Significant other/nearest friend or relative not residing with you: _____

_____

G. Your education and training

Dates		Schools	Special classes?	Adjustment to school	Did you graduate?
From	To				

H. Employment and military experiences

Dates		Name of employer	Job title or duties	Reason for leaving
From	To			

I. Family-of-origin history

Relative	Name	Current age (or age at death)	Illnesses (or cause of death, if deceased)	Education	Occupation
Father					
Mother					
Brothers					

(cont.)

Sisters				
Stepparents				
Grandparents				
Uncles/aunts				

J. Significant nonmarital relationships

	Name of other person	Person's age when started	Your age when started	Your age when ended	Reasons for ending
First					
Second					
Third					
Current					

K. Marital/relationship history

	Spouse's name	Spouse's age at marriage	Your age at marriage	Your age when divorced/widowed	Is spouse remarried?
First					
Second					
Third					

L. Children (Indicate those from a previous marriage or relationship with "P" in the last column. Indicate stepchildren with "S.")

Name	Current age	Sex	School	Grade	Adjustment problems?	P? S?

This is a strictly confidential patient medical record. Redisclosure or transfer is expressly prohibited by law.

You might also add client information questions relevant to your setting or practice, such as language spoken in the home, sources of income, living situation, and so on.

Obtaining Client Clinical Information

FORM 25   As noted earlier, the client clinical information form (Form 25) asks for more personal and detailed information, and so perhaps it should not be mailed to the client or completed when others are present. It should normally be completed during the first interview, but because it is useful to have this information *before* the first interview, it can be completed in the waiting room if you decide the client would not be uncomfortable doing so. I have seen forms like this one entitled "Application for Psychological Services."

Question 2 in section C of this form asks about medications for identified psychiatric conditions, which is appropriate for this screening form. More information on all medications is sought in section B (question 3) of Form 26.

Section E asks about various kinds of abuse and neglect. Do not let anyone skip this section, but do use judgment in inquiring. When adults disclose their abuse as children, it is painful for everyone involved. It shatters our assumptions about the world as a safe place, and so professionals often avoid asking about it (Becker-Blease & Freyd, 2006). This mirrors the silence of the victims, who were groomed by perpetrators not to tell anyone (Veldhuis & Freyd, 1999). Clients may find that being asked straightforwardly on a form is normalizing (because it is apparently common enough to be on a printed form), relieving (because someone cares enough to ask and presumably will attend to this information), or frightening (because the pain will be reexperienced), but it can be therapeutic if handled well (see Ullman, 1999; Sullivan & Cain, 2004). We *must* ask about abuse; see Section 3.9.

In section G, questions 3–6 ask about the "CAGE" criteria for alcoholism, described by Ewing (1984). Depending on the client's answers, your observations, and any referral information, you may want to complete the chemical use survey (Form 27). These questions are widely used, but may not be the most sensitive measures of change or of dependence. There are a few dozen brief and validated substance abuse screening tools available for different populations (who have different abuse patterns and base rates), so you should select one or two for your typical clientele.

Some possible additional questions (the first two of which are from Eugene Snellings, CSW, ACP, of Baton Rouge, LA) are:

- List five things you like about yourself.

- List five things about yourself that you would like to change.

- What are your major strengths?

- Have any anniversaries of important or stressful events in your life occurred recently or are any due to occur soon?

Client Information Form 2

Note: **If you were a patient here before, please fill in only the information that has changed.**

A. Identification

Name: _____ Date: _____

B. Chief concern

Please describe the main difficulty that has brought you to see me: _____

_____

_____

_____

C. Treatment

1. Have you ever received psychological, psychiatric, drug or alcohol treatment, or counseling services before?
   ❏ No   ❏ Yes   If yes, please indicate:

When?	From whom?	For what?	With what results?

2. Have you ever taken medications for psychiatric or emotional problems?   ❏ No   ❏ Yes   If yes, please indicate:

When?	From whom?	Which medications?	For what?	With what results?

(cont.)

FORM 25. Client clinical information form (p. 1 of 4).   From *The Paper Office.* Copyright 2008 by Edward L. Zuckerman. Permission to photocopy this form is granted to purchasers of this book for personal use only (see copyright page for details).

D. Relationships in your family of origin. Please describe the following:

1. Your parents' relationship with each other: _____

_____

_____

_____

2. Your relationship with each parent and with any other adults present: _____

_____

_____

_____

3. Your parents' physical health problems, drug or alcohol use, and mental or emotional difficulties: _____

_____

_____

_____

4. Your relationship with your brothers and sisters, in the past and present: _____

_____

_____

_____

E. Abuse history: ❑ I was not abused in any way. ❑ I was abused. If you were abused, please indicate the following. For kind of abuse, use these letters: P = Physical, such as beatings. S = Sexual, such as touching/molesting, fondling, or intercourse. N = Neglect, such as failure to feed, shelter, or protect. E = Emotional, such as humiliation, etc.

Your age	Kind of abuse	By whom?	Effects on you?	Whom did you tell?	Consequences of telling?

F. Present relationships

1. How do you get along with your present spouse or partner? _____

_____

_____

_____

2. How do you get along with your children? _____

_____

_____

_____

(cont.)

3. Your important friends, past and present:

Names	Good parts of relationship	Bad parts of relationship

G. Chemical use

1. How many cups of regular coffee do you drink each day? _____ How many cups of tea? _____ How many sodas with caffeine (Coke, Pepsi, Mountain Dew, Dr. Pepper, Orange Crush, etc.)? _____ How many "energy drinks"? _____ How often do you use NoDoz or similar pills? _____ .

2. How much tobacco do you smoke or chew each week? _____

3. Have you ever felt the need to cut down on your drinking? ❑ No ❑ Yes

4. Have you ever felt annoyed by criticism of your drinking? ❑ No ❑ Yes

5. Have you ever felt guilty about your drinking? ❑ No ❑ Yes

6. Have you ever taken a morning "eye-opener"? ❑ No ❑ Yes

7. How much beer, wine, or hard liquor do you consume each week, on the average? _____

8. Are there times when you drink to unconsciousness, or run out of money as a result of drinking? _____

9. Have you ever used inhalants ("huffing"), such as glue, gasoline, or paint thinner? ❑ No ❑ Yes If yes, which and when? _____

10. Which drugs (not medications prescribed for you) have you used in the last 10 years? _____
_____
_____

Please provide details about your use of these drugs or other chemicals, such as amounts, how often you used them, their effects, and so forth: _____
_____
_____

H. Legal history

1. Are you presently suing anyone or thinking of suing anyone? ❑ No ❑ Yes If yes, please explain:
_____
_____

2. Is your reason for coming to see me related to an accident or injury? ❑ No ❑ Yes If yes, please explain:
_____
_____

3. Are you required by a court, the police, or a probation/parole officer to have this appointment? ❑ No ❑ Yes If yes, please explain: _____
_____
_____

(cont.)

4. List all the contacts with the police, courts, and jails/prisons you have had. Include all open charges and pending ones. Under "Jurisdiction," write in a letter: F = federal, S = state, Co = county, Ci = city. Under "Sentence," write in the time and the type of sentence you served or have to serve (AR = accelerated or alternate resolution, CS = community service, F = fine, I = incarceration, Pr = probation, Po = parole, O = other, R = restitution).

Date	Charge	Jurisdiction	Sentence	Probation/parole officer's name	Your attorney's name

5. Your current attorney's name: _____ Phone: _____

6. Are there any other legal involvements? _____

_____

_____

I. Other

Is there anything else that is important for me as your therapist to know about, and that you have not written about on any of these forms? If yes, please tell me about it here or on another sheet of paper:

_____

_____

_____

_____

Please do not write below this line.

- -

J. Follow-up by clinician

Based on the responses above and on ❑ interview data   ❑ records I reviewed   ❑ other information
I have requested the client to complete and/or I have completed the following forms:

❑ Chemical use survey

❑ Suicide risk assessment summary and recommendations

❑ Mental status evaluation report

❑ Other: _____

This is a strictly confidential patient medical record. Redisclosure or transfer is expressly prohibited by law.

- List any major problems or stressful events that other family members or close friends are currently dealing with.

- What solutions have you tried for the problems that bring you here?

Pediatricians and family practice physicians are being requested by their respective organizations to ask patients routinely whether they keep guns in the house, whether their friends do, and what safety precautions are being taken. Some may see this as intrusive and others as preventative of violence. You might add such questions to Form 25.

Obtaining Client Medical Information

Gathering health-related and medical information about a client in psychotherapy has several goals:

- A key goal is making sure the client does not have an undiagnosed or untreated medical condition that is causing the psychological symptoms you observe; this presentation is called "psychiatric masquerade." (For a summary of medical conditions that may result in such "masquerade," see Zuckerman, 2005.) It is not always possible to place the cause of symptoms into clear organic *or* psychological categories. By being sensitive and informed about the psychological presentation of medical conditions, the competent therapist (medical as well as nonmedical) can make appropriate medical referrals for evaluation and treatment. A prime resource is Taylor (2007).

- Second, mental health clinicians can contribute to the psychological management of clients' medical conditions. For example, diabetes has painful and complex management needs that are often resisted, despite the well-known health and life threats its poor management presents. Psychological interventions can greatly facilitate patient compliance, and so can enhance both physical functioning and the quality of life.

- Through gathering health information, clinicians may also be able to discover and thus to treat psychophysiological disorders with specific interventions. For example, temperature biofeedback can be very effective for migraine and Reynaud's phenomenon. More general techniques, such as stress management or family therapy, can be helpful for hypertension and irritable bowel syndrome.

- Psychological techniques can lessen suffering from physiological conditions such as chronic pain, which often can be effectively managed with hypnosis or behavioral treatments.

- Depression and anxiety may be hidden in the presentation of medical complaints or frequent help-seeking patterns. When they are discovered their treatment becomes possible, and the reduced overutilization of medical resources (called "medical cost offset") becomes a very significant financial benefit.

There are other benefits of behavioral medicine for specific conditions; these are too numerous to describe here, but they are well worth the efforts of the professional therapist.

FORM 26   The purposes and functions of Form 26, the brief health information form, are as follows: (1) to gather basic information on the client's health status; (2) to document that this infor-

Brief Health Information Form

A. Identification

Client's name: _____ Case #: _____ Date: _____

B. History

1. Starting with your childhood and proceeding up to the present, list *all* diseases, illnesses, important accidents and injuries, surgeries, hospitalizations, periods of loss of consciousness, convulsions/seizures, and any other medical conditions you have had. (Describe pregnancies in section E.)

Age	Illness/diagnosis	Treatment received	Treated by	Result

2. Describe any allergies you have.

To what?	Reaction you have	Allergy medications you take

3. List *all* medications, drugs, or other substances you take or have taken in the last year—prescribed, over-the-counter vitamins, supplements, herbs, and others.

Medication/drug	Dose (how much?)	Taken for	Prescribed and supervised by

(cont.)

FORM 26. Brief health information form (p. 1 of 3). From *The Paper Office*. Copyright 2008 by Edward L. Zuckerman. Permission to photocopy this form is granted to purchasers of this book for personal use only (see copyright page for details).

4. Have you done any kinds of work where you were exposed to toxic chemicals?

Date	Kinds of chemicals	Kind of work	Effects

C. Medical caregivers

1. Your current family or personal physician or medical agency:

Name	Specialty	Address	Phone #	Date of last visit

2. Other physicians treating you at present or in last 5 years:

Name	Specialty	Address	Phone #	Date of last visit

D. Health habits

1. What kinds of physical exercise do you get? _____

_____

_____

2. How much coffee, cola, tea, or other sources of caffeine do you consume each day? _____

_____

_____

(cont.)

3. Do you try to restrict your eating in any way? How? Why? _____

_____

_____

4. Do you have any problems getting enough sleep? _____

_____

_____

E. For women only

1. At what age did you start to menstruate (get your period): _____

2. Menstrual period experiences:

   a. How regular are they? _____

   b. How long do they last? _____

   c. How much pain do you have? _____

   d. How heavy are your periods? _____

   e. Other experiences during period? _____

3. Please list all of your pregnancies:

Your age	What happened with this pregnancy?			Problems?
	Miscarriage	Abortion	Child born	
1.				
2.				
3.				
4.				
5.				
6.				

4. Menopause:

   a. If your menopause has started, at what age did it start? _____

   b. What signs or symptoms have you had? _____

   _____

F. Other

Do you use tobacco?   ❑ Yes   ❑ No   If yes, how many cigarettes/cigars/other (circle all that apply) per day?: _____

Have you ever injected drugs?   ❑ Yes   ❑ No   Ever shared needles?   ❑ Yes   ❑ No

Have you had HIV testing in the last 6 months?   ❑ Yes   ❑ No   If yes, results: _____

Are there any other medical or physical problems you are concerned about? _____

_____

_____

_____

Note: Significant aspects of family medical history should be recorded on "Client Information Form 2."

mation was gathered; (3) to support consultation with the client's medical caregivers; and (4) to assess psychobiological conditions for intervention.

Many detailed checklists and forms for gathering health-related information about clients are available from the medical arts publishers. These ask clients to indicate their symptoms, histories, surgeries, and similar medical data. However, those who cannot interpret this data probably should not acquire it. The brief form offered here does not ask for details, but only for general problem areas (to be further investigated by both medical and psychological means), diagnoses that have been already established, and the name of the client's physician.

If you want a more formal assessment of symptoms or health, a very complete form with 236 simple questions in eight areas is the Health Problems Checklist (Schinka, 1989), available from Psychological Assessment Resources (www3.parinc.com). As noted above, there are many psychobiological conditions, which require careful analysis by those expert in both the mind and the body. Whether you are a physician or not, consultation with the client's primary care physician is appropriate both before and during your treatment. Of course, make certain not to make such a contact before getting the patient's agreement and a signed release.

A word about **medication** in particular is in order here. Is it proper for psychologists and other nonphysicians to discuss medications with clients? Littrell and Ashford (1995) argue that both ethically (there is a requirement for coordination of treatment) and legally (co-treating nurses and pharmacists already do it), nonphysician therapists can and should discuss medications with clients. Many prescription medications are taken by people who become therapy patients, and these may cause psychiatric symptoms, which may mislead the unwary professionals assessing or treating these persons. Meyer and Fink (1989) offer some helpful ideas for nonphysicians in obtaining a full and accurate medication history:

❑ Ask the patient to bring all current and recent medications to the introductory or intake session.

❑ Review with the patient all medications: prescribed, borrowed, over-the-counter, recently discontinued, recreational. Many clients are taking several medications (prescribed, over-the-counter, borrowed from others, bought on the street, or mail-ordered); using a variety of herbals, teas, extracts, and supplements (to treat disorders, feel better, improve sexual performance, lose weight, gain muscle mass, etc.); eating only "natural" foods; and adhering (or trying to adhere) some kind of diet (Elkins et al., 2005). In your thinking, the term "interactions" should include all possible relationships. For each drug or other substance, obtain the dose, schedule (both prescribed and actual), source, side effects noted, efficacy, and other comments. Ask the patient to tell you of any future changes in medications.

❑ Review the possible psychiatric side effects of each medication. There are excellent online resources about medications' effects and side effects, with current and complete information. For example, www.drugs.com has enormous information of all kinds, including lists of side effects and interactions. Similar sites are www.rxlist.com and health.discovery.com/encyclopedias/checker/checker.jsp; the latter includes herbals and foods. For those using personal digital assistants (PDAs), www.epocrates.com is the best downloadable source of drug information, and it is also accessible online.

However, no list is complete; effects are variable; and drugs interact. There is no substitute for a consulting relationship with a well-informed, sensitive psychiatric physician and/or pharmacist.

❏ Continually evaluate for the presence of psychiatric conditions or symptoms.

❏ If a psychiatric condition is present, consider whether its onset appears to correlate strongly with the onset of or change in the medication.

❏ If such a correlation exists, obtain a release of information and contact the patient's physician or help the patient to do so.

❏ Seek out the consultation and provide the physician with a thorough evaluation of all the relevant factors (psychological, social, stress-related, developmental, etc.) that you are able to evaluate.

Again, Form 26 is designed to meet the documentation needs of the nonmedical psychotherapist, so it only asks about health status and records the medical resources available to the client. This form is not a substitute for a medical evaluation or any appropriate consultations with physicians.

Assessing Chemical Use

FORM 27 The purposes and functions of Form 27, the chemical use survey, are as follows: (1) to screen all new clients for chemical use problems, such as dependence, abuse, or withdrawal; (2) to document that information on these issues was sought, whether and how much information was obtained, and that options were weighed; and (3) to assist with the formulation of the case in its full biopsychosocial context.

Chemical use is a complex biopsychosocial phenomenon, and so there is no checklist (no matter how large) that will substitute for a comprehensive evaluation by an experienced clinician. If you want interview questions, there is a very complete set of questions to evaluate most aspects of chemical use in Zuckerman (2005). Form 27 can be given to clients to complete when there is any indication—from the referrer, from your observations, or in responses to your screening interview questions—that chemical use may be a problem.

Because of the denial and shame centering around chemical use problems, it is especially important to get objective or confirmatory data beyond what the client tells you. Try to interview a friend or family member of a person suspected of drug or alcohol misuse. Later in this chapter, Form 36, the chemical user's case formulation, is provided to aid you in summarizing all of your findings, formulating the case in a biopsychosocial context, and planning treatment for a client with a substance use problem.

Because chemical use problems can be understood from many perspectives, Form 27 offers several ways to document the findings; you can add or delete elements according to your preferences. (For example, you could add other chemicals to the list in section A, such as heroin or methamphetamine.) Furthermore, the individual's patterns of use/overuse/misuse/abuse may change with availability, resources, setting, decision, treatment, and aging, and may involve cross-addictions, temporary substitutions or preferences, and many other factors, so a detailed and individualized history is desirable. Obviously, the central

Chemical Use Survey

Name: _____ Date: _____

In order to treat you effectively, I need information about the ways you and your family have used alcohol, drugs, and/or other chemicals that can affect you psychologically. So please answer these questions fully.

A. What have you used?

1. Think about any and all chemicals you have used, and indicate how much you used (amount) and how often. Then indicate all the effects it had on you (mental, physical, family, legal, etc.).

Chemical	Age started	Last use	Over the last 30 days		See question 3, below
			Amount and how often	Effects/consequences	
Caffeine					
Tobacco (smoked or chewed)					
Alcohol					
Marijuana/THC					
Cocaine/crack (snorted, injected, or smoked)					
Inhalants ("Huffing")					
LSD					
Prescribed pills					
Others: Specify					

2. Write "P" above next to your primary drug of choice.

3. For each chemical you currently use, what causes you to stop? Enter one or more of these letters in the last column above: A = The money runs out. B = I use up my supply. C = Personal choice. D = Unconsciousness. E = Achieved my purpose. F = Other reasons: _____

4. What are or were your sources of money for buying the chemicals you have used? _____
_____

B. Which of these have you had? ❑ Blackouts ❑ Withdrawal symptoms ❑ Cravings ❑ Overdoses
❑ Detoxification in a hospital ❑ Tolerance ("Could not get high no matter how much I took")
❑ Preoccupation (spent lots of time finding and using chemicals) ❑ Failed attempts to cut down or control use
❑ Other problems: _____

(cont.)

C. Family patterns of chemical use

Please describe the chemical(s) used by family members.

	Name	Chemical	Age started	Last use	Over the last 30 days Amount and how often	Effects
Father						
Mother						
Brothers/ sisters						
Spouse/ partner						
Other relatives						

Please add any other information you think is important: _____

_____

D. Treatment for chemical use

Dates From	To	Agency/provider	Type of program*	Voluntary? (Yes or no)	Length of treatment	Methods used	Participation in aftercare programs (No/Which?)	Effects of treatment†

*In the fourth column, use these codes: AA/NA = Alcoholics Anonymous/Narcotics Anonymous; O = Outpatient counseling; ID = Inpatient detoxification; IT = Inpatient treatment (e.g., 28-day); O = Other.

†In the last column, use these codes: W = made situation Worse; N = No change; U = better Understanding of addiction; R = Reduction of use; BA = Brief abstinence (up to a month); LA = Long-term abstinence (several months or more); O = Other effects

F. Self-description of use

1. Would you say you ❑ are a social drinker? ❑ are a heavy drinker? ❑ have alcoholism? ❑ have a drinking problem? Or how would you describe your use? _____

_____

2. Would you say you ❑ are a recreational drug user? ❑ have a drug problem? ❑ have an addiction? Or how would you describe your use? _____

_____

G. Other

Has your drinking/drug use caused you any spiritual problems? _____

_____

_____

This is a strictly confidential patient medical record. Redisclosure or transfer is expressly prohibited by law.

dynamic of denial will significantly affect your information gathering. Therefore, follow your clinical intuition and the client's lead (or avoidances) in history taking to get all the relevant facts.

Obtaining Financial Information

FORM 28   The purposes and functions of Form 28, the financial information form, are as follows:

1. It collects all the essential data you need for evaluating the client's insurance benefits, and thus the true costs to you and to the client of your services.

2. It allows you to decide whether a client can afford your charges. If you do not use it before seeing the client, you should discuss fees and resources early in the interview, to avoid engaging anyone in a process and relationship that must then be disrupted. That is why it is best to mail this form to new clients or to give it to them while they wait for their first visit.

Do not trust clients to understand their coverages or the technicalities of today's insurance marketplace. When they come in, ask for and take photocopies of any insurance wallet cards they have. With those numbers and a Social Security number, you can call the insurer(s) to verify their coverage. Try not to start therapy without such verification.

You may need to make some changes to this form. For example, if your state has a special name for its health insurance program, or you see a lot of patients covered by Tricare or another specific carrier, you may need to change some of the wording of this form.

Sections F, G, and H of Form 28 are condensed legal statements addressing these issues, respectively: release of records to an insurer, accepting of financial responsibility, and assignment of benefits to you. If you are going to use other forms for these purposes (such as Form 29 about paying for services, or the letter in Section 2.5 about assignment of benefits), you do not need to include these three sections here.

Finally, the question asking for the secondary insurance company (question 2 in section D) is for "coordination of benefits," in which insurers set priorities about who will cover services first. Ideally, the secondary insurer will cover any remaining amount due you.

Assuring Financial Responsibility

FORM 29   The purpose of Form 29, the agreement to pay for professional services, is to formalize a client's (or someone else's) assumption of financial responsibility for therapy and other services. You may wonder "Isn't the client's stated promise to pay sufficient?" Simon (1992) indicates that an oral contract is valid and enforceable in simple circumstances where a client makes a simple promise such as "I will pay for his [or her] treatment," but where there is a condition such as "I will pay if he [or she] fails to pay," a written contract is needed. The client may harbor hidden assumptions—for example, that he or she will pay only if the problem is cured, or that he or she will need only a few sessions, or that psychotherapy services will be fully paid for by insurance or the government. Presenting this form (or the first paragraph as part of another form) brings these assumptions to the surface for resolution and clarification.

Financial Information Form

I truly appreciate your choosing to come to me for psychological help. As part of providing high-quality services, we need to be clear about our financial arrangements.

- If you have health insurance, it may pay for a part of the cost of your treatment here. To find out if this is so, my staff and I need the information requested below. We will explain any part of this form that you do not understand.

- If you have no health insurance coverage, or do not intend to use it, please check here ❑ , complete sections A and E below, and return this form to me or my secretary.

A. Patient's name: _____ Birthdate: _____ Soc. Sec. #: _____

Address: _____ Home phone: _____

(If the patient is a dependent) Insured's/policy holder's name: _____ Occupation: _____

Employer: _____ Work phone: _____

Address of employer: _____

B. (If applicable) Spouse's name: _____ Birthdate: _____ Soc. Sec. #: _____

Occupation: _____ Employer: _____ Work phone: _____

Address of employer: _____

C. If you (or your spouse) have any of these kinds of insurance, please fill in the numbers and names for each one.

1. Blue Cross/Blue Shield

   Name of subscriber (if different from patient): _____

   Identification/agreement/policy #: _____ Group or enrollment #: _____

   Plan #/code or BS #: _____ Effective date: _____

   Location of plan: _____ Reciprocity #: _____

   Phone: _____ Provider's phone: _____

2. Commercial health insurance carrier/company

   Name of company: _____ Policy holder (if different from patient): _____

   Policy #: _____ Certificate #: _____

   Phone: _____ Provider's phone: _____

   Address to send claims: _____

3. Health maintenance organization (HMO)

   Name of HMO: _____ Policy holder (if different from patient): _____

   Authorization #: _____ Agreement #: _____

(cont.)

FORM 28. Financial information form (p. 1 of 3).   From *The Paper Office*. Copyright 2008 by Edward L. Zuckerman. Permission to photocopy this form is granted to purchasers of this book for personal use only (see copyright page for details).

Phone: _____ Provider's phone: _____

Address to send claims: _____

4. Medical Assistance

List all numbers: _____

(*Note:* Copayments by you are required.)

5. Medicare

Agreement # with any letters: _____

Railroad Medicare/Mine Workers Medicare: _____

6. Workers' compensation insurance

Name of company: _____

Policy #: _____ Certificate #: _____

Address to send claims: _____

Phone: _____ Treatment authorized by: _____ Date of accident: _____

7. Do you or your spouse have any other insurance coverage that applies here (Tricare, motor vehicle insurance for an injury, etc.)? If yes, check here ❑ and fill in an empty section above.

D. For each kind of insurance you intend to use, you and I will have to make two decisions. First, we have to decide who will find the information to answer the questions below. Will you do this, or do you want this office to do it? The information will come either from your company's benefits office or from the insurance company. Then, when we have this information, we have to examine the treatment choices allowed by the coverage you have.

1. Company: _____ Effective date of coverage: _____

   Deductible: $_____ ❑ per person or ❑ per family? ❑ per fiscal year or ❑ per calendar year or ❑ per policy year? ❑ per diagnosis?

   How much of this deductible has been used so far? $_____

   Benefit: _____% of ❑ charges ❑ Usual, customary, and reasonable (UCR) ❑ Maximum charge of $_____
   ❑ Other benefits: _____

   Percent reduction, if any, for mental health? _____%

   Limitations: Number of visits: _____ Monetary limits: $_____ per _____

   Lifetime limits: $_____

   Is outpatient group psychotherapy covered? ❑ Yes ❑ No

   Must a physician refer the client? ❑ Yes ❑ No

   Is psychological testing covered? ❑ Yes ❑ No

   Does any rule about preexisting conditions apply here? ❑ No ❑ Yes: _____

   Are there any other limitations (such as conditions not covered, service settings, maximum per-session charges, need for DSM or ICD diagnostic codes or CPT service codes)? _____

   _____

   _____

   _____

(cont.)

2. Company:_____ Effective date of coverage:_____

Deductible: $_____ ❏ per person or ❏ per family? ❏ per fiscal year or ❏ per calendar year or

❏ per policy year? ❏ per diagnosis?

How much of this deductible has been used so far? $_____

Benefit: _____% of ❏ charges ❏ Usual, customary, and reasonable (UCR) ❏ Maximum charge of $_____

❏ Other benefits: _____

Percent reduction, if any, for mental health? _____%

Limitations: Number of visits: _____ Monetary limits: $_____ per _____

Lifetime limits $_____

Is outpatient group psychotherapy covered? ❏ Yes ❏ No

Must a physician refer the client? ❏ Yes ❏ No

Is psychological testing covered? ❏ Yes ❏ No

Does any rule about preexisting conditions apply here? ❏ No ❏ Yes: _____

Are there any other limitations (such as conditions not covered, service settings, maximum per-session

charges, need for diagnostic codes or service codes)? _____

_____

_____

_____

E. If you do not have insurance, how will you pay for services from this office? _____

_____

_____

_____

F. I give this office permission to release any information obtained during examinations or treatment of this patient that is necessary to support any insurance claims on this account and secure timely payments due to the assignee or myself.

G. I understand that I am responsible for all charges, regardless of insurance coverage.

H. Assignment of benefits

I hereby assign medical benefits, including those from government-sponsored programs and other health plans, to be paid to the therapist above. Medicare regulations may apply. A photocopy of this assignment is to be considered as good as the original.

_____   _____
Client's (or parent/guardian's) signature,   Date
indicating agreement to all of the statements above

_____
Printed name

Agreement to Pay for Professional Services

I request that the therapist named below provide professional services to me or to _____, who is my _____, and I agree to pay this therapist's fee of $_____ per session for these services.

I agree that this financial relationship with this therapist will continue as long as the therapist provides services or until I inform him or her, in person or by certified mail, that I wish to end it. I agree to meet with this therapist at least once before stopping therapy. I agree to pay for services provided to me (or this client) up until the time I end the relationship.

I agree that I am responsible for the charges for services provided by this therapist to me (or this client), although other persons or insurance companies may make payments on my (or this client's) account.

I have also read this therapist's "Information for Clients" brochure and agree to act according to everything stated there, as shown by my signature below and on the brochure.

_____   _____
Signature of client (or person acting for client)   Date

_____
Printed name

    I, the therapist, have discussed the issues above with the client (and/or the person acting for the client). My observations of the person's behavior and responses give me no reason to believe that this person is not fully competent to give informed and willing consent.

_____   _____
Signature of therapist   Date

❑ Copy accepted by client   ❑ Copy kept by therapist

If any of the following situations apply, make certain to get a responsible person's signature before you become too involved in treatment:

- A noncustodial parent brings a child in for services. Legal and physical custody are not identical. Before beginning therapy, therefore, ask for the paperwork supporting the legal authority to give permission to treat. States' rules differ, but the safest way is to get permission to treat from both parents unless treatment is court-ordered.

- A divorcing spouse whose assets are likely to be in dispute or inadequate to pay for services comes for treatment.

- An adolescent without assets seeks your services.

- Treatment is going to be long or expensive, and you want someone besides the client to share the cost.

- You suspect that the client isn't sincere in offering to pay for your services.

- You feel that the client doesn't fully appreciate the responsibility involved.

Note that a statement indicating acceptance of financial responsibility is included at the end of the financial information form (Form 28, section G): "I understand that I am responsible for all charges, regardless of insurance coverage." It is always a good idea to repeat this point, and if you have any doubts about the client's full appreciation of this point, Form 29 can then be used.

Form 29 indicates that the client has read and agreed to the client information brochure (see Section 4.2), because the client cannot be expected to assume financial responsibility without knowing basic information about therapy (its duration, probable costs, etc.). It is best to include this form with the preappointment package; if it is offered in the waiting room before the first visit, it should be accompanied by the brochure.

The American Academy of Family Physicians has a brief document similar to Form 29 online (www.aafp.org/fpm/20040400/samplepaymentpolicy.doc). This document cleverly includes definitions of the terms and procedures involved in using health insurance.

Problem Checklists

It isn't that they can't see the solution. It's that they can't see the problem.
—G. K. CHESTERTON

People come for "help" for many reasons (physician referral, threat of divorce, intolerable pain, desire for the cure of symptoms, need for answers or advice, support for their views, failure of previous efforts, etc.) and with many different understandings of the cause and possible cure of their difficulties. It has been shown repeatedly that the more closely client and therapist agree on the nature, cause, and methods of relieving the presenting problem, the better the outcome of therapy. Yet the professional's role often involves relabeling or reformulating the "referral reason" into something he or she understands and has the skills to relieve.

The intent of problem checklists is to offer new clients the widest range of possible choices and ask them to select from among these. This allows the exploration of all concerns early in therapy. If you simply ask, "What brings you here today?", you will get an abridged list of items, probably emphasizing the most recent and most memorable events (critical incidents). Or you might get the "referral reason," which is simply the "problem" defined by another professional, or a request for a specific treatment method (such as hypnosis). Although clients may come seeking a particular kind of therapy, this should be a professional's well-considered decision.

For precise information and documentation of symptoms or conditions, thousands of specific tests, checklists, and scales are available, and I encourage their valid use. An excellent starting point is the volume by Fischer and Corcoran (2006). For an emphasis on a child or teen's functioning, rather than symptoms, the Child and Adolescent Functional Assessment Scale (CAFAS) offers eight sub-scales and an overall dysfunction score. It has been widely used, offers a full list of strengths, and is very comprehensive although therefore long (vinst.umdnj.edu/VAID/TestReport.asp?Code=CAFAS). A very simple yet quite large form for adolescents, with 208 questions in 12 areas, is the Personal Problems Checklist (Schinka, 1984); this is available from Psychological Assessment Resources (www3.parinc.com).

FORM 30
FORM 31
The checklists offered here are labeled to avoid excessive pathologizing of the client's experience. The adult's version (Form 30) is called a checklist of "concerns" rather than "problems." The child's version (Form 31), called a checklist of "characteristics," offers both problematic and helpful behaviors so that you will have at least some positives to build upon, and is to be completed by parents or caregivers.

You can, of course, tailor these two lists to your own practice by adding some items; if you do so, I would also suggest removing some, so that the lists do not become burdensome for clients. For example, if you do more behavioral health work, you can add "Headaches," "High blood pressure," "Pain management," etc., and delete less relevant items. You can modify the format as well, by asking for a rating of severity or duration for each problem checked. Or you can ask patients to "Circle any of the following if they were a concern in the past, and underline those that are presently of concern to you."

Susan Lentulay, MA, of Erie, PA, suggests modifying the list of concerns to collect information on the intensity, frequency, duration, and impact of the symptomatic behaviors listed. Her format for recording these data uses vertical columns:

Instructions: Mark an × for each concern that applies to you and how it affects you.

(Name of concern)	How severe is this?			Life areas affected:			How long has this lasted?		
	Mild	Moderate	Severe	Work/ school	Home family	Social	2 weeks or less	3 weeks to 6–10 months	A year or longer

Lentulay also adds two areas to the list of concerns: "personal traumas" and "health problems."

Adult Checklist of Concerns

Name: _____ Date: _____

Please mark all of the items below that apply, and feel free to add any others at the bottom under "Any other concerns or issues." You may add a note or details in the space next to the concerns checked. (For a child, mark any of these and then complete the "Child Checklist of Characteristics.")

❑ I have no problem or concern bringing me here
❑ Abuse—physical, sexual, emotional, neglect (of children or elderly persons), cruelty to animals
❑ Aggression, violence
❑ Alcohol use
❑ Anger, hostility, arguing, irritability
❑ Anxiety, nervousness
❑ Attention, concentration, distractibility
❑ Career concerns, goals, and choices
❑ Childhood issues (your own childhood)
❑ Codependence
❑ Confusion
❑ Compulsions
❑ Custody of children
❑ Decision making, indecision, mixed feelings, putting off decisions
❑ Delusions (false ideas)
❑ Dependence
❑ Depression, low mood, sadness, crying
❑ Divorce, separation
❑ Drug use—prescription medications, over-the-counter medications, street drugs
❑ Eating problems—overeating, undereating, appetite, vomiting (see also "Weight and diet issues")
❑ Emptiness
❑ Failure
❑ Fatigue, tiredness, low energy
❑ Fears, phobias
❑ Financial or money troubles, debt, impulsive spending, low income
❑ Friendships
❑ Gambling
❑ Grieving, mourning, deaths, losses, divorce
❑ Guilt
❑ Headaches, other kinds of pains
❑ Health, illness, medical concerns, physical problems
❑ Housework/chores—quality, schedules, sharing duties
❑ Inferiority feelings

(cont.)

FORM 30. Adult checklist of concerns (p. 1 of 2). From *The Paper Office.* Copyright 2008 by Edward L. Zuckerman. Permission to photocopy this form is granted to purchasers of this book for personal use only (see copyright page for details).

- ❑ Interpersonal conflicts
- ❑ Impulsiveness, loss of control, outbursts
- ❑ Irresponsibility
- ❑ Judgment problems, risk taking
- ❑ Legal matters, charges, suits
- ❑ Loneliness
- ❑ Marital conflict, distance/coldness, infidelity/affairs, remarriage, different expectations, disappointments
- ❑ Memory problems
- ❑ Menstrual problems, PMS, menopause
- ❑ Mood swings
- ❑ Motivation, laziness
- ❑ Nervousness, tension
- ❑ Obsessions, compulsions (thoughts or actions that repeat themselves)
- ❑ Oversensitivity to rejection
- ❑ Panic or anxiety attacks
- ❑ Parenting, child management, single parenthood
- ❑ Perfectionism
- ❑ Pessimism
- ❑ Procrastination, work inhibitions, laziness
- ❑ Relationship problems (with friends, with relatives, or at work)
- ❑ School problems (see also "Career concerns . . . ")
- ❑ Self-centeredness
- ❑ Self-esteem
- ❑ Self-neglect, poor self-care
- ❑ Sexual issues, dysfunctions, conflicts, desire differences, other (see also "Abuse")
- ❑ Shyness, oversensitivity to criticism
- ❑ Sleep problems—too much, too little, insomnia, nightmares
- ❑ Smoking and tobacco use
- ❑ Spiritual, religious, moral, ethical issues
- ❑ Stress, relaxation, stress management, stress disorders, tension
- ❑ Suspiciousness
- ❑ Suicidal thoughts
- ❑ Temper problems, self-control, low frustration tolerance
- ❑ Thought disorganization and confusion
- ❑ Threats, violence
- ❑ Weight and diet issues
- ❑ Withdrawal, isolating
- ❑ Work problems, employment, workaholism/overworking, can't keep a job, dissatisfaction, ambition

Any other concerns or issues:

- ❑ _____
- ❑ _____

Please look back over the concerns you have checked off and choose the one that you most want help with. It is:

_____

This is a strictly confidential patient medical record. Redisclosure or transfer is expressly prohibited by law.

Child Checklist of Characteristics

Name: _____ Date: _____

Age: _____ Person completing this form: _____

Many concerns can apply to both children and adults. If you have brought a child for evaluation or treatment, first please mark all of the items that apply to your child on the "Adult Checklist of Concerns." Then review this checklist, which contains concerns (as well as positive traits) that apply mostly to children, and mark any items that describe your child. Feel free to add any others at the end under "Any other characteristics."

- ❑ Affectionate
- ❑ Argues, "talks back," smart-alecky, defiant
- ❑ Bullies/intimidates, teases, inflicts pain on others, is bossy to others, picks on, provokes
- ❑ Cheats
- ❑ Cruel to animals
- ❑ Concern for others
- ❑ Conflicts with parents over persistent rule breaking, money, chores, homework, grades, choices in music/clothes/hair/friends
- ❑ Complains
- ❑ Cries easily, feelings are easily hurt
- ❑ Dawdles, procrastinates, wastes time
- ❑ Difficulties with parent's paramour/new marriage/new family
- ❑ Dependent, immature
- ❑ Developmental delays
- ❑ Disrupts family activities
- ❑ Disobedient, uncooperative, refuses, noncompliant, doesn't follow rules
- ❑ Distractible, inattentive, poor concentration, daydreams, slow to respond
- ❑ Dropping out of school
- ❑ Drug or alcohol use
- ❑ Eating—poor manners, refuses, appetite increase or decrease, odd combinations, overeats
- ❑ Exercise problems
- ❑ Extracurricular activities interfere with academics
- ❑ Failure in school
- ❑ Fearful
- ❑ Fighting, hitting, violent, aggressive, hostile, threatens, destructive
- ❑ Fire setting
- ❑ Friendly, outgoing, social
- ❑ Hypochondriac, always complains of feeling sick
- ❑ Immature, "clowns around," has only younger playmates
- ❑ Imaginary playmates, fantasy
- ❑ Independent
- ❑ Interrupts, talks out, yells
- ❑ Lacks organization, unprepared

(cont.)

FORM 31. Child checklist of characteristics (p. 1 of 2). From *The Paper Office*. Copyright 2008 by Edward L. Zuckerman. Permission to photocopy this form is granted to purchasers of this book for personal use only (see copyright page for details).

- ❑ Lacks respect for authority, insults, dares, provokes, manipulates
- ❑ Learning disability
- ❑ Legal difficulties—truancy, loitering, panhandling, drinking, vandalism, stealing, fighting, drug sales
- ❑ Likes to be alone, withdraws, isolates
- ❑ Lying
- ❑ Low frustration tolerance, irritability
- ❑ Mental retardation
- ❑ Moody
- ❑ Mute, refuses to speak
- ❑ Nail biting
- ❑ Nervous
- ❑ Nightmares
- ❑ Need for high degree of supervision at home over play/chores/schedule
- ❑ Obedient
- ❑ Obesity
- ❑ Overactive, restless, hyperactive, out-of-seat behaviors, restlessness, fidgety, noisiness
- ❑ Oppositional, resists, refuses, does not comply, negativism
- ❑ Prejudiced, bigoted, insulting, name calling, intolerant
- ❑ Pouts
- ❑ Recent move, new school, loss of friends
- ❑ Relationships with brothers/sisters or friends/peers are poor—competition, fights, teasing/provoking, assaults
- ❑ Responsible
- ❑ Rocking or other repetitive movements
- ❑ Runs away
- ❑ Sad, unhappy
- ❑ Self-harming behaviors—biting or hitting self, head banging, scratching self
- ❑ Speech difficulties
- ❑ Sexual—sexual preoccupation, public masturbation, inappropriate sexual behaviors
- ❑ Shy, timid
- ❑ Stubborn
- ❑ Suicide talk or attempt
- ❑ Swearing, blasphemes, bathroom language, foul language
- ❑ Temper tantrums, rages
- ❑ Thumb sucking, finger sucking, hair chewing
- ❑ Tics—involuntary rapid movements, noises, or word productions
- ❑ Teased, picked on, victimized, bullied
- ❑ Truant, school avoiding
- ❑ Underactive, slow-moving or slow-responding, lethargic
- ❑ Uncoordinated, accident-prone
- ❑ Wetting or soiling the bed or clothes
- ❑ Work problems, employment, workaholism/overworking, can't keep a job

Any other characteristics:

❑ _____

Please look back over the concerns you have checked off and choose the one that you most want your child to be helped with. Which is it? _____

This is a strictly confidential patient medical record. Redisclosure or transfer is expressly prohibited by law.

If you have clients complete Form 30 or 31 before the first meeting, you can follow up those items checked to clarify exactly what is understood by each term and what difficulties are being presented.

Finally, I should note that under "Abuse" I have included cruelty to animals, which is illegal in all states and highly correlated with violence against humans. For more information or resources, contact the Latham Foundation (www.latham.org).

Obtaining Developmental Information

FORM 32

When the client is a child, collecting developmental history is essential. Much basic history information can be obtained on a form such as Form 32, the child developmental history record. However, more information will be required when there is a significant clinical problem with a child, and this additional and more detailed information is better acquired during an interview. The purposes and functions of Form 32 are (1) to gather and record information about major historical issues in development and (2) to support the later summarization of information to support treatment planning and initiation. Some items are adapted from a very complete set of forms by Robert E. McCarthy, PhD, of Myrtle Beach, SC.

5.5   Phase 4: First Meeting with a New Client

Should you use a questionnaire or checklist to ensure that you have missed nothing in the range of possible presenting symptoms, or should you rely on your interviewing skills ("clinical flags") and the conscientious patient to discover all of the important aspects of the case? Each approach has advantages and disadvantages, and so I have chosen to offer materials to support a combination approach, which is a multistep process.

Step 1. Use standard questionnaires to capture all the presenting problems, such as the two client information forms (Forms 24 and 25), the two checklists (Forms 30 and 31), and the child developmental history record (Form 32). At least some of these forms can be filled out by the client before the first meeting.

Step 2. Do an interview to follow up on the presenting problems in more detail, so that you and the client can come to a shared understanding of their nature and priority, and can establish a positive alliance.

Step 3. Because there may be other clinical issues that the client has not identified or was unwilling to indicate initially, do a survey interview with questions directed at some areas of known importance to all patients. The intake interview questions and guide (Form 33) provides structure when structure is desired, without imposing it.

Step 4. Follow up any new concerns with detailed interviewing methods. A very complete list of questions, organized according to clinical symptoms or syndromes, can be found in the *Clinician's Thesaurus* (Zuckerman, 2005).

Step 5. Use very specialized and focused questionnaires, behavioral schedules, and check-

Child Developmental History Record

A. Identifications

1. Child's name:_____ Birthdate:_____ Age:_____

   Person(s) completing this form: _____ Today's date: _____

2. Mother's name:_____ Birthdate:_____ Home phone:_____

   Address: _____

   Currently employed: ❑ No ❑ Yes, as: _____ Work phone: _____

3. Father's name:_____ Birthdate:_____ Home phone:_____

   Address: _____

   Currently employed: ❑ No ❑ Yes, as: _____ Work phone: _____

4. Parents are currently ❑ Married ❑ Divorced ❑ Remarried ❑ Never married ❑ Other:_____

   Child's custodian/guardian is: _____

5. Stepparent's name:_____ Birthdate:_____ Home phone:_____

   Address: _____

   Currently employed: ❑ No ❑ Yes, as: _____ Work phone: _____

B. Development

Please fill in any information you have on the areas listed below.

1. Pregnancy and delivery

   Prenatal medical illnesses and health care: _____

   _____

   _____

   Was the child premature? _____ Weight and height at birth: _____ _____

   Any birth complications or problems? _____

   _____

   _____

2. The first few months of life

   Breast-fed? _____ If so, for how long? _____

   Any allergies? _____

(cont.)

FORM 32. Child developmental history record (p. 1 of 3). From *The Paper Office.* Copyright 2008 by Edward L. Zuckerman. Permission to photocopy this form is granted to purchasers of this book for personal use only (see copyright page for details).

Sleep patterns or problems: _____

_____

_____

Personality: _____

_____

_____

3. Milestones: At what age did this child do each of these?

Sat without support: _____   Crawled: _____

Walked without holding on: _____   Helped when being dressed: _____

Ate with a fork: _____   Stayed dry all day: _____

Didn't soil his or her pants: _____   Stayed dry all night: _____

Tied shoelaces: _____   Buttoned buttons: _____

4. Speech/language development

Age when child said first word understandable to a stranger: _____

Age when child said first sentence understandable to a stranger: _____

Any speech, hearing, or language difficulties? _____

_____

_____

C. Health

List all childhood illnesses, hospitalizations, medications, allergies, head injuries, important accidents and injuries, surgeries, periods of loss of consciousness, convulsions/seizures, and other medical conditions.

Condition	Age	Treated by whom?	Consequences?

(cont.)

D. Residences

1. Homes

Dates		Location	With whom	Reason for moving	Any problems?
From	To				

2. Residential placements, institutional placements, or foster care

Dates		Program name or location	Reason for placement	Problems?
From	To			

E. Schools

School (name, district, address, phone)	Grade	Age	Teacher

May I call and discuss your child with the current teacher? ❑ Yes ❑ No

F. Special skills or talents of child

List hobbies, sports; recreational, musical, TV, and toy preferences; etc.: _____

_____

G. Other

Is there anything else I should know that doesn't appear on this or other forms, but that is or might be important?

_____

_____

_____

This is a strictly confidential patient medical record. Redisclosure or transfer is expressly prohibited by law.

lists only when the presentation is very complex or detailed documentation is essential. These syndrome-specific materials are beyond the scope of this book.

Step 6. Summarize and organize your data, using the forms provided in Section 5.6 for suicide risk, chemical use, and overall case formulation.

The purposes and functions of the forms presented in this section and in Section 5.6 are as follows: (1) to enable you to identify and assess the client's problems in clinical terms and decide how to intervene; (2) to document your assessment so that it is concise, accessible, productive, and professional; and (3) to help you begin building a productive therapeutic alliance.

Preparing the Client for the Intake Interview

Some routine and some critical information has to be exchanged, and organizing this process is advantageous for both sides. You can streamline the process by specifying what information clients need to provide to you (by mailing your intake forms); giving them enough time to collect and record the information; encouraging the noting down of any questions and areas of uncertainty; and (during the first interview) complimenting them on the quality of their work and emphasizing that their efforts are both appreciated and augur well for the therapy enterprise.

Since most people get "nervous" in a professional's office, they will fail to disclose important material or to pursue answers to their questions. If you appear rushed, this will compound the problem—so make it clear to clients that you will not be interrupted by phone calls or by your staff members, and remind them how much time you have made available. For some clients, you might encourage them to take notes and support this with paper, pens, and a clipboard: "Write down what you think is most important in what we say today, the answers to your questions, and my recommendations and suggestions." If you have any doubts about the clarity and fullness of the communication, say, "I want to be sure we are understanding each other, so tell me what you remember about. . . . "

Another way to collect many of these data is to have the client write his or her own history, using a comprehensive outline given by you. Joan Anderson, PhD, of Houston, TX, suggests that this is especially useful in any case you expect may go to court, because you will have the data in the client's own words (and usually his or her handwriting as well).

Using the Intake Interview Questions and Guide

FORM 33

Rather than use a printed form (which always seems to have either too much or too little space) for recording the responses to interview questions, you can ask the questions from the intake interview questions and guide (Form 33) and record the client's responses, numbered to correspond to the questions asked, on plain lined filler paper (see Section 1.4). As each question is answered, you can cross out its number on the form. Irvin P. R. Guyett, PhD, of Pittsburgh, PA, has used his laptop computer while interviewing patients and found that it is not as distracting as one might expect. It allows the answers to be placed under the questions, and wastes no space when the answers are printed out for the chart. Here are a few more suggestions about the use of Form 33:

Intake Interview Questions and Guide

Client's name: _____ Date: _____ Interviewer's initials: _____

❑ OK to thank referrer?   ❑ Yes   ❑ No   ❑ Entered into phone book   ❑ Entered into birthday book

Introductory questions

1. Who suggested that you come to see me? _____ Referral code:_____

2. What is the problem, in your own words? How do you see the situation?

   a. Symptoms—frequency, duration, intensity, latency, recurrence, course; distress caused.

   b. Change efforts.

   c. Why help is being sought *now*—precipitants, stressors, consequences; contexts, relevant history; needs, goals, strengths.)

Essential information

3. Previous psychological episodes, treaters, and treatments.

   a. For what?

   b. Where/by whom?

   c. Treatment?

   d. When (from–to)?

   e. Outcome?

   f. Satisfaction/difficulties? (Especially follow up any hints of problems/abuse by therapists—e.g., dual relationships, sexual intimacies, litigation.)

   g. Release(s) for records signed?

4. History of abuse. (Interview partners separately: Disagreements and decisions; verbal, emotional, physical, sexual abuse; marital, elder, childhood, family-of-origin abuse; kinds of violence; coping and protections; actions taken against abuser; fears, danger.)

5. Follow-up of responses to client information forms.

   a. Health problems. (Injuries, illnesses, allergies, eating patterns, exercise, sleep, sex; all current medications; last exam by an MD?)

   b. Legal history. (Involvement with the law/police, arrests; charges lodged—civil and criminal, not paying bills,

(cont.)

FORM 33. Intake interview questions and guide (p. 1 of 2). From *The Paper Office*. Copyright 2008 by Edward L. Zuckerman. Permission to photocopy this form is granted to purchasers of this book for personal use only (see copyright page for details).

fraud, violence; consequences, sentences; litigation anticipated, pending or in past, especially against therapists; lawyer's name and phone number.)

c. Family of origin. (Make genogram. Parents: ages, health, education, etc. Sibs: number, ages, relationships, etc. Important friendships. For all relatives: issues of abuse, affection, control, discipline, expectations, aspirations, personalities, mental health, religion, schooling, occupations, marriages, legal issues.)

d. Substance use history. (For client, family of origin, current family: Alcohol, drugs—street and prescription, chemicals, caffeine, tobacco; current and past use.)

e. Current relationship/family situation. (How client met current partner; attraction, love; family's role; duration, transitions, stressors, and affectual tone of relationship; number and ages of children; problems with or concerns about children.)

Optional questions

6. What changes do you hope therapy will lead to? (Realism, readiness to change, changes of self vs. others, consistency with therapist.)

7. What do you want to change about yourself? (Locus of responsibility, control.)

8. How will therapy help you make these changes? (Understanding, sophistication, dependence.)

9. What do you think a therapist should be like?

10. How long do you think these changes will take? (Realism of time frame.)

11. What are your major strengths? (Abilities, resources, education, employment, personality, feelings, habits, relationships.)

12. What have been your major crises of the last 1–5 years, and how have you handled them? (Precipitants, coping mechanisms/skills, defenses.)

13. What are your goals? (Ambitions, family situation and satisfaction, school/work situation and satisfaction.)

14. What persons, ideas, or forces have been most useful or influential to you in the past?

15. When are you happy? What are the positive factors in your life right now? (Hobbies? Sports? Family? Security?)

16. What spiritual or religious issues are important to you? How does your culture, heritage, etc., influence you?

17. Is there anything we haven't talked about that is relevant or important, or that you feel I should know about?

18. Examiner's confidence in accuracy of information obtained (high, adequate, marginal, poor).

19. Quality and intensity of alliance (positive, meshing; positive, building; neutral, cautious; negative, distant/ guarded; negative, hostile/suspicious).

20. [Add other questions that seem called for or appropriate.]

- Just before "Introductory Questions," the form lists the item "Entered into birthday book." This pertains to the sending of birthday cards, which may be appropriate for some child clinicians.

- The introductory questions repeat some of those of the client information forms (Forms 24 and 25), and so it may not be necessary to ask these again. However, if it has been a while since the first contact, they can be asked as a way of reestablishing rapport and making sure you and the patient agree on the problems to be dealt with. You may also discover changes that have occurred since the earlier contact. Finally, if you have doubts or concerns about what the client indicated earlier, ask these questions again to gain more detailed information or check for inconsistencies.

- As always, you should add or delete questions to this form to suit your clientele or practice. Having the forms on the CD makes this easy. If you prefer to use a written questionnaire, you can rephrase, reformat, and delete some of the questions in Form 33 for your clients to complete in writing.

As you interview a client, it may be clarifying for both you and the client to record relevant information by constructing a genogram or family tree. A photocopy of this can be given to the client at the end of the interview, either as homework or as a way to assist with further history gathering.

Collecting Information from Young Adults

FORM 34   Form 34 is designed to be acceptable to and productive with adolescent clients, who are often reluctant to divulge information, unfamiliar with the ability to keep information confidential, hostile to seeing a "shrink," and otherwise resistant. It asks initial questions, which are then followed up during the interview for more detailed information. For example, the question "Do you party?" is a lead into alcohol consumption, sexual activity, use of contraception, and so forth. Alternate phrasings for the question "Why do you think you are here?" include: "Do you understand why you are coming here?", "Are you coming here because of a problem that is mainly someone else's?" If so, ask, "Whose?", or "What is the problem?" This form is based on one designed by Nora Fleming Young, PhD, of Mayer, AZ, and is adapted here with her kind permission. The confidentiality statement at the top may need to be modified for your state and the young person's age.

Special Considerations for Interviewing a Child

During your interview of a child patient or his or her caregiver(s), you might want to consider collecting data and your impressions about these points:

Social Context

1. Relationship between this child and each parent or significant adult.

2. Ways affection is shown and emotions are expressed and controlled.

Young Adult Information Form

Note: Unless there is a serious risk of injury to you or someone else, the information on this form is confidential. It will not be discussed with your parents without your consent.

Your name: _____ Today's date: _____ Your age: _____

Your address: _____ Phone #: _____

Health

How tall are you? _____ How much do you weigh? _____ What do you consider your ideal weight? _____

What physical or medical problems do you have now, or have you had in the past? _____

_____

Family

Birth parents' names: _____ and _____

Address: _____ Phone #: _____

Present parents'/guardians' names: _____ and _____

Address: _____ Phone #: _____

How would you describe your parents' relationship? _____

What kinds of problems are you having with:

    Parents/stepparents/guardians?

    Parents' live-in friends or boyfriends/girlfriends?

    Brothers or sisters (or stepbrothers or stepsisters)?

(cont.)

FORM 34. Information form for young adults (p. 1 of 3). Adapted from a form devised by Nora Fleming Young, PhD, of Mayer, AZ, and used by permission of Dr. Young.—From *The Paper Office*. Copyright 2008 by Edward L. Zuckerman. Permission to photocopy this handout is granted to purchasers of this book for personal use only (see copyright page for details).

School

Which school do you go to? _____ Grade level/year: _____

How are your grades? _____

Problems in school? _____

Work

Do you work? _____ If so, where? _____

Problems there? _____

Friends

Who are your close friends (names and ages)?

Do you have a serious one-on-one relationship now? _____

Do you party? _____ If so, when and where? _____

Previous counseling

1. With whom? _____ When? _____

    For what? _____

    With what results? _____

2. With whom? _____ When? _____

    For what? _____

    With what results? _____

Concerns

Would you like information or answers on: ❑ Sex ❑ Alcohol ❑ Drugs (If so, which? _____)

   ❑ Birth control ❑ Relationships ❑ Other: _____

Is religion important to you and/or your family? _____ If so, in what ways? _____

_____

What worries or upsets you?

_____ *(cont.)*

315

What makes you happy?

Why do you think you are here? Please tell me in your own words.

What would you like to see happen or change because of this counseling?

What would you like me to let your parents know?

What else is important for me to know?

What would you like me to ask you about?

Signed: _____ Date: _____

3. Parenting skills. (Empathy, appropriateness of expectations, methods of control/discipline, by whom.)

4. Chores expected and performance.

5. Autonomy. (Age-appropriateness; allowances; selection of clothes, friends, music; etc.)

6. Relationships with siblings, relatives.

7. Social skills. (Friendships, peers, older vs. younger playmates, skill level.)

8. Social context. (Cultural, ethnic, religious, economic, immigrant, etc.)

9. Other.

Parental Understanding of Problem(s)

1. Parent's view of child's main problem.

2. Parental efforts to handle, change, or cure the child's problems.

3. Parental ideas of what the school or consultant can do for the child.

A complete and practical guide to collecting and using information on child clients is Braaten's (2007) *The Child Clinician's Report-Writing Handbook*, which is part of the Clinician's Toolbox series.

The Evaluation of Mental Status

FORM 35   The purposes of Form 35, the mental status checklist, are as follows: (1) to record observations about the customarily noted aspects of functioning in a systematic way; (2) to document the client's current mental status for baseline and treatment planning; and (3) to help a treating therapist, who may not be experienced in comprehensive and precise mental status evaluations, to document later observations.

There is no paper substitute for a comprehensive evaluation by an experienced clinician, because mental status is a complex biopsychosocial phenomenon. There are more formal brief mental status tests, such as the Folstein et al. (1975) Mini-Mental State, and clinical neuropsychological evaluation instruments, such as the Halstead-Reitan.

This form does not offer the interview questions that would produce the data it summarizes, because there are so many possibilities. It is adapted from Zuckerman (2005), which contains detailed resources for evaluating and describing mental status: a large collection of mental status questions in all categories, and hundreds of words and phrases describing all aspects of cognitive functioning commonly evaluated in a mental status evaluation.

Mental Status Evaluation Checklist

Directions: Rate current observed performance, not reported, historical, or projected. Circle the most appropriate descriptive terms in part C, and feel free to write in others. If an aspect of mental status was not assessed, cross out the heading. Write additional observations, clarifications, and quotations in part D.

Client: _____ Date: _____ Evaluator: _____

Highest grade completed _____ GED? _____ Special education for _____?

Primary occupation: _____ Other: _____

A. Informed consent was obtained about:

❑ The recipient(s) of this report ❑ Confidentiality ❑ Competency ❑ HIPAA ❑ Other:_____

B. Evaluation methods

1. The information and assessments below are based on my observation of this client during:

    ❑ Intake interview ❑ Psychotherapy ❑ Formal mental status testing ❑ Group therapy

    ❑ Other: _____

2. We interacted for a total of _____ minutes.

3. Setting of the contact: ❑ Professional office ❑ Hospital room ❑ Clinic ❑ School ❑ Home ❑ Work

    ❑ Jail/prison ❑ Other: _____

C. Mental status descriptors (Circle all appropriate items)

1. Appearance and self-care

Stature	Average Small Tall (For age, if a child)
Weight	Average weight Overweight Obese Underweight # pounds: _____
Clothing	Neat/clean Careless/inappropriate Meticulous Disheveled Dirty Appropriate for age, occasion, weather Seductive Inappropriate Bizarre
Grooming	Normal Meticulous Neglected Bizarre
Cosmetic use	Appropriate Inappropriate for age Excessive None
Posture/gait	Normal Tense Rigid Stooped Slumped Bizarre Other: _____
Motor activity	Not remarkable Slowed Repetitive Restless Agitated Tremor
Other notable aspects:	_____

2. Sensorium

Attention	Normal Unaware Inattentive Distractible Vigilant
Concentration	Normal Scattered Variable Preoccupied Confused Anxiety interferes Focuses on irrelevancies
Orientation	×5 Time Person Place Situation Object
Recall/memory	Normal Defective in: Immediate/short-term Recent Remote Amnesia Confabulation

(cont.)

FORM 35. Mental status evaluation checklist (p. 1 of 2). From *The Paper Office*. From Zuckerman (2005). Copyright 2005 by Edward L. Zuckerman. Adapted by permission. Permission to photocopy this form is granted to purchasers of this book for personal use only (see copyright page for details).

3. Relating

Eye contact	Normal Fleeting Avoided None Staring
Facial expression	Responsive Constricted Tense Anxious Sad Depressed Angry
Attitude toward examiner	Cooperative Dependent Dramatic Passive Uninterested Silly Resistant Critical Hostile Sarcastic Irritable Threatening Suspicious Guarded Defensive Manipulative Argumentative

4. Affect and mood

Affect	Appropriate Labile Restricted Blunted Flat Other: _____
Mood	Euthymic Irritable Pessimistic Depressed Hypomanic Euphoric Other: _____

5. Thought and language

Speech flow	Normal Mute Loud Blocked Paucity Pressured Flight of ideas
Thought content	Congruent mood and circumstances Incongruent Personalizations Persecutions Indecision Suspicions Delusions Ideas of reference Ideas of influence Illusions
Preoccupations	Phobias Somatic Suicide Homicidal Guilt Religion Other: _____
Hallucinations	Auditory Visual Other: _____ Content: _____
Organization	Normal Logical Goal-directed Circumstantial Loose Perseverations

6. Executive functions

Fund of knowledge	Average Above average Impoverished by: _____
Intelligence	Average Below average Above average Needs investigation
Abstraction	Normal Concrete Functional Popular Abstract Overly abstract
Judgment	Normal Common-sensical Fair Poor Dangerous
Reality testing	Realistic Adequate Distorted Variable Unaware
Insight	Uses connections Gaps Flashes of Unaware Nil Denial
Decision making	Normal Only simple Impulsive Vacillates Confused Paralyzed

7. Stress

Stressors	Money Housing Family conflict Work Grief/losses Illness Transitions
Coping ability	Normal Resilient Exhausted Overwhelmed Deficient supports Deficient skills Growing
Skill deficits	None Education Communication Interpersonal Decision making Self-control Responsibility Self-care Activities of Daily Living
Supports	Usual Family Friends Church Service system Other: _____ Needed: _____

8. Social functioning

Social maturity	Responsible Irresponsible Self-centered Impulsive Isolates
Social judgment	Normal "Street-smart" Naive Heedless Victimized Impropriety

D. Other aspects of mental status

_____

_____

_____

This is a strictly confidential patient medical record. Redisclosure or transfer is expressly prohibited by law.

This report reflects the patient's condition at the time of consultation or evaluation. It does not necessarily reflect the patient's diagnosis or condition at any subsequent time.

5.6   Phase 5: Summarizing the Intake Information

During the previous phases of the intake process, you have collected data about the client from the client, your observations, forms, and perhaps other sources. Now it is time to review, sift, and integrate those data. This section offers three forms to assist with this process.

Summarizing Chemical Use and Suicide Risk Data

FORM 36
FORM 37
The processes of assessing clients' chemical use and suicide risk have already been discussed in Sections 5.4 and 3.10, respectively. Form 36, the chemical user's case formulation, and Form 37, the suicide risk assessment summary and recommendations, are designed to assist you in summarizing and integrating all the relevant information in cases where one or the other of these factors plays a significant role.

Formulating the Whole Case

When the information presented by a new client has been collected, the data must be organized for the making of clinical decisions. What should be the disposition of the case: Should the client be referred elsewhere, be sent for further assessments or consultations, receive treatment from you, or be sent to a specialized treatment program? If treatment is appropriate, what should be the goals, and what methods should be used? A treatment plan is needed.

FORM 38
The purposes and functions of Form 38, the intake summary and case formulation, are to gather and formulate the findings so as to (1) prioritize the client's most important and immediate problems; (2) facilitate all appropriate referrals for evaluation or treatment; (3) support consultations and coordination with other professionals; (4) document the need for services to funding sources (e.g., health insurers and MCOs); (5) concentrate the data needed to develop a treatment plan; and (6) provide for continuity and comprehensiveness of care. If your patient requires MCO approval, complete this first and then see Form 39, the individualized treatment plan for MCOs, at the end of Section 6.1.

Section D, part 1, of Form 38 offers checkoffs for the assessment of risks. Some of the items can be expanded if your setting needs greater precision, as in these examples:

---

a. *Suicide*:   ❑ Not assessed   ❑ No indications   ❑ Passive death wish   ❑ Ideation without plan

❑ Threat   ❑ Preoccupation   ❑ Plan   ❑ Prior gesture   ❑ Prior attempt

❑ Plan without means   ❑ Access to means   ❑ Other: _____

b. *Homicide*:   ❑ Not assessed   ❑ No indications   ❑ Ideation without plan   ❑ Threat

❑ Identifiable victim   ❑ No identifiable victim   ❑ Preoccupation   ❑ Plan

❑ Prior attempt   ❑ Plan without means   ❑ Access to means   ❑ Other: _____

Chemical User's Case Formulation

Based on the data collected during this evaluation process, here are my conclusions. (The best descriptors are checked.)

A. Identification

Name: _____ Date: _____ Case #: _____

B. Observations

Client was intoxicated at interview	❏ Not at all	❏ Possibly	❏ Mildly	❏ Clearly	❏ Hung over
Consumption history was	❏ Acknowledged	❏ Minimized	❏ Denied,	❏ but confirmed	
Legal consequences were	❏ Acknowledged	❏ Minimized	❏ Denied,	❏ but confirmed	
Financial consequences were	❏ Acknowledged	❏ Minimized	❏ Denied,	❏ but confirmed	
Health consequences were	❏ Acknowledged	❏ Minimized	❏ Denied,	❏ but confirmed	
Spiritual consequences were	❏ Acknowledged	❏ Minimized	❏ Denied,	❏ but confirmed	
Vocational consequences were	❏ Acknowledged	❏ Minimized	❏ Denied,	❏ but confirmed	
Familial consequences were	❏ Acknowledged	❏ Minimized	❏ Denied,	❏ but confirmed	

What brought the patient in now? _____

_____

The patient's goals (and their realism, comprehensiveness, resources needed): _____

_____

_____

C. Degree of identification/denial as having alcoholism/addiction

❏ Denies any intemperate use; denies need for treatment

❏ Minimizes consequences of drinking/use

❏ Is "treatment-wise" or "just going through the motions"

❏ Identifies self as "alcoholic/addicted," "in recovery"; has made sobriety his or her first priority

❏ Is willing to and did do whatever is necessary to maintain sobriety, has a positive and optimistic attitude toward the future

D. Stage in the progression of the disease (for alcoholism only)

❏ None   ❏ Prealcoholism   ❏ Prodromal   ❏ Crucial   ❏ Chronic   ❏ Periodic excessive drinking

❏ Blackouts   ❏ Sneaking drinks   ❏ Loss of control over drinking   ❏ Remorse and rationalization

❏ Changing the pattern of drinking   ❏ Morning drinking   ❏ Benders/binges   ❏ Defeat

(cont.)

E. Personal variables

Gender/sex role training   ❑ Not relevant ❑ Minimal ❑ Important ❑ Crucial

Social class   ❑ Not relevant ❑ Minimal ❑ Important ❑ Crucial

Ethnicity   ❑ Not relevant ❑ Minimal ❑ Important ❑ Crucial

Self-esteem/sense of efficacy   ❑ Normal ❑ Control in other life areas ❑ Helpless/passive/defeated
❑ Blames others/denial ❑ Self-destroying

Impact of abuse   ❑ None ❑ Mild ❑ Significant ❑ Severe/prolonged

Attitude toward treatment   ❑ Eager for ❑ Hopeful ❑ Neutral ❑ Pessimistic

Other: _____

F. Social variables

Residence   ❑ Comfortable, stable ❑ Unstable ❑ Temporary ❑ None

Employment   ❑ Regular ❑ Irregular ❑ Tenuous ❑ None

Friends   ❑ No friends ❑ No abusers ❑ Some abusers ❑ Only abusers

Addiction of close relatives   ❑ Not relevant ❑ Minimal ❑ Important ❑ Crucial

Spouse/significant other   ❑ None ❑ Supportive ❑ Uncooperative ❑ Not involved ❑ In denial
❑ Enabling ❑ Codependent ❑ Addicted

Family involvement   ❑ None ❑ In denial ❑ Cooperative ❑ Exhausted ❑ Punitive

Support system for sobriety   ❑ Excellent, stable, broad ❑ Some ❑ Minimal ❑ Counterproductive

Other factors: _____

G. Diagnosis (DSM-IV or ICD diagnosis is on intake summary)

❑ Abstaining ❑ In recovery ❑ Social drinking/controlled drinking ❑ Heavy drinking ❑ Problem drinking

❑ Uncontrolled drinking/alcohol addiction/compulsive drinking ❑ Other: _____

❑ "Dry drunk" syndrome ❑ At risk ❑ Addiction ❑ Cross-addiction

H. Additional assessments needed

❑ Mental status exam ❑ Neuropsychological ❑ Neurological ❑ Medical ❑ Educational/vocational

❑ Diagnostic evaluations for presence of concurrent psychiatric disorders

❑ Assessment of relationship/marital/sexual difficulties ❑ Assessment of risk for suicide, homicide, abuse, violence

I. Prognosis

The prognosis, with treatment as specified in the individual treatment plan, is considered to be as follows:

1. For participation in and benefit from treatments: ❑ Optimistic ❑ Good ❑ Guarded ❑ Poor ❑ Negative

2. For improvement of symptoms: ❑ Optimistic ❑ Good ❑ Guarded ❑ Poor ❑ Negative

3. For recovery to previous level of functioning: ❑ Optimistic ❑ Good ❑ Guarded ❑ Poor ❑ Negative

4. For growth and wellness: ❑ Optimistic ❑ Good ❑ Guarded ❑ Poor ❑ Negative

This is a strictly confidential patient medical record. Redisclosure or transfer is expressly prohibited by law.

This report reflects the patient's condition at the time of consultation or evaluation. It does not necessarily reflect the patient's diagnosis or condition at any subsequent time.

Suicide Risk Assessment Summary and Recommendations

Client's name: _____ Date: _____

This assessment is based on information collected from the following:

❑ My interview(s) with these persons: On these dates:

    ❑ The client

    ❑ Family members: _____ _____

    ❑ Friends: _____ _____

    ❑ Other people: _____ _____

❑ Reading of records (specify): _____

_____

❑ Knowledge from previous client contacts of the risk factors this client and situation present

❑ Other sources: _____

It is my professional judgment that this person currently presents the following risk of suicide:

❑ Almost nonexistent	No direct or indirect evidence for suicidal ideation, rumination, or behaviors from client or others. (It is against strongly held beliefs; the client has many or valued reasons for living.)
❑ Low	Only passive/death wishes (tired of living/pain; fleeting ideation).
❑ Moderate	Ideation without plan, means, motivation (ambivalence, wondering, considering).
❑ Significant/likely	Persistent ideation, making plans, acquiring means. (The client has made statements, rehearsals, threats, gestures or low-lethality/symbolic/ineffective attempts. The client has discussed suicide.)
❑ Very high	Serious/high-lethality attempt is likely in near future. (The client has arranged some affairs, has acquired some means, and has some plan of action and privacy.)
❑ Acute and immediate	Persistent and preoccupying thoughts, continual efforts. (The client has acquired high-lethality means and is deliberate and focused. The client has one or more effective plans of action and the necessary privacy.)

(cont.)

Therefore, I recommend the following interventions:

❑ No intervention is needed at present.

❑ Reevaluate by this date: _____

❑ Consultation with these people or organizations:

❑ Relatives: _____

❑ Other professionals: _____

❑ Mental health authorities: _____

❑ Law enforcement authorities: _____

❑ Other: _____

❑ Changes to therapy or new therapeutic interventions:

❑ Confrontation and concerned discussion by client's therapist to explore issues and motives

❑ No-suicide contracting

❑ More intensive psychotherapy

❑ Changes in medications

❑ Intensive family interventions and support

❑ Crisis intervention team

❑ Partial hospitalization with intensive treatment

❑ Psychiatric inpatient hospitalization: ❑ Voluntary ❑ Involuntary

❑ Contacts with police or other authorities

❑ Other recommendations: _____

_____

_____

_____   _____
Signature   Date

_____
Printed name

A copy of this form should now be sent to: _____

Intake Summary and Case Formulation

Where space is insufficient, use an asterisk and write the information on additional pages.

A. Basic information

Client: _____ Date: _____ ID #: _____

Purpose of this intake: ❑ New client evaluation ❑ Readmission; previous intake on _____

❑ Consultation; copy to be sent to _____ ❑ Reevaluation or review

❑ Other purpose: _____

B. Dynamics of difficulties

Presenting complaint(s): Thoughts, behaviors, emotions	Stressors Acute/chronic	Strengths/resources

C. Present level of functioning/limitations/impairment (describe specific impairments at left, and rate degree of functional impairment at right with GAF number [100 = none, 70 = little, 30 = significant, 10 = incapacitated] or use descriptors):

Area of functioning	GAF rating
1. School/work functioning: _____	_____
2. Intimate relationship/marriage: _____	_____
3. Family/children: _____	_____
4. Social relationships: _____	_____
5. Psychological/personal functioning: _____	_____
6. Other areas: _____	_____

(cont.)

FORM 38. Intake summary and case formulation (p. 1 of 3). From *The Paper Office.* Copyright 2008 by Edward L. Zuckerman. Permission to photocopy this form is granted to purchasers of this book for personal use only (see copyright page for details).

D. Assessment conclusions

1. Assessment of currently known **risk factors**:

   a. *Suicide*: ❑ Not assessed   ❑ No known behaviors   ❑ Ideation only   ❑ Plan
      ❑ Intent without means   ❑ Intent with means

   b. *Homicide*: ❑ Not assessed   ❑ No known behaviors   ❑ Ideation only   ❑ Plan
      ❑ Intent without means   ❑ Intent with means

   c. *Impulse control*: ❑ Not assessed   ❑ Sufficient control   ❑ Moderate   ❑ Minimal   ❑ Inconsistent

   d. *Adherence to treatments*: ❑ Not assessed   ❑ Full adherence   ❑ Minimal nonadherence
      ❑ Moderate adherence   ❑ Variable   ❑ Little or no adherence

   e. *Substance abuse/dependence*: ❑ Not assessed   ❑ None/normal use   ❑ Overuse   ❑ Abuse
      ❑ Dependence   ❑ Unstable remission   ❑ Full, sustained remission

   f. *Current physical or sexual abuse*: ❑ Not assessed   ❑ No   ❑ Yes   Legally reportable? ❑ Yes ❑ No

   g. *Current child/elder neglect*: ❑ Not assessed   ❑ No   ❑ Yes   Legally reportable? ❑ Yes ❑ No
      If yes, client is   ❑ Victim   ❑ Perpetrator   ❑ Both   ❑ Neither, but abuse exists in family

   h. *If risk exists:* Client ❑ can ❑ cannot meaningfully agree to a contract not to harm ❑ self ❑ others ❑ both

2. **Urgency** estimate   ❑ Emergency; immediate interventions   ❑ Serious disruption of functioning; act in next 24 hours   ❑ Treatment needed; act soon/routine   ❑ Wait for: _____

3. **Diagnoses**—Current best formulation: Name (indicate which is primary diagnosis with "P")

   Code #
   ❑ DSM-IV-TR
   or ❑ ICD?

   Axis I _____   _____

   Axis II _____   _____

   Axis III—Significant and relevant medical conditions, including allergies and drug sensitivities:

	Condition	Treatment/medication (regimen)	Provider	Status
1.	_____	_____	_____	_____
2.	_____	_____	_____	_____
3.	_____	_____	_____	_____

   Axis IV—Psychosocial and environmental problems in last year; overall severity rating: _____

   ❑ Problems with primary support group   ❑ Problems related to the social environment

   ❑ Educational problems   ❑ Occupational problems

   ❑ Housing problems   ❑ Economic problems

   ❑ Health care access problems   ❑ Other problems: _____

   ❑ Problems related to interaction with the legal system/crime

   Axis V—Global Assessment of Functioning (GAF) Rating: Currently: _____   Highest in past year: _____

   V Codes—Other problems that may be a focus of clinical attention: _____

   _____

   (cont.)

E. Recommended program of coordinated liaisons, consultations, evaluations, and services

1. Psychotherapy: ❑ Cognitive ❑ Behavioral ❑ Family/systems ❑ Insight-oriented ❑ Play therapy ❑ Support/maintenance ❑ Environmental change ❑ Focal group ❑ Clinical hypnosis ❑ Biofeedback ❑ Other: _____

   CPT code(s) to be used: _____

2. Support groups: Twelve-Step program: ❑ AA ❑ NA ❑ Overeaters ❑ Gamblers

   ❑ Other community support groups: _____

   Psychoeducational groups: ❑ Parenting skills/child management ❑ Communication skills

   ❑ Stress management ❑ Assertiveness ❑ Women's issues ❑ Other: _____

   Ancillary services: ❑ Pain clinic ❑ Back school ❑ Physical therapy ❑ Other: _____

3. Legal services: ❑ Offender program ❑ Substance abuse/dependence ❑ Other: _____

   ❑ Victim support ❑ Referral to emergency services/advocates: _____

4. **Referrals for continuing services**

Referred to	For (kind of service)	Date of referral
	Psychotropic medications	
	Physical medical care	
	Psychiatric evaluation	
	Patient education	
	Nursing care	
	Educational/vocational services	
	Occupational/physical therapy	
	Other: _____	

5. **Further assessments,** based on current clinical evaluation, are needed to answer these concerns or rule out these possible coexisting conditions:

   ❑ Psychological presentation/symptoms of medical condition

   　　Likely possible sources: ❑ Thyroid ❑ Diabetes ❑ Alcohol/drug misuse ❑ Circulatory problem

   　　❑ Neurological problem ❑ Poor nutrition ❑ Medication interactions ❑ Toxin exposure

   　　❑ Other: _____

   ❑ Sexual dysfunctions　　　　❑ Factitious disorders　　　　❑ Substance abuse/dependence

   ❑ Psychophysiological disorders　❑ Learning disabilities　　　❑ Genetic disorders/counseling

   ❑ Other: _____

6. **Documents to be obtained** (have requests for records completed and signed, photocopied, and placed in client's file so that receipt can be assured):

Type of record	Source	Date of first request
❑ Medical/physician/hospital		
❑ School		
❑ Agency		
❑ Other: _____		

7. **Other needed resources and services:** _____

_____

For the section E, you could substitute a statement or checklist with options of the services you have available, in order of intensity of service/need:

E. Recommended level of care

- ❑ Emergency/immediate psychiatric hospitalization
- ❑ Regular psychiatric hospitalization
- ❑ Residential treatment center
- ❑ Inpatient medical detoxification
- ❑ Inpatient substance abuse/dependence program
- ❑ Specialized inpatient program for:_____
- ❑ Group or supported housing
- ❑ Partial hospitalization/day treatment program
- ❑ Structured/intensive outpatient program for:_____

Or, depending on the likely needs of your clientele, you can add these to the present section E:

Residential care: ❑ Shelter   ❑ Partial hospitalization   ❑ Inpatient 24-hour hospitalization
   ❑ Group home   ❑ Family support   ❑ Other:_____

Educational/vocational services: ❑ Agency evaluation   ❑ GED classes   ❑ Work hardening
   ❑ Sheltered workshop   ❑ Special school services   ❑ Other:_____

Economic supports: ❑ Welfare/AFDC   ❑ Soc. Sec. Disability   ❑ Other:_____

Or other categories of risk can be added:

Self-injury: ❑ Not assessed   ❑ No indications   ❑ Ideation without plan   ❑ Threat
   ❑ Preoccupation   ❑ Plan   ❑ Prior injuries:_____   ❑ Access to means

Isolation: ❑ Self-preoccupation   ❑ Avoidance   ❑ Seclusion   ❑ Self-neglect   ❑ Refuses supports
   ❑ Harm or injury from neglect   ❑ Other:_____

In the "self-injury" category, you need to distinguish acts of suicidal intent from body modification (tattooing, piercing, scarification), sexual or power exchange activities (knife play, slave and master, etc.), and acts motivated by psychopathology (relief of psychic pain through self-cutting and blood).

Another revision you could make is that you could add or substitute a visual scale for each of the risks in Section D, part 1:

When compared with this practice's/agency's typical patient population, the risk this client presents is judged at this time to be:

Very low   Low   Medium   High   Very high

Among other changes you might make to this form, DSM-IV-TR (American Psychiatric Association, 2000) has proposed three axes for future study; it may be useful to start using these now, so that outcome changes on these can be scored in the future. They should go at the end of section D, part 3 ("Diagnoses").

Social and Occupational Functioning Assessment Scale (SOFAS: 0–100): Currently: _____ Past year: _____

Global Assessment of Relational Functioning (GARF) Scale (0–100): Currently: _____ Past year: _____

Defensive Functioning Scale (DFS): List up to seven defenses, most prominent first:

_____

_____

Predominant current defense level: ❑ High adaptive ❑ Mental inhibitions ❑ Minor image-distorting ❑ Disavowal ❑ Major image-distorting ❑ Action ❑ Defensive dysregulation

CHAPTER 6

Planning and Then Documenting Treatment

After intake and assessment have been completed and recorded, the next clinical and record-keeping tasks are planning treatment, documenting its progress, and finally case termination. This chapter of *The Paper Office* covers these aspects in detail.

6.1 Treatment Planning

A good plan today is better than a perfect plan tomorrow.
—General George S. Patton

The whole subject of treatment planning is in flux. There is neither a widely accepted set of essentials for a plan, nor any universally accepted format in use. The following general guidelines, as well as the forms and formats offered in this chapter, are intended to provide ideas and a framework rather than to be prescriptive or final.

Issues

Some therapists working today resist the planning of treatment, because they believe it interferes with the immediacy and spontaneity they value in therapy. It also seems to require the prediction of what they see as unpredictable—the evolving, branching dance of client and therapist, problem and intervention.

The research has not resolved the question of whether a planful or a spontaneous approach is better, and it may never. Funding sources, manualized treatment methods, and clinical experience all suggest that at least some degree of organization is beneficial. However, as Hare-Mustin et al. (1979) point out, goal setting is extraordinarily difficult for some situations: when a client is unable to be specific; when children do not conform to their parents' goals (e.g., obedience); when spouses/partners have conflicting goals; when the client's goals stem from an ineffective conceptualization of the problem; when the client's symptomatic behaviors seem understandable or even socially acceptable to the therapist; and so forth.

Developing a treatment plan jointly with each client requires the kind of thoughtful, comprehensive, insightful effort that ensures successful therapy. It can be a productive focusing of therapeutic time. This process can be used cooperatively to involve the client in planning, homework/self-monitoring, revision of methods, and overall evaluation. Such a model of joint decision making strengthens the connections among consultation, planning, treatment, and evaluation. It also implements beliefs in mutuality and equality.

In addition, a treatment plan serves to limit distractions from the central goals. Without a plan, sequence, or map, both you and your client can easily be distracted from what is most important. You can both easily lose your "vision" in the welter of data, intercurrent events, levels of analysis, and so on, and fail to integrate the immediate into the important. As the saying goes, when we are up to our ears wrestling alligators, it is hard to remember that we came here to drain the swamp.

Guidelines for Treatment Planning

Typically, a client comes in with complaints or problems, some ideas of their causes, and some desired outcomes. His or her presentation is reformulated by the therapist within a framework that allows for intervention and change. The therapist's favorite (or even just familiar) methods are offered to the client, and change is assessed irregularly and mainly unreliably. A more systematic and yet realistic sequence for treatment planning would proceed as follows:

- **Identify and assess** all the current problematic or symptomatic behaviors, affects, or cognitions. First, list, with the client, the major problems and related effects of these problems on his or her life. Review all areas of functioning. Prioritize these concerns. Chapter 5's forms support this process, and formats for a problem list are offered in Section 6.2.

- **Define the outcomes desired**—both long-term "goals" and short-term "objectives." Some view the relationship between goals and objectives as analogous to strategic and tactical efforts in military terms. One way to seek objectives is to ask, "If we are to achieve this long-term goal by this specific date [such as next year], what smaller steps would have to be accomplished and by when [such as next month]?" These smaller steps, or objectives, are usually more behavioral, measurable, and concrete than goals. For a simple and yet reliable and valid way of assessing the accomplishment of goals, see the discussion of goal attainment scaling later in this section.

- **Consider the interventions and resources needed** to achieve the goals. The selecting and sequencing of interventions is the responsibility of the therapist.

- **Provide reliable ways to evaluate** the client's current status, progress, and outcomes.

These steps are considered in more detail below.

Systems and Formats of Treatment Planning

If you are seeking a comprehensive system of planning treatment, consider the following models. Some are more comprehensive or more detailed than others, and some will suit your setting or needs better. They are presented here roughly in the order of their complexity.

The PIC Treatment Plan

A simple, practical, and unique format is described by Levenstein (1994a). It has the advantages of coordinating treatment plans and progress notes, and of addressing obstacles to the progress of treatment. After a comprehensive evaluation, the clinician does the following:

1. Identifies the primary issues, and formulates a tentative explanation of how the problems occurred.

2. Gives a formal diagnosis (DSM-IV-TR).

3. Creates the goal plan (in essence, the treatment plan).

4. Assigns a target date for each goal.

The format for the goal plan uses the acronym "PIC":

- P is for the problem (current behavior) or goal (desired end state).

- I is for the intervention(s).

- C is for the indicators of change (specific, overt behaviors to be tracked, how they will be assessed, and by whom).

With the addition of R for resistance or obstacles (Levenstein, 1994b), this format can be easily adapted for progress notes. See Section 6.2 for various types of progress notes.

The Problem-Oriented Record

The problem-oriented record (POR) is a comprehensive and logical method that is widely used in medicine. It is discussed in detail in Section 6.2.

Individualized Treatment Plan for Managed Care Organizations

Managed care organizations (MCOs) require that an individualized treatment plan be developed the first or second session. Form 39 (see below) will assist you in developing such a plan.

Impairment Profile

Goodman et al. (1992) cleverly suggest using a patient impairment profile to document and communicate treatment needs, to develop a rationale for treatment and a treatment plan, and to predict outcome of care. The list of impairments (in their Appendix A) becomes a common language for helpers from different disciplines. When combined with a severity rating, it suggests an appropriate level of service or care. They add outcome objectives, selections from a list of interventions (their Appendix B), and progress measures to assess the effectiveness of treatment (basically, changes in the ratings of severity). Their system is neat and complete, but requires a new model—that of impairments.

As another example of an impairment-based approach, the World Health Organization has been working on an *International Classification of Functioning, Disability and Health* (ICFDH). This is likely to substantially replace the DSM for most psychotherapy and rehabilitation, so it is well worth your monitoring and support. It can be searched, browsed, and downloaded at www3.who.int/icf.

Other Approaches

Arthur E. Jongsma, Jr., has produced a large series of books called *Treatment Planners, Progress Notes Planners*, and *Homework Planners*, as well as a computer program to aid in the development of treatment. They offer very specific language for these topics and, though somewhat generic, can be used to create more tailored plans.

James A. Kennedy has developed a planning and outcome evaluation system based on DSM-IV-TR's Axis V, called the Kennedy Axis V. It addresses seven "universal functional domains": (1) psychological impairment; (2) social skills; (3) violence; (4) activities of daily living/occupational skills; (5) substance abuse; (6) medical impairment; and (7) ancillary impairment. (See www.kennedymd.bigstep.com for more information.) Although such a system is comprehensive, anchoring of scores is always problematic.

Other Points in Planning Treatment

Taking Account of Resistance

Everybody wants to be happier. No one wants to change.
—ANONYMOUS

If a treatment plan is to be truly effective, it must anticipate and respond to the obstacles to change. A great deal of the elegance and effectiveness of psychotherapy is found in its sophistication about handling "resistance." Here are some questions I like to ask a client in the course of planning treatment; the client's responses to these questions can be built into the plan, and can thus increase the chances of a successful outcome.

- "What would happen if you were to make the changes you say you want? How would these changes affect your partner, family, and friends? What would be the negative consequences?" (This question identifies demotivators, obstacles, and blind spots.)

- "What are the blockages/obstacles to change?" (This lets you see how the client conceptualizes the work to be done.)

- "What has not worked in the past?" (This might keep you from repeating unsuccessful approaches.)

- "What *has* been helpful in the past in dealing with these problems?" (You can then build on these.)

- "When were there situations like this, but you were able to manage them successfully?" (This is a solution-focused approach.)

- "Who are your best allies in helping you deal with problems like these?" (This question identifies the client's social and other supports.)

- "Who do you know who has successfully dealt with these same problems?" (This identifies potential role models.)

- "What do you think is necessary to make things better, and how long might each of these take?" (This question explores the client's conceptualization of treatment, so that you can blend into it or work to change it.)

Coordinating Treatment Efforts

If treatments must be simultaneous, you will need to communicate the relevant information among providers. Traditionally, case and team conferences have borne this function; however, unless they are very well organized (see, e.g., Doyle & Straus, 1993; Kelsey & Plumb, 2004), they have been demonstrated to make poor decisions (Meehl, 1973) and waste everyone's time and a lot of money. Consider alternatives like a client-oriented newsletter, with a title such as "Nancy's News," which could be circulated by e-mail and posted to a password-protected website. Perhaps the simplest way to create a group and share information can be found at www.groups.yahoo.com. PORs (see Section 6.2) are a paperwork improvement, but there is no reason not to be creative.

Evaluating Outcomes with Goal Attainment Scaling

How can you evaluate the changes a client makes? The methods of planning described earlier generally use symptom reduction as the criterion of change. However, alternative, more flexible models exist. The best-known one is "goal attainment scaling," which is a very simple but powerful method of documenting progress toward goals (Kiresuk et al., 1994). It consists of the following components:

1. Specifying at least five goals. Goals can be described in *any* terms or areas; this is a major strength of this method.

2. Specifying a date in the future when progress toward the goals is to be evaluated.

3. Defining possible outcomes, in observable terms, at five levels for each goal. These five levels are as follows (slightly reworded):

    −2 = The worst outcome that is likely to occur.

    −1 = An outcome less successful than expected.

0 = An outcome that achieves the expected level of success.

+1 = An outcome more successful than expected.

+2 = The most favorable outcome thought likely.

4. At the previously decided point or points in time, the level of attainment of each goal is scored.

5. A simple statistical test (Student's t-test) can be applied to this score to decide how likely it is to have happened by chance. Scores can be compared over time, across clients, or across programs.

Some difficulties will arise if expectations are low and the true cause of the change cannot be determined. But the method is simple, easily learned (as by a client), and widely applicable. Its greatest advantage is that it can be applied to almost any kind of goal, and is thus independent of any theory or orientation.

Formulating Treatment Plans for Managed Care Organizations

We should not let the current and substantial differences between the objectives of MCOs (see Section 3.11) and those of clinicians obscure the commonalities. Thoughtful planning of treatment interventions is always desirable and in the patient's best interest.[1]

Keeping an eye on treatment plans is managed care's preferred method for tracking "quality and appropriate care," says Scott Harris, PhD, codirector of the Center for Behavioral Health Care in Los Angeles. "It provides a structured mechanism for periodic review and authorization, monitoring providers for appropriateness, competence, and effectiveness."

Harris provides the following guidelines for writing a treatment plan (with special attention to the expectations of MCOs):

1. **Comprehensive overview.** Provide a full profile of the patient. Outline both the nature of the crisis and the focus of treatment.

2. **Goals and progress.** State treatment goals in measurable, behavioral terms. Indicate specific progress to be made within a given time period. Link clinical improvement to specific interventions and detail a predischarge level of progress.

3. **Action.** [The plan should] reflect the thinking, planning, and actions taken by the therapist with the patient. Interventions must promote change and movement through the therapy.

---

[1]The following passage, including the remarks and guidelines by Scott Harris, PhD, is reprinted from "Ten Steps to Create a Successful Treatment Plan" (1993). Copyright 1993 by Ridgewood Financial Institute. Reprinted by permission.

4. **Timeliness.** Treatment planning must correspond with the [MCO's] authorization as well as the clinician's billing. Without coordinated documentation, a delay in claims processing and reimbursement may result. That means frustrating phone calls and, perhaps, filing the claim a second or third time.

5. **Benefit awareness.** Know the limits and structure of the specific benefit being administered by the managed care firm. Some benefits may include only 3 to 5 sessions, while others allow as many as 50.

6. **Alternative services.** Show that you are aware of, and willing to refer to, other levels of care such as day treatment, hospitalization, etc., as well as other resources that complement and reinforce treatment goals. This may mean specifying patient involvement in 12-step programs, support groups, parenting classes, or medication consultations with a psychiatrist.

7. **Professional liaisons.** Specifically state the role of other professionals essential to the outcome of the case.

8. **Crisis and other potential red flags.** Understand, identify, and plan for potential crisis situations. Responses and steps for crisis intervention need to be clearly detailed for cases involving potential suicide or child abuse. Use case managers as resources.

9. **Chemical dependency.** Address and plan treatment for potential or existing chronic chemical dependency problems.

10. **Copies.** Always keep copies of treatment plans and authorizations. This prevents multiple frustrations when you learn that a plan has not been received, or received and then lost.

FORM 39 Form 39 is an individualized treatment form for MCOs that will enable you to follow these guidelines. Its purposes and functions are (1) to serve as a checklist to assure that all evaluations and treatments have been considered; (2) to document the recommendations for treatment; (3) to support consultation with MCO reviewers to assess needed level of care and "medical necessity"; and (4) to enable you to initiate the first phase of treatment.

To simplify record making, this form is similar to Form 38. Thus, after summarizing your understanding of a case on Form 38, you can easily reuse that material to create a treatment plan suitable for MCOs on Form 39. Your letterhead must contain any additional identifying information that the MCO requires (provider number, supervisor, credentials, license number, etc.).

You can make various changes to Form 39. For example, see the suggestions in Section 5.6 for changes to Form 38. In addition, you can elaborate on crisis management under heading E:

Individualized Behavioral/Mental Health Treatment Plan

This is for ❑ Preauthorization for initial certification ❑ Concurrent review for reauthorization of care

Date current episode of treatment began: _____ Date of last plan: _____

A. Identification

Client's name:_____ Soc. Sec.#:_____ ID#:_____

Membership #:_____ Date of birth:_____ Sex:_____

Group name/#:_____ Certificate #:_____

Name of subscriber/member, and address (if other than client):_____

Release-of-records form(s) signed: ❑ Yes ❑ Not yet

B. Administrative

1. Case manager's additional suggestions for treatments and resources:

Date	Name	Suggestions

2. Services:

Sessions requested	CPT code	Date of request	Start of sessions	Number of sessions authorized	Date of authorization	Date of next review

C. Present level of functioning/limitations/impairment (describe specific impairments at left, and rate degree of functional impairment at right with GAF number [100 = none, 70 = little, 30 = significant, 10 = incapacitated] or use descriptors):

	Area of functioning	GAF rating
1. School/work functioning:	_____	_____
2. Intimate relationship/marriage:	_____	_____

(cont.)

FORM 39. Individualized treatment plan for managed care organizations (p. 1 of 4). From *The Paper Office.*

3. Family/children: _____ _____

4. Social relationships: _____ _____

5. Psychological/personal functioning: _____ _____

6. Other areas: _____ _____

D. Assessment conclusions

1. Assessment of currently known **risk factors**:

   a. *Suicide*: ❑ Not assessed ❑ No known behaviors ❑ Ideation only ❑ Plan
      ❑ Intent without means ❑ Intent with means

   b. *Homicide*: ❑ Not assessed ❑ No known behaviors ❑ Ideation only ❑ Plan
      ❑ Intent without means ❑ Intent with means

   c. *Impulse control*: ❑ Not assessed ❑ Sufficient control ❑ Moderate ❑ Minimal ❑ Inconsistent

   d. *Adherence to treatments*: ❑ Not assessed ❑ Full adherence ❑ Minimal nonadherence
      ❑ Moderate nonadherence ❑ Variable ❑ Little or no adherence

   e. *Substance abuse/dependence*: ❑ Not assessed ❑ None/normal use ❑ Overuse ❑ Abuse
      ❑ Dependence ❑ Unstable remission ❑ Full, sustained remission

   f. *Current physical or sexual abuse*: ❑ Not assessed ❑ No ❑ Yes   Legally reportable? ❑ Yes ❑ No

   g. *Current child/elder neglect*: ❑ Not assessed ❑ No ❑ Yes   Legally reportable? ❑ Yes ❑ No
      If yes, client is ❑ Victim ❑ Perpetrator ❑ Both ❑ Neither, but abuse exists in family

   h. *If risk exists:* Client ❑ can ❑ cannot meaningfully agree to a contract not to harm ❑ self ❑ others ❑ both

2. **Urgency** estimate ❑ Emergency; immediate interventions ❑ Serious disruption of functioning; act in next 24 hours ❑ Treatment needed; act soon/routine ❑ Wait for: _____

3. **Diagnoses**—Current best formulation: Name (indicate which is primary diagnosis with "P")   Code #
   ❑ DSM-IV-TR or ❑ ICD?

   Axis I _____ _____

   Axis II _____ _____

   Axis III—Significant and relevant medical conditions, including allergies and drug sensitivities:

	Condition	Treatment/medication (regimen)	Provider	Status
1.	_____	_____	_____	_____
2.	_____	_____	_____	_____
3.	_____	_____	_____	_____

   Axis IV—Psychosocial and environmental problems in last year; overall severity rating: _____

   ❑ Problems with primary support group   ❑ Problems related to the social environment

   ❑ Educational problems   ❑ Occupational problems

   ❑ Housing problems   ❑ Economic problems

   ❑ Health care access problems   ❑ Other problems: _____

   ❑ Problems related to interaction with the legal system/crime

   Axis V—Global Assessment of Functioning (GAF) rating: Currently: _____ Highest in past year: _____

   V Codes—Other problems that may be a focus of clinical attention: _____
   _____

   (cont.)

E. Treatment plan (if additional problems are to be addressed, use copies of this page)

Problem number	Behaviors to be changed	Interventions (who does what, how often, with what resources; modality, frequency, duration)	Observable indicators of improvement	Sessions to achieve the indicator	Discharge level of problem behaviors

(cont.)

F. Cooperative treatment planning

Our signatures below mean that we have participated in the formulation of this treatment plan, understand and approve of it, and accept the responsibility to carry out our parts of the plan fully.

_____   _____

Signature of client (or person acting for client)   Date

_____   _____   _____

Signature of service provider   Provider number   Date

This is a strictly confidential patient medical record. Redisclosure or transfer is expressly prohibited by law.

This report reflects the patient's condition at the time of consultation or evaluation. It does not necessarily reflect the patient's diagnosis or condition at any subsequent time.

Plans for possible crises:

Crisis	Risk level (1–10)	Intervention	Resources
❑ Suicide			
❑ Homicide			
❑ Violence			
❑ Substance abuse			
❑ Child or other abuse			
❑ Impulse dyscontrol			
❑ Noncompliance			
❑ Other: _____			

Under each problem in section F ("Behaviors to be changed," "Interventions," "Observable indicators of improvement," "Sessions to achieve each indicator," and "Discharge level of problem behaviors"), you can substitute one of a number of alternative formats:

- "Goal," "Interventions," "Observable indicators of improvement," and "Time frame."

- "Target symptoms," "Target date," and "Expected outcome."

- "Diagnosis-related symptoms," "Symptom-related goals," "Interventions," and "Target date."

- "Short-term objectives," "Target date," "Long-term goals," and "Target date."

Also, consider adding this: "Special concerns or approaches because of ethnic, cultural, religious, racial, language, or similar issues."

About Managed Care Organizations' Own Checkoff Forms

Several of the large MCOs now use their own checkoff-type forms, at least for reauthorizations. Although this reduces the MCOs' processing costs (compared to having a human read and understand a narrative), they may increase your vulnerability, for several reasons:

1. You have to reduce complex issues and judgments to only a few options. The list of symptoms, signs, or impairments may allow you only to indicate their presence or absence, or to rate them as mild, moderate, or severe. These may not reflect the variations accurately. The few boxes for indicating substance use may force you to report use that is not problematic or not currently problematic.

2. The choices presented on these forms may not fit your goals or aims very well. For example, the Outpatient Review Form from Value Options offers these four choices: "Reasons for continued treatment: . . .   ❑ Remains symptomatic   ❑ Maintenance

❑ Prepare for discharge within coming month   ❑ Facilitate return to work" (see www.valueoptions.com/providers/clinforms.htm). A similar form from Mutual of Omaha offers under "Treatment Plan" these: "____ Improved functioning/symptom reduction and discharge from treatment; ____ Transfer to support groups or self-help and discharge from treatment; ____ Provide ongoing supportive counseling and maintain stabilization of symptoms; ____ Provide ongoing medication management; and ____ Other: _____" (see www.mutualofomaha.com/healthcareprofessionals/index.html).

3. The choices presented may not fit a client very well. The forms do not allow more than two Axis I diagnoses. When you are seeking more treatment sessions, each symptom has to be neatly rated as either "worse," "same," "improved," or "resolved." What degree of progress are you agreeing to with "improved," and are you ever sure a symptom is cleanly "resolved"?

4. The data can more easily be entered into computerized databases and thus accidentally disclosed, shared with other organizations, and used for profiling providers.

5. The choices may not be mutually exclusive or accurate. For example, doesn't the intended use of a selective serotonin reuptake inhibitor as an "antidepressant," "mood stabilizer," or "other" depend on the patient's situation and not the drug's "class"?

In light of these risks, I suggest not only the usual thoughtfulness and attempts to foresee the consequences, but also recording comments and qualifications in your case notes.

A form titled "Universal Outpatient Treatment Report Form," which addresses confidentiality and treatment concerns much better than most MCOs' forms do, has been developed by the American Psychiatric Association. It is available as a download (see www.psych.org/edu/other_res/lib_archives/archives/200108.pdf; see especially pages 7 and 8).

6.2   Documenting Treatment's Progress

Change is certain. Progress is not.
—E. H. CARR

After treatment has been planned and initiated, records of its implementation need to be kept. The treatment-planning formats offered earlier in this chapter often include ways to monitor the progress of the case. This section discusses those and other options in more detail. Specifically, it discusses the following options for keeping treatment records:

- The rules on notes from the Health Insurance Portability and Accountability Act (HIPAA), with sample forms.

- Guidelines for note taking, including when and how to take notes.

- The problem-oriented record (POR), including a POR progress note form.

- Structured progress notes for individual and for group therapy.

- Client-generated records.

Note Taking: Guidelines and Suggestions

Most clinicians write without a guiding framework for recording, and so their notes only partially describe the important facts of their therapy. Such notes will not protect these therapists or support understanding of their therapy. If this description applies to you, find or invent a system you can live with—one that makes sense for your way of working, helps you do your job, and protects you. The following ideas may help.

When to Write Notes

It's best to take notes immediately after a session. This allows for perspective on the whole session, as well as for the identification of themes and the most important events. Make certain to schedule enough time and to include this time in your charge to the client.

Writing notes during a treatment session saves time, but may lead to incompleteness and (because of lack of reflection or excess brevity) later incomprehensibility. It also reduces eye contact and rapport with the client. One position is to "Never take notes when an individual is talking about his feelings, or discussing matters which are sensitive, emotionally laden or difficult to express" (Wilson, 1980, p. 7). Other therapists find that taking notes uses little time, is seen as thoroughness, and gives them time to consider what is happening and to weigh their responses. However, saying "Let me just make a note of that," or even the minimal cue of writing after a client says something, may reinforce that topic, mood, or pattern even when you don't want to increase symptomatic behavior. If a client becomes uneasy, discontinue your note taking and offer to share the notes with him or her.

Two additional possibilities for taking notes during a session are as follows:

- Take notes about the major issues in a "headline" or "telegraphic" format, leaving space. As soon as the session is over, write in the details and your well-considered formulations. You can certainly use a shorthand method or Speedwriting™, which essentially omits all vowels. However, notes that are illegible or too telegraphic will not serve to defend you by demonstrating your assessments, thought processes, and decision making, and will not support any of the other functions of clinical notes.

- Take real-time notes of things you suspect you will forget or any factual data that you may not remember accurately without a reminder (Wilson, 1980, p. 7).

Do not wait till the end of the day to take notes. Writing so far removed from the experience can lead to contamination of your memories of one client by those of other clients or events, as well as to other errors or distortions in your recollections. This is not fair to you or your clients.

By the way, *not* keeping notes is not an option; you are ethically required to have such records. (See Section 1.4 for information on record-keeping obligations.) And, whatever note-taking schedule you adopt, always keep your notes current. Periodically, or at case closing, you can revise your working notes into formal records.

Two Kinds of Clinical Notes:
Routine Progress Notes and Psychotherapy Notes

The HIPAA Privacy Rule considers clinical records to be of two main kinds. The first consists of the "medical chart" or "official records." I will call the part that therapists typically create "routine progress notes." The second kind of record has been defined by HIPAA and is therein called a "psychotherapy note." This latter category is given special privacy protections. HIPAA restricts its use and disclosure, even to clients, beyond that of other protected health information (PHI). As explained by the Secretary of the Department of Health and Human Services (DHHS),

> . . . *rationale for providing special protection* for psychotherapy notes is not only that *they contain particularly sensitive information,* but also that *they are the personal notes of the therapist, intended to help him or her recall the therapy discussion* and are of little or no use to others not involved in the therapy. Information in these notes is not intended to communicate to, or even be seen by, persons other than the therapist. Although all psychotherapy information may be considered sensitive, we have limited the definition of psychotherapy notes to only that information that is *kept separate by the provider for his or her own purposes.* It does not refer to the medical record and other sources of information that would normally be disclosed for treatment, payment, and health care operations [TPO]. (Emphasis added. This and all other quotations about psychotherapy notes in this discussion that are not otherwise directly attributed come from "Standards for Privacy . . . ," 2000, pp. 82497, 82622–82623, 82652–82654.)

The special status of psychotherapy notes was partly a response to the many state laws establishing psychotherapist–patient privilege, and partly a response to the 1996 U.S. Supreme Court decision in *Jaffee v. Redmond* (518 U.S. 1, 1996), which held that statements made to a therapist during a counseling session were protected against civil discovery under the Federal Rules of Evidence. In HIPAA, psychotherapy notes are similarly protected. Only further court decisions and laws will clarify the extent of this privacy protection.

In a clarification, the Secretary of the DHHS said that the term "counseling," as used in the law, was to be interpreted to include psychotherapy: "We do not intend to limit the practice of psychotherapy to any specific professional disciplines." HIPAA is thus completely discipline-neutral and applies to all professions, but only mental health professionals can create psychotherapy notes.

Therapists can choose to create or not to create psychotherapy notes. The distinctions between them and routine progress notes are legally defined, and so some conditions must be met if you wish to create psychotherapy notes that have these special protections. Below I review each kind of note in terms of the dimensions along which they differ: their contents; their location; whether their release can be made a condition of receiving services or payment; the type of authorization needed to disclose them; rules on redisclosure; and access to them by clients and lawyers.

A Comparison of Routine Progress Notes and Psychotherapy Notes

Definition and Contents

Routine progress notes: By exclusion, these contain all the other usual contents of mental health notes. Since these notes are part of the regular record, they are used and disclosed for TPO, so an MCO or insurer may have **all of the following information:**

> Medication prescription and monitoring
> Counseling sessions
>> Start and stop times (or duration)
>> The modalities of treatment (types)
>> Frequencies of treatment furnished
>> Summaries of
>>> Diagnosis
>>> Functional status
>>> Treatment plan
>>> Symptoms
>>> Prognosis
>>> Progress to date
>>> Results of clinical tests

Psychotherapy notes: According to Section 164.501 of HIPAA, psychotherapy notes are those "recorded (in any medium) by a health care provider who is a mental health professional documenting or analyzing the contents of conversation during a private counseling session or a group, joint, or family counseling session."

Their content is clarified as follows: "These process notes capture the therapist's impressions about the patient, contain details of the psychotherapy conversation considered to be inappropriate for the medical record, and are used by the provider for future sessions. . . . [They] contain sensitive information relevant to no one other than the treating provider."

For instance, psychotherapy notes might include sensitive information about others in the client's life; fantasies and dreams; process interactions; the therapist's tentative formulations, hypotheses, or speculations; themes; and so on. So whereas psychotherapy notes have special status, the huge amount of information in routine progress notes does not.

Location

Routine progress notes: These are part of the client's regular health care record or chart. Nothing more specific is offered.

Psychotherapy notes: "These are separated from the rest of the individual's medical record" (HIPAA, Section 164.501).

Conditioning of Services

Routine progress notes: Failure to consent to a release of these notes for TPO is an allowable reason to deny services. Denying TPO is called "conditioning" upon consent.

Psychotherapy notes: Failure to authorize the release of psychotherapy notes cannot be a reason to deny services or payment from a health plan. The intent of disallowing "conditioning" is to prevent the release of highly personal information to insurance companies and other nonclinical operations. Thus clinicians can prevent the access by some payers to some information.

Type of Consent Needed to Release

Routine progress notes: Under HIPAA, only the initial consent form is required, although state rules usually require more. See Sections 7.3 and 7.5 for more.

Psychotherapy notes: The release of these notes to an insurer or health plan is *not* authorized by the consent form of DHHS. A covered entity (CE) can rely on the previously signed notice of privacy practices (NPP) consent form and does not need an authorization to "use and disclose psychotherapy notes, without obtaining individual authorization, to carry out its own limited treatment, payment, or health care operations as follows: (1) Use by the originator of the notes for treatment, (2) Use or disclosure for the covered entity's own training programs for its mental health professionals, students, and trainees, and (3) Use or disclosure by the covered entity to defend itself in a legal action or other proceeding brought by the individual." A special authorization is required for all uses beyond these, according to Section 164.508(a)(2) of HIPAA.

Redisclosure. "Redisclosure" is the forwarding by a second to a third CE (such as a successor therapist) of records created by a first CE and released to and now in the possession of a second CE.

Routine progress notes: Redisclosure is permitted. Once the generic consent is signed, HIPAA allows any CE to send these notes to any other CE.

Psychotherapy notes: Redisclosure is not automatically permitted. A second client authorization is required for one CE to disclose psychotherapy notes to another CE.

The routine redisclosure of PHI is a much looser privacy safeguard than most states' laws, and so the state laws are likely to preempt HIPAA. If the state law does not address redisclosure, HIPAA will prevail.

Client Access

Routine progress notes: Clients have rights to access, copy, and amend these, because they are part of their medical records.

Psychotherapy notes: There is no right of client access. It is allowed but not required; it is a choice by the notes' writer.

Discoverability in Litigation

Routine progress notes: These are routinely discoverable.

Psychotherapy notes: These are probably not routinely discoverable. It depends on several factors, including the type of suit or charges, the venue, previous decisions, and other factors. Consult your legal counsel.

Note that no client authorization is required for disclosure of psychotherapy notes when a client brings legal action against his or her therapist, according to Section 164.512(e) of HIPAA. This is logical because the alternative is to have to ask the now-suing client to cooperate and sign an authorization to release the notes. The HIPAA regulations only go so far as allowing release of these notes to the therapist's lawyer for preparing a defense.

Requirements and Conditions for Using Psychotherapy Notes

First, the two kinds of notes must be separated. But how "separate" must these notes be? HIPAA doesn't say. In the absence of guidance, you are free to develop your own methods. Develop ways to distinguish the two kinds of notes easily, in order to prevent an accidental disclosure of psychotherapy notes (which would be a prosecutable violation of the client's privacy). Certainly use different sheets of paper (do *not* put each type of notes on each side of a single page). Perhaps keep them in different files if they are in the same file drawer or computer. You might keep psychotherapy notes by hand on paper, and all other information in a computer. Or use a different name or code for each type, so they are not easily confused or accidentally combined.

Second, the information in psychotherapy notes must be kept nowhere else.

> The final rule makes it clear that *any notes that are routinely shared with others,* whether as part of the medical record or otherwise, *are, by definition, not psychotherapy notes,* as we have defined them. (Emphasis added)

> However, the requirement that psychotherapy notes be kept separate from the medical record and solely for the use of the provider who created them *means that the special protection does not apply to the same information in another location.* (Emphasis added)

> Because of the restricted definition we have adopted for psychotherapy notes, we do not expect that members of a team will share such information. *Information shared in order to care for the patient is, by definition, not protected as psychotherapy notes.* (Emphasis added)

Third, the form of the information is irrelevant.

> We do not require the notes to be in a particular format, such as hand-written. They may be typed into a word processor, for example. Copying the notes into a different format, per se, would not allow the information to be accessed by a health plan.

Other Points about Psychotherapy Notes

- Authorizations to release psychotherapy notes will be very rare.

We anticipate *these authorizations will rarely be necessary*, since psychotherapy notes do not include information that covered entities typically need for treatment, payment, or other types of health care operations. (Emphasis added)

- An authorization for the release of psychotherapy notes cannot be combined with other authorizations except those for other psychotherapy notes, according to 164.508(b)(3)(ii) of HIPAA.

- Psychotherapy notes can still be released without an authorization to Social Security disability and to workers' compensation, but not to Medicare.

Deciding Whether to Keep Psychotherapy Notes

1. Look at your current records. Find a dozen notes that are typical and of good quality. Ask these questions:

   a. Is there material that you believe you must record, and yet you don't want it shared with . . .

      - The client, because it lists your working hypotheses and was of value only at one time? Remember, clients have no access to psychotherapy notes unless you give it.

      - Insurance companies or others who are not required to protect its confidentially as carefully as your profession requires you to do?

      - Anyone else, because it is too sensitive and potentially damaging to the client or to others?

      - Other treaters, because they are not and will not be doing the kind of work you are with the client?

   b. But you . . .

      - May want to share the information with professional students for training.

      - Find value and meaning in these notes as you review them.

   If you answered yes to any of these, then the information should be kept separate in psychotherapy notes.

2. If, on the other hand, you mainly record the formalities of the therapy (such as your interventions and the client's responses), you may feel comfortable in disclosing this to an insurer or other CE, and so you have no need for records beyond the routine progress note.

3. Another possibility is to keep psychotherapy notes for some clients, but not all. Perhaps you want to see only some information about some types of clients more fully protected; for those clients, create and label psychotherapy notes. Creating such notes for only some clients may not have to be explained in a courtroom, but doing so for only some sessions may look suspiciously like destroying notes.

4. If you are not getting requests for intrusive case summaries and similar versions of your notes, keep just psychotherapy notes for simplicity, and provide a summary in a letter.

5. A variation would be to keep only psychotherapy notes, don't release them, and in the rare situation when you have to or wish to share PHI, generate a simple routine progress note by using a checklist form.

Examples of the Two Types of Notes

Here are examples of the two types of notes, made about treatment of the same client with comorbid panic disorder and narcissistic personality disorder.

Routine Progress Note

7/16/08

Sess #8   45 mins   Individual p/t—cog-behav. using Foa's manual.

Revwd HmWk and diary. 2 panics; used breathing → shorter duration, milder sx. Praised client. Revwd relaxation methods and practiced Deep Musc Rlx × 10 mins; 7 SUDS → 3. Syst desent hierarchy 4, step 6 was achieved at 2 SUDS. Discussed role of dysfunctional thoughts in generating client's depression. Revised HmWk.

Psychotherapy Note

7/16/08

Sess #8   45 mins   Individual p/t interpersonal insight-oriented.

Cl consulted Dr. Smith re breast enlargement surg. Recognizes superficiality, submission to male cultural definitions, as well as social power gain. May be door to core issues. Successful contract on her project. Deflected realistic praise from boss and me but will address next time (3rd recurrence). Saw new associate of husb.—triggered fears of loss of attractiveness producing 2 panics. Saw husband's pattern of withdrawal in this week's business trip, leading to worry and anxiety.

Summary: Advantages versus Disadvantages

The main advantages of keeping psychotherapy notes are the fact that the client has no access to them; that you don't have to reveal them to insurers, and that you can think for the record in terms of both clinical hypotheses and risk management, but need not reveal this content.

The main disadvantages are that psychotherapy notes require maintaining separate records; are likely to be discoverable in some legal proceedings; and don't protect the kind of information that must be placed in the routine notes.

Format for a Psychotherapy Note

To meet legal requirements, psychotherapy notes must be identified as HIPAA-authorized and must be explicitly labeled "Psychotherapy Notes." They must record information not in the rest of the chart, and kept separate from the rest of your records. There is no special format for psychotherapy notes, so by adding the paragraph below to your current method of note taking, you are likely to meet the labeling requirements.

Psychotherapy Note

Name of client: _____ Case/ID #: _____ Page #: _____

NOTICE: This page is a psychotherapy note under the HIPAA regulations. It must not be included in or attached to any other part of the client's health care records except other psychotherapy notes. Any information recorded here that is also in the rest of the client's records is not protected. Date and sign every entry. Some disclosures will require a special authorization.

Process Recording in Social Work

The logic of process notes, as commonly used by social workers, overlaps with that of the logic of psychotherapy notes. Typical process recording includes the following:

- An almost verbatim record of what each person said, in a format like C (Client): . . . and W (Social Worker): . . .

- Notes on the client's nonverbal behaviors.

- The worker's feelings and reactions to the client.

- Observations and analytical thoughts about the client's internal processes and the events of the interview.

- A section headed "Diagnostic Summary" or "Worker's Impressions," which summarizes the worker's analytical thoughts and understandings.

- A section headed "Social Service Plan," "Casework Plan," "Comprehensive Service Plan," or (more recently) just "Treatment Plan."

This format is helpful with a confusing case or for documentation for training and supervision.

Process versus Progress Recording in Family Therapy

Should you record process or record progress/content for family therapy? Brock and Barnard (1988) have this to say:

> Historically, clinical case notes have been more content oriented than process oriented. Process notes are more specific regarding systemic notions such as the family's rules, roles, evident communications styles, and patterns that appear to be operational: Attending to the organization and structure of a family in notes lends itself to the development of direction, goals, and possible interventions, for the therapist. Merely recording the content of who said what and where the session left off ignores such systemic information and may, in fact, get in the way of the therapist's appropriately conceptualizing the family in systemic fashion. We can all be entranced and diverted by stories. (pp. 139–140)

More is said later in this section about keeping notes in family or couple therapy.

A Basic Format for Routine Progress Notes

FORM 40

Because therapists have different needs for making progress notes, I have supplied two versions. A version designed to shorten record-making time by using check boxes as much as possible is offered later as Form 43. The form here (Form 40) is designed to supply all the HIPAA-required information *and no more* when you are sending PHI to a MCO. However, depending on your clientele, your local legal situation, or the MCOs you deal with, you may want to add any of the following components:

- You can provide **diagnoses** on all five axes of DSM-IV-TR.

- You can elaborate on **patient education** as follows:

Patient education offered re: ❑ Diagnosis, symptoms, disorder ❑ Adherence ❑ Expectations of progress ❑ Interpersonal dynamics ❑ Psychodynamics ❑ Medication effects ❑ Development ❑ Community resources ❑ Other: _____

If you are a prescriber, you might substitute this for "Medication effects":

❑ Medication: Adherence, rationale, usage, possible side effects, precautions

---

- You can provide more detail about **substances used:**

Substances used (for each, indicate: none, N; denies, D; current use, U; episodic use, E; abusing, A; dependence, Dep; in active recovery, R):

Tobacco _____   Caffeine _____   Alcohol _____   Over-the-counter drugs/herbals/supplements _____
Street drugs _____   Other: _____

Case Progress Note

Name of client: _____ Date: _____ Page #: _____

Starting time: _____ A.M./P.M. Ending time: _____ A.M./P.M.

Intended schedule: Biweekly   Weekly   2 4 6 8 12 weeks   PRN

Diagnosis (DSM-IV-TR/ICD): _____ Code #: _____

Diagnosis (DSM-IV-TR/ICD): _____ Code #: _____

GAF score today: _____   Other measures: _____

Target symptoms	Change since _____ date
_____	_____
_____	_____
_____	_____
_____	_____

Treatment provided: _____
_____

Treatment planned: _____
_____

Medications: Changed? ❏ No ❏ Yes to _____ side effects/adverse reactions: _____
_____

Prognosis (circle one):   Guarded   Improvement   Recovery   Fluctuating   Other: _____

Notes: _____
_____
_____

Person completing this form:

_____
Signature/initials

_____   _____
Printed name   Title

FORM 40. Case progress note.   From *The Paper Office*. Copyright 2008 by Edward L. Zuckerman. Permission to photocopy this form is granted to purchasers of this book for personal use only (see copyright page for details).

- You can describe the **medical necessity of treatment** as follows:

Medical necessity of treatment is to   ❑ Maintain level of functioning   ❑ Reduce/control symptoms
❑ Prevent relapse   ❑ Continue progress toward treatment's goals   ❑ Cope with increased psychosocial stressors   ❑ Other: _____

- You can add these lines:

Plan of care: Renewal of authorization from _____ needed by _____

Reviewed treatment plan with   ❑ client   ❑ caregiver   Changes made: _____

- For the section "Other measures" you can use instruments tailored to the presenting or chief symptoms such as the Yale–Brown Obsessive Compulsive Scale for obsessions/ compulsions or the Beck Depression or Anxiety Inventories. All represent improvements over the GAF's vague anchor terms.

- If you wish to enter any datum on every note, assigning a code requires less recording time and space. Examine your current notes to decide what might be coded. For example, you might use this code for "Change since __ date": <<, much worse; <, worse; 0, no change; >, improved; >>, greatly improved. For "Treatment provided," to record the modalities of treatment, you might use MM for medication monitoring, F for family therapy, C for conjoint, I for individual, and G for group. You could add a subcode (sm for stress management, resoc for resocialization/social skills, etc.). If you need to record who was present, you might code F for father, M for mother, Sn for son, Ss for sister, and so forth. Or you might prefer to use the SOAP format (to be discussed later in this chapter).

- In the space for "treatment planned," you might enter homework or changes in the treatment plan separately, or use a code here as well.

- I have included a section for medications, but you might keep track of them on a separate sheet, or simply indicate who is responsible for medication for this client.

A Checklist of Tips for Clinical Notes

Although notes should be concise, they must also be coherent, accurate, current, relevant, and handled in ways to assure and maintain confidentiality. If you are going to record more than skeletal information, your narratives should be guided by these principles.

❑ All entries should be dated, sometimes timed, and signed. A signature may be unnecessary when the notes are in your handwriting, but initials should indicate, where a particular note ends. Every page should have the client's name on it.

❑ Make sure your notes are readable. Do not try to hide anything, or everything you noted will be looked at with suspicion.

❑ It is best to avoid nonstandard or idiosyncratic abbreviations and acronyms. If you must use them, keep a list of them somewhere in your records so you won't forget what they stand for, and so a court won't misinterpret your intentions.

❑ Make subheadings of the session's notes for clarity. <u>Underline important information if you will have to search for it later.</u> (See how well it works?) Number issues and subjects in your notes. You can also circle some numbers. If you use a problem list, you can cross-reference each entry to a problem (by its number P1, P2, etc.). See the discussion of the POR, below.

❑ Whenever confusion might arise, write paragraphs giving full explanations, which are better than phrases or cryptic notations.

❑ Use behavioral and sensorial language, rather than imprecise, subjective, general statements. Use words that help the reader visualize; make your words a camera. Terms such as "No change" or "Improving" are too open to varying interpretations.

❑ Ignore set lengths as required on a printed form. Write as complete a note as necessary to achieve the record's purpose (Wilson, 1980, p. 113), but no more.

❑ The sources of all information recorded should be indicated. Never state as fact what a client reported. Use direct quotations whenever possible to indicate the client's experiences and thought processes. Separate your judgments and conclusions from the facts and observations. A simple and practical notation scheme is as follows:

> All unmarked notations are the client's ideas and reports.
> Quotes from the client can be indicated by standard double quotation marks: " ".
> Statements from others reported to you by the client can be indicated by both double and single quotes " ' ' ".
> Words in parentheses are (your statements to the client).
> Words in square brackets are [your unspoken hypotheses or conclusions]. Consider using HIPAA-compliant psychotherapy notes for these.
> Also, you can use HW for homework assignments and Rx for topics to cover in the future.

❑ Do not make entries criticizing another caregiver, no matter what, and do not enter anything about liability, professional insurance, or attorney contacts in progress notes.

❑ Never alter your notes. Never erase, write over, or "white out" anything you have written. Draw a single line through an error, date and initial it, and either write in the correct information (if there is space) or indicate where you placed the correct information in the record. If you later want to add anything to your notes—that is, to amend them—do it by indicating that there is a change and where in the chart the new material or changes can be found. Date and initial the indication, and write out the full amendment on the current page of notes: For example, "My present recall differs, in that . . . " or "I was misinformed at that time, and now believe . . . ". If you later recall something you did not record earlier, you can write it with a notation that it is "Prior knowledge [or understanding or recollection] presently recorded."

❑ Do not add comments near a previously recorded entry in your notes. This may also appear to be tampering with the record. Instead, write notes at their chronological place with today's date, and cross-reference them to the original location in your notes (Gutheil, 1980). For example, "August 1: In rereading my notes of July 4, I note that I neglected to mention the fireworks, which . . . ".

What to Write Down: Guidelines

There are legal risks to be considered in excluding anything from your notes (Fulero & Wilbert, 1988). For example, omitting material on sex may leave you with little defense against an accusation of impropriety during a session. Releasing records with premature diagnoses or speculations could be the basis of a malpractice claim. This is why, even before the passage of HIPAA, some therapists have kept dual records—one set of psychotherapy notes not to be released, in order to protect both themselves and their clients, and a second set of routine progress notes to be released upon request or court order. However, keep in mind that **no record is secret,** even as the obligation remains to try to keep information private. If you work in a setting covered by federal law, the Privacy Act of 1974 (Public Law 93-579) and the Freedom of Information Act of 1974 (Public Law 93-502) give clients rights of access to all your notes about them. Furthermore, state law or case law, or just filing a suit against you, will also give them access (Fulero & Wilbert, 1988). Obviously these laws and decisions have had to be integrated with the *Jaffee v. Redmond* (1996) decision and the HIPAA rules (see above), which effectively deny patients access to your "psychotherapy notes," although they may be discoverable. The best advice is the most cautious: Create records with the expectation that they will be read by someone else and should be clear when read years later. Your clients may someday see your notes, so consider their psychological and legal implications. The best policy may be to write your records so that all will be well when a client or a client's parents read your notes.

Since you can't record everything, you need to choose what to note while bearing in mind the purpose of the record. I suggest the following priorities.

First, make a record of your clinical decision making for your own later review. Ask yourself, "Will I need to know this later? For the next session? Later in treatment or after treatment, for another purpose?" If having this information will not change some aspect of treatment, do not bother to record it. In particular, when there is a change in the patient's condition (a new problem develops or is recognized, there is a response or a lack of response to adequate treatment, etc.), be sure to record any event or decision that preceded it.

Klein et al. (1984) (as summarized in Soisson et al., 1987) recommend the documentation of *all* significant decisions during therapy. Specifically, the record should include the following:

1. What the treatment choice is expected to accomplish (goals, objectives).

2. Why you believe it will be effective (a rationale).

3. Any risks involved and why they are justified.

4. Which alternative treatments were considered.

5. Why they were rejected or delayed.

6. Any steps taken to improve the effectiveness of the chosen treatments.

7. Evidence of informed consent provided by the client's statements or your own observations supporting the client's consent.

8. The rationales for any referrals made.

Make a record of your clinical decision making for self-defense. A useful rule of thumb may be "If it might make a mess, make a note." In a similar vein, Gutheil (1980, p. 482) intelligently suggests that when taking any risky actions, you should "think out loud for the record" so that if the unfortunate happens, it can be traced only to an error in judgment and not to negligence. The following specific pointers may be helpful:

- Explicitly note where information isn't clear.

- Document all clinically significant events, such as nonroutine calls, missed sessions, and consultations with other professionals (Soisson et al., 1987).

- When forensically significant events or possible malpractice situations are anticipated, the record should be written from the perspective of future readers (Gutheil & Appelbaum, 2000), especially unfriendly readers. An example of such a situation might be a suicidal patient.

- Emergency treatment situations are responsible for a disproportionately large share of malpractice claims, and so should be documented with extra care (Gutheil & Appelbaum, 2000). Get full consultations, and document any resistance from significant others, so that responsibility can be placed accurately (Cohen, 1979).

- Your statements about the limitations of a treatment should be noted; its success should not be guaranteed, and excessive optimism should be shunned to avoid responsibility for a failure (Gutheil & Appelbaum, 2000).

- Do not hesitate out of modesty to record a client's statements of appreciation for your work or successes and improvements during therapy. Similarly, regularly asking about any concerns clients might have and recording their comments on the progress of treatment will both allow you to refer to these comments when things are not going well and can serve as a defense against a complaint.

What Not to Write Down: Guidelines

Do not record anything that is unnecessary for or irrelevant to treatment. I suggest that you generally exclude the following:

- Excessive detail.

- Gossip and hearsay.

- Emotional statements, editorializing, or hunches.

- Moral or personal value judgments (especially negative ones) about the client or others (e.g., "fat," "lazy," "weak," or "stupid").

- The client's political, religious, or other personal beliefs.

- Difficulties you had with other professionals or agencies in this client's case.

- Names of paramours (use initials?) or specific indicators of affairs.

- Reports of most illegal activity in the past.

- Incriminating information about illegal activity in the present (e.g., details of drug use).

- Medical diagnoses or other judgments that your training and experience do not qualify you to make.

- Most sexual practices.

- Insulting, embarrassing, or overly critical statements.

Special Considerations for Keeping Notes in Family or Couple Therapy

If you see several members of a family, or a couple, you will have particularly complex decisions to make about record keeping.

You can keep separate records (separate pages) on each person involved in a conjoint session, so that you do not have to release all the records when just one client is involved. Confidentiality can then be maintained. Margolin (1982) offers an extensive and thoughtful discussion of the privacy issues in marriage and family therapy. On the other hand, separate records create a fiction that there were not several interacting people in the room. Because the family members' issues involve each other, separate notes on each person cannot be considered truly independent and so cannot logically be read separately.

The suggestion that all participating members must give permission for the release of the record seems logical. However, this must be implemented before the therapy is begun, by means of a paragraph in your client information brochure and paragraphs in your release-of-records forms. Two problems arise: You are initially asking family members to agree to conditions for the release of records whose content they do not know, because the therapy and the records of it have not happened yet. This cannot be considered informed consent. Second, problems may arise when one member does not consent to the release that another member seeks. Therefore, include in your practice brochure a statement allowing any adult to release the records of his or her family or couple sessions.

The Problem-Oriented Record

When you are documenting the progress of a case, the challenge is to record treatment-relevant information in an accessible form. However, clinicians, because of their differing training and interests, may record such diverse topics as the process of therapy, the symptoms of a disorder, the relationship with the client, the contents of interactions and outside events, the goals of recovery or growth, or many other possibilities.

In this diversity, the word "problem" has become a label acceptable to clinicians of many disciplines and backgrounds. Lawrence Weed (1971) invented a record-keeping method when he found that the information necessary to treat a patient was being recorded in medical charts in too many places to be useful. Instead of being entered under arbitrary topical or discipline-based headings ("Intake," "Diagnoses," "Social History," "Psychological Evaluations," "Nursing Notes," "Consultant's Reports," etc.), all notes were to be keyed to numbered problems. This method is called the "problem-oriented record" (POR), the "problem-oriented medical record," the "Weed system," or "SOAP notes." It is widely used in medicine and has been adapted to the psychotherapy setting.

As slightly modified for the psychotherapy context (see Grant & Maletzky, 1973, and Sturm, 1987), the format consists of four main components: (1) the problem list, which remains on top of the chart and which serves as a table of contents to it; (2) the database of history and findings; (3) the initial treatment plan; and (4) progress notes, or the continuing record of the clinician's observations and understanding of the patient. Each progress note entry is recorded in the "SOAP" format (see below) and is cross-referenced to a problem on the problem list by number. Therefore, all the information in the chart is organized around problems. All evaluations and their results are thus tied to their sources and their implications for treatment. To find all of the information in the chart about a concern, the reader has only to look for its problem number on all pages.

The Problem List

FORM 41

The problem list is simply a numbered listing of all problems identified by you or the client and used as a guide to the POR system. Forms 41, 42, and 43 offer several ways to identify problems. Once created, the list is placed on top of the chart to serve as a table of contents for the continuing record. Problems are defined at their current level of understanding, and are rewritten and renumbered as they become better or differently understood. Problems can be added and, when resolved, closed by making an entry and by not reusing that number. Added to this listing should be a psychiatric diagnosis with all axes considered; an evaluation of difficulties with activities of daily living; and a description of all functional impairments. Form 41 permits you to create a problem list for a POR.

The Database

The database consists of the following usual and expected psychological topics, with each entry tied to the list of problems:

- Chief complaint.

- Mental status examination results.

- Social situation—personal, familial, environmental factors.

Problem List for a Problem-Oriented Record (POR)

Client: _____ Page #: _____

		Problems currently active	Problems now inactive	
Problem number	Date problem recognized	Problem title/formulation	Prob. # where problem is now included, *or* →	Date problem resolved

This is a strictly confidential patient medical record. Redisclosure or transfer is expressly prohibited by law.

FORM 41. Problem list for a problem-oriented record (POR).   From *The Paper Office*. Copyright 2008 by Edward L. Zuckerman. Permission to photocopy this form is granted to purchasers of this book for personal use only (see copyright page for details).

- Personal and social history.

- History of other medical and psychological conditions and their treatments.

- Records obtained from other treaters.

- Results of testing, or other relevant data.

The Paper Office does not provide separate forms for all of these, because they can be recorded in whatever format and size you may prefer. However, Chapter 5 includes forms and guides for recording most of this information.

The Initial Treatment Plan

Psychological interventions usually require the consideration of many dimensions simultaneously, and so a treatment plan is necessary. See Section 6.1 for suggested treatment plan formats and essentials. The POR treatment plan is simply a listing of therapeutic responses to each currently recognized and defined problem. It is the starting point for treatment, and is modified or added to through changes in the progress notes as the case progresses. The plan may include every kind of treatment by anyone (patient education, collection of more information, treatment of and by others, etc.), as well as the usual therapies.

Progress Notes Using the SOAP Format

"SOAP" is an acronym for four kinds of information that needs to be documented for each problem addressed during each client meeting. This is where the POR shines. Every note begins with the problem number for cross-reference and completeness, and continues as follows:

- S is for subjective data—the client's reports of complaints, symptoms, efforts made, changes, and difficulties. S also includes notes of the statements of others.

- O is for objective data—your observations and the observations of others; measurable signs (especially changes); the results of psychological testing of the client; and his or her observable behaviors, appearance, and social situation.

- A is for assessment—your conclusions, diagnoses, interpretations, impressions, judgments, case formulations, and analyses of the meaning of the data.

- P is for the plan of treatment (both immediate and future), as created by you and by the others concerned. Diagnostic studies, patient education, and follow-up would also be placed here.

FORM 42 Form 42 is a photocopiable form for making POR progress notes according to the SOAP format, and Figure 5 is a completed example of this form. Of course, you can make various changes both to the SOAP format and to Form 40. First, progress notes can be made

POR Progress Note Form

Client: _____ Page #: _____

Problem number	Date of note	Problem status*	Progress notes**

*Problem status codes: C = continuing focused treatment; R = problem resolved; I = inactive problem; IT = inactive due to ongoing treatment; D = treatment deferred; N = newly identified problem; ReDf to # = problem redefined or combined with another problem whose number is indicated.

**Each entry must be related to a problem number; coded S for subjective, O for objective, A for assessment, or P for plan; and signed.

This is a strictly confidential patient medical record. Redisclosure or transfer is expressly prohibited by law.

POR Progress Note Form

Client: ___Last name, First name_____   Page #: ___1___

Problem number	Date of note	Problem status*	Progress notes**
1. Depression	9/9/07	C	S: No suicidal thoughts this week More energy—started painting project Fears of being fired Spouse confirms more optimism O: Increased facial expressions, more hand and arm gestures, faster movements BDI score = 9 A: Lessened depression P: Maintain or add treatments as follows: —Spousal reinforcement for activities as scheduled —Cognitive therapy 1/week —Continue meds —Consider adding new group activity—9/23/07 —Reevaluate medication—10/9/07 *Anna F. Therapist*

*Problem status codes: C = continuing focused treatment; R = problem resolved; I = inactive problem; IT = inactive due to ongoing treatment; D = treatment deferred; N = newly identified problem; ReDf to # = problem redefined or combined with another problem whose number is indicated.

**Each entry must be related to a problem number; coded S for subjective, O for objective, A for assessment, or P for plan; and signed.

FIGURE 5. Completed sample of a POR progress note form.

"SOAPIER," which is well suited for the current direction of psychotherapies. Use the SOAP format as described above, and then add the following:

- I is for intervention or implementation of the plan—what you have done to, for, or with the patient relative to this problem. In this version you would put the longer-term goals into the plan (P), and use implementation (I) for the shorter-term objectives.

- E is for evaluation/effectiveness of the intervention—that is, the outcomes of intervention, positive or negative. These, of course, could be recorded under S and O, but in this framework they are separated for greater specificity.

- R is for revisions of the plan if it was ineffective. Again, these could be recorded under P as a new plan, but using this new heading makes the changes more salient.

An alternative to the SOAP format is to use a "DAR" format:

- D is for data.

- A is for the action you take based on this data.

- R is for the response of the patient or other.

The Expanded POR

The expanded POR is simple, flexible, and comprehensive. It can be written in paragraphs devoted to these topics:

1. The problem.

2. The outcome or goal sought; foci of treatment (immediate and long-term issues); measurable performances or operationalizations of levels of progress.

3. The client's strengths or assets.

4. The client's liabilities, or the barriers to change in the client or elsewhere.

5. The treatment(s)/methods used: What, when, by whom? (Include interventions/methods/means/modalities, resources required, staff members and others involved, frequency of contacts, expected dates of achievement, dates of review.)

6. The means and dates of evaluation.

Advantages of the POR

- The POR is a complete record. It is logical and tidy. The information in it is accessible to other care providers, supervisors, or reviewers, and is easily defended in court.

- The POR is a means of keeping the focus of treatment on the client's larger concerns ("keeping your eye on the ball"). It is all too easy to go along with the client's desire to avoid change; to be distracted by interesting and possibly relevant side paths; or to avoid doing the hard work of being a therapist ("It's not fun any more"). The POR can help you keep such distractions to a minimum.

- The POR can keep both of you focused when the going gets confusing or slow, by keeping the horizon in view and allowing you to mesh the immediate and lively with the long-term and important.

- At another level, the problem list, treatment plan, and SOAP notes are the map of the territory of the client's life situation.

Disadvantages of the POR

- The POR format tends to oversimplify the complexity of psychotherapy's understandings and interventions.

- It can lessen the attention paid to the client's strengths and resources.

- Because it is person-focused, rather than focused on the person in his or her situation, context, or system, it may underemphasize the client's relationships. Environmental and case management interventions may be overlooked as a result.

- Its weakest point is defining what exactly is a problem. The good news, however, is that problems can be described at whatever level of understanding is currently available, and redescribed when they are understood differently. Simply close a problem entry with a cross-reference to the newer definition.

Two Structured Progress Note Forms

A Structured Form for Individual Clients

FORM 43

The structured progress note form (Form 43) is an efficient way of recording a client's progress when you do not use either the POR system described above or the basic case progress note (Form 40). The purposes of this form are (1) to document the progress of your treatment and the client's response to it; (2) to enable you to do this with as little time and effort as possible; and (3) to support evaluation of the treatment by you, the client, and other interested parties.

Form 43 is designed to be rather broadly useful for many kinds of treatment; it offers choices that may fit many practices, but you can enter specifics to fit your practice under the headings. This form is based loosely on an excellent one from Ronnie M. Hirsch, PhD, of New York, NY. If you need a more elaborate form, the "Professional Progress Notes" form from Psychological Assessment Resources (www3.parinc.com) is similar, but more elaborate in its coverage and evaluation of such risk areas as suicide potential, referrals needed, health problems, and allegations of sexual improprieties. In addition, its manual is a very thorough resource regarding record keeping and the use of good records as a malpractice risk reduction method. It is recommended.

Progress Note

If a checkbox (❑) is insufficient, enter a letter and write additional comments on a separate page.

A. Client and meeting information

Client:_____ Date:_____ Case #:____

Starting time: _____ A.M./P.M. Ending time: _____ A.M./P.M.

❑ Cancelled and was rescheduled for _____ ❑ Did not show or call

Others present: _____ Meeting was: ❑ Scheduled ❑ Crisis contact

Meeting #:_____ of _____ authorized on this date _____ with provider #:_____

Meeting place: ❑ Office ❑ By phone ❑ Clinic ❑ Hospital ❑ Client's home ❑ Workplace

Modality: ❑ Individual therapy ❑ Family ❑ Group ❑ Couple ❑ Consultation ❑ Other: _____

B. Topics/themes discussed

Notes

❑ Homework assignments _____

❑ Relationship(s) _____

❑ Stressors _____

❑ Identity/role _____

❑ Work problem _____

❑ Alcohol/drug problem _____

❑ Childhood/family of origin _____

❑ Sexual problem _____

❑ Parenting _____

❑ Dream(s) _____

❑ Other _____

C. Treatments/interventions/techniques

❑ Interpretation _____

❑ Behavioral _____

❑ Cognitive _____

❑ Homework _____

❑ Family _____

❑ Relationship/role play _____

❑ Problem solving _____

❑ Support _____

❑ Psychoeducation/bibliotherapy _____

(cont.)

FORM 43. Structured progress note form (p. 1 of 2). From *The Paper Office*. Copyright 2008 by Edward L. Zuckerman. Permission to photocopy this form is granted to purchasers of this book for personal use only (see copyright page for details).

D. Assessments

1. Symptoms

Target symptom/concern/complaint	Current severity rating*	Change since last evaluation (enter a check mark)					
		Much worse	More severe	No change	Less severe	Much improved	Resolved /absent

*Rate from 0 to 10 as follows: 0 = not a problem/resolved; 5 = distressing/limiting; 10 = disrupting, harm/risk.

2. Mood: ❑ Normal/euthymic ❑ Anxious ❑ Depressed ❑ Angry ❑ Euphoric
   Affect: ❑ Normal/appropriate ❑ Intense ❑ Blunted ❑ Inappropriate ❑ Labile

3. Mental status: ❑ Normal ❑ Lessened awareness ❑ Memory deficiencies ❑ Disoriented
   ❑ Disorganized ❑ Vigilant ❑ Delusional ❑ Hallucinating ❑ Other: _____

4. Substances used: Tobacco ____ Caffeine ____ Alcohol ____ Over-the-counter drugs ____
   Herbals/supplements ____ Street drugs ____ Other _____
   (For each, indicate: N = none; D = denies; U = current use; E = episodic use; A = abusing; Dep = dependence; R = in active recovery)

5. Suicide/violence risk: ❑ None ❑ Ideation only ❑ Threat ❑ Rehearsal ❑ Gesture ❑ Attempt

6. Sleep quality: ❑ Normal ❑ Restless/broken ❑ Delayed ❑ Nightmares ❑ Oversleeps

7. Participation level: ❑ Active/eager ❑ Variable ❑ Only responsive ❑ Minimal ❑ None ❑ Resistant

8. Treatment compliance: ❑ Full ❑ Partial ❑ Low/noncompliant ❑ Resistant ❑ Denial of disorder

9. Response to treatment: ❑ As expected ❑ Better than expected ❑ Much better ❑ Poorer ❑ Very poor

10. Global Assessment of Functioning (GAF) rating from 100 to 0 is currently: _____

11. Other observations/evaluations: _____

E. Changes to diagnoses: ❑ None or _____

F. Changes to treatment plan: ❑ None or _____

If treatment was changed, indicate rationale, alternatives considered/rejected/selected in notes.

G. Follow-ups

❑ Next appointment is scheduled for next ❑ week ❑ month ❑ 2 months ❑ 3 months ❑ as needed.

❑ Referral/consultation to: _____ For: _____

❑ Call/write to: _____ For: _____

H. Clinician's signature: _____ Date: _____

This is a strictly confidential patient medical record. Redisclosure or transfer is expressly prohibited by law.

To tailor Form 43 even more specifically to your practice, you might want to delete the "Next appointment . . . " or "Symptoms" items and add "Instructions, suggestions, directions" under "Treatments . . . " (as suggested by Muriel L. Golub, PhD, of Tustin, CA). If you work in an agency setting, you might want to add such options as "Chart reviewed," "Case consultation," "Treatment team meeting attended," or "Aftercare planning meeting." Specific target symptoms can be added to the listing, as well as a section on medications.

If it better suits your model of psychodynamics, you could add a section on stressors and coping like this to Form 43:

Stressors and coping

Stressor	Current sever-ity rating*	Changes in severity?	Current level of coping/functioning†	Changes in coping level?	Coping skills employed

*Rate from 0 = not a problem to 10 = very severe, continuous, omnipresent, preoccupying.
†Rate from 0 to 10 as follows: 0 = much less able to cope; 5 = no change from last meeting/evaluation; or 10 = much improved level of coping.

If you wanted to add more on mental status, you could remove the "Symptoms" section and use the space to add checkoffs from Form 35, the mental status evaluation checklist.

A Structured Form for Group Therapy

FORM 44

In keeping notes about the progress of individual clients in a therapy group, a simple checklist reduces the paperwork burden. You can use either Form 43, which contains several sections not in this one, or Form 44, which records more information about interventions, interactions, and participation in the group. You can, of course, add items from Form 43 to Form 44—for example, the "Symptoms," "Stressors and coping," "Global Assessment of Functioning," and/or "Changes to diagnoses" items.

Client-Generated Records

When clients take notes, or make drawings or flow charts of their problems' causes and interactions, they bring additional cognitive resources to bear on their issues. These can be especially valuable activities; when accompanied by at-home review, they should be encouraged.

- Diaries of associations, dreams, and relationship interactions in dynamic therapies help the client to see connections. Similar records are called "client memoranda" in social work, and "diaries," "logs," and "frequency counts" in behavioral therapies.

- There are many kinds of affect and behavior checklists to help identify situations for

Group Therapy Progress Note

Client and group information

Client: _____ Date: _____ Meeting attended is #: _____ for this client.

Group's name: _____ Time: _____ A.M./P.M.

Location: _____ # present: _____

Leader(s): _____ Signature(s): _____

_____   _____

Assessment of client

1. Participation level: ❑ Active/eager ❑ Variable ❑ Only responsive ❑ Minimal ❑ Withdrawn

2. Participation quality: ❑ Expected ❑ Supportive ❑ Sharing ❑ Attentive ❑ Intrusive ❑ Monopolizing
   ❑ Resistant ❑ Other: _____

3. Mood: ❑ Normal/euthymic ❑ Anxious ❑ Depressed ❑ Angry ❑ Euphoric ❑ Other:_____
   Affect: ❑ Normal ❑ Intense ❑ Blunted ❑ Inappropriate ❑ Labile ❑ Other: _____

4. Mental status: ❑ Normal ❑ Lessened awareness ❑ Memory deficiencies ❑ Disoriented
   ❑ Disorganized ❑ Confused ❑ Vigilant ❑ Delusional ❑ Hallucinating ❑ Other: _____

5. Suicide/violence risk: ❑ None ❑ Ideation only ❑ Threat ❑ Rehearsal ❑ Gesture ❑ Attempt

6. Change in stressors: ❑ Less severe/fewer ❑ Different stressors ❑ More/more severe ❑ Chronic stressors

7. Change in coping ability/skills: ❑ No change ❑ Improved ❑ Less able ❑ Much less able

8. Change in symptom severity: ❑ Same ❑ Less severe ❑ Resolved ❑ More severe ❑ Much worse

9. Other observations/evaluations:_____
   _____

Modes of interventions/treatments

❑ Support ❑ Clarification ❑ Education ❑ Exploration ❑ Problem solving ❑ Limit setting ❑ Role play
❑ Socialization ❑ Orientation ❑ Reminiscence ❑ Reality testing ❑ Activity ❑ Confrontation
❑ Other: _____

Topics/themes/critical incidents

❑ Relationship(s) ❑ Work problems ❑ Alcohol/drug problems ❑ Parenting ❑ Abuse
❑ Childhood/family of origin ❑ Sexual ❑ Homework assignments ❑ Process ❑ Logistics/structure
❑ Other: _____

Further comments: _____

_____

This is a strictly confidential patient medical record. Redisclosure or transfer is expressly prohibited by law.

FORM 44. Structured progress note form for group therapy. From *The Paper Office*. Copyright 2008 by Edward L. Zuckerman. Permission to photocopy this form is granted to purchasers of this book for personal use only (see copyright page for details).

clinical interventions. In rational–emotive behavior therapy, the use of antecedent–behavior–consequence analyses will reinforce teaching in the session and build a pattern for approaching stressful situations.

- I have asked some patients to keep their notes in a three-ring binder, which they may call "The Book of My [or Our] Therapy" and use for many purposes. The binder can also house handouts; notes the patients have made from assigned readings; notes taken and questions raised during reviews of audiotapes of their therapy sessions; observations of their family members, friends, or television characters; online searches and readings; news stories and magazine articles; self-study and journal writings; poetry and artwork; and many other items. When such materials are collected in one place, they are much more likely to be reviewed (and therefore to generate awareness and change) than if they are scattered in space and time.

- One of the most intriguing options is described by Albeck and Goldman (1991): The client and therapist coauthor a progress note after each session—a process these authors call "codocumentation." By reviewing each other's views and experiences, both parties benefit, and a supervisor who reads both could be of great assistance to the therapy.

- There are guides for diary writing as therapy, usually called "journal keeping" or just "journaling." Some clients may find "scrapbooking" valuable as a way to explore topics and document history.

Evaluating Each Therapy Session

FORM 45

When the rapport is not strong, or you suspect the client has some unarticulated reservations, or you believe that the client lacks the social skills to address these issues face to face, you can use the questions in Form 45 to collect immediate feedback. Such a questionnaire can be offered at any point in treatment and can be used repeatedly—for example, after the 3rd, 8th, 15th, and 20th sessions. It can be distributed (perhaps mailed, with a stamped, self-addressed return envelope) every 5 sessions, but if you start doing this with a patient you must continue, because he or she will expect it and may hold comments for the form.

Review the four sets of questions offered here (A, B, C, and D); revise, edit, and select from them to suit your practice and style; decide on and consistently use a first- or third-person pronoun to refer to yourself as the therapist; and then try it with your next three clients. When it is satisfactory, incorporate it into your routines for every patient, examine your data, and you will become a scientist/practitioner.

6.3   Case Termination

If we can turn neurotic pain into normal misery we have done a lot.
—SIGMUND FREUD

The most important clinical issues in the termination of therapy are the maintenance of gains made and, more generally, the prevention of relapse. However, a lack of clear goals may prevent both client and therapist from knowing whether therapy is finished. Therapy

Session Evaluation Questionnaire

Initials of client: _____   Initials of therapist: _____   Date: _____

A. These questions focus on the benefits and the communications of the session.

Please list what you got out of this session.

What was the best part?

What suggestions do you have?

What points do you want to have considered in our next session?

What did I miss or underconsider?

What didn't you tell me?

What did you want to tell me or do today that we didn't get to?

What will you take with you?

Therapist's response to the comments/feedback above:

(cont.)

FORM 45. Session evaluation questionnaire for clients (p. 1 of 3).   From *The Paper Office.* Copyright 2008 by Edward L. Zuckerman. Permission to photocopy this form is granted to purchasers of this book for personal use only (see copyright page for details).

B. These questions focus on the therapeutic behaviors and qualities of the relationship.

Please rate each of these aspects of my behavior during this session on a 7-point scale where 1 means "not at all" and 7 means "very much," and feel free to add any comments or explanations.

	Rating	Comments
Asked the right questions.	____	
Basically grasped/understood my situation.	____	
Tuned in to where I needed help.	____	
Was there for me/I felt supported.	____	
Used me for his or her own problems/needs.	____	
Coerced me until I backed up.	____	
Worked well with my reluctances, fears, defenses.	____	
Encouraged me to go further.	____	
I felt close to him or her.	____	
Was warm/caring.	____	
Accepted me as I am.	____	
Supported hope and change.	____	
Confronted me when I needed it.	____	
Didn't panic when I felt confused or overwhelmed.	____	
Helped me clarify my feelings, goals, needs.	____	
Made constructive use of problems/negatives.	____	
His or her self-disclosure was helpful.	____	
I want to work with him or her again.	____	

This was a positive experience for me because:

This was a negative experience for me because:

Additional comments, please.

(cont.)

C. These questions focus on "learning" from the session.

1. How did you feel (for example, anxious, relaxed, tense, angry, afraid, excited—use single-word emotions, though you can use more than one)?

   a. Before the session: _____

   b. During the session: _____

   c. After the session: _____

2. What did you learn about yourself that was new and that you believe will aid you in dealing with your problems?

   a.

   b.

   c.

3. What did you relearn or have reinforced that you believe will aid you in dealing with your problems?

   a.

   b.

   c.

4. If you are able to implement these plans at this time, what specific short-term changes would occur in your life? What long-term ones?

D. These questions focus on the therapist's assisting the client to achieve benefits.

Using the 1–7 scale where 1 means "not at all" and 7 means "very much," please write a number next to each benefit and feel free to add explanations or anything else you think would be beneficial to our relationship.

	Rating	Comments
During this session you helped me to . . .		
Clarify my thoughts and feelings.	____	
Understand what I was feeling and why.	____	
Approach some difficult and scary issues.	____	
Overcome depression.	____	
Resolve problems in my relationships.	____	
Relate better to my spouse/partner or children.	____	

I really appreciate the time and effort you put into answering these questions, and I promise that I will consider your answers and will review these points at the start of our next meeting. Thank you.

should have a distinct ending even if its goals have not been accomplished. The absence of a message of closure is not only confusing to both parties, but can expose you legally. For example, if you agree to a client's decision for a premature termination or terminate a client for nonpayment of fees, it may be legally seen as negligent unless the client's welfare is protected. By far the most important point in termination, regardless of reason, is the client's welfare. The American Psychological Association's code of ethics (APA, 2002, Standard 10.10) addresses the termination of professional relationships.

Reasons for Terminating or Transferring a Patient

First, **you simply cannot terminate a patient in crisis or at high risk.** On the other hand, you can terminate a patient for any of the following reasons. In these situations, terminating or continuing treatment is your professional decision, whether the MCO or anyone else agrees.

- The patient has failed to pay fair and negotiated fees. Termination in such a case is often therapeutic as well.

- The patient is not cooperating with treatment. You must first try to work through the patient's resistance to treatment and document these efforts, but failure to follow an agreed-upon and appropriate treatment plan is very important.

- There are conflicts of interests, disruptive romantic thoughts, countertransference, or similar issues that you have not been able to resolve.

- The APA ethics code (APA, 2002) says that you are ethically obligated to terminate when there has been little progress. (See "No-Improvement Terminations," below.)

- Although this is not made explicit in the ethics code, you should terminate and transfer when another, and incompatible, therapist or therapy appears to be in the patient's best interest. The patient may need services you cannot offer, such as medical interventions, inpatient care, or neuropsychological rehabilitation.

- Your own needs may require you to terminate the patient (e.g., you are leaving the area).

For clients covered by MCO payments, you must be familiar with your contracts' provisions about referral and termination or you may create a legal liability for yourself. See "Continuity-of-Care Concerns," in Section 3.11 regarding these contract and legal issues of seeing a client after an MCO has terminated benefits: your ability to discuss limitations of the MCO with the client, to refer the client to out-of-network providers, and to continue seeing the client on a private pay arrangement while providing legitimate but noncovered services. As always, your first ethical obligation is to your client—not to an insurer, your community, or society at large. But bear in mind the legal contexts of contracts you have signed.

Termination issues are best dealt with early and continually in treatment. Remember that they are a major focus in the quite successful time-limited therapies. Be alert to your possible reluctance to terminate a successfully treated and functional patient who pays his or her bills reliably, is not difficult, and perhaps is pleasant to see. Being a responsible professional can be bittersweet.

How to Terminate Treatment in Different Situations

The options offered below are designed for five kinds of termination situations. The section on dealing with premature or early terminations is based upon ideas from the Philadelphia Society of Clinical Psychologists' Committee on Ethics (1988) and from Ewing (1990) and Barnett et al. (2000), both of whose discussions are brief and highly recommended. O'Leary and Norcross (1998) offer excellent guidance on making successful referrals. Kramer (1990) has written a thorough book on "bringing meaningful closure" to therapy and more recently Joyce et al. (2007) have addressed termination from a dynamic perspective.

Appropriate Terminations

When the therapy is finished and the termination is mutually agreed upon, document the following:

- The reasons for termination. (Ideally, the goals of therapy have been met, and the client no longer needs your services.)

- The client's reactions to the ending.

- Any continuity-of-care needs and plans.

- Any referrals.

- Any unfinished issues.

Although it's not required, you can send **a follow-up note** to each appropriately terminated patient, either 1 month after the end of treatment or 3, 6, or 12 months later. If you do so, keep a copy. A note could include the following:

- Your hope that all is going well for the patient.

- A clear statement that termination was necessary. You do not have to specify the reason, but might do so.

- A summary of treatment—start date, diagnosis/diagnoses, treatment modalities, progress, successes, high points, any unfinished work, or recommendations. You might include lessons learned, if doing so does not seem too preachy; it all depends on the relationship.

- A statement that "The door is always open" for additional work or for "checkups" or "booster sessions." Indicate that the patient only has to call, and that you will be pleased to see him or her again (if this is true).

- A reminder that you are most pleased to accept referrals from former patients, as these are almost always appropriate and successful.

- Your best wishes.

Some therapists may see such a note as purely self-promotional; you could, of course, deal with all these points in the final interview(s) instead of sending a note. It can be argued, however, that using the patient's paid time is more manipulative than using your (unpaid) time to construct the note. This note is not the place to indicate any unpaid balances due to you or difficulties with insurance reimbursement.

Premature or Early Terminations

Premature or early terminations are ethically complex. When you feel the therapy is not finished but the patient declines to continue, the arrangements should be made jointly if at all possible. Handle termination therapeutically, working through the patient's issues; also, document these points, your efforts, and the outcomes.

Here are some suggestions for the last few therapy sessions (or, if the patient cannot be dissuaded, just the last visit):

- Do not argue or defend any perceived attack on your abilities.

- Assert your concern for the patient/family.

- Affirm the patient's right to choose to terminate and to seek treatment elsewhere.

- Express your regret, respect for the patient's decision, and acceptance (not agreement).

- Specify the factual bases for your recommendation to continue therapy at this point. Indicate why you think it may be harmful to stop now, and describe any negative consequences you foresee.

- Encourage the continuation of therapy. You can point out the "honeymoon" or "flight into health" effects and describe how they don't last.

- Offer to resume therapy at any time in the future.

- Offer your assistance in finding another therapist. Perhaps make a referral to an agency, or provide the traditional three referral names. When you do refer or transfer a patient to someone else, ethically you must make sure the professional to whom you are sending the patient is qualified (by training, credentials, experience, licensure status, etc.) or you could be vulnerable to an ethics charge ("negligent referral").

- Offer your services for emergencies in the interim before the patient finds a new therapist.

- Offer to send your records, with the patient's signed consent, to another therapist.

- Record all this in your notes.

- If you think there is some risk involved in termination at this time, you may prefer to have the patient sign a release indicating that the termination is against your advice. This formality may also encourage the patient to reconsider. If the patient refuses to sign, note this too. (See Section 3.12.) Consider sending a letter by certified mail, with an even stronger recommendation to continue treatment somewhere.

Necessary Terminations

In some cases, you may feel that the therapy is not finished, but you are discharging or transferring the client for one or more of the following reasons: Your own needs require it (e.g., you are leaving the area); the client requires services you are not competent to provide (e.g., medications, inpatient admission); financial noncooperation or insurance limitations exist; or the relationship has deteriorated into counterproductivity. Perhaps you or the client have not been able to maintain a schedule or intensity of contacts that would support significant work and change, or the client has not performed or refused his or her responsibilities as specified in the agreed-to treatment plan and its revisions.

When any of these situations exists, one of your concerns is not being negligent. To assure that you are not, do the following:

- Give the client a list of the reasons for termination, and make a note of the fact that you have done this.

- Give reasonable notice of the end of treatment, and enter this into your notes as well.

- If the client fails to show for his or her last scheduled appointment, make at least one call or send one letter to discover the reasons for the no-show. Record these reasons or your attempts to terminate properly. Offer to meet at least once more to "wrap things up," but not to "look at where we were and where we are now," as this is an invitation to continue in therapy.

It is usually better to discuss the reasons for termination in person, but a call or letter may be your only possibility. Even when there is a face-to-face discussion, it is best to send a letter as well. Keep a copy. A "discharged from treatment" letter can include any of the points above, as well as a number of the following suggestions:

- Describe what you have done (such as evaluate the client, discuss diagnoses and treatments, read records, initiate treatment, make referrals, etc.).

- List some of the successes and high points, if possible.

- Indicate that the purpose of the letter is to confirm your final conversations, if you had such.

- Give the client your reasons for discharging him or her.

- Express your regret at the ending of an important relationship.

- Recommend continuance of therapy, if clinically appropriate: "Since your condition requires treatment . . ." or "I believe you can benefit from continued treatment." Encourage the client to seek services without delay (Simon, 1992).

- Indicate that the client should now consider "our" treatment over, and that you are not, in any continuing sense, the client's therapist.

- Indicate your availability during a specific transitional period. This not only is clinically and ethically appropriate, but will protect you from a charge of abandonment. You can say, "Because your condition requires treatment [or monitoring or follow-up], I will continue to be available to you only for essential clinical services for a brief transitional period. You must make such arrangements immediately, because I will only provide care for a period of _____ [1 week, 1 month, etc.]." Current opinion suggests that to be safe, you should continue to be available. "Only when another licensed professional has accepted the patient (and vice versa) does the original therapist's responsibility end" (Meyer et al., 1988, p. 50).

- Offer recommendations for treatment by someone else. As indicated above, giving three referral names is traditional (but not essential). You have an ethical obligation to know that these care providers are competent to help the client. It may be appropriate to say that you will make a suitable referral if one is desired.

- Indicate that when written consent has been given for doing so, you will send your records or a summary of their treatment to another therapist with whom the client enters treatment. Explain how long you will keep the client's records and how they can be accessed. See Section 1.6 on record retention.

- Remind the client that any balance due must be paid. Enclosing the bill makes this clearest, but sending it separately serves to separate the two issues if you want to.

- Offer your "best wishes"—the generic, can't-be-misread closing.

You should make an appropriate effort to follow up with the client, to ensure that you have done all you could to make a transfer go smoothly and cause no harm to the client.

No-Improvement Terminations

When there has been little or no improvement despite appropriate treatment, you must terminate (see APA, 2002, Standard 10.10a). After you have done your best, including having reevaluated, reconsidered, and made extra efforts to get things moving forward again, you should do the following:

- Consult a colleague. Be sure, though, that you have honestly prepared the case, recognized and dealt with your ego involvements, and can listen openly. Document this consultation. Modify treatment as suggested by the consultation.

- Try a different approach, with the client's permission.

- If there is still no improvement, you must terminate and refer. You must also terminate when the client is being harmed by the relationship, such as in irresolvable transference issues.

- Send a "discharged from treatment" letter as described above.

Reluctant Terminators

When you feel that a client is ready to terminate but the client is apprehensive or reluctant, you can encourage termination by recounting improvements and addressing resistances. If you have discussed progress and options as you went along in therapy or labeled your treatment as "time-limited," then your pushing for termination will not come as a surprise. Depending on the length and qualities of the therapy, this may take several sessions. Consider the process of termination very carefully and make a plan.

- Expect emotional reactions (relapses, development of "new problems needing immediate treatment," "wanting to be friends/business partners afterward," etc.) and process them. See Section 3.7 on dual relationships.

- Clearly indicate the reasons for termination, so that it cannot be seen as a result of the client's deficiencies. Say that termination is for the client's long-term good, that it is necessary because of managed care requirements, or whatever the truths are.

- When it is appropriate to do so, offer the client the names of up to three other therapists if he or she wishes to continue therapy.

6.4   The Case Closing Summary

It is best to set aside time after the last session with a client, to compose a summary while the case is still fresh in your mind. You might consider dictating a summary using the headings below, and not having it typed unless you need it, in order to save some costs. A complete narrative on each patient at the end of treatment is better. But just reviewing your notes and adding to them at the end, in the form of a summary, will be valuable.

I strongly recommend that you also send (with the client's permission, of course) a termination note to the case manager or reviewer at any MCO involved in the case and to the referral source when appropriate. Both of these have moral if not legal involvement, and everybody wants closure and likes to hear good news, even if only some of the goals were achieved.

Outline for Dictation

The following outline is very comprehensive and assumes that you have *not* been using the forms provided in this book.

A. Client information.

1. Client's name and some other basic information (e.g., date of birth, address).

2. Referral source and reason.

      3. Presenting problems (e.g., problem list) and severity ratings; levels of functioning.

      4. Dates of initial and final contacts, consultations, hospitalizations, referrals.

  B. Treatments.

      1. Planned treatments.

      2. Services you actually provided; perhaps a sentence or paragraph about each session by date, specifying:

         a. Problems presented/addressed, homework.

         b. Relationship qualities.

         c. Process, motivations.

  C. Narrative summary of therapy, including critical incidents, unresolved problems.

  D. Status of each problem at discharge/termination and severity ratings; levels of functioning.

  E. Information about termination.

      1. Reasons/rationale for termination.

      2. Was treatment prematurely discontinued? (If yes, indicate why.)

      3. Originator of the decision to terminate.

      4. Recommendations and suggestions of continuing care, if any.

      5. Did the patient accept your recommendations at discharge?

  F. Optional: Lessons you have learned.

A Termination Summary Form

FORM 46   Form 46 is quite different from but based on a form in Piercy et al. (1989) called "Family Termination Summary," by Larry Constantine, LCSW.

6.5   Assessing Client Satisfaction and Outcomes

Much has been made, especially by MCOs, of the value of satisfying the consumers of health care services. Consumers' answers to simple questions about the distance from the office to a bus stop or the furniture in the office apparently have been used to remove or "disenroll" physicians from MCOs' panels of providers.

Termination Summary

Client: _____ Case: _____ Date: _____

Signature(s) of therapist(s) : _____ _____

A. Reason(s) for termination

❑ Client failed to attend two consecutive appointments without canceling.

❑ Client failed to comply with treatment recommendations.

❑ Client was noncompliant with court order, probation, or other (specify) _____.

❑ Client could not be reached by phone and did not respond to letters sent.

❑ Planned treatment was completed.   ❑ Client refused to receive or participate in services.

❑ Client was unable to afford continued treatment or did not pay bills on time.   ❑ Client moved.

❑ There was little or no progress in treatment.   ❑ This is a planned pause in treatment.

❑ Client needs services not available here, and so was referred to: _____

❑ Other: _____

B. Source of termination decision. The decision to terminate was: ❑ Client-initiated

❑ Therapist-initiated   ❑ A mutual decision   ❑ MCO-affected   ❑ Other: _____

C. Treatment sessions

Referred on date: _____   Date of first contact: _____   Date of last session: _____

Number of sessions: Scheduled: _____ Attended: _____ Cancelled: _____ Did not show: _____

D. Kinds of services rendered

❑ Individual psychotherapy, for _____ sessions ❑ Couple/family therapy, for _____ sessions

❑ Group therapy, for _____ sessions ❑ Other: _____

E. Treatment goals and outcomes (code outcomes as follows: N = no change, S = some or slight [about 25% to 35%], M = moderate [about 50%], V = very good [about 75% to 100%], E = exceeded expectation)

Goal	Outcome

F. Last diagnosis/diagnoses: _____

_____

Other notable aspects of treatment outcome, change, or progress: _____

_____

_____

This is a strictly confidential patient medical record. Redisclosure or transfer is expressly prohibited by law.

For therapists, such measures do not have great clinical import. Summarizing eight studies, Pekarik and Wolff (1996) concluded: "Research has indicated that the correlations between satisfaction and other outcome measures are low to modest, with correlations generally ranging approximately from zero to .40" (p. 202). Pekarik and Guidry (1999) again found no significant relationship for those treated by private practitioners. Examining a different group of studies, Lambert et al. (1998) came to the same conclusion.

However, "Satisfaction measures have several virtues, including ease of administration, high face validity, and appeal as indexes of treatment acceptability" (Pekarik & Wolff, 1996, p. 202) and so there may be advantages to your collecting this information. First, it can help you present your practice to MCOs as caring and well liked by your clients; second, such data could be an alternative to having the MCOs impose their generic questionnaires on you and your clients; finally, a questionnaire tailored to your way of working and the kinds of problems you typically address could be part of a continual quality improvement program for your services.

Client Satisfaction Measures

The most widely used form for medical practices is the Client Satisfaction Questionnaire (CSQ-8; Larsen et al., 1979; available online at www.tchcoalition.org/ph/questionnaire.doc). However, based on their review of the literature, Pekarik and Wolff (1996) decided that a simpler set of four questions was sufficient:

> The client was asked, (a) "Overall, how satisfied are you with the services you received?"; (b) "Would you recommend this agency to others seeking help?"; (c) "If you were to seek help again, would you return to this agency?"; and (d) "How would you rate your therapist?" Ratings were obtained on 5-point Likert scales.

You could easily adapt or expand these questions to your practice. A 39-question version, developed for MCOs' uses, is available in Eisen et al. (1999).

If you design a client satisfaction measure of your own, make it one page long and completable in 5 minutes or less; enclose a stamped envelope addressed to you; and use a code to make it anonymous. Ask some colleagues to review your work and pilot-test it.

FORM 47 Form 47 contains a set of 20 questions, but these do not have any research support. Both Forms 47 and 48 are designed for use by groups or agencies, and so they include both space for a letterhead and the name of the treatment provider. If you are in solo practice, omit the "Therapist." Before sending out either questionnaire, enter the date of the client's last session and the therapist's name. The use of "6 12 24 ____" is to code the number of months after the end of treatment this letter is being sent. "Today's date" is to allow for the client's not completing and returning the form promptly.

Outcome Assessment Questionnaires

Clinicians in private practice have almost never done outcome evaluations. This is unfortunate both because it leaves the responsibility for the improvement of clinical work to distant researchers, and because it denies clients the benefits of systematic, data-based, tailored clinician self-improvement. To address this issue, Clement (1999) offers his own

Follow-Up Questionnaire I

ID #: _____

Therapist's name: _____ Today's date: _____

Date of last session: _____ 6 12 24 ____

What is your gender? ❑ Male ❑ Female How old are you? ____ years

For each question, please circle a number to show how much you agree with the statement. Use a scale from 1 = "I completely **disagree**" to 7 = "I completely **agree**." If the statement does not apply to you or your experience, please circle NA.

	Disagree Agree	
1. I was treated with courtesy and respect by the secretary/receptionist and other staff.	1 2 3 4 5 6 7	NA
2. I was treated with courtesy and respect by the therapist.	1 2 3 4 5 6 7	NA
3. I felt the therapist was appropriately concerned about my problem.	1 2 3 4 5 6 7	NA
4. The therapist seemed well trained and skilled in helping me with my concerns.	1 2 3 4 5 6 7	NA
5. The therapist helped me to be comfortable enough to express what I was thinking and/or feeling most of the time.	1 2 3 4 5 6 7	NA
6. I felt there were too many forms to fill out on my first appointment.	1 2 3 4 5 6 7	NA
7. The amount of time I had to wait for the first appointment was too long.	1 2 3 4 5 6 7	NA
8. The amount of time I had to wait between appointments was too long.	1 2 3 4 5 6 7	NA
9. I felt the fees for service were affordable.	1 2 3 4 5 6 7	NA
10. The hours for appointments were convenient.	1 2 3 4 5 6 7	NA
11. The location and accessibility of the office were convenient.	1 2 3 4 5 6 7	NA
12. I received the kind of service I wanted when I came for therapy.	1 2 3 4 5 6 7	NA
13. I received helpful information about resources in the community.	1 2 3 4 5 6 7	NA
14. I believe that any information I revealed will be treated confidentially.	1 2 3 4 5 6 7	NA
15. If the need to speak to someone arises again, I would return to this therapist.	1 2 3 4 5 6 7	NA
16. I would recommend this therapist to others.	1 2 3 4 5 6 7	NA
17. I felt that the visit(s) were useful.	1 2 3 4 5 6 7	NA
18. I experienced improvement in the condition or problems for which I sought services.	1 2 3 4 5 6 7	NA
19. In an overall, general sense, I was very satisfied with the services I received.	1 2 3 4 5 6 7	NA

20. How many therapy/counseling sessions did you have? ____

Please add any other comments you wish about your experience with us. Use additional sheets if you wish. Thank you very much for your time and efforts.

FORM 47. Client satisfaction follow-up questionnaire. From *The Paper Office.* Copyright 2008 by Edward L. Zuckerman. Permission to photocopy this form is granted to purchasers of this book for personal use only (see copyright page for details).

experiences and methods, which can be easily implemented by even the busiest practitioner. In addition, the books by Cone (2000) and Wiger and Solberg (2001) can be helpful, and there are computer programs to make data collection and analysis much easier. Many measures are available for assessing the outcomes of treatment; some (such as those concerning "quality of life") address overall functioning, and others are more focused on symptom change and relief. Because of the variety available, do an Internet search to find ones tailored to your needs. Form 48 is a set of questions exploring your ex-client's views of the changes brought by treatment rather than the setting of treatment (which is explored in Form 47).

FORM 48

A Cover Letter for These Questionnaires

The following cover letter can be used for mailing both satisfaction and outcome questionnaires to clients. Although your clients deserve the use of their names, anonymity has its benefits. If you choose to use the client's name on the cover letter and a code number on the questionnaire, make sure they are on different sheets of paper. Or, as in the letter below, you can use a "Dear Client" form of address.

Dear Client,

Would you please help us to improve our work by answering some questions about the services you received from us? We are interested in your honest opinions (whether they are positive or negative), and we welcome your comments and suggestions.

All your answers are completely confidential, because your name will not be used on this form. We will use only an ID number (not a Social Security number). To ensure confidentiality, please do not write your name on the questionnaire. None of your responses will be included in your treatment records. Returning this questionnaire will be regarded as giving your informed consent to participate in the survey. You can choose to withdraw from this research at any time and refuse to answer any questions. Doing this will not affect the care you might receive in the future from us. If answering any of these questions makes you uncomfortable, please skip the question.

Thank you for taking the time to provide us with your feedback. We really appreciate your help.

Sincerely,

_____

(Signature)

Follow-Up Questionnaire 2

Therapist's name: _____ Today's date: _____

Date of last session: _____   6   12   24   _____

What is your gender?   ❑ Male   ❑ Female   How old are you? _____ years

Please feel free to add further comments about each question (use the back of this form if necessary).

1. What was the main problem that caused you to seek treatment?

2. When this therapist's treatment ended, was this problem:
   ❑ Resolved, no longer a problem?   ❑ Better?   ❑ About the same?   ❑ Worse?

3. If this problem was not completely resolved, have you gotten treatment from anyone else?
   ❑ No.   ❑ Yes.   If you have, whom have you seen? _____

4. Are these problem now   ❑ Resolved, not a problem?   ❑ Better?   ❑ About the same?   ❑ Worse?

5. Did any other problems come up during this therapist's treatment?   ❑ No or not really.   ❑ Yes.

   a. If yes, what were these?

   b. Is this problem now   ❑ Resolved, not a problem?   ❑ Better?   ❑ About the same?   ❑ Worse?

6. What did the therapy or therapist do that was most helpful to you?

7. What have you learned (in therapy or from anyone or anywhere) about your original problems that has been helpful to you?

8. What did the therapist do that was not helpful to you?

9. What could the therapist have done that he or she did not do or did not do enough of?

10. Has your therapy helped your performance at work?

11. Has your therapy helped you deal with any family problems?

12. Has your therapy helped you deal with any problems with friends or social organizations?

13. Do you have other comments and suggestions?

14. How many therapy/counseling sessions did you have? _____

Thank you very much for your time and efforts.

CHAPTER 7

Confidentiality and Releasing Records

7.1 Understanding Confidentiality

> *Whatever, in connection with my professional service, or not in connection with it, I see or hear, in the life of men, which ought not to be spoken of abroad, I will not divulge, as reckoning that all such should be kept secret. While I continue to keep this Oath unviolated, may it be granted to me to enjoy life and the practice of the art, respected by all men, in all times. But should I trespass and violate this Oath, may the reverse be my lot.*
> —HIPPOCRATES (translated by Francis Adams; retrieved from classics.mit.edu/Hippocrates/hippooath.html)

Over the course of Chapters 5 and 6, we have considered what client records need to be created from the first contact to the ending of therapy. We have also touched on the mandates of the Health Insurance Portability and Accountability Act (HIPAA) for protecting the privacy and security of the client health information in those records. However, HIPAA's rules are only a basic minimum, and the actual practice of confidentiality in psychotherapy is complex.

Rubanowitz (1987) found that 80% of patients believe that all information (including financial data for insurers) is confidential. Since this is not true, you must explain what is confidential and what will be released. Because confidentiality is an almost universal concern, you have the responsibility to discuss it, and especially its limits, with every patient.

Basic Definitions

We use many words for the types of information discussed in this chapter: "sensitive," "secret," "personal," "private," "confidential," "privileged." However, only the concepts of "privacy," "confidentiality," and "privileged information" have legal standing in health care and so bear discussion here. "Protected health information" (PHI) as defined by HIPAA is also considered in relation to these.

Privacy is frequently considered a basic right granted, by implication, through the Fourth and Ninth Amendments and other sections of the U.S. Constitution. It is understood as the right of an individual to decide which of his or her thoughts, feelings, or other personal data will be shared with others. This right protects attitudes, beliefs, behaviors, and opinions. The individual can decide to divulge or to withhold; can decide when, how, and under what circumstances to share information; and can do so with regard to which particular others.

Confidentiality is a concept that exists within many professions. "Confidentiality is an ethical concept that prohibits the physician from discussing his patient with anyone except under compelling legal circumstances" (Sadoff, 1988, p. 41). In all states it has legal recognition, but it is not primarily a legal concept. It is an ethic based on a recognition of the potentially damaging nature of some of the information we therapists collect and record (Wilson, 1980), and on respect of the client's right to privacy.

Privileged communication (or just privilege) is a legal term for a right that belongs to the client, not to the therapist. However, it can be asserted by the therapist to protect the client (as when the therapist does not want to release the client's records) until the issues are discussed with a client, and the client then may assert the privilege. It is granted by state rather than federal laws and by state as well as federal court decisions (*Jaffee v. Redmond*, 518 U.S. 1996; see www.jaffee-redmond.org). It restricts a clinician or other person from disclosing, in an open court, or in other legal proceedings, information that was given with assumed confidentiality. The restriction can apply to spouses, attorneys, priests, and physicians, as well as to many psychotherapists. The legal bases for privileged communication are extensions of the state statutes concerning attorney–client privilege, which vary from state to state.

PHI does not match any of these exactly. The category of PHI was created by HIPAA as a preliminary federal effort to set a basic floor for privacy protection standards across the country. Recognizing that the states had already created classes of information and rules for access, HIPAA states that its rules apply ("preempt") other laws only where other laws are less protective of (less "stringent") or are silent in protecting privacy. As a result, PHI covers what is privileged, as well as most information already protected.

In summary, **all privileged communications are confidential, but not all confidential communications are necessarily privileged.** A Venn diagram would show three concentric circles—the largest being privacy, the middle confidentiality, and the smallest privilege. Gutheil (quoted in Reid, 1999, p. 91) offers this clever mnemonic: "PRivilege is the Patient's Right, while COnfidentiality is the Clinician's Obligation."

The rules protecting confidentiality are confused, confusing, and ambiguous, because they may vary depending on the following circumstances:

- The topics communicated. The abuse of children, and serious threats of harm, are generally not protected; sexual affairs, actions that ended a long time ago, or actions that were situation-specific are generally protected.

- The legal status of those present. Some of these are protected in different situations: spouse, boyfriend or girlfriend, public employee, child, employee, and cotherapist.

- Your credentials, discipline, and licensure.

- The state in which you practice. Credentialing laws, case law, legislation, regulations, and legal climate vary with jurisdiction. For example, Massachusetts law denies privilege to non-doctoral-level psychologists.

- Whether you are doing individual, couple, marital, family, or group therapy.

- A judge's discretion, evolving case law, and court decisions.

- Whether civil or criminal actions will be involved.

- Whether the legal actions are in federal or state courts.

- Whether HIPAA regulations have preempted your state's rules because they were less protective than HIPAA's, or whether HIPAA applies because your state had no previous rules applicable to the situation.

- Other factors unknown at present.

Exceptions to Confidentiality

Our confidentiality practices require us to balance ethical principles of nonmaleficence (harm avoidance—"Do no harm") against beneficence (doing good by, in some cases, protecting others from harm—Standard 5.05[a] in the American Psychological Association [APA, 2002] ethics code). This balancing must be done within the legal context of state and federal laws and regulations concerning particular clients (e.g., children, substance-abusing adults). In particular, the meaning of your actions can be very different when you are dealing with child clients rather than with adults.

In an online article about domestic violence, Brabeck and Brabeck (2002) articulate the reasoning processes involved:

> Reporting abuse without consent may communicate a lack of respect for the client and risks harming the therapeutic relationship, which is necessary for the client to safely explore the serious issues she raised. Breaking confidentiality may rob the client of the opportunity to gain insight into the reasons for her silence, to name the wrong done to her and to confront others with the truth, thereby gaining control over her life. Furthermore, the client may conclude that no one is trustworthy and continue her silence regarding the abuse. . . . Finally, if the psychologist has reason to believe that the client's family will abandon her or will retaliate against her, the psychologist's disclosure might put the client at risk. . . .
>
> On the other hand, by not reporting the abuse, the psychologist may collude with the client in keeping her silence and in letting the abuser maintain power and control over her, which violates her autonomy and may not be in her best welfare. . . . If the client perceives the psychologist as a person of authority, his or her participation in this system of silence may exacerbate the client's sense of powerlessness and hopelessness.
>
> The best option is for the psychologist to maintain confidentiality and use the therapeutic relationship as a vehicle to empower the client to report the abuse to appropriate authorities. . . .

Such a resolution might enhance the client's sense of autonomy, maintain the trust of the therapeutic alliance, end the self-silencing that the abuse fostered and restore the power of the client's voice.

What does the client want and need from the therapist? Most likely, the client wants to process the long-concealed distress and address myriad emotions including anger, shame, sadness, guilt and a host of other issues commonly experienced by victims of sexual abuse.

The common exceptions to the rules of confidentiality, according to Stromberg et al. (1988, p. 371 ff.) and Koocher and Keith-Spiegel (1998), are as follows:

1. **When a patient requests his or her own records.** HIPAA gave patients broad access to their medical records, because the laws about this varied across states and most were silent on it. The main concerns are (a) whether the patient would be harmed through too full a disclosure, and (b) the patient's inability to understand the record's wording or ideas. The options include providing a summary rather than the full records, or disclosure to a third party (a mental health professional competent to understand and explain the records' contents) agreed upon by the patient and the therapist. Most authorities believe that the therapist should review the records' contents with the patient, explaining and answering questions, and that this will result in increased trust and prevent the misuse of the information. Patient "requests often reflect clinical issues, such as patients wondering 'What is wrong with me?' or, 'What does my therapist think of me?' Usually it is sufficient to deal with these issues directly within psychotherapy without having to show patients their records" (Knapp et al., 1998, p. 19).

2. **When the patient consents to the release of records.** To truly consent, the patient must have been fully informed of all aspects and consequences of what is to be released. This is discussed in Chapter 4, and the client's understanding can be documented by a highly specific release form, such as Form 49 or 50. Problems may arise if the client does not know all of what is in a record. If you suspect that anything you are asked for should not be released, discuss the situation with the client. If the client agrees, he or she can revoke the release or sign a revised, more limited version.

   If the request is from a lawyer (e.g., it is a subpoena) and appears inappropriately broad, you can write a letter to both parties (the defense and the prosecution) saying that you need a more specific release or a court order, and let them decide what to do. If you or your clients are involved in a dispute and you are not comfortable with a subpoena you receive, seek a court ruling on the limits of what to disclose. You can ask the court to decide and can discuss it with the judge. If this is not productive, the professional affairs officer of your state professional association may be very helpful (if you have joined this group). If you have purchased a "lawyer consultation" or advice plan from your state association, such contacts there would be your next step, before hiring your own counsel.

3. **Certain laws require disclosure.** Child abuse or neglect, suspected or proven, is the most common situation legally requiring disclosure. The first fact that you must know is this: Are you a "mandated" reporter of abuse? Not all providers of services are, and state rules vary. Are those you supervise, who may have different credentials

or be in a different relationship with a child, mandated reporters? Does the child or the suspected perpetrator have to be your client, or is a spouse's/partner's report to you sufficient to trigger your required reporting? Does your state require the reporting of the abuse of an elderly or disabled person? You must know exactly what your state laws require, because you must act immediately (usually within 24 hours). Besides your state association, the Child Welfare Information Gateway (www.childwelfare.gov/systemwide/laws_policies/statutes/manda.cfm) has tables of information on definitions, immunity, penalties, and procedures by state. These documents must be downloaded but are very accessible. For further guidance, you can call your state reporting agency's hotline and discuss a "hypothetical" situation for advice.

As you consider your own state's rules about reporting child abuse, bear in mind the following key questions. Let me use myself as a psychologist licensed in Pennsylvania as an example. (The Pennsylvania statutes cited here are online at www.dpw.state.pa.us/ServicesPrograms/ChildWelfare/ChildAbuseAnnualRpts/ 2006ChildAbuseRpt/. First, **what is my relationship with the child?** Psychologists must have direct contact with a child who "comes before them in their professional or official capacity" (23 Pa. Cons. Stat. Ann. Section 6311) to be a mandated reporter. I must see the child in my work as a psychologist or the agency I am employed by must see the child directly for me to be a mandated reporter. In other states, you must simply learn about the abuse. Second, **who is the perpetrator?** I must report abuse by a parent, paramour, responsible person, or household resident, but need not if the perpetrator is a teacher, neighbor, or stranger, as these are simply criminal assaults. (I do still have some a moral obligation as a citizen to protect others.) Third, **what is abuse?** It includes "a. non-accidental physical injury; b. neglect of supervision, shelter, clothes, food or medical care and not due to conditions the parent had no control over; c. sexual abuse or exploitation; d. emotional abuse" (23 Pa. Cons. Stat. Ann. Section 6303). This last must be severe. Fourth, **when did it occur?** For a physical injury, it has to have been within the last 2 years, but the other types of abuse do not have time limits. Fifth, what if I am unclear about what has happened? **How much proof do I need to have before I report abuse?** The answer is none. I must report if I have a "reason to believe" or "reasonable cause to suspect" (23 Pa. Cons. Stat. Ann. Section 6311). This is a very low threshold, because the laws were deliberately written to protect the greatest number of children, and so they disregard my professional judgment or need for evidence. I should not do any exploring, questioning, or therapy. The state agency will do the investigation. Sixth, **whom should I report to and when?** I can phone 24 hours a day to a toll-free number. The law does not say when, but if the danger is high, I must call immediately. If the danger is past, I may take a day or so, but I cannot put it off too long. Seventh, **what if I am wrong?** In Pennsylvania, I have immunity for making a report in "good faith" (23 Pa. Cons. Stat. Ann. Section 6318(a–b). Eighth, **what if I don't make the report?** The first violation is a summary offense, and later ones are misdemeanors of the third degree (23 Pa. Cons. Stat. Ann. Section 6319). Anything else? Yes. Immediately consult with one or more colleagues and document everything you heard, saw, and did; what actions you considered; and why you chose the ones you did. This is especially important if you have decided not to report.

Laws differ, but these requirements on reporting abuse seem typical:

a. You usually must have seen an allegedly abused child, but many states require you to make a disclosure if you have reason to trust an adult client's report of his or her abusive behaviors. Even where you are not legally required to report this abuse (because the perpetrator, not the child, is your patient), you may have the ethical or civic duty to make a report in order to protect the child or to prevent violence.

b. Even professional students and your assistants may be required to make such reports.

c. Proof of abuse is not needed to make a report; generally, you have no discretion about investigating and do not need to investigate. This is a sticking point for many therapists, because they do not want to serve as "police," would prefer to make a decision in what they see as the best interests of the child or family, and do not trust an agency to make good decisions. In the area of child abuse, Taube and Elwork (1990) found that disclosing the mandatory reporting issue to patients led to fewer self-reports of child neglect and punishment behaviors by caregiver clients. Similarly, Berlin et al. (1991) found that the legal obligation for psychiatrists to report child sexual abuse in Maryland was counterproductive: The number of self-referrals for child abuse and the self-disclosure rate during therapy both went to zero, and the number of children identified as abused did not increase. It appears that we mental health professionals have failed to make our need for options clear to our legislators.

d. You generally must report even abuse that occurred some time ago, if the victim is still under 18 and thus is considered vulnerable.

e. Bear in mind, however, that a duty to report is not a release of information; the patient's privilege still holds, and you may have to assert it when the patient has not, even when your patient is the suspected perpetrator. To provide more than the information your state authorities legally require will require a release from the client.

Some states, such as Pennsylvania, require you to report impaired drivers as well. These may include drivers with epilepsy, hallucinations, disorientation, homicidal tendencies, or a history of accidents or near-misses (Knapp et al., 1998, pp. 70–73). In my opinion, if a client appears for a session too intoxicated to drive home, you have a moral if not a legal responsibility as a citizen to intervene by negotiating safe travel or reporting the client to the police. Because there is no identified victim or certainty of an incident, your duty to protect others may not come into play.

4. **When the patient is a litigant and sues you.** Privilege cannot be used as "both a shield and a sword." That is, the client cannot waive privilege and have only some facts supportive of his or her case opened to view (the sword), while protecting himself or herself from the import of other facts (the shield). Once privilege is waived, it is generally waived completely. These situations are, however, negotiated between lawyers and the court, and some material can be excluded if it is of no relevance and is potentially damaging to the client. However, if you have been formally accused of malpractice, you may generally reveal *only* the information necessary to defend

yourself—not everything you were told or recorded or received as records from others.

In regard to lawsuits or ethics complaints, be careful about what you reveal to whom. It is natural to want to complain to or seek support from friends, colleagues, or a trusted supervisor. But these are *not* privileged conversations, and these people can be subpoenaed to testify about what you told them. (If you need support when dealing with a complaint, get into therapy. Besides, conversations in therapy sessions *are* protected.) Although ethical complaints to professional organizations and licensing boards are evaluated in confidence, the information revealed is also not privileged. The amount of material revealed depends on the attorneys and investigators and on the local procedures.

5. **When therapy or evaluations are court-ordered.** In this situation, the results of your evaluation or records of your therapy will be sent to both sides, so you must fully inform the client of this before you perform these services. It would be a good idea to make a note that you have informed the client that anything he or she says during an evaluation may be included in your report (American Psychiatric Association, 1987). Interestingly, examinations done at the request of a client's attorney may be protected by attorney–client privilege, and so may be suppressed if they are unfavorable to the client. (See Section 4.6.)

6. **Any legal proceeding where a client's mental status is at issue.** Lawsuits over head injuries, custody battles, adoptions, or disability claims can bring the records you created into court. This can include allegations of emotional pain and suffering or having been involuntarily psychiatrically hospitalized. In addition, your testimony may be required by a judge.

7. **Parents have rights to information about the diagnosis and treatment of their minor children.** See Section 4.5 and below.

8. **If your client seriously threatens an identifiable person or persons.** This is future criminal behavior, and you may have the "duty to warn or protect" (see Section 3.9 for clarification of this). Note that except in South Dakota, therapists are not required to report past criminal behavior if it is not ongoing.

9. **You must disclose in emergencies**—for example, when a "patient's health is seriously or imminently at stake" (Stromberg et al., 1988, p. 400). Keep the information disclosed to a minimum—that is, what a competent patient would agree would be necessary. In an emergency, a patient's oral consent to disclose is acceptable, but the details should be carefully documented. If the patient is unable (not unwilling) to provide the information or to consent, break confidentiality only if withholding it would endanger the patient and if the local law permits or does not forbid such disclosure.

10. **Nonlicensed therapists do not have privilege.** This includes intern psychologists, most "counselors," and those in training whom you may supervise. In general, students (including psychology interns, trainees, or supervisees) are not specifically covered by statutes granting privilege (Koocher & Keith-Spiegel, 1998). The HIPAA regulations specifically allow sharing of PHI with students and supervisees. The reg-

ulations are extremely broadly worded, and apply HIPAA to all those included in the Medicare regulations (Title XI, 42 U.S.C. 1301, Section 1861[u]). As such they seem to include just about any of the "various licensed/certified health care practitioners," and this may conflict with your state's rules or profession's codes.

Other Points about Confidentiality and Its Limitations

To obtain reimbursement with Medicare and Medicaid clients, providers are required to disclose more than basic identifying data. Managed care organizations' (MCOs') reviewers ask for lots of clinical information, and a client has almost always (and without any awareness of its implications) signed a blanket release for an MCO when applying for coverage. If the HIPAA regulations apply in this situation, the "minimum necessary" disclosure of PHI (see Section 164.5029[b]) may apply. These rules require the MCO to identify exactly what information each of its levels needs and to seek only that information; they may not request the entire medical record. It even appears that workers' compensation insurers routinely expect release of *all* records you create; this may be quite problematic when a client's employer is self-insured, and so the company's benefits staff can see records and may have few safeguards for maintaining their confidentiality. Clients need to know what will be revealed before they use their insurance, and they usually expect to use it from the beginning. Therefore you must inform them of this at the start of treatment. The client information brochure (see Section 4.2) covers this, as does Handout 3.

The sharing of information among members of a treatment team or care providers within an agency is generally acceptable without a release when the client has consented to treatment that he or she understands to involve several persons or departments within the agency (American Psychiatric Association, 1987). The HIPAA regulations specifically support the sharing of patient information among members of the treatment team and any others providing treatment with no more than the basic consent obtained during notification of privacy rights (see Section 5.4). Again, it would be best to include this point in the efforts you make to inform the client. Be especially careful about nonclinical personnel's access to agency records.

When you talk to a consultant about a client, do not add details that might enable the consultant to identify the client (APA, 2002, Standard 4.06). This is especially important if the consultant may know the client personally or by reputation, or if a case involves sensitive disorders (e.g., child or drug abuse, sexual difficulties). The consultant rarely needs detailed knowledge; it cannot be unlearned; and it becomes a burden to the other that he or she does not need to carry. The courts call this "guilty knowledge," and it is a very useful concept in doing psychotherapy.

Unless it is very sensitive, you do not need specific permission to share information with a consultant from whom you are seeking professional advice when this relationship was explained to and approved by the client. If you want to be more careful—perhaps because you do not know the contents of what will be revealed—you might get an authorization signed at the first meeting with the client, or document the absence of consent. This does not cover informally discussing a case with several peers, and this kind of consultation is not usually privileged, so don't do it. It is best to share clinical information only when doing so benefits the client, or else you are on thin ice.

In most states, the fact that a person is a client is itself not privileged information (although you should certainly treat it as confidential). Similarly, the dates and number of appointments, as well as billing information, are accessible to the courts (Knapp, 1994). Turning a case over to a collection agency or going to small-claims court is not a breach of confidentiality if the client is notified that it may occur. This notification is best included in your client information brochure. However, the information shared with the court should be minimal, given simply to establish the debt's legitimacy (client's identity, dates of service, fees) (APA, 2002, Standard 4.05b). Moreover, communications, reports, and observations made for purposes other than treatment are not covered by privilege; these include communications for employment or insurance purposes (American Psychiatric Association, 1987).

Confidentiality rules apply even after the death of the client involved. The privilege passes to the executor or legal representative of the client in most states.

Finally, claims of "That's confidential" cannot be used to protect the therapist, only the client. Such claims cannot be used to conceal harmful practices, protect the autonomy of the therapist, avoid the scrutiny of peers, or defend a need to be "right" (Sweet, 1990, p. 7).

Confidentiality and Children

With a competent adult, the person seeking services and the recipient of those services are the same; however, when the recipient of assessment or treatment services is a child, there are two "clients." In this situation, to whom does the therapist owe the duty of confidentiality? Even when the ethical duty is to the child, the legal duty may be to the parents. The best resolution can be found by looking for the local answers to the following questions suggested by Morris (1993, p. 11):

1. Is a child in psychotherapy accorded legally protected privileged communication in your state?

2. If yes, what are the exceptions to privileged communications for a child in your state?

3. Is there a common usage lower age limit for children legally granting them privileged communication?

4. Is there legal precedent in your state that has tested the constitutionality of the privileged communication granted to children and adolescents?

The therapist should, of course, inform the child of all the limitations of confidentiality. For example, the child should be told that the therapist will be discussing the contents of each interview (in general ways) with his or her parents, and that nothing can be kept secret. If the therapist will be consulting with school or hospital personnel, the child should be told that as well. Morris (1993) recommends putting these points in writing and obtaining the dated signatures of parents and child. Obviously, the wording of both oral and written statements must suit the child's understanding and reading levels. (See Form 11 of this book for a written statement suitable for an older child or an adolescent.) In general, the approach to an older or "emancipated" adolescent is like that to an adult.

Parental access to information and records varies a great deal. State laws usually do not address this issue, but logic suggests that if you need parental consent to provide treatment, the parents have the right to access the records of that treatment, and vice versa. The most common exceptions to the need for parental consent to treatment are emergencies and cases in which minors have graduated from high school or are married. You could try to discuss the issues of confidentiality in the first session with both adolescent and parent present. Goldberg (1995) suggests, at least, reassuring the parents that you will inform them if their child is in imminent danger.

Confidentiality and HIV-Positive Clients

There are many benefits of confidentiality for HIV-positive clients (including reduced risk of discrimination), but these must be weighed against its possible social costs (such as the infection of third parties). The issues are complex because of the intersection of a legally imposed duty to protect, laws and ethics about maintaining confidentiality, and clinical case issues. Chenneville (2000) is an excellent guide to making decisions and should be consulted in these cases. Also, the APA has made efforts to enhance psychologists' ability to respond to those affected by HIV (see www.apa.org/pi/aids/hope.html). See also Section 3.9.

A Handout on the Limits of Confidentiality

Issues concerning confidentiality have been incorporated into the client information brochure (see Section 4.2), because the APA ethics code (APA, 2002, Standard 4.02b) requires a discussion of confidentiality's limits before therapy begins. The same section requires discussion of limits as new circumstances warrant it. If and when you believe your clients **HANDOUT 6** need more specific information, Handout 6 covers confidentiality issues in greater detail than does the brochure. I recommend offering this handout only to those who raise concerns after reading the more general brochure, or to those whose referral (e.g., by the courts) or history suggests its need. The issues can then be discussed in a therapy session. Another way to use it is to make it available with other client education materials in a three-ring binder in your waiting room, perhaps entitled "For Your Information."

Like the other handouts and forms in this book, Handout 6 can be photocopied and distributed to your clients. It is generic enough to be applicable to most practices, and addresses issues relevant to adult, child, and family therapy. However, it does not fully address the issue of secrets between spouses in marital therapy. See Margolin (1982) for a discussion of this thorny topic.

Before using this handout, check on alterations you may need to make because of your locality, your profession or credentials, or your preferred methods of practice:

- If you treat older children, you might consider amplifying what is said here about what you have to reveal to parents or guardians.

- Weigh what you have to reveal to third-party payers with whom you have contracts in your state. Handout 3 is a more specific informed consent handout for MCO patients. In addition, review the current rules on releasing records of Medicare patients.

- If you do group therapy, consider its confidentiality limitations.

What You Should Know about Confidentiality in Therapy

I will treat what you tell me with great care. My professional ethics (that is, my profession's rules about values and moral matters) and the laws of this state prevent me from telling anyone else what you tell me unless you give me written permission. These rules and laws are the ways our society recognizes and supports the privacy of what we talk about—in other words, the "confidentiality" of therapy. But I cannot promise that everything you tell me will *never* be revealed to someone else. There are some times when the law requires me to tell things to others. There are also some other limits on our confidentiality. We need to discuss these, because I want you to understand clearly what I can and cannot keep confidential. You need to know about these rules now, so that you don't tell me something as a "secret" that I cannot keep secret. So please read these pages carefully and keep this copy. At our next meeting, we can discuss any questions you might have.

1. **When you or other persons are in physical danger,** the law requires me to tell others about it. Specifically:

   a. If I come to believe that you are threatening serious harm to another person, I am required to try to protect that person. I may have to tell the person and the police, or perhaps try to have you put in a hospital.

   b. If you seriously threaten or act in a way that is very likely to harm yourself, I may have to seek a hospital for you, or to call on your family members or others who can help protect you. If such a situation does come up, I will fully discuss the situation with you before I do anything, unless there is a very strong reason not to.

   c. In an emergency where your life or health is in danger, and I cannot get your consent, I may give another professional some information to protect your life. I will try to get your permission first, and I will discuss this with you as soon as possible afterwards.

   d. If I believe or suspect that you are abusing a child, an elderly person, or a disabled person I must file a report with a state agency. To "abuse" means to neglect, hurt, or sexually molest another person. I do not have any legal power to investigate the situation to find out all the facts. The state agency will investigate. If this might be your situation, we should discuss the legal aspects in detail before you tell me anything about these topics. You may also want to talk to your lawyer.

   In any of these situations, I would reveal only the information that is needed to protect you or the other person. I would not tell everything you have told me.

2. In general, **if you become involved in a court case or proceeding,** you can prevent me from testifying in court about what you have told me. This is called "privilege," and it is your choice to prevent me from testifying or to allow me to do so. However, there are some situations where a judge or court may require me to testify:

   a. In child custody or adoption proceedings, where your fitness as a parent is questioned or in doubt.

   b. In cases where your emotional or mental condition is important information for a court's decision.

(cont.)

    c. During a malpractice case or an investigation of me or another therapist by a professional group.

    d. In a civil commitment hearing to decide if you will be admitted to or continued in a psychiatric hospital.

    e. When you are seeing me for court-ordered evaluations or treatment. In this case we need to discuss confidentiality fully, because you don't have to tell me what you don't want the court to find out through my report.

    f. If you were sent to me for evaluation by workers' compensation or Social Security disability, I will be sending my report to a representative of that agency, and it can contain anything that you tell me.

3. There are a few other things you must know about confidentiality and your treatment:

    a. I may sometimes consult (talk) with another professional about your treatment. This other person is also required by professional ethics to keep your information confidential. Likewise, when I am out of town or unavailable, another therapist will be available to help my clients. I must give him or her some information about my clients, like you.

    b. I am required to keep records of your treatment, such as the notes I take when we meet. You have a right to review these records with me. If something in the record might seriously upset you, I may leave it out, but I will fully explain my reasons to you.

4. Here is what you need to know about confidentiality **in regard to insurance and money matters:**

    a. If you use your health insurance to pay a part of my fees, the insurance company, the managed care organization, or perhaps your employer's benefits office will require me to provide information about your functioning in many areas of your life, your social and psychological history, and your current symptoms. I will also be required to provide a treatment plan and information on how you are doing in therapy.

    b. I usually give you my bill with any other forms needed, and ask you to send these to your insurance company to file a claim for your benefits. That way, you can see what the company will know about our therapy. It is against the law for insurers to release information about our office visits to anyone without your written permission. Although I believe the insurance company will act morally and legally, I cannot control who sees this information after it leaves my office. You cannot be required to release more information just to get payments.

    c. If you have been sent to me by your employer's employee assistance program, the program's staffers may require some information. Again, I believe that they will act morally and legally, but I cannot control who sees this information at their offices. If this is your situation, let us fully discuss my agreement with your employer or the program before we talk further.

    d. If your account with me is unpaid and we have not arranged a payment plan, I can use legal means to get paid. The only information I will give to the court, a collection agency, or a lawyer will be your name and address, the dates we met for professional services, and the amount due to me.

5. **Children and families create some special confidentiality questions.**

    a. When I treat children under the age of about 12, I must tell their parents or guardians whatever they ask me. As children grow more able to understand and choose, they assume legal rights. For those between the ages of 12 and 18, most of the details in things they tell me will be treated as confidential. However, parents or guardians do have the right to *general* information, including how therapy is going. They need to be

(cont.)

able to make well-informed decisions about therapy. I may also have to tell parents or guardians some information about other family members that I am told, especially if these others' actions put them or others in any danger.

b. In cases where I treat several members of a family (parents and children or other relatives), the confidentiality situation can become very complicated. I may have different duties toward different family members. At the start of our treatment, we must all have a clear understanding of our purposes and my role. Then we can be clear about any limits on confidentiality that may exist.

c. If you tell me something your spouse does not know, and not knowing this could harm him or her, I cannot promise to keep it confidential. I will work with you to decide on the best long-term way to handle situations like this.

d. If you and your spouse have a custody dispute, I will need to know about it. My professional ethics prevent me from doing both therapy and custody evaluations.

e. If you are seeing me for marriage counseling, you must agree at the start of treatment that if you eventually decide to divorce, you will not request my testimony for either side. The court, however, may order me to testify.

f. At the start of family treatment, we must also specify which members of the family must sign a release form for the common record I create in the therapy or therapies. (See point 7b, below.)

6. **Confidentiality in group therapy is also a special situation.**

In group therapy, the other members of the group are not therapists. They do not have the same ethics and laws that I have to work under. You cannot be certain that they will always keep what you say in the group confidential.

7. Finally, here are a few other points:

a. I will not record our therapy sessions on audiotape or videotape without your written permission.

b. If you want me to send information about our therapy to someone else, you must sign a "release-of-records" form. I have copies you can see, so you will know what is involved.

c. Any information that you tell me and also share outside of therapy, willingly and publicly, will not be considered protected or confidential by a court.

The laws and rules on confidentiality are complicated. Please bear in mind that I am not able to give you legal advice. If you have special or unusual concerns, and so need special advice, I strongly suggest that you talk to a lawyer to protect your interests legally and to act in your best interests.

The signatures here show that we each have read, discussed, understand, and agree to abide by the points presented above.

_____   _____
Signature of client (or person acting for client)   Date

_____
Printed name

_____   _____
Signature of therapist   Date

- Adapt section 1d to your state's rules about the basis for reporting abuse. States differ in requiring a "suspicion" standard or a "reasonable belief" standard. The suspicion standard requires a lower level of certainty to trigger the mandated reporting requirement. Also, states differ in their definitions of elder abuse. Usually elder abuse is defined more broadly than child abuse and includes financial exploitation (Sam Knapp, personal communication, October 2, 1996).

- Section 3a states that anyone you seek consultation from is "required by professional ethics to keep your information confidential." This is an ethical but not likely a legal requirement; you, the person seeking consultation, are not the consultant's client.

- Adapt section 3b to your state's rules and preferred practices about clients' access to records. This section says, "You have a right to review these records with me." The exact means of a client's access to his or her records varies with states and regulations. Sending actual copies allows for misinterpretation and risks revelations to other parties. Sending them to another mental health professional for interpretation may be safest.

  If HIPAA regulations on patient access to your records (Section 164.524) apply in your state, the patient does not have a right to read your psychotherapy notes (if you created them), although you may allow such inspection. HIPAA also grants clients the right to amend their records, so you might add: "If you find errors in my records, you can ask me to correct these by adding new information to the records." Patients do not have the right to "access, inspect, and copy" information related to legal proceedings, research, or some other areas. You can limit access when you decide that access is "reasonably likely to endanger the life or physical safety" of the patient or another person, or when access might similarly harm another person identified in the record. If you do allow access, the regulations specify timely access and procedures for review of such denials of access. You should modify the wording in section 3b to reflect these rules.

- If the HIPAA Privacy Rule applies in your state, you should modify section 4a to explain what will be in the routine office notes that the client's insurer will access. See Section 6.2 on the content of these notes as well as psychotherapy notes.

- Section 4b says, "I usually give you my bill . . . ". This may not be your policy, so adapt the wording.

- You could expand the policy stated in sections 5d and 5e on your becoming a witness in custody or divorce proceedings. Incorporate some possible alternatives:

  "I will not serve as a witness or provide records for such matters, and I ask you to agree that if such a situation arises, you will accept my policy. If you go to court, you will have to ask another professional to do any evaluations of yourselves, your children, and your relationship."

  "I ask you to agree that my records will not be requested in court by either party, and to keep this in mind during our therapy."

  "I will provide a summary, but not the actual records, to the court. My charge for this summary is $150 per hour of preparation time."

- Section 5f covers the question of which family members sign a release-of-records form.

The safest method of release for a family's or couple's records is to require the consent of all adults or participants, although this is also the most complex solution.

Because of the litigious and "paranoid" flavor of our times, you might add wording like this:

> "I do not sell or in any way make available your name or any of the information you provide to me to anyone without your permission. I will not even acknowledge that you are a client of my practice without your specific permission."

The general rule is this: **Make certain that the client is informed about all the likely implications and consequences of confidentiality.** A handout like Handout 6, and your detailed notes, should show that you have told the client what he or she needs to know to act in his or her own best interest.

7.2   Maintaining Confidentiality

Guidelines for Maintaining Confidentiality

- Encourage clients to ask questions about confidentiality concerns when they arise in therapy, and to resolve them before they make any risky revelations. When answering questions, be careful to promise very little specific protection; you cannot know how confidential you can keep a client's specific situation until you are told, and then it may be too late. Clients have rarely formulated their situations within the ethical or legal frameworks you are bound to live by.

- Many clinicians worry that disclosing the limits of confidentiality will inhibit the freedom of discussion necessary for effective therapy. Nowell and Spruill (1993), surveying rather naive college students, found that disclosing exceptions to total confidentiality did result in some inhibition of self-disclosure. However, they also found that offering a complete description of the limitations did not result in more inhibition than a brief, cursory description, which is now seen as essential. Standard 4.02 of the APA ethics code (APA, 2002) requires that the limits of confidentiality be communicated explicitly and in advance. The client information brochure (see Section 4.2) incorporates these kinds of notifications.

- If in doubt, consult. By itself, making this effort offers you some malpractice protection and you may learn how to protect your client. Document these consultations.

- Avoid giving legal advice on confidentiality, and refer complex questions to the client's attorney.

- Both ethics and HIPAA's Security Rule require you to assure the confidentiality of your computerized client records. (See also Section 1.5.) Your records could be read and copied by any of the following: your own staff; cleaning persons in your office when you are not present; anyone on your local or larger computer network (unless you have blocked access to client files); those entering through your always-on Internet high-speed digital subscriber line (DSL) or cable modem connection, or secretly sending you a program that sends your files to them (a "Trojan Horse" virus);

a thief who steals your computer; a repair person if it needs service or upgrading; legal wiretappers; those using video monitoring "security cameras"; and probably others.

In my opinion, passwords are insufficient protection, burdensome, and likely to be misused by being changed too infrequently or used on too many accounts. Also, there are easily available programs for breaking passwords. A better solution is to encrypt all your clinical files. The liability is that you will be using a password to decrypt these files. Use any of the free (e.g., Pretty Good Privacy) or more convenient moderately priced encryption programs that you can download. If you use DSL or a cable modem, use and keep current a "firewall" program. You can find all these at Shareware.com, Download.com, and others. For privacy tools for all kinds of electronic communication, see www.epic.org/privacy/tools.html, or do an Internet search for the latest tools.

- Do not gossip or otherwise talk lightly or casually about your patients. Famous patients, fascinating clinical phenomena, bragging, making the irresistible joke—all these are tempting conversational topics. We may try to gain points for ourselves at the expense of our patients, trusting that no one will figure out their identity or use the information. The best rule is *never* to discuss your patients or your work with your spouse, friends, or even other therapists, but only with a consultant or in a carefully prepared presentation. With such a rule, you won't have to keep deciding what to reveal, or feel the anxiety of uncertainty.

- Leave nothing with a client's name on it lying around anywhere—no folders, no letters, no phone notes, no unusable photocopies. Arrange your office and office procedures to prevent the viewing of charts, appointment books, telephone messages, computer screens, and the like by clients, salespersons, cleaning people, visitors, and other staff members. Lock your door, desk, and cabinet when you are out of the office. If you share an office, each therapist will need a locked record storage area.

- To be safest, develop a rule of never using a client's name in any conversation with anyone outside your consulting room. Never discuss clients, even for consultation or supervision, in any place (whether public or professional) where anyone not bound by your professional code could *possibly* overhear. Certainly do not do so in an elevator or taxi. Make the time for consultation and do it right. Words cannot be unsaid, and lawsuits are depressing.

- Train all members of your staff in all aspects of the maintenance of confidentiality. Make it clear to your staff that any kind of client information must not be casually or carelessly discussed (over lunch, in rest rooms, in elevators, etc.), including in the office. If other staff members, employees, or even other clinicians bound by confidentiality are present when you need to communicate, write the client's name down and point to it for your conversation. Similarly, do not allow your staff or office mates to refer to clients who phone or otherwise come up in conversation, except as "this client" or "he" or "she." Finally, make clear your intention to dismiss immediately anyone who breaks any of the rules of the office. (See below on staff training.)

- Be careful when you replay the answering machine, so that no one else can overhear. Instruct your staff to do the same. Use password-protected "mailboxes" for your voice mail.

- Assure yourself that your answering service also understands these rules and obeys them. Ask about the staff's training, offer some hypothetical situations, and perhaps call as someone else to test the service.

- Do not use a client's name in the waiting room unless you and the client are alone. It may seem odd, but you can just make eye contact and say, "Won't you please come in?" without mentioning the client's name. If it is a first appointment, saying "I'm Dr. Doe. Are you here to see me?" will serve the same purpose in a busy waiting area. If the office is used by professionals of other disciplines, such as dentists, they are likely to use clients' names freely; do not be swayed.

- In some cases, just revealing information in the presence of a third party (such as another therapist, an uninvolved professional, or perhaps even an employee) may void the legal protection of confidentiality. This also applies to your clients, so discourage them from saying private things when others (such as family or friends) are around. There is no privilege if the patient tells other people about the session, because that, too, means it is no longer actually held in confidence by the client.

  1. Did the patient intend the session to be confidential? The answer to this question often lies in the original reason for the session. If the patient has a regular, long-term relationship with the therapist (e.g., is being treated for a disorder), then the reason for the sessions are solely for the patient's private benefit, and clearly are intended to be confidential. However, many people contact psychologists in connection with some particular legal rather than psychological problem. Perhaps they are in the process of or contemplating divorce, are being evaluated as parents for custody or adoption purposes, have been raped or abused and are pressing charges, are fulfilling a condition of probation, or the like. In these cases, the courts are likely to find that the patient intended immediately or in the future to disclose the fact that he or she was undergoing treatment, in which case there is no evidentiary privilege.

  2. Was the session in fact confidential? There is no privilege if the FBI is lawfully wiretapping the session, or an undercover police officer is actually present in the room.

- *Never* discuss any kind of confidential matter on a wireless or cellular phone. Be aware that they are broadcasting devices and do not have the same protections (legal or technical) for confidentiality that wired phones do. Encryption programs for wireless phones are available.

- Make sure you have sufficient sound muffling in your office. You can achieve this with white-noise generators, an air deflector in the air conditioning ductwork, double-studded and double-wallboarded walls, a radio with several speakers (set fairly loud and not under the control of the clients in the waiting room), and heavily weather-stripped or carpeted doors.

- Even if a client's spouse is in therapy with the client, it is not appropriate to discuss the client's treatment in detail with the spouse. The law is frequently silent on the issue of the privileged status of what is said to spouses in marriage counseling, or to a therapist's assistants, staff, and employees, so you may not have protection. Court-ordered marriage counseling may be an exception to confidentiality, but check your local rules.

- Make explicit in your client information brochure how you will handle the confidentiality issues of family therapy.

- Keep separate sets of group therapy records. That is, keep a record for each individual in which other members are not identified, and a separate record for the group as a whole. See Form 12, the group therapy contract.

- Develop a clear plan to dispose of your records without breaking confidentiality. See Section 1.6.

Training Employees in Privacy Practices

If your office is large enough to employ others, you have to train them in your procedures and then monitor and supervise their work. HIPAA makes formal staff training in privacy policies and practices a requirement, and this is certainly a good thing. Training in security procedures should be included as well. This training must be completed by the time your practice becomes officially HIPAA-compliant. It must be done for new employees, should be repeated at intervals, and must be documented (see below). At the end of such training, a formal confidentiality agreement with each staff member can be signed as a good summary of the issues and reminder of the likely risks. Staff members *must* be trained in HIPAA, and *should* be trained in your local laws and your professional ethics to protect your clients and yourself. The checklist below can be used to organize your training of employees and can also be used as an employee agreement to maintain confidentiality. It includes the issues of greatest concern and likelihood, but you should add items to fit your practice and revise the contents over time.

A Checklist for Staff Training in Confidentiality

Below is a checklist of the issues of greatest concern and likelihood (and the sections of this book where you will find some guidance). It is presented here as an example only; you should add items to fit your practice and revise the contents over time. It can be used to organize your training of employees (permanent or temporary, part- or full-time), answering service personnel, or anyone else with access to your records. It can also be used as an employee agreement to maintain confidentiality. A few sentences are based on a form devised by Ginger Blume, PhD, of Middletown, CT. The HIPAA privacy rule specifies that you must train your staff in these issues (Section 164.530[b]) and must "have in place appropriate administrative, technical, and physical safeguards to protect the privacy of protected health information" (Section 164.530[c]).

Checklist for Staff Training in Confidentiality

When people come to this practice, they are likely to discuss very personal information that they want to remain confidential—that is, to be known only to themselves and the therapist or clinician who is treating them. Below we describe our office's rules designed to protect the confidentiality of all clients' health care information and any other confidential information in this office. You should assume that *everything* is confidential in this office and treat it accordingly.

As a condition of your employment, we require you to read, understand, and agree to comply with these rules.

A checkmark below indicates that this topic was discussed with those present on this date: _____.
I, _____, conducted this training.

❑ The codes of ethics and guidelines of my profession.

❑ The main malpractice and ethics issues and risks—confidentiality, dual relationships, billing, and

_____.

❑ Procedures and limitations on releasing any kind of records.

❑ Procedures for copying any kind of records.

❑ Responding to phone calls about clients (Section 7.3).

❑ The organization, handling, and storing of all material with patients' names—charts, forms, photocopies, faxes, voice mail boxes, computer screens, appointment books, phone messages and books, and so forth.

❑ Proper use of computer programs that contain client information, in order to maintain its privacy.

❑ Not using clients' names on the phone, in the waiting area, or anywhere else they could be overheard by unauthorized persons.

❑ Privately playing the answering machine or calling the answering service.

❑ Casual conversations and gossip about patients, in and out of the office.

❑ Computer security—passwords and encryption (Sections 1.5 and 7.2), backups, off-site storage, and the like.

❑ The fact that the confidentiality of a patient's information extends after the death of the patient or the professional, after my leaving this employment, and into the future indefinitely.

❑ The breaking of confidentiality rules as grounds for immediate dismissal.

❑ How to handle questions of ethics, confidentiality, access, and so forth raised by clients, by other professionals, or by situations.

My signature below indicates the following:

❑ I have read and discussed:

   ❑ The "Information for Clients" brochure (Section 4.2) or the other routes to informed consent (Sections 4.3–4.6).

   ❑ Other client education materials of this practice, such as the handout on the limits of confidentiality (Handout 6) and the Handout on managed care (Handout 3), as appropriate to my job functions.

   ❑ The notice of privacy practices (NPP) forms (Forms 21 and 22), the form for consent to privacy practices (Form 23), and the various release forms (Forms 49–54), as appropriate to my job functions.

❑ I have been informed about the issues and guidelines above, have had the opportunity to raise any questions, and have had my questions answered. I believe I understand the issues and concerns about confidentiality and related issues, and will ask _____ when any questions or concerns arise for me.

❏ I agree not to disclose any patient information to third parties, persons outside this practice/office/ organization, other patients, or anyone else unless authorized to do so in writing by a patient (or patient's guardian) and approved by my employing professional.

❏ If a breach of this agreement or the confidentiality of any records should occur, I agree to notify my employer immediately or within 24 hours of its discovery.

❏ I understand that any material breach of this agreement shall constitute good cause of my discharge from this employment. In addition, such breach may subject me to liability and legal damages.

Signature of employee	Printed name of employee

Signature of employee	Printed name of employee

Signature of employee	Printed name of employee

Creating Confidential Records

There are three methods of increasing the likelihood of confidentiality of your records:

1. Always abridge as much as possible. This means limiting the client information collected, recorded, retained, and reported. Do not put information of a sensitive nature into a report if it is not *clearly* necessary to the purposes of that report. For example, do not repeat a client's history from earlier reports or the reports of others, unless this is essential for your present purposes. If you do incorporate others' information, you are in effect releasing information sent to you in confidentiality—presumably with a limited and legal release—but without a legal release from the client. Simple as this rule is, it is broken frequently. You cannot control the destinies of your reports, and your primary responsibility is to your client. If the information is crucial and very sensitive, consider telling the referral source or other concerned persons orally.

2. Ensure the client's access to his or her records. (The rules about this access should be indicated in your client information brochure.) Access can further protect clients' privacy by (a) informing them of what information has been collected and how it is interpreted and used; (b) allowing them the opportunities to correct errors; and (c) allowing them to make informed decisions before releasing information. All of this is empowering to clients and thus protects them in a larger sense. It is also supported by federal law and perhaps by your local laws.

3. If a client is at risk from the information, write it in a protecting, discreet, thoughtful way.

A Quick Test

1. A physician calls to ask: "This is Dr. Jones. Did my patient, Joe Smith, whom I referred to you, come in?" How should you answer?

2. An attorney asks: "Did my client, Joe Smith, come in to see you?" How should you answer?

3. A caller asks: "Did my brother, Joe Smith, get to your office OK?" How should you answer?"

One or more of the following may run through your mind:

- "I don't want to be rude to this caller."

- "My first duty is to protect his privacy by concealing my patient's identity."

- "All three of us know Joe was supposed to be here, so where is the risk?"

- "Is there anyone who can overhear this conversation?"

- "Am I certain this is indeed Dr. Jones/Ms. Brown/Joe's sister?"

However mixed your reactions may be, unless you know the caller and are willing to take the risk of breaking confidentiality, the only acceptable answer to all three of these queries is this: "I'm sorry, but I cannot give you that information. If you will have the person [don't even use Joe Smith's name, as it could signal that he is known] sign a consent form releasing the information you want, I will check to see if he is known to us, and then I will be able to talk further with you or send you the information you want." Instruct the members of your staff today that they are never to take the risk of responding in any other way. As a way to soften the pain of refusal, you should explain the need for privacy, and you can offer to send the caller a copy of your release form.

7.3   Releasing Clients' Records

Note: See also Chapter 4 on informed consent.

The balance of this chapter offers a variety of more specific guidelines to help you answer questions such as these:

- How can you decide whether or not to honor a request for a client's records?

- How can you best protect the client's confidentiality when you do release your records?

- What legal elements must a request for the records of another professional contain?

The first of these questions is addressed here. Later sections include sample forms for requesting records from and releasing records to different requesters. The forms are designed to meet important legal and ethical guidelines.

A Pretest

How sophisticated are you in weighing the relevant issues in releasing records? Pope (1988e) offers the following fictional case history.[1] A 17-year-old married father of a 1-year-old child, living with his parents, comes in complaining of headaches. He is a full-time employee with insurance to pay for your testing. This is an unusual and complicated case, but not entirely unlikely. After you do the evaluation, you receive six requests for your records, from the following:

   (a) the boy's physician, an internist.

   (b) the boy's parents, who are concerned about his depression.

   (c) the boy's employer, in connection with a worker's compensation claim filed by the boy.

   (d) the attorney for the insurance company that is contesting the worker's compensation claim.

   (e) the attorney for the boy's wife, who is suing for divorce and for custody of the baby.

   (f) the attorney [for the boy], who is considering suing you for malpractice since he doesn't like the results of the tests.

   Each of the requests asks for: (a) the full formal report, (b) the original test data, and (c) copies of each of the tests you administered (e.g., instructions and all items for the MMPI).

   To which of these people are you legally or ethically obligated to supply all information requested? Partial information? A summary of the report? No information at all? (Pope, 1988e, p. 24)

Again, this is admittedly a complex situation, and Pope does not offer answers. Before reading further, take a pencil and paper and try to indicate which records you would send out and which you wouldn't, and to whom you would send them. My answers can be found at the end of this section (see pp. 394–395).

We still have to act in the real world. Records must often be shared among professionals for the benefit of clients, but breaches of confidentiality can destroy the trust essential for intimate work. The professions have therefore developed procedures for protecting the privacy of records. The following discussion shows how to evaluate a request for your client's records. In general, as in the case above, you need to weigh the needs of the requester against the ethical and legal requirements. These are described next.

---

[1]The passage below is reprinted, and the case history is taken, from Pope (1988e). Copyright 1988 by Division 42 of the American Psychological Association. Used by permission.

Ethical Considerations in Releasing Records

A release that authorizes you to "release and disclose all information and to discuss anything pertaining to this client and the client's progress" appears to be illegally vague and broad, and may be prohibited by HIPAA regulations concerning the "minimal necessary" disclosure rules (see Section 164.502).

The HIPAA Privacy Rule is not very restrictive about the confidentiality of your records. However, wherever your state's laws and court decisions are more stringent they will apply, and this does not remove the necessity for your complying with your profession's ethics codes. Therefore, I have inserted some information where it is most applicable.

The basic rule is that consent to release records must be *informed* and *voluntary*, and must be obtained from a *competent* person. These requirements are discussed in Chapter 4. Informed consent to release records requires that the client know and agree to the following:

- Which specific person wants the records (name, position, affiliation, function).

- What the records sought contain. Knowledge can come from the client's reading the materials, or from having the materials read and explained to him or her.

- Exactly what information is sought.

- Why this information is sought and exactly how it will be used. What decision(s) will be based on it?

- How the information in the records can be corrected or amended.

- Whether the requester can share this information with anyone else (e.g., consultants, treatment team members).

- What repercussions would follow from granting or withholding permission.

- That the client's consent is revocable except for information already released.

Do not confuse this full consenting process (becoming informed, acting voluntarily, having the mental capability to consent) with signing the HIPAA-required consent form acknowledging having learned about your privacy practices from your NPP (see Form 23). Also, remember that this consent form is not a release-of-records authorization, which you should always use.

Finally, this may seem obvious, but the client must believe that it is in his or her long-term best interest to release the records. For fuller comprehension, your release-of-records form should be available for the client to read; anything the client does not understand must be explained at his or her level of comprehension, and in his or her native language if necessary.

Legal Requirements for a Release of Records

The legal requirements for releasing records are set by the HIPAA regulations (Section 164.508) and by the Code of Federal Regulations (42 C.F.R. Part 2, Public Law 93-282, Sections 2.31(a) and 2.33, governing the confidentiality of alcohol and drug abuse patients' records). A valid release form must address all of the following:

- Name of client. Date of birth is also usually sought, as is Social Security number, because names are not unique.

- The name or title of the person or organization requesting disclosure of the record.

- Either the name or general designation of the program from which or person from whom the records are to be released.

- The extent or nature of the information to be disclosed. (A request for "any and all information" should never be made or honored.)

- The purpose of the request, why these records are needed, or how the PHI be used. (You may receive a request by error that was created for another proceeding.)

- The consequences of refusing to release the records (e.g., loss of reimbursement for medical costs or of disability benefits).

- The signature of the client (or his or her representative) and the date signed. (The signature must usually be given within 90 days of the time you receive the form.)

- Verification that the person signing is of legal age, or documentation of his or her "emancipation."

- A statement that the participant has the right to revoke, in writing, this authorization; a description of the means for doing so; and the exceptions to such revocation (e.g., that it is not retroactive and thus won't apply to what has already been disclosed).

- When, how, or on what condition upon which the consent will expire if not revoked earlier.

- A notice that after the PHI is disclosed, it may be redisclosed and thus is no longer protected by HIPAA regulations. Note that other federal laws forbid this redisclosure.

- A statement that the client does not have to agree to and sign the authorization. If this authorization is for your use, you need to state that your providing treatment, payment, enrollment, and so forth is not contingent (or "conditioned") upon the client's agreeing to the release of your or others' records according to HIPAA. Note that agreement is required for treatment in a research program, obtaining health insurance, and some other situations.

    There is a subtle difference here. Presumably all clients would agree to your *use* of their PHI. You can of course, treat them without their agreement to release your records to someone else. However, you should never treat a client who would not allow you to get others' records, for both therapeutic and risk management reasons.

The HIPAA rule above is designed to prevent nontreating covered entities (CEs) such as insurers from requiring the release to them of more information than is present in the routine progress notes.

- An indication that you will be paid directly or indirectly for this disclosure, if that is true. This pertains to the marketing restrictions created by HIPAA and rarely if ever applies to psychotherapists. (Please don't sell a list of your depressed patients to a travel agency, even though Hippocrates might have endorsed vacations to treat depression.)

For clarification about how some of these ideas are carried out, see the release forms in Sections 7.4 and 7.5. Additional criteria may be required by your state.

Eight Variations on the Theme of "Please Send Your Records"

Many different people may request your records in many different ways. Each request needs to be considered from an ethical perspective. The following discussion evaluates eight of these variations.

1. A Third Party's Routine Written Request for Records

Consider these usual bases for releasing information to a third party:

- A competent patient has requested release. The disclosure is necessary for the patient's continuing or comprehensive care by another provider or institution, for reimbursement, or for a needed consultation.

- A *surrogate* consent is received for a minor, for someone adjudicated incompetent, or for a dead person.

- A law requires disclosure (e.g., Medicare, mandatory child abuse reporting). See variation 2, below.

Now consider these possible bases against releasing information to a third party:

- The release form sent to you is faulty. It is missing some of the necessary contents of a proper release as listed above. As a courtesy, you could, if you are still in contact with the patient, use one of your releases (perhaps Form 49) to construct a proper release.

- The requester is someone you don't recognize, and you know nothing about the intended uses for this information. "Verify the requester's identity and official capacity" before proceeding, say Stromberg et al. (1988, p. 394).

- The information in your possession is not relevant to the request (e.g., it may not pertain to the request's purposes, the decisions to be made, the time period in question, or even the patient named in the request).

- Confidentiality law or privilege protects against release, and your general duty to protect confidentiality is not overcome by any recognized exception (see Section 7.1 for a list of exceptions).

- In family therapy, the "family" or "couple" cannot have legal confidentiality; only individual members have this privilege. Thus you will have to clarify and negotiate rules for release with each family member. Ideally, you have specified in your introductory materials that all members must sign a release.

- Is it completely clear that the patient is fully informed about all the information in the record and the effects of passing on all this information? If not, contact the patient directly to clarify the release. In one case in Pennsylvania, a patient sued (successfully at first) the psychologist whom she had specifically requested to write a letter to her employer seeking a less stressful job for her, after she had signed a release form. She sued for invasion of privacy and infliction of emotional distress. The psychologist probably would have received a dismissal (before going to the Court of Appeals) if he or she had had the patient see and authorize the release of the exact letter. It is best to have all records released be seen by the patient.

- Can you withhold records if you have not been paid for your services? The APA ethics code (APA, 2002) says in Standard 6.03 that "Psychologists may not withhold records . . . that are requested and needed for a client's/patient's emergency treatment solely because payment has not been received." Notice the qualifiers "emergency" and "solely." I believe the message is that you can indeed withhold records for nonpayment in nonemergency situations. You certainly would not withhold records in an emergency with serious consequences, but what if the request is being made only for the convenience of the patient (e.g., in support of a school transfer) and he or she is fully capable of paying you?

One last point: Should you type up your notes to make them actually readable? No, just send copies of your records in whatever shape they are in. "Redacting" them is not what you were asked for, and it would tempt you to make minor revisions (for clarification), which would create doubts about your veracity and integrity.

2. A Patient's Request to See His or Her Own Records

Who actually *owns* a patient's records? Hirsh (1978) says that "records are considered to be the property of the health care provider [who created them] or his or her employing agency [who paid the creator]. Generally, the consumer controls the dissemination of the records."

When a patient asks to see his or her own records, consider these points:

- What specific disclosures does the applicable state law require? Applicable laws may concern workers' compensation, disabilities acts, dual-diagnosis clients, substance abuse/dependence, your specific discipline, relationships with other mental health professions, and so forth.

- Consider why the patient wants these records and work from there. The request may conceal other needs, which can be resolved better through different methods.

- In general, offer to review the records with the patient, or offer a *précis* of the record. The issues are the impact on the patient of the disclosure of a diagnosis (which will require explanation and guidance for the patient to understand productively) and the impact of other information (see variation 3, below).

- Consider whether there may be errors in the record, which the patient has a right to see, correct, or amend. The client also has the right to add a statement of agreement or disagreement. These rights come from the Privacy Act of 1974 (Public Law 93-579); the HIPAA regulations; and, for drug and alcohol clients, the Drug Abuse Office and Treatment Act of 1972 (Public Law 92-255).

Clients' Access to Their Records under HIPAA. In the past, patients have had little real ability to examine their own medical records. HIPAA has given them some ability to "access, inspect, and copy protected health information" (under Section 164.524).

A patient has the right to access, inspect, and obtain a copy of the PHI that you created unless one or more of the following applies:

- The information was collected for use in a legal proceeding (civil, criminal, or administrative).

- The information is in your psychotherapy notes.

- The patient was an inmate of a correctional institution for which you work.

- The information was generated as part of a research project that is still ongoing, and prior to entering the research the client agreed to delay access.

- The information was collected by a health care provider who was promised anonymity, and the information would reveal the identity of this person.

Denial of access for any of the reasons above is not a reviewable decision.

Access requests must be in writing and must be acted on within 30 days (for records onsite, and 60 days for those off-site) or formally extended for another 30 days. If you wholly or partly deny the request, you have to provide the denial in writing, in plain language, containing the basis for the denial, explaining the rights and procedures for a review of the denial, and explaining how, if he or she chooses to do so, the patient can complain to you or the Secretary of the Department of Health and Human Services (DHHS) with names and phone numbers.

While the information would usually be in photocopied or printed form, it can be otherwise if the patient is amenable. You can provide a summary or explanation of the information if the patient agrees to this and to your fees for such a version. You can assess charges for copying and postage.

If you don't have the information sought by the patient but know who does, you must direct the patient there.

Amending a Client's Record. The HIPAA regulations (Section 164.526) describe how a patient may seek to amend, not "correct" records with PHI. You will provide a link, in the record, to the newer information.

You can refuse to amend your records (per HIPAA Section 164.526[d]) if one of the following is true:

- You didn't create the record. However, you may still amend it if you believe that the originator of the record is no longer available.

- The record would not otherwise be available for the patient to "access, inspect, and copy" it (see above).

- You believe that the record is accurate and complete.

You should tell clients that they may be able to amend their records if they have good reason and make a request in writing. You will have to act on such a request within 60 days and either amend the record or deny the request in whole or in part. In either case you must inform the patient. If you agree to amend, you must make efforts to provide this amended record to others who the patient has identified or others who "may have relied, or could foreseeably rely, on such information to the detriment of the [patient]." If you deny the request you must explain in plain language, in writing, the basis for the denial; the client's right to and the procedure for submitting a written disagreement; a statement that you will, if the client requests it, include in future disclosures the client's request for amendment and the denial you made; and an explanation, including names and phone numbers, of how the patient can complain to the covered entity or the Secretary of DHHS. The regulations allow you to limit the size of the client's request and to substitute a summary of the issues. Your records must indicate all of these exchanges and their outcome.

3. A Patient's Request to See His or Her Own Records, Which Contain Potentially Harmful Information

Access can be denied if it might harm the client. If, as a licensed health care provider, you come to believe that allowing the patient access to his or her PHI is likely to endanger the life, safety, or health of the patient or someone else, you can deny access. This denial can be appealed and reviewed by an additional licensed health care professional (see HIPAA Section 164.524[d][4]).

An example of a patient who could be harmed by information in his or her records is an adult with a history of childhood sexual or physical abuse where the patient may be unaware of or deny the abuse, but it is supported by records released to you.

Your plan in such a case should depend on the circumstances, your understanding of the patient, and the impact of the information. Traditionally, this "re-release" of records that are in your file but created by others was forbidden, but HIPAA allows such disclosures. State laws differ, and using an authorization form is somewhat protective. You could sidestep the issue by refusing to release to the patient records generated by someone else. This would require the patient to seek those records from their creators. However, you might not be acting in the patient's best interest, because those records would have to be released to someone, and this someone might not do as sensitive a presentation of the distressing information as you could. If you think the information will harm the patient, you can withhold it; this is called "therapeutic privilege." You may not have heard of this privilege, because it is getting rarer and should be invoked only in extraordinary circumstances (Stromberg & Dellinger, 1993). However, the HIPAA regulations have revived this concept and do allow you to restrict the information a client can access (see Section 164.524[a][3][ii]). In such a situation you are asking the patient to understand that some information would be upsetting, and to agree that he or she should be kept ignorant of this information (which seems to go against informed consent). You are also asking that if the information is presented to the patient, he or she will not hold you responsible for any damages (which seems to ask the patient to waive recourse from a harm he or she cannot anticipate—this again seems unfair). If the situation is touchy, go slowly and carefully; give full attention to maintaining the best possible relationship with the patient; document the issues, rationales, and choices made; and get consultation.

The following are some suggestions for proceeding:

- Decide whether it is "advisable and feasible to discuss the records with the patient prior to making them available in order to clarify matters" (Stromberg et al., 1988, p. 422).

- Then decide "which portions of the records should be revealed and which portions (if any) should not be" (Stromberg et al., 1988, p. 422).

- If the patient might be harmed, is there someone else (an advisor or family member) who can then represent the patient for the purpose of reviewing the record?

- If you decide that releasing certain information would not be in the patient's best interest if he or she were to read it, Woody (1988, p. 210) suggests that you should (1) obtain a release for that specific information, or (2) obtain a waiver from the patient of his or her right to have access to this report. You could also write a letter to the requester justifying your refusal to release damaging information, and base it on your local regulations. Here is an example:

  The regulations of the Pennsylvania Department of Health govern a patient's access to his or her records: "The hospital shall provide the patient, upon request, access to all information contained in his (or her) records, unless access is specifically restricted by the attending physician for medical reasons" (Pa. Code 103.22 (b) (15)).

  I have discussed the release of these records with my attorney, and in my considered professional opinion, this patient should not have access to the following parts of the records that are attached:

  1.

  2.

  3.

  I believe that the patient's coming to know the information contained in these parts will cause him or her to suffer mental anguish and pain without any balancing productive or beneficial effects. It is also, in my opinion, likely that reading this information will interfere with further treatment or cause the patient to lose gains already achieved.

  Because of these likely negative effects upon the patient, I strongly recommend that the information contained in these parts of the record not be disclosed to the patient. If you believe a situation arises in which it is absolutely necessary to disclose this information to the patient, I strongly recommend that this be done only by myself or a professional whom I designate, and not by you or any other person, professional, or organization who may obtain these records.

Prepare in advance for this possibility by adding language to your client information brochure. Section 4.2 includes this statement: "I may temporarily remove parts of your records before you see them. This would happen if I believe that the information will be harmful to you, but I will discuss this with you." Ideally, you have avoided using any language in the record that might exacerbate the emotional state of the client.

4. A Parent or Guardian's Request for Records

Parents and guardians have a right to know about minor children's status and progress. Traditionally, this has been a right to *information* about the children's treatment (not full access to all their *records*), but HIPAA gives full access. Remember, nevertheless, that you own (or your agency owns) the actual records.

Minors themselves, however, have few rights; so unless your state laws give them privilege, be careful what you write, and be diplomatic and therapeutic with the parents. (See also the forms for consent to treatment of children in Section 4.6.) Young children cannot claim confidentiality, but teens have "rights" to be respected. Be frank in advising children of their lack of these guarantees. You may also be able to negotiate with the parents to accept less information than they desire. Whether a parent is custodial or noncustodial usually makes no legal difference (Stromberg et al., 1993a).

If parents or guardians seem to be seeking more information than you think they or others need, try educating them before releasing the data. For example, explain that by their very nature, reports tend to focus on negatives or weaknesses (Sweet, 1990, p. 8). You can also explore the adults' motivations for seeking the records. Take into account parents' legal obligation to know in order to protect their children, as well as their emotional concerns for their children. If there is a difference of opinion about treatment, clarifying this through discussion, or perhaps sending records to another therapist for a "second opinion," may serve the parents' needs.

In custody cases, privilege may be overridden by the "best interests of the child." Try to get permission, at intake, to prevent your notes from being subpoenaed by one party if the other objects. The client information brochure (in Section 4.2) addresses this issue. And see Form 54 for a consent form for releasing information to family members.

5. A Subpoena[2]

If you receive a subpoena, do not release everything (or anything precipitously) just to be done with it. "A subpoena, which is a request for documents, is authorized by a court but actually is filled out and served by the attorney seeking the information" (Tepper et al.,

---

[2]Most of the quotations in this subsection are taken from Tepper et al. (1991). Copyright 1991 by the Pennsylvania Psychological Association. Reprinted by permission.

1991, p. 14). You have to *respond* to a subpoena, but you do not have to *comply* with it. Your options include sending the requested information; challenging the relevance or validity of the subpoena by seeking to "quash" it; refusing to comply on legal or ethical grounds (e.g., privileged communication or local laws, regulations, or precedents); or obtaining a protective order that would limit the information or materials to be provided to the court. You may also negotiate sending a summary, or revealing information only in a private meeting with the judge. If you are reluctant to comply immediately, contact the attorney who has requested your records and find out "what type of legal action is pending, and why these materials are being requested. Let the attorney know that you are not attempting merely to avoid complying with the request, but, rather, that you yourself have certain ethical and legal obligations you must satisfy before releasing any patient information" (Tepper et al., 1991, p. 14). If you are still reluctant, "After obtaining the written consent of your patient, contact [the patient's] attorney, explain the situation, and see if the two attorneys can come to an agreeable resolution" (Tepper et al., 1991, p. 14).

What happens if you do not comply with a subpoena? Tepper et al. (1991, p. 14) continue: "Since a subpoena is a court authorized request, non-compliance technically puts you in contempt of court. However, the requesting attorney still must go to a judge to seek further compliance with the subpoena. If you have outlined the grounds for your initial refusal, you later will be able to argue that you acted in a reasonable fashion." If the court orders you to provide the information, you can either comply or appeal to a higher court:

> A court order is a document signed by a judge, requesting that certain materials be provided to a party named in the order. A court order may follow a subpoena or may be issued on its own. By its very nature, a court order indicates that a judge has already authorized the request. You may or may not agree with what you are being requested to do; however, failure to respond to the court order may result in a contempt hearing in which you will be required to explain your behavior before the issuing judge. Nonetheless, if you continue to have questions regarding the court order, such inquiries also may be directed to the requesting attorney, the opposing attorney, or the Court itself. At this stage, a consultation with your own attorney [will] also become necessary. (Tepper et al., 1991, p. 14)

Woody (1991) suggests placing a specific statement in your client information brochure. Because it is so specialized, it has not been included in the brochure in this book (Section 4.2), but it may suit your practice. Woody's statement is as follows:

> Notice: In the event that a subpoena for records or testimony is received, the policy will be that (1) the client will be notified in writing and provided with a copy of the subpoena; (2) the client must either provide the practitioner with a written waiver of objection to the subpoena (an authorization form for honoring the subpoena will be provided) or indicate that an objection will be filed with the court (with a copy send to the practitioner); and (3) if an objection to that subpoena is to be filed, it is the responsibility of the client to have it filed with the court. (p. 126)

The APA's Committee on Legal Issues (2006) has recently offered guidance on coping with subpoenas and the releasing of client records and test data. This is an excellent overview and is highly recommended; also available online (www.edst.purdue.edu/cd/psychology/pdf/legalissues-2.pdf). Some further suggestions for dealing with a subpoena are as follows:

- Make sure that any request you receive, even a subpoena, is valid, is properly served, and offers enough time to respond to it (see above for the response options).

- If you release any subpoenaed information, you can charge for it and for your time to prepare it.

- Harry Corsover, PhD, of Evergreen, CO, suggests that when you receive a subpoena, you negotiate with the lawyer and offer him or her some report choices like these: (1) a full mental health treatment report for the whole treatment or a part of it; (2) responses to specific questions; or (3) a detailed, session-by-session summary. The fee for each depends on the time it takes to prepare.

6. A Request (Not a Subpoena) for Test Materials, Raw Data, or Protocols of Evaluation

Psychologists have resisted allowing the public, lawyers, or anyone untrained in their interpretation to see raw test data, such as protocols of answers given to test questions and the questions themselves. There are three rationales for maintaining such "test security":

1. The data would be misunderstood by anyone not trained in their use. The same would apply to X-rays or laboratory test results; only those qualified to interpret the client's responses or the conclusions drawn from them should have access. In fact, the publishers of all high-quality tests restrict who can purchase their materials, to ensure that only those who have the training to understand the tests' appropriate clients and limitations can buy them.

2. If the test questions became widely known, they would lose their discriminant validity. People seeking to present themselves as ill or incapable would learn how to "fake bad," and those wishing to conceal deficits and disorders would be able to "fake good." Disability evaluations, forensic testing, and academic assessments would lose the capability of distinguishing between people with and without psychological problems. Thus the tests' ability to provide useful information to society would be crippled.

3. The test materials are copyrighted by their creators, and so they may not be given away or made public in a way that would lessen their sales. The tests' authors have legal control over their distribution.

These three reasons are incorporated into the ethical prohibition in Standards 9.04 and 9.11 of the APA's code of ethics (APA, 2002). However, these standards recognize the complexities of releases made with client approval. Such complexities are also addressed in three online papers on test security (see www.nanonline.org/PAIC/Pages/PositionPapers.aspx). Current practice appears to compromise by distinguishing test *data* (which can be released, such as scores, protocols, and interpretations) from test *materials* (which are the questions, stimuli, scoring devices, etc.). A leading publisher of psychological tests, Pearson Assessments, has responded thoughtfully to HIPAA's rules about patient access to psychological tests (see www.pearsonassessments.com/catalog/hipaa.pdf). The policy of Multi-Health Systems, another major publisher of tests, is also available online (www.mhs.com/testdiscloser.asp?id=mhs). Do consult and keep abreast of further developments in this area.

Note: Forms for permission to test or evaluate a person are provided in Chapter 4 (Forms 17 and 18).

There are few if any laws about the release of records of evaluations (as opposed to the release of treatment records), but it is likely to be treated similarly by the courts (Stromberg et al., 1993a). In these situations, your ethical responsibility is to maintain "test security" for the valid evaluation of future patients. However, HIPAA grants clients the right to access and copy records containing PHI; test results and data are PHI. Tranel (1994, p. 35) suggests a simple strategy: Advise the attorney or other to hire a psychologist consultant "who is qualified by virtue of licensure, training, and experience, to receive the data" and send the data to this psychologist, with the patient's consent. Tranel also points out that this consultant "must operate under the same rules and standards of ethics and confidentiality" as you do. (See also Form 54.)

7. A Request to Which the Patient Does Not Consent

If the patient has not given his or her consent to a request for records (e.g., a subpoena from opposing counsel), discuss the issues fully with him or her to lessen any feelings of distrust and lower the risk of a HIPAA complaint or suit for improper disclosure. Discuss the implications of the request and your planned response with the patient; he or she may then decide to give consent. Knapp (1994) also suggests that you encourage the patient to consult an attorney for advice. Here are some other suggestions:

- If you do not get consent or a disposition of the request agreed to by the requester, obtain a court ruling on whether the release is proper. Let the judge be your guide.

- In the absence of consent or a court order to release the records, verify that there is a basis for the release.

- Perhaps the patient cannot give consent. He or she may be a minor or may be ruled incompetent because of a variety of factors (significant mental retardation; dementia; intoxication on drugs, alcohol, or medications; etc.). The person seeking your records must seek "substitute consent" from the patient's parent or guardian, or from the court of jurisdiction.

8. The Need to Share Records with a Consultant or Referrer

The principle about sharing records with a consultant or referrer is that if the patient has approved of the consultation or has accepted the referral to you or to another professional, you do not need a signed release (American Psychiatric Association, 1987). If you are operating under the HIPAA regulations, the client's initial consent allows full sharing of all relevant information among all treaters. However, if you have any doubts because of the kind or amount of material to be discussed or about the patient's understanding, get a signed release. (See APA, 2002, Standard 4.06.)

Guidelines and Considerations in Sending Records

- It bears repeating: Never send the originals of your records anywhere. The only exception might be a legal copying service arranged by your lawyer. And, speaking of lawyers, never let a patient's lawyer do any copying of your records.

- If you decide to release records, consider the extent of necessary disclosure, and ways to continue to protect confidentiality as much as possible.

- Never copy and send your whole record, because it may contain material irrelevant to the issues at hand. Ideally, you will be able to discuss the issues, costs and benefits, and implications of releasing records with a client. Hamberger (2000) offers many specific topics and language for such a discussion, and reports that about 60% of clients who originally asked to have their entire records released changed their minds after full discussions.

- Consider the likelihood that the patient may read the records, reports, or materials you are sending.

- Weigh the best way to organize and present the necessary information. For example, send written records instead of discussing the contents of the records over the telephone, because this will make it clearer what has and has not been disclosed. If a release must be oral, confirm in writing the contents released as soon as possible. Use fax only when you are sure of confidentiality (see Section 7.6).

- Prepare and retain careful documentation on the following:

  Your discussions with the patient and the patient's responses to the issues involved in the release, such as the content of your records and the nature of confidentiality.

  The information ultimately released, the release date, and the person or agency to whom or which it is provided. Record on the release before making copies (see below) which pages are included; what forms, letters, or notes are enclosed; and so on.

  Either the release signed by the patient (or his or her legal representative), or the response why a duty to disclose without consent seems to exist.

- Both release forms and requests for records to be released by another provider (see Section 7.4) should be prepared in triplicate—an original and two photocopies, each signed in ink (preferably blue, so that it is less likely the signature has been photocopied). These should be distributed as follows: one for the patient or his or her guardian; one for the party releasing the information; and one for the party receiving the information.

- Notifying the recipient that this is sensitive material is important and can be accomplished in several ways. You can use the more specific notices provided in Section 7.7; use your computer's printer to print them as labels on peel-off paper, or have your word processor put the notice in a "header" or "footer" on every page. Some therapists have had a rubber stamp made up with one of the confidentiality notices from

Section 7.7, which they then stamp on each page released. But note that a stamp for each page that says simply "Do not copy" or "Confidential" or "Personal and confidential" is probably not legally sufficient notification. In addition, enclose an explanatory, cautioning, and educational cover letter with all records you send. Form 51 can be used for this purpose.

- If you are asked to send the record to anyone whose credentials you don't know or recognize, write or speak to him or her and suggest that you could send the records directly to a different and more appropriately qualified professional for interpretation (with, of course, a new release form).

- Although discretion and sensitivity to the client's wishes in releasing information are appropriate (as in providing selective disclosure), providing false information (e.g., a different diagnosis than in the records) is unethical (Stromberg et al., 1988, p. 392).

- You can certainly charge for copying your records and sending them. A charge of $10 to $15 seems to be common, but do charge more if your efforts justify the cost. Make certain to include and clearly mark your federal tax identification number or Social Security number on your bill or you will waste a lot of time on the phone when requesters want to pay you. It seems fair to charge for records requested by non-health-care professionals who will make a profit from the record (e.g., lawyers, insurance companies). I would not charge for a record sent to the patient or his or her face-to-face health care provider (not an agency). If a patient requests that I send copies to several providers, I might send a single copy to the patient and let him or her arrange things.

- In summary, "the overriding rule is *'When in doubt, don't give it out!'* (The next rule, of course, is *'If still in doubt, call your redoubtable lawyer'*)" (Stromberg et al., 1988, p. 389; emphasis in original).

Comments on the Pretest

At the beginning of this section (pp. 382–383), I offered a case example from Pope (1988e) that raises many of the issues just examined. Would your answers now be different from your earlier responses? Here is my best understanding of this situation.

First, is this 17-year-old an adult in your state or is another's consent needed? Second, I would not send the tests' data or copies of the tests to anyone, citing in my cover letter both the inability of nonpsychologists (all of the requesters) to interpret the tests' data, and the ethical and professional need to maintain the security of the tests. I would also mention in this letter that if the requesters, after reading my letter or report, believed they had a need for the raw data or for test copies, I would consider releasing these to another sufficiently qualified psychologist who could interpret them for the requesters. I would add that they should arrange this.

Third, I would contact the young man and tell him of the requests I had received. The issue to be dealt with is the degree to which this man understood the content and implications of my report's contents. If he did not, he could not informedly release the report. I would suggest that he and I meet (at his expense) to discuss the contents, and that he consult his lawyer about the report's consequences in regard to each of the intended recipients, especially his own and the other attorneys.

Fourth, I would indicate to each requester that I would be willing to create a version of my report that might answer specific questions each might raise, but that since I did not know the requester's needs, I would be very reluctant to release a full report containing a great deal of material that was likely to be irrelevant to the requester's needs, might easily be misunderstood, and could embarrass my client. I would offer to produce these revised reports at my usual per-hour fee, to be paid by the requesters, in advance. As the requesters would probably not initially accept this proposal, I would telephone each one, attempt to clarify his or her needs for information, and discuss (in a general way) whether or not my report might contain information to meet their needs.

There are, to be sure, other concerns and responses.

7.4   Forms for Requesting and Releasing Information

Both the briefer form (Form 49) and the longer form (Form 50) provided in this section give you the option of using them either to have a client release your records, or to request records from another provider.

A Briefer Request/Release Form

FORM 49 Form 49 is a simple and multipurpose one-page document and should meet most of your needs. It can be used for a child or an adult; it can be used either to obtain or to release records; and it leaves spaces to write in some specifics.

A More Comprehensive Request/Release Form

FORM 50 I use Form 50 when I have little confidence in the ethical sophistication of the professional to whom I am sending it. It contains formal and legal language that may impress its recipient, and it cites all the regulations; it may thus educate (or intimidate) the recipient into following ethical practices, such as fully informing the client about what is to be released and what will be done with the information. This longer form has some useful additions and advantages over typical request/release forms:

- It meets the special standards for requesting/releasing drug and alcohol treatment records (see part C).

- It allows telephone contacts (see part D), which is a convenience.

- It includes a release of liability (see part H).

- It adds an authorization to make photocopies for sending multiple records or keeping some copies for later use (see part J).

- It documents the client's acceptance of the inevitable and not foreseeable risks of trans-

Request/Authorization to Release Confidential Records and Information

I hereby authorize:

Person or facility: _____

_____

Address: _____

_____ Phone: _____

to release information from records about _____, born on _____,

and whose Social Security number is_____, for the following purpose(s):

❑ Further mental health evaluation, treatment, or care   ❑ Rehabilitation program development or services

❑ Treatment planning   ❑ Research   ❑ Other: _____

These records concern the time between _____ and _____.

In the boxes below, the information to be disclosed is marked by an ×; the items not to be released have a line drawn through them; page numbers are indicated when appropriate; and written dates indicate when those records were mailed to the requester.

❑ Intake and discharge summaries _____   ❑ Medical history and evaluation(s) _____

❑ Mental health evaluations _____   ❑ Developmental and/or social history _____   ❑ Educational records _____

❑ Progress notes, and treatment or closing summary _____   ❑ Other: _____

Select only one:

❑ Please forward the records to the address in the letterhead at the top of this form.

❑ Please forward the records to the address written above.

HIV-related information and drug and alcohol information contained in these records will be released under this consent unless indicated here: ❑ Do not release HIV-related information.   ❑ Do not release drug and alcohol information.

I have had explained to me and fully understand this request/authorization to release records and information, including the nature of the records, their contents, and the likely consequences and implications of their release. This request is entirely voluntary on my part. I understand that I may take back this consent at any time within 90 days, except to the extent that action based on this consent has already been taken. This consent will expire automatically after 90 days from the date on which it is signed, or upon fulfillment of the purposes stated above. I understand that if the person or organization that receives this information is not a health care provider or health insurer the information may no longer be protected by federal privacy regulations.

_____   _____   _____
Signature of client   Printed name   Date

_____   _____   _____   _____
Signature of parent/   Printed name   Relationship   Date
guardian/representative

I witnessed that the person understood the nature of this request/authorization and freely gave his or her consent, but was physically unable to provide a signature.

_____   _____   _____
Signature of witness   Printed name   Date

❑ Copy for patient or parent/guardian   ❑ Copy for source of records   ❑ Copy for recipient of records

FORM 49. Briefer form for requesting/releasing confidential records and information.   From *The Paper Office*. Copyright 2008 by Edward L. Zuckerman. Permission to photocopy this form is granted to purchasers of this book for personal use only (see copyright page for details).

Request/Authorization to Release Confidential Records and Information

A. Person or facility: _____

Address: _____

_____ Phone: _____

B. Identifying information about me/the patient

Name: _____

Address: _____

_____

Phone: _____ Birthdate: _____ Social Security #: _____

Parent/guardian (if applicable): _____

Address and phone of parent/guardian: _____

_____

C. I hereby authorize the source named above to send, as promptly as possible, the records marked by an × in the boxes below. (The items not to be released have a line drawn through them.) Page numbers are indicated where appropriate. Written dates (other than those regarding inpatient admission/outpatient treatment) indicate when those records were mailed to the requester.

❑ Inpatient or outpatient treatment records for physical and/or psychological, psychiatric, or emotional illness or drug or alcohol abuse:

    Date(s) of inpatient admission: _____ Date(s) of outpatient treatment: _____

    Other identifying information about the service(s) rendered: _____

❑ Psychological evaluation(s) or testing records, and behavioral observations or checklists completed by any staff member or by the patient.

❑ Psychiatric evaluations, reports, or treatment notes and summaries.

❑ Treatment plans, recovery plans, aftercare plans.

❑ Admission and discharge summaries.

❑ Social histories, assessments with diagnoses, prognoses, recommendations, and all similar documents.

❑ Information about how the patient's condition affects or has affected his or her ability to complete tasks, activities of daily living, or ability to work.

❑ Workshop reports and other vocational evaluations and reports.

❑ Billing records.

❑ Academic or educational records.

❑ Report of teachers' observations.

❑ Achievement and other tests' results.

❑ A letter containing dates of treatment(s) and a summary of progress.

❑ HIV-related information and drug and alcohol information contained in these records will be released under this consent unless indicated here: ❑ Do not release.

❑ Other: _____

(cont.)

FORM 50. Requesting or releasing confidential records and information (p. 1 of 2). From *The Paper Office.*
Copyright 2008 by Edward L. Zuckerman. Permission to photocopy this form is granted to purchasers of this book for personal use only (see copyright page for details).

D. Select only one:

    ❑ Please forward the records to the address in the letterhead at the top of this form.

    ❑ Please forward the records to the address written above.

E. I authorize the source named above to speak by telephone with the professional identified in part N about the reasons for my/the patient's referral, any relevant history or diagnoses, and other similar information that can assist with my/the patient's receiving treatment or being evaluated or referred elsewhere.

F. I understand that no services will be denied me/the patient solely because I refuse to consent to this release of information, and that I am not in any way obligated to release these records. I do release them because I believe that they are necessary to assist in the development of the best possible treatment plan for me/the patient. The information disclosed may be used in connection with my/the patient's treatment.

G. This request/authorization to release confidential information is being made in compliance with the terms of the Privacy Act of 1974 (Public Law 93-579) and the Freedom of Information Act of 1974 (Public Law 93-502); and pursuant to Federal Rule of Evidence 1158 (Inspection and Copying of Records upon Patient's Written Authorization). This form is to serve as both a general authorization, and a special authorization to release information under the Drug Abuse Office and Treatment Act of 1972 (Public Law 92-255), the Comprehensive Alcohol Abuse and Alcoholism Prevention, Treatment and Rehabilitation Act Amendments of 1974 (Public Law 93-282), the Veterans Omnibus Health Care Act of 1976 (Public Law 94-581), and the Veterans Benefit and Services Act of 1988 (Public Law 100-322). It is also in compliance with 42 C.F.R. Part 2 (Public Law 93-282), which prohibits further disclosure without the express written consent of the person to whom it pertains, or as otherwise permitted by such regulations. I understand that if the person or organization that receives this information is not a health care provider or health insurer the information may no longer be protected by federal privacy regulations. It is in compliance with the Health Insurance Portability and Accountability Act (HIPAA) of 1996, Public Law 104-191.

H. In consideration of this consent, I hereby release the source of the records from any and all liability arising therefrom.

I. This request/authorization is valid during the pendency of any claim or demand made by or in behalf of me/the patient, and arising out of an accident, injury, or occurrence to me/the patient. I understand that I may void this request/authorization, except for action already taken, at any time by means of a written letter revoking the authorization and transfer of information, but that this revocation is not retroactive. If I do not void this request/authorization, it will automatically expire in 90 days from the date I signed it.

J. I agree that a photocopy of this form is acceptable, but it must be individually signed by me, the releaser, and a witness if necessary.

K. I have been informed of the risks to privacy and limitations on confidentiality of the use of electronic means of information transfer, and I accept these.

L. I affirm that everything in this form that was not clear to me has been explained. I also understand that I have the right to receive a copy of this form upon my request.

M. Signatures:

Signature of client	Printed name	Date

Signature of parent/ guardian/representative	Printed name	Relationship	Date

I witnessed that the person understood the nature of this request/authorization and freely gave his or her consent, but was physically unable to provide a signature.

Signature of witness	Printed name	Date

N. I, a mental health professional, have discussed the issues above with the patient and/or his or her parent or guardian. My observations of behavior and responses give me no reason to believe that this person is not fully competent to give informed and willing consent.

Signature of professional	Printed name	Date

❑ Copy for patient or parent/guardian   ❑ Copy for source of records   ❑ Copy for recipient of records ferring information by electronic means, such as fax, e-mail, and other methods not yet common (see part K). Informed consent to this is an ethical responsibility (see APA, 2002, Standard 4.02c).

- It offers your opinion that the signer is competent (see part N).

As always, you can tailor this form to your needs in various ways. You may want to add any other specific records you regularly request to the list in part C.

Other changes you can make to Form 50 include the following:

- If you are not doing treatment, you might want to change the wording at the end of part F to indicate your need and the uses or purposes of the disclosure of the records.

- Releases must have time limits. The one in part I says "90 days," but if that is insufficient, you can replace it with this sentence: "It shall be valid no longer than is reasonably necessary to meet the purposes stated above, and not to exceed 1 year."

- You can add one or both of these sentences to part L: "I further understand that I have the right (granted by HIPAA) to inspect and copy any of the information I request/ authorize for release," and/or "This therapist and I have explored the likely consequences of waiving the privilege of confidentiality."

- In the signatures section (part M), you might want to consider that the older a child is, the more his or her wishes should be considered and honored. So even if your state does not legally give power to an adolescent, you might want to make him or her a participant by having him or her sign the form.

- For some additional protection, you might include a statement like this: "I understand and agree that in no event shall [the releaser] be liable to me, or my heirs, executors, or assigns, for any reason arising from [the releaser's] disclosure or release of my records by acting in good faith and depending on this authorization." A very inclusive authorization form, which asks for everything to be released, is available online at www.highmarkmedicareservices.com/partb/forms/index.html, download the "HIPAA Compliant Authorization For The Release of Patient Information Pursuant To 45 CFR 164.508."

Forms 49 and 50 can even be made interactive by inserting language like that below. (However, I do not know whether this has been tested in a legal setting.)

I, _____ request and authorize the two parties listed below to release to each other all information and records either party may have created (about my history, symptoms, diagnoses, functioning, treatments, prognoses, etc.). These parties are:

_____ and _____

7.5   More Specific Forms for Releasing Information

A Release-of-Records Cover Letter

It is standard practice to provide a cover letter to accompany any records you send to another professional or organization; this informs the recipient of his or her legal and ethical responsibilities. Or, if for some reason you cannot release a patient's records as requested, you must, of course, write a letter to explain the reason for the refusal.

FORM 51   The letter provided as Form 51 can serve either of these purposes. Its thoroughness can save you effort and impress medical record sophisticates (such as registered record librarians, some physicians, and defense lawyers). However, you may have to modify it to suit your setting, local laws, and practice. For example, if you operate in Pennsylvania, you can add the following protected-information disclosure notices after the one provided for drug and alcohol disclosure. If you work elsewhere, substitute your local versions.

Psychiatric disclosure—55 Pa. Code Section 5100.34. This information has been disclosed to you from records whose confidentiality is protected by state law. State regulations prohibit you from making any further disclosure of this information without the prior written consent of the person to whom it pertains.

HIV disclosure—the Confidentiality of HIV-Related Information Act (1990). This information has been disclosed to you from records protected by Pennsylvania law. Pennsylvania law prohibits you from making any further disclosure of this information unless further disclosure is expressly permitted by the written consent of the person to whom it pertains or is authorized by the Confidentiality of HIV-Related Information Act. A general authorization for the release of medical or other information is not sufficient for this purpose.

The information in records can become outdated, inaccurate, and misleading, and releasing it can be harmful to the client's interests. The APA's record-keeping guidelines (APA, Committee on Professional Practice and Standards, 2007) and ethics code (APA, 2002, Standard 9.08) require that when this is the case, you clearly indicate their limited utility or invalidity.

Also, if you don't keep records for a prolonged period, you could substitute the following for the current first option under "I am unable to comply . . . ":

❑ My office policy is to retain patients' records for 12 years and then destroy them. In accord with this policy, the records you have asked for no longer exist. I can state only that this person was treated by me between the dates of _____ and _____.

FORM 52   Sometimes you will be specifically requested to send the results of a psychological evaluation to another professional or agency. Form 52 can be used as an authorization form for this purpose. This form is modified from one by Ruth H. Sosis, PhD, of Avondale, OH, and is adapted with her kind permission. (Note that, like Forms 49 and 50 but unlike the other forms in this section, Form 52 can also be used to *request* information.)

Re: the following patient: _____ Date of birth: _____

Dear Sir or Madam:

Regarding the information you requested in a request-for-information form or consent-to-release-records form dated
_____:

❑ Please find attached the records or information you requested on the above-named patient. The charge for copying these records is $_____. Please forward this amount with the same courtesy, trust, and dispatch as my staff and I have used in collecting and providing this information to you. Thank you.

   Also, please note the following points:

   1. *Protected-information disclosure notice: Drug and alcohol disclosure.* This information has been disclosed to you from records whose confidentiality is protected by state and federal law. Federal regulations (42 C.F.R. Part 2, Sections 2.31(a) and 2.33) and state regulations prohibit you from making any further disclosure of it without the specific written consent of the person to whom it pertains, or as otherwise permitted by such regulations. A general authorization for the release of medical or other information is not sufficient for this purpose. These regulations provide for a fine of up to $500 for the first offense and up to $5,000 for each subsequent offense.

   2. This is strictly confidential material and is for the information of only the person to whom it is addressed. I can accept no responsibility if it is made available to any other person, *including the patient.* Redisclosure or retransfer of these records may be prohibited, and such redisclosure may subject you to civil and criminal liability.

   3. Federal and state rules restrict use of this information to criminally investigate or prosecute any alcohol or drug abuse patient.

❑ I have completed the form or forms you sent and have enclosed them.

❑ You have sent a form for me to complete, which will take some of my professional time. If you wish this done, please forward, in the next 10 days, the sum of $_____ to pay for the additional service.

❑ According to my records, this information was sent to you on _____. If you have not received it, please investigate. Call this office and send another copy of your request-for-information form.

❑ Enclosed are the remaining records you requested. The other records were sent to you on _____.

❑ I am unable to comply with your request for these records, because:

   ❑ All records are destroyed after 7 years following the date of the last visit. Records of minor patients (14 years and younger) are retained for 7 years after they are no longer minors. Enclosed is the only available information.

   ❑ The records you are seeking are not complete at this time. I will send the records as soon as they are completed.

   ❑ No authorization or release was enclosed with your request. I cannot release records without such an authorization or release.

(cont.)

FORM 51. A release-of-records form letter (p. 1 of 2).   From *The Paper Office.* Copyright 2008 by Edward L. Zuckerman. Permission to photocopy this form is granted to purchasers of this book for personal use only (see copyright page for details).

❑ After a thorough search of our files, my staff and I are unable to locate any record on this person with the information you provided. Please check to see whether he or she may have used another name, or a different spelling, or other different identifying information. If you can provide additional identifying information, I will search our records again. I certify that, to the best of my knowledge, no such records with the present information exist in our files.

❑ I have not provided service to this person during the time period covered by the release.

❑ I did not originate the records you requested, and so cannot release them.

❑ The information you requested is not available here. You might try contacting: _____.

❑ The authorization enclosed was deficient because it is or was:

   ❑ Not dated, or not dated after treatment ended.

   ❑ Dated more than 90 days prior to the receipt of your request.

   ❑ Not sufficiently specific. Please indicate exactly what information is needed.

   ❑ Not legally adequate.

   ❑ For a minor patient, but had no signed authorization by one or both parents or a guardian. (If the latter is the case, proof of guardianship is also required.)

   ❑ For an emancipated minor, and so a parent's or guardian's signature is not acceptable.

   ❑ Signed by someone other than the patient. Such authorizations must be signed by the patient unless the patient is physically or mentally unable to do so.

   ❑ Signed illegibly, and so I am unable to verify that it is the signature of the patient.

❑ Your request/authorization/consent-to-release records form does not conform to the requirements of state/federal regulations covering the release of confidential records. Because of the nature of the information contained in this record, a general medical consent form cannot be accepted. Specifically, it _____
_____.

   ❑ I have enclosed a form for you to execute.

❑ The patient is deceased, so an authorization must be signed by the next of kin or the administrator of the estate, and appropriate documentation is required (i.e., death certificate/short form, proof of being the executor of the patient's estate, letters of administration, or power of attorney).

❑ It is our policy that this information is not released directly to patients or families because of the potential for its misinterpretation, misuse, or misunderstanding. Because it may have been generated to address psychological distress and psychopathology, there may be only slight or no attention paid to strengths and positive characteristics of the client. Statements in it require interpretation and explanation by an appropriately trained and licensed professional. If you want this information released, please send the name and address of a professional who would understand this information and a suitable request-for-information form or consent-to-release records form.

❑ Other reason: _____.

If you have any questions, please do not hesitate to contact me. If you need additional information, please return this letter with your second request for information or records.

Sincerely yours,

Request/Authorization for Release of Evaluation Information

Client: _____

Address: _____

Phone: _____ Birthdate: _____ Social Security #: _____

Regarding the administration of psychological tests, I give my permission to (select only one):

❑ the professional named in the letterhead at the top of this form, or

❑ _____

of _____

_____

to release the results of the tests taken by me/the patient, in order to:

❑ Assist with treatment planning

❑ Document a need for services

❑ Support an application for _____

❑ Other: _____

and to send these records to (select only one):

❑ the professional named in the letterhead, or to

❑ _____

of _____

_____

I hereby release the person or organization sending these records and results from any liability associated with administering, scoring, interpreting, evaluating, reporting, or transmitting the results of these tests.

I understand that the records, information, or results will not be given to me by the evaluator.

_____	_____	_____
Signature of client	Printed name	Date

_____	_____	_____	_____
Signature of parent/ guardian/representative	Printed name	Relationship	Date

I witnessed that the person understood the nature of this request/authorization and freely gave his or her consent, but was physically unable to provide a signature.

_____	_____	_____
Signature of witness	Printed name	Date

❑ Copy for client or parent/guardian   ❑ Copy for source of records   ❑ Copy for recipient of records

FORM 52. Request/authorization for release of evaluation information.   Adapted from a form devised by Ruth H. Sosis, PhD, of Cincinnati, OH, and used by permission of Dr. Sosis.—From *The Paper Office*. Permission to photocopy this form is granted to purchasers of this book for personal use only (see copyright page for details).

Releasing Information to an Attorney

FORM 53

The sending of records or reports to a client's attorney should be accompanied by the same consent elements as the sending of records to anyone else. In addition, the release form offered here as Form 53 authorizes your deposition, testimony, and other ways of sharing information. It also adds wording designed to protect you and to assure payment in a legal case where deferring (part of) your payment may be necessary but is not contingent on the outcome of the case.

When lawyers have sought raw test data and test materials for their own psychologist consultants to examine, there are often few problems, because both psychologists are more or less equally trained and bound by the same code of ethics. However, lawyers have often sought such materials to cross-examine psychologists—test by test, question by question, and even interpretation by interpretation.

The proper procedure is to release such materials (with the written consent of the client) only to those qualified to interpret them. Ask the attorney for the name and qualifications of his or her psychologist consultant, and ask that this person sign a statement such as "I agree to protect the test materials in accordance with the principles set forth in the APA Ethical Principles of Psychologists and Code of Conduct." For all other cases, such as a subpoena signed by a judge or a court order, you will have to explain your concerns to the judge and try to negotiate a release that maintains the tests' security. Excellent initial guidance can be found in APA, Committee on Legal Issues (2006).

Incidentally, you should not accept contingency fees, in which you will get paid only if the client wins a judgment. That arrangement could prejudice your professional opinion, make it appear worthless, and compromise your reputation. You can be certain that opposing counsel will ask you whether your fee is contingent. If so, this will be used as a means of disparaging your findings. The number of similar evaluations and testimonies you have done can also be used to present you either as inexperienced or as a possible "hired gun" if you do a lot of testifying.

The third paragraph of this form waives all confidentiality and requires discussion with the client and his or her attorney. The general principle is that confidentiality cannot be waived partially, so once it is waived, all contents of the record are available to both sides. As noted earlier in this chapter, confidentiality cannot be used as "both a shield and a sword"; that is, you cannot release only the evidence that favors your client's side. (However, courts frequently will suppress irrelevant information when asked to do so.) Therefore, all the contents of the record and the implications of those contents should be fully explored before the decision to release is made.

Releasing Information to the Patient's Family

What should a therapist tell the patient's family about the patient? There is always the potential for conflict between a family's legitimate right to information about its members and the therapist's obligation to keep information confidential (Zipple et al., 1990). For example, the spouse of a patient may ask a question, or the adult child of an older patient may inquire. Unless the issue of who has a right to know is clarified, staff members may refuse to provide simple and nondisruptive information about a patient to an appropriate

Authorization to Release Confidential Information to an Attorney

I do hereby authorize you, the clinician named in the letterhead above, to furnish to _____,
my attorney, at _____,
with a full report of your examination, diagnosis, treatments, prognosis, and any other records concerning me/the
patient named _____ in regard to the accident/incident/condition
for which I/the patient sought your services, which began on _____.

I authorize you, the clinician, to answer any and all questions or other requests for information from my attorney
regarding my/this patient's treatment by you, and to appear and to testify regarding my/this patient's treatment and
records at depositions or in court or any administrative proceedings.

I completely waive and release any rights of confidentiality I may have concerning these records and information,
and agree to hold the clinician harmless and to indemnify him or her from any and all claims made against him or her in
connection with the release or transfer of these records and information as here authorized.

I understand and accept that I am directly and fully responsible to you, the clinician, for all bills submitted for services you render to me/this patient, and that this agreement is made solely for your additional protection and in consideration of your awaiting payment. I understand that submission of your reports or other written materials may be contingent upon settlement of this account. And I further understand that such payment is not contingent on any
settlement, judgment, or verdict by which I/this patient may eventually recover monies, and that I am responsible for
this payment.

I hereby authorize and direct my attorney to pay directly to you such sums as may be due and owing to you for
mental health/psychological/counseling services rendered to me/this patient, by reason of any other settlement, judgment, or award that may be paid to you, my attorney, or me/the patient as the result of the injuries/incident/condition
for which I have/the patient has been evaluated or treated, or any other litigation on my/the patient's behalf. I hereby
state my intention and desire that you be paid at the time you provide services, no matter what is common practice or
the legal decisions made.

I affirm that everything in this form that was not clear to me has been explained to my satisfaction.

A photocopy of this release is to be considered as valid as the original.

_____   _____   _____
Signature of client   Printed name   Date

_____   _____ _____ _____
Signature of parent/   Printed name   Relationship   Date
guardian/representative

I witnessed that the person understood the nature of this request/authorization and freely gave his or her consent,
but was physically unable to provide a signature.

_____   _____   _____
Signature of witness   Printed name   Date

For the Attorney:

The undersigned, being attorney of record for the above-named patient, does hereby agree to observe all the
terms described above, and also agrees to withhold such sums from any settlement, judgment, or award as may be necessary to adequately protect the above-named clinician or otherwise to guarantee reimbursement.

_____   _____   _____
Signature of attorney   Printed name   Date

Please date, sign, and return one copy to the clinician's office and keep one copy for your records.

❏ Copy for client or parent/guardian   ❏ Copy for clinician   ❏ 2 copies for attorney

---

family member, because "We do not reveal patient information" (Marsh, 1995). This response has apparently become more widespread with common misunderstandings of the HIPAA regulations. However, Section 164.510 (b)(1)(i) of HIPAA does allow release of PHI which is "directly relevant to . . . the individual's care or payment . . . [or] to the individual's health care" to a "family member, other relative, or close personal friend . . . or any other person identified by the individual" without an authorization and based solely on the consent form signed with the NPP. Getting a form such as Form 54 signed early in treatment can lessen problems. If you intend to release significantly different information to different persons/relatives, use several versions of this form.

FORM 54   Form 54, adapted from Marsh (1995), can empower both the patient and family by making the process and content of family communications more explicit and informed. It sets boundaries, specifies contact persons, and then allows you to negotiate the exact information to be supplied with all parties.

7.6 Confidentiality When Faxing Records or Sending E-Mail

Faxing Records

If you send clinical information by facsimile machine, you risk compromising its confidentiality. It could be mistakenly sent to the wrong person or department by misdialing; It could be seen by inappropriate people at the receiving end; and/or it could be read by those at your end who should not have access, such as untrained workers. You should make the rules of confidentiality (see Section 7.1) part of the orientation of *all* new hires in your practice. For those whose services you use on a shared or part-time basis, some refresher training should be provided. You, the professional, are the only one who will be held responsible for violations.

In 1992, Barton Bernstein, an attorney in Dallas, TX, suggested adding a paragraph to your intake forms to let clients know that you may be faxing clinical data to their MCOs ("Legal Issues," 1992). A warning like this has been included in the client information brochure in this book (see Section 4.2) and is part of the APA code of ethics (APA, 2002, Standard 4.02c). Many fax machines have ways to send this kind of warning as part of their built-in "cover sheet." Here is a warning in ordinary language that can be added to your fax cover sheet:

Confidentiality Warning!!

This communication may be **confidential and legally privileged.** If you are not the person to whom it is addressed, do not read, copy or let anyone else besides the addressee see it. Please respect the confidentiality of this personal information and respect the federal and state laws that protect its confidentiality. If this has been transmitted to you by mistake, we ask you to extend the courtesy of calling us back at the voice number listed above and telling us what went wrong.

Thank you very much.

Authorization to Release Confidential Information to Family Members

Name of patient: _____ Date of birth: _____ Social Security #: _____

I understand that the purpose of this release is to assist with my/this patient's treatment by improving communication between professional service providers or agencies and the important individual(s) in my/the patient's life. To further this goal, I authorize this specific service provider, therapist, case manager, or _____,
to release the below-specified information regarding me/the patient to the individual(s) listed below, and to receive information from them. I have been informed of the risks to privacy and limitations on confidentiality of the use of electronic means of information transfer, and I accept these.

The information to be disclosed is marked by an × in the boxes below, and any items not to be released have a line drawn through them:

❑ Name of therapist   ❑ Name of case manager   ❑ Name(s) of treatment program(s)

❑ Admission/discharge information   ❑ Treatment plan   ❑ Scheduled appointments   ❑ Progress notes

❑ Compliance with treatment   ❑ Discharge plans   ❑ Treatment summary

❑ Psychological evaluation   ❑ Medications   ❑ Other: _____

This information is to be disclosed to these persons, who have the indicated relationship to me/the patient:

_____	_____
Name of person	Relationship
_____	_____
Name of person	Relationship
_____	_____
Name of person	Relationship

I understand that I may revoke this release at any time, except to the extent that it has already been acted upon. This release will expire on   ❑ 1 year from this date,   ❑ upon my discharge from treatment by this agency or by the person specified above, or   ❑ under these circumstances: _____

_____	_____	_____
Signature of client	Printed name	Date
_____	_____	_____
Signature of parent/ guardian/representative	Printed name	Relationship	Date

I witnessed that the person understood the nature of this request/authorization and freely gave his or her consent, but was physically unable to provide a signature.

_____	_____	_____
Signature of witness	Printed name	Date
_____	_____	_____
Signature of witness (a second witness is needed if person is unable to give oral consent)	Printed name	Relationship	Date

❑ Copy for patient or parent/guardian   ❑ Copy for provider/therapist/case manager   ❑ Copy for family member

FORM 54. Authorization to release confidential information to family members.   Adapted from Marsh (1995). Copyright 1995 by the Pennsylvania Psychological Association. Adapted by permission.—From *The Paper Office*. Permission to photocopy this form is granted to purchasers of this book for personal use only (see copyright page for details).

The following more legalistic version is based on the article cited above ("Legal Issues," 1992).

Confidentiality Warning!!

The information contained in this fax message is intended only for the personal and confidential use of the designated recipient or entity named above. As such, this communication is **privileged, confidential, and exempt from disclosure under applicable law.** If the reader or actual recipient is not the intended recipient or an agent or employee responsible for delivering it to the intended recipient, you are hereby notified that you have received this document in error, and that any review, dissemination, distribution, or copying of this message is strictly prohibited by federal and state laws with civil and criminal penalties. If you have received this communication in error, we apologize for any inconvenience. We would appreciate your notifying us immediately by phone and then return the original to us by the U.S. Postal Service at the address listed above.

Thank you.

Using E-Mail with Clients

E-mail is not secure; many copies are kept on servers as the e-mail is transmitted through the Internet, and these are not always deleted. It is also not secure from others with access to one's e-mail mailbox or computer. Therefore, it has become almost universal for psychologists to add a disclaimer at the end of all e-mail messages, such as the ones indicated above for faxes.

If you decide to use e-mail, at least do the following:

- Unless you have fully automated backups of your e-mails, print out all exchanges and place them in the client's chart. HIPAA's Security Rule requires you to have procedures for protecting the confidentiality of such messages over time.

- Fully explain the risks e-mail poses to confidentiality, and get a signed agreement to its use for each kind of risky or potentially embarrassing information, before sending any such information.

- Explain to the client the following issues and get written informed consent: how often you will pick up e-mails, and ways to contact you more rapidly and assuredly; how e-mails might be released; whether you will use the material in training or supervision; and how the absence of the usual contextual information acquired in face-to-face meetings can lead to misunderstandings, and how you and the client will address these.

- Before using e-mail with a client, make certain that there will not be a problem with confidentiality at the client's end. For example, family members may share the client's computer, or the client may be unable to set up a password-protected e-mail address. Document the client's agreement.

- Develop a password system to verify the client's identity as the sender of each e-mail. Code words may be sufficient if changed often, but electronic signature guarantees would be very advantageous.

- Acquire and deploy an encryption program. There are many free and simple programs available. If, during a private face-to-face meeting or even over the telephone, you and the client select a password to use to encrypt and decrypt messages, this method will provide very substantial privacy. No method is unbreakable given sufficient time and resources, but very protective programs are available for about $50 that will encrypt e-mails, your computer's files, portable drives, and so on.

Despite its risks, there are some rather safe uses for e-mail with clients, even without encryption.

- It may be suitable for sending out intake and informational material, but not for having a client return forms with clinical information (PHI).

- It can be safe for administrative or logistical purposes with most clients: confirming and rescheduling appointments, sending information about resources, answering simple questions, supplying blank data-recording forms, and the like. Allowing cancellation of sessions via e-mail may lead to its overuse when clients are under time pressure, however.

- With caution, it can be substituted for some appointments with current active clients who cannot come to some meetings due to bad weather and other transportation limitations; for clients who have moved to another location and have not yet arranged a follow-up therapist; for clients who have disabilities or are home-bound due to illness; and the like.

- You can correspond with, educate, and refer those who find you through your writings or an Internet search about your specialties. Or you can respond to an e-mail inquiry from a potential client with directions to your website for more information.

Moreover, e-mail (with security measures taken) may have valuable clinical leverage. Consider the following possibilities:

1. For clients who do not do homework because of anergic depression, having them send brief daily e-mails about their activities can focus their thinking and increase their motivation to complete other assignments. A therapist and client can decide whether the therapist will confirm receipt of the e-mails or whether all communication will take place during the next session. (This suggestion and the second one come from Dorothy Ashman, MA, of Bloomsburg, PA, and are used with her kind permission.)

2. For clients with dissociative identity disorder, it is likely that only a few of the alters will have time to speak during any single session. Other alters, co-conscious or not, may be very frustrated at their lack of contact with the therapist. These alters can send their questions or comments about the session by e-mail once they are home. This can provide additional information about what is going on within the client. In reply, the therapist can include the original text so that the answer makes sense both to the alter who sent the e-mail and to the other alters, some of whom may not have been co-conscious when the e-mail was written. This facilitates the sharing of information between the alters in the same way that journaling does. At times the therapist may choose to exclude the original text, because the information would be better shared with the other alters during a face-to-face interaction at a later date.

3. For a client who makes unnecessary phone calls but takes poorly to boundary setting over this, allowing the client to leave e-mails may meet some need, even if the client knows that the therapist may not respond and certainly won't respond immediately. The contents of the messages can be addressed in the next session. (This suggestion and the fourth one come from Kathie Rudy, PsyD, of Great Neck, NY, and are used with her kind permission.)

4. For a client who cannot yet handle the intense intimacy of a full session or of frequent contacts, alternating face-to-face sessions with telephone or e-mail sessions can help to maintain contact by titrating the affect and allowing different kinds of work to be done in each mode. This approach can help manage the obstacles of what would otherwise be overwhelming and disorganizing affects such as shame.

For a review of the ethical aspects of using e-mail, an article by Drude and Lichstein (2005) is highly recommended. The discussion above concerns e-mail with clients, but the issues raised by online therapy, case consultation with an e-mail list, and other electronic communications are too complex to discuss properly here. For more on online case consultations, see Dvoskin (2006), and for the ethics of online therapy, see Childress (2000). The best general resource is the International Society for Mental Health Online; its website (www.ismho.org) is a great starting point for information and creative ideas about online clinical services, research, and organizations.

7.7   Confidentiality Notifications

I believe that a stamped note on each page of a report warning "Do not make copies," "Do not redistribute," or merely "Confidential" does not provide enough information for the reader to make decisions about how to store and use the pages. As a simple and inexpensive alternative, I suggest notices like those given below. These notices include explicit rationales and warnings, so records are less likely to be misused and their confidentiality breached. You can edit one of the notices below or create your own version; you can then place it on the paper in various different ways:

- You can type it onto each page of every document you send out.

- If you use a word processor, it can be printed on every page of reports you create by adding it, from a "glossary" entry, as a "header" or "footer" on each page.

- You can photocopy it onto a sheet of labels, and then stick a label onto each page or onto the first page of records or reports you send out.

- You can make a rubber stamp with the notice's text and use it on each page of records you release.

The sample notices follow; as indicated below, many are from Zuckerman (2005). (*Note:* Your state may have additional requirements for the release of HIV information or drug and alcohol information, as Pennsylvania does. If so, you may need to add the exact phrasing or citation of the appropriate laws to your releases.)

Permission to send these records to you/the addressee has been given to me in writing by the concerned patient or his or her guardian. You do not have the legal right to share these records with any other person, agency, organization, or program unless you first obtain written permission to do so from the subject of these records or his or her guardian.

CONFIDENTIAL PATIENT INFORMATION

WARNING: This report may contain sensitive client information. You must protect this document as confidential medical information. Please handle, store, and dispose of properly.

This is privileged and confidential patient information. Any unauthorized disclosure is a federal offense. Not to be duplicated. (Zuckerman, 2005, p. 86)

This information has been disclosed to you from records protected by federal confidentiality rules (42 C.F.R. Part 2, P.L. 93-282) and state law (e.g., Pennsylvania Law 7100-111-4). These regulations prohibit you from making any further disclosure of this information unless further disclosure is expressly permitted by the written consent of the person to whom it pertains or as otherwise permitted by 42 C.F.R. Part 2. A general authorization for the release of information is not sufficient for this purpose. The federal rules restrict any use of the information to criminally investigate or prosecute any alcohol or drug abuse patient. (Zuckerman, 2005, p. 86)

This report may contain client information. Release only to professionals capable of ethically and professionally interpreting and understanding the information it contains. (Zuckerman, 2005, p. 86)

It is inappropriate to release the information contained herein directly to the client or other parties. If this information is released to interested individuals before they are afforded an opportunity to discuss its meaning with a trained mental health professional, it is likely that the content of the report may be misunderstood, leading to emotional distress on the part of the uninformed reader. (Zuckerman, 2005, p. 86)

This information is not to be used against the interests of the subject of this report. (Zuckerman, 2005, p. 86)

Persons or entities granted access to this record may discuss this information with the patient only insofar as necessary to represent the patient in legal proceedings or other matters for which this record has been legally released. (Zuckerman, 2005, p. 86)

For a Child:

The contents of this report have/have not been shared with the child's parent(s)/guardian. She/he/they may review this report with the evaluator or his/her specific designee. Copies of this report may be released only by the evaluator or his/her departmental administrator, or in accord with the school district's policy. (Zuckerman, 2005, p. 86)

The information contained in this report is private, privileged, and confidential. It cannot be released outside the school system except by the examining psychologist/evaluator/creator of this report, upon receipt of written consent by the parent or guardian. Not to be duplicated or transmitted. (Zuckerman, 2005, p. 86)

7.8   Complaints and Reports of Privacy Violations

Take any and all complaints or reports of problems seriously. They can be the harbingers of ethics complaints, licensing board actions, or worse. Act immediately.

As part of your NPP (see Section 5.4), you must mention a complaint procedure for clients to report violations of their own or others' privacy. While more general complaints are not necessarily the same things as reports of privacy violations it is simpler and more convenient to combine the two types and have them both addressed by the privacy officer. Also, having a complaint mechanism is part of good client relations and a valuable means of heading off more serious problems.

A Sample Complaint Form

FORM 55 In the sample complaint form provided here (Form 55), I have combined a variety of problems that might arise, and have deliberately avoided the use of the word "complaint." Having a client file this form is the second step, after the client has talked to the privacy officer, in resolving a complaint.

Although HIPAA does not require anonymity to be offered, it is always a good policy, and Form 55 incorporates it.

Online Complaint Filing

The third step in resolving a complaint of a privacy violation is having the client file a complaint with the Office of Civil Rights, which is responsible for investigating complaints of HIPAA privacy violations. A form and fact sheet are available online in both English and Spanish (www.hhs.gov/ocr/generalinfo.html).

Complaints on paper can be sent to Privacy Complaints, P.O. Box 8050, U.S. Department of Health and Human Services, Centers for Medicare and Medicaid Services, 7500 Security Boulevard, Baltimore, MD 21244-1850.

Is There a Problem?

If you are not satisfied with your experiences in our office, we want to hear from you.

If you have a problem with anything about our practice, first speak with one of our staff. If the problem is with your insurance, bills, or payment, talk to _____, who is our _____. If the problem is with your therapy, talk to your therapist. If you believe there has been a violation of the confidentiality or the privacy of your records, speak to our privacy officer, _____, to help us clarify and fix the situation. If you don't know whom to talk to about a problem, ask our privacy officer for assistance.

If you are still not satisfied or the problem continues ,please fill out this simple form so we can investigate it. We will try our best to fix it, and to repair any damage that has been done. Bringing a problem to our attention will not in any way limit your care here or cause us to take any actions against you.

If you wish to remain anonymous, you do not have to fill in the lines marked with an asterisk (*). But if you want a response from us, please do complete those items. Thank you.

*Client's name: _____ *Date of birth: _____

*Client's address: _____

*Phone: _____ *Identification #: _____

What is or was the problem? _____

_____

_____

What would you like to see done about the problem? _____

_____

_____

_____   _____
*Signature of client or his or her personal representative   Date

_____   _____
*Printed name of client or personal representative   *Relationship to the client

_____
*Description of personal representative's authority

Note: If a name is given on the form, a response must be made to this person within 30 days from when you, the privacy officer, receive this form. Indicate action(s) taken on a separate page.

_____   _____   Version #____
Privacy Officer   Phone

FORM 55. A sample complaint form. From *The Paper Office.* Copyright 2008 by Edward L. Zuckerman. Permission to photocopy this form is granted to purchasers of this book for personal use only (see copyright page for details).

APPENDICES

Resources

Appendix A. Books on Practice Development and Marketing

Ackley, D. C. (1997). *Breaking free of managed care*. New York: Guilford Press.

> Although Ackley explains the poisonous consequences of managed care with precision, the best parts of the book are those identifying and challenging the thoughts and assumptions of therapists that keep them from leaving managed care dependence. He demonstrates the value of psychology to clients and to businesses, and inspires us to follow him.

Barnes, D., & Kaye, J. (1999). *Independent practice for the mental health professional: Growing a private practice for the 21st century*. New York: Brunner/Mazel.

> This book addresses a variety of topics, all very briefly: marketing, networking, managed care, legal issues, office planning/procedures, and solo or group practice.

Cole, P. H., & Reese, D. (2004). *Mastering the financial dimension of your practice: The definitive resource for private practice development and financial planning*. New York: Brunner-Routledge.

> Written by two therapists, this book educates readers about financial thinking and planning. It also addresses the dynamic meanings of money and of independent practice, as well as the customary and mistaken money strategies of therapists. It guides readers through creating a financial plan and carrying it out.

Grodzki, L. (2000). *Building your ideal private practice: A guide for therapists and other healing professionals*. New York: Norton.

> Like a great coach, Grodzki guides you to a blueprint for practice and a business vision. She emphasizes getting support and maintaining optimism, attracting clients with your own message, expanding your services, avoiding pitfalls, and staying successful over time.

Grodski, L. (2003). *Twelve months to your ideal private practice: New skill sets, essential exercises, and tools for success*. New York: Norton.

> The great coach returns with monthly guidance about balancing life with work and handling other real-world issues. For each month, she provides exercises, skills sets, and action plans to keep you moving. Do the work and you will succeed.

Harris, S. M., Ivey, D. C., & Bean, R. A. (Eds.). (2005). *A practice that works: Strategies to complement your stand alone therapy practice.* New York: Routledge.

Descriptions of 23 specializations written by those in each niche practice. Innovative and enthusiastic, but short on the size of the market, scientific bases, and moving from where you are to where you want to be.

Heller, K. M. (1997). *Strategic marketing: How to achieve independence and prosperity in your mental health practice.* Sarasota, FL: Professional Resource Exchange.

If you shy away from "marketing" but know you need to do something, Heller will help you understand, design, and implement a strategy that will enhance your work.

Hunt, H. A. (2005). *Essentials of private practice: Streamlining costs, procedures, and policies for less stress.* New York: Norton.

Utterly practical guidance on "how to do it better." Advice on reducing overhead, dealing with insurance, creating more efficient telephone procedures, and establishing collection policies. Solid nuts and bolts.

Kase, L. (2005). *The successful therapist: Your guide to building the career you've always wanted.* Hoboken, NJ: Wiley.

If you have always wanted to think like an MBA, the first 200 pages will teach you leadership, marketing, financial planning, and operational planning. The last 120 pages cover five practice areas: coaching, forensics, teaching, administration, and other fields.

Kolt, L. (1999). *How to build a thriving fee-for-service practice: Integrating the healing side with the business side of psychotherapy.* San Diego, CA: Academic Press.

Kolt combines exercises in awareness and attitude change with tools for surveying community needs, developing specialty practices, marketing ideas, selecting an office, presenting public seminars, and using practice data for decision making. Excellent.

Lawless, L. (1997). *Therapy, Inc.: A hands-on guide to developing, positioning, and marketing your mental health practice in the 1990s.* New York: Wiley.

Lawless covers the basics of marketing, with good specific advice, exercises, and examples of marketing materials. She addresses issues of professional identity, stages of a therapist's career, and making the transition to a more viable model of practice in the managed-care-dominated world.

Lawless, L., & Wright, J. (2000). *How to get referrals: The mental health professional's guide to strategic marketing.* New York: Wiley.

Just what the title says. Chapters are about types of referrers, such as lawyers, physicians, educators, religious leaders, and managed care representatives. Each chapter provides explanatory and background information, discusses needs, and suggests methods and materials to use in approaching referrers.

LoPresti, R. & Zuckerman, E. L. (2004). *Rewarding specialties for mental health clinicians: Developing your practice niche.* New York: Guilford Press.

This book discusses almost 40 niches that are financially viable, scientifically supported, not entangled with managed care, and enterable without going back to graduate school. It takes the generalist into specifics of medical care, couple and child work, business, forensics, work with underserved populations, and developing areas. For each niche, it describes what the work is like, what skills are transferable, where to learn new ones, where to start, and so forth.

Mart, E. G. (2006). *Getting started in forensic psychology practice: How to create a forensic specialty in your mental health practice.* Hoboken, NJ: Wiley.

Just what the title says. This book tells you how to go about it, comprehensively.

Morgan, W. D. (2006). *Today's private practice: Strategies for building a thriving managed-care free psychotherapy practice.* Havertown, PA: Golden Hill.

> How to find, explore, and exploit a niche market for psychotherapy and many related functions (e.g., coaching). The author describes how he left managed care, redeploying his therapy skills from a medical illness approach to one of skill building and problem solving.

Pope, K. S., & Vasquez, M. J. T. (2005). *How to survive and thrive as a therapist: Information, ideas, and resources for psychologists in practice.* Washington, DC: American Psychological Association.

> A quarter of this book contains excellent questions and advice; the rest presents and discusses American Psychological Association (APA) guidelines. The book covers topics like finding an office, insurance, clients, and an attorney; using computers; writing a professional will; and responding to a complaint. Some checklists are provided.

Stout, C. E., & Grand, L. C. (2005). *Getting started in private practice: The complete guide to building your mental health practice.* Hoboken, NJ: Wiley.

> Comprehensive coverage of financing, startup, fee setting, risk minimization, marketing, niching, self-care, presentations, customer service skills, and many other topics. Solid information, excellently presented. Superb.

Zur, O. (2006). *The complete fee-for-service private practice handbook.* Sonoma, CA: Zur Institute.

> This book addresses 57 topics, albeit too briefly.

Appendix B. Readings in the Law, Ethics, and Malpractice

Bernstein, B. E., & Hartsell, Jr., T. L. (2000). *The portable ethicist for mental health professionals: An A–Z guide to responsible practice.* New York: Wiley.

> Very readable and practical guidance.

Bersoff, D. N. (Ed.). (2008). *Ethical conflicts in psychology* (4th ed.). Washington, DC: American Psychological Association.

> Excerpts of more than 100 articles from many sources and perspectives, with well-considered commentary. Very instructive.

Bongar, B. (2002). *The suicidal patient: Clinical and legal standards of care* (2nd ed.). Washington, DC: American Psychological Association.

> Realistic standards of care, sophisticated risk management strategies, risk estimators, legal action guidelines, postvention methods, and a review of the literature.

Fisher, C. B. (2003). *Decoding the ethics code: A practical guide for psychologists.* Thousand Oaks, CA: Sage.

> A volume by the lead author of the APA ethics code's 1992 revision.

Gutheil, T. G., & Appelbaum, P. S. (2007). *Clinical handbook of psychiatry and the law* (4th ed.). Philadelphia: Lippincott Williams & Wilkins.

Haas, L. J., & Malouf, J. L. (2005). *Keeping up the good work: A practitioner's guide to mental health ethics* (4th ed.). Sarasota, FL: Professional Resource Press.

> Comprehensive, readable, and compact—yet full of practical advice and a usable model for ethical decision making. Very highly recommended.

Jacob, S., & Hartshorne, T. (2007). *Ethics and law for school psychologists* (5th ed.). Hoboken, NJ: Wiley.
Very thorough coverage of the special areas and considerations of school practice.

Knapp, S., & VandeCreek, L. (2003). *A guide to the 2002 revision of the American Psychological Association's ethics code.* Sarasota, FL: Professional Resource Press.

Koocher, G. P., & Keith-Spiegel, P. (2008). *Ethics in psychology and the mental health professions: Standards and cases* (3rd ed.). New York: Oxford University Press.
A standard text in ethics. Lots of cases, addressing all the areas of concern, and highly readable.

Nagy, T. F. (2005). *Ethics in plain English: An illustrative casebook for psychologists* (2nd ed.). Washington, DC: American Psychological Association.
Lots of cases make understanding the issues much easier.

Pope, K. S., & Vasquez, M. J. T. (2007). *Ethics in psychotherapy and counseling: A practical guide for psychologists* (3rd ed.). San Francisco: Jossey-Bass.
Highly recommended. It is up-to-date, well reasoned and integrated, very comprehensive, readable, and practical. Written by experts in the field.

Rave, E. J., & Larsen, C. C. (Eds.). (1995). *Ethical decision making in therapy: Feminist perspectives.* New York: Guilford Press.
At least two experts respond to each dilemma using the Feminist Therapy Institute's code of ethics and more traditional ethical approaches.

Reid, W. H. (1999). *A clinician's guide to legal issues in psychotherapy, or proceed with caution.* Phoenix, AZ: Zeig, Tucker.
Reid combines a lively style with his contentions and advice based on "the standard of practice" and stable and durable ethical principles. Highly recommended.

Wheeler, A. M., & Bertram, B. (2007). *The counselor and the law: A guide to legal and ethical practice* (5th ed.). Alexandria, VA: American Counseling Association.
A presentation of the laws and guidelines that apply especially to counselors.

Woody, R. H. (2000). *Child custody: Practice standards, ethical issues, and legal safeguards for mental health professionals.* Sarasota, FL: Professional Resource Press.

Appendix C. Professional Liability Insurance Resources

General Information

Margaret A. Bogie is a licensed property and casualty insurance consultant who has worked with mental health professionals for years. She has written extremely informative papers on professional insurance topics, which are available at www.americanprofessional.com (go to the "Shopping Tips" menu).

You may find a list of insurance terms to help you understand policies not written in "plain English" at www.aishealth.com/ehealthbusiness/ehealthterms.html.

Last but not least, **read your policy carefully.** Know and understand it. Call and ask the agent or agency any questions. Pay special attention to the many important exclusions.

Sellers of Insurance

This list is current as of May 2008.

American Professional Agency, 95 Broadway, Amityville, NY 11701; 516-691-6400 or 800-421-6694; www.americanprofessional.com

> Coverage is available for students and for members of all the mental health professions.

American Psychological Association Insurance Trust (APAIT), 750 First Street, N.E., Suite 605, Washington, DC 20002-4242; 800-447-1200; www.apait.org

> The APAIT offers many kinds of insurance besides professional liability, but only to APA members. It stands as an intermediate and marketing organization. Under "Resources" on the website are several booklets and sample forms. The site's "Risk Management" menu includes a course, *Assessing and Managing Risk in Psychological Practice: An Individualized Approach* (Book alone $40, Course and book $90 APAIT-insured psychologists, course and book $140 for others). There are two online courses on the Health Insurance Portability and Accountability Act (HIPAA)—one on the Privacy Rule and one on the Security Rule—with similar pricing (see Appendix G). The somewhat dated *HIPAA Primer* can be downloaded by anyone.

American Psychotherapist Professional Liability Insurance Program (APPLIP); www.applip.com

> Besides occurrence-based policies, the APPLIP offers directors' and officers' insurance and coverage for just about any kind of organization. The plan administrator is J. J. Negley Associates, P.O. Box 206, Cedar Grove, NJ 07009; 973-239-9107 or 800-845-1209; www.jjnegley.com.

CPH and Associates, 727 S. Dearborn, Suite 312, Chicago, IL 60605; 800-875-1911; www.cphins.com

> This company offers occurrence-based policies, a "loss assistance hotline," and coverage to all disciplines and healing professions.

Healthcare Providers Service Organization (HPSO), 159 E. County Line Road, Hatboro, PA 19040-1248; 800-982-9491; www.hpso.com

> HPSO offers both occurrence-based and claims-made policies for all kinds of mental health professionals. Some policies have unique features.

Rockport Insurance Associates, P.O. Box 1809, Rockport, TX 78381-1809; 800-423-5344 or 361-790-9043; www.rockportinsurance.com

> This company offers occurrence-based policies. Its professional liability policies include premises liability coverage. The coverage for legal fees is in addition to the liability limits. The website's "Risk Management" menu includes some brief checklists on managing specific risks (such as dealing with violent patients, maintaining confidentiality, and gaining informed consent).

Appendix D. Practice Guidelines from Professional Organizations

Because practice guidelines are continually being developed and revised, a printed list may quickly become outdated. Instead, please go to these sites for links to the most recent guidelines.

Assessment Psychology; www.assessmentpsychology.com/practice.htm

> This is a metasite with links to hundreds of rich sites related to psychology, including sites for professional organizations, guidelines, and other resources about practice. William E. Benet, PhD, PsyD, maintains the site.

Ken Pope, PhD; www.kspope.com/ethcodes/index.php

A true labor of love, Pope's site has links to more than 100 codes of ethics from all the mental health professions and others; copies of his and other's publications on ethics; and links to other resources.

Appendix E. Dealing with Managed Care Organizations

Multimedia Resources

The National Coalition of Mental Health Professionals and Consumers, P.O. Box 438, Commack, NY, 11725; 888-SAY-NO-MC (888-729-6662) or 631-424-5232; www.nomanagedcare.org

The major anti-managed care organization, with a history of successful advocacy and ingenious alternatives.

- Under "Helpful Resources" on the website is a superb set of links to national and other organizations for consumers and professionals.

- The National Coalition has also published a *Mental Health Consumer Protection Manual: A Guide to Solving Problems with Insurance and Managed Care*. "Many consumers are finding that the strategies in the manual are useful for dealing with managed care problems within all of healthcare. Those who cannot afford the cost may obtain a copy at no cost." (See the address above.)

Newsletters

Psychotherapy Finances, 14255 U.S. Highway 1, Suite 286, Juno Beach, FL 33408; 800-869-8450; www.psyfin.com

Not anti-managed-care.

The website offers several dozen articles from both newsletters on marketing and practice issues (click on the "Articles" box at the top) and many useful links.

Books

Browning, C. H., & Browning, B. J. (1996). *How to partner with managed care: A "do-it-yourself kit" for building working relationships and getting steady referrals*. New York: Wiley.

Very comprehensive, clear, positive, and practical advice on dealing with MCOs.

Clement, P. W. (1999). *Outcomes and incomes: How to evaluate, improve, and market your psychotherapy practice by measuring outcomes*. New York: Guilford Press.

This is a book of measures that will enable those in private practice to evaluate their outcomes; it explains how to use this information for marketing and for dealing with MCOs.

Corcoran, K., & Vandiver, V. (1996). *Maneuvering the maze of managed care: Skills for mental health practitioners*. New York: Free Press.

Heavily researched and clearly written, it offers background and direction, as well as forms and procedures.

Davis, S. R., & Meier, S. R. (2000). *The elements of managed care: A guide for helping professionals*. Belmont, CA: Wadsworth.

A very brief (110-page) introduction to managed care.

MacKenzie, K. R. (Ed.). (1995). *Effective use of group therapy in managed care*. Washington, DC: American Psychiatric Press.

> Just what the title says.

Poynter, W. L. (1994). *The preferred provider's handbook: Building a successful private therapy practice in the managed care marketplace*. New York: Brunner/Mazel.

> This book mainly concerns how to market your private practice to MCOs.

Poynter, W. L. (1998). *The textbook of behavioral managed care: From concept through management to treatment*. New York: Brunner/Mazel.

> This book helps clinicians to evaluate and restructure their practices in the managed care context. It covers assessment, goal setting, treatment, reauthorization, and patient satisfaction.

Zieman, G. L. (1998). *The handbook of managed behavioral healthcare: A complete up-to-date guide for students and practitioners*. San Francisco: Jossey-Bass.

> The author says that this book includes "the history of managed care, annotated samples of a provider contract and a credentialing application with a managed care company, and extensive appendices including a glossary and resources regarding managed care information."

Appendix F. Resources for Supervision and Consultation

Bernard, J. M., & Goodyear, R. K. (2004). *Fundamentals of clinical supervision* (3rd ed.). Boston: Pearson Education.

> The standard textbook, with additional materials for teaching graduate students to be supervisors.

Brantley, A. (2000). A clinical supervision documentation form. In L. VandeCreek & T. L. Jackson (Eds.), *Innovations in clinical practice: A source book* (Vol. 18, pp. 301–307). Sarasota, FL: Professional Resource Press.

> If you wish to use a structured format for documenting supervision, Brantley offers a clever and efficient two-page form that should cover all bases.

Campbell, J. (2000). *Becoming an effective supervisor: A workbook for counselors and psychotherapists*. Philadelphia: Accelerated Development.

> This is a workbook that integrates theory and research across disciplines and offers many practical resources.

Falender, C. A., & Shafranske, E. P. (2004). *Clinical supervision: A competency-based approach*. Washington, DC: American Psychological Association.

Falender, C. A., & Shafranske, E. P. (2007). Competence in competency-based supervision practice: Construct and application. *Professional Psychology: Research and Practice, 38*(3), 232–240.

> Both of these publications are highly recommended—not just for the model proposed, but for the sophisticated thinking behind the model.

Haber, R. (1996). *Dimensions of psychotherapy supervision: Maps and means*. New York: Norton.

> Haber offers both a metaphor (maps) and consideration of the practical matters and methods of psychotherapy supervision, all from a family systems perspective.

Hamilton, J. C., & Spruill, J. (1999). Identifying and reducing risk factors related to trainee–client sexual misconduct. *Professional Psychology: Research and Practice, 30*(3), 318–327.

> In terms of ethics, these authors specifically address how supervisors can reduce the likelihood of trainee–client sexual misconduct.

Williams, A. (1995). *Visual and active supervision: Roles, focus, technique.* New York: Norton.

Williams covers the roles inherent in the supervision process, and encourages being both systematic and creative.

There are also two journals: *The Clinical Supervisor* from The Haworth Press (www.haworthpressinc.com) and *Counselor Education and Supervision* from the American Counseling Association (www.counseling.org)

Appendix G. Resources on Record Privacy and Security

American Psychological Association (APA) Practice Organization; www.apapractice.org/apo/hipaa.html

The APA Practice Organization offers its members several online publications and other resources on HIPAA compliance. The publications include *Getting Ready for the HIPAA Privacy Rule: A Primer for Psychologists* (2002, coauthored with APAIT) and the *HIPAA Security Rule Primer* (2005); both are large booklets with solid information. An online program titled the *HIPAA Security Rule Online Compliance Workbook* (2005) is a response to the HIPAA Security Rule's requirement for a HIPAA policies and procedures manual. It explains the issues and offers questions for you to type in narrative responses. At the end, the program collects everything into a printable manual. When I took it, the program offered minimal suggestions to guide responses. The course is available to APA Practice Organization members and APAIT insureds for $99, to other APA members for $139, and to nonmembers of APA for $159. A similar program, the *HIPAA Privacy Rule Online Compliance Course* (2003), is available to APA Practice Organization members, APAIT insureds, and dues-exempt APA members for $225, to other APA members for $375, and to nonmembers of APA for $600.

Center for Medicare and Medicaid Services; www.cms.hhs.gov

The CMS (yes, not CMMS) website offers educational information about HIPAA for professionals and citizens.

Start with the HIPAA—General Information Overview page (www.cms.hhs.gov/HIPAAGenInfo/01_Overview.asp).

For more on the Security Rule, the site offers six downloadable, highly readable "Security Materials" pamphlets (www.cms.hhs.gov/EducationMaterials/04_SecurityMaterials.asp#TopOfPage).

Health Privacy Project at Georgetown University; www.healthprivacy.org

The Health Privacy Project has developed a number of papers to help you find your state laws on privacy. You can find its collection of documents under "Health Privacy 101." These include an excellent introduction to the topic, rather complete summaries of the laws of each state about privacy, materials on federal laws and documents, and other resources.

Model State Public Health Privacy Project; www.critpath.org/msphpa/privacy.htm

Some states have adopted very comprehensive privacy laws, and others have their laws fragmented under dozens of pieces of legislation. If you are interested in a model state privacy law, have a look at this site.

Three Wishes Press; www.threewishespress.com

My book *HIPAA Help: A Compliance Manual for Psychotherapists* is available at this site. It contains resources, guidelines, and a decision worksheet, as well as forms, handouts, and materials for dealing with future developments of HIPAA.

References

Ackley, D. C. (1997). *Breaking free of managed care: A step-by-step guide to regaining control of your practice.* New York: Guilford Press.

Adams, S., & Orgel, M. (1975). *Through the mental health maze.* Washington, DC: Health Research Group.

Alabama Psychological Association. (n.d.). *Client–therapist intimacy: Appropriate and inappropriate conduct.* Montgomery: Author.

Albeck, J. H., & Goldman, C. (1991). Patient–therapist co-documentation: Implications of jointly authored progress notes for psychotherapy practice, research, training, supervision, and risk management. *American Journal of Psychotherapy, 3*(3), 317–334.

Allen, M. H., Serper, M. R., & Elfenbein, C. (1994). Psychiatric principles. In L. R. Goldfrank, N. E. Flomenbaum, N. A. Lewin, et al. (Eds.), *Goldfrank's toxicologic emergencies.* Norwalk, CT: Appleton & Lange.

American Professional Agency. (1992). *Important information concerning your professional liability claim.* Amityville, NY: Author.

American Professional Agency. (2006). *Claims made psychologists' professional and office liability policy.* Retrieved from www.americanprofessional.com/sitemap.htm

American Psychiatric Association. (1987). APA guidelines on confidentiality. *American Journal of Psychiatry, 144,* 1522–1526.

American Psychiatric Association. (2000). *Diagnostic and statistical manual of mental disorders* (4th ed., text rev.). Washington, DC: Author.

American Psychiatric Association. (2006). *The principles of medical ethics with annotations especially applicable to psychiatry* (2006 ed.). Washington, DC: Author. Retrieved from www.psych.org/psych_pract/ethics/ppaethics.cfm

American Psychological Association (APA). (2002). *Ethical principles of psychologists and code of conduct.* Retrieved from www.apa.org/ethics/code2002.html

American Psychological Association (APA). (2003). Guidelines on multicultural education, training, research, practice, and organizational change for psychologists. *American Psychologist, 58,* 377–402. Retrieved from www.apa.org/pi/multiculturalguidelines.pdf

American Psychological Association (APA). (2006). *Advancing colleague assistance in professional psychology.* Retrieved from www.apa.org/practice/ACCA_Monograph.pdf

American Psychological Association (APA), Committee on Ethics. (1988). Trends in ethics cases, common pitfalls and published resources. *American Psychologist, 43,* 564–572.

American Psychological Association (APA), Committee on Legal Issues. (2006). Strategies for private practitioners coping with subpoenas or compelled testimony for client records or test data. *Professional Psychology: Research and Practice, 37*(2), 215–222.

American Psychological Association (APA), Committee on Professional Practice and Standards. (1996). Twenty-four questions (and answers) about professional practice in the area of child abuse. *Professional Psychology: Research and Practice, 26*(4), 377–385.

American Psychological Association (APA), Committee on Professional Practice and Standards. (1998). *Guidelines for psychological evaluations in child protection matters.* Retrieved from www.apa.org/practice/childprotection.html

American Psychological Association (APA), Committee on Professional Practice and Standards. (2007). *Record keeping guidelines.* Retrieved from www.apa.org/practice/recordkeeping.html

American Psychological Association (APA), Committee on Women in Psychology. (1989). If sex enters the psychotherapy relationship. *Professional Psychology: Research and Practice, 20,* 112–115.

Anderten, P., Staulcup, V., & Grisso, T. (1980). On being ethical in legal places. *Professional Psychology: Research and Practice, 11,* 764–773.

Appelbaum, P. S. (1993). Legal liability and managed care. *American Psychologist, 48*(3), 251–257.

Appelbaum, P. S. (1996). Suits against clinicians for warning of patients' violence. *Psychiatric Services, 47*(7), 683–684.

Barge, B. N., & Fenalason, K. I. (1989). *Dealing effectively with malpractice litigation.* (Available from Human Factors Department, Risk Management Services Division, St. Paul Companies, 385 Washington St., St. Paul, MN 55102)

Barnett, J. E., Cornish, J. A. E., Goodyear, R. K., & Lichtenberg, J. W. (2007). Commentaries on the ethical and effective practice of clinical supervision. *Professional Psychology: Research and Practice, 38*(3), 268–275.

Barnett, J. E., Hillard, D., & Lowery, K. (2001). Ethical and legal issues in the treatment of minors. In L. VandeCreek & T. L. Jackson (Eds.), *Innovations in clinical practice: A source book* (Vol. 19, pp. 257–272). Sarasota, FL: Professional Resources Press.

Barnett, J. E., MacGlashan, S. G., & Clarke, A. J. (2000). Risk management and ethical issues regarding termination and abandonment. In L. VandeCreek & T. L. Jackson (Eds.), *Innovations in clinical practice: A source book* (Vol. 18, pp. 231–245). Sarasota, FL: Professional Resource Exchange.

Barnett, J. E., & Yutrzenka, B. A. (1994). Nonsexual dual relationships in professional practice, with special applications to rural and military communities. *Independent Practitioner, 14*(5), 243–248.

Bates, C., & Brodsky, A. (1993). *Sex in the therapy hour: A case of professional incest.* New York: Guilford Press.

Beahrs, J. O., & Gutheil, T. G. (2001). Informed consent in psychotherapy. *American Journal of Psychiatry, 158*(1), 4–10.

Beck, A. T. (1986). Hopelessness as a predictor of eventual suicide. *Annals of the New York Academy of Sciences, 487,* 90–96.

Beck, A. T., Kovacs, M., & Weissman, A. (1979). Assessment of suicidal intention: The Scale for Suicide Ideation. *Journal of Consulting and Clinical Psychology, 47,* 343–352.

Beck, A. T., Schuyler, D., & Herman, I. (1974). Development of suicide intent scales. In A. T. Beck, H. L. P. Resnik, & A. I. Lettieri (Eds.), *The prediction of suicide.* Bowie, MD: Charles Press.

Beck, I. C. (1982). When the patient threatens violence: An empirical study of clinical practice after *Tarasoff. Bulletin of the American Academy of Psychiatry and the Law, 10,* 189–201.

Beck, I. C. (1990). The potentially violent patient: Clinical, legal, and ethical implications. In E. A. Margenau (Ed.), *The encyclopedic handbook of private practice* (pp. 697–709). New York: Gardner Press.

Beckham, E. E. (1992). Predicting patient dropout in psychotherapy. *Psychotherapy, 29,* 177–182.

Beeman, D. G., & Scott, N. A. (1991). Therapists' attitudes toward psychotherapy informed consent with adolescents. *Professional Psychology: Research and Practice, 22*(3), 230–234.

Bennett, B. E., Bryant, B., VandenBos, G. R., & Greenwood, A. (1990). *Professional liability and risk management.* Washington, DC: American Psychological Association.

Berk, M., Rubin, R., & Peck, S. (1994). *Super-pak practice builders: Forty forms for psychotherapists.* Island Park, NY: Private Practitioners Group.

Berkowitz, S. (1995). Common questions and answers regarding process notes. *Massachusetts Psychologist Quarterly, 39*(2), 4–12.

Berlin, F. S., Malin, H. M., & Dean, S. (1991). Effects of statutes requiring psychiatrists to report suspected sexual abuse of children. *American Journal of Psychiatry, 148*(4), 449–453.

Bindrim, P. (1980, July). Group therapy: Protecting privacy. *Psychology Today,* pp. 24–28.

Boedecker, A. L. (1995). Practicing with integrity: Responding to a malpractice suit. *Networker: Newsletter of the New Hampshire Psychological Association, 7*(7), 2–3.

Bogie, M. (2002). *Shopping tips.* Retrieved from www.americanprofessional.com/shopping.htm

Bongar, B. (1992). Effective risk management and the suicidal patient. *Register Report, 18*(6), 1–26.

Bongar, B. (2002). *The suicidal patient: Clinical and legal standards of care* (2nd ed.). Washington, DC: American Psychological Association.

Bouhoutsos, J., Holroyd, J., Lerman, H., Forer, B. R., & Greenberg, M. (1983). Sexual intimacy between psychotherapists and patients. *Professional Psychology: Research and Practice, 14,* 185–196.

Braaten, E. (2007). *The child clinician's report-writing handbook.* New York: Guilford Press.

Braaten, E. B., Otto, S., & Handelsman, M. M. (1993). What do people want to know about psychotherapy? *Psychotherapy, 30*(4), 565–570.

Brabeck, M., & Brabeck, K. (2002). Ethics rounds: Reporting past abuse, Part II. *Monitor on Psychology, 33*(7). Retrieved from www.apa.org/monitor/julaug02/ethicsrounds.html

Branscomb, L. (1996, Winter). Clinical advantages of the extended psychotherapy disclosure form: A feminist ethical perspective. *Georgia Psychologist,* pp. 46–49.

Broadman, K., Erdmann, A. J., Jr., & Wolff, H. G. (1949). *Manual: Cornell Medical Index Health Questionnaire.* New York: Cornell University Medical College.

Brock, G. W., & Barnard, C. P. (1988). *Procedures in marriage and family therapy* (2nd ed.). Boston: Allyn & Bacon.

Brodsky, S. L., & Schumacher, J. E. (1990). The impact of litigation on psychotherapy practice: Litigation fears and litigaphobia. In E. A. Margenau (Ed.), *The encyclopedic handbook of private practice* (pp. 664–676). New York: Gardner Press.

Caldwell, C. B., & Gottesman, I. I. (1990). Schizophrenics kill themselves too: A review of the risk factors for suicide. *Schizophrenia Bulletin, 16*(4), 571–584.

Campbell, C. D., & Gordon, M. C. (2003). Acknowledging the inevitable: Understanding multiple relationships in rural practice. *Professional Psychology: Research and Practice, 34*(4), 430–434.

Cantor, D. (1999). Ensuring the future of professional psychology. *American Psychologist, 54*(11), 922–930.

Cervantes, N. (1992). Ethical responsibility of therapists: Spousal abuse cases. *Psychotherapy Bulletin, 26*(4), 12–15.

Charles, S. C. (1985). Doctors and the litigation process: Going against the grain. *Child and Adolescent Psychotherapy, 3,* 219–222.

Charles, S. C., Warnecke, R. B., Nelson, A., & Pyskoty, C. E. (1988). Appraisal of the event as a factor in coping with malpractice litigation. *Behavioral Medicine, 14*(4), 148–155.

Charles, S. C., Wilbert, J. R., & Franke, K. J. (1985). Sued and non-sued physicians' reactions to malpractice litigation. *American Journal of Psychiatry, 142*(4), 437–440.

Chenneville, T. (2000). HIV, confidentiality, and duty to protect: A decision-making model. *Professional Psychology: Research and Practice, 31*(6), 661–670.

Childress, C. (2000). Ethical issues in providing online psychotherapeutic interventions. *Journal of Medical Internet Research, 2*(1), e5. Retrieved from www.jmir.org/2000/1/e5

Ciarlo, J. A. (1979). Awareness, use, and consequences of evaluative data in a community mental health center. *Community Mental Health Journal, 15*(1), 7–16.

Claiborne, C. D., Berberoglu, L. S., Nerison, R. M., & Somberg, D. R. (1994). The client's perspective: Ethical judgements and perceptions of therapist practices. *Professional Psychology: Research and Practice, 25*(3), 268–274.

Clement, P. W. (1999). *Outcomes and incomes: How to evaluate, improve, and market your psychotherapy practice by measuring outcomes.* New York: Guilford Press.

Cohen, R. J. (1979). *Malpractice: A guide for mental health professionals.* New York: Free Press.

Cohen, R. J. (1990). The professional liability of behavioral scientists. In E. A. Margenau (Ed.), *The encyclopedic handbook of private practice* (pp. 651–663). New York: Gardner Press. (Original work published 1983)

Cone, J. (2000). *Evaluating outcomes: Empirical tools for effective practice.* Washington, DC: American Psychological Association.

Confidentiality of HIV-Related Information Act, 35 P.C.S.A. 7601 et seq. (1990).

Corning, A. F., Malofeeva, E. V., & Bucchianeri, M. M. (2007). Predicting termination type from client–therapist agreement on the severity of the presenting problem. *Psychotherapy: Theory, Research, Practice, Training, 44*(2), 193–204.

Cross, H., & Deardorff, W. M. (1987). Malpractice in psychotherapy and psychological evaluation. In J. R. McNamara & M. Appel (Eds.), *Critical issues, developments, and trends in professional psychology* (Vol. 3, pp. 55–79). New York: Praeger.

Cull, J. G., & Gill, W. S. (1988). *Suicide Probability Scale.* Los Angeles: Western Psychological Services.

Curlin, F. A., Odell, S. V., Lawrence, R. E., Chin, M. H., Lantos, J. D., Meador, K. G., et al. (2007). The relationship between psychiatry and religion among U.S. physicians. *Psychiatric Services, 58,* 1193–1198.

D'Avanzo, C. E., & Geissler, E. (2003). *A pocket guide to cultural health assessment* (3rd ed.). St. Louis, MO: Mosby.

Dana, R. H. (2005). *Multicultural assessment: Principles, applications and examples.* Mahwah, NJ: Erlbaum.

Dattilio, F. M. (2002). Board certification in psychology: Is it really necessary? *Professional Psychology: Research and Practice, 33*(1), 54–57.

Dauser, P. J., Hedstrom, S. M., & Croteau, J. M. (1995). Effects of disclosure of comprehensive pretherapy information on clients at a university counseling center. *Professional Psychology: Research and Practice, 26*(2), 190–195.

DeBell, C., & Jones, R. D. (1997). Privileged communication at last?: An overview of *Jaffee v. Redmond. Professional Psychology: Research and Practice, 28*(6), 559–566.

Derman, K. H., & Connors, G. J. (1999). Strategies for preparing clients for treatment: A review. *Behavior Modification, 23*(1), 129–151.

Doverspike, W. F. (1997). Informed consent forms. In L. VandeCreek, S. Knapp, & T. L. Jackson (Eds.), *Innovations in clinical practice: A source book* (Vol. 15, pp. 201–214). Sarasota, FL: Professional Resource Exchange.

Downey, D. L. (2001). Therapeutic touch in psychotherapy. *Psychotherapy Bulletin, 36*(1), 35–39.

Doyle, M., & Straus, D. (1993). *How to make meetings work.* New York: Berkley.

Drude, K., & Lichstein, M. (2005, August). Psychologists' use of e-mail with clients: Some ethical considerations. *The Ohio Psychologist,* pp. 13–17. Retrieved from www.kspope.com/ethics/email.php#copy

Durana, C. (1998). The use of touch in psychotherapy: Ethical and legal guidelines. *Psychotherapy, 35*(2), 269–280.

Dvoskin, J. A. (2006). Internet consultation. *Newsletter of the American Psychology–Law Society, 26*(2). Retrieved from www.ap-ls.org/publications/newsletters/aplsnews.sum2006.pdf

Dwyer, J., & Shih, A. (1998). The ethics of tailoring the patient's chart. *Psychiatric Services, 49*(10), 1309–1312.

Eimer, B. (1988). A patient's guide to psychotherapy. In P. Keller & S. Heyman (Eds.), *Innovations in clinical practice: A source book* (Vol. 7, pp. 499–501). Sarasota, FL: Professional Resource Exchange.

Eisen, S. V., Shaul, J. A., Claridge, B., Nelson, D., Spink, J., & Cleary, P. D. (1999). Development of a consumer survey for behavioral health services. *Psychiatric Services, 50*(6), 793–798.

Elkins, G., Marcus, J., Rajab, H. H., & Durgam, S. (2005). Complementary and alternative therapy use by psychotherapy clients. *Professional Psychology: Research and Practice, 42*(2), 232–235.

Employee Retirement Income Security Act. 29 U.S.C. § 1001 *et seq.,* 29 C.F.R. § 2509 *et seq.* (1974).

Epstein, R. S., & Simon, R. I. (1990). The Exploitation Index: An early warning indicator of boundary violations in psychotherapy. *Bulletin of the Menninger Clinic, 54*(4), 450–465.

Everest Reinsurance Company. (1999). *Mental health practitioners' professional liability coverage.* Retrieved from www.rockportinsurance.com/about-the-policy.htm

Everstine, L., Everstine, D. H., Heyman, G. M., True, R. H., Prey, D. H., Johnson, H. G., et al. (1980). Privacy and confidentiality in psychotherapy. *American Psychologist, 35*(9), 828–840.

Ewing, C. P. (1990). Legal issues in terminating treatment. In E. A. Margenau (Ed.), *The encyclopedic handbook of private practice* (pp. 720–236). New York: Gardner Press.

Ewing, J. A. (1984). Detecting alcoholism: The CAGE questionnaire. *Journal of the American Medical Association, 252,* 1905–1907.

Fine, M. A., & Kurdek, L. A. (1993). Reflections on determining authorship credit and authorship order on faculty–student collaborations. *American Psychologist, 48*(11), 1141–1147.

Fischer, C. T. (1994). *Individualizing psychological assessment.* Mahwah, NJ: Erlbaum.

Fischer, J., & Corcoran, K. (2007). *Measures for clinical practice and research: A sourcebook* (4th ed.). New York: Oxford University Press.

Folman, R. (1990). *Legislative action on therapist misconduct: Implications for clinical training and treatment.* Address presented at the annual convention of the American Psychological Association, Boston.

Folstein, M. F., Folstein, S. E., & McHugh, P. R. (1975). Mini-Mental State: A practical method for grading the cognitive state of patients for the clinician. *Journal of Psychiatric Research, 12,* 189–198.

Foster, S. (1996, January). The consequences of violating the "forbidden zone." *Counseling Today,* pp. 25–53.

Freud, S. (1958). Further recommendations on the technique of psychoanalysis: On beginning the treatment. In J. Strachey (Ed. and Trans.), *The standard edition of the complete psychological works of Sigmund Freud* (Vol. 12, pp. 121–144). London: Hogarth Press. (Original work published 1913)

Fulero, S. M. (1988). *Tarasoff*: Ten years later. *Professional Psychology: Research and Practice, 19*(2), 184–190.

Fulero, S. M., & Wilbert, I. R. (1988). Record-keeping practices of clinical and counseling psychologists: A survey of practitioners. *Professional Psychology: Research and Practice, 19*(6), 658–660.

Garber, B. D. (1994). Practical limitations in considering psychotherapy with children of separation and divorce. *Psychotherapy, 31*(2), 254–261.

Garfield, S. L. (1986). Research on client variables in psychotherapy. In S. L. Garfield & A. E. Bergin (Eds.), *Handbook of psychotherapy and behavior change* (3rd ed., pp. 213–256). New York: Wiley.

Garfield, S. L., & Wolpin, M. (1963). Expectations regarding psychotherapy. *Journal of Nervous and Mental Disease, 137,* 353–362.

Glassman, J. B. (1998). Preventing and managing board complaints: The downside of custody evaluation. *Professional Psychology: Research and Practice, 29*(2), 121–124.

Goldberg, R. (1995, October). Ethical dilemmas in working with children and adolescents. *Pennsylvania Psychologist Update,* pp. 7–9.

Goode, T. D. (2000). *Promoting cultural diversity and cultural competency: Self-assessment checklist for personnel providing services and supports to children with special health needs and their families.* Retrieved from gucdc.georgetown.edu/nccc7.html [2001, April 20].

Goodman, M., Brown, J., & Deitz, P. (1992). *Managing managed care: A mental health practitioner's survival guide.* Washington, DC: American Psychiatric Press.

Goodwin, R., Gould, M. S., Blanco, C., & Olfson, M. (2001). Prescription of psychotropic medications to youths in office-based practice. *Psychiatric Services, 52,* 1081–1087.

Gottlieb, M. C. (1993). Avoiding exploitative dual relationships: A decision-making model. *Psychotherapy, 30*(1), 41–48.

Gottschalk, L. A., Mayerson, P., & Gottlieb, A. A. (1967). Prediction and evaluation of outcome in an emergency brief psychotherapy clinic. *Journal of Nervous and Mental Disease, 144,* 77–96.

Grant, R. L., & Maletzky, B. M. (1973). Application of the Weed system to psychiatric records. *Psychiatry in Medicine, 3,* 119–129.

Graziano, A. M., & Fink, R. S. (1973). Second order effects in mental health treatment. *Journal of Consulting and Clinical Psychology, 40,* 356–364.

Grisso, T., & Appelbaum, P. S. (1998). *Assessing competence to consent to treatment: A guide for physicians and other health professionals.* New York: Oxford University Press.

Grosch, W. N., & Olsen, D. C. (1994). *When helping starts to hurt.* New York: Norton.

Group for the Advancement of Psychiatry (GAP). (1990). *Casebook in psychiatric ethics.* New York: Brunner/Mazel.

Grunder, T. M. (1980). On the readability of surgical consent forms. *New England Journal of Medicine, 302,* 900–902.

Gue, D. G. (2002). The HIPAA Security Rule (NPRM): Overview. In *HIPAAdvisory.* Richardson, TX: Phoenix Health Systems. Retrieved from www.hipaadvisory.com/regs/securityoverview.htm

Gustafson, K. E., & McNamara, J. R. (1987). Confidentiality with minor clients: Issues and guidelines for therapists. *Professional Psychology: Research and Practice, 18,* 503–515.

Gustafson, K. E., McNamara, J. R., & Jensen, J. A. (1994). Parents' informed consent decisions regarding psychotherapy for their children: Consideration of therapeutic risks and benefits. *Professional Psychology: Research and Practice, 25*(1), 16–22.

Gutheil, T. G. (1980). Paranoia and progress notes: A guide to forensically informed psychiatric recordkeeping. *Hospital and Community Psychiatry, 31,* 479–482.

Gutheil, T. G. (1992). Approaches to forensic assessment of false claims of sexual misconduct by therapist. *Bulletin of the American Academy of Psychiatry and the Law, 20,* 289–296.

Gutheil, T. G. (1993). Letter to the editor. *Hospital and Community Psychiatry, 44*(10), 1005.

Gutheil, T. G., & Appelbaum, P. S. (2000). *The clinical handbook of psychiatry and the law* (3rd ed.). Philadelphia: Lippincott Williams & Wilkins.

Guy, J. K., Brown, C. K., & Poelstra, P. L. (1992). Safety concerns and protective measures used by psychotherapists. *Professional Psychology: Research and Practice, 23*(5), 421–423.

Haas, L. J., & Malouf, J. L. (1995). *Keeping up the good work: A practitioner's guide to mental health ethics* (2nd ed.). Sarasota, FL: Professional Resource Exchange.

Haas, L. J., Malouf, J. L., & Mayerson, N. H. (1986). Ethical dilemmas in psychological practice: Results of a national survey. *Professional Psychology: Research and Practice, 17,* 317–321.

Hamberger, L. K. (2000). Requests for complete record release: A three-step response protocol. *Psychotherapy, 37*(10), 89–97.

Handelsman, M. M. (1990). Do written consent forms influence clients' first impressions of therapists? *Professional Psychology: Research and Practice, 21*(6), 451–454.

Handelsman, M. M., & Galvin, M. D. (1988). Facilitating informed consent for outpatient psychotherapy: A suggested written format. *Professional Psychology: Research and Practice, 19*(2), 223–225.

Handelsman, M. M., Kemper, M. B., Kesson-Craig, P., McLain, I., & Johnsrud, C. (1986). Use, content, and readability of written informed consent forms for treatment. *Professional Psychology: Research and Practice, 17,* 514–518.

Hansen, I. C., Green, S., & Kutner, K. B. (1989). Ethical issues facing school psychologists working with families. *Professional School Psychology, 4,* 245–255.

Hansen, N. D., Randazzo, K. V., Schwardz, A., Marshall, M., Kalis, D., Frazier, R., et al. (2006). Do we practice what we preach?: An exploratory survey of multicultural psychotherapy competencies. *Professional Psychology: Research and Practice, 37*(1), 66–74.

Hare-Mustin, R. T., Marecek, I., Kaplan, A. G., & Liss-Levinson, N. (1979). Rights of clients, responsibilities of therapists. *American Psychologist, 34,* 3–16.

Harpaz-Rotem, I., & Rosenheck, R. A. (2006). Prescribing practices of psychiatrists and primary care physicians caring for children with mental illness. *Child: Care, Health, and Development, 32*(2), 225–238.

Haspel, K. C., Jorgenson, L. M., Wincze, J. P., & Parsons, J. P. (1997). Legislative intervention regarding therapist sexual misconduct: An overview. *Professional Psychology: Research and Practice, 28*(1), 63–72.

Hatchett, G. T., & Park, H. L. (2003). Comparison of four operational definitions of premature termination. *Psychotherapy, 40*(3), 226–231.

Hawkins, I. L., & Bullock, S. L. (1995). Informed consent and religious values: A neglected area of diversity. *Psychotherapy, 32*(2), 293–300.

Health Insurance Portability and Accountability Act (HIPAA) of 1996, Pub. Law No. 104-191, 110 Stat. 1936 (1996).

Herron, W. G., & Sitkowski, S. (1986). Effect of fees on psychotherapy: What is the evidence? *Professional Psychology: Research and Practice, 17*(4), 347–351.

Higuchi, S. A. (1994). Recent managed care legislative and legal issues. In R. L. Lowman & R. I. Resnick (Eds.), *The mental health professional's guide to managed care* (pp. 83–118). Washington, DC: American Psychological Association.

Hillard, J. R. (1995). Predicting suicide. *Psychiatric Services, 46*(3), 223–225.

Hines, P., & Hare-Mustin, R. (1978). Ethical concerns in family therapy. *Professional Psychology, 9*, 165–171.

Hirsh, H. L. (1978). Will your medical records get you into trouble? *Legal Aspects of Medical Practice, 6*, 46–51.

Hirshfeld, R., & Davidson, L. (1988). Risk factors for suicide. In A. I. Frances & R. E. Hales (Eds.), *American Psychiatric Press review of psychiatry* (Vol. 7, pp. 307–333). Washington, DC: American Psychiatric Press.

Holstein, R. (2007, Winter). Make them (managed care) an offer they won't refuse: How to negotiate a raise. *Independent Practitioner*, pp. 23–24.

Hurvitz, N. (1976). Marital problems following psychotherapy with one spouse. *Journal of Consulting Psychology, 31*, 38–47.

Hussey, W. R. (1986). How to use small claims court for collections. In L. G. Ritt & S. R. Heyman (Eds.), *Innovations in clinical practice: A source book* (Vol. 5, pp. 245–256). Sarasota, FL: Professional Resource Exchange.

Jaffee v. Redmond, 518 U.S. 1 (1996).

Jensen, J. A., McNamara, J. R., & Gustafson, K. E. (1991). Parents' and clinicians' attitudes toward the risks and benefits of child psychotherapy: A study of informed-consent content. *Professional Psychology Research and Practice, 22*(2), 161–170.

Jobes, D. A. (2006). *Managing suicidal risk: A collaborative approach.* New York: Guilford Press.

Jobes, D. A., & Berman, A. L. (1993). Suicide and malpractice liability: Assessing and revising policies, procedures, and practice in outpatient settings. *Professional Psychology: Research and Practice, 24*(1), 91–99.

Joyce, A. S., Piper, W. E., Ogrodniczuk, J. S., & Klein, R. H. (2007). *Termination in psychotherapy: A psychodynamic model of processes and outcomes.* Washington, DC: American Psychological Association.

Kachorek, J. (1990). Record keeping. In E. A. Margenau (Ed.), *The encyclopedic handbook of private practice* (pp. 96–112). New York: Gardner Press.

Kaplan, A. I. (1990). Nonsexual dual relationships: Protecting the psychologist. *Illinois Psychologist, 28*(3), 25, 30.

Katz, E. C., Brown, B. S., Schwartz, R. P., Weintraub, E., Barksdale, W., & Robinson, R. (2004). Role induction: A method for enhancing early retention in outpatient drug-free treatment. *Journal of Consulting and Clinical Psychology, 72*(2), 227–234.

Keith-Spiegel, P. (1977, September). *Sex with clients: Ten reasons why it is a very stupid thing to do.* Paper presented at the annual convention of the American Psychological Association, Washington, DC.

Kelsey, D., & Plumb, P. (2004). *Great meetings!: Great results* (rev. ed.). Portland, ME: Hanson Park Press.

Kertay, L., & Reviere, S. (1993). The use of touch in psychotherapy: Theoretical and ethical considerations. *Psychotherapy, 30*(1), 32–40.

King, J. H., Jr. (1977). *The law of medical malpractice.* St. Paul, MN: West.

Kiresuk, T., Smith, A., & Cardillo, J. E. (Eds.). (1994). *Goal attainment scaling: Applications, theory, and measurement.* Hillsdale, NJ: Erlbaum.

Kleespies, P. M., Deleppo, J. D., Gallagher, P. L., & Niles, B. L. (1999). Managing suicidal emergencies: Recommendations for the practitioner. *Professional Psychology: Research and Practice, 30*(5), 454–463.

Klein, J., Macbeth, J., & Onek, J. (1984). *Legal issues in the private practice of psychiatry*. Washington, DC: American Psychiatric Press.

Knapp, S. (1992a, April 16). *Record keeping*. Handout presented at workshop, Practicing Safely and Ethically in the 1990s, Pittsburgh, PA.

Knapp, S. (1992b, April). Medicare update. *Pennsylvania Psychologist Update*, p. 7.

Knapp, S. (1994). *Pennsylvania law and psychology*. Harrisburg: Pennsylvania Psychological Association.

Knapp, S., & Tepper, A. M. (1992, May). Caught in the middle: The parent, child and psychologist triangle. *Pennsylvania Psychologist Quarterly*, p. 16.

Knapp, S., & VandeCreek, L. (1981). Behavioral medicine: Its malpractice risks for psychologists. *Professional Psychology: Research and Practice, 12*, 677–683.

Knapp, S., & VandeCreek, L. (1983). Malpractice risks with suicidal patients. *Psychotherapy: Theory, Research, and Practice, 20*, 274–280.

Knapp, S., VandeCreek, L., & Tepper, A. (1998). *Pennsylvania law and psychology* (3rd ed.). Harrisburg: Pennsylvania Psychological Association.

Kobayashi, M., Smith, T. P., & Norcross, J. C. (1998). Enhancing adherence. In G. P. Koocher, J. C. Norcross, & S. S. Hill III (Eds.), *Psychologists' desk reference* (pp. 23–60). New York: Oxford University Press.

Koocher, G., & Keith-Spiegel, P. (1998). *Ethics in psychology: Professional standards and cases* (2nd ed.). New York: Oxford University Press.

Koss, M. P. (1979). Length of psychotherapy for clients seen in private practice. *Journal of Consulting and Clinical Psychology, 47*, 210–212.

Kovacs, A. L. (1987). Insurance billing: The growing risk of lawsuits against psychologists. *Independent Practitioner, 7*, 21–24.

Kramer, S. A. (1990). *Positive endings in psychotherapy: Bringing meaningful closure to therapeutic relationships*. San Francisco: Jossey-Bass.

Kremer, T. G., & Gesten, E. L. (1998). Confidentiality limits of managed care and client's willingness to self-disclose. *Professional Psychology: Research and Practice, 29*(6), 553–558.

Kruger, J., & Dunning, D. (2002). Unskilled and unaware—but why?: A reply to Krueger and Mueller (2002). *Journal of Personality and Social Psychology, 82*(2), 189–192.

Lambert, W., Salzer, M. S., & Bickman, L. (1998). Clinical outcome, consumer satisfaction, and ad hoc ratings of improvement in children's mental health. *Journal of Consulting and Clinical Psychology, 66*(2), 270–279.

Larsen, D. L., Attkisson, C. C., Hargreaves, W. A., & Nguyen, T. D. (1979). Assessment of client/patient satisfaction: Development of the general scale. *Evaluation and Program Planning, 2*, 197–207.

Legal issues: How to avoid problems with cellular phones and fax machines. (1992). *Psychotherapy Finances, 18*(2), 3.

Levenstein, J. (1994a). Treatment documentation in private practice: I. The PIC treatment plan. *Independent Practitioner, 14*(4), 181–185

Levenstein, J. (1994b). Treatment documentation in private practice: II. PIRC progress notes. *Independent Practitioner, 14*(5), 233–237.

Lewis, B. J. (2004, Spring). When the licensing board comes a'calling: Managing the stress of licensing board investigations. *Independent Practitioner*, pp. 121–124.

Ley, P. (1982). Studies in recall in medical settings. *Human Learning, 1*, 223–233.

Liberman, B. (1990). Letter to the editor. *Independent Psychologist, 10*(4), 5.

Lidz, C. W., Meisel, A., Zerubavel, E., Carter, M., Sestak, R. M., & Roth, L. H. (1984). *Informed consent: A study of decisionmaking in psychiatry*. New York: Guilford Press.

Lipman, A. J. (1995). Treating borderline personality disorder. *Contemporary Psychology, 40*(10), 996–997.

Littrell, J., & Ashford, J. B. (1995). Is it proper for psychologists to discuss medications with clients? *Professional Psychology: Research and Practice, 26*(3), 238–244.

LoPresti, R. L., & Zuckerman, E. L. (2004). *Rewarding specialties for mental health clinicians: Developing your practice niche*. New York: Guilford Press.

LoVerde, M. E., Prochazka, A. V., & Byyny, R. L. (1989). Research consent forms: Continued unreadability and increasing length. *Journal of General Internal Medicine, 4*(5), 410–412.

Mallory, S. D., Gert, B., & Culver, C. M. (1986). Family coercion and valid consent. *Theoretical Medicine, 7,* 123–126.

Maramba, G. G., & Nagayama Hall, G. C. (2002). Meta-analyses of ethnic match as a predictor of dropout, utilization, and level of functioning. *Cultural Diversity and Ethnic Minority Psychology, 8*(3), 290–297.

Margolin, G. (1982). Ethical and legal considerations in marital and family therapy. *American Psychologist, 37*(7), 788–801.

Marine, E. C. (n.d.). Retrieved from www.americanprofessional.com/risk_html

Maris, R. W., Berman, A. L., & Silverman, M. M. (2000). *Comprehensive textbook of suicidology.* New York: Guilford Press.

Marsh, D. T. (1995, January). Confidentiality and the rights of families: Resolving possible conflicts. *Pennsylvania Psychologist Update,* pp. 1–3.

McArdle, E. (2003, August 18). Small firm specializes in patient abuse by therapists: Far more common than many suspect. *Lawyers Weekly USA.* Retrieved from www.speroandjorgenson.com/lwusa.htm

McGee, T. F. (2003). Observations on the retirement of professional psychologists. *Professional Psychology: Research and Practice, 34*(1), 388–395.

McGoldrick, M., Giordano, J., & Garcia-Preto, N. (Eds.). (2005). *Ethnicity and family therapy* (3rd ed.). New York: Guilford Press.

Meehl, P. E. (1973). Why I do not attend case conferences. In P. E. Meehl (Ed.), *Psychodiagnosis: Selected papers.* Minneapolis: University of Minnesota Press.

Meek, C. (1987). Suggestions on the collection of fees. In P. A. Keller & S. R. Heyman (Eds.), *Innovations in clinical practice: A source book* (Vol. 6, pp. 271–276). Sarasota, FL: Professional Resource Exchange.

Meek, C., Keller, P. A., & Ritt, L. G. (1985). A collection of office forms. In P. A. Keller & L. G. Ritt (Eds.), *Innovations in clinical practice: A source book* (Vol. 4, pp. 345–360). Sarasota, FL: Professional Resource Exchange.

Meiselman, K. C. (1990). *Resolving the trauma of incest.* San Francisco: Jossey-Bass.

Meyer, J. D., & Fink, C. (1989). Psychiatric symptoms from prescription medications. *Professional Psychology: Research and Practice, 20*(2), 90–96.

Meyer, R. G., Landis, E. R., & Hays, J. R. (1988). *Law for the psychotherapist.* New York: Norton.

Miller, I. J. (1998). *Eleven unethical managed care practices every patient should know about (with emphasis on mental health care).* Retrieved from www.nomanagedcare.org/foyer.htm

Miller, I. J. (2000). *Dealing with insurance refusal to pay for couples therapy.* Retrieved from www.psychotherapistguild.com/refusal.html

Miller, I. J. (2001). Protecting privacy with the absence of records. *Independent Practitioner, 21*(2), 78–79.

Miller, M. C., Jacobes, D. G., & Gutheil, T. G. (1998). Talisman or taboo: The controversy of the suicide-prevention contract. *Harvard Review of Psychiatry, 6*(2), 78–87.

Moline, M. E., Williams, G. T., & Austin, K. M. (1998). *Documenting psychotherapy: Essentials for mental health practitioners.* Thousand Oaks, CA: Sage.

Monahan, J. (1993). Limiting therapist exposure to *Tarasoff* liability: Guidelines for risk containment. *American Psychologist, 48*(3), 242–250.

Monahan, J., Steadman, H. J., Silver, E., Appelbaum, P. S., Robbins, P. C., Mulvey, E. P., et al. (2001). *Rethinking risk assessment: The MacArthur study of mental disorder and violence.* New York: Oxford University Press.

Montgomery, L. M., Cupit, B. E., & Wimberley, T. K. (1999). Complaints, malpractice, and risk management: Professional issues and personal experiences. *Professional Psychology: Research and Practice, 30*(4), 402–410.

Morris, R. J. (1993). Ethical issues in the assessment and treatment of children and adolescents. *Register Report, 19*(1), 4–12.

Morrison, J. K., Fredrico, M., & Rosenthal, H. J. (1975). Contracting confidentiality in group psychotherapy. *Journal of Forensic Psychology, 7,* 1–6.

National Center for Health Statistics. (1988). *Vital statistics mortality data: Multiple cause-of-death detail.* Hyattsville, MD: U.S. Department of Health and Human Services.

National Center for Injury Prevention and Control. (2005). Web-based injury statistics query and reporting system (WISQARS). Retrieved from www.cdc.gov/ncipc/wisqars/default.htm

Negley, E. T. (1985). Malpractice prevention and risk management for clinicians. In P. A. Keller & L. G. Ritt (Eds.), *Innovations in clinical practice: A source book* (Vol. 4, pp. 243–251). Sarasota, FL: Professional Resource Exchange.

Norris, M. P., Molinari, V., & Rosowsky, E. (1998). Providing mental health care to older adults: Unraveling the maze of Medicare and managed care. *Psychotherapy, 35*(4), 490–497.

Nowell, D., & Spruill, J. (1993). If it's not absolutely confidential, will information be disclosed? *Professional Psychology: Research and Practice, 24*(3), 367–369.

O'Leary, B. J., & Norcross, J. C. (1998). Making successful referrals. In G. P. Koocher, J. C. Norcross, & S. S. Hill III (Eds.), *Psychologists' desk reference* (pp. 524–526). New York: Oxford University Press.

O'Neill, P. (1998). *Negotiating consent in psychotherapy.* New York: New York University Press.

Orchowski, L. M., Spickard, D. A., & McNamara, J. R. (2006). Cinema and the valuing of psychotherapy: Implications for clinical practice. *Professional Psychology: Research and Practice, 37*(5), 506–514.

Orlow, E. (2001, December). Requirements for parental consent for psychological services for children in Pennsylvania. *Pennsylvania Psychologist Update,* p. 3.

Orne, M. T., & Wender, P. H. (1968). Anticipatory socialization for psychotherapy: Method and rationale. *American Journal of Psychiatry, 124,* 1202–1212.

Ownby, R. L. (1991). *Psychological reports: A guide to report writing in professional psychology* (2nd ed.). Brandon, VT: Clinical Psychology.

Paniagua, F. A. (2005). *Assessing and treating culturally diverse clients: A practical guide* (3rd ed.). Thousand Oaks, CA: Sage.

Pargament, K. (2007). *Spiritually integrated psychotherapy: Understanding and addressing the sacred.* New York: Guilford Press.

Pargament, K. I. (1997). *The psychology of religion and coping: Theory, research, and practice.* New York: Guilford Press.

Parsons, I. P., & Wincze, I. P. (1995). A survey of client–therapist sexual involvement in Rhode Island as reported by subsequent treating therapists. *Professional Psychology: Research and Practice, 26*(2), 171–175.

Patten, C., Barnett, T., & Houlihan, D. (1991). Ethics in marital and family therapy: A review of the literature. *Professional Psychology: Research and Practice, 22,* 171–175.

Pearlman, L. A., & Saakvitne, K. W. (1995). *Trauma and the therapist.* New York: Norton.

Pekarik, G. (1985). Coping with dropouts. *Professional Psychology: Research and Practice, 16*(1), 114–123.

Pekarik, G., & Guidry, L. L. (1999). Relationship of satisfaction to symptom change, follow-up adjustment, and clinical significance in private practice. *Professional Psychology: Research and Practice, 30*(5), 474–478.

Pekarik, G., & Wolff, C. B. (1996). Relationship of satisfaction to symptom change, follow-up adjustment, and clinical significance. *Professional Psychology: Research and Practice, 27*(2), 202–208.

Philadelphia Society of Clinical Psychologists, Committee on Ethics. (1988, January–February). Ethical issues in psychotherapy termination. *Pennsylvania Psychologist,* p. 10.

Piercy, F., Lasswell, M., & Brock, G. (1989). *AAMFT forms book.* Washington, DC: American Association for Marriage and Family Therapy.

Pomerantz, A. M. (2000). What if prospective clients knew how managed care impacts psychologists' practice and ethics?: An exploratory study. *Ethics and Behavior, 10*(2), 159–171.

Pomerantz, A. M., & Handelsman, M. A. (2004). Informed consent revisited: An updated written question format. *Professional Psychology: Research and Practice, 35*(2), 201–205.

Pope, K. (1988d). Avoid malpractice in the area of diagnosis, assessment, and testing. *Independent Practitioner, 8*(3), 18–25.

Pope, K. (1988e). More on avoiding malpractice in the area of diagnosis, assessment, and testing. *Independent Practitioner, 8*(4), 23–24.

Pope, K. S. (1987). Preventing therapist–patient sexual intimacy: Therapy for a therapist at risk. *Professional Psychology: Research and Practice, 18*(6), 624–628.

Pope, K. S. (1988a). Dual relationships: A source of ethical, legal and clinical problems. *Independent Practitioner, 8*(4), 17–25.

Pope, K. S. (1988b). How clients are harmed by sexual contact with mental health professionals: The syndrome and its prevalence. *Journal of Counseling and Development, 67,* 222–226.

Pope, K. S. (1988c). Fee policies and procedures: Causes of malpractice suits and ethics complaints. *Independent Practitioner, 8*(4), 24–29.

Pope, K. S. (1989a). Malpractice suits, licensing disciplinary actions and ethics cases: Frequencies, causes, and costs. *Independent Practitioner, 9*(1), 22–26.

Pope, K. S. (1989b). Therapists who become sexually intimate with a patient: Classification, dynamics, recidivism and rehabilitation. *Independent Practitioner, 9*(3), 28–34.

Pope, K. S. (1992). Responsibilities in providing psychological test feedback to clients. *Psychological Assessment, 4*(3), 268–271.

Pope, K. S. (2000). Therapists' sexual feelings and behaviors: Research, trends, and quandaries. In L. Szuchman & F. Muscarella (Eds.), *Psychological perspectives on human sexuality* (pp. 603–658). New York: Wiley.

Pope, K. S. (2003). *Fallacies and pitfalls in psychological assessment: 7 examples.* Retrieved from www.kspope.com/fallacies/assessment.php

Pope, K. S. (n.d.). *Informed consent in psychotherapy and counseling: Forms, standards and guidelines, and references.* Retrieved from www.kspope.com/consent/index.php

Pope, K. S., & Bouhoutsos, I. (1986). *Sexual intimacy between therapists and patients.* New York: Praeger.

Pope, K. S., Geller, J. D., & Wilkinson, L. (1975). Fee assessment and outpatient psychotherapy. *Journal of Consulting and Clinical Psychology, 43*(6), 835–841.

Pope, K. S., & Vasquez, M. J. T. (2005). *How to survive and thrive as a therapist: Information, ideas, and resources for psychologists in practice.* Washington, DC: American Psychological Association.

Pope, K. S., & Vasquez, M. J. T. (2007). *Ethics in psychotherapy and counseling: A practical guide* (3rd ed.). San Francisco: Jossey-Bass.

Pressman, R. M., & Siegler, R. (1983). *The independent practitioner: Practice management for the allied health professional.* Homewood, IL: Dow Jones-Irwin.

Purcell, R., Powell, M. B., & Mullen, P. E. (2005). Clients who stalk psychologists: Prevalence, methods and motives. *Professional Psychology: Research and Practice, 36*(5), 537–543.

Quinn, V. (n.d.). *Professional therapy never includes sex.* (Available from California Department of Consumer Affairs, 1020 N Street, Sacramento, CA 95814; single copies available at no charge)

Ragusea, S. A. (2002). A professional living will for psychologists and other mental health professionals. In L. VandeCreek & T. L. Jackson (Eds.), *Innovations in clinical practice: A source book* (Vol. 20). Sarasota, FL: Professional Resource Exchange.

Reid, W. H. (1999). *A clinician's guide to legal issues in psychotherapy or proceed with caution.* Phoenix, AZ: Zeig, Tucker.

Reis, B. F., & Brown, L. G. (2006). Preventing therapy dropout in the real world: The clinical utility of videotape preparation and client estimate of treatment duration. *Professional Psychology: Research and Practice, 37*(3), 311–316.

Reynolds, W. M. (1991). *Adult Suicidal Ideation Questionnaire.* Odessa, FL: Psychological Assessment Resources.

Richards, P. S., & Bergin, A. E. (2000). *Handbook of psychotherapy and religious diversity.* Washington, DC: American Psychological Association.

Rollnick, S., Miller, W. R., & Butler, C. C. (2008). *Motivational interviewing in health care: Helping patients change behavior.* New York: Guilford Press.

Rosenthal, M. B. (2000). Risk sharing and the supply of mental health services. *Journal of Health Economics, 19*, 1047–1065.

Rubanowitz, D. (1987). Public attitudes toward psychotherapist–client confidentiality. *Professional Psychology: Research and Practice, 18*, 613–618.

Rudd, M. D., Dahm, P. F., & Rajab, M. H. (1993). Diagnostic comorbidity in persons with suicidal ideation and behavior. *American Journal of Psychiatry, 150*, 928–934.

Sadoff, R. L. (1988). Record keeping in private practice. In F. Flach (Ed.), *Psychiatric risk management*. New York: Directions in Psychiatry.

Sahid, J. R. (1998). *Practice Strategies, 4*(11).

Satler, J. M. (1977). The effects of therapist–client racial similarity. In A. S. Gurman & A. M. Razin (Eds.), *Effective psychotherapy: A handbook of research* (pp. 250–288). Elmsford, NY: Pergamon Press.

Saunders, T. R. (1993). Some ethical and legal features of child custody disputes: A case illustration and applications. *Psychotherapy, 30*(1), 49–58.

Schinka, J. (1984). *Personal Problems Checklist*. Odessa, FL: Psychological Assessment Resources.

Schinka, J. (1989). *Health Problems Checklist*. Odessa, FL: Psychological Assessment Resources.

Schlosser, B., & Tower, R. B. (1991). Office policies for assessment services. In P. A. Keller & S. R. Heyman (Eds.), *Innovations in clinical practice: A source book* (Vol. 10, pp. 393–405). Sarasota, FL: Professional Resource Exchange.

Schoenfeld, L. S., Hatch, J. P., & Conzalez, J. M. (2001). Responses of psychologists to complaints filed against them with a state licensing board. *Professional Psychology: Research and Practice, 35*(5), 491–495.

Sederer, L. I., & Libby, M. (1995). False allegations of sexual misconduct: Clinical and institutional considerations. *Psychiatric Services, 46*(2), 160–163.

Seligman, M. E. P. (1995, November). The effectiveness of psychotherapy: The *Consumer Reports* study. *Consumer Reports*, pp. 734–739.

Shea, S. C. (2002). *The practical art of suicide assessment: A guide for mental health professionals and substance abuse counselors*. New York: Wiley.

Shuman, D. W., & Foote, W. (1999). *Jaffee v. Redmond*'s impact: Life after the Supreme Court's recognition of a psychotherapist–patient privilege. *Professional Psychology: Research and Practice, 30*(5), 479–487.

Simon, R. I. (1992). *Clinical psychiatry and the law* (2nd ed.). Washington, DC: American Psychiatric Press.

Simon, R. I. (1999). The suicide prevention contract: Clinical, legal, and risk management issues. *Journal of the American Academy of Psychiatry and Law, 27*(3), 445–450.

Simon, R. I. (2008, February 1). Is it a "true" emergency?: Suicidal patients' access to their psychiatrists. *Psychiatric Times, 25*(2). Retrieved from www.psychiatrictimes.com/ showArticle.jhtml?articleID=206504179

Small, R. F., & Barnhill, L. R. (Eds.). (1998). *Practicing in the new mental health marketplace: Ethical, legal, and moral issues*. Washington, DC: American Psychological Association.

Smith, E. W. L., Clance, P. R., & Imes, S. (Eds.). (1998). *Touch in psychotherapy: Theory, research, and practice*. New York: Guilford Press.

Smith, M. L., & Glass, G. V. (1977). Meta-analysis of psychotherapy outcome studies. *American Psychologist, 32*, 752–760.

Soisson, E., VandeCreek, L., & Knapp, S. (1987). Thorough record keeping: A good defense in a litigious era. *Professional Psychology: Research and Practice, 18*, 498–502.

Sonne, J. L. (2006, Fall). Nonsexual multiple relationships: A practical decision-making model for clinicians. *Independent Practitioner*, pp. 187–192.

Soreff, S. M., & McDuffee, M. A. (1993). *Documentation survival handbook for psychiatrists and other mental health professionals: A clinician's guide to charting for better care, certification, reimbursement, and risk management*. Seattle, WA: Hogrefe & Huber.

Sparks, W. A., Daniels, J. A., & Johnson, E. (2003). Relationship of referral source, race, and wait time on preintake attrition. *Professional Psychology: Research and Practice, 34*(5), 514–518.

Spayd, C. S., & Wiley, M. O. (2001, April). Closing a professional practice: Clinical and practical considerations. *Pennsylvania Psychologist Update*, p. 8.

Sperry, L., & Shafranske, E. P. (Eds.). (2004). *Spiritually oriented psychotherapy.* Washington, DC: American Psychological Association.

Staal, M. A., & King, R. E. (2000). Managing a multiple relationship environment: The ethics of military psychology. *Professional Psychology: Research and Practice, 31*(6), 698–705.

Standards for privacy of individually identifiable health information. (2000, December 28). *Federal Register, 65,* 8246–82829. (Retrieved from www.access.gpo.gov/su_docs/fedreg/a001228c.html)

Steenbarger, B. N. (1994). Duration and outcome in psychotherapy. An integrative review. *Professional Psychology: Research and Practice, 25*(2), 111–119.

Stout, C. E., Levant, R. F., Reed, G. M., & Murphy, M. J. (2001). Contracts: A primer for psychologists. *Professional Psychology: Research and Practice, 32*(1), 88–91.

Straussner, S. L. A. (Ed.). (2001). *Ethnocultural factors in substance abuse treatment.* New York: Guilford Press.

Stromberg, C. D., & Dellinger, A. (1993, December). Malpractice and other professional liability. In *The psychologist's legal update, 3.* Washington, DC: National Register of Health Service Providers in Psychology.

Stromberg, C. D., Haggarty, D. I., Mishkin, B., Liebenluft, R. F., McMillan, M. H., Rubin, B. L., et al. (1988). *The psychologist's legal handbook.* Washington, DC: National Register of Health Service Providers in Psychology.

Stromberg, C. D., Lindberg, D., Mishkin, B., & Baker, M. (1993a, April). Privacy, confidentiality, and privilege. In *The psychologist's legal update, 1* (p. 8). Washington, DC: National Register of Health Service Providers in Psychology.

Stromberg, C. D., Schneider, J., & Joondeph, B. (1993b, August). Dealing with potentially dangerous patients. In *The psychologist's legal update, 2* (p. 10). Washington, DC: National Register of Health Service Providers in Psychology.

Stuart, R. B. (1975). *Treatment contract.* Champaign, IL: Research Press.

Sturm, I. E. (1987). The psychologist and the problem-oriented record (POR). *Professional Psychology: Research and Practice, 18,* 155–158.

Sue, D. W. (2003). *Overcoming our racism: The journey to liberation.* San Francisco: Jossey-Bass.

Sue, D. W., & Sue, D. (2008). *Counseling the culturally different: Theory and practice* (5th ed.). Hoboken, NJ: Wiley.

Sullivan, C. M., & Cain, D. (2004). Ethical and safety considerations when obtaining information from or about battered women for research purposes. *Journal of Interpersonal Violence, 19,* 603–616.

Sullivan, T., Martin, W. L., & Handelsman, M. M. (1993). Practical benefits of an informed-consent procedure: An empirical investigation. *Professional Psychology: Research and Practice, 24*(2), 160–163.

Swartz, H. A., Zuckoff, A., Grote, N. K., Spielvogle, H. N., Bledsoe, S. E., Shear, M. K., et al. (2007). Engaging depressed patients in psychotherapy: Integrating techniques from motivational interviewing and ethnographic interviewing to improve treatment participation. *Professional Psychology: Research and Practice, 38*(4), 430–439.

Sweet, J. J. (1990). Further considerations of ethics in psychological testing: A broader perspective on releasing records. *Illinois Psychologist, 28*(4), 5–9.

Tarasoff v. Regents of the University of California, 131 Cal. Rptr. 14, 551 P.2d 334 (1976).

Taube, D. O., & Elwork, A. (1990). Researching the effects of confidentiality law on patients' self-disclosures. *Professional Psychology: Research and Practice, 22*(1), 72–75.

Taylor, L., & Adelman, H. S. (1989). Reframing the confidentiality dilemma to work in children's best interests. *Professional Psychology: Research and Practice, 20,* 79–83.

Taylor, R. L. (2007). *Psychological masquerade: Distinguishing psychological from organic disorders* (3rd ed.). New York: Springer.

Teisman, M. (1980). Convening strategies in family therapy. *Family Process, 19,* 393–400.

Ten steps to create a successful treatment plan. (1993, August). *Managed Care Strategies, 1*(6), 5–6.

Tepper, A. M., Rinella, V. J., Jr., & Siegel, A. M. (1991, November). Subpoenas and court orders in the everyday practice of psychology. *Pennsylvania Psychologist Quarterly*, pp. 14–15.

Thomas, J. T. (2007). Informed consent through contracting for supervision: Minimizing risks, enhancing benefits. *Professional Psychology: Research and Practice, 38*(3), 221–231.

Thorn, B. E., Rubin, N. J., Holderby, A. J., & Shealy, R. C. (1996). Client–therapist intimacy: Responses of psychotherapy clients to a consumer-oriented brochure. *Ethics and Behavior, 6*(1), 17–28.

Thorn, B. E., Shealy, R. C., & Briggs, S. D. (1993). Sexual misconduct in psychotherapy: Reactions to a consumer-oriented brochure. *Professional Psychology: Research and Practice, 24*(1), 75–82.

Tips from an attorney on how to handle lost, stolen or damaged records. (1998). *Practice Strategies, 4*(3), 2, 7.

Tishler, C. L., Gordon, L. B., & Landry-Meyer, L. (2000). Managing the violent patient: A guide for psychologists and other mental health professionals. *Professional Psychology: Research and Practice, 31*(1), 34–41.

Tracy, M. (n.d.). *An ounce of prevention now will pay off later for psychiatrists, their practices.* Retrieved from www.prmsva.com/risk_management/An_ounce_of_prevention.htm

Tranel, D. (1994). The release of psychological data to nonexperts: Ethical and legal considerations. *Psychotherapy: Theory, Research, and Practice, 25*(1), 33–38.

Ullman, S. E. (1999). Social support and recovery from sexual assault: A review. *Aggression and Violent Behavior: A Review Journal, 4,* 343–358.

Vaccarino, J. M. (1978). Consent, informed consent, and consent forms. *New England Journal of Medicine, 298,* 455.

Van Horne, R. A. (2004). Psychology licensing board disciplinary actions: The realities. *Professional Psychology: Research and Practice, 35*(2), 170–178.

Veldhuis, C. B., & Freyd, J. J. (1999). Groomed for silence; groomed for betrayal. In M. Rivera (Ed.), *Fragment by fragment: Feminist perspectives on memory and child sexual abuse* (pp. 253–282). Charlottetown, Prince Edward Island, Canada: Gynergy Books.

Vespia, K. M., Heckman-Stone, C., & Delworth, U. (2002). Describing and facilitating supervision behaviors in counseling trainees. *Psychotherapy: Theory, Research, Practice, Training, 39*(1), 56–65.

Vinson, J. S. (1987). Use of complaint procedures in cases of therapist–patient sexual contact. *Professional Psychology: Research and Practice, 18*(2), 159–164.

Wagner, L., Davis, S., & Handelsman, M. M. (1998). In search of the abominable consent form: The impact of readability and personalization. *Journal of Clinical Psychology, 54*(1), 115–120.

Walfish, S., & Ducey, B. B. (2007). Readability level of Health Insurance Portability and Accountability Act notices of privacy practices used by psychologists in clinical practice. *Professional Psychology: Research and Practice, 38*(2), 203–207.

Walters, G. C., Solomon, G. S., & Walden, V. R. (1982). Use of the MMPI in predicting persistence of male and female patients. *Journal of Clinical Psychology, 38,* 80–83.

Weed, L. L. (1971). *Medical records, medical education and patient care: The problem-oriented record as a basic tool.* Chicago: Yearbook Medical.

Weiner, B. A., & Wettstein, R. M. (1993). *Legal issues in mental health care.* New York: Plenum Press.

Weiner, I. (1989). On competence and ethicality in psychodiagnostic assessment. *Journal of Personality Assessment, 53,* 827–831.

Wendorf, D., & Wendorf, R. (1985). A systemic view of family therapy ethics. *Family Process, 24,* 443–353.

Widiger, T. A., & Rorer, L. G. (1984). The responsible psychotherapist. *American Psychologist, 39,* 503–515.

Wiger, D. E., & Solberg, K. B. (2001). *Tracking mental health outcomes: A therapist's guide to measuring client progress, analyzing data, and improving your practice.* New York: Wiley.

Wilcoxon, A., & Fenell, D. (1983). Engaging the non-attending spouse in marital therapy through the use of therapist-initiated written communication. *Journal of Marital and Family Therapy, 9,* 199–203.

Wilkinson, A. P. (1982). Psychiatric malpractice: Identifying areas of liability. *Trial, 18*(10), 73–77, 89–90.

Willbach, D. (1989). Ethics and family therapy: The case management of family violence. *Journal of Marital and Family Therapy, 1,* 43–52.

Williams, M. (1992). Exploitation and inference: Mapping the damage from therapist–patient sexual involvement. *American Psychologist, 47*(3), 412–421.

Williams, M. H. (2000). Victimized by "victims": A taxonomy of antecedents of false complaints against psychotherapists. *Professional Psychology: Research and Practice, 31*(1), 75–81.

Williams, M. H. (2001). The question of psychologists' maltreatment by state licensing boards: Overcoming denial and seeking remedies. *Professional Psychology: Research and Practice, 32*(4), 341–344.

Wilson, S. J. (1980). *Recording guidelines for social workers.* New York: Free Press.

Woody, R. H. (1988). *Fifty ways to avoid malpractice: A guidebook for mental health professionals.* Sarasota, FL: Professional Resource Exchange.

Woody, R. H. (1991). *Quality care in mental health: Assuring the best clinical services.* San Francisco: Jossey-Bass.

Woody, R. H. (1997). Valuing a psychological practice. *Professional Psychology: Research and Practice, 28*(1), 77–80.

Woody, R. H. (1999). Bartering for psychological services. *Professional Psychology: Research and Practice, 29*(2), 174–178.

Woody, R. H. (2000). *Child custody: Practice standards, ethical issues, and legal safeguards for mental health professionals.* Sarasota, FL: Professional Resource Press.

Wright, R. H. (1981a). Psychologists and professional liability (malpractice) insurance. *American Psychologist, 36,* 1485–1493.

Wright, R. H. (1981b). What to do until the malpractice lawyer comes: A survivor's manual. *American Psychologist, 36,* 1535–1541.

Younggren, J. N. (1995). Informed consent: Simply a reminder. *Register Report, 21*(2), 6–7.

Younggren, J. N. (2002, May). *Ethical decision-making and dual relationships.* Retrieved from www.kspope.com/younggren.html

Younggren, J. N., & Gottlieb, M. C. (2004). Managing risk when contemplating multiple relationships. *Professional Psychology: Research and Practice, 35*(3), 255–260.

Zhu, S., & Pierce, J. P. (1995). A new scheduling method for time-limited counseling. *Professional Psychology: Research and Practice, 26*(6), 624–625.

Zipple, A. M., Landle, S., Spaniol, L., & Fisher, H. (1990). Client confidentiality and the family's need to know: Strategies for resolving the conflict. *Community Mental Health Journal, 26,* 553–545.

Zuckerman, E. L. (2004). Computerized billing and office management programs. In G. P. Koocher, J. C. Norcross, & S. S. Hill (Eds.), *Psychologists' desk reference* (2nd ed., pp. 670–673). New York: Oxford University Press. (Reprint available at www.nationalregister.org/development_Zuckerman.html)

Zuckerman, E. L. (2005). *Clinician's thesaurus* (6th ed.): *The guide to conducting interviews and writing psychological reports.* New York: Guilford Press.

Zuckerman, E. L. (2006). *HIPAA help: A compliance toolkit for psychotherapists for maintaining records' privacy and security, managing risks, and operating ethically and legally under HIPAA* (rev. ed.). Armbrust, PA: Three Wishes Press. (Available at www.threewishespress.com)

Zuckerman, E. (2007). *Reference listing of psychiatric diagnoses from ICD-9-CM.* Armbrust, PA: Three Wishes Press. (Available at www.threewishespress.com)

Index

Note: The titles of figures, forms, and handouts are shown in **boldface.**

Feedback Form

Dear Fellow Clinician,

This book is the result of many therapists' efforts to assist their peers in coping with the rapid and complex ethical and legal developments in the independent practice of psychotherapy. Continuing changes will make parts of *The Paper Office* obsolete in a few years, and so I intend to revise it to meet the evolving needs of therapists for ethical and legal forms and procedures. Please help me keep it useful and relevant by sending me your suggestions and modifications. You will receive credit in the revised editions, as well as a **free copy of the next edition,** for a significant contribution.

Edward L. Zuckerman, PhD
P.O. Box 222
Armbrust, PA 15616-0222
thepaperoffice.com

First, would you please tell me about your professional life?

Name: _____

Mailing address: _____

_____

Your professional title: _____ Degree(s): _____ Areas of practice

you specialize in: _____

Highest relevant credential(s): ❏ Licensed ❏ Registered ❏ Certified ❏ National Register ❏ ABEPP

❏ ACSW ❏ NBCC ❏ MFCC ❏ Other: _____

Member of this (these) national association(s): ❏ AACD ❏ AAMD ❏ AAMFT/MSCC ❏ ACSW ❏ ANA

❏ APsychologA ❏ APsychiatA ❏ APsychNurseA ❏ ACS ❏ NASP ❏ None ❏ Other: _____

❏ Division(s) of this (these) national association(s): _____

Member of your state's professional association: ❏ Yes ❏ No ❏ No state association

Years in private practice when you bought this book: Full-time: _____ years. Part-time: _____ years.

What were the biggest obstacles to your entering private practice? _____

_____

What have been your biggest problems in private practice? _____

_____

Which ethical or legal problems or questions seem most pressing to *you* right now? _____

_____

Now, please tell me about *The Paper Office:*

What is your overall evaluation of the book? _____

_____

_____

What specific changes would you suggest?

Increase: _____

_____

Decrease or eliminate: _____

_____

What forms not included were most useful to you? _____

_____

_____

What forms do you still need? _____

_____

Instructions for Installing and Using
The Paper Office's Forms on Your Computer

Using the Forms

The forms and handouts in this book are offered in two formats on the CD, .pdf (Portable Document Format) and .rtf (Rich Text Format). All of them are in .pdf format so you can print them out to look just as they do in the book. Almost all have been included in the .rtf format as well so that you can tailor them to your practice. The .rtf versions retain the formatting seen in the printed versions (such as bold and italic, tabs, check boxes, etc.), although not always exactly as it appears in the book. The .rtf files can be opened by all current word-processing programs including those in various "works," "office," or "suite" collections. The .pdf versions can't be modified but will print just like the forms in the book. To use a form, simply double-click on its name and the appropriate application will open the file (your word processor or Adobe Acrobat Reader). You are then ready to work.

For Windows Computers

Insert the CD, open Windows Explorer, and under "Folders" on the left side of the directory select your CD drive by clicking on the drive letter once. The contents of the CD will be shown on the right side of the directory, under "Name." You will see four folders; double-click on the one entitled "Windows," where you will find two folders, one called "PDF" and one called "RTF." Copy the folders from the CD by highlighting them and hitting Control + C or by using Edit, Copy from the drop down menu. Paste them into a folder where you can find easily find them, perhaps by creating a new folder on your hard drive called Paper Office. You may want to put the .rtf versions in a folder where you keep your word processing files.

Installing Adobe Acrobat Reader on a Windows Computer

If you do not have Reader or have an earlier version and would like to upgrade to version 8, insert the CD, open Windows Explorer and under "Folders" on the left side of the directory select your CD drive by clicking on it once. The contents of the CD will be shown on the right side of the directory. You will see four folders; double-click on the one entitled "Read Me" (a text file) and check the system requirements for version 8. To install it, double click on the folder called "Adobe Acrobat Readers," and then on the file entitled "AdbeRdr812_en_US.exe." This will install the latest version of Adobe Acrobat Reader onto your computer. Older and different versions can be downloaded from www.adobe.com/products/acrobat/ readstep2_allversions.html. Here you will find various versions for downloading.

For Macintosh Computers

Insert the CD, and when the icon for the CD, labeled "Forms from The Paper Office 4" appears on the desktop, double-click to open its directory. Copy the whole folder entitled "Forms for Mac" to your desktop by clicking on it once to highlight it, dragging the folder's icon to the desktop (or another location if you prefer), and releasing the mouse button. The computer will tell you which files it is copying. Inside the new folder, "Forms for Mac," which is now on your hard disk, are the forms in two versions, each in a separate folder: the forms in .rtf (Rich Text Format) are for all word processors, so you can modify them, and the forms in .pdf (Portable Document Format) are for viewing and printing in Adobe's Reader program. Because of copyright restrictions, you may not modify some forms without permission of their authors (as indicated at the bottom of the printed form in the book), so these appear only in .pdf form.

Installing Adobe Reader on a Macintosh Computer

If you do not have Adobe Reader (or "Acrobat Reader") or have an earlier version and would like to upgrade to version 8, insert the CD and open the Read Me file on the CD to check the system requirements. If your computer does not meet these requirements, go to the Adobe website (www.adobe.com) and download an earlier version such as 7. To install version 8, double-click on the folder called "Adobe Acrobat Readers," and then copy the file entitled "AdbeRdr812_en_US_ppc.dmg" by dragging it from the directory onto your desktop. Double-click on the file on your desktop and follow the instructions to install the program. Older and different versions can be downloaded from www.adobe.com/products/acrobat/ readstep2_allversions.html.